HIDE AND SEEK

HIDE AND SEEK

THE SEARCH FOR TRUTH IN IRAQ

CHARLES DUELFER

PublicAffairs

New York

Copyright © 2009 by Charles Duelfer

Published in the United States by PublicAffairs™,
a member of the Perseus Books Group.
All rights reserved.

Printed in the United States of America.
No part of this book may be reproduced in any manner whatsoever without
written permission except in the case of brief quotations embodied in critical
articles and reviews. For information, address PublicAffairs, 250 West 57th
Street, Suite 1321, New York, NY 10107.

PublicAffairs books are available at special discounts for bulk purchases in the
U.S. by corporations, institutions, and other organizations. For more
information, please contact the Special Markets Department at the Perseus
Books Group, 2300 Chestnut Street, Suite 200, Philadelphia, PA 19103, call
(800) 810-4145, ext. 5000, or e-mail special.markets@perseusbooks.com.

Designed by Brent Wilcox
Text set in 11.5 point Adobe Caslon

A CIP catalog record for this book is available from the Library of Congress.
ISBN-13: 978-1-58648-557-3
First Edition

10 9 8 7 6 5 4 3 2 1

To the memory of

SFC Clint Wisdom and SGT Don Clary

who gave their lives saving mine;
And to all those who gave so much in
the pursuit of truth in Iraq.

When the stars threw down their spears,
And water'd heaven with their tears,
Did He smile His work to see?
Did He who made the lamb make thee?
  —"The Tyger," William Blake, 1757–1827

CONTENTS

PREFACE

Iraq didn't need to be this bad. Still, something had to be done. That much is clear.

Six years after the invasion, sufficient time has now passed to make a reasoned, nonpolemical assessment of the course the United States followed in Iraq. Moreover, we are at a transitional point.

President George W. Bush decided to implement regime change in Iraq by force and spent much of his presidency trying to control the aftermath. President Barack Obama is now the first president since Richard Nixon who has not had to reckon with Saddam Hussein. President Obama's legacy, however, will be shaped by the uncertain outcome in Iraq. It may be a bright spot or a terrible stain. Post-Saddam Iraq remains an unstable country in an unstable region—and the stakes are still very high. As the United States withdraws, it will become clear whether the central government has coalesced with enough gravity to replace the force that Saddam used to maintain a unified Iraq. If not, divergent subnational interests, combined with Iranian meddling, may produce further disintegration or lead to another more authoritarian central government.

It can be said that primary responsibility for the future of Iraq is now up to the Iraqis. Those words have been said before, but the change in the U.S. administration gives them more meaning. The central Baghdad government must now broaden its support, reinforce its electoral mechanisms, and achieve an acceptable division of power and resources or it will collapse. The signs are not hopeful. Washington will not and cannot save it. Tehran cannot save it.

The immediate transition from the Saddam regime to something else is now over and a new phase has begun. This presents a moment to assess how we got here and perhaps to inform future decisions in Washington, Baghdad, Tehran, and elsewhere.

This book examines the events that led to the tragedy in Iraq from the perspective of someone who witnessed firsthand the array of issues both in Washington and in Baghdad. It is easy to forget now that there were very few Americans who knew anything firsthand about the Saddam regime immediately prior to the invasion. Today there are thousands of Americans who have been to Iraq. In the decade prior to the invasion, I was virtually the only senior American official who regularly dealt with the regime. As a result of my position as Deputy Chairman of the UN disarmament organization called UNSCOM, I became quite familiar with the perspectives and personalities of Saddam's top leaders.

At the same time, I was in regular contact with the senior levels in Washington. Clearly, neither side saw the universe the same way. Both made incorrect, sometimes fatally incorrect, assumptions about how the other would act or react. The absence of communication and understanding on both sides facilitated bad decision making. I did not appreciate how little current knowledge of Iraq existed in the government and therefore how unique my experience was until I witnessed the ill-informed decisions that have made the current circumstances so costly.

From this background, I have attempted to convey both major and less obvious dynamics that shaped the course of events and decisions that got us to the present point. The reader will also, hopefully, continue to consider *and reconsider* individual conclusions about how we came to be where we are.

It was clear by 2001, as the Bush administration was gradually establishing itself in Washington, that something had to be done about the Saddam regime. Sanctions were crumbling. Legally, they depended upon consensus in the United Nations Security Council that Iraq had not complied with the UN strictures concerning WMD. Operationally, they depended upon enforcement by key nations on the Security Council and among countries surrounding Iraq. In 2001, a decade after the sanctions had been imposed, both elements were collapsing.

The Oil-for-Food program had evolved into a massively corrupt process that Saddam had skillfully leveraged to his advantage. Russians, including at the highest level of government, were making profits and actively violating sanctions. Russia was pressing Baghdad's case in the Security Council to reduce and eliminate sanctions. Syrians were profiting from and aiding the transit of prohibited materials to Iraq. The UN was hosting a process that did not stop illicit trade and had only retarded the reemergence of Saddam's threat. Moreover, the arrangement was not sustainable and Saddam knew it. He took a long view. Saddam and his regime were reemerging as a considerable regional power and even a global power, by virtue of their impact on the oil markets.

The United States, led by its new administration, faced a choice among three general options. Washington could attempt through diplomatic efforts to sustain as many constraints on Iraq as possible for as long as possible, and hope for the best. The "best" would mean, in effect, a slow collapse of containment. Maybe we'd get lucky and Saddam would drop dead.

A second course would recognize that the time had come for a concrete decision concerning Iraq. Washington could consider some sort of accommodation or dialogue with the regime aimed at the goal of moderating its behavior directly, bilaterally. Unspoken would be the objective of manipulating the succession process from Saddam in a direction favorable to the United States.

Finally, Washington could take tangible actions to create the conditions to implement the long-standing policy of "Regime Change," on the basis that since Iraq—under Saddam—was again a growing threat to American interests, we should act.

The first option—muddling through—is frequently followed in government because it is easier to do nothing and remain on the same course. Changing strategy always entails political and material costs, and the future benefits are often hazy. In the context of Iraq, the cost of stringing out sanctions as long as possible, however, was relatively cheap in the short term. But by 2001, it was becoming obvious that the sanctions path was leading to nowhere.

Saddam was successfully manipulating people and governments in 1999–2002—when the price of oil averaged well under $30 a barrel. Imagine the effects as oil prices climbed to $100 a barrel. The billions of dollars the Saddam regime produced in illicit income before 2003 would instead have been tens of billions. Saddam channeled that illicit income into rebuilding his security services, regime structure, and weapons programs, including prohibited ballistic missiles. He corrupted not only his own government but also the UN and some of its member states.

The problem posed by the Saddam regime was not diminishing. We now know he retained his aspiration for WMD. Saddam told us after the war that he would "do whatever is necessary" to respond to comparable threats from his neighbors such as Iran and Israel. However, even without WMD, Saddam could have caused many other major problems.

President Bush sized up this problem and concluded the Saddam regime was unacceptable to U.S. security and something had to be done. This strategic decision was defensible—especially in the post-9/11 world. It was time to act, not to "muddle through."

The Bush administration did not give serious consideration to the option of addressing the Saddam threat indirectly by establishing a relationship with the regime as a path to modifying or removing it. The political costs of such a shift in the long-held U.S. policy of regime change would have been high. There would also be a negative effect on relations with other countries in the region—notably Israel. While such a course was, in theory, possible (Baghdad made regular approaches through me and others seeking dialogue with Washington), the realities in Washington made this low-cost approach impossible. The United States could not, or would not, consider an option of establishing overt relations with Baghdad in support of a covert objective of regime change. In the world of international politics, this would require the equivalent of delicate brain surgery and *the U.S. government cannot do brain surgery*. At best, it can conduct a surgical air strike.

This left the option of forced regime change. But even this tougher route did not need to be so costly. Critical steps to implement that decision were ill-considered or badly executed. Changing a regime is a huge and profoundly political step, yet lead responsibility was placed in the Pentagon. The political civilian leadership in the Office of the Secretary of Defense (OSD) guided the military planning *and* the postwar planning within a fractious interagency environment that lacked unity of purpose and unity of direction.

In the postinvasion political debates much has been made of the lack of intelligence about WMD. The WMD assessments were clearly wrong. *But the far more important error was in understanding the political and societal circumstances inside Iraq.* Leaders in the White House and especially the Department of Defense were extraordinarily ignorant about Iraq. They were either unaware of their own ignorance or decided that knowledge was unimportant and could be supplied by the best guesses of select Iraqi exiles—predominantly the Iraqi National Congress (INC), which was built by and around Ahmad Chalibi (who also declared confidently that WMD stocks were in Iraq). *There was far better information within the intelligence community on internal Iraqi dynamics.* However, the political leaders did not solicit the intelligence community for deeper analysis on such matters. Administration leaders pressed the intelligence community for information on Iraq's WMD and links to al-Qaeda, but did not ask about the viability of imposing external opposition groups on Iraq. In fact, the CIA was explicitly blocked from participating in postconflict planning.

Only this ignorance can explain the two most costly sweeping postwar decisions—the order on de-Baathification of Iraqi society and the dissolution of the army and all security-related organizations. These decisions were a reversal from what Iraqis had been led to believe would be U.S. policy. They excised any hope from millions of Iraqis who could do the most good or the most harm to U.S. efforts to secure a better post–Saddam Iraq. *Ignorance, virtually elective ignorance in this case, was very costly.*

While our government tries to keep a separation between intelligence and policymakers, in practice this is neither possible nor desirable. In the simplest example, an administration must ask questions of the intelligence community regarding matters it deems important. Yet, the simple act of asking a question shapes the answer and underlying analysis. Asking if there is a link between Saddam and al-Qaeda is a natural question. Posing that question posits a hypothesis. Answering, however, requires targeting resources and time to test the hypothesis. Analysts' eyes and ears are tuned to see data that may support or contradict this connection. Being tuned to that question distracts from other things. *But that's where balance, judgment, and trust among leaders in the policy and intelligence communities must come into play. On the subject of Iraq in 2002–2003, there was little of either.*

The intelligence community is the only part of the U.S. government whose ultimate goal is to seek out truth. Regarding Iraq, the intelligence community fell far too short of what reasonably could be expected. In the aftermath of the established errors in assessing Iraq WMD, the intelligence community has undergone externally imposed changes (such as the creation of the Director of National Intelligence structure) and also numerous internally directed reviews. One feature of these changes has been further emphasis on the training of analytic tradecraft for new analysts. In this context, I have had the opportunity to lecture on the experiences and lessons from Iraq. Each lecture is an opportunity to rethink the history and the dynamics of U.S. and Iraqi policies and intelligence judgments.

Underlying the many points that can be made, one fundamental element is certain. The key events and the sequences of those events were understood entirely differently depending on whether they were observed from Washington or Baghdad. Perspectives were so different in Washington and Baghdad that I came to doubt that a common reality existed. Assessments and predictions were far off the mark—on both sides. Analysts can see, in retrospect, how mistaken assumptions shaped mistaken assessments. Critical thinking lapsed, but in understandable ways. The clear bias to see evidence that confirms a hypothesis was overwhelming. Even when there were only crumbs of evidence, analysts "saw" what they thought was the truth, but it was not. They "saw" what they expected to see. American analysts made assumptions by projecting the logic of Washington onto Baghdad. However, what was logical in Washington was not always logical in Baghdad. The differences between the two could be enormous.

Intelligence analysts routinely face these challenges. At the time of this writing there is a debate between those who see Russia's incursion into Georgia as a sign of renewed strength, military and political, and those who see it as a sign of great weakness. Both views are tenable, but they cannot both be right. No doubt a similar debate about U.S. intentions exists in the Kremlin.

In retrospect, it is obvious that analysts had too little direct contact or experience. The Iraq WMD analysts had little, if any, experience in the political or societal context of those programs in Iraq. In my lectures I portray the weakness of making assessments about an environment they know only through electronic screens. Analysts should have a tactile feel for their subjects. How do words read or spoken in the secure air-conditioned vaults of the intelligence community relate to the dust, tension, and chaos of Iraq? Except for some former military recruits, most new analysts have no personal experience with any of the conflicts or emotions of much of the rest of the world. Most of the students have experienced no immediate physical conflict in their lives. The closest they may come to experiencing the feelings of sectarian violence may be in competing with another shopper for a parking space at the local mall.

For my part, I am at a loss to convey the visceral feeling of being proximate to some sublime truth in the midst of the heat, violence, and fear in Baghdad. Edging closer to insanity seemed sometimes to bring some greater understanding. Cool analysis does not always produce truth. The Internet does not transmit those insights. There are atavistic instincts that drive events that are not obvious when the world is experienced through a computer screen.

There is a further challenge for intelligence analysts, even if they are able to understand the worldview of their subject. Such understanding is useless if they cannot communicate it to those making choices for the government. An analyst who confidently grasped how Baghdad viewed the universe must be able to convey that to his customers. Decision makers need to listen and be able to understand in abbreviated form things in which they may have no experience.

Consider the analyst whose task it may be to observe and understand the meaning of Michelangelo's statue of David. To condense this subject into the time and space constraints imposed for the President's Daily Brief, the analyst reduces the subject to its basic elements and presents the equivalent of a stick figure. No president, nor any other reader, will not be able to appreciate how little of the reality has been put before him. While training and teaching in the intelligence community are helpful, it would also pay substantial dividends for policymakers to educate themselves in the language, tradecraft, and procedures of intelligence collection and analysis. They could better understand the virtues and shortcomings of the products they receive.

Intelligence will inevitably be imperfect and the process of acting on it flawed. Leaders must exercise their judgments and act not just on the basis of data served up by the intelligence community but also on that of their own experience and that which is commonly available from other sources. The damnable act of political leaders is to stop asking questions themselves or, worse, to inhibit reasonable efforts to explore for more facts and deeper understanding. Complete truth is unattainable, but progressively more detailed knowledge and progressively better questions mark progress. Failure is when the pursuit is halted, not managed.

A difference between the failures of intelligence and the failures of policy is that intelligence failures are usually discernible at some point. We now know where assessments on Iraq went wrong. Policy judgments are not so concretely judged. Evaluating policy actions requires comparison with alternative futures, which, by their nature, are speculative. It is not a feckless exercise, however. Saddam made some pretty clear blunders. If he had not invaded Kuwait in 1990, Iraq would be very different today—as would the United States. The question of whether the alternatives to an invasion of Iraq to remove Saddam would have yielded a better future can be debated, and that debate can help illuminate some features of governance that might inform future leaders. In the case of Iraq, the question that emerges from this consideration is, Was there any other way to remove Saddam? In this case, the answer, as described above, is yes, but the U.S. government is not sufficiently dexterous or focused to accomplish lower-cost, longer-term solutions.

The conclusion is that American leaders and the American people must assume that a foreign policy objective must be *so important that it is worth doing very badly*—because it is probable that the U.S. government *will, in the event, do it very badly.* Good intentions are not enough. Our good intentions, when acted upon, have done much damage.

Nevertheless, errors, even blunders, have a moral component. For all the similarities between the misperceptions and ill-conceived actions in both Baghdad and Washington, there is a vast moral distinction between them. Washington's actions, even when wrong, have been categorically different from Saddam's. The U.S. government, because it is constitutionally responsive to its citizens, cannot depart far from the collective sense of what is the "right" or moral foundation to its policies and actions. The controversies surrounding Abu Ghraib prison erupted because the United States is concerned about the moral component of its actions. There was never any debate over Abu Ghraib prisoner treatment when Saddam was running it—and it was a scene of horrors throughout his reign. Saddam's regime was virtually immune from any such self-examination or doubt.

A third party in this modern tragedy is the United Nations. It is not a single unitary actor, but an amalgam of its component members. The UN and especially the UN Security Council played a critical role in the Iraq issue. History points to the weaknesses of the UN Security Council system more than to its strengths. It is better at urging norms of behavior than at enforcing them. The latter may never be possible, especially in circumstances where states' interests diverge. Saddam astutely maximized the differences of interests among the Security Council members. Council members—particularly the pivotal permanent five members—moderated their enthusiasm for enforcing resolutions if it was no longer in their interest. For the Bush administration, taking the Iraq issue to the UN produced the convoluted efforts to demonstrate that Iraq was not fully compliant with UN resolutions (and it was not), but even then, there was no consensus among council members on action. The UN will remain a very imperfect and limited tool in circumstances affecting the interests of major powers.

What we learned from Iraq is broadly applicable to other circumstances. Policymakers, intelligence analysts, and citizens will, I hope, extrapolate many conclusions beyond what I have sketched here. I highlight one of many. The broadest problem underpinning U.S. decisions regarding Iraq was the paucity of information and understanding. In retrospect, the cost to the United States of severed relations with Baghdad during more than a decade was extraordinarily high. The absence of even limited dialogue produced growing ignorance. As a UN official, I was in a unique position to visit regularly senior officials in both Baghdad and Washington. I stayed current on perspectives in both governments. That sort of knowledge, more broadly experienced, would have softened the collision between the two countries.

The present book is not in any way intended to shape or interpret the information of the 2004 Comprehensive Report on Iraq WMD (and its addendum)—commonly referred to as "The Duelfer Report." That report was written to portray carefully the facts regarding the Saddam regime's relationship with WMD over time. It stands alone.

Instead, I have reflected here on my observations of the interactions between the various parties, drawing together the events as seen from both sides and placing them in the context of the recent history of Iraq and the United States. Since I knew the players on both sides well, particularly on the Iraqi side, I have tried to explain their circumstances. The actions of some individuals were truly despicable; yet there were also many talented Iraqis who were caught in a horrible system. The United States during its invasion and occupation incarcerated both good and bad Iraqis. Responsibility and authority over these prisoners have largely been transferred to the government of Iraq. Unfortunately, some good Iraqis remain in prison for questionable reasons probably having to do with the politics of the new government.

Sadly, the risks to Iraqis and their families remain. The participants often lived in fear of their lives, and many still do. I have had to camouflage the identities of most of the Iraqis mentioned in this book, with the exception of those who are already well known or dead. I have also used partial names for current and former CIA colleagues except where they have explicitly agreed otherwise.

This manuscript, per the direction of the Office of the Director of National Intelligence, was reviewed by all relevant agencies of the U.S. government for security purposes. (This process took well over nine months and substantially delayed publication.) Their review does not imply their agreement with the content.

I have included some elements of dialogue in this text. I do not pretend to recall these verbatim. However, they are intended to reflect accurately the substance and tone of selected exchanges.

In this light, it is risky to write about the "truth" in such a complicated series of events. My effort is to seek truth. There will be, inevitably, errors of fact or degree in my description of events. But I hope the broad direction of the narrative comes close to reflecting a picture that Iraqis and Americans can both recognize and perhaps even agree on.

CHAPTER 1

Knowledge Is Costly

On a Saturday morning in January 2005, I was driving from Kansas City airport to Atchison, Kansas. I was on my way to meet with families of servicemen who died with me, and for me, in Iraq. Passing through the Kansas countryside, I was turning over the questions I would try to answer, "What happened?" and "Why?" The first was straightforward. It was the second that I could only begin to answer.

If there is going to be a happy ending to the story of America's entanglement with Iraq, it has not yet been written. So far, it is the story of good intentions fatally implemented. A fundamentally good objective was fundamentally undermined by grave mistakes, and even incompetence, in execution. There are ideals blended with egos, blunders, false assumptions, and monumental waste. This story takes place at the intersection of countries, clans, economic interests, and serendipity. In sum, it is a concentrated dose of the human condition—a tragedy. We can learn from this experience. The world will certainly have many opportunities to make the same mistakes again, to relive the kind of unhappy days endured along the way in Iraq.

One such day was Monday, November 8, 2004. Baghdad was cool, the sky overcast with low clouds. The heat of summer and the harsh contrasts between light and shadow were replaced with soft, bland colors—gray above, tan or beige everywhere else.

I was in Baghdad leading the effort to investigate Iraq's weapons of mass destruction (WMD) as head of the Iraq Survey Group (ISG).

Baghdad was not new to me. I had been going there regularly through the 1990s, and CIA director George Tenet had personally asked me to lead the mission the previous January.[1] The hotly contested U.S. presidential elections had taken place six days earlier. President George W. Bush won a second term over John Kerry, and doubts about a major change in political direction were settled.

Intentionally or not, President Bush had staked his presidency on the Iraq war. It was the central issue in the 2004 campaign, and weapons of mass destruction were the central reason the American electorate thought we went to war. When asked about WMD, President Bush would say he would wait for Duelfer's report. Now, that was all over.

I presented the Comprehensive Report of the Special Advisor to the Director of Central Intelligence on Iraq's WMD to Congress a month before the presidential election. The question of WMD in Iraq was a pivotal issue. I had committed to deliver the report before the election for two reasons. The first was practical. I could not sustain the range of talent needed for this task in Iraq. We had to manage intelligence collection, reporting, and analysis with a constantly fluctuating body of people. Experts, case officers, technical collection staff—everyone—came and went, but the problem of producing the report stayed with me. The only person who was present from the beginning to the end of the Iraq Survey Group was the army chaplain. Civilians did not come out to Baghdad and hang around any longer than they were required. Conditions were Spartan, and the security situation was getting progressively worse. I had scheduled a surge of civilian analysts during the spring and summer of 2004, but they were departing in August and September. If the report wasn't finished by then, it never would be.

The second reason I reported prior to the election was to assure credibility. The intelligence community had lost a lot of stature over Iraq. If the report was not completed until after the election, it would have been impossible to avoid suspicion that the timing was for political expediency—to spare the administration. I wanted the Comprehensive Report to be rock solid and invulnerable to accusations of political motivation. Too many had put too much into the effort.

I had made a round of political consultations before coming out to Baghdad. During a meeting with Senator Carl Levin, with him sizing me up over his half-frame reading glasses, I described my goals to assemble a factual account of Iraq WMD programs and to find any stockpiles. I emphasized that my only instruction from either the president or George Tenet was to find the truth.

When I asked him if he had any advice, he observed that I would have to tread a very fine line. Senator Levin pointed out that there already seemed to be a tendency for the White House to place blame on the CIA for providing bad prewar intelligence on which war decisions were made. He was clearly saying I might easily find myself in political crossfire among multiple belligerents.

There were some loose ends that could not be resolved by the time I reported to Congress on October 6, so I returned to Baghdad to run these questions down with a residual team from the ISG. The goal was to provide some subsequent annexes that would address leftover issues.

I had no intention of prolonging the ISG as an organization. It was expensive and it was not intended to have an open-ended mission. I felt it should wrap up at the end of the year. Moreover, with the election past and the bulk of the WMD issues settled, there was little attention or resources available—particularly in the face of a growing insurgency. As far as my CIA colleagues on the ground in Iraq were concerned, I was engaged in archaeology. Who cared about WMD when there were insurgents killing Americans? I thought the ISG would now wind down and end with a whimper.

My deputy, John, and I met at our shared office at the headquarters of the ISG following a routine breakfast at the contractor-operated dining facility.[2] Handsome and deceptively youthful, John has an easy grin, sandy hair, and the athletic build of a runner. He mixes easily with everyone, and his distinctive laugh will provoke a smile in the next room. John was the guy in school who was always popular—and smart, though he did not flaunt it. He was a great intermediary with the dozens of experts who flowed through our operation. I could be caustic at times in my comments about the quality of work or the absence of experience reflected in some efforts. John would correctly and carefully convey appreciation for every effort and then attempt to redirect the work if it was at all off track. He also had a strong background as an experienced CIA Iraq WMD analyst (a Ph.D. in analytic chemistry), and as it turned out, he had a knack for the operational side of our business as well, which is too rare in the CIA.

There is a schism between operations officers (those who go out in the field and recruit agents or conduct other collection activities) and analysts (those who synthesize information from all sources, try to make sense out of it, and create the assessments used by policymakers). Operations officers tend to have their own culture and (secret) universe, while the intelligence analysts tend to be more academic in temperament and attitude. One is predisposed to action; the other, to observation. I wanted to combine both. At ISG, we had them working side by side in the field—to great effect. Overall, we were a large team—at our peak roughly seventeen hundred—which included security, support, and transportation.[3] Most members of the team were military; the senior officer was a very smart and very supportive army major general named Keith Dayton. We worked remarkably well together, partly because our personalities meshed and partly because we had as clear a goal as anyone else did in Iraq—to find the truth about the regime's WMD programs.

ISG headquarters were located at a separately secured area adjacent to the Baghdad International Airport in a former palace known as the "Perfume Palace." The site was called Camp Slayer after the first unit to occupy the site following the invasion: a chemical battalion nicknamed the "Dragon Slayers." The palace derived its name from an inscription above the entrance, taken from the Koran and referring to the beauty of perfume.[4] On the top floor were my office and that of Major General Dayton. His was large, pristine, and staffed with aides and executive officers Colonel Robert Adams and the more cerebral Navy Commander Robert Kettle.

By contrast, the office John and I shared was a mess of clutter and dust. I was responsible for the former; Iraqi storms brought the latter. The room had only one tiny glass window with bars. Still, the dust blew in from unseen cracks and holes. Dust coated every surface.

Pigeons skulked on the sill of my window. Their numbers seemed to grow over the months, as did my hatred of them and their brainless bobbing and cooing. Their tiny eyes were peepholes into nothing. I would have preferred Poe's raven—something with dignity or foreboding echoes of "nevermore." I wanted to shoot the pigeons with our omnipresent M-4 rifles or Glock pistols. The grinding pressure in Baghdad magnified such irritations.

This pit of an office had been the crucible containing the efforts to produce the thousand-plus-page, three-volume report on Iraq WMD. The room was littered with classified debris. Numerous piles of drafts of hundreds of pages lay around. Ultimately, we burned out two industrial-strength paper shredders disposing of these tailings.

One of the remaining issues that I sought to resolve was the reported movement of WMD to Syria before the war. Without completely running this down, I worried that uncertainty would fester and infect the overall results of the WMD report and confuse the debate over the war. I had no expectation that any WMD material had reached Syria and had stated this both in my report to Congress and directly to the White House (when National Security Advisor Condoleezza Rice had inquired about it).

I had personally pressed this question with the senior Iraqi officials in custody who had created the close links between the Saddam and Bashar al-Assad regimes. We had plenty of concrete evidence of smuggling everything but WMD through Syria. The most senior Syrian officials certainly supported (for a price) the transit of weapons and prohibited materials into Iraq, but we could confirm no evidence of WMD going to Syria.

Nevertheless, a couple of Iraqis I hoped to track down were reportedly involved in driving trucks with something "sensitive" into Syria. The Iraqis worked for a company related to Saddam's son Uday, and we wanted to talk to them to identify concrete times and locations where they moved their suspect cargo.

We knew that Syrian cooperation with the Saddam regime was high and that senior Syrian officials had benefited personally from helping Iraq elude sanctions. Syria was also the conduit for much of the illicit support provided from Russia. Iraq had paid handsomely for such assistance. It was not unthinkable that Iraq might have moved selected incriminating equipment over Syria's border. It was clear that many top former regime officials had scurried to Syria during the war. Saddam's presidential secretary, Abed Hamid Mahmud (arguably the second-most-powerful individual in Iraq), went there and returned, only to be captured by U.S. forces in June 2003. Abed described many incriminating things about the Iraq-Syrian relationship, but had no knowledge of WMDs shipped to Syria. Other senior Iraqis, such as Deputy Prime Minister Tariq Aziz, likewise claimed no knowledge of such movement and strongly denied the possibility. I personally thought it was more likely that the regime was moving gold, cash, or expensive and difficult-to-obtain machine tools out of the country. But we didn't know for sure.

In that political postelection atmosphere, John and I gathered up the usual things to go to a meeting near the U.S. Embassy inside the so-called Green Zone. One of the few advantages to working in Iraq (for civilians, anyway) was the ability to wear sensible clothing. Blue jeans and light hiking boots were most common, though I preferred Teva sandals in hot weather. This day, John had a greenish beige T-shirt and khaki pants. There is a certain "deployment chic" for civilians, especially CIA officers overseas. L. L. Bean is the Brooks Brothers equivalent for this set. It was simple to pick out our officers from the crowds deplaning at airports on their way to Iraq or Afghanistan. By contrast, the military had standard-issue everything—from weapons to helmets. CIA had different weapons, haircuts, cars, and rules.

John had a red poppy pinned to his black Kevlar vest. It had been given to him by the British deputy commander, Major (later, Lieutenant Colonel) Henry Joynson for the approaching Remembrance Day on November 11, when the British commemorate all their war dead since World War I.

In addition to wearing body armor for the ride down the airport road, I brought my usual blue canvas satchel with the briefing book for the upcoming Senate Oil-for-Food hearings, a Glock pistol, a small digital camera, and a Sony Discman—the typical items for a day in Baghdad.

The convoy to make the trip from the airport was organized by the military security unit. As was their practice, the convoy consisted of several vehicles. The first and last vehicles were up-armored HMMVs with a .50-caliber machine gun. Two class 6 armored Suburban vehicles formed the two middle vehicles and were manned by a five-man personal protection detail from the Kansas National Guard. The first Suburban was driven by Army Specialist Steve Nelson, and the front passenger shotgun position was taken by Sergeant Jon Johnson. The second Suburban, the follow car, was driven by Specialist Don Clary, and in the front right seat was the team leader, Staff Sergeant Clint Wisdom. In the back watching the rear was Specialist Nathan Gray.

At 0900, the detail and its vehicles were ready at the door of the Perfume Palace when John and I came out and headed for the first armored Suburban. Protocol would have the senior person in the right rear seat. John, unaware of the protocol, got in that side because he happened to be closer to that door. I hesitated a second, recognizing that the team trains with a certain order in mind, but I gave it no further thought and climbed in the left side.

The convoy started off, first making its way around the lake immediately in front of the Perfume Palace. It then passed down the road leading to the exit from Camp Slayer. Just beyond the walls of Camp Slayer was the neighborhood called "Jihad" and the bombed facilities of the Special Republican Guard (SRG).

Overhead, a blimplike aerostat floated silently at the end of a long tether. Suspended beneath it were visual and nonvisual sensors to monitor the area and rapidly locate insurgent firing positions from the surrounding neighborhood and along the airport road. From the ground looking up at the balloon, I felt like a crab on the sea floor gazing quizzically up an anchor line and seeing the bottom of a boat drifting above. It irritated me that the aerostat floated languidly above our chaos below. The object also served as a target for those in nearby neighborhoods to take potshots at with their AK-47s. The rounds would fall short, but would come plinking down in Camp Slayer.

A year and a half earlier, I had regularly driven alone through the area in an unarmored vehicle. I knew the streets and homes. Now it was a lawless no-man's-land, home to insurgents of various stripes. Its transformation was stark.

❖

I surmise that on the same gray morning, at sunrise, a young man in his early twenties was nervously pacing outside an old red Kia sedan. He had no doubt said his prayers. He was in the driveway of a home with another, older man whom he knew only by the name "Khadam." Iraqi homes are normally surrounded by a wall, and a solid metal gate rolls across the drive. The older man waited with a cell phone. It rang. After a very brief conversation, the man hung up. He turned to the youth and said, "Allah is with you. They are on the way." They embraced, and then the youth got behind the steering wheel. "Khadam" looked into his eyes one last time and then rolled the driveway gate open for the car to exit.

As we traveled, John and I talked about our upcoming meeting and how we might get a commitment for re-contacting sources that could help resolve the Syria question. We passed the exit checkpoint of the airport. There were the usual number of local Iraqis along the road and adjacent houses. Some were outside on roofs. At least one had a cell phone.

The airport access road is about ten kilometers long. In Saddam's time, it was lined with trees and walls. Access was strictly limited, and the road was carefully guarded since it passed by two key palace areas. There were carefully manicured fields and much wildlife. The remains of Saddam's private gazelle herd (he favored their meat) had been quickly eliminated. Too many people possessed too many weapons, and there were no rules of engagement regarding gazelles.

The trees too were now gone, lopped down to reduce the cover for anyone seeking to attack. The road had a wide, formerly landscaped area that divided the east- and westbound carriageways. At one point on the approach to the airport stood a twenty-foot-tall statue of a man with wings and representing Ibn Firnas. In 875 A.D., at age sixty-five, he strapped on mechanical wings and attempted to fly. Iraq had many such monuments to its historical achievements in the arts and sciences. The airport, built by Saddam to highlight Iraq's technical achievements, was meant to open in time to welcome a planned Baghdad meeting of the Organization of Islamic States in 1980. A

French firm had designed the terminals, and modern facilities were created, including a special separate terminal for arriving foreign delegations and other VIPs. Saddam, however, elected to invade Iran in that year, and the conference, for which so much effort had been expended, was cancelled.

By 2004, the airport highway was a dirty and wreckage-strewn road with an absurd mix of taxis, private cars, armored cars for U.S. officials, Bradley fighting vehicles, HMMVs, and an occasional M-1 tank—all rushing to their destinations. The Americans nervously watched approaching cars. Iraqis in a hurry took their lives in their hands if they decided to pass a military convoy. Anxious young gunners with no experience in Arab countries (or any foreign countries, for that matter) had to make instant decisions about whether to fire upon (or "light up") passing vehicles they considered possible threats.

Unmarked U.S. vehicles were also at risk. I had often been in armored BMWs driven by Blackwater contract security guards who felt they should speed as fast as possible and pass all the dumb "big army" vehicles. In their view, the faster you went, the less time you were exposed. From the army gunner's point of view, a fast-moving BMW was a fast-approaching threat. On more than one occasion, a young enlisted kid manning a .50 cal drew down on my vehicle and was about to open up before the BMW waved identification. Innocent Iraqis were regularly killed in similar mistakes. Eventually, convoys placed large signs on the rear vehicle, warning other vehicles not to pass or risk deadly force.

Still, accidental killings occurred regularly. In any country other than Iraq, there probably would have been greater outrage over such deaths. However, a population used to the brutality of Saddam and its unpredictability had a store of fatalism that diffused much of the anger that might otherwise have boiled over.

The initial optimism in the spring of 2003, when it was hoped that the world's only superpower, which had rid Iraq of its dictator, would doubtless fix everything, had vanished. It was once assumed that since the United States could make a missile that would fly into a specific window of Saddam's Palace after having been launched from thousands of miles away, then Americans could certainly fix Iraq's water and electricity and make a viable government. But Iraqis quickly learned that the world's last superpower had no idea what to do in Iraq. Many were convinced that the stupid decisions were made on behalf of the external opposition leaders. Many Iraqis were convinced the United States simply came in to take the oil. Where was the government? America's "freedom" brought chaos and death.[5]

A colleague of mine, the only other person I knew who could drive from one side of Baghdad to the other without getting lost, said with bitter disillusionment about our own government, "We are finding, fixing, and eliminating all pockets of cooperation." This was less than three weeks after Baghdad had fallen.

I recalled a long conversation I'd had in May 2003. It was in the private home of a friend in the neighborhood John and I were passing in the armored Suburban. I was discussing the methods of Saddam's control over Iraq with an Iraqi colonel from the Directorate of General Security (DGS). He had been in charge of controlling local political aspects of Iraq under Saddam. At one point in the conversation, he said, "You know, before the war, we thought that the United States could not take casualties. This was a basis for our thinking on defeating the Americans. We believed the Americans were too soft and could not accept many deaths. This was wrong."

I asked, "What makes you now think that was incorrect?"

This colonel, who had described to me in great detail how Saddam distributed rewards and punishments to control Iraq, replied simply, "If you cared about casualties, you would never have disbanded the army or fired all Baathists."

Finally, he looked at me deeply and went on, "You know, to rule Iraq, you will have to become Saddam." These two comments echoed continuously in my mind.

The insurgency and simple, non-ideological crime had filled the vacuum created by the removal of Saddam's regime. In time, external jihadists also moved in. Iran quickly learned that Iraq was an opportunity, not a threat. Iraqis learned that you did not have to be smart to be the last superpower. It was not difficult to attack the Americans, and there were lots of reasons to do so. Americans were seen as facilitating Shia rule. They had emasculated the Iraqi Army.

Hundreds of thousands of young Iraqis now had no jobs or sense of self-worth or identity. How better to reassert strength than by shooting Americans? Even the electricity was still down. After the 1991 war, everyone recalled that Saddam had restored electricity within weeks.

In a city and culture prone to see conspiracy, it was easy to understand the power of rumors. Lines at gas stations were hours, and sometimes days, long. How could this be if Iraq had the second-largest oil reserves after Saudi? Someone must be taking the oil and gas.

"Khadam" and his ilk could offer a cause, a belief set, to youths they sought to recruit: the injustice of the American infidels, the duty and heroism of sacrificing oneself for the jihad, the protection of Islam from the Westerners who sought to steal oil and corrupt the Arab world. Moreover, Americans offered no meaningful alternative that the jihadists could discern. There was no competing ideology preached at Friday prayers. There was no spiritual or economic hope. The Iraqi leaders the United States was seen to be importing or supporting were known as crooks or opportunists who lacked power. Allah was not on their side.

Americans did not understand Iraq. They did not know the neighborhoods. They had no defense against someone who was committed to a cause to the point of dying. Still, there must have been some nervousness as the young man drove the short distance to the entrance to the airport road. He must have thought about his parents and his brothers and sisters. Would they be told of his fate? He carried no identity on him, and the car was not his. Soon he would be in heaven with nothing left on this earth. The dirty red Kia looked like any other Iraqi car merging with the traffic.

The airport road ran through the heart of the decay that had become Baghdad. John and I passed the overpass to the al-Amiriya section of Baghdad. There were wrecked hulks of destroyed cars and vehicles. The guard rails had been bulldozed. This removed the threat from artillery rounds hidden in back of the rail and detonated by cell phones or garage door openers, a tactic popular for several months at the end of 2003 and early 2004. Other tactics replaced them.

Detritus of war and decay passed by the windows quickly. I scanned my briefing book for the upcoming hearings, but could not concentrate. Concentration was not easy in Baghdad. The convoy passed another overpass and on-ramp to the airport road, which merged from the right.

I saw our driver glance in the rearview mirror, and I began to sense something from the right, a car, a driver, traveling a bit too close, a bit too fast.

The protection detail behind us was from the Second Battalion of the 130th Field Artillery of the Kansas National Guard. They were trained as a Multiple Launch Rocket System (MLRS) battalion—artillery rockets. There was no need for MLRS in Iraq after the conventional conflict had ended in May 2003. Instead, there was a need for security forces, a function that most of the unit now found itself performing. They manned guard towers and other fixed positions. The personal protection detail was a special group, and the duty was good. But the unit was looking forward to redeploying back to Kansas in a couple months. Downtown Baghdad was definitely not Kansas.

Specialist Don Clary kept the follow car tight behind our lead Suburban. Clary was twenty-one, a big guy with a sense of humor. He was close to his sister Kristi, who stayed in touch via e-mail from Troy, Kansas. Clary had become hooked on the deals offered on e-Bay. He had just ordered a guitar. Staff Sergeant Clint Wisdom was in the front passenger seat. He was thirty-nine and the team leader. His wife, Janet, and daughter were back in Atchison, Kansas. The daughter was recently married and pregnant. He liked fishing and could be seen fishing in the lake surrounding the Perfume Palace in the evenings. He lived up to his name and conveyed confidence to the team. Specialist Nathan Gray had just been accepted for a position on the Horton Police Force. The force had only five police officers, and he was worried that they would not hold the position for him after he had been called up with the rest of his Kansas guard unit. His wife, son, and infant daughter waited for him in rural Lancaster, Kansas.

Gray saw the red Kia come down the on-ramp as they passed under the overpass. It gradually accelerated and was catching up in the right lane. There were many other cars in the flow of traffic. At that time of the morning, many Iraqis used the airport road to get into Baghdad quickly. It was 0915, still cloudy and dull. The remaining date palms that stood in the area separating the inbound and out-bound airport roads were ragged and covered with dust.

Gray mentioned the Kia to Wisdom, who turned to look. Wisdom was not comfortable with the acceleration of the Kia. It was making its way past them, and the driver was watching the Suburbans, not the road ahead. Suddenly, the Kia moved to get ahead of them and began to cross toward their lane.

The Kia driver knew his target. He had been told by "Khadam" to aim for the first Suburban. He had to be careful because he could not ac-celerate very quickly with the weight of the several artillery shells in the car; they were about a hundred pounds each. The Kia rode low on its shocks, and he did not want to scare the Americans off or blow out a tire.

Wisdom probably noticed that the car was riding too low—and that there was only one nervous-looking person in it. Clary and Wisdom responded by driving faster and trying to force the Kia off to the side. Clary pushed the gas pedal down, accelerated, and steered to-ward the Kia.

In the covering HMMV, the gunner was watching the traffic and saw the Kia passing them. The Iraqis are crazy drivers. They all have beat-up cars, and it was clear why. What was the Kia doing? It was pretty far ahead. The Suburban was moving toward it. Maybe they knew what to do. The HMMV gunner wondered, If I light up this one, odds are it is just some kid late for work.

I did not have time to process what followed: an instantaneous spasm, during which chaos tore into the car. A violent compression wave blew the armored windows into the car. I felt it inside my head.

Whatever had been outside to the right and behind was gone. Our Suburban was hurled forward. A heavy, inch-thick plate of bulletproof window flew into John's armored vest and landed in his lap. I glimpsed red on John's chest, but was relieved to see it was the poppy still pinned to his chest.

Our driver, Specialist Steve Nelson, kept the wheel straight, and somehow, the vehicle kept going forward. His training taught him to get off the X. The X was the term used by security teams to indicate the site of the attack. Presumably, this comes from figuring that the attackers have a plan with an X marking the spot where they intend to kill you. Survival chances go up the further and faster you get away from the X.

We veered to the left in the direction of a Bradley fighting vehicle that had been positioned in an open area between the inbound and outbound airport roads. As we approached, the Bradley rapidly started up and moved off. No help from it. John looked OK. The two guys up front seemed OK. The Suburban was a battered wreck. We had rolled to a stop in the middle of the desolate area vacated by the Bradley. Doors opened. Everyone had weapons out. The combination of adrenalin and anger produced a desire to fire, but there were no targets. I felt a sense of surprise that we were basically OK, while the vehicle was completely demolished. John called on his radio. Sergeant Jon Johnson called on his radio. No response. We stayed close to the shelter of the Suburban, as small-arms fire had become a tactic that often accompanied suicide car bombs. There was some small-arms firing, and we realized our follow car was gone. We were on our own and exposed. It seemed eerily quiet, but then I realized my hearing was dulled. Across the broad (perhaps fifty meters) median, heavy traffic continued in the opposite direction. No traffic followed on our side of the road.

Behind us, almost out of sight, was the twisted wreckage of the second Suburban. It had been flung several meters into the median area, killing Don Clary and Clint Wisdom and gravely injuring Nathan Gray.

VBIED is the acronym for vehicle-borne improvised explosive device. One reality behind the acronym is that each VBIED represents a young kid who has been convinced to kill himself by someone like "Khadam," under whose influence he has fallen. His mind has been filled with some concoction of toxic feelings or ideas that lead him to commit his life to a single moment of destruction. The power of this poison is enormous. This twisted ideology has been used to generate an arsenal of suicide bombers.

Such youths, channeled into a destructive urge that advances the goals of their elders, are used as weapons. Every VBIED is a youth lost to a family. It is a youth so won over, so seduced by the words of others (who churn through such malleable minds) that they drive their cars against cars or army vehicles in hopes of killing a few other humans.

With exactly the opposite objective, Wisdom, Clary, and Gray committed their lives to preserving life. They were committed to the positive side of humanity. The contrast could not have been greater.

Large VBIEDs, like the Kia with several 155-mm artillery rounds, leave little behind. Typically, all that is left of the driver is a head blown through the windshield, usually flattened somewhat and propelled a long distance from the site of the explosion. The Kia engine block flew three hundred yards.

As we began to walk warily around the remains of the Suburban, John said to me, "This isn't worth it." It was a question more than a statement. But it was a vital one and one that we would discuss over the next weeks. In fact, the question will linger forever.

The answer began with at least two parts. One was the U.S. Constitution. As CIA officers, we had sworn to uphold the Constitution. Our government is founded on ideas and principles, not individuals or regimes. We were there, at the most basic level, because of the Constitution. Over the next few days, I printed off a copy of the Constitution from the Internet. It had been ages since I had read it. John did the same. It is an impressive document and worth upholding.

The second part is that the president, the commander in chief, wanted the truth of the WMD question to be understood. We were there to find and record as much truth as possible, and this was a worthy cause. It might save others greater pain later. These were at least two compelling reasons for being there in the middle of the airport road.

But was the war itself worth it? Was the chaos we sparked worse than the tyranny of Saddam? Have we created circumstances that will lead to a Middle East under the control of radical Islamists who will be more threatening than Saddam? Or have we created circumstances in which governments more responsive to their citizens will now take hold and evolve into a stable and viable region? These are harder questions that will be answered only with the passage of more time, if ever. Survivors of the war and the families of those who died certainly ask such questions and will have their own answers.

For my part, I am able to pen these words only because of the positive actions of Clint Wisdom, Don Clary, and Nathan Gray. On the Baghdad airport road that November morning, while looking for truth, I saw the best and worst of humanity collide.

On the wall of the entrance to CIA headquarters is the oft-quoted biblical inscription: "Ye shall know the truth, and the truth shall set you free" (John 8:32). The price of knowledge can be very high. Complete knowledge is impossible, but not to strive for it brings its own perils; the price of ignorance can be higher. Indeed, as the early U.S. decisions in Iraq reflect, ignorance about your own ignorance—to the point of willful ignorance—is the costliest error of all.

CHAPTER 2

Cradle of Conflict

Tragedy in Iraq did not start with the invasion ordered by President Bush in March 2003. The piece of geography we now call Iraq has a rich history. Mesopotamia, the historical name for the region between and around the Tigris and Euphrates, is known as the "cradle of civilization." Geology made it rich in resources. This attracted humans, who competed over this rich territory. Mesopotamia is also the cradle of war. City-states were built; empires grew; and science, technology, and the arts flourished. With equal regularity, wars were waged, winners glorified, and the vanquished were slaughtered or enslaved.

Iraqis and especially Iraqi leaders are imbued with this history. American leaders are not. This disparity of historical roots and perspective is an elemental cause for the mutual misunderstanding, major miscalculations, and mistaken assessments on both sides.

Iraq's geological story begins hundreds of millions of years ago, when events in the Mesozoic Era (which lasted almost 200 million years, beginning 250 million years ago and ending 65 million years ago) created the conditions that placed fossil fuels there. At that time, the planet had a single huge continent (Pangaea) surrounded by a large ocean. Pangaea was roughly centered over the equator—on the side of the globe where Africa is presently located. The earth was an imperfect, spinning sphere with a nonuniform distribution of mass on its outer crust—especially where Pangaea was located. The crust covering the molten outer core was out of balance. Centripetal forces of the spinning earth acted to even out this imbalance left from the earth's creation. Tectonic plates formed and inched apart. The unitary continent of Pangaea divided into separating segments. The area that is now Iraq was, even then, an area fracturing along unique lines. The plates carrying North America, Eurasia, and Africa were all pulling apart at the point where the Red Sea, Great Rift Valley, and Arabian Gulf are so prominent. The earth's plates are still drifting apart—Iraq moves a couple of centimeters further away from the United States every year.

In the Mesozoic Era, the globe was warmer, there were no polar ice caps, and the seas were higher. Large reptiles, mammals, and birds inhabited the Pangaea land mass, and fish and coral filled the seas. This life produced, over time, plant and calciferous material that accumulated at the bottoms of what were then shallow seas. Life was good— at least for a while.

Somewhere around 250 million years ago, something really bad (even by modern Iraqi standards) happened. An environmental cataclysm produced a mass extinction that some call the "Great Dying." This killed off an estimated 90 percent or more of marine species and roughly 75 percent of terrestrial vertebrate species. The geologic record points to a few mass extinctions, but this appears to have been the most extensive. During the Jurassic and Cretaceous periods, the biomass from this die-off was transformed, under the right temperature, pressure, and amount of time, into fossil fuel. These reserves of oil have lain in pools near the surface of Iraq ever since. Dinosaurs were trudging over ground that was incubating petroleum—until they met their end in yet another mass extinction 65 million years ago.[1]

In much more recent geologic history—just a couple million years ago—the continents were close to their current locations. Climates were changing. The last ice age was winding down. Equatorial Africa was warm and hospitable to new, reevolved life. Mammals were the dominant species, and hominids evolved out of Africa. The hominids spread north, adapting to the land and conditions they found. Around 500,000 years ago, one species, *Homo erectus*, appears to have figured out how to make fire. Rivers were forming from the water patterns evolving from the warming climate.

this region. Technology was improving, most visibly in the weapons and armor used by invading armies.

In 637 A.D., Arabs regained control of the region for the first time in almost a thousand years. This was concurrent with the birth and spread of Islam. The Prophet Mohammed dictated the Qur'an (Koran) in 610 in Mecca. The religion spread into Mesopotamia, but when Mohammed died in 632, the issue of successor caliphs, who combined both spiritual and political leadership, divided the followers. Again, like the dividing tectonic plates below the earth's surface, conflict played out in Iraq with those who became known as Shia supporting only a line of succession from a direct relative of Mohammed. The first caliphs were friends and companions of Mohammed, but not related by blood. The first lasted two years and died, possibly of poisoning. The next two survived ten and twelve years, but were assassinated. During this time, there were continuous battles and other conflicts to eliminate apostasy.

The fourth caliph was the first to be related to Mohammed. Ali ibn Abi Talib was a cousin of Mohammed. Although he was the first to be recognized by the Shia, he too was assassinated. Ali was buried in Najaf, Iraq, now one of the holiest sites in Shia Islam. After Ali was killed, a battle between the next caliph and a small Shia group led by Hussein, the son of Ali, took place in 680 at Karbala. The vastly outnumbered Shia were defeated, and Hussein was beheaded. And on it went.

The Abbasid Dynasty assumed control of the region that is Iraq in 750, and Baghdad was founded in 762 by Caliph Abu Ja'far al-Mansour. The reigns of the succeeding caliphs waxed and waned, but Baghdad was not really sacked until the Mongol invader, Hulagu Khan (grandson of Genghis), raided in 1256. In the fashion that made Mongolians famous, they really pillaged the city.

During what Europeans call the Middle Ages, Mesopotamia was mostly occupied by Turks and battling Persians. The Crusades in the twelfth century introduced regular battles with Europeans. Saladin, who was born in Saddam's home area of Tikrit, made a name for himself by building an empire and defeating the Crusaders in many major battles, including recapturing Jerusalem from Crusader control.

The Ottomans ruled from the fifteenth century until after World War I, in 1917, when the British were mandated to rule. Britain empowered a constitutional monarchy in 1922 and named the nation Iraq, under King Faisal.

Among the things that were learned in World War I was the importance of oil (the mechanized forces needed petroleum, not horse feed) and that chemical weapons could be very useful against massed troops and especially troops who were otherwise protected in trenches.

In 1927, the Iraq Petroleum Company (a British-dominated consortium of European oil companies) drilled a well in the Kirkuk area. A gusher emerged, sprouting fifty feet in the air and spilling 95,000 barrels of oil per day for over a week before it could be controlled. The geology of the Mesozoic Era had just met twentieth-century human technology and economics. And so the fate of modern Iraq was set. The monarchy was given full independence by the British in 1932, although the British reoccupied Iraq during World War II. The occupation lasted until 1958, when Faisal II and Crown Prince Abdul-Illah were assassinated and a military junta took power under Abdul Karim Qasim. Saddam Hussein participated in an attempt to assassinate Qasim in 1959, but failed. Four years later, Qasim was killed in a coup staged in a combined effort of the Baath Party and the military. The new government was headed by Abdel Salam Arif, who subsequently drove out the Baathists while consolidating his power. When he died in a helicopter crash, his brother General Abdel Rahman Arif carried on until he was ousted by the Baathists under Major General Ahmed Hassan al-Bakr and his deputy Saddam Hussein on July 17, 1968. This date became Iraq's National Day until 2003.

Versions of this record have been imprinted in the psyches of Iraqis, none more so than Saddam Hussein. Saddam considered himself the latest in a long line of great Iraqi leaders who pursued greatness through the promotion of Iraqi arts, engineering, military conquest, and acquisition of the spoils. The battles, methods, and achievements of Saladin, Nebuchadnezzar, and Hammurabi formed ideals for Saddam and his regime. In the context of the history in Mesopotamia, nothing could be more normal.

Saddam took over as president in 1979, eleven years after the Baathist coup. He had been the true power behind Hassan al-Bakr for years when al-Bakr, then sixty-seven years old, resigned for "health reasons." Saddam had worked his way through the Baathist Party, which had grown, building on the sentiments of Arab nationalism germinating since the 1950s. Riding this wave, he gathered around him those whom he could trust or who were indebted to him. The cost of getting to his position was offset by the greater achievements he would bring as leader of the greater Arab nation. He achieved his goal of being the leader of the Arab nation of Iraq and had to strengthen his position, which to him was synonymous with strengthening Iraq.

Saddam had an uncanny ability to understand what motivated those around him—both positively and negatively. He dispensed reward and punishment easily and, like so many leaders before him, identified himself with the country. Hammurabi once said, "The people treat me as their father and I bring them order." Saddam said virtually the same thing in his speeches to the Iraqi people.[3]

Saddam clearly identified with the preceding renowned Mesopotamian leaders. Saladin was revered for his defeat of Crusaders, who when captured were sometimes enslaved, but were more regularly beheaded in large numbers. Saladin would perform beheadings himself, as the occasion demanded.

Saddam saw himself as part of a long tradition. Force necessarily accompanied the growth of the empire and allowed greater glory. It provided the basis for economic growth and the arts and sciences. Saddam was engaged in the pursuit of historical greatness for himself and Iraq. He did not see himself as a wicked, brutal dictator. He did not think he was an enemy of Allah.

Saddam set the tone early in his presidency. Just days after becoming president, he called an extraordinary general meeting of the Baath Party leadership. It was videotaped and later televised. The al-Khuld Hall, in what is now the Green Zone, was filled with over two hundred Baathist leaders. Saddam, still only forty-two years old, sat in a chair on the stage as General Secretary Abdel Hussein Mashhadi confessed to the existence of coup plotting under the previous president al-Bakir. Saddam requested that Mashhadi read the names of coconspirators. As each of sixty names was read, security officers took the terrified accused away. Saddam affected a tear or two when those particularly close to him were taken out. Throughout the proceedings he was casually smoking a cigar. About one-third of those removed were executed. Some of the remaining "unaccused" were given the physical task of killing their former political colleagues. The rest were imprisoned.

The participants in the regime knew the nature of the regime from the start. Other political organizations like the Iraqi Communist Party faded fast.

Saddam must have thought, "This is how they—Nebuchadnezzar or Saladin—would have done it."

The early period of his political experience shaped Saddam's thinking in ways that preordained later tragedy. In 1979, international dynamics were changing. There was much turmoil, especially in the Middle East. However, what seems obvious now was anything but obvious at the time. This is the chronic pretension of history. What is beyond doubt is that the region combined historic animosities, cross-border tribal and religious tensions, vast resources (which are of value only if outsiders can obtain them), competition by global powers, and the egos of leaders not particularly responsive to their citizens.

From the perspective of Baghdad, and more particularly in the eyes of Saddam, turmoil was not necessarily a threat, but an opportunity. Saddam was not interested in the status quo. His visions for himself and Iraq were grander. In contrast, Washington typically prefers the international status quo. Why not? The United States is at the top, so stability is good and instability is bad. But that is not the view of everyone else, and it wasn't Saddam's.

As seen from Baghdad, part of the turmoil was the Jimmy Carter presidency. While Carter is noted now for his international expertise, his international experience when he was president was limited. He seemed naively idealistic while learning on the job and playing catch-up with world events.

A founding member of the Organization of Oil Exporting Countries (OPEC), Iraq had been using its oil wealth since the Arab oil embargo in 1972 to fund infrastructure improvements like highways, canals, schools, and hospitals. Iraq had also been on a buying spree for military hardware to include fighter aircraft (mostly French) and thousands of tanks (Russian), SCUD missiles, artillery, and helicopters. Under both Bakr and Saddam, Iraq also sought to develop the capacity to produce weapons, not just to buy them. The growth of a large military industrial complex for many weapons and ammunition resulted. The oil wealth did not cover the expenditures, but countries were willing to extend plenty of credit. National debt grew as the armed forces expanded.

Saddam took over the presidency as Iraq's neighbor and America's regional ally, Iran, was about to turn upside down. The monarch, Shah Mohammed Reza Pahlavi, was a great friend of the United States (indeed, without the United States, he would not have been in power). There were many Iranian students studying in the United States, and Iran was permitted to buy advanced U.S. military equipment, including the top-of-the-line F-14 Tomcat Fighter aircraft.

But the Shah had become increasingly dictatorial and was aging. Conservative religious clerics incited students fed up with what they saw as a foreign-imposed rule. In assisting the Shah into power, the United States had short-circuited moves toward democracy.

In Washington, President Jimmy Carter's primary concerns were to introduce an emphasis on human rights as a factor in international relations and to strive toward the goal of eliminating all nuclear weapons from the planet.[4] Like most foreign policy experts, Carter focused on the U.S.-Soviet balance. He did, however, recognize that energy and access to oil were critical. Still, with the exception of the Israel-Egypt peace talks, he never seemed to master international affairs. This was evident in the Persian Gulf. Iran had been for years one of the two pillars in the region (Saudi Arabia was the other). At first, Carter criticized Iran for its human rights record. This undermined the Shah, who was already under pressure. Then, over New Year's Eve 1977 to New Year's Day 1978, he visited the Shah in Tehran and called Iran "an island of stability in one of the more troubled regions of the world" at exactly the moment that Iran was boiling over domestically. Rouhollah Mousavi Khomeini (to be forever known as Ayatollah Khomeini) led the conservative clerics in denouncing the Shah. Khomeini had been living in exile in the key Shi-ite holy city of Najaf—in Iraq—for the previous thirteen years. The Shah had exiled Khomeini in 1964, when the cleric condemned the Shah's corruption and his subservience to Israel and the United States, and compared him to the Umayyad caliph, Yazid.

The comparison was loaded. Caliph Yazid was the third successor after the death of the Prophet Mohammed and was particularly re-viled by the Shia branch of Islam. He was considered a corrupt tyrant who had betrayed the Prophet's message when he defeated (and be-headed) Hussein Ali, Mohammed's grandson, precipitating the split in Islam between Shia and Sunni.

From Najaf, Khomeini was in contact with fellow Shia clerics in Qom, Iran, providing inspiration and guidance. There was a continu-ous flow of communications and pilgrims between the two cities. The power of religion and ideas easily permeated geographic borders—ultimately, with dramatic results.

In September 1978, Anwar Sadat, Menachim Begin, and Carter produced the Camp David Accords. At the same time, on the margins of the UN General Assembly meeting in New York, the foreign min-isters of Iran and Iraq met to discuss a problem that signaled things were coming unglued elsewhere in the region. The Iranian foreign minister asked the Iraqi foreign minister to expel Khomeini from Najaf. Baghdad agreed and told Khomeini he must give up his politi-cal activity or leave. He left Iraq on October 3, 1978, for Paris. It would be a short stay.

Saddam had done deals with the Shah before. Baghdad had a long-standing conflict with rebellious Kurds in the north of Iraq. A people famously without any homeland but residing largely in western Turkey, northern Iraq, and northwestern Iran, the Kurds had been fighting against central governments (and among themselves) for years. Iran had been supporting the Kurds with arms and other re-sources in their battle against the Iraqi Army. This was simple power politics by the Shah. The Kurdish insurgency was a distraction for Saddam; it required him to locate troops in the north. The Shah, meanwhile, wanted more control over the vital Shatt al-Arab water-way in the south, which controls access to Iraq's only ports (and oil tanker loading). The ongoing border dispute between Iraq and Iran was sometimes violent.

In 1975, Baghdad agreed to a deal whereby the Shah would abandon support for the Kurds, and Saddam conceded (temporarily, as it turned out) on the border issue in the Shatt al-Arab. The Shah made an enemy of many Kurds by this sellout. Some, particularly the group now known as the Patriotic Union of Kurdistan (PUK), headed by Jalal Talabani (who also became president of Iraq in 2005), developed a strong relationship with the Shah's opponents. Partly motivated by revenge, the PUK and Talabani enthusiastically supported the revolutionary followers of Ayatollah Khomeini.

Saddam was aware of the fragility of the secular leadership of the Shah and the power of the clerics, particularly Khomeini. What's more, Saddam had to account for Shia religiosity in Iraq. He understood the various Shia clerics and senior ayatollahs and kept them divided. He did not want the equivalent of an Ayatollah Khomeini in Iraq developing a combination of political and religious power. At the same time, he dealt with the Kurds by feeding their natural divisions.

The Shah lasted only three more months after Khomeini was expelled from Iraq, yet this regional conflict did not rise to the top of Carter's foreign policy agenda until it really blew up. U.S. focus was still on U.S.-Soviet affairs. Carter and Communist Party Chairman Leonid Brezhnev signed the Salt II Treaty on June 18, 1979. By September, Carter had the lowest approval rating of any president in decades. On November 4, 1979, the U.S. Embassy in Tehran was taken over. Thus ensued the hostage crisis that consumed the rest of his presidency. A month later, on December 4, Carter announced his hopeless reelection bid.

A couple weeks later, the Soviets invaded Afghanistan. This was no surprise to anyone, except possibly Carter, who seems to have judged that the importance of SALT II to Brezhnev would outweigh the impulse to militarily secure Afghanistan as a client state. Invasion would scuttle the prospects for ratifying the treaty in the U.S. Senate, where it had never been viewed favorably.

The intelligence community had watched the Soviet actions closely. Analysts monitored all the expected indicators, like military support flights and both military and political communications. They provided solid warning to the White House. Hawks in the Carter administration saw the Afghanistan invasion as an opportunity to tie down the Soviets. His national security advisor, Zbigniew Brzezinski, purportedly said, "That secret operation was an excellent idea. It had the effect of drawing the Russians into the Afghan trap and you want me to regret it? The day that the Soviets officially crossed the border, I wrote to President Carter: We now have the opportunity of giving to the USSR its Vietnam War."[5] The Soviets stayed and bled for ten years. Bagram was a major Soviet airbase from 1979 to 1989.

Covert support for any Afghan opponents or warlords, as long as they were shooting at the Soviets, was fine. The United States encouraged regional countries to support these efforts financially or with matériel. The Saudis and others pitched in. The United States even provided the sophisticated shoulder-fired antiaircraft Stinger missiles to offset Soviet helicopter and aircraft advantages. This aid was all funneled through Pakistan.

Saddam viewed the world in 1980 as an opportunity for Iraq. The Soviets, who supplied him with arms and a small nuclear reactor (as did French Prime Minister Jacques Chirac in 1975), were now tied up in Afghanistan. Washington reacted publicly to the Soviet invasion by not seeking SALT II ratification and not attending the Moscow Olympics; it reacted privately by funding the mujahedeen. The UN Security Council was split between two veto-bearing members.

Saddam was acutely aware that the Shah's regime had crumbled and fundamentalist clerics were trying to take over. A Shia theocracy in Tehran would be a much greater threat to Saddam than the Shah, if it solidified. The Khomeini clerics could have dangerous influence over the Shia-dominated south of Iraq. The potential vulnerability Saddam had to the Shia became suddenly clear when the Iraqi Dawa Party, long supported by Iran, attempted to assassinate Tariq Aziz, the foreign minister at the time, at Mustansiriya University in Baghdad on April 1, 1980. Saddam also understood that the key institution that would oppose Khomeini was the Shah's secular military. Khomeini had to eliminate that element for his Shia theocracy to take root. From Saddam's perspective, this was a window of vulnerability on the part of Iran.

On a couple of occasions, I personally discussed with Aziz the attempted assassination. He was convinced that the Iraqi Shia Dawa Party, which took credit for the grenade attack on him, was acting with the strong support of Iran. It was part of the provocations he believed Saddam was confronting. Aziz acknowledged that Iraq also backed Iranian dissidents called the Mujahidin-e Khalq (MEK), who would episodically conduct raids in Iran.

The day after the attack on Aziz, Saddam went to Mustansiriya University to give a speech that put Iran and its supporters on notice. He referred to the famous defeat of the Persians by the forces of the Caliph Umarr, the second caliph to succeed the Prophet. In circa 636, a few years after the death of Mohammed, Islamic forces crushed larger numbers of Persians at the battle of al-Qadisiyah (located near today's Hilla in Iraq). Saddam said, "In your name, brothers, and on behalf of the Iraqis and Arabs everywhere we tell those Persian cowards and dwarfs who try to avenge al-Qadisiyah that the spirit of al-Qadisiyah as well as the blood and honor of the people of al-Qadisiyah who carried the message on their spearheads are greater than their attempts."[6] Saddam began a crackdown against the Dawa Party.

Saddam made membership in the Dawa Party punishable by death and expelled tens of thousands of Shia of Iranian origin. Deportations of Iraqi Shia to Iran reached about 400,000, according to a 1985 estimate of the UN High Commission for Refugees in Tehran.[7] Saddam ordered the arrest and execution of Mohammed Baqr al-Sadr (and his sister), who was a senior Iraqi Shia cleric and one of the early organizers of the Dawa Party in the 1950s. Baqr al-Sadr had studied with Khomeini while Khomeini was residing in Najaf. Now, Saddam made him a martyr. (He was succeeded by his cousin, Mohammed al-Sadr, a noted cleric who was subsequently assassinated in 1999. Mohammed al-Sadr was the father of present firebrand Moqtada al-Sadr.)

It was also at this time that 'Abd al-Aziz al-Hakim left Iraq for Iran. He, too, had been a student of Mohammed Baqr al-Sadr, and his family had suffered the consequences of opposing Saddam and his secular Sunni-dominated government. Al-Hakim formed the Iraqi external opposition group called the Supreme Council for Islamic Revolution in Iraq (SCIRI).[8] This group, too, was largely based in Iran and was certainly supported by Ayatollah Khomeini and his successor, Ayatollah Khameni, in opposition to Saddam's secular government.

In April 1980, Saddam understood that the growing threat posed by the Dawa Party and Shia opposition would balloon under the theocracy Khomeini was creating in Iran. For Saddam, this was an opportunity to act while Iran was weak and the superpowers distracted. With the Iranian revolutionaries holding American hostages, Washington was helpless. The futility was even more pronounced when on April 24, 1980, President Carter's rescue attempt failed badly with a crash between a helicopter and a C-130 aircraft at a location named Desert One.

From Saddam's view, the Iranians were in chaos and were close to being Washington's biggest enemy. The Shah's military leadership was being removed, and the lines of authority disrupted at a moment when Iraqi forces were as strong as they had ever been. With the two superpowers distracted, Saddam must have asked himself, "What would Saladin do in these circumstances? What would Nebuchadnezzar do?"

Saddam decided they would have engaged in preemptive war. If the Soviets could invade Afghanistan, why couldn't he invade Iran? A quick and inexpensive military victory against Iran to recover the Shatt al-Arab access and other concessions seemed logical. Inaction was too risky. As Khomeini solidified his power, so too would grow the power of the Dawa Party with Iranian support.

Twenty-six years later, committing the crime for which he was ultimately convicted and hanged, Saddam conducted a series of atrocities in the town of Dujail. Few outside Iraq were aware that the violence was retribution for a Dawa-organized assassination attempt against him there in 1982.

Dawa members also were responsible for bombing the American and French embassies in Kuwait in 1983, although current Iraqi Dawa members say those Dawa bombers had been co-opted by Iran. One Dawa Party member who escaped and was convicted and sentenced to death in absentia was to reemerge in the Iraqi Parliament in 2006 under Jawad al-Maliki. Maliki himself was deputy head of the Dawa Party before becoming the Iraqi prime minister and President Bush's partner in building democracy in Iraq. Saddam was hanged by the order of Prime Minister Maliki, and the videos recorded the frenzied witnesses chanting the name of Mohammad Baqr al-Sadr. Revenge was served cold.

Throughout the 1980s, the U.S. policy was described as "tilted" toward Saddam's Iraq and against Iran. This was no small incline, and Tehran knew it. The Iranians supported the Dawa Party actions against the United States and other Western powers that supported their enemy, Iraq. The plague of terrorist acts against the United States in Lebanon, including the hostages taken in Beirut, as well as attacks against other symbols of American power had common threads running through revolutionary Iran. I spent much time working a variety of State Department antiterrorism activities and task forces in response to Iranian-backed terror attacks. It was in response to these acts that the State Department created and led a secret Emergency Support Team that would respond to terrorist actions, especially hijackings, around the world. At various times, we ran joint training exercises in the Middle East, Southeast Asia, the Caribbean, and elsewhere. Among the lead terrorist bad guys were the Iranian surrogates and groups backed by Iran, including the Dawa.

On Friday, June 14, 1984, hijackers took over TWA Flight 847, and for the next two weeks, a drama played out over the international media as the aircraft went to Beirut then to Algiers and back to Beirut. The hijackers demanded the release of hundreds of Shia prisoners held by Israel and the release of the Dawa prisoners held by Kuwait. The image of a hooded hijacker holding a semiautomatic pistol to the head of pilot John Testrake became emblematic. During the ordeal, navy diver Robert Stetham was beaten and shot in the head, and his body was dumped on the tarmac at Beirut International Airport, all on international television.

This hijacking, one of the most prominent of the 1980s, concentrated the Reagan administration's policies on terrorism. In the end, Israel released prisoners because they were going to be released anyway. The Dawa prisoners were not released. Neither were any of the other U.S. hostages held in the Bekaa Valley by Hezbollah or other Iranian-backed groups.

The strenuous efforts by Washington in 2002 to establish links between Saddam's regime and the present headline terror group, al-Qaeda, must have confused Baghdad. Baghdad would have recalled the terror acts committed by some Dawa members in the 1980s (with apparent support from Iran) against the United States.

Today, Washington has facilitated the Dawa Party's assumption of power in Baghdad, wittingly or not. Washington now accepts Dawa as a moderate group, just as Washington came to accept Yasir Arafat, who was on our threat list during the 1980s. Time moves on, and memories, at least in Washington, are short. Saddam's long memory contributed to his miscalculations. Dawa Party members have a memory as well. In the spring of 2003, more than one former regime member told me that they had seen their names on death lists circulated by Dawa elements in the chaos following the invasion.

So by his own irresistible rationale, on September 22, 1980, Saddam's forces invaded Iran. He elected to execute a preemptive war that he calculated would go quickly. If he waited, his enemy would only get stronger. His war of choice was based on a logical strategic assessment, but it turned into a costly disaster.

Initial advances were stalled as young Iranians responded to the national threat. Iraq's army was better organized, better led, and better equipped. Saddam had bought thousands of tanks, armored vehicles, and artillery pieces. He had hundreds of aircraft and helicopters. By these measures, he had three to five times the military capacity that Iran had. Invasion forces, however, don't have knowledge of the terrain they are occupying, and the invasion was a great recruiting tool for the Khomeini regime. And ultimately, the demographic disparity played a huge role. Iraq's population was around 13.5 million, about half that of Iran's. (Both have since doubled.)

Like World War I, a deadly ground war of attrition developed and lasted until 1988, when a UN-brokered ceasefire was agreed on. Saddam declared a victory against the Persians and built some of Baghdad's more memorable monuments, including the famous pairs of huge crossed swords at either end of the ceremonial parade area in the Green Zone. At the bottom of the swords are thousands of Iranian helmets from the battlefield. Virtually every American who has passed through Baghdad these days has a picture of those swords.

Hundreds of thousands died on both sides. Hundreds of thousands more were injured and maimed. Saddam was explicitly supported by the West with weapons sales and economic aid. Two major factors underlay this bias. First and foremost was that Iraq was fighting a clear enemy of Washington. The Khomeini regime had humiliated both the Carter and the Reagan administrations. Iraq was fighting Washington's enemy. It was a classic war by proxy.

The second reason was economic. The United States and the rest of the West have a vital interest in keeping access to gulf oil. It would be a major setback to have the Khomeini regime controlling not only Iran's oil reserves (which are comparable in scale to Iraq's) but also the Shatt al-Arab and choke points in the lower gulf, through which vulnerable tankers ceaselessly sailed. Washington could not afford for Baghdad to lose. This message was made clear to Baghdad by U.S. Secretary of State George Shultz to Tariq Aziz in personal meetings and even by Donald Rumsfeld, acting as a special envoy to Saddam Hussein in December 1983.[9]

Iraq also offered huge business opportunities through the 1980s. Western interests competed for Iraqi business to replace what they had lost in Iran. Saddam was spending billions on weapons, agriculture, and infrastructure. He bought thousands of tanks from the Russians and hundreds of jets and air defense systems from the French and Russians. By 1983, the French were anxious to sell him their top fighter, the Super-Etendard, and their Exocet missiles. (The Iraqis fired an Exocet missile at the USS *Stark* and killed a number of U.S. sailors on May 17, 1987. Saddam apologized and paid a high compensation figure of $27 million.) He bought turn-key arms-manufacturing plants. Most of the acquisitions were on credit.

Saddam had an instinctive understanding of power and leverage. He would have grasped as obvious the American expression "If you owe the bank a thousand dollars, they own you. But if you owe the bank a million dollars, you own them." The U.S. State Department estimated in 1983 that Iraq was spending about $12 billion annually on military imports and $6 billion on commercial imports while earning only $6 billion from oil sales. Baghdad was also getting billions in aid (mostly loans) from the other Gulf States and was going deeper and deeper into debt. This was the Iranian strategy: to simply burn Iraq out of resources and bodies.

Iran had one resource that it applied with ruthless abandon. The country had hundreds of thousands of young men. By motivating these youth through religious zeal, the clerics organized massive human wave attacks against Iraqi positions. These were not the tactics of a conventional army. Tens of thousands found the martyrdom that the clerics described. The Iraqi Army, though better equipped, could not match this force conventionally.

Tariq Aziz described the Iraqi dilemma to me many times. The first was in 1994, at a dinner the Iraqis hosted for Swedish diplomat Rolf Ekeus and me in New York during one of his visits to the United Nations to discuss the UN disarmament process. I was seated next to Aziz, and he turned to me to say, "You know, Mister Duelfer, the Persians initiated the use of nonconventional weapons against us in the 1980s war." It was the first time I had heard the suggestion that the mass application of fanatical suicidal forces would be equated with WMD.

Aziz had thick-lensed, dark-rimmed glasses that made him appear slightly bug-eyed, and it was difficult to read his eyes from the side. That night, he was also surrounded by the usual cloud of smoke from an ever-present Cohiba cigar. He was not an imposing person physically, and he gave very little away. It was very rare that he would open a discussion. In an official meeting, he would typically call on the other side to begin.

Aziz knew I was familiar with the U.S.-Iraq relationship during the 1980s. He also knew that Ekeus and I were trying to account for Iraq's chemical weapons and that things didn't add up. What he said, though, was surprising because I had not yet gotten in the practice of thinking about how the world looked from Baghdad. I was expecting Aziz to say that Iran had begun using mustard rounds against Iraqi positions.

"The religious fanatics who took over in Tehran would preach to the very young men—boys, really—in Iran. Their message was that they would reach paradise instantly if they died in battle. They would be serving Allah, and Allah would reward them."

Aziz went on: "They brainwashed these youths, saying that they would have many virgins when they reached paradise and so they threw themselves in suicidal waves against Iraqi forces. Our army had to respond by killing them in the thousands with machine guns and canons. It was an inhuman act by the mullahs."

It was hard to argue with him. The human wave attacks were incredible. I had read the intelligence reports and wondered how kids could do such things. What was it like to try to run across the southern Iraqi marshes with memories of home and family interrupted by sudden flashes of hot metal or a suffocating cloud of chemical agents?

Thousands threw their lives away in short dashes into the Iraqi fire. But the Iraqi lines fell back. Aziz was tacitly acknowledging a point that Iraq would not state publicly—that Iraq had used chemical weapons to repulse the Iranian human-wave attacks. Aziz argued that there was little difference in the horrendous damage inflicted by bullets, land mines, and artillery rounds tearing through flesh and the effects of chemical agent. It was the same argument the British and Germans had used to explain gas attacks in World War I.

In 1983, Washington made an explicit decision that it was necessary to keep the Straits of Hormuz open, militarily if necessary. This was inscribed in National Security Decision Directive 114 (NSDD-114), which was signed by President Reagan on November 26, 1983. Five months later, on April 5, 1984, following a tour of the region by Special Envoy Donald Rumsfeld, Reagan signed NSDD-139, requiring a plan to prevent Iraqi defeat in the Iran-Iraq War. In the summer and fall, an interagency study of ways to help Iraq was conducted. At the time, it was clear that Iraq was already using chemical weapons. Washington wrestled with its concern over chemical weapons, but its priority was clear—and the Iraqis, especially Saddam, got this message from the top.

When Rumsfeld met with Saddam in December 1983 as a presidential envoy, he delivered a letter from President Reagan. Chemical-weapons use was not mentioned. Rumsfeld only raised the issue of chemical weapons with Tariq Aziz in a later, lower-level meeting so that Washington would be on the record as objecting to their use. But both Rumsfeld and, later, George Shultz made clear that the use of these weapons would not block the improving relations between Iraq and the United States.[10]

The United States could not completely ignore the use of chemical weapons, however. It made a public condemnation in March 1984, but when, shortly thereafter, the United States learned that Iran was massing troops for another wave of attacks in the central front where Iraq was unprepared, the knowledge was shared with Iraq. One of the reactions was a statement by Saddam's army chief of staff, General Nizar Khazraji, who was quoted on February 22, 1984, as saying that the Iranians should know that "for every harmful insect, there is an insecticide capable of annihilating it, whatever their number." Clearly, Iraq valued our intelligence. In fact, U.S. intelligence was used by Iraq to target the chemical munitions against Iranian troop concentrations. Inevitably, the Iraqis believed they could ignore any concerns expressed about chemical-weapons use.

I met later with General Khazraji in Amman, Jordan, on May 16, 1996, after he had defected from Iraq. I was with UNSCOM colleagues. Khazraji was clear that the weapons worked both on the battlefield and as a deterrent. Militarily, Iraq had needed them. Iraq used 101,000 artillery rounds and aerial bombs filled with chemical agent. From Baghdad's perspective, chemical weapons saved the day.

Washington's thaw with Baghdad continued through the 1980s. The Iranians had counterattacked Iraq and occupied territory on the Iraqi side of the Shatt al-Arab. In November 1983, Ambassador Nizar Hamdoon arrived in Washington to head the Iraqi interest section, which was then housed in the Algerian Embassy. (Formal diplomatic relations between the United States and Iraq were suspended after the Six Day War in 1967.) Within a year, on November 26, 1984, full diplomatic relations were reestablished and Ambassador Nizar Hamdoon took office in the Iraqi Embassy. That same day, Foreign Minister Tariq Aziz was welcomed by President Reagan at the White House. Iraq was America's new friend in the region.

CHAPTER 3

Shaping Regime Perspectives

Ambassador Nizar Hamdoon was articulate and shrewd. He was cautious by nature, which had a lot of survival value in Iraq. Hamdoon was born in 1944 to a Sunni family. He emphasized to me that he studied in Baghdad at a school run by American Jesuits and graduated from there in 1960. His English was very good. In high school at the age of fifteen, he had joined the Baath Party in the aftermath of the popular coup by Abdul Karim Qasim, which toppled the monarchy in 1958. Hamdoon insisted that he was not a fervent Baathist, but a kid joining something that had broad popular appeal. What does a fifteen-year-old know? He added that the theoretical doctrine of the party was not the problem; the problem was the purposes to which Saddam later put the party infrastructure.

Hamdoon went on to earn a degree in architecture and city planning at the University of Baghdad. He had a brief period in the military and spent much of his time in the 1970s working for the Baath Party headquarters. I was never clear what he did there, but had heard from other Iraqis that he was in Lebanon running agents against Syria—not a friend to Iraq at that time. It was unproven, but believable. He certainly seemed familiar with that sort of business. On the other hand, Hamdoon also spent some time at the Iraqi Ministry of Culture and Information. He was quite conversant about Iraqi history and art.

When Hamdoon first came to Washington, he had not had much exposure to the West, but he was a very fast learner. He was quick to engage with other diplomats, the press, and businesspeople. He became very smooth very quickly. A regular visitor to the U.S. State Department's Near Eastern Bureau, Hamdoon became close to the key officials there. Those officials had to deal with the daily issues surrounding the Iran-Iraq War, and Hamdoon did everything possible to support the rationale for favoring Iraq. The year before Hamdoon arrived, Iraq was removed from the list of countries that sponsored terrorism. This made it eligible for some U.S. aid and exports. This occurred even as the State Department first confirmed that Iraq had used chemical weapons against Iran.

When full diplomatic relations with Baghdad were restored, Hamdoon was a close witness to the harmonization. Relations between the two countries were strong enough to handle disagreements, including those over chemical-weapons use.

In Washington, Hamdoon used the Iraqi Embassy resources to good effect. He hosted formal and informal gatherings at the embassy, and he circulated among the think tanks whose scholars help shape the trends in official Washington. Hamdoon was particularly quick to understand the role of the press; he immediately befriended some of the nation's most powerful journalists.

There were perhaps a dozen Iraqi diplomats who were skilled in translating the policies and rhetoric emanating from Saddam and his immediate lieutenants into terms that were understandable and more soothing to Washington and other Western ears. Nizar Hamdoon was one of these.

Also, Hamdoon could deliver. He knew U.S. businesses wanted access to Iraqi markets. He arranged the meetings and access. Iraq needed to import grain, especially rice. The United States needed oil, which increasingly came from Iraq. Throughout the 1980s, the relationship deepened, despite the clear horrors on the battlefield and at home in Iraq.[1]

At this time, I was in the Political Military Bureau of the State Department and found myself working on a wide assortment of so-called regional security issues, the off-the-front-page activities that were overshadowed during the Reagan years by the continuing major threat from the Soviet Union. More often than not, this involved providing military guidance or assistance in areas of turmoil. My office was known as the "little Pentagon" in the State Department. The secretary of state at that time, George Shultz, wanted his own office of military and security experts who could provide him direct links with the Pentagon and other government elements both in Washington and in the field. The State Department had a policy role and control over some resources—usually categorized as "security assistance."

Our shop was intended to straddle the world of people who could write clever memos and cables with those who could make things happen on the ground. It was a good place to be if you wanted to turn words into action. Write a short memo one day, and by the end of the week, find yourself in the middle of a desert or a jungle delivering military equipment or training.

There were also a set of real activists at the top. Besides George Shultz, Caspar Weinberger was secretary of defense, and the president's longtime friend, Bill Casey, was head of the CIA. Since then, the ability to translate ideas into action within the national security bureaucracy has become much slower.

We had some very talented and experienced military officers, some civilian political military experts, and a few adaptable Foreign Service officers (FSOs). We planned the unexpected at times, and at other times, the unexpected hit us. There was an annoying pattern that coups and hijackings (quite common in the 1980s) occurred on Fridays and inevitably wrecked weekends as staff would man the Operations Center "task forces" to organize the responses.

During the night of August 31, 1983, just before the beginning of Labor Day weekend, I was on duty in the Operations Center after some routine Beirut shelling, when some initially garbled reports announced that a Korean Airlines flight, KAL 007, had gone down somewhere near Soviet airspace. Intelligence was indicating it was shot down. A week later, I accompanied the U.S. ambassador to the United Nations, Jeanne Kirkpatrick, to the UN Security Council as her intelligence expert when she played the intercepted Soviet air defense communications with the fighter aircraft that shot down the passenger Boeing 747. It was an event that drew the attention of the world.

I had spent an unexpectedly frenetic week analyzing the interceptor aircraft tracks, the passenger flight path, aircraft inertial navigation systems (it was off course, probably because the crew punched the wrong initialization numbers into a keypad), the flights of other U.S. government aircraft in the area, and the radar track of the aircraft's spiraling descent into the sea with 269 passengers—including a U.S. congressman. It was obvious the Soviets ordered their fighter aircraft to shoot, as the pilot reported, "the target is destroyed." That much was simple. The deeper truth, as always, was harder. Did they think they were shooting an intelligence aircraft? Was it a bureaucratic bungle?

Just six months earlier, President Reagan had called the Soviet Union the "Evil Empire." This action seemed to justify the description. Anti-Soviet feelings peaked again, and détente was set back. By the same token, political factors drove how the event was interpreted and handled in Moscow. The Soviets did not acknowledge it was an accident by a civilian airliner to stray over its territory, nor a mistake on their part to shoot it down.

In the Soviet delegation at the Security Council was a political officer named Nikita Smidovich. Ten years later, fate put us together as close colleagues at UNSCOM. Brilliant and hardworking, Nikita had a mind that seemed predisposed to disassemble events and look for underlying reasons. This underlay a key difference in our perspectives. Nikita was never convinced that things sometimes just happened. For him, there was always a reason. Conversely, I had become used to an environment in Washington that was, to a large extent, out of anyone's control. The only explanation was often, "shit happens." If there was a leak in the *Washington Post*, Nikita would search for the reason for the leak, believing that it must have a purpose. I suspect that he, and many other non-Americans, found it difficult to accept that so much that the world's last superpower does is out of anyone's control.

During our time together as UNSCOM inspectors, Nikita and I analyzed many points of the U.S.-Soviet confrontation with some nostalgia. Long evening discussions of how opponents viewed the same event revealed to us that any single event was not, in fact, the same to both observers.[2]

Though Nikita and I never said it expressly, neither his long experience in Moscow nor my experience in Washington offered much hope that anything other than continuing tragedy would come from the reflexive mechanisms of international bureaucracies. Still, we could reminisce about the confrontation over KAL 007 and the playing of the intelligence tapes, which seemed so momentous at the time, but, in retrospect, were so minor.

Nikita recalled with amusement how his ambassador made a show of not listening to the KAL 007 tape or watching the video transcript as it played in the hushed Security Council chambers. What was so critical then between two powers poised to launch thousands of nuclear weapons (or smallpox, as it turns out) all over the globe had shrunken in perspective to a pimple. A common observation Nikita would make about many issues after a long discussion or analysis was, "It doesn't really matter."

In the end, this particular tragedy was the product of an accident combined with incorrect assumptions and misperceptions. The Soviets claimed the aircraft was on an intelligence mission and the Soviet Air Defense would have suffered if they had not responded to the "American transgression." Of course, there is a long history of U.S. overflight of the Soviet Union and intelligence probing. The Reagan administration utilized this incident to support its depiction of the Soviet threat. The intelligence data was incomplete on both sides, and the politicians on both sides filled in the gaps with their interpretations on intent.[3]

In addition to the Soviet-Afghanistan War and the Iran-Iraq War, there was an assortment of regional conflicts that the United States became involved in, usually in ad hoc ways, during the 1980s. Insurgencies in El Salvador, Nicaragua, Suriname, and the Philippines were ongoing. Africa had an insurgency in Mozambique, war in Angola, and a civil war in Ethiopia. The United States invaded Grenada, Libya

invaded Chad, and of course, Israel invaded Lebanon. Terrorism was
also a regular ongoing concern. In the early to mid-1980s, it seemed as
if the average time between significant hijackings or bombings was
only weeks. Airliners were hijacked and hostages taken. Bombs were
placed in airplanes, airports, nightclubs, and embassies in Europe and
the Middle East. Frequently, the terror either took place in, or was
linked to, groups operating out of the convoluted mess in Lebanon.
The Palestinians were a major source of instability; Iran and Libya
were another. However, all this turmoil paled in comparison with the
dominant risk—thermonuclear war. If we got that wrong, tens or hundreds of millions would have been killed.

It was my luck to be involved in many of these, either in Washington or in the field. Our offices were papered with the customized
CIA maps of each of these conflicts. Satellite imagery, then treated
as highly classified and compartmented information, was a specialized tool that was a daily window into denied areas. Who, then,
would ever have imagined that twenty years later, anyone could look
at relatively high-resolution imagery from something called Google
Earth?

Among the maps that were taped to our office walls were detailed
maps of Beirut and Lebanon. Factions battled there for a variety of
reasons. Palestinians and Arafat were the bad guys then. Iran and
Hezbollah were stirring the pot. Evacuating embassies in the middle
of some mess was not unusual in the 1980s. Our office had the planning down to a routine. Then the U.S. Embassy and Marine barracks
in Beirut were blown up, and this raised concerns to a new level. The
battleship *New Jersey* lobbed sixteen-inch shells into positions in the
Shouf Mountains outside Beirut. A marine from my office was on the
ground providing range corrections. Hezbollah positions in Baalbek
were identified on imagery and targeted very carefully because of their
proximity to the tallest surviving columns from the Roman Empire.
Terrorism, as we confronted it then, was overseas, usually in the Middle East, and mostly related to the political circumstances surrounding
Palestine or Iran or both. We did not recognize the Islamic religious
theme that motivates the actors today, although it was embedded in
Hezbollah and Dawa.

The head of state most loathed by the United States in the 1980s was Libya's Muammar al-Qaddafi, who was both extremely dangerous and often inexplicable. Qaddafi made Saddam look pretty good by comparison. Tariq Aziz once asked me informally, "Why doesn't the United States go to war with Qaddafi?" It was a fair question.

At the age of twenty-seven, Qaddafi had taken over Libya and abolished the preceding monarchy in September 1969, when King Idriss was in Turkey for medical treatment. (Saddam's Baathist Party had taken over in Baghdad just a year earlier.) Qaddafi officially renamed the country the "Great Socialist People's Libyan Arab Jamahiriya." He called himself the "Brother Leader and Guide of the Revolution." On taking over, he also promoted himself to "Colonel Qaddafi." He had studied at both a Libyan military academy and the British Army Staff College in the 1960s.

Qaddafi's declared intention was to create a utopian pan-Arab society with a new political system rooted in an incomprehensible notion of social contract he deemed the "Third Universal Theory." He inscribed his ideas in *The Green Book*.

Qaddafi was all over the map. He was involved in supporting a long list of revolutionaries or terrorists around the globe—from the Irish Republican Army to Daniel Ortega's Sandinistas. He supported the Japanese Red Army and Palestinian groups like Black September. He hosted terrorist training camps.

Qaddafi thought Libya, under his leadership, should unite with Egypt and Sudan. At one point, he organized twenty thousand Libyans, who would march fifteen hundred miles to Cairo to demand unification. (Egypt, then under Sadat, blocked them at the border.) He threatened Egypt militarily, laid acoustic mines in the Red Sea, sent TU-22 bombers to hit Sudan, plotted the assassination of the U.S. ambassador to Cairo, bombed various places in London and other European capitals, and smuggled explosives regularly around the world in diplomatic pouches for a range of purposes. His "Libyan People's Bureaus" were accredited as embassies. In 1984, there was a standoff around the Libyan People's Bureau in London after the occupants had fired on anti-Qaddafi demonstrators and killed a London policewoman.

Like Saddam, Qaddafi had spent a lot of his oil revenues on military equipment, largely from France and the Soviet Union. Also like Saddam, he bought thousands of tanks and hundreds of fighter jets, bombers, radars, SCUD missiles, mines, antiaircraft missiles, and ships. Throughout the Carter presidency, the United States was selling lots of commercial goods to Libya and buying most of its oil. In one of the odder events of the time, Qaddafi sent an intermediary to persuade the president's brother, Billy, to visit Libya, where the Libyans tried to entice him to do business and to convince the president to release ten C-130s, whose delivery had been blocked.[4] The intermediary found Billy at the gas station he operated in Georgia, and Billy agreed to come to Tripoli with some of his friends as guests of Qaddafi. By most accounts, he had a memorable time. The president did not release the C-130s and finally gave up trying to improve relations with Qaddafi in December 1979, when a mob attacked the U.S. Embassy in Tripoli in support of the Iranian revolution. The rioters burned the embassy down, but did not take hostages. The last diplomats were finally withdrawn in May 1980.

There was constant friction over coastal borders, with the U.S. Navy regularly challenging extensive areas in the Gulf of Sidra—areas that Qaddafi claimed were his. Crossing his declared "Line of Death" regularly was part of the navy's job to make the point globally that self-declared maritime borders would not be accepted. At that time, Qaddafi was competing on the world stage in a way that has been forgotten today. Qaddafi marched to some personal, internal drummer that no one else could hear. He supported terrorists and insurgent groups and spent his oil wealth on weapons. He had huge domestic projects and, of course, a WMD program. His themes were not theologically based; they were not even pan-Arab in nature. It was really about Qaddafi, and Qaddafi was no friend of the United States or his neighbors, Tunisia, Egypt, and Chad. He was a megalomaniac strongman, and his example was studied closely by the recently empowered president of Iraq, who seemed almost sensible by comparison.

In 1980, Qaddafi deepened his entanglements in Chad by sending his army in a full invasion. The border area with Chad had been in dispute over the years, but no one really cared, since the area was barren desert.[5] Nevertheless, Qaddafi's view of the universe in 1980 saw it as an opportunity, and he ordered his army to support a Chadian group. He subsequently withdrew in 1981, only to reinvade in the summer of 1983.

We watched it all closely, because of Qaddafi's aggressive actions in Africa and around the globe. It was no great surprise when our morning intelligence briefer said phlegmatically, "Well, Libya has invaded Chad."

I responded with a "Huh?" and then thought for a second. "How can they tell?" I asked. Northern Chad is quite empty. The logistic lines would have to be very long just to get to southern Libya. Then they had to pass down the trails through the desert of northern Chad. For what? Didn't they learn there was nothing in it the last time?[6]

Chad was then and still remains among the top ten poorest countries on the planet. The per-capita income in 1983 was around a hundred dollars. The phone numbers in the capital were composed of three digits. The northern two-thirds of the country is a vast desert landscape dotted very occasionally with places that have names on a map. In the seventeenth century, important caravan routes passed through Chad to places more prosperous, like Timbuktu (which used to be a kingdom worth the trip). Not much has changed since then, except the trade routes vanished.

Chad does have some known oil reserves in the south, but in the 1980s, no one was thinking of investing to build the necessary pipelines to transport the oil to a coast. The huge political instabilities in Chad and the surrounding countries would have made such construction exceedingly difficult. Southernmost Chad does have some agriculture, but it is hard to imagine wanting to invade and occupy Chad for economic reasons.

France had traditionally kept a military presence in the region as part of its legacy of colonialism. Paris paid serious and close attention to its former African colonies—much more so than London, Bonn, or Rome did. Washington was content to let Paris take the lead. We were not especially pro-Chad. But we were anti-Qaddafi. And so I found myself in Chad. The White House was determined to oppose Qaddafi, but purposefully stayed in back of the French. Our guidance was to be supportive to the Chadian government in opposing the Libyans, but to coordinate with the French. This, I found, left room for a lot.

Chad's president at the time was the less-than-holy Hissène Habré. He and his key military leaders were Gorane tribesmen from the north, so the Libyan occupation of the north was a great affront to them personally. Habré's interests suddenly coincided with Washington's.

So, just after Libya invaded in 1983, I had the opportunity to organize the emergency provision of a variety of training and weapons to the Chadians. I knew my way around the assortment of U.S. agencies that had the simple weapons and the expertise to train locals on their use. The policymakers readily agreed that supporting Chad against another Qaddafi adventure was useful, especially if it helped drain the support of the Libyan Army for his gonzo leadership. Libya had a population of about four million at the time, and while its military had plenty of equipment, its personnel were not numerous. Since most of the army came from the cities along the coast (where most of Libya's population resides), the soldiers did not relish being stuck in the dusty "towns" in northern Chad. So, supporting Chad militarily made a lot of sense, though Hissène Habré was no democratic idol. Democratic idols were not the objective in the 1980s.

This approach was the same as the strategy and tactics we applied to Iraq against Iran, just on a much lower scale, a point noticed in Baghdad. Ultimately, however, the Chad action was much more successful.

In my first of what were to become, in an odd way, routine trips to Chad, I flew out with another political-military guy and a load of ten jeeps mounted with 106-mm recoilless rifles (and both regular high-explosive ammunition and fléchette rounds). Days earlier, I had been in the State Department Operations Center conference room, where the policy types were discussing aid to Chad. The Pentagon representatives were typically reluctant to part with any of their equipment. My unfair impression was that they believed it was always too good to use. We had to pry it out of their grasp. What we wanted for the Chadians was simple, easy-to-use equipment that was highly mobile.

Since the U.S. military was largely focused on the Soviet Union at that time and defense contractors had little incentive to make anything that was simple or didn't break, not much equipment of U.S. origin was useful. We identified material that had been in the Army Reserve inventory since Vietnam. The equipment was redundant, so the Pentagon agreed to hand it over, and the cargo was soon loaded onto an aircraft that I met at Dover Air Force Base.

Our C-141 mission flew first overnight to Dakar, Senegal. After twelve hours on the ground, we were to depart on a night flight arriving at the capital, N'djamena, at dawn the next day.

There is something exciting about going into a situation when you are largely on your own and do not have a clear idea when or exactly how you would get out. My colleague and I knew there would be a series of support missions going into and out of Chad, and our plan was to be on one of the outbound flights. Going in, all we really knew was that it would be weird and unpredictable and a lot more interesting than writing memos. In an odd way, these situations become normal.

There is a normalcy to political chaos. You see the same kinds of people and dynamics. Often, it's wasteful, ugly, and stupid on a large scale. But there is the attraction of excitement combined with the sense that an individual can make on-the-ground decisions that may make a positive difference. Maybe.

By midmorning the next day, we were on the ground at the N'djamena Airport, quickly unloading the cargo. The airport had a small tower, a single story "passenger" terminal, and a couple of hangars. All had substantial war damage. There was a lot of discarded and derelict aircraft and airline equipment. It was already hot, and the wind stirred up the dust. The crew set up a tactical satellite radio, which required unpacking a small dish antenna and aiming it at a satellite. It was hi-tech then, but clunky by today's standards.

I got a room at the Hotel Tchadienne. Most of the windows had been shot out during the recent fighting. There was dirt and dust everywhere, but the room had a metal framed bed and a small wooden desk and chair. It was hot and humid, but did not smell too bad. The hotel was located on the bank of the Chari River, the wide, slow-moving river that separates Chad from Cameroon. There were hippos in the river. One beast had lumbered up the riverbank and made its way into the hotel pool. No one else was about to use the pool, even without the hippo. The hippo didn't stay long, either.

The key person we worked with on the ground was Habré's aide, or chef de cabinet, Orozi Fodeibou. We got to know him, and his younger brother, quite well. Orozi appeared about thirty and was fairly tall, maybe six feet. He was lanky, as are all the northern Chadians. Orozi's face had the usual vertical scars on his cheekbones and a very lean, sculpted look. His skin was taut and a lighter shade than the deep black of the southern tribes. Orozi could be goaded into a smile, but could also produce a deadly cold stare. I liked him. He drove us around N'd-jamena in a white Toyota sedan with a folding stock AK-47.

The next day, I met a guy who was described as the chief Chadian "interrogator." It was the first time I had met this type of person. He was only about five foot seven, and he was not as lean as most of the Gorane tribesmen. But what I cannot describe is the look in his eyes. Whatever he saw when he looked at me was nothing I could imagine. When his eyes held mine, I felt as if he had my spinal cord somehow exposed to the raw air and with just a flick of his hand could send the feeling of the barbs on the rusty fishing spears ripping across my brain. I shook his hand. He smiled.

Later, I wondered what I had touched. On a subsequent trip a couple years later, I had occasion to sleep in a house near a guarded government building. Across the distance, I heard shrieks that sounded human but that might have been from an animal. Or was there, at some level, no difference? I thought of the interrogator. I would meet others like him. For some reason, I always wondered what these people did when they got old. How did they live with what they had seen and done? One thing I knew, I would not want to be a Libyan and fall into his hands.

The part of Chad that Libya occupied was desert. It had a clarity that felt quite good. The horizon was sharp and well defined. Light and shadow brought sharp contrast and sharp definition to objects—unless there was a dust storm, when everything was lost in confusion.

The Chadians who formed the bulk of Habré's army were northern tribesmen who were not well trained (or trained at all), but would make good use of the wheeled vehicles like jeeps and Toyotas with various weapons mounted on them. They would sweep in on the fixed Libyan positions and ultimately make the enemy positions untenable. The challenge in supporting the Chadians was to find suitable equipment. Direct-fire weapons were easy: point and shoot. Rocket launchers like the Soviet-designed RPG-7s were great. Mortars were too abstract. It was difficult to get the fighters to hang around long enough to listen to the instructions.

Simplicity was also good because the Chadians would use equipment until it broke. Broken equipment tended to stay broken. Desert tracks and roads were littered with abandoned military vehicles. The N'djamena Airfield had an assortment of old aircraft that had not moved in years or decades. Common to all these artifacts were their flat tires.

Repeatedly, I would be drawn to examining these depopulated machines and would stare at the minute features of the materials, especially the tires. The tough, black rubber would slowly, over years, fade to the ambient drab gray or beige that predominated in the desert heat. The desert heat would suck out the material's fluidity. The rubber would slowly harden from the outside inward. The surface cracked into hundreds or thousands of small, linear slits. Each slit offered tiny glimpses into the dark, interior of the substance. Inside, if you could look close enough, was the original deep ebony black material. And this image was just the same as the satellite images of this area of Chad. The dried wadis scratched dark lines across the gray flatness of the desert. Both looked the same. But they had different meanings.

The conflict with Libya lasted four years, during which time the French cut a deal with Qaddafi whereby they would withdraw and he would withdraw. The French pulled their aircraft out, and Qaddafi moved his forces around, though he did not really withdraw (but neither did he move to take the capital). The Libyans built up sizable bases in northern Chad at great expense. At Faya Largeau, Fada, and Wadi Doum, Libya established fixed positions and defended them with current Soviet military equipment, including MI-25 helicopters, SA-6 and SA-13 air defense missiles, radar, and armor. Much of this

Soviet equipment was of interest to the U.S. intelligence community because the U.S. Defense Department remained obsessed with the Soviet Union.

The biggest base, Wadi Doum, lived up to its name when the Chadians overran it in 1987. They swarmed over the base with dozens of vehicles, including many Toyota Land Cruiser pickups with Chinese-manufactured 12.7-mm machine guns or 40-mm grenade launchers mounted in the truck beds. The Libyans were overwhelmed. They fled into the desert, but most—hundreds—were captured or killed. The Chadians did the same at the other two Libyan bases in Chad, Fada and Faya Largeau.

Left behind was virtually all their Soviet equipment. This was a great opportunity. At that point, military intelligence on Soviet equipment was in short supply and there was funding available to acquire such intelligence. So a perfect way to provide the Chadians with financial support would be to buy their captured Soviet equipment (which they could not use), and then the Chadians could buy the equipment they did need. And that's what happened, with one further complication. I had to go to Paris to negotiate what amounted to a time-sharing agreement with French Major General Henrion. I managed to get on pretty well with the French both in Chad (where there was a mix of regular military, intelligence, and Foreign Legion personnel) and in Paris at the Foreign Ministry. The French wanted to share in the exploitation of the equipment. We paid for it, but so what? We made the deal, which was good for everyone except the Libyans. (Even the Soviets got to sell more equipment to Libya.)

The Chadians then went further. They attacked a Libyan base in southern Libya. Same tactics, same results, except that most of the Libyans fled the base when the Chadians swept in. I spoke afterward to one of the Chadians who led the raid. He said his guys only briefly occupied the base. The Libyans had deserted. The Chadians found a couple of Russians and ordered them into a truck, with the intention of bringing them back to N'djamena. The Russians hesitated. When ordered into the truck again, the Russians still did not move. So, the Chadians killed them. They then withdrew from the base to the surrounding hills, where they intended to spend the night. The Libyans who had fled returned to the base. Not long after, Libyan aircraft bombed the base—with a chemical agent, according to the Chadian. Thinking the Chadians were still at the base, the Libyans gassed their fellow countrymen instead.

It was 1987, the same time at which Saddam was using chemical agents against Iran.

I was never sure why Habré had wanted to strike in Libya, except maybe because he could. It definitely infuriated the French. They thought the United States was behind it. We certainly gave Chad some vehicles, including some well-armed dune buggies—the real road warriors.[7]

The Chad-Libya conflict was typical of the conflicts and dynamics of the time. It was not so much that the United States had a strong interest in, or affinity with, the Chadians, but that we strongly objected to the actions of Qaddafi. Terrorist incidents were frequent and graphic. Libya was directly behind many of them or provided support. The Labelle Disco bombing in West Berlin in April 1986 was the last straw for the Reagan administration, which conducted a bombing raid against sites in Libya with the thinly disguised goal of killing Qaddafi. He survived, but got a strong message. France, despite our cooperation in Chad, did not cooperate and refused overflight clearances to the U.S. aircraft originating from bases in the United Kingdom. Without these clearances, the F-111 bombers had to fly three hours longer. It was rumored that word of the attack was leaked in advance to Tripoli, from the request put to Paris for the flight clearances.

Libya was an important market for France, which wanted to be very independent of the United States. French oil companies had strong interests in the Libyan fields—especially after the United States unilaterally declared an embargo on Libyan oil and the export of U.S. oil technology to Libya in 1982.

The U.S. raid in 1986 created limited damage. I examined the bomb damage assessments from satellite imagery. Given the overall Libyan infrastructure, it did not amount to much. The key point was that Qaddafi survived (though an adopted daughter was reportedly killed in the strike at the Qaddafi quarters). Still, the attack definitely rattled the cage. I wondered at the time if Qaddafi's hearing was damaged and if this was why he did not appear for a while. Twenty-one years later, the new president of France, Nicolas Sarkozy, visited Qaddafi after the release of six foreign medical workers who had been under a death sentence for allegedly infecting Libyan children with HIV. Qaddafi met Sarkozy in the presence of the international press in front of a residence that had been targeted in the April 1986 raid. If you looked carefully at the pictures and video, shrapnel holes in walls were evident in the background.

The effect of this raid on modifying Qaddafi's behavior was limited. Two years after the raid, Pan Am 103 was destroyed over Lockerbie, Scotland, in a Libyan plot.[8] The brother of a marine colonel in my office was on board.

The Chadian conflict with Libya would be a footnote in U.S. history, but for one thing. The episode was scrutinized by Saddam Hussein, who made many assumptions about U.S. behavior based on the evidence in Chad.

Saddam correctly judged that how the United States (and the rest of the world) reacted to Qaddafi would be a guide to how they would react to him. He was in the adjacent region, and at almost each moment in the Libyan story, there is a parallel moment in the Iraq story. The differences tended to be in the magnitude of the forces, be they political, financial, or military. The general equations of power were the same, but the factors in the case of Iraq were larger. Iraq had three times the population, more oil, more weapons sales, and a bigger war with Iran. Of course, in the 1980s, Saddam had a real threat in the form of Iran, while Qaddafi had only token threats and enemies of his own creation. Neither Chad nor Tunisia nor Sudan nor Egypt was going to topple the government in Tripoli. The nature of Qaddafi's delusional leadership was different from Saddam's. It some ways, Qaddafi was crazier, but he modified his behavior in ways that allowed him to survive. Qaddafi also had a much more compliant domestic population to satisfy—if for no other reason than Libya's population is much smaller and has fewer underlying divisions of religion and tribes.

By the end of the decade, Saddam's experience left him certain that nothing the United States was likely to do should inhibit his regional ambitions. Moreover, Saddam saw that the United States had toyed with, but never really punished, Qaddafi. Later, an Iraqi translator told me a parable in the context of some limited strikes on Iraqi radar sites: If you hit a camel to get it to obey, you must beat it and beat it until it cries. If you stop too soon, it will bite you when you stop.

A second, almost simultaneous adventure in U.S. foreign policy also sent Saddam a confusing message: the Iran-Contra scandal.

In 1986, Lieutenant Colonel Oliver North was the energetic, creative, and perhaps too-unguided marine officer on the National Security Council (NSC) staff charged with the terrorism account. He was also the White House godfather of the Nicaraguan Contras. Under NSC heads Bud McFarlane and, later, Admiral John Poindexter, he had created a lot of running room for himself. North also developed a close relationship with Bill Casey at the CIA. The lieutenant colonel worked the bureaucracy and used the power of his White House mantel to good effect, both in Washington and around the world. His attitude of "damn the bureaucracy, we have a mission to accomplish" resonated with principals who were frustrated with the bureaucratic Lilliputians.

North presented himself as the go-to guy for the president's critical national security issues. He was a powerfully connected fixer, confident that right was on his side.

I had some interactions on both terrorism and Central American issues with North. I was predisposed to agree with him that the bureaucracy could be a threat to our own national security. I could also see how a lieutenant colonel (a GS-14 equivalent in the civil service ranks, which is to say, a midlevel action officer) could be seduced and swept away by the effects of working at the White House and communicating directly with a CIA director predisposed to compartmented, clandestine activities.

Prevalent among North's supporters was a mind-set that those who argued caution were wimps and should be cut out. And these cautious ones were. But Washington operates by laws and political considerations. Actions will be judged not just by the standards of the moment, but by future standards—often unpredictable standards. There are great risks for activists in government. Even those who charged out shortly after 9/11 to fight the global war on terrorism with youthful enthusiasm and disdain for caution may learn that later judgments may be less forgiving. The facts may also change. Extraordinary renditions, seen as justified once the gloves were off after 9/11/2001, are now seen in different light. There were the same concepts and pressures during the fight against what was, in many ways, a more regularly violent spate of terrorism in the 1980s.

Oliver North did not get in trouble because he acted against the United States. He got in trouble because the U.S. system—legal and political—is slow and sluggish. North wanted the United States to act quickly, cleverly, and forcefully. If it seemed unwilling, he would do it himself with the encouragement of Casey and Casey's immediate superiors, National Security Advisor John Poindexter and, ultimately, President Reagan. The State Department issued him a diplomatic passport in the alias "Willie B. Goode" for his travels to try to deal with Iran on the hostages their surrogates held in Lebanon.[9]

Of North's many activities, the one that blew up was the scheme to sell weapons to Iran to get that country to facilitate the release of hostages held by Hezbollah in Lebanon. The receipts were to be used to buy arms for the Contras outside congressional-imposed restrictions that had limited such aid. A number of things were wrong with this all-too-clever idea. It certainly undermined the declared U.S. policy of not negotiating with terrorists. Two features of this episode struck the Iraqis, as I later learned. One was that it was contrary to the repeated public statements by the United States. Baghdad was also getting the message that we did not particularly object to weapons being supplied by intermediaries. The second and more important observation from Baghdad concerned the leverage the Hezbollah hostage-takers derived over the huge superpower. Saddam learned that hostage taking was a very potent tool, one he would use later. American desperation to free hostages could tie the United States up in knots.

At the same time, Saddam realized that chemical weapons allowed him to thwart the Iranian manpower advantage, and Iraq narrowly escaped defeat and fought to a bloody standstill. Hundreds of thousands died. Saddam accumulated a debt through purchases of weapons, food, and civil infrastructure on credit from the West, Russia, and China. Although the first two years of the war did not do huge damage to the major growth and development that had occurred in the 1970s, by 1983–1984, Saddam had burned through his reserves and become dependent upon assistance from other Gulf States (particularly Kuwait and Saudi Arabia), which also could not afford to risk any expansion of the Iranian Revolution. The mid-1980s also became a period of crisis for OPEC. In 1985, the organization could not agree on production cuts to support prices, given the ongoing war between key members. The Saudis took a decision to roughly double their production. They did this to generate more revenue to support their cash needs, which were driven up by financial support to Iraq, and also to drive down the price, which would hurt Iran, whose production capacity was limited. They played economic warfare. Prices fell radically, roughly from $27 per barrel in 1985 to $15 in 1986.[10]

Diminished oil revenues had an effect on the combatants. In late 1986 and continuing through the end of the war, oil production and shipping became critical targets for both Iran and Iraq. What became known as the Tanker War began, with each side trying to interdict the other's shipping and neutrals being put at considerable risk. This drew the United States even further onto the side of Iraq. The U.S. Navy patrolled to protect shipping and prevent Iran from closing down the gulf and, in particular, the Straits of Hormuz. The Iranians had suicide boats, mines, and Silkworm cruise missiles, as well as a limited air force (they were unable to sustain much activity with the U.S.-built F-14s, purchased by the Shah, due to the lack of spare parts).

In 1987, there were often engagements with regular Iranian naval forces and the Iranian Revolutionary Guard. U.S. Special Forces operated from special vessels and barges to counteract Iranian Boghammar assault vessels (Swedish-manufactured, very-high-powered coastal patrol boats). I had colleagues who raided an Iranian oil platform that had been used to coordinate military attacks against shipping. Night operations using very quiet modified Hughes 500 helicopters surprised Iranian forces. The United States was more than just tilting at this point.

The Persian Gulf is a small arena for opposing militaries to fight in. In an era when aircraft and missiles measure distances between targets in minutes and warheads can devastate vessels, warning and reaction times are critical. On July 3, 1988, the USS *Vincennes* was patrolling and mistook an Iranian civilian Airbus for a threat aircraft. The Americans fired two Standard II missiles, which destroyed the target. Years later, the United States paid compensation.

Only when the Soviet empire collapsed would the United States decide it was more concerned about regional threats and would react more vigorously. The office I ran at the State Department Political Military Bureau during the 1980s was responsible for the rest of the world, or in our acronym-infected terminology, the ROW. This was how non-Soviet and non-NATO conflicts were dismissed. But by 1989, that prioritization was changing. Saddam's next major move was based on a worldview that had always contained a far different perspective than Washington's. Additionally, Washington had changed, but Saddam had no way of knowing this. And so he miscalculated again, badly.

CHAPTER 4

Negative Feedback Loop: Saddam's Miscalculations

For Saddam, the Iran-Iraq War was a grand, historic struggle. There was glory in struggle, and its magnitude suited Saddam's grandiose sense of self. Saddam was a costar on the stage with the globe's leaders.

At the end of the war, in 1988, to the outside world it seemed as though Iraq had achieved virtually nothing but disaster. The borders and access to the gulf were basically unchanged, despite the huge cost. But Saddam saw it differently. Iraq (and he embodied Iraq in his mind) had prevailed. It was a victory. Anyone in Iraq who said otherwise was in trouble.

Saddam ended the war with an army of about a million men and enough equipment to make it bigger than the army of any member of NATO except the United States. It was the world's fourth-largest standing army. Saddam had also created a massive domestic arms industry—and a massive debt.

During the 1980s, Iraq had made use of extensive U.S. loan guarantees through the Commodity Credit Corporation (CCC), as well as through irregular loans from the Banca Nazionale del Lavoro (BNL). In October 1989, Secretary of State James Baker pushed for an additional $1 billion program. There were also hundreds of millions of dollars of

Export-Import Bank (EXIM) loan guarantees, which had been pushed by George H. W. Bush, then vice president. The scandal surrounding the BNL loans and associated kickbacks and bribes anticipated the same Iraqi tactics a decade later with the UN Oil-for-Food program.

The Iraqi population anticipated a peace dividend. Saddam expected some forgiven debts from foreign creditors and a resurgence in oil revenues. In his view, Iraq had defeated the Persians to the benefit of all Arabs. Iraq deserved to be rewarded.

I discussed this period with Tariq Aziz many times. I slowly came to understand what he would say, even though my objective reality was very different. To Aziz, Saddam led the Iraqi nation and people, who were proud of their heritage as builders, scientists, poets, and warriors. They were energetic and deserved to lead the Arab world—in their view. The neighboring Gulf States, particularly the Kuwaitis and Saudis, were led by slow, lethargic tribes that happened, through the accident of birth, to be born on reservoirs of oil. Accidental wealth allowed them to buy friends and buy off their enemies. By history, tradition, and culture, however, they were not leaders.

Saddam was not grateful for the financial support he received from Kuwait and Saudi Arabia; he hated it. They were paying him to fight their battle against the Persians, as he saw it. What was worse, they were now keeping the price of oil down, just as they had during the later stages of the war, with the effect of not just controlling Iran, but also diminishing Iraq. Saddam could not regain his wealth without higher oil prices. His infrastructure was greatly damaged, and this limited oil production. With the prices low, incentives for Western oil companies to finance greater infrastructure reconstruction were limited. In effect, by keeping up their production, Kuwait and Saudi Arabia were cementing their regional supremacy.

There was a negative feedback loop on oil prices, as far as Saddam was concerned. Countries with limited production capacity could not pump more to make up revenues as prices fell. Saudi Arabia, Kuwait, and United Arab Emirates could, and did. And the more they pumped, the more prices tended to fall. Iraq and Iran were boxed in.

There was a special meeting of OPEC in March 1990 to address the issue of quotas, but no conclusion emerged and prices remained low. Baghdad was furious, but no one, at least in Washington, paid much attention.

In addition, there were disputes of rights to the lucrative Rumaila oil field and accusations by Iraq that Kuwait was drilling at an angle ("slant drilling") to get at oil that properly was under the Iraqi sector of the fields. Baghdad declared that Kuwait had stolen $2 billion of oil. After the Iraqis had given their blood to defeat the Persians, Kuwaitis, it seemed, were stealing from them.

April 1990 was a pivotal month in what would soon be the next phase of Iraq's modern-day tragedy. Exactly a decade after the Dawa movement had attempted the assassination of Tariq Aziz, spurring Saddam toward his invasion of Iran, Saddam again gave an aggressive speech that exposed his willingness to thrust out in any direction—and he announced that he had new, more powerful chemical weapons. He threatened to "make fire eat half of Israel if it tries to do anything against Iraq."[1]

Later, when UNSCOM was investigating the Iraqi WMD programs, I learned that Iraq had in fact just recently test-fired a modified SCUD missile *with a live chemical-agent warhead.* (U.S. intelligence did not know this in 1990.) Saddam had also ordered the Muthanna State Establishment to restart production of chemical munitions, and by the end of the 1991 war, it had produced 25,000 chemical munitions. Nevertheless, on April 12, 1990, Senator Bob Dole and a party of five other senators from agricultural states met with Saddam and provided a message from President George H. W. Bush addressing human rights and WMD and assuring the Iraqi president that Washington wanted better relations.

Four days later, Bob Gates, then deputy national security advisor under Brent Scowcroft, chaired a National Security Council "Deputies Committee" (made up of the deputies of the NSC agencies—they tended to do the real work of policy formulation and execution) to consider whether any action should be taken to address Saddam's statement. No action was taken. Gates commissioned an options paper that would be discussed a month and a half later. There was no direction to act quickly. Within the following twelve months, Saddam would invade Kuwait and lose another disastrous war, and in April

1991, the UN Security Council would approve a ceasefire resolution that would invoke coercive sanctions and disarmament. This, in fact, set the stage for yet another war twelve years later.

At an Arab summit meeting held in Baghdad on May 28, 1990, Saddam demanded from the Gulf States that their loans to Iraq be forgiven ($35 billion at the time) and that Iraq should be returned to its economic position of 1980. In essence, the latter was a demand for an additional $10 billion.

Saddam's recent experience was that the United States was supportive. Washington had made clear that it could not afford to have Iraq lose the war with Iran. And by all its actions of recent years, Washington had demonstrated that whatever it said (and that was not much) about Baghdad's use of chemical weapons and the destruction of Kurdish towns, it would not block the emerging relationship. President Bush had signed a Persian Gulf policy directive, NSD-26, on October 2, 1989. It declared that normal relations between the countries would serve long-term U.S. interests. The United States would propose economic and political incentives for Iraq to moderate its behavior. The directive also mentioned that illegal *use* (not possession) of chemical or biological weapons would lead to economic and political sanctions. Sanctions would also result if Iraq breached International Atomic Energy Agency (IAEA) safeguards. NSD-26 went on to say the United States should look for opportunities to participate in Iraqi reconstruction, especially in the energy sector. Finally, the U.S. government should consider sales of nonlethal military assistance. On Friday, October 6, 1989, Tariq Aziz met with Secretary Baker at the State Department, where Baker promised more CCC loan guarantees.

In Baghdad, Nizar Hamdoon (who had returned to be deputy foreign minister in September 1987) provided his assessment of Washington's direction. His view was based on close relations and extensive informal opinions he heard from now senior Americans. Hamdoon was confident that the United States wanted to develop further its links with Baghdad. When I saw him in the 1990s in New York in the Iraqi UN mission, his office displayed many pictures of himself and senior American officials. The most prominent one was a picture of Hamdoon and Bill Clinton. It was signed, "All best wishes, Bill."[2]

Such was the background for Saddam's assessment of regional dynamics. He saw two main powers—Iraq and Iran (in addition to Turkey and, of course, Israel). When he spoke with senior Iraqi ministers about the other Gulf States, the ministers basically described these states as just oil reservoirs with Bedouin tribesmen sitting on them, thinking that they were real countries. The disdain was not disguised. The Iraqi view was that these Bedouin would find they had to deal with Iraq, not Iran.

In 1989 and 1990, Iraq's dialogue with Kuwait went from bad to worse. At one point, Tariq Aziz described to me the insolence of the Kuwaiti side when its negotiator dismissed the Iraqi side with a statement of "talk to my hat."

Saddam had a massive army and weapons of mass destruction. He had oil reserves, but just could not get out of his current financial straps. The war with Iran cost Iraq roughly a half trillion dollars, figuring direct costs, GNP losses, and destroyed oil infrastructure. Iraq owed billions to its neighbors Kuwait and Saudi Arabia, and billions to its Western backers for arms, infrastructure, and food. And Iraq owed the Soviets, now clearly in decline, billions for weapons acquisition and training. Saddam was the local Gulliver held down by the Gulf Lilliputians. He needed another struggle to survive.

In the spring of 1990, Saddam's speeches became still more bellicose. He began to threaten Kuwait, but Kuwait gave nothing in the negotiations. By July, according to senior Iraqis I spoke with later, the military was moving almost unstoppably.

Saddam had no reason to believe that if the United States did react, it would be anything other than a limited bombing raid such as what Reagan had authorized against Qaddafi. The United States had not acted militarily in any serious way when Iran humiliated it by seizing its embassy in Tehran or when more hostages were seized in Lebanon. Only limited U.S. air strikes were conducted against Libya in response to the bombing of a disco in Germany. Nor did the United States react militarily when Pan Am 103 was blown up in December 1988 (the Libyan connection took much longer to nail down definitively). What's more, the United States had largely ignored Iraq's massive use of chemical weapons and the gassing of Kurdish villages and their complete razing, which was no secret and showed up perfectly well in satellite imagery.

I remember these images. Satellite imagery is antiseptic. The black-and-white pictures did not really communicate what happened on the ground. It was one of the growing appreciations I acquired as an analyst in Washington, reviewing pictures and words and comparing them to the reality when later I stepped physically into the "ground truth" presented in those same picture frames.

Aerial photography showing bomb damage may show crater impact points. It may show a collapsed roof. On the ground you see the ring of shrapnel holes perforating the sides of buildings at a human level. From aerial imagery, you see a vehicle-mounted cannon of some sort. On the ground, you may see that it is a recoilless gun with fléchette rounds—a gun that fires thousands of slivers in a lethal cloud that can pin bodies to trees in a way that no artist would paint St. Sebastian. Fear does not show up on satellite imagery. Objective assessments based on countable things that show up on film were idealized in Washington. It was a remote kind of truth. Truth on the ground or truth in other people's minds, I came to see as different. Only when Halabja was gassed and pictures and video of the victims were widely seen in the West was there some shift in the calculations of reality in Washington.

Saddam knew the reality on the ground. He knew what a razed village was and the terror it would instill. It was one of his methods of government. Saddam had done it, and Washington had accepted it. He concluded that the last superpower was pragmatic—like the Russians and French and other non-Arab powers that did business in Iraq. The United States had become a major consumer of Iraqi oil during the 1980s.[3]

Why would Saddam think that the United States would do anything that could ultimately threaten his regime? The only way the Russians, the Europeans, and even the Americans could hope to recoup their loans to Iraq would be if he got free of the economic choke that he saw Kuwait and Saudi Arabia applying. He would have gotten away with it, too, had the Soviet Union not just dissolved. But the overarching dynamics of the world—certainly those that would govern how the United States behaved—had radically changed, marked by the destruction of the Berlin Wall in late 1989. American forces were no longer fixed in place by the Soviet threat. The NATO-Warsaw Pact balance had the effect of *locking down* the vast majority of U.S. forces. This is easy to forget now, but for the United States to use any sizable military force "out of area," meaning out of the NATO context, was virtually impossible. Small, minor operations, like Grenada or bombing Beirut or Libya, were one thing. Deploying major air and ground forces to some non-NATO contingency was not seriously anticipated, except for Korea, where U.S. forces remained, guarding the border between North and South Korea.

For Saddam (and, if one could imagine, Saddam's intelligence analysts), recent history would be a very misleading indicator for the future. The world dynamics were in flux and Saddam, looking from Baghdad, miscalculated the implications for the United States. He would make a similar mistake in 2002.

Even Nizar Hamdoon, Baghdad's most savvy diplomat in the ways of Washington, did not grasp the shifting dynamics of post–Soviet American policy.

Hamdoon had enjoyed extraordinary success in winning access in Washington. George Shultz acknowledged this success as a reason for what appears in retrospect to have been perhaps ill conceived support for Iraq: "It was a notable example of the power of diplomacy and of the difference that a deft ambassador can make."[4] Or, perhaps, hearing what you want to hear at the time.

As deputy foreign minister, Hamdoon also met with Secretary of State Baker on March 24, 1989, shortly after the Bush administration had come to power.[5] Still, he could not have appreciated the changed circumstances in Washington at the end of 1989. And, even if he had, Hamdoon was viewed suspiciously in Baghdad (and particularly by Saddam), precisely because he had become so immersed in the ways of Washington.

Years later, on Monday, June 3, 1996 (when he was the Iraq UN ambassador and I was at UNSCOM), Hamdoon and I had lunch at a Manhattan restaurant called the Captain's Table. We talked about how relations between Iraq and America had shifted, and he gently commented upon a dilemma he faced in 1989 and 1990. In essence, he said that he knew Washington was different with the new president and the end of the Soviet Union. But he could find no way to convey that to his leadership. His leaders had been out of touch for so long, if he stated fully what he thought it would be received very badly. He lamented the difficulty of communications.

At the time of this luncheon, there had been no diplomatic relations between Washington and Baghdad for several years, and I had increasingly found myself in a somewhat similar circumstance. There was no one in Washington who had any recent direct knowledge of Baghdad or its regime.

"Mister Duelfer," he asked me, "is it not very strange that now, if I pass Ambassador Burleigh [Peter Burleigh, then a deputy U.S. ambassador at the UN and previously a senior member of the Near East Bureau at the State Department responsible for Iraq during the Iran-Iraq War], he cannot even say hello?"

Washington was in a muddle about Iraq in July 1990. But Saddam was not; he was focused on action. He would break out of his economic and regional cage.

On the Iraqi National Day, July 17, 1990, President Bush sent Saddam a congratulatory letter proclaiming the goal of better relations. According to the U.S. ambassador to Iraq, April Glaspie, when she met with Saddam a week later, he said that he "had been touched by President Bush's letters."[6]

Touched maybe, but not appeased. In his National Day address, a major event watched carefully by the regional audience and others seeking a window into Baghdad, Saddam made one of his most bellicose speeches ever. He directly threatened his neighbors and explicitly referred to Iraq's chemical weapons. He said Iraq had defended the Arab States against the Persians and then been stabbed with a poison dagger.[7] The day before, in a memorandum to the secretary general of the Arab League, Saddam had equated Kuwait's actions with military aggression toward Iraq.

Saddam's military was going forward with its preparations to invade and occupy Kuwait. Saddam saw no reason to hesitate. While he expected that the United States would react, it was a matter of degree. He summoned Ambassador Glaspie to see him at noon on Wednesday July 25, 1990 (a week before the invasion), which was highly unusual.

Saddam, with Tariq Aziz present, referred to the potential military threat the United States could launch. He made his statement in a way that should have drawn some reaction, but Glaspie did not react to it. According to Glaspie's reporting cable, Saddam said, "Iraq knows the USG [U.S. government] can send planes and rockets and hurt Iraq deeply." The Iraqi transcript of the meeting says the same. There was no response from Glaspie saying that the American response would be much more than mere bombing. Her silence was ambiguous. Glaspie had no instructions on this point and certainly did not say, "Mister President, let me be clear: If you go into Kuwait, the United States will deploy hundreds of thousands of troops."[8]

Glaspie heard Saddam reiterate that he was pursuing negotiations and that he wanted good relations with the United States. She decided things were not critical and left Baghdad for her annual home leave. Washington did not choose to bolster its message to Iraq after her encounter. (Secretary Baker would be certain later, in his final meeting with Tariq Aziz before the war, not to repeat this mistake. He was absolutely unambiguous about the use of force and the U.S. reaction should Saddam use chemical weapons.)[9]

None of Saddam's advisors told him that if Iraq invaded Kuwait, the United States would build a thirty-two-nation coalition and deploy a half-million soldiers to the region to expel Iraq from Kuwait. Such a reaction was utterly removed from any recent experience. This was Iraq's major intelligence failure.

In a debriefing session after the war, Saddam stated that he had already decided to go into Kuwait to "take their resources" before his meeting with Glaspie. He also said that he and his advisors judged that the United States could not risk casualties. This was a recurrent theme in discussions of Iraqi calculations. They judged that the U.S. public would not support long-term costs or casualties. This assumption shaped many of Saddam's decisions. It was not unreasonable. Saddam knew he had chemical and biological weapons but no nuclear weapon yet. He calculated he did not need one. This was another mistake on his part.

Two weeks later, on August 2, 1990, Saddam unleashed the Iraqi Army and Republican Guard divisions that had been mobilized to the Kuwaiti border. Iraqi forces swarmed into Kuwait and quickly occupied the entire country, looting and pillaging whatever they could. It was ugly. The Saudis were terrified Saddam would press on into Saudi Arabia. Washington woke up.

President Bush was determined to react with international support. He had served as a CIA director, a UN ambassador, an ambassador to China (technically, a senior representative, since at the time the United States had not established formal diplomatic relations), and a vice president. He understood the international system as well as had any incoming president. Around him, he had a team composed of longtime supporters and professionals. Yet, as vice president under Reagan, he had also been part of the U.S. tilt toward Iraq.

Bush was cautious and did not immediately realize that a full military response would need to be prepared. He was the transitional president from the Cold War international dynamics to the ill-defined "New World Order." The normal handrails and gauges for evaluating international risks and balances were out of calibration. Saddam's bold invasion of Kuwait exceeded the limits for gradual retuning. Leaders had to decide in a flash what they were going to do.

The Iraq invasion of Kuwait was bad, but how bad? It was less than a Cuban Missile Crisis, which had directly threatened the United States, but where did the Iraqi action fit? Saddam clearly bet that the United States would not see it as a major, direct challenge. It was Saddam's bad luck to have chosen a moment when British Prime Minister Margaret Thatcher happened to be visiting President Bush in Colorado. Thatcher had gone through the experience of the Argentine invasion of the Falkland Islands (or Islas Malvinas, if you are Argentine) in 1982. She had galvanized the British response and built a military response that prevailed in a distant conflict.

While President Bush may have been reflective at first about how vigorous a statement to make, Thatcher made clear to him that the United States and the United Kingdom could not allow Iraq's act to stand. She sharply helped President Bush focus his priorities.

At the same time, Secretary of State James Baker happened to be in Mongolia. Baker, an old pro in Washington, had been sculpting a new relationship with Moscow. Mikhail Gorbachev and his foreign minister, Eduard Shevardnadze, were working their way through a transition. The crisis in Iraq, oddly, provided an opportunity for Washington and Moscow to consider how to work together in this new environment. Baker and Shevardnadze understood they were not just dealing with the Iraq crisis, but restructuring international dynamics. Baker's instincts were to broaden participation in the response to Iraq, which exactly matched President Bush's experience.

The UN Security Council reacted swiftly with the imposition of sanctions and an oil embargo on Iraq (UNSCR 661) on August 6, 1990. These measures were linked to Iraq's withdrawing from Kuwait. As pressure mounted and the reaction on the part of the United States became more explicit, Saddam gave a speech attacking foreign countries that occupied holy places. Shortly thereafter, he began rounding up foreigners and ordered embassies to close in Kuwait. Saddam declared that hundreds of foreigners in Kuwait and Iraq would remain as "guests" to protect high-value facilities from "outside aggression." Saddam had hostages—just as the Iranians, Hezbollah, and others had taken them.

President Bush had a very difficult time amassing the consensus to prepare for war, both internationally and domestically. The buildup of forces in the region was a massively expensive effort. Some military advisors, notably Colin Powell, then chairman of the Joint Chiefs of Staff, urged caution about how to react. He questioned if the White House really understood the level of military effort that would be required to dislodge the Iraqi occupation and asked, Was it worth it for Kuwait? His reaction was exactly what Saddam expected of the U.S. administration in general.

The Gulf States had been very cautious about accepting U.S. forces prior to Saddam's invading Kuwait. Now it was another story. But bedding down all the aircraft, basing ships, and building up mechanized ground forces to the levels General Norman Schwarzkopf required was time-consuming and very expensive. Congress was reluctant; the international community was reluctant. What was termed Desert Shield—the deployment to deter Iraq from going further into Saudi

Arabia—was doubled in size in November, when planners began to realize that expelling Iraq from Kuwait would take more ground forces. Congress became even more unwilling.

Saddam's assessment about the American reaction seemed for a while to be not far off the mark. Congress was not questioning the intelligence, which was out there in plain sight. The world was watching as Iraq rampaged through Kuwait. Iraqi troops were pillaging and raping in that long tradition. Saddam gave a grotesque television interview with the Western hostages he had taken. There was no ambiguity about the facts. The case for war did not rest on intelligence assessments. It did not depend on a single human source's claims about WMD. The intentions of the regime were clear. Saddam stated categorically that he had WMD. He said he would not retreat from Kuwait.

Yet it was not until November 29, 1990, that the UN passed a resolution authorizing the use of force if Iraq did not withdraw by January 15, 1991. Many were not sure it was in their interests to see this situation resolved militarily.

Last-gasp efforts were made at negotiation by a number of parties. In December, Texas oilman Oscar Wyatt flew to Baghdad with former Texas Governor and Secretary of the Treasury John Connally to meet with Saddam. The meeting was arranged through Wyatt's Iraqi oil business counterparts, who had lucrative shared interests. The net result was relatively good publicity for Saddam as he agreed to the release of hostages.[10]

The Russians, who had a lot to lose, also sought to mediate. Foreign Minister Yevgeny Primakov, an Arabist who was well known to Saddam, met with Bush in the White House and said that they should make one last attempt at negotiation. Primakov made clear that Saddam would fight even a doomed battle rather than capitulate, if he was not given a respectable alternative. Out of respect for Gorbachev, additional time was given for the Russian efforts. The Russians had large stakes in Iraq and eight thousand citizens there at the time of the invasion. They had trained the Iraqi Army and intelligence services.

At the end of November, Washington also offered to have a meeting between Secretary Baker and Tariq Aziz. This was done as much to win over congressional support as anything. The meeting finally took place on January 9, 1991, in Geneva—a week before the UN deadline expired. Only after that meeting did Congress debate a use-of-force resolution. After three days of debate, by a slim 52 to 47 margin, the Senate voted to authorize the use of force. Twelve years later, in strong contrast, the Senate vote on October 11, 2002, authorizing war was a lopsided 77 to 23.

In late 1990, Washington was deeply concerned that a token withdrawal would be offered by Iraq and would be sufficiently attractive to cause some members of the coalition to argue for more time for diplomatic efforts. In a break during a meeting while I was at UNSCOM in March 1994, I asked Tariq Aziz why Iraq did not make some token adjustment in its position. Did the Iraqis not know how tenuous the support in Congress was before the final vote? Did they not know how easily the coalition could be divided?

Aziz merely replied, "Our leadership knew you were intent on going to war anyway. The talks in Geneva were not serious. They were for appearances. You said you would bomb us back to the Stone Age. You see, you failed. We are a strong country. We have survived. Your government did not." He meant that George Bush lost his reelection. Saddam did not.

I pressed him a bit in his area of responsibility: "But from *your* perspective, could you not see that even small withdrawals would have strengthened your hand? Could you not have had a negotiation on the allocation of oil resources?" He shrugged. I suppose I should have known better than to even ask. Iraq's "leadership" had its perspectives, and even at tremendous cost, a struggle was preferable to Saddam's perceived loss of dignity.

From our perspective and probably the perspective of the tens of thousands of Iraqis who died in the war and under the next twelve years of sanctions, it was another monumental blunder by Saddam. More mistakes lay ahead.

It was instantly understood that the UN Security Council would be a focus of action. President Bush had been U.S. ambassador there in 1971–1973. There was no debate within the administration about involving the Security Council.

My window into the war was from the glass cage that was the State Department Operations Center. Undersecretary Bob Kimmit, Secretary Baker's lead on the Iraq crisis, wanted me in Washington to run the State Department Operations Task Force for what was about to be a war. I did not see much daylight for six weeks.

Running a task force is a thankless coordination activity. The key is to make sure all information about all aspects of an ongoing crisis gets to the correct person. There is continuous information—military, intelligence, diplomatic, consular, press, congressional, and so on—which must flow to the secretary. I suppose it requires some judgment about whether a particular report is nonsense (many are) or whether it is worth waking someone up. One of the downsides of crises in the Middle East was the eight-hour time difference. Latin American crises have the advantage of being in the same or similar time zones, and bad things didn't always happen in the middle of the night.

So I spent the 1991 war in a facility that reminded me of an ant farm I had as a kid. Besides the overexposure to fluorescent light bulbs, I remember one moment in particular. Early in the evening on January 17, 1991, the second day of the war, I received a critic alert (this was a National Security Agency urgent message) that ballistic missiles had been launched. Moments later, the secure line from the Pentagon rang with an alert that it had a satellite warning of a launch in the direction of Israel.

Instantaneously with those two messages, I realized the danger. I was a child during the Cuban Missile Crisis, when nuclear war seemed to be a real possibility. The United States regularly conducted nuclear exercises that strove to simulate a real event. Though there were some mistakes and miscalculations, it seemed a pretty remote possibility that someone might order a nuclear weapon launched. Nevertheless, I had no idea how Israel might react to a missile attack. Everyone was aware of Israel's reported nuclear capacity—certainly including Saddam. This event just seemed to turn the corner from the predictable to the wildly unpredictable.

We did not know what was on the warheads of Iraqi missiles. We knew they had chemical capabilities. We did not know for sure about nuclear. Prior to the war, there had been some intelligence reports about radiological weapons, if not actual nuclear weapons. Whatever was on the warhead of the Iraqi missile, it was going to provoke a crisis for Israel.

I woke up Bob Kimmit at home on his secure line.

"Bob," I said, "we have a critic and IR [infrared] data about at least one missile launch en route to Israel. This looks like a good report . . . not a false alarm. For what it's worth, this would be a good time for the president to call [Prime Minister Yitzhak] Shamir . . . like in the next five minutes."

Kimmit was sharp even in the middle of the night: "Got it." Click.

The Iraqis did not launch their chemical SCUD warheads. Still, the SCUDs did cause huge political problems—much more than military. And the power of potential WMD use was evident. The Israelis had to prepare for possible chemical attacks. They distributed gas masks and sealed apartments with plastic. It was terror, and as the Israelis reminded us regularly, it was always their policy to retaliate. Of course, this was what Saddam wanted. He wanted to lure Israel into the conflict with the hope that the other Arab nations would then divide from the coalition. Saddam almost succeeded. While his missiles did not cause many direct fatalities (only two in Israel, though one SCUD hit a barracks in Dhahran, Saudi Arabia, killing twenty-eight Americans), the fear and disruption throughout Israel was substantial. It was a very tough argument to block the Israelis from attacking Iraq, even if the SCUDs did not have chemical warheads. The United States provided Israel with satellite missile warning data and Patriot missile batteries and dedicated a substantial portion of U.S. aircraft sorties to SCUD hunting (around 2,500 sorties). Also, U.S. and UK special operations forces deployed in the western Iraq desert to search for SCUD launchers. These efforts failed to destroy any SCUDs, but they helped to keep Israel out of the war.

In 2004, we asked the commander of the Iraqi SCUD force about a few very curious SCUD warheads. On a couple of occasions, the SCUDs had only *concrete* warheads. Our experts speculated that these were kinetic-energy warheads intended to strike bunkers at the Israeli nuclear facility at Dimona. Instead, the commander stated that "the Leadership" intended to emulate the struggle of the Palestinians who, during the intifada, threw stones at the heavily armed Israeli soldiers. Saddam was demonstrating solidarity with the Palestinians. It was not an explanation we would have anticipated. I could not imagine a CIA missile analyst writing a paper explaining the mysterious concrete warheads as Saddam's symbolic message of throwing stones at the Israelis.

Iraq, of course, was decisively defeated. Thirty-nine days of intense bombing of the Iraqi positions wore away matériel and morale. It is no wonder that Iraqi troops surrendered in droves to any advancing force . . . even in one case to a circling, unmanned drone aircraft. The rapid ground attack lasting one hundred hours precipitated a frenzied retreat from Kuwait.

On April 3, 1991, the UN Security Council passed UNSCR 687—the formal ceasefire resolution ending the war with Iraq and setting the terms for the lifting of the embargo and sanctions. It had been an eventful year for Saddam. He crystallized the "New World Order" at the expense of the Iraqi population. It was almost exactly a year after Saddam had welcomed Senators Bob Dole and Alan K. Simpson to his palace in Baghdad with their message of friendship from President Bush (April 12, 1990). Iraq had been crushed militarily by a broad coalition and now had to verifiably destroy its WMD and the means for their production. In addition, Iraq had to accept UN weapons monitoring to assure that the programs were not reconstituted. Only when the newly created arms inspection organization UNSCOM and the IAEA (for nuclear matters) verified full Iraqi compliance would the Security Council consider lifting the oil embargo and sanctions on Iraq. This was not arms control. This was coercive disarmament, like the Treaty of Versailles imposed on Germany after World War I. And likewise, it was doomed to failure.

CHAPTER 5

The UN Resolves . . .

Those drafting UN Security Council Resolution (UNSCR) 687 in the spring of 1991 were largely unaware of the attempt after World War I to create a similarly coercive mechanism.

The drafters of the Treaty of Versailles represented a coalition that had defeated a country, but were not occupying it. They linked political and economic incentives to the verification of German disarmament by an international group they called the Inter-Allied Control Commission (IACC). The German government responded exactly as the Iraqis did seventy-one years later. They obfuscated, they blocked, they moved things around, they did all they could to inhibit the inspectors. Politically, the Germans worked to divide the coalition around them. They worked deals with the Russians, for example, to produce weapons in Russia, out of sight of the inspectors. As the attention and interests of the coalition diverged (the United States never ratified the treaty, and it pulled out of the inspection system), the position of the inspectors became progressively weaker. They became frustrated as they were caught between the German High Command, who wanted to preserve as much of their military capacity as possible, and the Allied political leaders, who became progressively more concerned about domestic economic issues. Even France, which had been the most stalwart (understandably, since it was the most likely victim of future conflict), chose to accommodate an end to inspections after a few years and a change in leadership in Paris.

The original inspection reports of the IACC are eerily similar to UNSCOM reports. It almost appeared that Iraq had studied the previous efforts and learned from them. Or, more likely, it was simply that international dynamics played out the same way under similar circumstances.

The IACC lasted about the same length of time as UNSCOM lasted, and ended before its mission, as defined in the Treaty of Versailles, was accomplished. Coercive disarmament as a method of containment can buy some time, but nothing more.

The drafters of UNSCR 687 were pleased that they appeared to contain Saddam in an internationally agreed-upon web. However, it could not last forever. As Charles de Gaulle reportedly said in the 1960s (referring to a treaty between France and Germany): "Treaties are like roses and young girls. They last while they last."

The members of the Security Council had scrambled to create the ceasefire resolution—sort of. They had informal meetings and consulted between long lunches, dinners, and receptions. A text was drafted in Washington and circulated around capitals. Washington was by far the dominant player since it had expended most of the effort to win the war. Nevertheless, others, particularly the French, used their leverage (the potential to veto any draft) to the fullest. They had lost a major market in Iraq, and that was quite a sacrifice. Only after a long period of refusal and great reluctance, they provided information to the Coalition air forces about the Iraqi air defense system that they had sold to Saddam (called Kari, which backward is the French spelling of *Iraq*).

The French had opposed creating a new inspection organization to disarm Iraq. They believed the International Atomic Energy Agency (IAEA), then headed by Hans Blix, was the appropriate body. They did not recognize the distinction between what the IAEA monitored (a nuclear treaty that parties join voluntarily) and the coercive disarmament obligation being forced on a vanquished aggressor state. The agreed-on compromise that Washington established was a new organization reporting directly and uniquely to the UN Security Council for all matters except judgments about Iraq's nuclear program. The argument for separating nuclear matters turned on the fact that Iraq was a party to the Nuclear Non-Proliferation Treaty (NPT). The NPT was the raison d'être for the IAEA. Of course, Iraq had earlier broadly violated the treaty, and the IAEA monitoring regime had not detected its violations.

The new organization labored under the title of United Nations Special Commission on Iraq, known everywhere as UNSCOM. The commission had one key point of leverage. The Security Council vested the UNSCOM chairman (or deputy) with the power to officially designate sites for inspection in Iraq—whether they were related to nuclear matters or anything else. This was UNSCOM's most potent tool.

Resolution 687 was the core document that guided inspections. At the time, it was the longest resolution the Security Council had ever passed. It was complicated and written in typical UN language; it was verbose. Participants at the time had no expectation that the procedures it established would frame an ongoing crisis into the next millennium.

The unspoken assumption among the council representatives was that Saddam's regime would soon collapse and a new government would be dealt with on new terms. In March and April 1991, Saddam was confronted with a massive Shia uprising. His army was defeated, though not destroyed, as many thought. Washington was not alone in thinking Saddam would not survive. There was an unspoken expectation that Iraqi oil would be back on the market in months, not years. Part of that assumption was that Saddam would be gone, as part of some sort of Iraqi natural-selection process following the loss of a war.

A few fundamental aspects of the terms of Resolution 687 (and its later companion, Resolution 715) would determine the relationships between Iraq, the UN inspectors, the Security Council, the UN secretary general, and key Security Council governments. First, lifting of the sanctions and the oil embargo on Iraq was linked to verification by UN inspectors of Iraqi WMD disarmament. This was a switch. The sanctions had originally been imposed as a quick response to the Iraqi invasion of Kuwait in August 1990. On August 6, 1990, the Security Council passed Resolution 661, which imposed sanctions and an embargo on Iraq to force it to withdraw from Kuwait. Resolution 687 made explicit that sanctions would be continued to force Iraqi WMD disarmament.

Also fundamental, the resolution was a *ceasefire* resolution. It was not a peace treaty. If the Security Council determined that Iraq was not in compliance with the terms of the resolution, it would be in "material breach," and in principle, military actions against Iraq could be resumed to enforce compliance. Of course, the words on paper appear clear. Circumstances on the ground are different. A constant question lurking over all subsequent work would be: How uncooperative would Iraq have to be to merit a reaction, including the use of force, from the Security Council? If an inspector was blocked from entering a government building that may or may not contain anything relevant, would the Security Council agree to restart a war? Saddam became quite adept at knowing how far to push. And incrementally, the standards moved in his favor.

Also important to later events, Resolution 687 clearly put the burden of proof on Iraq. The resolution declared that Iraq must make a full declaration of its WMD programs and their disposition, which the UNSCOM inspectors would *verify*. UNSCOM was not envisioned by the Security Council to be required to seek and find concealed WMD. The concept was that Iraq would be required to make a complete, detailed accounting, which would be confirmed by UNSCOM and reported to the Security Council. Only then would economic restraints be removed.

The resolution also provided, in principle, extremely broad powers to the inspectors. They had the explicit right to go anywhere, anytime, under any circumstances, to sites they declared necessary. Iraq had to make available all information, documents, people, facilities, and so on—whatever the inspectors commanded. The inspectors were mandated to use any tool they judged applicable, and they were to have total access.

However, the inspectors would be examining a defeated nation— not an occupied country. This meant that rights on paper were not necessarily enforceable in practice.

The reporting hierarchy was also important. Iraq was to provide to UNSCOM its evidence in the form of a verifiable written declaration on the disposition of its prohibited WMD programs. It was up to UNSCOM to evaluate the declarations and report to the Security Council. Moreover, UNSCOM had decision authority over what materials and facilities qualified for destruction because of their past role in WMD programs. Iraq hated this reporting structure and tried, with increasing success over time, to change it.[1]

The Security Council mandated that UNSCOM would have an executive chairman and a deputy executive chairman. Informally, it was agreed that a suitable non-American would have the chairman position, but that the deputy would be an American. UN jobs are often filled this way. The council informally agreed that since the United States had taken the lead in the war and had the greatest amount of resources to contribute to the inspection regime (including intelligence, equipment, and transportation), it was appropriate that the United States should have a major role.

The Security Council picked Swedish Ambassador Rolf Ekeus to be the executive chairman. Although he was not Washington's first choice, Ekeus, who was then the Swedish representative to the Office of Security and Cooperation in Europe (OSCE) in Vienna, was a consensus candidate agreed on by the permanent members of the UN Security Council. (The United States, the United Kingdom, France, Russia, and China—the so-called Permanent Five, or P-5—are the only members that have permanent positions on the council and that can individually veto any proposal. They also formed the original nuclear club.) It turned out to be a good match. Ambassador Ekeus agreed to take the position and commute from Vienna. The assumption was that the job would last a few months and then he would return to Vienna. This was the working assumption as the rest of the staff for UNSCOM was assembled. No one expected to have to move to New York permanently.

There were no precedents for implementing Resolution 687, so Ekeus defined the roles as he went along. He headed to New York to begin quickly assembling a team of inspectors. The first American deputy was Bob Gallucci, who was a career civil servant at the State Department and who had been detailed to a teaching position at the National Defense University. He became the link to Washington when Ekeus needed U.S. support. Gallucci also kept Washington abreast of what UNSCOM was doing.

Ekeus quickly surrounded himself with a team that would be loyal to him and included a range of very sharp analysts from various countries, as well as a British special assistant and a British-trained UN lawyer. They provided records and drafts of all documents and drafted notes of all Ekeus's meetings (which he proofed to make sure they recorded the reality he saw). Ekeus also brought on a tough and shrewd Philippine UN secretary who could manipulate the convoluted UN bureaucracy. Ekeus knew he had to get inspections started quickly. The longer they waited, the more Iraq could conceal. He also did not want the IAEA under fellow Swede, Hans Blix, to get there first. These two politically prominent Swedes were very competitive. And Ekeus wanted to distinguish himself by being more resolute in enforcing disarmament.

While aware of the need for U.S. support, Ekeus did not want to be strictly dependent upon it. He wanted independent control. For example, the United States offered to provide aerial surveillance with a U.S. Air Force U-2.[2] Ekeus saw the benefit, but wanted control. The result, after much discussion, was that the United States would fly U-2 reconnaissance flights over Iraq on missions for UNSCOM. They would be UN flights, the U-2 would have a UN tail number, and UNSCOM would notify the Iraqis with the necessary flight notifications (so that they would not fire on the aircraft). The surveillance imagery would be provided to UNSCOM for its own purposes, but with agreed-on controls on its distribution (e.g., it could not be taken into Iraq). This was the first inevitable link between UNSCOM and the national intelligence services of supporting countries—of which the United States was the most prominent. As Iraq became a more difficult subject to penetrate, as it became more difficult to know the extent of their programs, and as it became harder and harder to know what the truth was, such "intelligence" activities evolved in ways that would appear contrary to the normal image of UN activities.

The early steps in the process established by the Security Council were critical and set the pattern for confrontation and grudging, gradual compliance. This cycle of confrontation followed by an increment of compliance or greater revelation about Iraq's WMD programs contributed to a mind-set of perpetual disbelief on the part of the inspectors. Iraq made initial declarations that were partial, deceptive, or outright lies in key aspects. The blockages and limits Iraq imposed on inspectors' access to people, places, and documents fueled the conclusions that Iraq was continuing to conceal its WMD programs. The pattern of deceit and obfuscation produced calluses in the mind, and ultimately, the true status of Iraq's WMD stocks and programs became unrecognizable and unacceptable.

Iraq made its first formal declarations about its WMD programs as required by UNSCR 687 on April 18, 1991. It declared it had fifty-three SCUD-type missiles, some chemical weapons, and no biological-weapons or nuclear-weapons program. We learned much later that Saddam had chaired a meeting of the regime's top leaders, the Revolutionary Command Council (RCC), to discuss how Iraq should handle the new resolution. Saddam established that his top priority was to get rid of sanctions. At the same time, he viewed the extensive Iraqi military-industrial establishment as a point of pride and power. His direction was to give up as little as necessary to satisfy the UN. Precise steps of implementation were up to his son-in-law, Hussein Kamel (the senior Iraqi in charge of building the military industries in Iraq).

Kamel, who prided himself on directing the development of Iraqi military industries (especially those that produced WMD), took pleasure in exercising his power over the senior Iraqi technocrats. I never met any of them who spoke well of Kamel. Privately (particularly after he was killed in 1996), they said he was stupid. Much of the responsibility for the early blunders by Iraq in trying to conceal weapons programs and material that was readily uncovered by UN inspection activity was Hussein Kamel's. No Iraqi could have anticipated how intrusive and zealous UNSCOM inspectors would be. Kamel's arrogant and uncooperative instructions to deceive led Iraq down a path that required increasingly complicated lies, one building on the next, until the entire deception would suddenly collapse.

It was natural that Baghdad approached the initial encounters with the UN inspectors as a negotiation of sorts. The Iraqis' view seemed to be that if they offered the UN inspectors something, we would be satisfied and go away. There were repeated discussions with senior Iraqis on how to implement the resolutions, and the point that took Iraq years to appreciate fully was that the resolution said *all* WMD and associated production capacity had to be identified and eliminated. That was categorical to me. *All* meant *all*. It was as simple as that.

I gradually appreciated that Tariq Aziz and the other senior ministers did not see things so literally. Consciously or not, they were driving toward a mutually satisfactory description of the WMD situation that would be declared reality. It was one of the many things I learned from the Iraqis about my own thought patterns. I had approached the process with the assumption that there *was a single objective reality* that we as weapons inspectors would describe.

The first inspection teams went into Iraq in June 1991. They were sent to inspect obvious WMD-related sites. One team, a nuclear group led by David Kay, who at that time worked for IAEA Director Hans Blix, had been tipped off by the United States about a site containing nuclear-related materials. When the inspectors approached the site, the Iraqis blocked them and drove away with what turned out to be calutrons on trucks.[3] The calutrons were part of Iraq's clandestine uranium enrichment program. Though very brief (lasting only five days), it was a telling inspection. Iraq had violated the Nuclear Non-Proliferation Treaty. This exposed the failure of the IAEA to detect both the Iraqi nuclear program before the war and recent Iraqi lies about the country's nuclear activity after the war. Additionally, the Iraqis were blocking the inspectors, in direct confrontation to the UN Security Council demands. So began the UN inspection experience in Iraq.

The Security Council reacted to Saddam's defiance by "deploring" it and sending Ekeus and Blix to Baghdad on a high-level mission to discuss the matter. They met with Aziz and other Iraq ministers, but did not meet with Saddam. To Saddam, Ekeus and Blix were not exactly American cruise missiles or bombers. They weren't even Americans, but peripatetic Swedish arms controllers whose own country hadn't fought a good war in centuries. This implicitly communicated a couple of messages. First, Saddam deduced that he could blatantly ignore or obstruct the UN Security Council ceasefire resolution and that the United States would not seek to recommence serious military action. More basically, there was no existential risk to his regime by defying the UN.

The second message was that the United States had allowed *itself* to be contained by the UN Security Council. Many in Washington had great difficulty in understanding this concept. Throughout the entire UN Security Council involvement in Iraq, Washington thought it was all about containing Saddam. But from other permanent members of the Security Council, Saddam understood that the members were often as concerned about containing the United States. This was a lever that, over time, Iraq used increasingly successfully to divide the Security Council.

Ekeus and Blix offered to the international community an aura of nonpartisan objectivity. Sweden was not a party to the conflict. The two Swedes were held in high regard among those who populated the diplomatic set and who engaged in UN and other multinational negotiations to foster world peace. Ekeus and Blix were process-oriented. They were lawyers.

The transcripts of Iraqi internal conversations, found in 2003, showed that the Iraqis believed that Ekeus was saying one thing to them and another to others. They were correct. In fact, I was amazed they understood anything from what Ekeus said at times. I am convinced Ekeus would intentionally speak with progressively more accented English (dubbed "Swenglish" around UNSCOM) when issues were difficult and his position uncomfortable. Sometimes, I would be asked afterward for some gentle clarification—to which I would have to say I could not improve on his exposition of his position, while thinking that I had no clue what he was saying but that these poor bastards were going to be jerked around for a long time by it. Over time, Aziz, no slouch when it comes to obfuscation or outright lying, tried to get Ekeus to agree to written understandings of procedures and accomplishments to pin him down.

The Security Council routinely passes resolutions making demands it cannot enforce and then routinely takes no responsibility for such failures. Duly, when Ekeus and Blix reported back to the Security Council, it passed another resolution (UNSCR 707), which was even more explicit in demanding full disclosures by Iraq and full access to documents, sites, and people. Iraq outright rejected it. Saddam saw it for what it was, something akin to a New York City parking ticket under the windshield of a car with diplomatic plates.

At this early critical stage of the inspection process, when Saddam's hold on power was far from absolute, he concluded that the UN was not a threat to his regime. He would deal with the sanctions over time. And he would either satisfy or outlast the inspectors. How hard could that be? Iraq was assuming there would be some relatively cursory inspections and it would destroy only the obvious SCUDs and chemical weapons. Iraq underestimated the persistance of the inspection process.

During the next year, there were additional confrontations over access and Iraq made revisions to the declarations of its WMD activities. There was also internal violence by the regime against the Kurds in the north of Iraq and the Shia in the south. Kurdish refugees teemed into Turkey, fleeing from Iraqi forces that were stamping out regime opposition. There was also an effort to "Arabize" the oil-rich area around the northern city of Kirkuk. Secretary of State James Baker visited the Kurdish area on April 8, 1991, and saw the mass of displaced humanity that resulted from Saddam's iron-fisted response to retain power. Baker was, by his own record, shocked.[4] He instigated a humanitarian response largely drawing on the U.S. military in an operation called Provide Comfort. As part of this action, the United States, the United Kingdom, and France established a no-fly zone north of the thirty-sixth parallel. They justified it under a UN resolution (UNSCR 668), although this was never agreed to by the rest of the Security Council members—particularly Russia.

The Shia in the south were abandoned. Saddam crushed any opposition ruthlessly. Many Shia fled to Iran to join the hundreds of thousands of Iraqi Shia refugees who had either fled or been expelled from Iraq during the previous decade. Only in August 1992 did the United States, the United Kingdom, and, for a time, France create a southern no-fly zone, originally south of the thirty-second parallel but raised in 1996 to the thirty-third, which is not far south of Baghdad. The no-fly zones generated an ongoing level of conflict outside the UN context, since the Security Council did not explicitly agree with them. Baghdad saw them as primarily a conflict with the United States and its partner, the United Kingdom. France barely participated. As is so often the case in their policy, the French wanted to have it both ways, and they got it. The Iraqis certainly saw Paris as their best avenue of political support on the Security Council, save the Russians.

In September 1991, Iraq tried to block UN inspectors from using their own helicopters. Eventually, Iraq relented. Later in September, inspectors acting on American intelligence conducted an inspection at a building in central Baghdad identified as Project Petrochemical-3. In it they found a large collection of documents related to Iraqi nuclear-weapons development. Iraq seized many of the documents from the inspectors and blocked the people from leaving the grounds with other documents. A four-day standoff ensued before the inspectors were permitted to leave, and only then after the president of the Security Council threatened enforcement action by some Council members (i.e., the United States and the United Kingdom).

On October 11, 1991, the UN Security Council passed a resolution (UNSCR 715) detailing an intrusive, unlimited monitoring system for Iraq. The intent was to verify that Iraq did not reconstitute its WMD programs—in perpetuity. This was the second fundamental requirement levied upon Baghdad—the Iraqis had to disarm and accept permanent intrusive monitoring, or sanctions would stay on, permanently. Iraq declared the resolution unlawful and refused to acknowledge it.

In April 1992, Iraq called for an end to UN surveillance flights (the flights of U-2 aircraft by the United States performed for UNSCOM) and implied it might fire upon them. Later that month, Aziz appeared before the Security Council and informed the council that Iraq had more weapons than previously declared, but it had unilaterally destroyed them. He declared that Iraq had thus complied fully with the UN Security Council resolution and it was the obligation of the Security Council to lift the sanctions.

In July 1992, inspectors were blocked from entering the Ministry of Agriculture. After the Security Council declared that this was a material breach of the ceasefire resolution, the Iraqis permitted the inspectors access. They found that materials (weapons development archives, we later learned) had been removed.

In January 1993, Iraq denied access by UNSCOM aircraft bringing inspectors to Iraq. This, after much Security Council debate, produced a brief bombing exercise in which U.S., UK, and even French aircraft participated (this was the last enforcement activity by the French). There was little significant damage.

Each confrontation tested the limits of the will and consensus among Security Council members to maintain the inspection commitment articulated in Resolution 687. Saddam was trying to erode it by attrition.

In the middle of the early tests of strength, President Bush surprisingly lost his 1992 reelection bid, despite having won a recent decisive military victory. He was challenged on the economy, and Ross Perot sapped a big chunk of the president's support. Saddam could never have predicted this outcome, but it certainly supported his strong view that the war was not over and he had not lost. Saddam looked at Bush's loss as his victory.

With the change in administration, I found that the new managers in the State Department wanted to put their own person in the position I occupied. I was not a political appointee, just a so-called politico-military expert who happened to rise to a sufficiently senior position in the State Department to be politically interesting. I was simply asked by the Clinton appointees to go find some other place in the government (or anyplace else) to work. Not pleasant, but better than suddenly being without a paycheck, or worse, as Iraqi government officials might point out. The area in which I was working had changed. The types of operations I conducted or was involved in during the 1980s would never happen again. The trend, all over the federal bureaucracy, was for individual responsibility to shrink. As layers increased, the ability to make a decision diminished. *Doing something* meant writing a memo. Memoranda can be important, but clever writing needed to lead directly to action, in my mind. That was happening less and less. It appeared to me that the number of things our government could do was getting smaller, not larger, as the number of people and dollars were added.

It turned out that the position of deputy executive chairman of UNSCOM was open because the temporary incumbent had moved on to an arms-control negotiation. I met with Ambassador Ekeus. We got along, and I began what became a six-and-a-half-year "temporary" assignment at the UN. I commuted to Washington on weekends via the Delta Shuttle. During the week, I commuted between Manhattan and Connecticut on the New Haven Railroad. And I traveled to Baghdad. The State Department system was glad to have me out of the way, though I was still a U.S. government employee with the same security clearances.

It took time to learn the complexities of the UN and the UNSCOM procedures in dealing with Iraq. It took no time to figure out that Ekeus had built an organization that was like a wheel and spokes. It was not a layered management system. Everything went to him or some of the people he trusted throughout the organization. As deputy, I had rank, but I had to demonstrate my value to both Ekeus and the senior long-term inspectors. Ekeus needed a link to Washington and to senior levels in Washington. This I could easily deliver. If Ekeus decided he wanted to go to the White House, I could arrange that.

Washington, of course, had a major stake in both UNSCOM and Ekeus, since it had fought and won the war with Iraq and did not want some international bureaucrat to screw things up. Ekeus was sensitive to this and carefully balanced Washington, the rest of the UN Security Council, and Baghdad.

The Clinton administration inherited the Iraq problem and essentially decided it was a problem that could be managed but not solved. Managing it meant containing Saddam until something else happened. Perhaps we would get lucky and he would simply drop dead. It wasn't much of a policy.

Shortly after I accepted the position of deputy chairman of UNSCOM, I had lunch in the White House mess (i.e., the small navy-run restaurant in the West Wing basement) with Martin Indyk. At the time, Indyk was the top Clinton NSC person for the Middle East (he would go on to become U.S. ambassador to Israel just after his friend Yitzhak Rabin was assassinated). I asked for the meeting to get his sense of where the White House thought we were headed with

Iraqi disarmament and Iraq generally. Indyk had authored a concept of "dual containment," which was the simple-sounding policy of containing the external ambitions of both Iraq and Iran. The primary tool for containing Iraq was the UN sanctions and oil embargo.

We discussed how we got to where we were in Iraq. Many aspects I knew in detail from my experiences during the Iran-Iraq War days. Indyk said the administration wanted a new regime in Iraq, but that it would have to come from within. I pointed out that Saddam had certainly survived the greatest threat to his regime, the postwar chaos in 1991, and was now stronger internally than ever. The other trend I highlighted was that support for sanctions was diminishing internationally. Baghdad was successfully pointing to the suffering of the innocent Iraqi people "caused" by the UN sanctions. There was also the powerful incentive to get Iraqi oil back on the markets with lucrative reconstruction contracts. Support for the UN sanctions was weakening, and pressure was growing on UNSCOM to clear up the disarmament business. Already some UN Security Council members were blaming the incompleteness of the disarmament work on UNSCOM, rather than on Iraq.

Indyk put his two index fingers down on the tablecloth and slowly drew two parallel lines. He said in his Australian-accented English that the two lines represented support for sanctions and support for Saddam. The hope was that support for Saddam would crumble before support for sanctions did. What I took away was that Iraq was a problem too hard and too dicey to actively try to fix. Therefore, a policy based on hope and measures designed to buy time was implemented; it was not an unwarranted tactic. There are only so many things an administration or a president can spend time and capital on. Iraq was a problem the administration put in the category of "too hard" and "too expensive," so let's kick the can down the road.

UNSCOM was the tool for ridding WMD from a very dangerous regime. The problem was, if we were successful, then the UN Security Council Resolutions said the sanctions would be lifted. No one really believed Saddam would change stripes and become a responsible member of the international community. No one really believed the UN monitoring system would inhibit his aspirations for WMD forever. And no one really believed that once the Security Council lifted sanctions, there would be the collective will to reimpose them. So Washington retained a paradoxical policy of strongly supporting UN-SCOM and, at the same time, declaring its desire for regime change in Baghdad. This confused Baghdad (among others) to the end.

On Monday, November 8, Ekeus and I flew to Washington for a series of meetings, including a White House session with Sandy Berger, President Bill Clinton's deputy national security advisor (National Security Advisor Tony Lake had bronchitis) and Jim Woolsey, the director of Central Intelligence. There were also stops at the Pentagon and State Department. I began a practice of arranging such meetings every couple of months.[5]

Three issues were prominent. First, Ekeus was setting Washington on notice that if Iraq accepted monitoring (as Tariq Aziz had been hinting), then it was only a matter of time until the question of lifting sanctions would have to be confronted in the Security Council. Both Berger and Peter Tarnoff (number three at the State Department) expressed concern about how long it would take to set up a monitoring system that was tough. They stated explicitly that they were in no hurry.

The second issue concerned how many SCUD missiles were left in Iraq. UNSCOM was concluding that there were very few, if any, SCUDs. The CIA's assessment was that there were 150 or more left. Nikita Smidovich was in charge of the UNSCOM missile investigation. He was very rigorous and had real data from both the Russians, who sold the SCUDs to Iraq, and the Iraqis, who bought and used them. His missile team included experts from the United States, Germany (which had inherited a number of SCUDs from the former East Germany), France, and the United Kingdom. Nikita had just completed the most extensive inspection campaign ever conducted in Iraq. Largely at U.S. urging, a team of dozens had conducted no-notice inspections at every real or imagined missile-related site in Iraq. We inspected every location the United States and other intelligence sources could identify. UNSCOM also brought into Iraq a helicopter outfitted with ground-penetrating radar that the United States provided. Nikita's inspection team, dubbed "Cabbage Patch," operated in Iraq for almost a month. And found nothing.

We asked Woolsey and his analysts if the intelligence community was still holding to its SCUD estimate and on what basis the numbers had been calculated. They stuck to the higher figure and justified it because of uncertainty over the number that Iraq claimed to have expended in the Iran-Iraq War. On the basis of *an analysis of communiqués issued during the war by both sides*, they thought that about 100 to 150 were missing—particularly from the early years of the war.

This struck me as pretty lame, but if that was the best data they had and they were obliged to tell their leaders a number, then it was understandable. The problem is, analysts frequently are placed in a position to create an estimate even though they have junk data. During the Iran-Iraq War, many SCUDs were fired in very low trajectories and were less visible to the technical collection systems the United States then had available. UNSCOM suggested that Iraq was using SCUDs against very short-range targets. The U.S. analysts thought this would be an inefficient use of SCUD missiles. Why use a valuable long-range missile against short-range targets? The U.S. analysts were missile experts, not Iraq experts. Iraq might choose to use SCUDs for all sorts of "inefficient" purposes. Some missile nerd sitting in front of a computer would not be able to incorporate the "Iraq" part of the calculation. He or she had forgotten, or did not factor in, the nonsensical (in our view) concrete warheads.

What also struck Ekeus about the U.S. estimate was that the analysts had virtually no evidence of the existence of these hundred-plus SCUDs. No pictures, no tracks, no secret test flights. So the CIA simply assumed Iraq was very good at hiding them. It was typical of the suspicions that surrounded weapons in Iraq: No one wanted to be the first to suggest that, in fact, they were not there.

In the end, UNSCOM simply asked some of the Russian technicians who supported the Iraqis in the 1980s in using the SCUDs (often, it seems, the Russians actually fired them). The technicians confirmed rates of fire along the lines of those Baghdad was declaring. There was no cunningly concealed stockpile. UNSCOM staff was beginning to get a sense of the good and bad of U.S. intelligence.

It took months, if not years, before the official U.S. intelligence estimate was reduced to be in line with UNSCOM. Analysts found it very hard to change their assessments. That is human nature. Conventional wisdom was that Iraq would cheat. It was also assumed Saddam had every incentive to cheat. Therefore, the assessment was that he was cheating. The analysts just couldn't show exactly how. If a U.S. missile analyst had stood up in 1992 and asserted that Saddam didn't have any SCUDs, because we had not seen any, he or she would have been put in a padded cell.

This type of mistake was repeated regularly for the next decade, including through the production of the National Intelligence Estimate of October 2002 and the dramatic and dramatically wrong Powell presentation on the Iraq WMD threat to the UN Security Council on February 5, 2003. It was not cooking the books; it was just piling wobbly assessments on top of wobbly assessments based on extrapolations from a few possible "facts" at the bottom, facts derived from the eyes of an American analyst who may well have never seen an Iraqi.

Also, it was manifestly clear to the intelligence community that the Clinton administration had a very strong incentive to find Iraq in violation of the UN resolutions. Some officials said flat out to Ekeus that they were not anxious for Iraq to be found in compliance, although if UNSCOM rigorously concluded this, then Washington would reluctantly accept it. At the end of the meeting, Woolsey asked what the CIA could do to help UNSCOM. I knew it was already doing a lot. Nevertheless, Ekeus asked for any data that might help on inspection sites. Woolsey suggested that there were twenty to twenty-five Iraqi presidential facilities where something might be found. Hardly revelatory, it conveyed how little the new administration understood.

Finally, there was a third point that Ekeus raised with Sandy Berger at the White House and with the undersecretary of state, Peter Tarnoff. Tariq Aziz had asked Ekeus privately if it would help in Washington if Baghdad made a significant contribution to the Middle East peace process or assisted in the struggle against "Islamic fundamentalists." Aziz also suggested Iraq could assist by resettling Palestinian refugees from southern Lebanon (where they provided a recruitment pool for Hezbollah against Israel) in Iraq. Tarnoff said simply that the United States would not mix the issue of disarmament with anything else.

Iraqis regularly approached me with similar entreaties over the years. It genuinely mystified them that the United States would be so categorical in refusing any dialogue with the regime on such issues. Aziz made such offers multiple times and even suggested that they could help with information on terrorism such as the 1993 World Trade Center bombing. There would have been great logic to this, except that these offers were overlooking the impact of Saddam. U.S. policy was to contain Saddam and wait for regime change, not to make him into an international peacemaker.

As long as UNSCOM was not satisfied that Iraq had complied, then the justification for keeping sanctions remained. The pattern of behavior Iraq established with UNSCOM from the outset made it possible to defer dealing with the implicit paradox of U.S. policy for several years, even though the sanctions would inevitably become less sustainable as time went by. Iraq was blatantly noncompliant as long as it rejected totally UN Resolution 715, which mandated ongoing monitoring.

In the meantime, I was able to get support from Washington for almost every conceivable operation we came up with—to a point. I kept Washington informed of UNSCOM's work and had no conflict of interest in being part of the UN structure, since it was the strong policy of the United States to support the UNSCOM's mission. Therefore, anything I did for UNSCOM was consistent with the interests of my country.

CHAPTER 6

UNSCOM:

The Great Game

In late November 1993, during a visit to UN headquarters in New York, Tariq Aziz announced that Baghdad had finally accepted the second fundamental UN resolution (UNSCR 715) calling for a permanent monitoring system to be established by UNSCOM and the IAEA in Iraq.[1] One of the most secret and paranoid regimes on the planet had opened the door to what would become the most intrusive and extensive monitoring system ever deployed. Conflict was inevitable.

Having accepted this resolution, Iraq pressed UNSCOM to accomplish its objective as quickly as possible. We began designing and building monitoring systems for each type of WMD—ballistic missiles, chemical weapons, biological weapons, and nuclear (under IAEA leadership). Ekeus delegated the management of this to me, and over the course of the next year, we installed an extensive system in Iraq with a headquarters at a building provided by Iraq and called the Canal Hotel.[2]

While the overall direction of the monitoring system was done from UNSCOM headquarters in New York, a sizable permanent staff was now required in Baghdad—roughly 120 people—including weapons experts, communications staff, support staff, linguists, helicopter teams, and vehicle maintenance teams.

To establish the scope of monitoring, we conducted a major baseline survey of all facilities in Iraq that had any potential application to WMD activity. These included industrial, military, and medical sites, and universities. Detailed information was collected on staffing, material consumption, power usage, production, and laboratory equipment. Further, Iraq was required to regularly—quarterly or even monthly—fill out extensive questionnaires on the activities at sites of interest. It was very labor-intensive on both sides.

We also deployed a series of sensors and monitoring cameras. There were roughly 120 cameras at sites around Iraq, and the cameras were linked by microwave to the monitoring headquarters (where a three-hundred-foot tower was erected to receive signals from remote locations), now dubbed the Baghdad Monitoring and Verification Center (BMVC). Chemical air samplers were positioned outside selected facilities. Samples would be examined in a laboratory in the BMVC to test for prohibited materials. Frankly, the samplers did not operate well, but I figured they served as a deterrent as long as the Iraqis did not know how unreliable they were.

UNSCOM also conducted a concerted helicopter surveillance program of all monitored sites. We had a German helicopter unit of CH-53s succeeded by a Chilean team using Bell Huey helicopters. We arranged to fly over most of Iraq (some areas, like palaces, were off-limits). These operations were complicated and required the precision and logistics akin to military operations—many of our team leaders were military officers. Coordinating transportation through Iraqi airspace to avoid being shot down by either the Iraqis or the United States was not simple.

For their part, the Iraqis recognized that this activity would be their highest security threat. The Mukhabarat—the Iraqi intelligence service—already targeted UNSCOM inside and outside Iraq; now there would be an even larger effort, including the elite Special Security Organization (SSO), run by Saddam's son Qusay. Iraq created a direct counterpart organization for the UNSCOM monitoring system called the National Monitoring Directorate (NMD) under a beleaguered brigadier general named Hussam Amin. Its declared intention was to facilitate the UN inspectors' work and to serve as the interface with the Iraq government. Anything the inspectors requested was funneled through the NMD. If UNSCOM requested documents, the demand went through NMD. If UNSCOM was going to inspect a site, NMD staff would accompany the team to "assure access." Anyplace UN-SCOM went, NMD sent along such "minders." The Iraqis said the NMD would facilitate movement and avoid problems with the various Iraqi security forces. This was partly true. But NMD was also intended to prevent the inspectors from finding anything that Iraq did not want them to find and to keep complete records of what UN-SCOM was told or otherwise learned.

Conflict came early and often. The UN inspectors wanted to achieve surprise inspections to monitor Iraq. The SSO wanted no surprises and probably was successful 99 percent of the time.

The NMD kept the book on the WMD story that Iraq presented to UNSCOM. Their experts were like the people responsible for continuity in movie production. If they shoot a scene in a room in the morning and flowers are on a table, they check to make sure flowers are on the table if they shoot another scene in the same room later. Iraq had a far more complex version of the same problem. The NMD kept track of everything that everyone told the UN, and it tried desperately to keep the stories straight and consistent. It was not easy, and there were notable failures.

The NMD's other major task was to monitor individual inspectors. UNSCOM had basically two sorts of inspectors. There was a small core group—on the order of fifty—who were permanent members of UNSCOM (or who participated in so many temporary inspections as to be considered regular fixtures). In addition, there were experts who were recruited for short periods (a couple of weeks was typical), during which a specialized inspection might be conducted. Over the seven years of UNSCOM's work in Iraq, more than a thousand individuals at one time or another served in such a capacity.

Iraq kept records of every inspector. It knew who it could influence and who it could not. The Iraqis tried to figure out who were spies and who were not. They monitored calls and radio traffic and inspected hotel rooms and offices. If you could imagine it, they did it. It was a great game, but one with great pressures on both sides.

While pressures on inspectors were significant, the consequences of this game for the Iraqis were far greater. The population suffered, and the government officials, if they erred, could pay an enormous price. We inspectors could always go home. The Iraqis could not leave.

Iraqis knew any comments made to inspectors could become known to their superiors. Rooms were bugged. Phone calls and radios were monitored. Some of our inspectors took advantage of this monitoring by injecting false information into telephone conversations over the open phone line to New York headquarters. They would describe things that were not as they had in fact occurred. Or, inspectors would discuss fake future inspections to improve our chances of achieving a surprise site inspection.

Throughout 1994, we conducted numerous interview sessions with all manner of individuals who had a role in the WMD program—from the chiefs to the bottle-washers. We knew it would be extremely difficult for the Iraqis to keep their WMD story consistent. The details would trip them up. Our inspectors were technically very well informed, and we sharpened their questioning skills with a few tutorial sessions from the FBI.

The interview process was effective, but very uncomfortable. The Iraqi technicians were caught in a vise, knowing implicitly that much depended upon getting the answers correct. The NMD minder might even correct a response, interrupting to insist the poor fool was confused. Watching some of these terrified individuals was not pleasant. The threat to them did not come from our side, but from their own.

I never really discussed it with the Iraqis at the time, but death always seemed present in these meetings. When individual Iraqis had been helpful to us (intentionally or not), we would make certain that the NMD knew we might seek to reinterview the person, in the hope that might protect the person. There were, however, a couple of individuals who were reported to have suffered unfortunate ends (heart attacks, car accidents) and became "unavailable."

Sitting across the table for so many hours over so many years, I found it impossible not to consider that through the accident of birth, those on the other side of the table had to face decisions I had never confronted. Had I been born in Iraq and pursued an interest in public policy or engineering, what paths would have been open? If you were moderately successful, you would rise to a point where pursuit of your interest required an accommodation of some sort with the government. Do you continue with your career, incrementally becoming more deeply involved and indebted to the regime? Iraqis faced decisions about accepting offers of study abroad, knowing there would be an obligation upon return to work on regime priorities. If you elect not to do something, it may affect not just your future but also that of your relatives. If you grow up constantly surrounded by the regime, do you see with any clarity what it is doing? The luxury of our choices was never more apparent.

Longtime UNSCOM inspectors who spent a lot of time in Iraq, not just one or two visiting inspections, understood the nature of the dilemma faced by Iraqi scientists and technicians. There was little satisfaction in our position of superiority in the dialogue. We did not achieve that superiority because we were better as individuals.

Saddam typically mixed a measure of acceptance of UN requirements with a measure of threat. In 1994, Iraq warned UNSCOM that the commission must declare the monitoring system complete in a scheduled report to the Security Council on October 7, 1994, or Iraq would reconsider all cooperation. It was clearly premature to declare the monitoring system operational.

I was focused on creating a system of inspection with a sufficient probability of detecting Iraqi violations—*even after sanctions were lifted*. That was the high standard we were meant to achieve, yet we were not even close on biological weapons and I was dubious in the chemical-weapons area. UNSCOM had leverage at that time to set the standards and precedents for inspection activity. If monitoring were prematurely declared adequate, we would find it very difficult to ask later for measures that were more intrusive.

When it looked as if Ekeus might grant Iraq's request in October, I came very close to resigning. I had enormous respect for Ekeus; he had to balance the politics (including the French and Russian pressures to accommodate Iraq) while I focused on the strict capabilities of the monitoring system. In the end, we included the purposefully vague term "provisionally operational."[3] The French and Russians had been hoping for a more positive statement in this UNSCOM report to argue that Iraq had fulfilled its requirements for monitoring and they could now press for the lifting of sanctions. Apparently, they had been making such promises to the regime. Baghdad recognized that UNSCOM had cut off this path, and the very next day, Iraq began moving forces, including Republican Guard units, to southern Iraq, where they could menace Kuwait.

This move forced President Clinton to redeploy aircraft (at considerable expense) to the region. In contrast, it cost Saddam very little to threaten Kuwait.

Saddam had gone too far with the bellicose troop movements for the Russians and French to defend him in the Security Council. The United States and the United Kingdom put forward a new resolution (UNSCR 949) passed by the full council, which demanded that Iraq return its forces to their original locations and not take any action to increase its military strength in the south. Russia, in an effort to help Iraq, sent Foreign Minister Kozorov to meet with Saddam. After that meeting, Iraq agreed to return its forces. Russia also pressed Iraq to agree to recognize the border with Kuwait officially. According to Tariq Aziz and other senior Iraqis after the war, the Russians said that if Iraq took these steps, Russia would press the council to move forward on removing sanctions. Baghdad was subsequently disappointed by Moscow's inability to deliver.

This was the first time that I truly understood an important point: The reality UNSCOM described was not the reality the UN Security Council wanted. The council wanted a less contentious version.

UNSCOM plowed ahead, meanwhile. It ran a chemical destruction plant from 1992–1994 at the massive Iraqi chemical establishment in the desert west of Baghdad. Called Muthanna State Establishment, this secret Iraqi facility contained dozens of buildings and bunkers, many of them built by German construction companies. At the height of the Iran-Iraq War, it was churning out mustard blister agent and sarin nerve agent around the clock.

It was an amazing place. In production, it must have looked like a scene from a James Bond movie. UNSCOM, using the facilities at hand and at minimal cost (under $5 million, which compares favorably to the U.S. dismantlement program costing billions), destroyed 28,000 munitions, 480,000 liters of agent, 1.8 million liters of liquid chemical precursors, and a million kilograms of solid precursor chemicals. Some containers and munitions were too volatile to attempt to destroy. They were gingerly placed in a huge bunker that reminded me of the Great Pyramid at Giza. I visited the storage bunker once before it was finally, and permanently, sealed. Outfitted in full protective gear, breathing air from scubalike tanks, and carrying a chemical detector that progressively blinked warnings of the lethal environment, the Dutch team chief, Cees Wolterbeck, and I examined the interior with its leaking sarin rounds, barrels with toxic agents, and assorted contaminated equipment. It was a dark, lethal junkyard. UNSCOM had successfully removed a substantial amount of chemical-weapons capability from the world scene.

UNSCOM first established a full-time biological-weapons team in 1994, headed by a wonderful man named Richard Spertzel. He brought together a number of experts, including David Kelly of the United Kingdom. Spertzel and Kelly initiated a superb investigation that gnawed away at Iraqi denials of any offensive biological-weapons production until 1995, when Baghdad finally conceded it had been lying since 1991. Baghdad's successful concealment highlighted UNSCOM's neglect of the biological program for the first three years of its work. We behaved a bit like a children's soccer team, on which the mass of players simply chases the ball. We had been pursuing missiles and chemical weapons because we could see them.

Ironically and again underlining the cycle of misperception, when UNSCOM did vigorously investigate Iraqi biological-weapons programs in 1994, Iraq concluded that the United States had *purposely* delayed such efforts as a method of prolonging the sanctions regime. Tariq Aziz said later that Baghdad assumed the U.S. rationale for not pushing the biological-weapons investigations was to prolong the UNSCOM process and, thus, sanctions. Baghdad was wrong. UNSCOM did not investigate biological weapons sooner because it was busy doing other things. Aziz was correct, however, in his judgment that the United States certainly did not want to accelerate the lifting of sanctions, but that others, including Russia and France, did.[4]

The hunt for the truth behind Iraq's biological-weapons program contained one of the best examples of the convoluted stories the Iraqis would be forced to invent—reinforcing disbelief over anything they declared. Regarding biological weapons, Iraq presented a rationale I called the *progressive idiocy theory.*

Our inspectors were interested in the import by Iraq (from the United Kingdom) of materials known as *growth media.* In microbiological work, specially constituted organic material is used to cultivate specific microorganisms. In a crude sense, a growth medium is the bread on which you can grow mold. In hospital laboratories and universities, it is commonly used to do tests or experiments, but it is used in small quantities—a kilogram lasts a long time.

UNSCOM found that Iraq had imported forty-two tons of growth media. This discovery prompted an exchange, which went something like this:

"We just have one simple question for you related to the baseline we are establishing for biological-weapons monitoring." The Iraqis, led by then Oil Minister Lieutenant General Amer Rasheed, become immediately suspicious. Cigarettes are lit on their side of the table. They wait for more.

"Well, you see, we understand that Iraq imported some growth media in the late 1980s, and we don't know where it went."

Iraqi eyes brighten a little bit, and Rasheed answers, "Ah, well, we have many very good hospitals and universities, and they require various types of growth media for their research and diagnostic medical work."

The inspector, relieved, says, "Oh, that's good. Now I understand. And you could give us a list of those hospitals and universities so we will know where our monitors should visit?"

Rasheed, also relieved, readily agrees. "Of course, of course. Husam, make sure the list is assembled and provided." His deputy performs like one of those bobblehead toys, nodding agreement to whatever Rasheed commands.

But the inspector is not done. "There is just one complication, however. Iraq purchased forty-two tons of growth media. These labs would only use a few hundred kilograms at most."

This produces a moment of silence and head twists, mostly away from the senior Iraqi. Then there is a burst of Arabic conversation between the senior Iraqi and his deputy. Hands wave. Shoulders shrug. More cigarettes are lit. A guy appears sheepishly from a side door with a diversionary tray of small tea glasses. He serves them as Rasheed continues his animated conversation with his deputy.

Finally, "Ah, well, it seems there was a mistake. You must understand that while Iraq is an advanced country at the senior levels, we are still a third-world country at the lower levels. We have been fortunate with resources, however. At the time we purchased the growth media, we had resources, and medical facilities had priority."

Now comes the progressive idiocy part.

The senior Iraqi continues, "We had clerks who would fill out the purchase voucher for the requested growth media. A lab would request a few kilos. That clerk would pass the voucher to his supervisor, who would review it. The supervisor would judge that if such a small amount was important, then a larger amount would be better. He would change the amount from, say, ten kilos to one hundred kilos."

If it weren't Iraq, and if these sorts of things did not happen with some regularity, the inspectors might have looked incredulous.

Warming to his theme, Rasheed adds, "The supervisor then passed the voucher to the deputy procurement manager for his review, and he exercises his judgment that if one hundred kilos is good, then a thousand is better still. That way, we will not run out. Our suppliers are not always reliable. Don't forget, some countries made it difficult for Iraq to purchase even medical supplies."

The inspector picked up the lead. "Ah, so then the top manager finally issues the purchase order for the final amounts totaling forty-two tons."

"Yes!" The minister says, almost shouting in triumph.

"I am frankly relieved to hear that. I won't tell you what I had been thinking," replies the chief inspector. "Then I guess there's just one simple thing to close this out."

The minister stares straight across the table and awaits the next sentence.

"Where did it all go? You can show us where the growth media is now. I suppose there's about forty-one tons in some warehouse?"

The minister is caught. This is the moment he desperately hopes UNSCOM will agree on an acceptable lie. It is in everyone's interest to agree, isn't it? The Iraqis have to have a story of where the growth media went. Thinking on his feet, the minister explained that this would not be possible.

"You see, after the war there were riots everywhere. You know this. Some would say the rebellion was encouraged by certain governments, but that is not our subject."

He goes on, "The rioters broke into every warehouse they could. The medical warehouses were unguarded, since they did not have important weapons. So the rioters broke in and destroyed everything they could use. They destroyed the growth media."

The process goes on a little longer. The UNSCOM inspector says, again, "Mr. Minister, thank you very much for that. That's a relief. I won't tell you what I was beginning to think. But just so we can close out this matter, could you just provide the documents for the warehouse receipts and disposition of the growth media?"

At this point, Rasheed looks both furious and worried. Without any consultation with his underlings, he declares that the rioters had destroyed the files and records as well. His deputy, seeking to aid the situation, speaks for the first time: "Yes, and in addition to the rioters, there was a truck transporting boxes of records traveling through Baghdad, and the boxes fell off."

This, finally, is not a mutually acceptable truth.

With progressively improbable explanations like this, coupled with reinforcement from defectors claiming that Iraq was concealing WMD, it became increasingly difficult for UNSCOM to believe Iraqi declarations that no WMD existed.

In December 1994, the former head of Iraqi Military Intelligence, Major General Wafiq Samarrai, fled Baghdad and took refuge in the northern Kurdish part of Iraq, which was not under the control of the central government. When Samarrai defected, Ahmed Chalabi had offices in Salahuddin for his Iraqi National Congress (INC).

The INC positioned itself to be a clearinghouse for defectors. In the mid-1990s, the INC was receiving U.S. support, which it used for, among other things, facilitating the escape of former regime officers. Samarrai came to my attention via a tiny press article picked up by our public affairs officer, Ewen Buchanan. It struck me that this Iraqi general was someone who could tell us a lot.

So in February, with my UNSCOM colleagues Nikita Smidovich, our Russian missile expert, and Tim Trevan, Ekeus's British special assistant, we traveled commercially to Ankara, Turkey, and, after meetings with the U.S. Embassy, flew on to Diyarbakir, where the United States had a military base. Tim, Nikita, and I were flown in a pair of Blackhawk helicopters to Zakho, and there we met up with a Danish UN guard contingent that was protecting relief efforts in Kurdistan. They drove us to Dohuk, where U.S. officers had arranged with the INC to bring Samarrai.[5]

The ride to Dohuk was slow. I enjoyed traveling with Smidovich. How far we had come from the day when he and I were in the Security Council and our respective delegations were bitterly attacking each other over the downing of the KAL 007 airliner! Now we both observed an independent tragedy, and I watched his reactions to the scenes we passed by. Kurdistan was recovering slowly from the assaults of Saddam and the battles between the Kurdistan Democratic Party (KDP), headed by Massoud Barzani, and the Patriotic Union of Kurdistan (PUK), led by Jalal Talabani. Smuggling was a major economic engine that Barzani and Talabani were fighting to control. Oil came by land in every imaginable vehicle that could be converted to carry barrels or tanks. The creative welders of the auto and truck garages of Iraq were a marvel. The lawlessness was also a marvel. The guys with guns collected taxes. The money supported either the PUK or the KDP. Flying over the border crossing point near Zakho, you could see hundreds of trucks lined up to make the crossing to Turkey. To me, it was a scene out of *Mad Max*, where chaos ruled in a trashed industrial wasteland. To Smidovich, I am sure it wasn't a scene out of a movie. Russia and the Soviet Union had experienced lawless chaos. Nikita could see deeper into Iraq more easily and more accurately than I could.

After some coordination problems were resolved, we got to the correct house. Wafiq Samarrai arrived with his son Mohammed at about 1430 in the afternoon. Mohammed, about seven years old, sat politely and silently for the next six hours of our discussions. Wafiq spoke very little English, and we made use of an INC guy named Bahzad, who translated.

Wafiq knew of UNSCOM and our general interests. He had been directly involved in military intelligence during the Iran war and knew generally about the use of WMD against Iranian targets. He described in detail contingency plans to use chemical weapons against Tehran when Iranian troops were advancing across the Shatt al-Arab. Iraq intended to use TU-22 bombers to deliver conventional high-explosive bombs to shatter city windows. Then it would attack with chemical weapons so the agent would penetrate the buildings.

Samarrai did not have direct access to information about WMD capabilities after the Iran war. He stated confidently, however, that many SCUD missiles remained. He did not know exactly where. People he knew said there was a site northwest of Samarra (his hometown) with hidden missiles. He said that Iraq had also retained many hidden documents. Many were distributed to people's homes, where inspectors would not look. Samarrai also said that the Mukhabarat was responsible for much of the biological-weapons program. (This turned out to be accurate in ways we did not know until Iraq Survey Group investigations in 2003.)

Samarrai told us that Saddam ordered an inventory of all weapons after the Kuwait war and that this document (created in mid-May 1991), if we could get it, would tell us the inventories of the weapons we needed to account for. This was very useful information, of course, and we later confirmed that such a document was created. He told us where there was a safe with key documents, probably including this one. If we could inspect that office in a surprise inspection, we could get this key document.

Samarrai confirmed that Iraqi intelligence was very good at getting information about UNSCOM and other countries. He said they gave a lot of money to other country officials (he alleged that the Russians—including Primakov—were key recipients).[6] The Mukhabarat spent a lot on such officials, he emphasized. (This point predated the Iraqi manipulation of the Oil-for-Food program, but clearly anticipated the tactics used there.)

In the end, the long trip was worthwhile, but inconclusive. Like many defectors, Samarrai knew some things directly, such as the existence of the inventory documents, but his other statements were not concrete. He certainly contributed to our skepticism about Iraqi declarations. The INC also began what ultimately became a pattern. It spurred Samarrai to write public letters to the UN, newspapers, and others, declaring that Iraq had WMD hidden and that UNSCOM had missed much. This undermined his credibility, because he was clearly "trying to influence as well as inform," as an intelligence reporting officer would describe. Samarrai was the first prominent defector who would contact the INC and whom the INC would promote for its own ends—which was to build support for the INC and Chalabi's plans for getting rid of Saddam. Chalabi later asked for a meeting with Ekeus in New York. Chalabi made the case that his position in northern Iraq provided him access to a stream of departing Iraqis, some of whom could have useful information for UNSCOM. That was logical, and we agreed to keep in touch.[7]

UNSCOM had the Iraqis in a corner with their refusal to admit any offensive biological-weapons program. Their denials were becoming ever more ludicrous. Saddam finally gave instructions that Aziz should make a deal with UNSCOM—if the commission gave a positive report to the Security Council in June 1995, saying that the missile and chemical-weapons areas were in satisfactory shape, then Aziz would be authorized to admit to offensive biological-weapons programs.

The Iraqis had foreshadowed this deal to me at a meeting in early May, when they had finally offered some new information admitting they had produced the sophisticated nerve agent VX in large quantities, not laboratory amounts—tons, not ounces. Two weeks later, when Ekeus met with Aziz in Baghdad on May 29, Aziz made the deal explicit. Give a good report in June, and "I will satisfy you on

BW [biological weapons]." And if not, the threat was they would end the process completely.

I did not like this deal. We knew some parts of the Iraqi declarations were flat wrong, and I was still tied to the assumption that there was a single objective reality and our purpose was to find it. But we were being squeezed to declare a reality that was acceptable to multiple parties, Baghdad and the Security Council. Ekeus wanted language that straddled the demands of Iraq with the technical facts we possessed. The report was sufficiently positive to buy us support in the Security Council from the French and Russians. Ekeus, who was an accomplished pianist, was attempting to play the Security Council and Iraq like a piano. In the June report, he played the notes of a dirge with the lightness of a lullaby.

Ekeus, however, found some of the keys he hit in the council were connected to notes he did not see. He had commented in the press about how the Security Council might react when Iraq complied with certain weapons requirements, hinting that sanctions might be lifted. Washington worried (correctly) that he might be telling the Iraqis that they could force the United States to confront lifting the sanctions and embargo on Iraq if Baghdad met some standards of cooperation, as described by him. This provoked a rare but stern message from Madeleine Albright on June 28, 1995: "I am also concerned about your credibility. To put it bluntly, the Council will *not* act soon to implement paragraph 22 (unless Iraq quickly reverses its position on non-WMD issues). If you continue to lean so far forward on 22, you put yourself in the position of seeing your advice ignored and rebuffed by the Council."[8]

Her reference was to paragraph 22 of Resolution 687, which describes the lifting of the oil embargo once UNSCOM reports it is satisfied with Iraq's work. Albright was clearly telling Ekeus to stick to the technical issues, not Security Council politics. This incident illustrated the concern in Washington over keeping the constraints on Iraq and the bind Ekeus was in, trying to satisfy the council members while seducing Baghdad to continue cooperating with UNSCOM.

In a report to the Security Council the previous April, we had declared that the monitoring system was finally operational. French

Ambassador Jean-Bernard Merimee proceeded to declare that even if there were some "loose ends" in understanding Iraq's previous WMD programs and stocks, they could be compensated for in the monitoring process.[9] Iraq's friends in the council glossed over the fact that once sanctions were lifted, Saddam lost all incentive to cooperate with any monitoring. *And no one believed the Security Council would find the will to reimpose sanctions, once the participating countries were all making money again. Yet no country could verbalize this silent fact as an argument for not lifting sanctions. The resolution providing the sanctions linked their suspension only to favorable reports by UNSCOM on disarmament and its monitoring system, not to disbelief about future Iraqi compliance.*

This fatal flaw in the original resolution was ignored as a matter of convenience in the aftermath of the war. Quite simply, no one really thought the process would go on this long with Saddam still in power.

By 1995, with Saddam seemingly firmly in place, many wanted to declare the UN process successful and get on with business and restore Iraq to a more normal status. The Russians were deeply interested in Iraq's ability to pay back the roughly $7 to $9 billion in debt it owed for weapons purchases. France wanted access to the oil fields. Both France and Russia, through their embassies in Baghdad and in New York, attempted to coordinate their strategies in the Security Council to create conditions for lifting sanctions. In fact, they were discussing a draft Russia-French resolution to lift the oil embargo.[10]

Lending moral background to these motivations was the growing damage to the Iraqi population. Iraq pointed to the effects of sanctions on children, in particular. Baghdad regularly declared that the sanctions were killing hundreds of thousands of children. UNICEF and other aid organizations validated the trend if not the magnitude. There was no doubt that health conditions had plummeted.

Saddam used this lever as he used the lever of hostages in other circumstances. He pinned the responsibility for the death of his population on the refusal of the Security Council to lift sanctions and insisted that the refusal was shaped by the United States and its deliberate attempts to prolong the sanctions and its failure to acknowledge that Iraq had disarmed.

The Iraqis found the June report sufficiently positive that Aziz summoned Ekeus back to Baghdad. On July 1, 1995, with his usual fully inflated arrogance, Aziz presented ten points describing that Iraq did, after all, have an offensive biological-weapons program. Aziz suggested that Iraq had chosen not to reveal its existence before because it had all been eliminated and Baghdad was concerned that Washington would find this an excuse to attack Iraq again. Aziz stated that Iraq had produced botulinum toxin and anthrax at a facility called al Hakam. Large quantities of concentrated agent had been produced, but had never been put in weapons. Aziz also declared that all the agents had been destroyed in October 1990, before the war against Kuwait.

This was progress, but still nonsensical. Why would you destroy your weapons *before* you go to war? And the denial of ever putting agents in weapons did not seem consistent with Iraq's own track record of extensively using chemical weapons in the 1980s.[11]

Days later, Saddam took the offensive again. In his annual July 17 National Day speech, he threatened the Security Council that Iraq would cease all cooperation. Saddam practiced the threat-reward strategy domestically and internationally. He had offered cooperation with UNSCOM. He had accepted the hated monitoring system and had conceded more about his previous weapons programs. He accepted the border with Kuwait as the Russians had strongly advised. Now he demanded that the Security Council act to lift sanctions or Iraq would cease all work with the council. This speech was followed a few days later by Iraqi Foreign Minister Mohammed al-Sahaf's declaring during a visit to Cairo that Baghdad had established a deadline of August 31 for the council to act. Saddam calculated that he need not be too worried about serious military action. He knew the French and Russians were making his case. He was ratcheting up the pressure.

In this heated summer, Tariq Aziz requested that Ekeus come to Baghdad yet again on August 4 to receive the "full, final, and complete declaration" of Iraq's biological-weapons program. Though the declaration was still skimpy, Aziz repeatedly warned Ekeus that the deadline for the council to act on the sanctions was serious. Aziz said that he had no responsibility for the biological-weapons portfolio—that it was the responsibility of Hussein Kamel. Aziz said that the next time, Ekeus might have to meet with Kamel. This turned out to be prescient, but in an unexpected way.

On Monday, August 7, Ekeus returned to New York from this latest browbeating from Aziz. That evening, the day before the anniversary of the end of the war with Iran—a day of celebration for the regime—some very wild parties were organized by some of the closest, and hence most powerful, family members. Booze, women, guns, and competing egos clashed. Events transpired that no American analyst could have predicted, nor understood. Yet they were transformative for Baghdad.

In circumstances that apparently developed out of competition over a particular woman, Uday, the psychotic son of Saddam, shot Saddam's half brother Watban Ibrahim al-Tikriti badly in the leg. The highly inebriated collided with the highly uninhibited. The shootings also included a number of bystanders.

Watban had recently been relieved of his position as interior minister by Saddam. Saddam explained later, "What was I to do? He would drive around Baghdad at night, drunk, and shoot out traffic lights. Is this behavior acceptable for the minister of interior?" Watban was still morose from his demotion and drowning his sorrows when Uday, similarly out of control, laid claim to the desired woman.

The injured from all factions were taken to the same primary hospital for the inner circle, Ibn Sina. The fracture lines in the family spread rapidly. Hussein Kamel, the son-in-law responsible for the development of Iraq's military industry and WMD and frustrated by the chaos of the regime, left for Jordan. He saw himself as a potential future replacement for Saddam.

Kamel's entourage included his wife, Raghad, who was Saddam's daughter, his brother Saddam Kamel and his wife Rana, who was also a daughter of Saddam, as well as their children and some cousins. It was a huge defection. Half of Saddam Hussein's immediate family and one of its highest officials had voted with their feet. King Hussein of Jordan granted them asylum and provided them a place to live.

Baghdad was shocked. Saddam's grip on power depended on the loyalty of those closest to him—his family. He had to move swiftly to restore control and repair the damage to his image.

Not the least of the immediate problems for the regime was the impact upon the WMD work with the UN. General Amer Rasheed was given responsibility for sorting out much of the aftermath. He told me later that millions of dollars were missing. And there were boxes of documents that would change the WMD picture Iraq had presented to UNSCOM. Baghdad quickly concluded that Hussein Kamel, as head of the Iraqi WMD efforts, would be sharing whatever he knew with the Americans. Within a week, Rasheed called UN-SCOM to invite Ekeus yet again to Baghdad to receive new information. It was clear the Iraqis wanted to get to Ekeus before he spoke to Hussein Kamel.

In the meantime, the CIA formed a task force of analysts and operations officers to debrief Kamel. They made many requests to King Hussein for access to Kamel and his entourage and were able to have limited discussions. The initial news on WMD was modest. The king was also being lobbied by Baghdad to send Kamel's group back. Already, Iraqi emissaries had been dispatched to talk to Kamel to get him to return, but he refused to meet with them. Ekeus traveled yet again to Baghdad to meet with Tariq Aziz on Wednesday, August 17. Aziz said there was more information and declared that one person had been responsible for withholding information from the UN—namely Hussein Kamel. He was in charge of the WMD programs and he had given orders, Aziz said soberly. It was all Kamel's fault. (Although, curiously, Aziz said it had been his own decision to hold back on the biological weapons.)

Aziz and his colleagues now volunteered still more information. Aziz admitted that they had made biological weapons, not just agent. They provided many more details on their activities to destroy weapons secretly in 1991. The most interesting revelation was that shortly before the 1991 war, the Iraqis had pursued a shortcut to making a nuclear weapon by diverting material from the nuclear reactors under IAEA monitoring. At that time, the Iraqi regime believed it would complete a weapon before the end of 1991.

In light of the new information, Aziz considerately suggested that, naturally, it would take some time for UNSCOM and the IAEA to verify the matter and thus Iraq would suspend its deadline (then only one week off) for the Security Council to act on lifting sanctions. In fact, Amer Rasheed later declared that UNSCOM could take as long as necessary. Saddam had instructed that all information must be provided. Anyone who withheld information would be executed. The statements made by the Iraq side were good, an excess of cooperation almost, but where were the documents? Iraq had offered none.

On August 20, Ekeus was anxious to get out of Iraq and started out to meet the UNSCOM aircraft at the Habbaniya Air Force Base, about a hundred kilometers out of Baghdad. In a twist that was weird even by Baghdad standards, the head of the National Monitoring Directorate, Brigadier General Hussam Amin, came to Ekeus and asked that he delay his departure. There was something Amin wanted to show him. Amin was even more beleaguered than usual and even more plaintive. Still, Ekeus demurred. Baghdad was a hot, oppressive place, and once you get your mind in the mode of getting out, it was not easy to turn around.

But Hussam was insistent and babbled some story about a chicken farm that belonged to Hussein Kamel. He said, his eyes shifting to the ground, "You see, Ambassador Ekeus, we have received information from a girlfriend of the criminal Hussein Kamel. She said that there may be something of interest to you at his chicken farm. And if so, you should see this before you depart. Let us take you there now."

Accompanying Ekeus was the UNSCOM lawyer, John Scott. Scott was a retired UN lawyer, born in England and raised in South Africa. I deeply admired him and depended on his boyish enthusiasm, which had somehow survived a lifetime of exposure to the UN bureaucracy. He had an unfailing appreciation for the absurdity, but also the inevitability, of the UN system.

Yet even in Scott's experience, this tale proffered by Hussam Amin was singular. As Scott listened to this pitch, he could not contain himself and blurted out the obvious: "That's absurd. You mean to say some unknown girlfriend approaches the Iraqi authorities about a chicken farm, with something—you don't know what—related to the WMD or the UN?"

Amin had not survived this long in the regime by being creative. He followed orders, no matter how idiotic. I always suspected he was not stupid, just crushed by authority. He replied, "Yes. You see, Mister Scott, that is just the way it is. Now, please, it is very important that we investigate this matter together."

Ekeus knew it was ridiculous, but also recognized that despite how much he wanted to get out of Iraq, they had to play along. Ekeus called me later that day, when he finally got to Bahrain. He was exhausted, but amazed as he related the charade he had been through.

At Hussein Kamel's chicken farm, they were led to a building secured by a lock (apparently quite new), which the Iraqis dramatically broke off. Inside were dozens of metal boxes the shape and size of foot lockers, filled with documents. One box was filled with obviously interesting biological-weapons data, including videos and photos (e.g., testing on donkeys and beagles, but not humans). Most of the boxes contained documents related to the nuclear program. This was Iraq's striking concession and revelation that it had, in fact, been lying about not having any further documents. The artifice for revealing them now was that Hussein Kamel had been hiding them without authorization. This was the reality they wanted us to share. It was Kamel's fault, not the regime's. It, too, was not a mutually acceptable truth.

UNSCOM staff from Baghdad secured the documents, and Ekeus belatedly boarded the UNSCOM aircraft and departed once again. The documents were brought to the UNSCOM building in Baghdad as quickly as possible and then removed from Iraq.[12] There were roughly a million and a half pages.

Studying them confirmed much of what Iraq had declared, but revealed more. For example, Iraq manufactured a substance called *aflatoxin* as a biological-weapons agent. This was weird to our weapons experts, who came from military or scientific backgrounds. Aflatoxin causes liver cancer. Its effects are long term and will not affect the course of a battle. Exposure may prevent a lieutenant from ever becoming a colonel, but there was no obvious military rationale for this agent. The only rationale we could imagine—and the Iraqis never acknowledged—was to cause long-term effects in targeted populations, who would never even know they had been exposed. Iraq also had planned on poisoning lakes in Iran during the Iran-Iraq War, according to Hussein Kamel. It was also working on an agent (wheat smut) that would kill agricultural crops, according to Kamel.

Then there were videos. The Iraqis videotaped some of their biological- and chemical-weapons tests on animals. The videos are not pretty, especially if you like beagles or donkeys. The experiments were pretty rudimentary, and the test arrangements almost amateurish. In some, animals were staked at measured distances from a center point, where a 155-mm chemical round was detonated. The poor creatures were mostly blown up. The agent was salt in the wound at best.

The videos convey the gruesome reality of the chemical and biological weapons Iraq produced. UNSCOM was extremely careful not to release the videos publicly. If they had been, the grotesque spasms of dying animals would have been played endlessly on television news around the world. Baghdad would have concluded that UNSCOM was not upholding its obligation to protect information and behave objectively. Certainly some council members would have agreed. The videos did not reveal anything Iraq had not already declared with respect to their WMD efforts.

In 1998, I made a similar decision during inspections of Saddam's presidential compounds. My team found jail cells with abundant evidence of torture and a bullet-riddled wall with surrounding ground dimpled with what appeared to be graves of recently executed prisoners. General Amer Rasheed, who himself seemed surprised, requested that these features not be recorded in my reports since they bore no relationship to WMD. I satisfied myself that there was no WMD connection, such as chemical or biological testing on humans, and then agreed with Rasheed's rationale that such matters were not part of UNSCOM's WMD mandate. They were evidence of the nature of the regime, but not of WMD.

As UNSCOM experts inventoried the chicken farm documents, there was a recognition that certain sorts of documents were not present. We were convinced the gaps were not accidental, but were evidence that other documents were being withheld. For example, there was a lacuna having to do with chemical and biological agent fabrication records. The data collected through experience in producing agents is very valuable and cannot be learned from textbook formulae. This acquired knowledge is vital, and anyone who produced agent would record such information. There was none in the files provided. More telling, there were no documents from the Ministry of Defense. Not one. It seemed odd that the ministry would have no documents concerning the most critical weapons systems.

This fact, and the clear evidence that these documents had been systematically retained and concealed, forced us to conclude that there was a government-directed system to retain WMD materials, if not weapons themselves. And the documents provided no evidence that the system was terminated. We certainly did not believe that it was all Hussein Kamel's fault.

Ekeus's next stop was to meet with Hussein Kamel himself. Ekeus asked Jordan to arrange such a meeting. On the evening of August 22, in a three-hour session, Kamel described aspects of the WMD programs that had not been admitted previously by Iraq but also confirmed some important parts. He was in a position to know a great deal, but he was not good with some details. Kamel mixed his answers about WMD programs with disparaging comments about the regime and Tariq Aziz. He claimed he had been frustrated with the regime for many years and tried to change it from within.

Kamel did not dispute Iraq's contention that it had eliminated chemical and biological weapons. He said Iraq had done more on uranium enrichment, particularly centrifuge enrichment and at different locations.

Kamel also described efforts to obtain missile gyroscopes and to develop indigenous rocket engines, and he declared that Iraq had retained two SCUD launchers. He made it clear that they intended to restart long-range missile production. He finally stated that certain production equipment was concealed at the house of a relative, Major Izzadeen al-Majid, who accompanied Kamel to Jordan. (Izzadeen, we later learned, was in the Eighth Battalion of the Special Republican Guard and was in charge of hiding material.)

He mentioned certain new aspects of the biological-weapons program, such as agents to destroy crops and research on viral agents. In the chemical-weapons field, he stated that Iraq had filled some bombs with VX at the very end of the Iran-Iraq War, but had not used them. He acknowledged that an Egyptian scientist had initially helped the Iraqis make mustard agent. Overall, the impression was that they had reluctantly destroyed existing weapons, but had been struggling to retain the ability to restart the programs by concealing documents and certain equipment, as well as certain development activity that would not be detected. In answer to questions on the production of chemical weapons, he said Iraq had used the facilities to produce pesticides, not chemical agents. However, the capacity to restart the programs was clearly preserved wherever possible.

The UNSCOM debriefing of Kamel was consistent with what he told CIA debriefers. The Ekeus meeting, however, had begun with a big surprise.

When Ekeus first entered with his group, Kamel immediately demanded to know the identity of the interpreter and was very agitated. Upon hearing the name, Kamel asked where he was from. At the response (Syria), Kamel demanded that the interpreter leave. Then, working through a Jordanian interpreter, Kamel declared that Iraq had been paying the UNSCOM interpreter for some time. This immediately hardened Ekeus's view that the Iraqis were seeking to defeat UNSCOM, not work with it.[13]

I had also been one of the "hardliners" in UNSCOM concerning the control of information and the threat of Iraqi (and other) attempts to penetrate and defeat our sensitive inspections. Others considered me paranoid. But UNSCOM could not effectively conduct surprise inspections if someone was informing Iraq in advance about our plans. So I became the person who tried to manage operational security and keep tabs on who was likely to be working for whom. I learned things about my colleagues that I neither wanted to know nor cared about knowing, as long as their objectives were in consonance with UNSCOM objectives. The commission was filled with bright, energetic people mostly loaned by the governments of their various countries, but some staff did have motives that were at variance with

UNSCOM. Many worked for the intelligence services of their home countries. Some were using aliases. Mostly, I didn't care, as long as the people supported the UNSCOM mission, or could at least do no harm. UNSCOM was organized around a clear mission, and for the most part, we formed a great team.

I cared about only two things. First, was the person doing something against the United States via his or her position in UNSCOM? Clearly, some people were using their position in UNSCOM to gain access to U.S. intelligence sources and methods. It was obvious that the U.S. intelligence community worked closely with UNSCOM (as did a few other countries). UNSCOM inspectors knew that in the State Department and CIA, there were offices that directly supported Iraq disarmament work. There was also a special office established in Bahrain called Gateway, which provided intelligence and logistic support as needed and requested by UN inspectors. Many countries were interested in this, some for their own purposes and some as a way of assisting Iraq. For example, one night a French UNSCOM staffer was found riffling through and copying U-2 imagery in the UNSCOM offices.

The second aspect that concerned me was whether someone was working to help Iraq thwart our efforts. We were obviously Iraq's most important target, and Iraq had highly skilled agents and lots of money. What's more, in the UN context, selling UNSCOM secrets to Iraq was not a crime. While Iraq's paying UN staff officers at UNSCOM (as distinguished from officers loaned by governments to UNSCOM) for information might seem to be spying, within the UN context it was not. It was breaking rules, but not laws. UNSCOM could not arrest someone for working for the Iraqis (or for falling into a nonprofessional relationship with an Iraqi intelligence officer). You couldn't even fire the person, as it turned out. The best we could do was to maneuver those who were suspected or known to be assisting Iraq into positions where they would not have access to critical information. This was the course we took with the interpreter identified by Kamel, even though we could not confirm that he was the individual Kamel knew to be supporting Iraq.

The Ekeus meeting with Kamel revealed some interesting information that was new and some that supported Iraq's line about destroying the bulk of weapons in 1991–1992. But could he be trusted? We knew he aspired to return to Iraq as its new leader. It would not be unreasonable for him to wish to have WMD when he got back. Ekeus was very cautious in crediting Kamel's statements. In the end, we needed admissions and hard evidence from the regime in Baghdad, not from its defectors.

I was aware, but unable to divulge at the time, that Kamel had had a brain tumor. It had been removed surgically, but I always wondered if the surgery had affected him. In a decision even more bizarre than his initial move to defect to Jordan, Kamel decided to return to Baghdad, believing that Saddam would forgive him and all would return to the status quo ante. All but one member of his entourage—Major Izzadeen al-Majid, who was traveling out of Jordan when Kamel made his decision—returned on February 20, 1996. As soon as they crossed the border, Saddam's two daughters were separated from Kamel's group by regime officers. Within a couple days, at the end of Ramadan, it was announced that both women had divorced their respective husbands. After the Eid al-Fitr holiday, family members attacked the villa (belonging to Kamel's sister) in Saydia, where Hussein Kamel and his brothers and father were staying. Ali Hasan al-Majid (aka "Chemical Ali," who was executed in 2001) is said to have organized the assault on those who "disgraced" his family. It was a long and bloody fight, but the outcome was certain. The brothers and several of their family members, including children, were killed. Major Izzadeen's wife and children, who had also gone back to Iraq, were killed as well.

Saddam later said it surprised him, as well, that Hussein Kamel had returned to Baghdad.[14]

The episode, with its cycle of deception, misperception, and miscalculations, left UNSCOM and the Security Council with a reinforced view that Iraq had not and would not come clean on its WMD programs. These events bought the Clinton administration more time for its policy of containment through sustaining the UN sanctions.

The events in Baghdad during the summer of 1995 could never have been anticipated by U.S. intelligence analysts. The chaotic internal actions by senior regime members had international implications, but without any contact with Iraqis in the regime, they were unfathomable in Washington. I suspect that even if the United States had had an inside-the-regime source who reported the crazy machinations, the source would have been disbelieved.

In retrospect, with today's better understanding of the underlying instability in Saddam's regime, the prospect of his possession of a nuclear weapon—nearly realized in 1990—is even more unnerving.

CHAPTER 7

Targeting Concealment

The Hussein Kamel defection disturbed Ekeus because Kamel's revelations contradicted UNSCOM's favorable reports from the previous spring—statements on the full operational capability of our monitoring system and statements that we had accounted for the majority of Iraq's past WMD programs. In fact, we had been successfully deceived. Moreover, the evidence suggested not only that there was a concerted governmental system to conceal from UNSCOM important material, but also that there continued to be significant retention of material. Ekeus was now determined to deal with Iraq's "concealment" mechanism.

In early September 1995, Ekeus and I met with our top UN-SCOM inspectors, Nikita Smidovich, Rachel Davies (a former U.K. Defense Intelligence Service officer), and Scott Ritter (a former U.S. Marine intelligence officer). We discussed the need to begin a much more intrusive strategy for inspecting in Iraq.

At that meeting, we understood we would be starting down a new path for the UN, and for international work anywhere. UNSCOM would be spying on Iraq. We would be using virtually every technical collection technique sophisticated countries used to obtain information about their opponents. The only area we ruled out was directly recruiting agents. The goal was to either peel back the layers of untruth ourselves or simply cause Iraq to decide to be completely forthcoming. It left us exposed since the Security Council had, by a resolution, placed the burden on Iraq to prove it had complied. By going down this path, we knew we were implicitly allowing the burden to shift to UNSCOM to prove the Iraqis were cheating.

Our collection strategy was selected based on the fact that in Baghdad, decisions and control came from the top. Therefore, we decided to focus on the most senior institutions and people—from Saddam's presidential office to the top security organs. The most important secrets would be known by the most important decision makers. In classic operational intelligence planning, we would design a collection plan that coincided with an inspection. We would pick a site, take every measure possible to conduct a surprise inspection, and have in place tools to watch the reactions before, during, and after the inspection. A key technique we decided to employ was to get inside Iraqi communications. This was an idea that UNSCOM staff had toyed with years earlier, but Ekeus had ruled out. Now he agreed to the concept of listening to Iraqi reactions to our inspections with the equivalent of police scanners. After all, crime reporters use them to get a leg up on local news events. Why shouldn't UNSCOM inspectors listen to see where the Iraqi security guys were moving in reaction to inspections?

Ekeus knew that collecting communications would be far more sensitive than our aerial reconnaissance. It depended upon secrecy not just for political reasons, but also because it would work best if Iraq did not anticipate it. As with many UNSCOM inspection techniques, the more the Iraqis knew, the more they could circumvent them. So we had to guard the technique from not only Iraq, but also the Security Council governments that would inform Iraq. The Iraqis later told me some members were competing with each other to help Iraq out. So, we could not inform the Security Council itself of our new tactics. Nor could we inform the secretary general or most of the UNSCOM staff, since they either had no need to know, lacked experience in keeping anything secret, or would inform their home governments, which might then share information with Baghdad. Secrecy would be awkward, but necessary. In the end, Ekeus agreed that we should go ahead with what became increasingly sophisticated inspection and collection activities.

Planning meetings were held outside the UN building. We did not believe that our offices in the UN were secure. One night, a late-working UNSCOM staffer found a UN cleaning person wandering around the UNSCOM offices. The cleaner turned out to be a former Iraqi Army officer. Several of our planning meetings were held at the Princeton Club, which was sufficiently distant from the UN on West Forty-third Street. Others were held at a dingy place called the Turtle Bay Café. If we were meeting with U.S. intelligence, sometimes we would gather at a hotel room secured for the meeting, or in certain cases, we would meet at the secure offices of the U.S. Mission to the UN.

Ekeus also took a step to deepen our cooperation with Israeli intelligence. They had studied the Iraq WMD threat, and we had begun to hold technical discussions in 1994. Israel clearly had an interest in UNSCOM success, and Prime Minister Rabin had approved working with UNSCOM. Now we began to expand the dialogue to discussions on how to collect more information. We met with Major General Armidror, the deputy director of military intelligence, in a hotel selected by the Israelis. I had worked with Israeli military and Israeli intelligence officers in my previous capacity in Washington. These were people I knew and respected. They had their own separate agenda, but if interests coincided, they could be helpful.

Still, for Ekeus to accept Israeli intelligence assistance was a bold step. In the UN, the Israelis were not popular (to say the least), and if the Iraqis found out, they would paint UNSCOM as a tool of the "Zionists" as well as the United States, and this would drum up sympathy from the Arab countries. Therefore, this relationship became yet another aspect of UNSCOM's work that had to be strictly compartmented and kept confidential.

Indeed, Israel shortly proved very valuable. In early November 1995, it provided UNSCOM a tip about an ongoing effort by Iraq to import prohibited Russian missile gyroscopes. We quickly developed some very specific, "actionable" intelligence and approached the office of King Hussein of Jordan. Fortunately, Ekeus and I had just seen King Hussein at his suite in the Plaza Hotel a couple weeks earlier. Hussein, like dozens of world leaders, had come to New York for the celebration of the UN's fiftieth anniversary. He offered his help (and some very good insights into Saddam).

We took advantage of this to contact his immediate staff for assistance on an urgent matter that could not be discussed except in person. We sent Scott Ritter, who was energetically involved in many of UNSCOM's sensitive activities. He met with the king's aide, Brigadier Ali Shukri, and explained the data we had. The Jordanians reacted quickly. On November 10, 1995, Jordanian customs seized crates at the port of Aqaba, opened them, and found guidance units from Soviet SSN-18 submarine-launched intercontinental ballistic missiles. The units were destined for Iraq.

This incident was further evidence that Iraq's strategic intention was not to comply with the UN. It also undermined Russian efforts to advance Iraq's case in the Security Council.

We undertook an investigation that identified a key figure by the name of Wiam Gharbiyah, a Palestinian who had graduated from the University of Chicago in 1987 and had been making a living smuggling technology into Iraq. He had a contract with the Al Karama missile facility in Iraq and close ties to key Iraqi missile engineers. Gharbiyah also had good contacts in Russia. He made six trips to Russia as well as visiting the Ukraine to set up deals and arrange meetings with Iraqi missile engineers (who posed as Syrians or Jordanians). He had sessions with a variety of major Russian missile companies, like Energomash. We spent months trying to unravel a very complicated history that involved the Mukhabarat, Russian companies with government connections, front companies, and complicated banking transactions. The Iraqis let us interview Gharbiyah and, as was their current habit, attributed any transgressions to Hussein Kamel. They ostentatiously conducted several investigations of their own and gave us their conclusions.

After much pressure from Ekeus, the Russian government agreed to conduct an investigation itself. It was difficult for the Russians to refuse, since the guidance equipment we intercepted was from missiles that were dismantled after the Strategic Arms Reduction Treaty (START) agreements with the United States. After the Russian Federal Security Service (known as the FSB) conducted its investigation, we were simply informed that the Russian government was not involved. This result was not surprising. It might also be true, but subsequent investigations by the Iraq Survey Group revealed that Russian experts were working with Iraq on their missile programs almost up to the war. Clearly, Russian companies were almost continuously violating the sanctions. After the war, Iraqis stated that they assumed the Russian government approved the activities.

This incident hardened our views that Iraq had yet to come clean and indicated that Iraq's intentions concerning WMD were highly suspect. If Iraq was prepared to conduct these activities while under sanctions, it did not require a great imagination to believe the regime would reignite its weapons programs when sanctions were lifted. Hussein Kamel said as much. It was an increasingly obvious reality that no one apart from the inspectors would acknowledge. The prospect of monitoring Iraq successfully once sanctions were lifted looked very dubious to the UNSCOM inspectors.

At this time, the French made clear their interest in being more fully involved in UNSCOM. They offered to provide some of the security cameras for the monitoring center in Baghdad, which seemed like a good idea to me. It turned into a fiasco. And, after a year and a half of effort, Thomson-CSF—then a nationalized French company—had installed ten cameras for internal security in our monitoring center. Unfortunately, the cameras did not work, but Thomson-CSF[1] billed us a million dollars, anyway.

The French also pressed to be part of the concealment investigation. They had an intelligence officer who was fluent in Arabic and a good inspector. But we knew he would report everything he learned about UNSCOM to Paris. From my contacts with Iraqis, I also knew that the French were providing information to Baghdad—information that did not help UNSCOM. So my message to the French was simple. If they helped us in ways that would hurt them *badly* in their relations with Iraq should Iraq learn of their actions, then I would agree to their participation.

The French never met that condition, and we never let the French fully in. This was classic French international behavior. I had had many opportunities to work with them earlier in my career, in Chad and in some arms-control efforts. French interests were always mixed. They would keep a foot in every camp and, in this way, remain independent. The French were also indicative of the problem of trying to exert disarmament measures through the Security Council. France had its own interests and Iraq could play to them—successfully. It was annoying but inevitable.[2] For France, its position as a permanent member of the Security Council, with veto authority, was vital and gave it leverage in the world that its economy did not. This was true for the other veto-wielding members, including the United Kingdom, China, and Russia. Each country tended to behave in different ways to maximize its leverage—recognizing that the Security Council was the essential tool for the country to contain not Iraq, but the last superpower, the United States.

The decision to go forward with the concealment investigation inspections also meant I had to convince Washington to provide support. Much has been written about the U.S. intelligence involvement in UNSCOM. Many have drawn the conclusion that the CIA hijacked UNSCOM. My perspective was quite different. In fact, the argument could be made that over time, UNSCOM hijacked the CIA (and the White House and State Department). Certainly, many offices in the CIA were opposed to the more inventive UNSCOM collection ideas and it was a struggle on my part to secure assistance. UNSCOM had two huge levers—we were in Iraq and the CIA wasn't, and what we said would determine the future of the oil embargo and sanctions, the foundation of U.S. containment policy.

My regular, day-to-day contact at the CIA was an officer named Larry Sanchez. Sanchez would become a good friend and colleague over the years ahead. He had experience in intelligence analysis, operations, and how the bureaucracy in Washington worked. Sanchez had become accustomed to receiving requests for assistance from UNSCOM, and he regularly delivered. The formal process was from UNSCOM to the U.S. Mission, to the State Department, and then to the CIA.

There was a big difference in the velocity of UNSCOM and the velocity of the U.S. bureaucracy. At the commission, we could agree on a strategy, identify inspection targets, establish an inspection team, coordinate material and transport, and launch in as little as ten days—or roughly about the length of time it would take an action memorandum to be drafted and cleared among the various offices within the State Department and get into the system to go to the secretary of state. And that was just the State Department. It could not keep up with UNSCOM, and when UNSCOM depended upon U.S. support, the department could be a drag.

For the concealment inspections, I briefed Sanchez and an assortment of other U.S. officials on what UNSCOM wanted to do and what we wanted from the United States. One request was for aerial reconnaissance timed to coincide with inspections on the ground. That was not too hard. The hard part was our request for the capability to collect communications. Initial reaction at staff levels in the CIA was that it was crazy. I was told to forget it. At higher policy levels, they had a tough debate about how much they really wanted to help UNSCOM. Was it in their interest to help? And to give this type of intelligence to a UN body was risky. Congress had sharply criticized the CIA for sharing classified information with the UN in Somalia. Documents had been lost. To move this forward, Sanchez set up a visit for Ekeus and me to try to get the CIA involved at the top.

On November 17, 1995, Ekeus and I flew to Washington for meetings at CIA headquarters. We had lunch with senior staff who worked on Iraqi WMD, and after lunch, we met with Director of Central Intelligence (DCI) John Deutch. We discussed the U-2 program. (Deutch was very concerned about our use of the imagery—particularly that UNSCOM might share it without consulting Washington.) Ekeus also requested more support and any information that could be shared. Deutch nodded politely.

I am not sure he really understood what Ekeus was saying. Afterward, I was asked to interpret what Ekeus meant to say.

It did not have much effect. Although the policy in Washington was that UNSCOM should be assisted, on a practical level we received only grudging support to our expansion of tactics under the concealment investigation. UNSCOM had planned its first concealment inspection for early December, but we did not get the equipment we expected. Over the Thanksgiving weekend, Ekeus and I discussed this and decided that we should cancel the inspection rather than launch it ineffectively. The cancellation communicated to the White House that the bureaucracy was not supporting us.

At CIA headquarters the following Monday, I met with George Tenet, who was deputy DCI at the time. I had known Tenet when he was a National Security Council (NSC) staffer and could be candid with him.

I said, "George, I know this is a pain in the ass and breaks a lot of crockery, but it will yield big dividends if we get it right. Our goal is to get as deep into the Iraqi decision process as possible. So far as I know, the White House still thinks supporting UNSCOM is good U.S. policy. At least that's what Lake and Berger seem to be saying. We are on the ground in Iraq, and you're not. You might as well help us go as far as we can."

Tenet asked, "What's the holdup?"

"I believe I'm getting the old rope-a-dope treatment from NE [the regional office in the Directorate of Operations in CIA]. They don't really want to have anything to do with the UN, they will get nothing out of it, and it's not their idea. We thought we would get equipment and training in time to conduct this inspection and got only half-assed responses."

I suggested that the British or Israelis would step up if the CIA did not. The participation of the British offered some help. I explained that if the United States could provide equipment and training, the Brits could provide technical assistance on the ground.

At this moment, contrary to later accusations of the infiltration of UNSCOM by members of the U.S. intelligence community, they wanted to stay away. I was trying to recruit them. At the end of our conversation, Tenet seemed to appreciate that I was not presenting just a problem, but also a solution. He would look into it.

Two weeks later, on December 4, I was back at CIA headquarters discussing the arrangements for going ahead with the concealment investigation with U.S. support. It was a sensitive meeting about how UNSCOM would handle the U-2 information (with more constraints). I suggested that more responsive, perhaps near-real-time, imagery would be very helpful to our collection plan. If we inspected a site and an Iraqi convoy fled an adjacent point, it would be good to see the site in U-2 prints provided two weeks later, but it would be better to know immediately or within hours. Deutch rolled his eyes at this.

We went on to discuss going forward with the communications collection requested by Ekeus at our earlier meeting. Tenet had evidently gotten the bureaucracy to turn around. Deutch confirmed they were prepared to go ahead, but basically said it was my ass if it blew up. There was a long list of legal, policy, and operational risks that were entailed, and specific authorization further up the food chain was required. I had a pretty good idea of how complicated it would be to get approval.

Deutch had looked at recent CIA history in Iraq and seen dead agents. The two Americans who wandered into Iraq from Kuwait were thrown into Abu Ghraib prison to cook until (then) Congressman Bill Richardson trekked to Baghdad and talked Saddam into letting them out. Deutch and the others were calculating the risk: If blown, this activity could produce American hostages in Iraq, and if one of them was identified as a CIA person, the operation could end very badly—and be counterproductive for containing Saddam via sanctions.

The White House would have to approve this new type of collection, and it did.

I met with Larry Sanchez after the meeting. He would be the CIA coordinator. He laughed thinking about what we were going to do. He would have to stitch together operations officers, technical operations people, and analysts. It made sense, but was new territory for the agency bureaucracy. The U.S. intelligence community was unconsciously becoming dependent on UNSCOM for Iraq information. Ultimately, the commission became virtually the only source of Iraq WMD information, and this affected all future assessments.

Flying back to New York, I wondered where this adventure would end. A lot was at stake, and I was beginning to appreciate more fully the willingness of Ekeus to engage in some very aggressive activity. At the heart of this was that recurrent question, What is the truth? Given the tough shell Iraq presented, UNSCOM had to invent new tools to get inside.

Two days later, I met with Tom Piccard, the senior FBI agent for national security matters in New York. I had been seeking a closer working relationship with the bureau for a couple reasons. It was the

FBI's job to keep an eye on foreign threats in the United States. They had New York wired and knew who was zooming whom. That included the Iraqi Mission to the United Nations. We had lots of anecdotal reports about Iraqi approaches to UNSCOM and other UN staff working on Iraq inspection activity. Piccard agreed to keep an eye on things, but did not promise much. Later, John O'Neill took over from him. I knew O'Neill from Washington, where he had worked on counterterrorism. He was an energetic, charismatic character who cut a wide swath through New York. His face reminded me a little bit of Richard Nixon, but his personality could not have been more different. I met with him regularly and was amazed at the stuff the bureau could get away with. He agreed to watch for evidence of leaks to Iraqis. The FBI rode the Iraqis pretty hard.

One day, the deputy Iraqi ambassador, Sayeed Hassan al-Musawi, and I were meeting for coffee in the UN as we did regularly. We had become a regular feature of the UN landscape, and more than one delegate had approached with the comment, "If you two can get along, why can't Washington and Baghdad?"

On this particular day, Musawi, who never looked happy (UNSCOM staff perversely dubbed him "Mr. Sunshine"), looked particularly glum. He said, "Mister Duelfer, you know your people follow us, and sometimes it is too much."

This was not a topic that related to UNSCOM, and I looked completely blank. "Well, Mister Duelfer," he explained, "your people hit my car today, and it will be very expensive to fix." I suggested that some crazy New York driver might be responsible. Musawi shrugged, unconvinced, and moved on to UN matters.

The next time I saw O'Neill, I mentioned the incident, and he dissolved in laughter. "Yeah, one of our guys was doing a close follow and it got too close. Sideswiped the guy. You know him?"

"Well, you know he's not one of the Mukhabarat guys," I replied. "Musawi is not a regime thug. He was a geography professor who studied in Paris before Tariq Aziz recruited him to the Iraqi Foreign Service. He's a Shia from the southern town of Amara."

But O'Neill clearly didn't care about biographical details. He was just sending a message to the Iraqis. They were in his town, not theirs.

His eyes were rolling. Stupidly, I said one more thing: "Look, John, just keep in mind, what you do to these guys here, well, they will return the favor to me when I am in Baghdad." That seemed to be the funniest thing O'Neill had heard in weeks.[3]

We closed out 1995 with three key meetings. On the evening of December 12, Ekeus, John Scott, and I met with Tariq Aziz, who had come to New York to try to repair the damaged Iraqi position in the Security Council. It was a typically long meeting with Aziz at the Iraqi Mission. Ambassador Nizar Hamdoon sat silently observing the performance of Aziz. For Hamdoon, there was safety in silence. Aziz was trying to restore some support among Iraq's sympathizers in the Council. The year that had begun so well for Iraq had come unglued after Hussein Kamel's defection.

Tariq Aziz opened the meeting with his usual command that Ekeus start. Ekeus stated that the prohibited guidance equipment intercepted in Jordan was "very disturbing." Further, we had learned that many items had already gone into Iraq, and there were extensive contracts with the Iraqi government. Aziz lit his Cohiba at this point, and a cloud of smoke enveloped him. A portrait of Saddam loomed over his left shoulder as I faced him. I wondered if he felt Saddam looking at him. Aziz declared that Iraqis were throwing these devices in the Tigris even now. "Hmmm . . . that's not good," I was thinking. "We'll have to fish them out somehow to account for them."

Ekeus moved to another problem—Iraq had carried out a covert surface-to-surface missile program based on the SA-2 Soviet air-defense missiles. There had even been flight tests that we had missed completely and that Iraq had not declared. Ekeus listed a range of other newly discovered problems. Aziz treated them dismissively. Nevertheless, Aziz blithely promised to satisfy Ekeus that all the problems would be solved.

On December 18, we met with Ambassador Madeleine Albright in advance of a meeting at the White House. We saw Albright regularly, and while she was always very tough on Iraq, especially in her public statements, I never had the impression that she possessed deep knowledge. Her focus was on keeping the Security Council in support of sanctions.

Shortly before Christmas, on December 20, Ekeus and I made another trip to see Tony Lake at the White House. Lake, I suspect in the hopes of getting us in and out quickly this time, preemptively said he was assured by DCI John Deutch that our problems would be solved and that we would get what we needed to collect against Iraq during inspections. Ekeus thanked him and went into a discussion of how helpful the Israeli assistance had been. He noted that Prime Minister Rabin had decided to provide information to UNSCOM himself. Initially, it had been information about past Iraqi activities, but now the Israelis were stepping up to "the next phase" and providing information about current activities, or real-time information. This real-time information had produced the interception of the guidance equipment in Jordan. Ekeus then went on to warn that UNSCOM would be challenging the most sensitive parts of an evil regime. Lake said the United States was committed to providing the technical collection we needed and he understood where we would be going with it.

On Friday night, March 8, 1996, we launched our first concealment inspection. Nikita Smidovich was the chief inspector. I went out to Baghdad concurrently with the team for some talks with senior Iraqis and to provide some cover for the team. The first site was the headquarters of the primary government-run construction company (called al Fao). We chose to inspect at night on Friday, which is the equivalent of Sunday in the West—a day off. It had been our practice to inspect only during regular hours. We had three reasons to break that practice: (1) we wanted to surprise the Iraqis; (2) we believed the site would be politically sensitive, and we therefore figured it would be easier and less intrusive to inspect when few if any employees were there; and (3) we could not allow sanctuaries in time or space for the Iraqis. We had to be able to conduct surprise inspections at night as well as in the day, if we were to prevent prohibited activities. We were now exercising the full rights of access clearly written in the resolutions. We could and would search anytime, anywhere.

The Iraqis were upset, to say the least. They were accustomed to the nonintrusive monitoring inspections and were thrown off by this surprise. It turned out our information on al Fao was dated. Something had definitely changed at the building, but the site was still very sensitive to the Iraqis, and Nikita and his team were blocked from entering. Hours passed before members of the team got in. Iraqi employees entered and left carrying things we could not inspect. I met with senior Iraqis during the standoff to explain our decision to exercise more intrusive inspections as was our right and to inform them that Iraq's lack of cooperation would be reported to the council.

We had succeeded in stirring the pot. Hopefully, our collection plan would let us learn more about Iraqi reactions. The day after I returned to New York, the Russian counselor at their UN mission, Gennadi Gatilov, came to see me. His message was that Russia "understood" that UNSCOM was *going* to conduct a night missile-site inspection later in the week and Russia believed this would be needlessly provocative. The situation with Iraq was delicate, and we should take that into account. Ambassador Ekeus (who was not in New York) should be made aware of Russian views. Gatilov went on to say that Russia did not want to dictate or impose its will on the commission. Nevertheless, Gatilov made clear that Russian support in the Security Council for UNSCOM actions would be affected if there were additional intrusive inspections.[4]

It was not surprising that Russia was so explicitly taking the Iraqi side (as we later learned, Iraq believed it was paying handsomely for this support). I was more interested in Russia's belief that it had solid advance knowledge of our inspection plans. It clearly was trying to obtain such information. I knew Russia's information did not come from Nikita Smidovich, but I suddenly appreciated that Nikita was in a very awkward position. UNSCOM objectives were diverging from Russia's objectives. The information Russia had obtained was false data we had put out as part of a deception plan to throw off the Iraqis. Nikita's team did attempt to inspect the Special Republican Guard (the most elite and loyal of Saddam's forces, which, we assumed, would have operational control of WMD-related material). Our helicopter surveillance was blocked, access was blocked, and Iraqi vehicles departed the sites without stopping. These confrontations were to become the norm for the next two years.

UNSCOM inspections were akin to military operations without weapons—at least on our side. The concealment team inspections always had an operations officer with a military background. The ops officer had to plan driving routes, assure helicopter surveillance missions, build inspector teams for entry and perimeter security, and set up a communications plan. Teams had to arrive on site at the correct time, particularly if aerial surveillance was planned. This was not simple, and with our more complex collection, the plans became even more complicated. Many people around the globe were keyed to the timelines laid out for these inspections.

We planned more intrusive inspections of key security and leadership sites through 1996 and 1997. Our collection plans strove to "get inside the Iraqi decision loop"—jargon for being able to act before the Iraqis could react and put defensive measures in place. In simple language, to catch them before they could remove the documents and materials we were convinced they were concealing. We progressively deployed more sophisticated equipment and personnel to Baghdad to collect more rapidly and be able to immediately adjust our inspections in response to observed Iraqi actions.

After the first concealment inspections, I made a few trips to discuss the results with Tenet, among others. On Wednesday morning, April 10, I flew to Washington to meet with NSC staff and later with Tenet to debrief him on our operations and to ask for some further assistance. He agreed to meet with me again a week later. During the intervening weekend, I was back in the Washington area and went skydiving—a long-standing hobby. On the last jump of the day from a Cessna 206, we were starting to climb out at 10,000 feet when one jumper's canopy deployed prematurely. He was pulled off the plane and struck the horizontal stabilizer (tail), which caused the plane to spin and ripped off the tail. I was lodged on the lower side of the wing, but was able to get off without hitting the propeller. The pilot eventually got out by about 8,000 feet, but one jumper was crammed into the rear fuselage as the plane spun into the ground. Airplane crashes get to the news media quickly. TV crews showed up at this site, and the story was on the Washington evening news. To the news reporters, it sounded like a weird event, and I suppose it was. I lost a fellow jumper, but it's an activity where that happens. Participants judge that the experience is worth the risk—just like driving down the interstate, where the slightest swerve into the oncoming traffic can produce the same effect as falling out of an airplane.

A couple days later, I was back down in Tenet's office. He was just shaking his head at me in response to what he had heard about the airplane crash. I was worried that the story would color how actors in Washington would respond to my assessments of operational risk associated with UNSCOM activities.[5] Tenet and the CIA generally made risk assessments every day. At some point, trust in people means a lot, and I did not want Tenet to mistrust my judgment about risk—particularly considering our activities in Iraq. I took some time to explain the incident and did my best to differentiate the risk attendant to skydiving and the types of risks we would be incurring in Iraq. It was a relevant discussion. Much in intelligence analysis and operations is based on judgment. If Tenet did not trust me, he would not support taking the risks associated with UNSCOM in our collection activities. The CIA has lots of opportunities to take risks, more than most other government agencies have, and when things go wrong, they can go wrong in a really big way.

Tenet bought in. He would continue to help us over the next two years (both as deputy and subsequently when Tenet became director in 1997) with our increasingly intrusive and complicated technical collection. He remained, however, very concerned about hostages.

As we assessed the Iraqi reactions to our inspections, we determined we needed to get feedback from our collection faster. If the U.S. intelligence systems could see a convoy of trucks moving while inspectors were delayed by Iraqis at a checkpoint, it would be good to know this immediately.

For one inspection, my Washington colleagues got a suite in a New York hotel, where secure communications could link them to U.S. national systems. Selected UNSCOM staff holding U.S. security clearances could get quick readouts of what was happening on the ground and use that data to redirect inspection teams. Of course, daylight in Iraq was the middle of the night in New York, so the hotel suite was buzzing with visitors at odd hours. I'm not sure what the hotel desk thought, but the staff there did not ask.

The Defense Department also helped by providing real-time U-2 imagery. The U-2 flew out of a base in Saudi Arabia and at that time had flown with an old film-type camera for UNSCOM. The department now agreed to fly a camera that could beam its images electronically to a ground station. Since the U-2 could loiter over certain areas and flew very high, it could provide very broad coverage. If inspectors triggered an Iraqi reaction in an adjacent area, we could pick it up with the U-2 imagery. That worked a couple times, and we used some of the imagery to demonstrate to the Security Council examples of Iraqi actions that provoked our suspicion about their compliance. The problem was the U-2 was very complicated to fly and often had mechanical issues that scrubbed missions while the ground inspections went forward. And, of course, the Iraqis knew when it was flying overhead, because we gave them notifications of upcoming missions and they had a surprisingly good air-defense radar system to track all aircraft that entered their airspace.[6]

At one point, I asked Tenet if he could get us a Predator UAV. Predators have become common now, but in 1996–1997, there were only a couple, and those were committed to the Balkans. The U.S. military also questioned their value. The air force hated them, because they had no pilots. For our purposes, a Predator would have been great. It would have allowed us to put aerial eyes on sites, with a very long loiter time. It was asking for too much, too soon. A decade later, I would have wide access to UAVs, which proved invaluable for multiple missions in Iraq.

Blocked inspections became regular events. In 1996 and 1997, we conducted several concealment inspections with Scott Ritter usually at the head of the team. He became popular in the media for his confrontations with Iraqis in the field. Ritter was convinced that the Iraqis were deceiving UNSCOM systematically and that if we had enough support, we would crack their walls of deception. We did pretty well, but generated progressively more controversy in the Security Council. Ekeus tried to moderate our aggressive inspections according to the ebb and flow of support in the Security Council. Over time, the United States became wobbly as well. Still, our efforts were clearly showing that the Iraqis were hiding something—we just could not be certain that it was WMD.[7]

Ritter was convinced we would catch them eventually. We had access to Iraqis who had defected and taken up residence in European countries; some of the defectors were quite explicit in their descriptions of concealed, ongoing WMD work. We had obtained copies of ongoing contracts for missile-related work. Later, we would even work with some governments to covertly videotape Iraqi weapons-procurement meetings, including ballistic missiles, in Europe.[8] It was clear Iraq was violating sanctions—with assistance from other governments. But, was it building WMD?

Ritter has since become a strong critic of the U.S. Iraq policies and the interaction of the intelligence community with UNSCOM. At the time, however, he was energetic in aggressively pursuing UNSCOM inspection activities. He had a great deal of latitude and resources. Ritter became very close to the Israeli intelligence services, which, I suspect, knew how to take advantage of his penchant for action and his desire to be in the "club" of intelligence operatives. Both Ekeus and I supported his work, as it produced results. But I think I may have been blind to something that became overzealousness. I was given a memorable hint that Ritter's worldview may have been a little different from mine.

Ritter and I were meeting with British intelligence officers in London. I had flown overnight to London from New York, and Ritter had arrived from one of his regular trips to Tel Aviv. We met near the Strand Hotel. It was early, and we shared a table in a coffee shop. Still bleary from the overnight flight, I was stirring my coffee and, perhaps, inadvertently hypnotizing myself as I stared at the circulation of the coffee. The previous day, I had had coffee with an Australian and noticed he stirred his coffee in the opposite direction . . . I was wondering stupidly if there was something to the Coriolis effect and maybe Australians stirred their coffee backward . . . well, my mind was not sharp.

By contrast, Ritter was excited and emphatically (he was rarely anything else) describing the Iraqi concealment system based on the new information from Israel. It was too much for me at that moment.

"Scott, look, this is Duelfer," I said. "I know what we know. I know what we think we know. And I know there is a lot that we just 'assess.' There is a lot in your concealment model that we have just made up because we think it makes sense. You don't have to con me."

Ritter straightened, thinking I was challenging his approach, and declared, "This is right, I know it is. I have never been wrong."

The last statement woke me up. Ritter was a character I found appealing. But he was high maintenance; key people in Washington thought he was not reliable. I had spent a lot of my time and credibility arguing on his behalf in policy and intelligence circles. Now I began to wonder if maybe they knew something I didn't. In any case, I could just see the reaction of the faces of some cabinet officers if they heard the inspector who was at the point of UNSCOM-Iraq confrontations stating categorically he had never been wrong.

"Scott, do me one big favor," I now asked him. "Please, never say you are 'never wrong' in Washington."

I think he understood, but I also think he was absolutely convinced he was right. Ritter would be the subject of many discussions I had with Iraqis long after UNSCOM was gone. He was a character that they did not understand or fully trust—even when he espoused their cause and when many thought he worked on their behalf. The one thing we knew for certain was that no Iraqi who behaved like Ritter would have survived in Saddam's Iraq.[9]

While Ritter dominated news reports on UNSCOM inspection standoffs, there was scant attention to the underlying dynamics at the time. It was clear the Iraqis were not allowing inspectors the full access the resolutions demanded. But were they hiding WMD?

In any case, it was also becoming very obvious that the Security Council was not able to force Iraq to comply. At the same time, the council and Iraq were agreeing on the sale of Iraqi oil through the Oil-for-Food program, which was finally agreed on in December 1996. Many members of the Security Council would now have an interest in the continued export of Iraqi oil and Iraq's import of permitted materials. Agendas and priorities of individual council members were straying in different directions. With the strongly competing interests among council members, UNSCOM was caught in the middle, unable to declare that Iraq had complied with the stringent WMD disarmament standards established by the UN Security Council.

Different permanent members of the council wanted UNSCOM to declare very different things. Russia and France were anxious for UNSCOM to state that Iraq was compliant enough and the monitoring system good enough that the sanctions should be lifted.

The United States and the United Kingdom saw Saddam as an irredeemable security risk who could never be trusted, and therefore the containment via sanctions were essential as long as he was in power. Left uncontained, Saddam would inevitably instigate regional conflicts that would require U.S. intervention (as the last superpower) to fix. The United States had no confidence that once sanctions were lifted, they could ever be reimposed. It believed, therefore, that if the sanctions were removed, the UNSCOM monitoring system would soon be ignored by an economically resurgent Saddam.

This dilemma in the Security Council was becoming more obvious. It was like watching someone with a toupee sliding out of position—people saw it but remained silent. The Iraq resolutions were becoming transparently unexecutable, but no one wanted to acknowledge this publicly. There was much concealment of some untreatable truths by the Security Council. What remained to be seen was how long UNSCOM could continue pressing its efforts before something gave way among the conflicting objectives in the council, Baghdad, and Washington.

CHAPTER 8

The End of UNSCOM

In June 1997, Ambassador Ekeus resigned to become the Swedish ambassador to Washington. Secretary General Kofi Annan selected Australian Ambassador Richard Butler to become the new chairman of UNSCOM. Ekeus had recommended Butler, who had a great deal of experience as the Australian ambassador to the UN and in previous international disarmament areas.

Dealing with Iraq, however, was different, and Butler came in at an extremely difficult time. The Security Council was fracturing, and Iraq was losing patience. The UNSCOM issues were driven by details that were very difficult to assimilate for someone new (and of course, the Iraqi side knew the details perfectly).

As Butler had a very steep learning curve, the Iraqis set out to take advantage of him, if at all possible. In Butler's first formal meeting in Baghdad, Tariq Aziz tried to come on to him with a friendly, "have a cigar with me" attitude. The UNSCOM experts and I had long since lost any expectation of candor from the senior levels in Baghdad, especially Aziz. Butler, on the other hand, appeared receptive to Aziz's proposals for swiftly closing out a range of issues. The new chairman's attitude dismayed UNSCOM experts, who felt they were witnessing the dissolution of their hard-fought positions. Before the next session with Aziz, I wrote a pointed note to Butler with some strong comments on the day's meeting. I tried to help him get a quick grasp of the reality in Iraq. This was not European-style arms control. The guys on the other side of the table—Cohiba cigars or not—had directly or indirectly killed lots of people. Their motives and actions would be different, and these Iraqis would quickly take advantage of any perceived softness or weakness. "You have to grab them by the throat and feel the pulse of the carotid artery under your thumb. Apply pressure and don't let go." I think Butler concluded Aziz was going to be difficult, but I suspect Butler also reckoned he had in me a difficult deputy who would be second-guessing him.

Butler quickly came to his own harsh assessment of the regime and employed his own style and judgments. Whatever he may have first thought, it did not take him long to become very antagonistic. In turn, the Iraqis treated him with disdain, painted him as under the control of Washington, and tried to undermine him in the Security Council via the Russians and French.

Butler did, indeed, become very close to the U.S. administration—sometimes too close, in my opinion. The Clinton administration seduced him with close attention and began to take advantage of him for domestic political purposes. Butler gave great television interviews. He always had a crisp, Australian, no-nonsense answer to even the most complicated question. It usually pointed out the wickedness of the Saddam regime, and this suited the White House. Butler was not the type of person to try to cover up the underlying problems. As he realized the contradictory objectives of the Security Council members, he vocalized them in clear terms. He did not let the council pretend fundamental problems did not exist. He pushed UNSCOM to continue to dig out the truth and exercise the inspection rights the council had given in its resolutions.

Within three months of Butler's taking the job, Iraq was pushing to limit cooperation and UNSCOM was pushing against those limits with intrusive inspections. In September 1997, Butler approved a plan we had been developing to flood Iraq with a large number of inspection teams, aiming to overwhelm Iraq's ability to monitor and control them all. We succeeded. There were several blockages and confrontations, which produced clear evidence of Iraqi deception activities—though again, we could not tell exactly what they were concealing.

The next month, Iraq began a counteroffensive seeking to divide the council. The Iraqi deputy ambassador, Sayeed Musawi, asked to see me on October 29. We met regularly, no matter how bad the relations were. There was usually something useful to discuss, but if not, we would simply have coffee and escape our respective headaches for a half hour.

This time, Musawi told me Tariq Aziz was about to declare that Iraq would no longer accept American inspectors and would no longer assure us that UNSCOM U-2 missions would be safe over Iraq. Saddam must have personally approved and probably suggested this tactic. It was typical: an aggressive action that just went too far, even for Iraq's friends in the Security Council.

Butler responded by ceasing all inspection work by all nationalities unless Iraq permitted the Americans. He made the point that *Iraq* could not be allowed to pick the inspectors, whether by nationality or by any other factor.

Two weeks later, Iraq demanded that all American UNSCOM staff in Baghdad leave by road to Jordan immediately. We discussed this internally. Butler took a strong stand: all in or all out. The Russians hated this, but had to support it. The Iraqis had crossed the line. After negotiations between Moscow and Baghdad, Iraq relented.

In exchange, however, the Russians were going to put as much pressure on UNSCOM as possible. They demanded changes to commission procedures and at one point recommended that instead of a single American deputy (i.e., me), it would be more "efficient" to surround Butler with five deputies, one from each of the permanent members of the Security Council. Butler fended this off.

However, Russian Ambassador Sergei Lavrov was successful in forcing Butler to accept a Russian "political advisor" on his executive staff. The advisor's role was clearly to represent Moscow's interests and smoke out as much as possible about the intelligence UNSCOM was getting.[1]

All this pressure caused Butler to become still closer to the Americans. He also resolved to continue the very intrusive concealment inspections. The situation became progressively more antagonistic.

At that delicate moment, in January 1998, the news broke about Monica Lewinsky. President Clinton's intimate activities with a White House intern flooded the international media—including in Baghdad. It would have been funny if not for the serious, and unpredictable, consequences. I happened to be in Baghdad and very senior Iraqis, including Tariq Aziz, spoke to me on the margins of meetings to inquire what all this meant. I could only imagine what Aziz would be saying to Saddam when he asked for an explanation, and the implications for the Clinton administration. One thing I realized immediately was that the Iraqis sensed weakness. As the single senior American they got to see in Baghdad, I found it a very unpleasant moment.

The Lewinsky affair had an impact on the Iraqi issue over the next twelve months. For all the claims by then Secretary of State Madeleine Albright that decision making in the White House was unaffected, it must have drained the energy and time of senior American officials. Washington was clearly suffering from Iraq fatigue. At senior levels, there was exasperation expressed to me concerning the endless confrontations with the council, provoked by intrusive UNSCOM inspections. The White House, through Albright and the new UN Ambassador Bill Richardson, began requesting that Butler adjust the nature and timing of the intrusive inspections. Saddam was being counseled by Moscow that there was general weakness in the Security Council. Iraq certainly saw no reason not to press further with the council and with Secretary General Annan, and it did.

Annan was lured into direct involvement in the Iraq issue. This was a major achievement by Tariq Aziz. The deputy prime minister had been contending strongly that UNSCOM inspections and activities like the U-2 flights were simply an extension of U.S. policy toward Iraq. Iraq argued that the commission's demands to inspect the most sensitive areas of its government were intentionally provocative and without foundation. This argument was winning support with Russia, France, and, now, the secretary general.

Annan offered himself as a mediator. This gravely undermined UNSCOM and, in particular, Richard Butler. Annan and Butler did not see eye-to-eye, to say the least. The coterie around Annan advised him that Butler was causing needless friction and was a disruptive figure.

Still, Annan would not have stepped in if Washington had opposed this move. In the first instance, Washington was largely responsible for Kofi Annan's being the secretary general. The Clinton administration had vetoed a second term for the previous secretary general, Boutros Boutros Ghali. In his stead, Secretary Albright had strongly promoted Annan. He was a career UN staffer who had risen to the post of undersecretary general in charge of UN Peacekeeping.

The crisis over UNSCOM access to sites that Iraq declared sensitive and unrelated to the commission's objectives had drawn Clinton into the fray directly. On February 2, he was on the phone to Boris Yeltsin to try to get Russian support for a more robust line for Annan's approach to Baghdad. Clinton made clear that if the diplomatic track did not convince Saddam to cease delay and diversion, then it would be necessary to make good on the threat of force that backed the diplomacy. Albright followed up in a dialogue with Russian Foreign Minister Yevgeny Primakov.

With great fanfare, Annan traveled to Baghdad to negotiate procedures for inspections at sites Iraq declared sensitive or "presidential." Secretary Albright had met with him in New York before he left. She conveyed some "redlines" Washington did not want him to cross in his negotiations. Annan had no experienced Iraq inspectors with him. Certainly, he had no one from UNSCOM. He had lots of good intentions to save the world from conflict and to help relieve the suffering of the Iraqi people. He was buoyed by a gang of supporters and press on the private jet the government of France provided him to travel to Baghdad. He spent two days working on a draft Memorandum of Understanding with Tariq Aziz, and then, only after it was approved, Saddam consented to see him. The agreement was signed on February 23 by Tariq Aziz and Kofi Annan, not Saddam.

On the morning of February 24, Annan returned to UN headquarters in triumph. Throughout headquarters, the emergency speakers beckoned all staff to come to the foyer and welcome him back. There was much cheering by everyone but UNSCOM. Annan gave a press conference and declared that he was "impressed with Saddam's decisiveness" and felt "we did have a good human rapport. He said many times, 'I know I can do business with you. I know you are courageous and I know I can trust you.'"

Annan went on to brief the Security Council on his triumph. In the course of his briefing, he referred to UNSCOM inspectors at one point as behaving like cowboys. Therefore, he had agreed that inspections of presidential sites would include a team of ambassadors to accompany the inspectors under the direction of the undersecretary for disarmament affairs. They would assure that UNSCOM would respect the dignity of Iraq and behave appropriately.

While Annan was traveling back to New York, Tariq Aziz thought he could improve on a couple of the seven paragraphs in the agreement and sent a letter dated February 23, the same day of the signed Memorandum of Agreement, stating how Iraq would interpret the agreement. It set some limits on the objectives and procedures. This was not a good sign for Annan, who was busy saying he could do business with the Iraqis. His office desperately tried to keep the letter's existence quiet and get Baghdad to "take it back."

On Saturday morning, February 21, while Annan was in Baghdad, I stopped by the White House for a private hour with National Security Advisor Sandy Berger. He wanted to hear my take on the back-and-forth on inspections. I reiterated our conviction that Iraq was actively working to defeat our inspections from achieving the necessary access to confirm there were no prohibited materials and activities. Of course, we were being very aggressive and going to some very sensitive places.

To illustrate this from Iraq's perspective I said, "Look, if you were Saddam's National Security Advisor, a guy named Abed Hamid Mahmud, you could never be sure that Scott Ritter wasn't going to show up at the West Wing gate demanding to search your safe, or else report you to the Security Council." (In fact, we would later try to do just that.) I went on: "That's pretty intrusive, but that's what we believe we need to do to get to the truth, and the resolutions explicitly permit that."

Berger was trying to see where it all ended. "But then what happens?"

"Well," I shrugged, "they either give us free rein to inspect long enough that we become confident they really do not have and will not rebuild WMD. Or they eventually throw us out, and it's crunch time. I know you probably don't want to hear this, but it is my view that UNSCOM needs to hold a mirror up to the Security Council and show the council the reality that it is not enforcing the resolutions it passed and Iraq is outlasting it."

"You don't think there is a way Baghdad will accept inspections and monitoring, with some new procedures for presidential sites?" Berger asked.

"No. Not over time. UNSCOM has been at this for six years. Every year, we have found Iraq has been holding something big back. Saddam can outlast the Security Council. We, the United States, cannot sustain our forces around him forever, and it is only under force that he accepts the inspections. The council is sick of UNSCOM. And, I fear, Washington is beginning to view UNSCOM and Iraq as two sides of the same coin. If the council tells us to go away, that's great. But it won't; it wants us to say we can do monitoring and inspections the way Iraq wants. I don't think you will get UNSCOM to agree to that."

Berger had a real problem that could not be kicked down the road much further. Iraq was becoming more hostile, and the issue was becoming inflamed domestically. My simple objective was to be clear about what our inspections could and could not do, especially over the long run. And under the circumstances, I made clear I felt the inspection process was running into a brick wall. We could not pretend it wasn't there.

I came out of the Berger meeting with an appreciation of how impossible the situation was for the people in the White House. They wanted UNSCOM to be able to do its job, but they didn't want to force the issue to the point of conflict. Yet they could not deal with an outcome in which UNSCOM gave Saddam a clean bill of health. They still wanted to avoid making a decision—but that was hardly a viable strategy.

When I heard the terms of Annan's agreement, I felt it was time to go. I drafted a resignation letter to Kofi Annan and shared it with a couple of colleagues. I commented on his effort to find workable procedures but stated my opinion that "neither you nor the Security

Council have been able to find the right mix of incentives and/or disincentives to cause Iraq to choose to fulfill its obligations. The current situation is that partial compliance is deemed acceptable by the international community." I went on to say, "We have learned from the experience of the IAEA in Iraq during the 1980s that ineffective monitoring may be *worse* than nothing since the presence of such activity offers a false security—which is often used to justify the sale of otherwise dubious dual-use equipment."

I judged that UNSCOM was exactly where the disarmament organization of the Treaty of Versailles had found itself after six years. The international community could not sustain the necessary pressure (which was perhaps impossible), and ultimately, it found a way of declaring success. I did not want the system to fail without all parties recognizing that it had failed and why it failed. By this time, I firmly believed that the Security Council, a disparate group with different and evolving agendas, could not sustain the will to force Iraqi acceptance of intrusive inspections and monitoring, essentially in perpetuity. I was very stubborn in my view (and Butler was of a like mind) that we should not allow the council to pretend it had an effective coercive monitoring system that would prevent Saddam from rebuilding WMD forever, when it did not.

As I was dithering over resigning, Richard Clarke, who was the top counterterrorism official at the NSC under Sandy Berger, asked to talk to me. He knew I was at the end of my rope at UNSCOM and had advice that I took as a message from Berger. Clarke said, "It won't do any good to resign. You could make a big splash in the press for two days and then you're gone. You will have no influence and someone else less competent will come in."

This part sounded like typical advice from Clarke. Stay in the game; you never know how it will turn out. I appreciated that. But I was also sick of the game. For almost five years, I had not lived in one place. What's more, I hated being part of some Security Council scam that I knew would not work. What kept me going was the team we had at UNSCOM. It had become a unit that had been through a lot together, and I did not want to see it bent to fit political expedients.

Then Clarke added something quite different: "And you know, of course, if you resign, you will never work in this town again." This was apparently the sting in the tail of the White House message. It was not a message I appreciated, but this was Washington, and I understood the types of people who populated the political positions. Ultimately, I decided to remain at UNSCOM and do what I could to highlight the failure by the Security Council to achieve the objectives of the ceasefire resolution. This was an "inconvenient truth" for all the Security Council governments, including Washington. But UNSCOM was not going to supply a politically expedient description of reality.

Only a month later, I found myself leading the UNSCOM team that would implement the presidential-sites agreement Annan had worked out. I was glad I stayed in the game. We made a good-faith effort to accomplish a baseline *inspection* (although Annan agreed with Aziz to call it a *visit*) that would serve a purpose for future monitoring. In practice, it was a farce.

Iraq had declared eight areas to be "presidential" and therefore off-limits to inspection. With the process agreed on by Annan, we would now have access as a "special group," though not for a regular inspection. Inspectors would go, accompanied by a party of twenty ambassadors and diplomats from all over the world—to observe that the inspection or visit was conducted properly and with the appropriate dignity. The accompanying swarm of diplomats was under the direction of a senior UN official, Jayantha Dhanapala. I headed the inspection team of nearly seventy inspectors divided into five subteams.

The sites were not trivial. In area, they totaled around thirty-five square kilometers, including over a thousand structures. Our teams had the limited objective of conducting the general survey of the sites and identifying each building as to general form and function. We had some specialized equipment to survey underground and take samples.

We immediately found ourselves highlighting the fissures in principle, which Annan's agreement had papered over. First, this circus was hardly a surprise inspection. Iraq had weeks to prepare while diplomats were identified and organized for their adventure out in the field. For most of them, it was like going on safari. They rode around in buses and watched as UNSCOM inspectors and Iraqi minders went about their rituals. (I did entice U.S. Ambassador Ryan Crocker to join me in climbing up the three-hundred-foot UNSCOM communications tower for a great view of Baghdad.)[2] The advance notice to Iraq had allowed the locations to be cleansed. There was not a single document in any of the buildings we entered, and there were only a couple token computers. Even the furniture was removed from most offices. You had to give credit to the Iraqis for an astonishingly thorough job of cleaning.

The most fundamental problem was that the Iraqi side had declared the presidential-sites inspection to be a onetime event. Once this exercise was complete, inspectors would never be coming back. My clearly stated view was that the visit only had utility as an initial survey mission so that future, true inspections could be better focused and easily accomplished. I made certain that this difference was well documented.

As the inspection teams spread out, they were tailed by dozens of minders as well as the diplomatic "dignity brigade" (as we called them). The diplomats had brand-new safari clothing or even jackets and ties (to display dignity in the hot Iraqi sun and in some very ratty sheds and warehouses). There were dozens of vehicles in the convoy; police screamed ahead to scatter the traffic out of the way. Everyone knew we were coming.

The Iraqis provided a large mix of minders from the Special Security Organization (SSO), the Mukhabarat, and the National Monitoring Directorate (NMD); these minders outnumbered the inspectors. I had at least six minders who followed me around. At one point, I walked up to the top of a wall that was about twelve feet high and a foot thick. It ran about twenty-five yards before it came to the side of a small shed. I walked across the top of the wall, and sure enough, a couple decided to follow me until they figured out this was a joke. I obviously was not trying to detect surveillance or lose them. They clearly had serious instructions to never let me out of their sight. A colonel with them was scared of heights. I think he wanted to shoot me for making him look wobbly in front of his men.

The only time any inspector was out of sight while in the presidential areas was to go to the bathroom. And then, the NMD immediately searched the bathroom afterward, presumably looking for any sort of surveillance device.

The head of the UN diplomatic group, Jayantha Dhanapala, was approached by General Amer Rasheed, who complained about our inspections taking global positioning system (GPS) coordinates at building corners. Rasheed declared that these would be given to the U.S. military and used to bomb Iraq. I said that the issue should be raised with me and proceeded to get in a vocal argument with Amer. Amer declared, "You know, Mister Duelfer, that you can survey the perimeter of the presidential areas, but not register the GPS coordinates of the building corners."

"No, Amer, we can do what we want with GPS. This is the way we are building our baseline inventory of buildings for this survey. We have blocked the area in sections on imagery-derived line diagrams. We are registering data on each building according to each site and including its location."

"We cannot accept that. You know full well your air force uses your UNSCOM data to bomb!" He had a point there, but the air force could have bombed without that data.

Getting louder, I shouted, "Look, General, do you really think the next satellite going over our heads doesn't see exactly where on this pathetic planet this pile of Italian marble sits? If Washington gets it in its head it wants to blow up this place, it can do so without a bunch of UNSCOM inspectors!"

The Iraqis regularly recalled to me that on January 17, 1993, the United States had bombed a facility in Zafaraniya called al Nida, using Tomahawk cruise missiles to hit three of four corners of the building. The building had been inspected by UNSCOM inspectors many times. The three targeted sections of the building had important equipment; the fourth untouched corner had nothing. Iraq concluded that UNSCOM inspection reports had provided information that informed U.S. military targeting. That one was hard to dispute.[3]

Amer started yelling back at me in a well-practiced shouting voice that all our inspectors were accustomed to.

I interrupted, "Excuse me, General Amer, I need a word with Jayantha over here." It suddenly dawned on me that to his gentle eyes, this dialogue probably didn't look like what the quietly polite and virtually inaudible Kofi Annan had in mind when he said inspections should respect the dignity and sovereignty of Iraq.

Dhanapala, a perpetually courteous, short, and very "diplomatic" Sri Lankan, had been gradually stepping back from the shouting match. I walked him a few steps further and said quietly and slowly, "Look, Jayantha, it always goes like this. Amer and I have been doing this for years. We shout and argue about stuff like this and then wind up agreeing on something. It's Iraq. And once you do it a few times, it's normal."

Amer and I resumed for a while longer and then agreed on a way of taking GPS readings at some distance from the buildings.

I walked through a few of the major buildings myself, including the Republican Palace, which five years later would become the headquarters of the Coalition Provisional Authority and, then, the U.S. Embassy. It was quite interesting to see these forbidden places that we had so carefully studied from aerial imagery. Some of our guys found the garage area where Saddam, in a fit of anger directed at his son Uday, had burned Uday's fleet of expensive vintage cars. We gave a close inspection to an underground command post we had previously known as Project 2000. It had been designed to survive bombings and had special air-filtration equipment in the event that chemical weapons were used against it.

Saddam's presidential secretary, Abed Hamid Mahmud, sought me out on several occasions. He had never before had direct contact with UNSCOM. Arguably the second-most-powerful man in Iraq, in charge of Saddam's security among other things, he came up to me while I was with an experienced Australian UNSCOM chief inspector named Roger Hill. We were looking at a map laid out on the hood of a Jeep Cherokee when a large, black Mercedes glided up. Out stepped Abed with a couple of guards and a translator.

He introduced himself needlessly. I said, "Well, I am Charles Duelfer, as you know, and this is Roger Hill." We shook hands.

"What's the problem?" Abed asked, gesturing to the map.

"We have to define the perimeters of the presidential area, and we have a few questionable areas," I replied.

"Where?" he asked.

Roger picked up with his Australian accent: "Here's one spot. See where this wall joins another from a separate building."

Abed declared, "That's out." I looked at Roger and shrugged, as though to say, well, if he says so. Roger moved on to another. Abed said, "In."

We went through all our questions in about five minutes. We had been expecting long hours of work with GPS handsets and haggling with less-senior Iraqis.

Then Abed signaled to one of his guards and pointed to the trunk of his Mercedes. The guard scurried off to open it. In my mind, I wondered what Abed would have in the trunk of his car. AK-47s, or RPGs? I was not expecting the guy to come back with a tray of chilled Pepsi-Colas, but he did. It would have made a great commercial.

We chatted for a while. I commented upon his pistol. It was a Tokarov with chrome plating. He drew it out and showed me.

"Look," he said. "It is inscribed by Qusay. Do you want to fire it?"

It was very tempting, but Roger's eyes were rolling. "Thanks," I said, "but I think our minders would get nervous. Another time." He smiled and eventually took his leave.[4]

Roger and I were still finishing our Pepsis when a white Mercedes rolled up containing General Amer Rasheed. I smiled and said, "We have solved all the problems of the perimeter." He was suspicious. Picking up on this, Roger ticked off the results.

Amer asked, suspiciously, "How do you know this?"

"Well, the presidential secretary, Abed Mahmud, stopped by to inquire if things were going smoothly. We said we were having trouble establishing some of the precise boundaries, and he said he could decide and he did."

Predictably, Amer exploded. "Abed can't even read a map," he shouted. "Come with me, and we'll go look at the areas and measure." Amer was correct. Abed did not get his job because he was the brightest bulb in Iraq.

The circus moved on from site to site over several days to Mosul, Lake Thar Thar, Jabul Makol, and Basra. On the long drive to Mosul, the convoy of UNSCOM vehicles, diplomat buses, and Iraqi minders constituted seventy vehicles. Overhead were both UNSCOM and Iraqi helicopters. At one point, the convoy pulled over to allow some laggards to catch up. It was evidently a very welcome opportunity for a large number of Iraqis to relieve themselves in the adjacent field. Probably a dozen were in the middle of the field generally pissing in the direction away from the road. An Iraqi MI-8 helicopter saw an opportunity and, before any of these Iraqis could react, swooped low over the field. The powerful downwash of the rotor had the desired effect on those in the field. The Iraqis were not without a sense of humor.

Saddam's secretary, Abed Mahmud, had one very serious, private conversation with me in Baghdad on April 2, 1998. He said that he wished me to tell the White House, Sandy Berger in particular, that he was open to dialogue and could be contacted through me if that was useful. Abed said I could always reach him through Ambassador Hamdoon in New York or the Iraqi ambassador in Amman—both of whom he trusted to pass any confidential messages. Iraq, he said, would be prepared to talk with the United States with no conditions and there was much that Iraq could offer. Iraq could be helpful with the Palestinian matter, perhaps accepting Palestinians in Iraq. There could obviously be oil deals and security arrangements. All was on the table. All that was needed was a dialogue. The United States could satisfy itself on WMD in Iraq if it would only open a dialogue with Baghdad. Abed concluded, "We can be your best ally in the region."

Abed would not have taken this step without explicit instructions from Saddam. (Years later, when I spoke with Abed in detention, he confirmed this.) I conveyed the message to Bruce Riedel, who ran Middle East affairs at the National Security Council. Riedel said that the NSC was then considering any new, even out-of-the-box options for Iraq. I wrote a one-page memo to Riedel, relating the Abed offer. I added for consideration the notion of replying with a message stating that if Iraq conveyed serious information about its WMD programs to the UNSCOM, then the United States would open confidential discussions at the ambassadorial level—perhaps Richardson in New York or elsewhere. I offered that this could be a way out for the United States, which appeared to be losing ground in the Security Council and headed toward a military confrontation that would not be successful. I noted that the problem was, of course, that any hint of dealing with Saddam would be dangerous in domestic politics and that there was the risk that Iraq would leak the dialogue to the French or Russians to further encourage them to terminate sanctions. I suggested that on balance, it was worth a try.

I never heard back, and neither did Baghdad. In my later sessions with Abed, who was in detention after the war, he asked why the United States could not come to terms with Baghdad. Why did it have to invade if all it wanted was to get rid of Saddam? I could not explain in any way that he could understand, nor did I want to.

Back in New York, I completed my report. Jayantha Dhanapala wrote a separate report. His was quite positive about the events. Mine was not. I highlighted some critical problems that the secretary general's staff thought or hoped could be diplomatically addressed. My report was focused on the strict characteristics required for monitoring Iraq. And from this perspective, the report had the tone of "the emperor has no clothes" in considering Annan's agreement with Baghdad.

UNSCOM continued to plan intrusive inspections, despite reluctance expressed from Washington. This coincided with a period when the technical support to UNSCOM from the United States was getting more advanced and the intelligence community was very concerned about Scott Ritter, who by then was becoming familiar to the media as the leader of some of our most provocative inspections. An active investigation of Ritter was under way, and the United States requested that only individuals with U.S., U.K., or Australian government security clearances be given the product of sensitive collection activity. We went along with this request, which left Ritter out. This was difficult, especially given his gung-ho personality. Ritter had achieved status far exceeding his former rank in the marines. The in-toxicating effect of dealing with the press and governments at high levels had pumped him up. Ritter was a proactive guy and hated what he considered the melting support by the Clinton administration.

At one point, he mentioned to me that he had seen to it that some very provocative UNSCOM sampling test results (that undermined Iraq's claims of never putting VX in missile warheads) got into the hands of people who would make the knowledge public. The idea was to force Washington to toughen up its support of UNSCOM. Sure enough, the VX story hit the front page of the *Washington Post* on June 23, 1998.

Years later, when I was discussing the end of UNSCOM with Iraqi officials, they made clear that this event was a turning point. Until that time, Iraqi senior leadership had thought that perhaps with some con-tinued cooperation, the United States would eventually go along with a positive finding by UNSCOM that Iraq had finally complied. How-ever, Iraq saw this newspaper story as a concerted move by Washington to fabricate evidence that would extend UNSCOM's investigations endlessly. Moreover, the complicated Iraqi declarations were now being evaluated by independent international experts in a series of meetings Butler had initiated to provide a "second opinion" to Security Council members who tended to doubt UNSCOM. Drawing on the same data UNSCOM had, the independent conclusions were pretty much the same—that is, Iraq's declarations could not be validated and sometimes were wrong.

Iraq saw this activity and the *Washington Post* VX story as an effort by Washington to cook the books.

At the same time, UNSCOM was accumulating experience that bred more doubt about Iraq. In one key case, an inspection team on July 18, 1998, found an inventory document for chemical weapons used during the Iran-Iraq War in an office in the air force headquar-ters. One of our most experienced chief inspectors, Gabriele Kratz-Wadsack (loaned to UNSCOM from the German army), had the document in her hands; the Iraqis seized it from her and would not re-turn it. The incident was not a total loss, since sharp-eyed American inspector Steve Black had already quickly and accurately copied down the figures. The importance of this was twofold. First, Iraq had been repeating that it had no more documents related to WMD. Second, the numbers did not conform to what Iraq had previously declared to us. The consumption of chemical-weapons bombs, according to this document, was thousands lower than Iraq had stated. This meant there were potentially thousands more chemical-weapons bombs to account for and potentially seven hundred more tons of agent. This was a major discrepancy, which we could not just write off to messy record-keeping. The differences were on the order of 30 percent.

In what turned out to be a final meeting, Butler led a visit to Baghdad during the first week of August 1998. With barely disguised contempt, Aziz addressed Butler: "You start."

Butler began with the summary of UNSCOM and Iraqi work on the outstanding issues that our analysts prepared. There was emphasis on the need for documents from Iraq to verify their declarations. Butler said we could not agree to "disarmament by declaration" without substantiation. As things stood, we could not verify what Iraq said, especially on VX, now that we had contradictory evidence.

Aziz took the floor, saying, "I am not surprised by what you say, Mister Butler. In our view and the view of every major fair nation, you must answer two questions: Are there weapons in Iraq? Is there a capability to produce weapons?"

"You promised me the work would be done honestly and quickly. UNSCOM has been neither quick nor honest," Aziz declared. He went on at length to state that the commission had almost completed its work in 1995 under Ekeus, but after Hussein Kamel, UNSCOM had opened a long series of minor issues to prolong the work. He said UNSCOM focused on the trivial, adding that the VX problem was illogical: "If we admitted anthrax, why wouldn't we admit VX?" Claiming the experts were just generating confusion, Aziz said the outside experts were people who did not know Iraq and that UNSCOM "brainwashed" them before they arrived in Baghdad.

Aziz went on to comment about individual UNSCOM experts. He singled out Nikita Smidovich as "one of the best experts in UNSCOM in confusion and procrastination." Amer Rasheed chimed in with a list of the "silly and trivial" questions to which UNSCOM demanded answers. Aziz concluded that there was a political decision to delay, not a technical case for delay.

The third-highest-ranking Iraqi WMD official, and in many ways the most articulate, was Dr. Amer al-Saadi. He was a presidential aide (with ministerial rank) who had held senior positions in the Military Industrial Commission. He then spoke to observe that UNSCOM was asking Iraq to "verify the unverifiable." He said, "Nothing is left, it is obliterated." It emerged that this was, in fact, the case. In the end, we had asked Iraq to prove the nonexistence of something—a task wholly dependent on trustworthiness. The Iraqis did not have WMD. But neither could we ever trust them.

Aziz said pointedly, "If you judge Iraq by Western standards, you will not reach the truth."[5]

There was a break in the meeting, and in the evening, when we recommenced, Aziz had a firm position: Iraq would no longer discuss the disposition of its past WMD programs. It had provided everything possible and necessary for UNSCOM to be satisfied. Iraq would not participate in any more inspection activity, other than monitoring designed to see that WMD programs were not restarted.

Aziz said at the time—and he told me again years later in prison at Camp Cropper—that it was clear to Iraq that the United States would not accept a report that could lead to lifting sanctions. Aziz said, "Therefore, we have a simple choice. Iraq could have sanctions with inspectors or sanctions without inspections." It chose without. The Iraqis did not know what military response they might be risking, but they knew they had support in the Security Council and in the secretary general's office. And with the domestic political crisis in Washington, the United States appeared weak.

The Iraqis had provided so many explanations over the years to explain their partial revelations that it became impossible for them to re-create a completely consistent and verifiable accounting of their WMD materials. Given the track record of past concealment and their reluctant admissions of key program elements, UNSCOM had no reason to give Iraq the benefit of the doubt. Moreover, we knew that Iraq's account was wrong at particular points and those points were more logically explained by a decision by Iraq to retain weapons than by the explanations Iraq offered, which were akin to "the dog ate my homework."

Baghdad had concluded that Washington must know the true status of Iraq's WMD, but would not acknowledge it. At that moment in August 1998, the question of truth was addressed, and we could not agree on a single truth. There were important interests seeking to validate different truths. Iraqi officials and civilians, Russians, the French, U.S. Republicans, U.S. Democrats, all had major stakes in what UNSCOM would declare.

Shortly after we returned from Baghdad, on August 26, 1998, Scott Ritter resigned in frustration with the reaction of Washington and the Security Council to Iraq's defiance of UNSCOM. Ritter's resignation letter declared that Iraq was not disarmed and the recent actions by the Security Council to downplay the significance of the Iraqi actions indicated the council would not enforce compliance with its own resolutions. He declared that Iraq had lied to UNSCOM and the world since day one. I certainly shared his frustration. I had said in an unguarded moment among some colleagues, "Madeleine Albright has blocked more inspections lately than Saddam Hussein." There were powerful forces at work, and UNSCOM was in the middle. Both Butler and I shared much of the sentiment Ritter expressed, but perhaps had slightly more understanding for the balancing acts political leaders have to perform.

Ritter stepped out of UNSCOM and directly into the world of the media. Within a week, on September 3, 1998, he appeared in front of a highly publicized joint hearing of the Republican-chaired Senate Foreign Relations and Armed Services committees. Senator John Warner, one of the most balanced and senior senators, said, "Major Ritter, you've leveled one of the most serious indictments against the top-level national security team of this country that has ever been done in contemporary times, in my judgment." He was referring to Ritter's specific complaint that Albright and Berger had requested that Butler remove Ritter as a chief inspector and had interfered with the conduct of UNSCOM inspections the previous spring.

Senator Warner went on to ask Ritter about the recent disclosures concerning VX, in particular: "The question of the discoveries you were making about VX gas, and there was a considerable amount of publicity given to that discovery, do you feel that that publicity was a factor in the decision that you allege that the secretary of state took?"

Ritter answered, "I believe that disclosure forced this administration to turn on the green light, which it had turned off back in April, concerning inspections of discovery."

Ritter evidently perceived the leaking of the VX laboratory analysis results to have successfully influenced the administration. No one seemed to consider the reaction in Baghdad to this leak.

The Republicans echoed Ritter's statements that Iraq remained a major WMD threat and the Clinton administration had blocked Ritter's inspections the previous April. Ritter became a vocal critic of the Clinton administration's Iraq policy.

Between August and November, there were a series of heated debates and conflicts in the Security Council to try to get a consensus whereby the Iraqis would accept full inspection activity again. On October 31, 1998, Baghdad announced an end to all UNSCOM activity, including monitoring inspections. Later that same day, President Clinton signed the recently passed Iraq Liberation Act, a bill that directed U.S. support for Iraq opposition groups, specifically, Ahmed Chalabi's Iraqi National Congress. This gave the first tangible substance to the previously stated objective of regime change as an administration objective.

Baghdad saw this act as a further indication that the United States was no longer serious about the UN disarmament process and lifting sanctions. The UN dialogue was getting nowhere on the readmittance of inspectors, and Clinton was getting close to launching air strikes.

Iraqi Ambassador Nizar Hamdoon worked intensely with the French and Russian delegations. He was also in contact with the secretary general's staff. Hamdoon was going out on a limb to draft with the Russians a letter, acceptable to the Security Council and Baghdad, that would permit inspectors back in. Later, Hamdoon told me he had difficulty communicating with Baghdad and was caught without instructions at times. The Russians apparently could reach their ambassador in Baghdad more readily, and that was, for the Iraqis and Russians, a more secure route. Hamdoon tried to put the best face on this effort. He said later he felt it would not work or endure, but argued that Iraq would be viewed more favorably by its supporters in the council if it made one last effort to work with the inspectors. At the last minute, he announced that Baghdad would agree.

Washington had to recall aircraft that were being positioned to attack.

The Security Council agreed to a month-long test of inspections. Then Butler would report whether Iraq had complied satisfactorily. It was the endgame playing out for inspections.

We sent in a wide range of inspection teams, including one to test access to sensitive presidential sites. The results were roughly the same. There were some obstructions, and we still had unanswered questions.

This was a very tense period. Butler had been in regular contact with both Madeleine Albright and Ambassador Richardson. He and I spoke at length on where all this was headed. The Security Council really wanted Butler to say everything was OK, that the mechanism it had created in 1991 would work, that Iraq was disarmed of WMD, and that we could monitor forever. The reality was that it was a fundamentally flawed and unstable system. The council could not force compliance without sanctions or military threat. The military threat depended on the United States, and sustaining a military posture around Iraq was expensive and impractical. The cost of maintaining the no-fly zones was very expensive. Butler understood all these dynamics. On December 15, 1998, he wrote a letter indicating that the level of cooperation Iraq provided was insufficient for UNSCOM to perform the task mandated by the UN Security Council.

Butler and I had discussed the content and tone of the letter. He had circulated a draft among the staff and asked for comments. He received no objections in the overall conclusions. Suggestions were made in tone. The U.S. Mission to the UN had passed along one request, that the message be clear. If the message was, "UNSCOM could work with Iraq," say it. If not, say that. If the administration was going to bomb Iraq, the White House needed clarity. Administration staff also asked for an early copy of the relevant text so they could send it to Air Force One carrying the president back from a visit to Israel.

On the evening of December 15, we began evacuating the UN-SCOM monitoring facility as a result of a meeting we had with the U.S. Mission in New York, where we were informed, in essence, that military action was imminent. We had an orderly but nervous period while the staff, for the last time, evacuated our carefully constructed and designed Baghdad Monitoring and Verification Center. As a last request, I asked our communications guy, a New Zealander named Roy Joblin, to leave the monitoring cameras on so we could watch from New York as long as they lasted. We also had a camera set up to view the interior of the monitoring center to note intrusions as they occurred. A few cameras remained active for several weeks. Each time we checked from New York, I felt like NASA contacting a probe on Mars and finding it was still operating.[6]

In the late afternoon of December 16, the Security Council met in its private chambers to discuss the crisis in Iraq and in particular Butler's report on Iraqi cooperation. The meeting was a continuation of discussions begun in the morning. Unlike most of these sessions, I did not have trouble staying awake in this one. I think even the well-fed diplomats at that table realized something was going to happen. Russian Ambassador Lavrov (later to become foreign minister) was particularly exercised. He was scathing about Butler's report and Butler personally. He declared that in a recent trip to Moscow, Butler had told Foreign Minister Sergei Ivanov that UNSCOM was close to resolving past issues. Now Butler was saying something else. Lavrov said harshly, "Either Butler was lying then, or he is lying now." It was about as blunt as it gets in the UN. Lavrov really did not care for Butler.

Suddenly a cell phone went off. I think it was Lavrov's, but in seconds, several other cell phones were ringing and the order of the meeting disintegrated as word spread that Baghdad was under attack. The American response called Desert Fox had begun, and the Security Council meeting ended. It was decided to reconvene in a public, televised session later that night.

I went back to the UNSCOM offices and checked on our staff who had evacuated to Amman and Bahrain. Butler went out to dinner with his security contingent and a couple of his advisors. I joined our experts in their offices.

The core of UNSCOM experts had been a close team for many years—a mix of nationalities and personalities. We knew this was the end. One of the cameras that still functioned was inside our empty and locked offices in Baghdad. It seemed likely that we would never see them again by any other means.

At 2130, the Security Council reconvened in public chambers. The debate was televised live. It lasted a couple hours and displayed for the world a deeply divided council. Some condemned the U.S. action; a few condemned Iraq.

When it was over, Iraqi Deputy Ambassador Musawi and I gravitated to each other in the hallway and found a quiet corner. It was approaching midnight. My country was bombing his country, and oddly, there was no one else I would have rather talked to at that moment. We both understood the inadequacies of the governments and UN that led to this circumstance. Musawi opened lightly.

"Well, you have really gotten your boss [Butler] into trouble now with the UNSCOM report." Musawi was referring to the pummeling by Lavrov and others. He continued, "The report is so unbalanced and unfair, I am glad. It makes our position easier."

I steered toward more pragmatic matters: "How do you interpret the position of the U.S. now?"

He said, "There is nowhere for Iraq to go in this process. What else can we do?"

I said, "Well, if you put three SCUDs on the table, that would signal serious intent." I told him that I personally believed that there were a small number of prohibited missiles left. If Baghdad declared them, at this point the Security Council might be inclined to declare success.

Musawi brought some notes out of his pocket. The United States had presented a démarche to them earlier, and he asked if there was anything new implied in it. I said, "It seems the same position, but if I learn otherwise, I will let you know."

Musawi then asked, "Do you think this bombing can lead us to a new start? Things would be so much better with an attitude of mutual cooperation. Otherwise, what is the point of this? Afterwards, perhaps there will be a moment when Washington will be able to talk to Iraq."

Inside, I agreed with Musawi. This bombing was the equivalent of some ritual bloodletting. It really would change nothing other than cause a recognition that the inspection process could not solve a political problem between Iraq and the Security Council and the United States. WMD and UNSCOM were surrogates for the real problem— Saddam. The possibility of dialogue after a bombing was a good thought, but reflected ignorance by Musawi on what was possible in Washington. A dialogue with the Saddam regime would be difficult for any U.S. administration, but especially one weakened by a pending impeachment trial.

"Maybe something will come of this," I said, but without hope.

As recently as a month before, both Hamdoon and Musawi had asked me if there could be a bilateral dialogue with Washington. I had passed these queries to the NSC and Ambassador Richardson. There was never any answer. The Clinton administration could not have a dialogue with Baghdad, even if it thought dialogue was a good idea. Clinton was in the midst of being impeached. A dialogue with the Saddam regime would have been used by the Republicans to shred the administration. I think Hamdoon understood this from his years in Washington, but he was instructed to ask, anyway. Each time I passed such entreaties to Washington, there was never any answer.

A decade later, now that we know the massive costs of removing Saddam, these options for dialogue—even with a tyrant—look much better. If nothing else, they were missed opportunities for Washington to gain more knowledge. As it was, I remained the only senior American with an extensive knowledge of the Iraqi leadership, and now that would be ending.

It was late in New York and would be early morning in Baghdad as Musawi returned to his office to contact his superiors. We shook hands. He still had no instructions prohibiting contact with me, but that would change. Musawi was a thoughtful observer. He was an unassuming Shia in the Iraqi mission. Later, Saddam would designate him as the ambassador to succeed Hamdoon. Almost exactly five years later, U.S. forces would locate Saddam hiding in a hole beneath a farmhouse in Tikrit. However, at that moment, all either of us knew was that things would soon be much different.

The United States (and the United Kingdom) conducted a limited bombing campaign, which had been carefully timed to begin between President Clinton's departure from Israel and the beginning of the Muslim holy month of Ramadan on December 20, 1998—roughly 100 hours. The raids also coincided with a critical House of Representatives decision to impeach President Clinton. The decision was delayed a couple of days as a result of the strikes, and three weeks later, an impeachment trial of the president was under way in Congress.

The trigger was pulled, and thirty or so targets associated with the previous WMD programs and current missile-development programs were hit. Little of consequence was destroyed on the ground, but the bombing killed UNSCOM and the illusion that the Security Council could implement its objectives. The council was in turmoil. There had been no vote authorizing the use of force. Washington argued it wasn't necessary. The Russians, French, and Chinese felt otherwise and were furious.

Kofi Annan said the bombing was a sad day for the UN and for the world. He said his thoughts were with the people of Iraq and the 307 UN humanitarian workers who remained in Iraq. Annan had staked his position on negotiating a resolution. He was of the clear view that peace at any price was better than war. By his actions, it was clear he thought a less rigorous and less intrusive inspection system would do.

Shortly after New Year's, I saw Musawi in the hallway of the UN. He stopped briefly to say, "If we knew that was all you would do, we would have ended this much sooner."

CHAPTER 9

Breaking Out: No Inspections, Crumbling Sanctions

The end of inspections in December 1998 was a triumph for Tariq Aziz over UNSCOM and the United States. Iraq was on a roll, gathering momentum that would accelerate the erosion of sanctions, if not cause their complete elimination. Iraq's illicit revenues went from about $250 million in 1998 to $2.6 billion in 2001.

Both Aziz and Nizar Hamdoon told me later that Baghdad had been pursuing two tracks to relief from sanctions. One was cooperation with the inspectors, albeit in minimalist, incremental steps, while testing the response from the Security Council and Washington, in particular.

The second track was to erode support in the Security Council for sanctions and to foster sanctions breaking. In 1998, Iraq finally concluded that Washington was not going to move on sanctions, no matter how much the regime cooperated. After the war, Aziz pointed explicitly to the VX leak to the press. "The leadership became convinced that the Americans would create more problems as old ones were resolved," Aziz said to me, adding, "Mister Duelfer, you know I visited Washington and we had practical relations with mutual respect. I flew to Andrews Air Base in my own 747. It would have been normal for governments to proceed with a dialogue. All governments

eventually change. We could have been on a different path now." He
was arguing that not only did Washington lose inspections in 1998,
but by not opening a dialogue, even a modest one, the United States
trapped itself so that war seemed unavoidable. Aziz's analysis failed to
take into account the political consequences for any administration in
Washington to open a dialogue with Saddam.

In 1998, it seemed Baghdad had no reason to regret ending cooperation with UNSCOM, except that there was no clear path to formal
cessation of the sanctions. The United States was still implacably opposed to the regime, as evidenced when Congress passed the Iraq Liberation Act, which mandated support to opposition groups. It was not
a coincidence that Iraq notified UNSCOM of the termination of
Iraq's cooperation on the day President Clinton signed the act.

The landscape in 1999 changed quite favorably for Iraq. Perhaps the
most salient reason was that the paradox of U.S. Iraq policy became
obvious. The Clinton administration demanded Saddam's compliance
with arms inspectors, but refused to acknowledge any possibility of
changing sanctions until Saddam was gone.

Over the years, the Iraqi deputy UN ambassador, Sayeed al-Musawi,
repeatedly asked me for my interpretation of what Washington would
do. He was especially inquisitive after Secretary Madeleine Albright
had made a speech on March 26, 1997, at Georgetown University, on
U.S. policy toward Iraq. Albright made clear that the United States
would not support lifting sanctions before there was a new government in Baghdad: "We do not agree with the nations who argue that
if Iraq complies with its obligations concerning weapons of mass
destruction, sanctions should be lifted. Our view, which is unshakable,
is that Iraq must prove its peaceful intentions." She then asked rhetor-
ically, "Is it possible to conceive of such a government under Saddam
Hussein?" Her answer was, "And the evidence is overwhelming that
Saddam Hussein's intentions will never be peaceful."

Hamdoon and Musawi were trying to explain what this meant to
Baghdad. The French and Russians and even the British were asked by
the Iraqis for their interpretation. Musawi said to me that the other Se-

curity Council members were telling Baghdad that it was just a position largely driven by domestic politics in Washington. The Republicans were challenging Clinton for being too complacent on Iraq.[1] I avoided giving Musawi any direct answer, but did say that Washington was difficult to predict, even by those at high levels in the administration.

Musawi replied, "Well, Mister Duelfer, there is a long tradition of UN resolutions on many subjects not being implemented. The implementation of sanctions against Iraq may be one of them." He suggested that the U.S. refusal to lift sanctions even if Iraq complied with disarmament measures was no different from other council members that violated the sanctions before they were officially lifted. Baghdad's view was supported by Moscow in practice.

In retrospect, I am surprised Iraq cooperated as long as it did, especially once the Oil-for-Food program began in December 1996. By the end of 1997, Iraq realized how much income it would derive from the Oil-for-Food program and how much support it could leverage from council members like Russia and France. At the same time, UNSCOM was drilling pretty deep into Iraq's security operations.

From the Iraqi perspective, it was difficult to comprehend why the vaunted CIA did not know the diminished status of their WMD programs, especially after they had been forced to reveal so much and there were so many defectors. On several occasions, senior Iraqis would say something like, "Mister Duelfer, we understand you must know the true extent of the programs. They are obliterated, and your people must know this. Why must you keep denying that?"

The Iraqis (and many other countries) have believed that U.S. intelligence has almost magical technical abilities to ferret out information. Hollywood fosters this impression. Indeed, there is some very interesting technology. But collecting data and accumulating understanding are two very different things. Generally, I found the Iraqis could not believe how little we really knew or how little we understood.

The extent of U.S.-Iraqi incomprehension was evident in a conversation I had with General Amer Rasheed while waiting outside a building in the Republican Palace area during the presidential palace inspections. The Iraqis had just built a freestanding wall about twenty feet high and thirty feet long set about twenty-five feet from the entrance to one palace building.

"General, may I ask you a question about this wall?"

"Yes, Mister Duelfer, of course," he replied. We were both relaxed and killing time while inspectors toured the building.

"What is the purpose of the wall?"

Amer assumed I knew the answer already, but said, "Well, you know, we have carefully studied your cruise missiles, and we know they are targeted by images. We thought a wall would confuse the imagery guidance system and possibly . . . possibly cause the missile to either detonate early or not at all."[2]

That sounded logical; it might even work. "Well, maybe," I admitted. "But that doesn't help with bombs."

Amer shrugged and then said, "May I ask you a question?"

"Sure."

"Mister Duelfer, why do you always blow up buildings?" he asked seriously.

Shrugging, I said, "It's in our genes. We're Americans, that's what we do. We blow up buildings." I was being facetious, but it was a fascinating question. Why *do* we always blow up buildings? One of the most interesting aspects of my work with the Iraqis was how much I learned of our own assumptions and characteristics, which, untouched by such a contrasting light or experience, go unnoticed.

We blow up buildings because our intelligence system is constructed around buildings. At its heart is an assumption that a building represents a capability or something of value. Satellites take pictures of facilities and photo-interpreters will assess the purposes of various buildings, be they hospitals, missile plants, or intelligence headquarters. Military campaigns designed to degrade the enemy's capabilities are largely based on buildings. Images are digitized and put into the computer guidance systems of cruise missiles (or GPS coordinates are entered), and the missiles, or aircraft, bomb the buildings. Then we conduct "battle damage assessment" based on imagery of damaged buildings.

The Iraqis had figured this out and took measures to dissolve the images we could see. They simply moved equipment, documents, or other valuables and dispersed them outside the facilities. They could put valuable machine tools out in a field, and we would not notice or target them, because there was no building to attract our attention. During the 1991 war, Iraqis quickly learned that the huge, German-built ammunition bunkers were large targets, and so they began to store ammunition, even chemical munitions, out in open areas that drew little attention in photographs viewed on a screen in an office cubicle thousands of miles away.

Of course, the same Iraqis who could deceive U.S. intelligence were capable of deceiving themselves as well. Although they were proud of their ability to conceal targets, they assumed our intelligence community must know they had no WMD. Our continued insistence that they might have WMD led to some strange questions that I would be asked, very confidentially. These questions suggested that even some very senior Iraqis thought that while *they* had absolutely no evidence that Iraq retained WMD, if the CIA was convinced that Iraq indeed had WMD, then maybe there was some very secret reserve that only Saddam and the CIA knew about.

Baghdad had successfully ended UNSCOM and built sympathy in the Security Council at a very low cost. While the Security Council clearly could not lift the sanctions without Iraq's accepting UN inspectors, the growing consensus was that a new, more "realistic" resolution had to be passed if the council were to achieve its objectives and Iraq were to comply. The Russians and French competed to lead this effort, and the Security Council began to debate how to proceed.

In early January 1999, just at the beginning of the Clinton impeachment trial, news leaks began spilling out about "spying," by and through UNSCOM, on Iraq. The general conclusion emanating from these stories was that the United States had co-opted UNSCOM. This was played up by Iraq and its supporters on the Security Council. Much of this was inspired by Scott Ritter, who had become increasingly vocal about the techniques used by UNSCOM in Iraq. There is an inexorable suction from the media for something new to be said, and Ritter provided them more and more. He seemed to be lashing out not just at the Clinton administration (cheered on by the Republicans in Washington), but also at his old organization, UNSCOM.

This began a feeding frenzy that suited many interests around Washington and the rest of the world. Republicans took political advantage of the disintegrating Iraq policy that left Saddam stronger. Parts of the Clinton administration (not consumed with the impeachment trial) tried to respond that the so-called spying showed how tough they were. Iraq was delighted because it painted the UNSCOM inspectors as evil CIA agents, a portrayal that gave Baghdad justification for not cooperating with UNSCOM. The French and Russians liked it because it supplemented their views that a more neutral body needed to be created to replace UNSCOM and Iraq needed a clear path out of sanctions. The two countries provided "intelligence" to Kofi Annan, showing that UNSCOM was conducting inappropriate activities at the behest of the United States.

Finally, the dust-up suited Annan because it tended to make his efforts in dealing with Saddam look more reasonable and undermined Richard Butler (who was barely civil to the secretary general after what Butler considered a Neville Chamberlain–like appeasement effort with Saddam). It was an agreeable reality for many interested parties.

Conveniently lost in this swirl of revelations about UNSCOM inspection techniques was Iraq's defiance in limiting UN-mandated access and the Security Council's inability to make Iraq comply fully with its own resolutions. The events of early 1999 allowed everyone, including Washington, to let UNSCOM take the fall. And take the fall it did.[3]

UNSCOM was a spy magnet. Charged with disarming the highly secretive regime of Saddam Hussein, the commission had access to what was called "a denied area" in U.S. parlance. It had to penetrate the shield and sword of the Iraqi security services. These roles made life interesting at UNSCOM, since in many cases, you never knew who was working for whom. The previously discussed concealment investigation teams were a special target, and we took reasonable precautions. Still, credible rumors suggested that UNSCOM phones were subject to monitoring by countries that would pass information to Iraq. In the same vein, multiple countries used UNSCOM inspections as a way of getting their nationals into Iraq for a variety of reasons beyond merely supporting UNSCOM. Iraq was the most pivotal issue for many governments, and their intelligence organizations responded.

Newspapers love spy stories, especially, it seems, when the president is being impeached. The *Washington Post* ran a couple of detailed articles that concentrated on Scott Ritter. There seemed to be a coincidence of interests by a new young *Post* reporter who fortuitously inherited the UNSCOM beat and Ritter as a source just when Ritter was bursting with tales to tell. However, Ritter was not alone. There was clearly someone, besides Ritter, who had access to classified, compartmented information and who revealed it. I do not know for certain, but it seemed then that some of the leaked stories conveniently served to bolster the argument that the Clinton administration was being aggressive against the Saddam regime—a charge being leveled by Republicans at the time. Moreover, any news story that deflected attention from the travails of the impeachment would have been positive for the politicians in the administration.[4]

The Clinton administration opened no investigation of what appeared to be a felony. Some of my colleagues in Washington had their suspicions about the source, and a politically motivated leak about UNSCOM activities would certainly not be beyond the young political appointees I observed. In my opinion, this whole period reflected the expediency that had befallen the Clinton administration while it wrestled with its own chaos. The decision not to initiate an investigation into the leaks highlighted to me the vagaries of our justice system as it relates to security issues. Some leaks get investigated relentlessly, and some don't, depending on the circumstances. (Illegal leaking also seems to be a nonpartisan tactic, as later events in the Bush administration would show.)

The aggressive UNSCOM actions taken in Iraq and the close collaboration with various national intelligence agencies were thoroughly justified, in my opinion. The Security Council had demanded that Iraq comply with its demands on complete disclosures as part of the ceasefire resolution. This was a coercive demand made after a major war. UNSCOM was what Iraq got instead of an invasion and occupation in 1991.

Of course, over time, Iraq tried to transform the agreement into something akin to arms control, and it bought the support of others, like Russia and France, both of which played minimal or no roles in the 1991 war. And the will of Security Council members flagged— even in Washington. But before that support slipped, UNSCOM caused Iraq to give up virtually all its weapons and production capacities. This was a direct result of the aggressive, intrusive actions by UNSCOM. By the same token, Iraq was not about to put up with such measures forever, as required by the Security Council's requirement for long-term monitoring.

The U.S. intelligence support to UNSCOM also broke new ground in Washington. Never before had such extensive and sensitive support been provided to an international organization. The U-2 surveillance was flown at the request of UNSCOM, and similarly, the collection of information in the invisible part of the electromagnetic spectrum was in support of, and requested by, UNSCOM. The commission did not have the technical capacity to collect, decrypt, and translate material. Others did, which meant they would get to see the material their technology collected.

In retrospect, the U.S. intelligence community had become *too* reliant upon UNSCOM. Our inspection reports offered incredible details about the Iraq WMD capacity, and we had direct access to facilities and people all over Iraq. The intelligence community had nothing independently that came close to this access. Therefore, it was caught flat-footed and largely blind when UNSCOM left Iraq in December 1998. Moreover, as time went on, uncertainty about Iraq's WMD potential naturally grew. The extent of this problem permeated the U.S. intelligence community in 1999, just as the UN Security Council was arguing over a new resolution. The United States had virtually no clue what Iraq was doing with WMD.

At UN headquarters in New York, discussions about Iraq lagged. The United States was in an extraordinarily weak position, and everyone knew it. Clinton escaped impeachment, but looked ridiculous from Baghdad. The spying stories made UNSCOM's position weak, and the commission was reduced to reviewing materials and information collected from outside Iraq.

I was in a particularly awkward position as the publicly identified senior American with complete knowledge of all U.S. and UNSCOM "spying" activities. Nevertheless, I actively worked to preserve the tough characteristics I felt necessary for any inspectors to credibly disarm and monitor Iraq. The State Department senior levels had all but abandoned UNSCOM. Albright, who had made her reputation by talking tough on Iraq years earlier, now relegated Iraq to others and became immersed with the Kosovo crisis. The only objective left for the administration seemed to be a mechanism to prevent sanctions from disintegrating completely. Ambassador Bill Richardson, to his great credit, stuck by us, but he could not do more than the White House would support.

Albright now needed Russian support or at least acquiescence for NATO actions in Kosovo. The disintegration of the former Yugoslavia drew strong interest from the Russians, who had substantial stakes and interests in Serbia. Russian UN Ambassador Lavrov made good use of Albright's needs in the Kosovo matters as leverage for Russian objectives with regard to Iraq.

Likewise, French support was required in the Security Council to achieve Kosovo objectives. As Washington and NATO edged closer to a bombing campaign, cooperation was required from both Russia and France. In the chess game at the UN Security Council, Washington (and London) would concede on UNSCOM, as long as Moscow and Paris would keep the sanctions. If Washington and London had to trade UNSCOM away for support on Kosovo, then so be it. The higher priority at that point was Kosovo. UNSCOM was last year's problem.

Within these overarching dynamics, during the spring of 1999, several drafts of resolutions to reconfigure the UN inspection system were floated. The Russians had a draft, as did the British. The French said they would work on both these drafts and, at the same time, had their own draft. Interestingly, the Russian draft would have retained the UNSCOM name, but mandated broader participation. The British version killed UNSCOM and replaced it with a new organization. At this point, in case anyone had any lingering doubts, it was now clear the Security Council would no longer be able to sustain the type of coercive inspection system that would cause Iraq to permanently and forever forsake WMD.

The Security Council debated for a year what a new inspection resolution should include. The only party feeling any pressure was the United States, which was desperate to keep a consensus to retain sanctions of some sort. Iraq was restoring its prestige, and business in Baghdad was booming.

Denied access to Iraq, UNSCOM staff was reduced, mostly to experts in New York. Butler requested the production of a compendium document that would summarize the status of work in each weapons area. This was completed at the end of January 1999. I directed a second project to design a monitoring system that would, based on our experts' judgments, meet the requirements of the resolutions. My goal was to leave a benchmark by which any future organization's monitoring system could be compared. The UNSCOM staff had developed a lot of expertise, and we spent substantial time on this analysis. I was concerned that the council would approve a diminished monitoring system that would not be robust. Already, in April 1999, proposals for a new inspection body talked about "reinforced monitoring," which was code for exactly the opposite, a diminished system. The French and Russians had been around Madison Avenue enough to know that whatever they proposed, they would call "reinforced."

Other activities of the staff included developing a data management system based on the numerous Iraqi sites UNSCOM had inspected over the years. This database was an extremely useful tool. It was based on sites in Iraq and incorporated photographs and other data, including visits, people, weapons programs, contracts, and interviews. In 1999, this was more advanced than it sounds now in 2009. The database was an up-to-date catalog on the Iraqi industrial base, military, security, and political structure. Over the years, UNSCOM had been provided some very sensitive data by individual countries. The data remained separately held. As it became clear that UNSCOM would be terminated and a new, more open organization was to be established, we began a process of returning or destroying sensitive data, which had been provided by some governments under the assumption it would be protected. It was doubtful that the UN-SCOM records would be secure in a new organization. This was done very quietly because of the concern that some council members were already overtly and covertly seeking to gain access to UN-SCOM records. One obvious step was to return U-2 imagery to the United States.

There was one ongoing collection activity that I continued. Some European countries received a large number of Iraqi asylum-seekers—tens of thousands, in some cases. We had established a confidential line of communication with the governments to keep an eye out for Iraqis with connections to the military-industrial complex or security services. For those governments, UNSCOM could provide useful validation of the claims these individuals made to support asylum requests.

Two particularly interesting cases arose. One was a former minder for UNSCOM inspectors—mostly for our chemical-weapons experts. His job was to accompany the teams wherever they went in Iraq. He indicated a couple of interesting points. First, he had been asked by the SSO to begin an affair with a female UNSCOM translator. He ducked that by passing the task on to another security officer, who, he said, successfully accomplished his mission. Second, the individual also told us that he was required to take a sealed carton of documents to his home for storage. This was a frequent occurrence since the Iraqis knew we had avoided inspecting any private homes, for the practical reason that there were simply too many and Iraq would have complained that this was an affront to its sovereignty and dignity. His information was very interesting, but did not point explicitly to prohibited weapons, only the well-known efforts to thwart UNSCOM inspectors from achieving surprise inspections.

A second individual was directly involved in the missile program. Nikita Smidovich and I traveled to the European country where he had become a refugee. Nikita had met with him once before. His information had checked out. For Nikita and me, this was a pleasant change from the usual trips to the Middle East. For my part, I was always bemused by the fact that I would be traveling with and trying to work out a puzzle jointly with this former Soviet official, whom I genuinely admired.

This session touched an area Nikita knew in great depth. The Iraqi described detailed aspects of the ongoing Iraqi missile programs, but did not establish that the range was explicitly beyond that permitted by the UN. He did, however, provide information concerning the people and mechanisms for bringing technology into Iraq and described how Iraq used companies in Jordan to accomplish some tasks. Iraq had even conducted some limited missile work at a site in Jordan.[5]

The defector's information, in retrospect, was very accurate—Iraq had significant ballistic missile programs under way. In 1999, however, there was nothing that UNSCOM or anyone else could do with it. In fact, we continued to receive information about much smuggling into Iraq for missile and other programs—especially with Belarusian, Ukrainian, Romanian, and Russian connections. Many of the reports turned out to be correct, once the Iraq Survey Group probed the regime's missile transactions in 2003–2004. But we did not get such explicit reports of WMD, other than ballistic missiles.

In July 1999, Richard Butler came to the end of his term at UNSCOM. He had an impossible job and, in the end, had to accept that his choices were limited to variations on how best to wind up UNSCOM. I believe he was correct to strive to make the parties realize there was neither the will nor the mechanism to sustain disarmament and intrusive monitoring against Iraqi obstruction. It was a bold position and, in the UN, rare. The UN, naturally, prefers to adjust process to accommodate conflicting views rather than highlighting a failed process in a way that leads to conflict. The secretary general of the UN worked for peace at any price. Butler, by his style and his sense of what was right, did not let any of the parties off the hook.

Butler entered the conflict at the most difficult time. (Conversely, Ekeus shrewdly or luckily left at a propitious moment.) Butler also tolerated a very difficult deputy—me. I had long experience with the Iraqis and our experts. In a way, maybe I knew both sides too well. I tried to serve as a mediator between Butler and the experts, who were used to the deep knowledge of Ekeus and had less patience with Butler's approach. I also tried to moderate the Clinton administration's attempts to influence Butler's pronouncements. The White House, no matter who happens to be there, can exert substantial influence, and there is a natural tendency for political interests to be interleaved with security interests. I made known my opinion that the White House was pushing Butler in ways that were beyond what was helpful for UNSCOM or, indeed, the United States. There were substantial domestic political motivations underpinning the administration's dialogue with Butler. This is not surprising, given the circumstances that mired the Clinton administration. As the Iraq crisis in late 1998 intensified, Albright and others requested that Butler not bring me to their sensitive meetings. I took that as a compliment.

Butler was a favorite with the media. He spent a lot of time on television. I learned a great deal from this. And I think the Iraqis, particularly Tariq Aziz, did as well. The popular reality created by television was one of great influence, even if it bore little relationship to a more analytical reality. Butler's Australian accent swayed the views of millions. If he said something, it sounded good and became a fact—even if the UNSCOM experts sometimes cringed when it did not accord with their facts.

The media covering the Iraq-UNSCOM-UN conflict sought out lots of former inspectors. It seemed as if everyone and his dog was a former UN inspector and lived off the briefest of inspection experiences for years. The demand to fill twenty-four-hour airtime creates a market for "experts," and more and more former UN inspectors took up microphones to help fill the void. Some of the least informed, and the most biased, became television favorites. The Iraqis hated this. At one point, Baghdad was so furious with a CNN special on UNSCOM concealment inspections that it threatened to throw CNN out of Iraq if the network did not modify the program. CNN had largely made its reputation by broadcasting live from Baghdad during the 1991 war. It could not afford to miss covering a war inside Iraq—and the Iraqis understood this. Consequently, the network complied with the regime's demands. The CNN producer was unhappy that journalistic independence had been compromised and that, as a practical matter, a business decision had shaped the content of its reportage. Baghdad was shrewd enough to know that journalists will trade independence for access, and it understood that shaping the image over the airwaves was becoming more important. Television performances were a strong factor in shaping the agreed-on reality.

On Monday, June 28, 1999, the remaining experts of UNSCOM at UN headquarters held a modest farewell for Butler. As one more moment in the slow dismemberment of UNSCOM, it was a low-key event with little participation from outside UNSCOM. Ambassador Butler had originally been appointed by the secretary general for a two-year period with the assumption that the Australian government would pay his salary. The conservative Australian government did not support Butler for the position and originally balked at paying his salary. Only after a strong intervention by Madeleine Albright did it agree. Kofi Annan, after two years of friction with Butler, certainly wasn't going to ask him to stay, nor was the Australian government going to suggest it.

The only other farewell event was a very generous reception hosted by U.S. Ambassador Richardson. The ambassador had always appreciated the fact that UNSCOM was caught in the middle of some tough pressures. He understood Butler and offered a counterpoint to the coarse, semipolitical requests made by Albright. Richardson did a good job of balancing policy concerns with people, and the recognition he gave Butler for his efforts was well done and well received.

I was left as the acting chairman of UNSCOM. It was a team I enjoyed, even though we knew the Security Council was going to dissect us. My goal in the time remaining was to leave a good system and legacy. Our experts analyzed existing data to crystallize the remaining questions about the Iraqi accounting of their previous WMD programs. We concluded a careful study of requirements for a monitoring system in January 2000.

Meanwhile, Baghdad was in the middle of an economic explosion. The Baghdad International Fair in November 1999 attracted hundreds of companies from all over the world seeking to get a piece of the Iraqi action. Baghdad made clear that it was only a matter of time before sanctions collapsed or were lifted and anyone who wanted business in the future better be a good friend now. Each successive Baghdad fair became grander. Years later, I asked one of my teams at the

Iraq Survey Group to examine the hotel records of the Rasheed Hotel (the Mukhabarat maintained them). They told a fascinating story of the business growth. By the end of 1999, commercial and government officials were swooning over the prospect of Iraqi contracts. The Rasheed Hotel was bursting with businessmen. Tariq Aziz's strategy was working quite well.

In 2004, Tariq Aziz recalled, "You see, it was not Iraq that was breaking the sanctions. The other countries were breaking the sanctions by providing Iraq what was needed. This was a natural evolution which we encouraged. Naturally, we would have preferred to do business with more Americans. We did have some Americans whom you know. But other countries were more pragmatic. It was in their interests to do business with Iraq. They understood as well that Iraq provided stability in this region. This period was a great success."

He was right.

Finally, on December 17, 1999—exactly a year after the Clinton bombing of Iraq—the Security Council finally passed a new resolution (UNSCR 1284) that made clear that there was an intention to lift Iraqi sanctions once Iraq accepted new inspections under new and less restrictive conditions. A new, more diverse organization was created: the UN Monitoring, Verification and Inspection Commission (UN-MOVIC). (Given that the Russians were a key force in shaping this to accommodate Iraqi concerns, the wags at UNSCOM suggested the correct pronunciation of the acronym UNMOVIC must rhyme with "Milosevic.")

French Ambassador Alain Dejammet explained his vote for the new resolution and organization:

> UNMOVIC will be very different from UNSCOM, and that is a good thing. The new Commission will follow the principles of professionalism, collegiality and universality. Those principles should guarantee its independence from all Member States and ensure that, like the IAEA and the Organization for the Prohibition of Chemical Weapons, it enjoys the respect of all, including Iraq. The Commission will have the same powers and duties as its predecessor; including the duty to abide by the Memorandum of Understanding

of February 1998 [this was the Kofi Annan–Tariq Aziz agreement]. But its behavior, its methods, its organization and its composition will have been reformed in depth.

The use of force to bring about the return of inspectors is neither desirable nor practicable, as shown by the experience of December 1998. The draft (until voted) resolution therefore had to include a mechanism for realistic incentives for the Iraqi authorities; this lies in the suspension, then the lifting, of sanctions.[6]

Dejammet clarified a couple of features. Aziz had for years been trying to metamorphose the coercive disarmament mechanism into an arms-control mechanism. The French and Russians were offering him one. Arms control under UNMOVIC replaced the forced disarmament agenda of UNSCOM.

The French ambassador also made clear that force would not be used against Iraq, only positive incentives. Baghdad, and especially Tariq Aziz, had reason to be very pleased with their efforts. The Clinton administration tried to state that this was a tough resolution that showed that the international community was committed to Iraqi compliance with disarmament. This was definitely not what it looked like to the Iraqis.

Aziz had just returned from a visit with Russian Premier Vladimir Putin and, being aware of the French view that force could not be used against Iraq, did not welcome the new moderated resolution. On Iraqi radio on December 18, he stated that the resolution was unacceptable to Iraq and did "not respond to Iraq's legitimate demand to lift the siege." He declared that Iraq would only accept immediate steps to "lift the siege without any additional restrictions and conditions."

The resolution required the secretary general to find a candidate to head the new organization. In a back-to-the-future moment, he asked Rolf Ekeus to return and so informed the Security Council in a letter dated January 17, 2000. Ironically, Ekeus had previously told me that in his opinion, the new resolution was a seriously flawed document that was a major retreat by the council and would leave the inspectors unable to do their job. Ekeus did not have to worry that it would become his problem. In the note transmitting Annan's decision to the council members, the president of the council said he would assume concurrence unless he heard objections by 12 noon on January 18. There were vociferous objections from the Russians and French (echoing the reaction of Baghdad). Annan quickly withdrew it and went on to suggest Hans Blix, the former head of IAEA. Blix was a much more tolerable candidate, and key members of the council gave agreement.

I stayed at UNSCOM until Blix arrived at the end of March. To his credit, Blix retained some long-term UNSCOM experts (though sometimes in unrelated or diminished jobs).

With the arrival of Blix, the system had achieved a stable situation and everyone was relatively happy. The Security Council had approved a new resolution and had a process in place for Iraq to continue to sell as much oil as it wanted. Washington had a mechanism that would prolong the sanctions in place, even if they were leaking massively. There was an election coming, and the administration did not want Iraq to be a prominent issue. Even Baghdad was relatively happy because money was flowing and sanctions were eroding. This translated into greater international influence, especially in OPEC. More importantly, Iraq's supporters, Russia and France, were now exercising more influence in the council, and there was no risk of further "enforcement" actions to force Iraq to accept inspectors.

After a thirty-day overlap with Blix, I left the UN for the last time, after six and a half years. I returned to Washington and met with Under Secretary Tom Pickering, then the senior career Foreign Service officer at the State Department. As the number three at the department and a former UN ambassador himself, Pickering followed Iraq closely. Since I was a career U.S. government civil servant still being paid by the State Department, I inquired if there were any positions that he thought I would be suited for. Pickering responded that unfortunately, this late in the administration, the department just wasn't sending up nominations for jobs that required Senate confirmation. It was a polite way of saying no. No one ever told me explicitly that I had burned my bridges with the State Department, but it was clear from my meeting with Pickering that whatever I did at the UN was not going to be rewarded or even tolerated at the State Department. Secretary Albright, while complimentary to me in person, was aware of my previous concerns about the U.S. support and use of UNSCOM. I was a reminder of the failure of Iraq policy.

My position was not, in fact, unusual for a career civil servant who becomes too senior without being politically aligned one way or the other. Moreover, the State Department is dominated by the Foreign Service, which has its own union and fiercely defends its primacy for senior positions in the department. It came as no surprise that the State Department wanted no part of someone with so much Iraq experience. I was also relieved. Former colleagues had warned me that the department had become quite stultifying. I would rather have gone back to Baghdad.

I had many years of experience working with Iraqis and their weapons programs at the UN and had unique, direct experience in Iraq with senior Iraqis. I figured that it would be interesting to do some academic writing on the subject. I suggested to Pickering that perhaps the problem of what to do with me could be solved by my placement as a scholar in residence someplace. He readily agreed, and I quickly found a position at the Center for Strategic and International Studies in Washington, in its Middle East Section directed at the time by Judith Kipper.

In addition to allowing me the time to write articles and longer pieces on Iraq and UNSCOM, I was able to keep up with the contacts I had made with a range of Iraqis. I also participated in various international conferences addressing Middle East issues. Being detached from the State Department, I was free from many constraints imposed on State Department and other U.S. government officials concerning contacts with foreigners. I was just another academic.

CHAPTER 10

Transition

Iraq was a minor issue in the 2000 presidential campaign. It did not separate the candidates. George W. Bush and Al Gore had similar declared positions: Saddam must comply with UN resolutions; regime change was desirable. The UN Security Council had been renewing the sanctions, and that kept "Saddam in his box," as the outgoing Secretary of State Madeleine Albright was fond of saying. The election of 2000 took place at a time that was remarkably quiet on the international front. The more polemical debates were over domestic issues and "values."

The only efforts to make Iraq a political issue seemed to come from the Iraq National Congress (INC). Ahmed Chalabi was trying to build more support among those Republicans who had been challenging Clinton for not taking tangible action to support the opposition in its efforts to depose Saddam. Chalibi had his own lobbyists. But there was no enthusiasm in Washington for mounting a major effort to unseat Saddam, who looked to be pretty well entrenched with remarkably strong security services. To anyone who looked carefully, there did not appear to be any substantial dissident groups ready to move *inside* Iraq proper (as opposed to Kurdistan, which had achieved de facto independence under U.S. military protection).

At the same time, life in Baghdad was improving for Saddam and even the rest of Iraq. The resources from the Oil-for-Food program were accumulating, and commerce was growing. In June 2000, Iraq agreed to reopen the pipeline to Syria in a decision that proved extremely lucrative for both countries. Syria had modest oil production, which primarily served its domestic requirements. Iraq, however, now sold oil to Syria at $6 off the market price, and Syria used that oil domestically and sold its own production at market price. The difference was split, with cash going into secret accounts for Baghdad. It was a great deal made easier by the death in June of longtime Syrian leader Hafez al-Assad. Relations improved further as Assad's son Bashar took over. As Tariq Aziz said to me later, in 2004, Iraq's economy was back by the end of 2000.

Iraq was also building international support from many sources—some quite unexpected. During the summer of 2000, former UNSCOM inspector Scott Ritter was in Iraq filming a documentary titled *In Shifting Sands: The Truth About UNSCOM and the Disarming of Iraq*. Ritter's views had evolved to the point where Aziz gave him access and support to make this documentary, which came out in 2001. It was first shown at the UN, where Ritter had made a name for himself as being tough on Iraq.

Ritter's documentary described Iraq as having been completely disarmed of any practical WMD. It accused the United States of having used the UN to keep sanctions on Iraq and intentionally provoking confrontation with Iraq through UNSCOM. Ritter carried this message broadly in his public appearances as well. While Ritter strongly denies he accepted any direct Iraqi support for his projects, the funding of his film project was from a private Iraqi American rumored to have connections with the former regime. In discussions with Mukhabarat officers after the war, they indicated that they tried to assist in broadening Ritter's exposure.

While I worked closely with Ritter for years at UNSCOM, I found his new perspective baffling. It struck me that perhaps he expected things to be black-and-white, not gray. In retrospect, Ritter was inclined to be categorical. People were right or wrong. Guilty or innocent . . . there was no "guilty with an explanation." He erased ambiguity. His pronouncements made great television sound bites, and there was a ready audience for his colorful expositions.

Sometime between his departure from UNSCOM, in August 1998, and 2000, his deductive logic seemed to change. Ritter stated to Richard Butler in his resignation letter from UNSCOM in 1998, "The sad truth is that Iraq today is not disarmed anywhere near the level required by Security Council resolutions. As you know, UNSCOM has good reason to believe that there are significant numbers of proscribed weapons and related components and the means to manufacture such weapons unaccounted for in Iraq today."

He also wrote: "Iraq has lied to the Special Commission (UNSCOM) and the world since day one concerning the true scope and nature of its proscribed programs and weapons systems. This lie has been perpetuated over the years through systematic acts of concealment."

By 2001, Ritter's message was different, as evidenced in his documentary. Its critique was largely of the United States, not Iraq. The Iraqis distributed copies of the Ritter film broadly. Iraq characterized it as a revelation that the wicked Americans had been lying about Iraq intentionally. This was illustrative of the changing international perceptions that Iraq was attracting in 2000 and 2001. These arguments also provided a moral underpinning for those who were interested in doing business with Iraq.

In Baghdad, the normal governmental functioning was being perverted by the processes that had evolved around the illicit revenues from the Oil-for-Food program. A growing number of normal financial budgeting processes became contorted because the revenues came into Iraq through front companies, hidden bank accounts, and all manner of corrupt systems. Reflecting a tradition of detailed record-keeping and order, the former finance minister, Hikmat Mizban Ibrahim al-Azzawi, complained bitterly about the corruption that took place, largely having to do with Uday and others around the president. A former director of the State Organization for Marketing of Oil (SOMO) also complained that the methods of allocating oil exports were so twisted by political interference that the six-month oil plans approved by the UN were oversold. Corruption was rampant. He pointedly said that the Kurdish leaders (who are now part of the new government in Baghdad) were competing over oil deals and were making profitable arrangements with the regime—while the U.S. Air Force was providing air cover to prevent the regime from going north.

The decision to use corruption as a tool of foreign policy by the regime (from their perspective, it made perfect sense) had a reciprocal effect on the regime's own mechanism of governing. But that poison was slow-acting and in 2000 the regime was riding a wave of euphoria while trumpeting the suffering of its own citizens to further justify the international community relieving sanctions, or ignoring them.

Around Iraq, new presidential palaces and two huge new mosques were being constructed. In the world economy, Iraq was playing a greater role. Within OPEC, Iraq acquired leverage as its oil exports were growing in volume and had the potential to grow much more. The UN had authorized a sizable portion of the Oil-for-Food revenues to be used for oil infrastructure improvements. Within the region, Saddam continued to be seen as the defiant actor single-handedly taking on the United States. He continued to speak loudly about his support for the Palestinians.[1] He railed against the no-fly zones. Saddam encouraged international support and successfully drew prominent individuals to Baghdad's cause.

The erratic and highly controversial Russian politician Vladimir Zhirinovsky made multiple highly publicized visits. Britain's controversial Member of Parliament George Galloway also made publicized visits and decried the sanctions and the policies of the United States and the United Kingdom. Both individuals were identified later in Iraqi documents as beneficiaries of Iraq's oil voucher system.

In late 2000, the Russian government was pursuing diplomatic efforts to move the Iraqis to accept inspectors under the softer disarmament resolution UNSCR 1284, passed the previous December. While Washington was otherwise occupied, Russia was taking the opportunity to push the Iraq issue forward in the Security Council. President Vladimir Putin's foreign minister, Sergei Ivanov, met with Tariq Aziz several times and even with Saddam and got the same answer: No.[2] Aziz said that "the leadership" (the term for a Saddam decision wrapped in a Revolutionary Command Council meeting) had established that there would be no consideration of a change in position on inspectors until the Security Council took tangible steps to remove sanctions, which were eroding even as the issue was debated.

Kofi Annan was also working to encourage the Iraqis to accept inspectors. He had met with the Iraqi Revolutionary Command Council vice chairman, Izzat Ibrahim al Duri, in Doha on the fringes of the Organization of Islamic States conference on November 12 and proposed further meetings on the subject. Annan was now directly involved.

At the same time, Iraq was gradually increasing the number of flights into and out of Iraq. It began domestic civilian flights to Mosul and Basra from Baghdad, and the United States accepted this new step and had to adjust its no-fly-zone procedures. Both Aziz and Iraqi Foreign Minister Naji Sabri said later that this was a period of substantial progress by the regime. They believed they had conducted successful diplomacy and that other members of the Security Council were taking on more responsibility. Spirits were very high among regime officials. Business and diplomacy were blossoming.

The Iraqis continued their efforts to shoot down any U.S. or British aircraft flying over Iraq. They had taken note of the F-117 stealth fighter that had been shot down over Kosovo.[3] Saddam wanted to do the same. Deals were being done with Belarus and other countries to acquire advanced air-defense systems. Syria acted as a willing partner in the transactions. Relatives of President Bashar were middlemen in the process and assured that export documentation would be provided. Saddam's presidential secretary, Abed Hamid Mahmud, was a key interlocutor in the transactions.[4]

Saddam's aggression was also returning. The previous June, he gave a pointed speech in which he declared he would not reduce the level of his weapons unless his neighbors did likewise. In fact, he was ordering the expansion of efforts to build ballistic missiles.

The November 2000 U.S. election, its result teetering back and forth, was an especially strange episode seen from Baghdad. Were there so few issues of real importance to the American people that they could not favor one or another candidate? Or were the American people so divided? Or did the American people not really care and basically decide to flip a coin? The television images of scruffy-looking people squinting nearsightedly at punched holes in the Florida ballots mystified observers in Iraq. This is the last superpower? And then, having the Supreme Court—a group of nine political appointees—decide who would be president must have seemed bizarre. There was lots of speculation—especially in Baghdad, where conspiracy theories are savored.

Perhaps most damaging to the United States was its image of weakness from Saddam's perspective. Since the Clinton bombing in December 1998, the U.S. administration was shrinking from Iraqi defiance of sanctions. Nothing Saddam saw in the 2000 election could have caused him to think that Washington would be any tougher under the next president, whenever he was finally chosen.

Saddam had his own elections. In 1995, he won 99.96 percent of the vote (he was the only candidate). He would do even better in his next election—on October 16, 2002, Baghdad announced he had received 100 percent of the votes.

Americans' ambivalence about their next leader (in December, the Supreme Court ruled five to four in favor of Bush) in no way signaled to Saddam how it might affect his fate. Exactly three years later, on December 13, 2003, Saddam Hussein would be pulled out of a hole by U.S. forces near Tikrit. The implications for Iraq could not have been predicted—certainly not in Baghdad. The U.S. Supreme Court vote led to Saddam's hanging as much as did the Baghdad court that condemned him in 2006.

All new U.S. administrations go through a transition period, when they place their political appointees into the leadership positions of the agencies of government. President George W. Bush picked his cabinet more rapidly than most and was able to get Senate confirmation of key positions very quickly on the same day he was sworn in. On January 20, 2001, Colin Powell and Donald Rumsfeld were confirmed as secretaries of state and defense. They joined the national security team of Dick Cheney, Condoleezza Rice, and George Tenet. It looked as though the experienced first string of the previous Bush administration had come together and at least the national security team of the new administration would hit the ground running. The top issues they thought they would contend with were Balkans deployments, national missile defense, the quadrennial defense review, Anti-Ballistic Missile (ABM) Treaty withdrawal, North Korea, and perhaps Iran and terrorism.

Policy divisions, however, began to surface quickly. With powerful secretaries of defense and state, as well as an active vice president, the relatively junior national security advisor, Condoleezza Rice, sought to "manage issues" rather than force decisions. This is a fair and equitable approach, but without strong National Security Council (NSC) muscle to force resolution of disputes, the bureaucratic tendency is to let issues fester. Bureaucrats would rather have no decision than lose a decision. In addition, in the early months of the administration, lower-level political jobs took longer to fill. The national security team was slow getting going.

The State Department became an ideological battleground right from the start. Secretary Powell selected his old friend Richard Armitage as his deputy and selected senior Foreign Service officer Marc Grossman for the number three job. None of them would qualify as kindred spirits to the so-called neoconservatives. But nominated to be the undersecretary for arms control and international security, with Powell's acquiescence if not enthusiasm, was John Bolton, a clear member of the neoconservative axis. During the first Bush administration, he was assistant secretary of state for international organizations—the bureau that handles the UN. I had come to know him at the time as a very bright and talented person whom you half expected to spit every time he said "UN." During the Clinton administration, he was a senior vice president at the American Enterprise Institute with other conservative voices, like Richard Perle. Bolton and I had been in touch on occasion to discuss the UN inspection process.

I attended Bolton's swearing-in ceremony at the State Department. Supreme Court Justice Clarence Thomas officiated. Thomas spoke warmly of their discussions at Yale Law School, where they were classmates. Colin Powell spoke, making light references to those who questioned whether Bolton and he could coexist in the same

State Department in the same administration. Powell was certainly closer in view to the more naturally liberal perspectives of most of the Foreign Service.

From my position as an outside observer at that time, I regularly heard from former State Department colleagues that Bolton was carefully isolated by the Foreign Service infrastructure and even Powell's office. I discovered just how poisonous the situation was when I visited various offices under Defense Deputy Secretary Paul Wolfowitz to give briefs on UN inspection processes and the UNSCOM findings. There, the civilian defense policy staff would refer to Bolton's office as "the American Interests Section" at the State Department.

This moniker alludes to the practice of having a non-American embassy represent the practical interests of the United States in a hostile country where the United States has no diplomatic relations and therefore no embassy (e.g., Cuba). It was a very funny quip, but reflected a crevice in philosophy and cooperation causing a major dysfunctional relationship in key parts of the government.

On Iraq, Bolton was completely cut out of the process within the State Department. Instead, Powell co-opted Bolton's own subordinate, John Wolf (whom Bolton had selected to be the assistant secretary for nonproliferation), to report around Bolton on Iraq UN inspection issues. This did not mean Bolton did not exert influence on the Iraq issue. He (and his immediate staff) touched other key points in the administration—particularly at the Office of the Secretary of Defense (OSD) and the vice president's office.

With this embedded turmoil in the team, prospects for moving ahead quickly with a revised Iraq policy were low. Upon assuming office, the Bush administration kicked off reviews of various national security policies. Iraq was one policy area. The National Security Council staff typically directed such studies. The NSC staff was in a bit of turmoil, as well. National Security Advisor Condoleezza Rice selected Zalmay Khalilzad as the top NSC staffer for the Middle East; he was responsible for the Iraq study review.[5] It moved very slowly through the summer of 2001. Khalilzad was not known for his expertise in management. Moreover, given the style established by Rice in running national security issues, he had no leverage to force consensus in interagency meetings. Before 9/11, Khalilzad's Iraq policy review was one of several responsibilities. It had to compete with a policy review of South Asia, including Pakistan, Afghanistan, and India. Rice thought it was important to finish the South Asia review before making decisions on al-Qaeda. So, where the Department of Defense could act alone, it did. Where the State Department could act alone, it did. Where coordination was required or where there was a difference of view, things stalled.

One issue that could not wait was the UN semiannual Iraq sanctions reviews. The matter fell strictly under State Department leadership. While Washington had been consumed with elections, Russia and France were pressing Iraq's case in the Security Council. Syria was establishing facts on the ground in the form of the agreed-on protocol allowing the opening of the oil pipeline to Syria. The Bush administration was playing catch-up, trying to fill the vacuum of U.S. leadership in the council—a vacuum that had grown as the Clinton administration wound down in 2000.

Secretary of State Powell received a briefing from the intelligence community on sanctions, even before he was confirmed. The impression one lead briefer had was that Powell appeared to think that getting the sanctions renewed would be a diplomatic task, but once it was accomplished, he could leave Iraq aside and "get on to more critical issues." Powell proceeded with revising sanctions, drawing largely on proposals from Clinton administration holdovers. They proposed something he called "smart sanctions" to replace the previous sanctions. The basic goal was to keep a consensus in the Security Council to retain sanctions on Iraq without committing to ending them. In addition, the proposal was characterized as a way to relieve the suffering of the Iraqi people and focus sanctions on the real target—the regime.

"Smart sanctions" changed the entire premise of the Security Council sanctions program from a *presumption of denial* of any given item contemplated for export to Iraq to a *presumption of approval*. Under the existing UN export mechanism, staff reviewed all proposed exports to see if they were permitted. The Powell proposal shifted the mechanism to review items only to see if they were on an explicit listing of prohibited items. Prohibited items would be weapons and so-called dual-use items that could have civil or military purposes (e.g., machine tools or large transport vehicles). This general approach was acceptable to Russia and France, but the list had to be negotiated. Baghdad immediately recognized this as a major retreat on the part of Washington.

Tariq Aziz later said that this reflected the success of his efforts internationally to draw attention to the unfairness of U.S. treatment of Iraq in the Security Council. Saddam had credited him with this forced shift in Washington, and it validated Baghdad's decision two years earlier to end cooperation with UNSCOM.

Baghdad also thought this move might signal that the new Bush administration was willing to deal with Iraq—along the lines of Nixon's going to China. After all, the alumni of the first Bush administration—Cheney, Powell, and Rumsfeld—were tough professionals who understood the practical applications of power and business, realists by virtue of their past dealings with Iraq. Aziz remembered well the visits of Rumsfeld to Baghdad as Reagan's representative in 1990 and 1991. Aziz assessed that the new team would have to deal with Iraq as the regional power it inevitably would be. He noted to the Iraqi press in an extensive dialogue on May 23, 2001, that Saddam had observed, "When they [the United States] term their new plan 'smart' sanctions they admit that their previous sanctions were stupid." The journalists quoted Saddam as saying the "Smart Sanctions" were the "kick of a dying mule" and Aziz responded that after this "kick" it was possible the United States could admit defeat as it had in Vietnam and things could change. He noted that the "aggression" of December 1998 had backfired and served only to remove UNSCOM.[6] In effect, Aziz was still anticipating that Washington would eventually come to terms with the Iraqi regime.

In 2004, both Presidential Secretary Abed Hamid Mahmud and Aziz said that the Clinton administration had been too weak to consider the steps they suggested in the message Abed passed through me to the White House in 1998. Three years earlier, they had thought that the new Bush administration might find such a pragmatic turn more acceptable. This was not an illogical speculation from their perspective, but it was wrong.

Saddam had a track record of miscalculating international dynamics and Iraq's power. In 1980, he miscalculated the difficulty in invading Khomeini's Iran. A decade later, he miscalculated the reaction to an invasion of Kuwait. The danger with Saddam was that he could readily act with little constraint. His form of dictatorship favored action. In 2001, he was doing quite well. His internal control had become better grounded in the decade since the uprisings following the Kuwait war. Saddam's controlling clique had settled down since the Hussein Kamel defection in 1995. His son Qusay was maturing and was a relatively effective head of the elite Special Security Organization.

Saddam's elder son, Uday, was still a problem, however. Following an attempted assassination in December 1996, he had been badly wounded in the left side and leg by automatic weapons fire while cruising in a Porsche (in the trendy Mansour section of Baghdad). He spent six months in Bin Sina Hospital and would never fully recover the normal use of his left leg.[7] Uday may also have suffered some brain damage; he would remain a wild card for Saddam.

But, overall, in mid-2001, things looked pretty good from Saddam's office window in the Republican Palace in Baghdad.

Then al-Qaeda attacked on September 11, 2001. The immediate reaction among regime leadership was that this was good because it served to demonstrate American weakness. To their surprise, it appeared that some ragtag fundamentalists had succeeded in destroying the two symbols of American capitalism in New York. Al-Qaeda, a collection of stateless ideologues, could hurt the last superpower.

Initially, regime leaders thought the 9/11 attacks would increase the momentum of support for Iraq in the Security Council as well as making America realize that it was not omnipotent and needed to be more pragmatic in the Security Council and the Middle East. Senior regime figures recalled later the entreaties they had made to the United States, explicitly calling out that they had offered to help counter Islamic fundamentalism. Saddam and his top aides thought this event might cause the United States to understand the importance of dealing with Iraq in terms of Iraq's providing stability for U.S. interests. Baghdad expected that Washington would have to take the first step toward a pragmatic reconciliation. It was wrong again in its judgment about Washington.

Only after some time did the notion that Iraq might be blamed for the 9/11 attacks dawn on Baghdad. Saddam knew he had no connection to Osama bin Laden and certainly did not share bin Laden's objectives. The Iraqi was very slow to understand that the action by bin Laden in fact put him at risk. After the war, Tariq Aziz said that the United States would have taken any opportunity to blame Iraq for anything. He said if there was a drought, Washington would blame Iraq. The Iraqi leaders came to see the reaction to 9/11 in the same way.

Within Baghdad, there was a debate concerning how to react to the World Trade Center destruction. The UN Iraqi ambassador, Mohammed al-Duri, requested instructions on what to say or do. Should Iraq express condolences? Foreign Minister Naji Sabri passed the question to the president's office and received from Presidential Secretary Abed a response that no condolences should be expressed. Sabri thought this was a mistake, but mainly because it would make Iraq look bad to the rest of the Security Council. It had nothing to do with sympathy for the United States. At the next Revolutionary Command Council (RCC) meeting with Saddam in the chair, Sabri asked to see the president afterward. Sabri said he raised this question personally with Saddam, who readily agreed that it was a human tragedy and that Iraq did not want to appear inhumane.

On September 10, 2001, Undersecretary of Defense Doug Feith and Assistant Secretary of Defense J. D. Crouch (later to become deputy national security advisor to Stephen Hadley) had been in Moscow to discuss the U.S. goals regarding a national missile-defense system and the termination of the ABM Treaty limiting missile-defense systems between the United States and Russia. It was the highest national security priority of the new administration. The goal was to develop and deploy a system estimated to cost over sixty billion dollars to defend against rogue nations launching ballistic missiles at the United States.

The next day, Manhattan was hit by hijacked aircraft—not missiles. Although Feith gave a brief press conference as he left Moscow to say that this did not undermine the importance of national missile defense, it certainly appeared that while Rumsfeld and his staff were working so hard to terminate the ABM Treaty, they had completely missed the real threat, which emerged not from a country, but from a terrorist organization.

Feith and his team made their way to Germany and were able to fly back to the United States on September 12 on a military KC-135 (U.S. airspace was closed to all civilian air traffic). Both Feith and Bill Luti, the deputy assistant secretary of defense for the Near East and South Asia, attested that this flight was a key moment in shaping thinking about next steps. As they flew home, they drafted papers on the U.S. policy implications of the attack. They absorbed the implications of President Bush's statement on 9/11 that the United States had been attacked and that *we were at war*. This was *not a criminal* act. The difference was momentous. The FBI would not take the lead as it had in other cases. The goal was not to collect evidence and prosecute the perpetrators according to criminal law. The president had put the United States on a war footing. This empowered the Pentagon within the Washington policy community. The Department of Defense would dominate the response to 9/11 because it controlled the vast majority of resources involved and because we were a nation at war. It is natural in wartime that the Defense Department has the lead in virtually all matters.

Even before the shift to a wartime operation, the State Department was not a prime player in the administration. This was underscored by the fact that Feith was in Moscow negotiating the end of the ABM Treaty. In other administrations, the State Department traditionally had the lead when discussing arms-control treaties.

On September 12, preemption was the thought not yet articulated by the president. The idea did, however, circulate among these key defense officials. They began to turn over the notion that in this new technological age, the United States could no longer "give up the first punch." Their thinking had gone from defending against a missile attack to carrying the fight forward.

The KC-135 approached Washington from the northeast. It diverted over Manhattan to circle over the remains of the World Trade Center. By all accounts, it was a powerful moment, and Feith and his colleagues were motivated to move ahead in the directions they believed were necessary not only to eliminate the enemy that caused this attack, but also to make sure other enemies were dealt with before they could attack the United States. Afghanistan was first on the list, but Iraq was next.

With the country at war, any notion of long, perhaps orderly, interagency debate about goals and tactics was dropped. It was discussed among the principals in various forums, formal and informal. From the president's own statements and from the comments, public and private, of his closest advisors, it is clear that he felt that the problem of Saddam Hussein had to be solved and that containment wasn't adequate. Shortly after 9/11 the president concluded that Iraq was a problem that could not be put off too much longer.[8]

So once it was clear the war in Afghanistan was going well, Bush turned back to Iraq. On November 21, just before Thanksgiving, he asked Rumsfeld to begin quietly examining the war plans for Iraq. The existing ones were old. New ones would take time, as these are extraordinarily complicated documents. A serious review would involve dozens or more officers. It could never remain confidential. Word would get out that Iraq war plans were being considered.

Another decision was also taken by the president, either consciously or not at this time. On Monday, November 26, during a Rose Garden ceremony for two rescued aid workers who had been held captive by the Taliban, Bush was asked about Iraq by the press:

Q. Does Saddam Hussein have to agree to allow weapons inspectors back into Iraq? Is that an unconditional demand of yours?

A. Saddam Hussein agreed to allow inspectors in his country. And in order to prove to the world he's not developing weapons of mass destruction, he ought to let the inspectors back in.

Q. And if he doesn't, Sir?

A. That's up for . . . he'll find out.

Q. Sir, what is your thinking right now about taking the war to Iraq? You suggested that on Wednesday [November 21], when you said Afghanistan was just the beginning.

A. I stand by those words. Afghanistan is still just the beginning. If anybody harbors a terrorist, they're a terrorist. If they fund a terrorist, they're a terrorist. If they house terrorists, they're terrorists. I mean, I can't make it any more clearly to other nations around the world. If they develop weapons of mass destruction that will be used to terrorize nations, they will be held accountable. And as for Mr. Saddam Hussein, he needs to let inspectors back in his country, to show us that he is not developing weapons of mass destruction.

That night, Secretary Powell was interviewed by Larry King of CNN. When asked about the president's statements, Powell said Saddam "should see it as a very sober, chilling message." Powell did not explain what the president meant, implying he was deliberately ambiguous, but said the president retained "all his options" if Saddam did not accept inspectors. Bush's linkage—that Saddam should allow UN inspectors into Iraq with the purpose of proving he had no WMD— was *a critical point*. It tied the president's reaction to the threat posed by Saddam to the Security Council's judgments about Iraq's compliance with the WMD disarmament provisions. Those judgments would be made by international inspectors, not Americans. A major U.S. security decision depended upon experts reporting to the Security Council under a resolution more accommodating to Iraq than the resolution that provided the UNSCOM mandate. It would be the Swedish former IAEA director, Hans Blix, who would make the relevant judgments. I was amazed the president had put such faith in a process that had been systematically run down.

No one I spoke with seemed to have any idea where the Bush statement came from.[9] It would shape the entire debate and drive the demand for intelligence on WMD, which was problematic since UNSCOM left Iraq three years earlier. I knew from my UNSCOM experience that finding demonstrable WMD in Iraq would be very difficult. The commission had deployed all sorts of tactics that Blix and his UNMOVIC team would never even dream of. In the end, UNSCOM could only demonstrate that Iraq was hiding *something*. We could not prove they were hiding WMD.

During December, I made it a point to see Ryan Crocker at State Department. Since returning from the UN, I had stayed in touch with the Near Eastern Affairs Bureau, mostly through Crocker. He and I had worked together during the first Gulf War, and he had been out to Iraq for the Presidential Palace inspections I ran in 1998.

Crocker was a deputy assistant secretary under Bill Burns, the assistant secretary for Near Eastern Affairs. I knew Burns as well, having worked not only with him, but also with his father, who was an army brigadier general detailed to the State Department in the 1980s. Both Bill Burns and Crocker knew of my political military experience and my work in Iraq, and I figured they might listen to my views.

I ran through how I saw the Iraq problem and in particular the risks of being trapped going down a path of UN inspections again. Crocker did not know how the president had come to demand that Saddam accept inspectors again. I wanted to try out an idea on him. I suggested a possible alternative rationale, which would initially be harder to sell at the UN, but which might be easier and more honest in the long run.

I reminded Crocker that on September 20, 1999, Kofi Annan had given a very bold speech at the UN General Assembly. Annan had taken on the question of sovereignty, which members of the UN had always treated as inviolable. He had stated that on the verge of the new millennium, conditions were changing the notion of the inviolability of the sovereign state. In essence, he said there were occasions when conditions made sovereignty secondary. Sometimes, intervention in another country was justified. This was radical in the UN context. The Chinese, for example, hated this notion.

Annan was speaking in the context of Rwanda and Kosovo as instances where mass murder was the consequence of inaction by the international community.

"Why not use Annan's argument with respect to Iraq?" I argued. "We could go through the UN process, even using his own words, and we would not be tied to the resolutions that are written only in respect to WMD. It is clear that Saddam has done massive, odious things to his own population."

"Besides mass murder," I added, "Iraq is a risk to its neighbors, it engages in genocide, and it shows no signs of redemption."

Crocker listened politely, but offered little response. Perhaps he thought my argument was too unlikely to be adopted. I emphasized that it would satisfy the desire to act in Iraq *with* international support. It would mean new resolutions, which might seem difficult. But I felt the real difficulty was to retrace the WMD inspections. That would be convoluted, and ultimately, Saddam could win those arguments.

Crocker was respected in the department, but he was not a decisionmaker. He said little about State Department deliberations except that Iraq policy was being driven by the OSD, which seemed enamored with the Iraqi National Congress. Crocker and the other Near Eastern Affairs staff who had dealt with the INC were not impressed, but went through the motions of working with them. The staff also went through the motions of thinking about a post-Saddam Iraq world.

Crocker and I did agree on one point, which was that the external Iraqi opposition would have no following in Iraq, even if Saddam fell. Crocker knew that new leaders in a post-Saddam era would have to come from within Iraq. He had lived in Baghdad in the 1980s, which gave him more recent experience than Ahmad Chalabi had.

State Department professionals resented the assumption of control of Iraq policy by the OSD. At the top, Powell was not encouraging a team effort to accomplish regime change. He was focusing on working in the UN. On any given day, I could hear harsh words about "opposing" departments and their prominent individuals. There was no dominant strategy around which to build a single team. It was Sunnis and Shias, but in Washington. They could never agree on a shared set of facts or strategy.

Later, on December 19, I met with John Hannah, a national security advisor to Vice President Cheney. I shared with Hannah my thoughts about the president's statement that Saddam must accept inspectors. He knew my views on the UN process, but I tried out the notion of using a different, non-WMD-based rationale for seeking support at the UN. He seemed curious, but skeptical, because starting a new line of argument would be time-consuming and because the argument might not prevail in the Security Council despite having originated from Kofi Annan.

Hannah seemed to think it was best to avoid the UN entirely. He readily agreed that having inspectors go back was a risk. I pointed out that as far as I could tell, no one who knew anything about inspections in Iraq was involved in the State Department process. He shrugged. Hannah was, as always, very discrete.

As a resident scholar at a think tank, I wrote an op-ed for the *Washington Post*, commenting on the president's demand of Saddam. The title was "Inspectors in Iraq? Be Careful What You Ask For."[10] Over the next few months, I wrote articles on the faults of coercive inspections in Iraq over any extended period. I subsequently realized that this was not the message Colin Powell wanted anyone to hear.

Apparently, Powell, and subsequently Tony Blair, argued that the president could achieve his objective of regime change with international support, if he chose to drive the Iraq issue through the UN. They stated that there was no way Saddam could comply with the UN disarmament resolutions. Powell had strong reservations about a military action to remove Saddam but said that it is better to go to war with allies than without, and with international support than without. He argued that if the United States pressed its case within the UN Security Council, with time it could have both.

Others in the administration thought Powell's real objective was to get the United States tied up in the UN so that a military option would be derailed. Powell clearly thought that the military option was fraught with too many uncertainties and that those who promoted it were unfamiliar with the costs and uncertainties involved.

Powell's case depended upon the assumption that there was no way Saddam could comply with the inspection requirements. This was an argument of convenience and was disingenuous at best. As far as I could tell, Powell did not know anything about inspections, nor did anyone on his immediate staff. It was also inevitable that Saddam would make any issues of noncompliance seem far too trivial to go to war over. This tactic had worked well with the Russians and French for almost a decade.

In retrospect, the arguments made by State Department that inspections would force Saddam to reveal his assumed WMD were as skewed as any of the erroneous WMD intelligence arguments. In some ways, they were worse because they were advanced by a State Department that knew or should have known that inspections were fundamentally flawed. And if the department did not know, it did not ask.

In contrast to the fighting among departments in Washington, Saddam did not suffer from the erosion of purpose caused by a bureaucracy that was at war with itself, first, and with Iraq, second. Foreign Minister Mohammed al-Sahaf did not dare undermine the explicit or implicit desires of Saddam as passed to Defense Minister Sultan Hasham Ahmad al-Tai. They would execute Saddam's guidance, and Abed Hamid Mahmud would make certain that they did. Condoleezza Rice did not have the authority, nor did she instill the fear of consequences that Abed Mahmud did for Saddam.

On January 29, 2002, President Bush delivered his second State of the Union message. He was at the height of his popularity, and the country welcomed his leadership. There had been success in Afghanistan, even if bin Laden remained free. It was assumed it was only a matter of time before the terrorist leader was captured or killed. The government looked competent and more unified than anyone would have expected after the 2000 election.

The president called direct attention to Iraq:

> Iraq continues to flaunt its hostility toward America and to support terror. The Iraqi Regime has plotted to develop anthrax, and nerve gas, and nuclear weapons for over a decade. This is a regime that has already used poison gas to murder thousands of its own citizens— leaving the bodies of mothers huddled over their dead children. This is a regime that agreed to international inspections—then kicked out

the inspectors. This is a regime that has something to hide from the civilized world.

States like these, and their terrorist allies, constitute an axis of evil, arming to threaten the peace of the world. By seeking weapons of mass destruction, these regimes pose a grave and growing danger. They could provide these arms to terrorists, giving them the means to match their hatred. . . .

I will not wait on events while dangers gather. I will not stand by, as peril draws closer and closer. The United States of America will not permit the world's most dangerous regimes to threaten us with the world's most destructive weapons.

There was applause.[11]

This speech was heard in Baghdad. It finally made Baghdad understand that the United States was going to be a *greater* threat to Iraq as a consequence of 9/11. *From Saddam's perspective*, he saw no particular link between 9/11 and Iraq. To him, it simply made the United States look vulnerable. Saddam did not know that some in the United States really did believe he was connected to 9/11. Tariq Aziz had been getting some hints from his dialogues with the French and Russian ambassadors. Now, the message in President Bush's speech was clear—Iraq was not a matter to be deferred. Bush was going to do something.

Saddam finally got it.

In early February 2002, Saddam convened a meeting of the RCC to discuss the Bush speech and the question of UN inspectors. It was Saddam's practice to let others speak on the designated topic first, and then, only at the end, would he speak. At this session, Aziz spoke in favor of admitting the inspectors immediately. He pointed out that this would allow their friends in the Security Council, France and Russia, to help them more.

Saddam finally agreed, but, in classic Saddam style, only if he got something tangible in exchange. He had been critical of Aziz (as had Vice President Taha Yasin Ramadan) because Iraq had given much to the UN and received nothing. Saddam instructed that Aziz begin a discussion with the UN, leading to the readmission of inspectors, but only if Iraq received something concrete on the lifting of sanctions.

This was a critical meeting, and the decision to negotiate played into Washington's hands. Both Aziz and Foreign Minister Sabri believed that Iraq should simply accept the inspectors and not yet try to argue for sanctions relief. After the war, they both told me this was Saddam's fatal mistake.

As Baghdad began its negotiation with the UN, Washington began a long dialogue with the Security Council members. The council understood that after 9/11, the United States was going to be difficult to contain. New major dynamics were set in motion. Washington was building a case in the international community to solve the Iraq problem by forcing Saddam on WMD compliance, or there would be military action to remove the regime. Since Iraq was blatantly not in compliance—it refused to admit inspectors, even though it claimed not to have WMD—the U.S. position gained traction.

The United States quickly established an ally with the United Kingdom. Prime Minister Tony Blair assured President Bush that he supported regime change. Sir David Manning, the British ambassador in Washington, D.C., made this clear to Rice on March 18. Later, on April 6, Blair visited Bush at his Crawford, Texas, ranch, where they confirmed strategic goals and discussed the requirements to get there.

Blair and Bush agreed that Saddam posed a strategic risk. It was, of course, an unlikely meeting of the minds. Blair was an urbane liberal, and President Bush was, well, not. The "special relationship" that has been a handrail for U.S. foreign policy for decades has been gripped by a range of prime ministers and presidents. It was held again in the case of Iraq, and British concerns tended to support the State Department positions over those who strove to pass over the UN quickly. While he had a shared appreciation of the strategic threat of Saddam, Blair had an even tougher job to bring along not only the British public, but his own Labour Party. Blair needed a legal rationale for effecting "regime change," and that required going through the UN. This bolstered the Powell tactic, which in combination with Blair's attitude muted the objections of the OSD and Vice President Cheney, who understood the risk that Saddam at the last minute would accept inspectors. This would open endless and uncontrollable delays, as Hans Blix and his team would have to be given time to pursue their work.

Still, it was felt that there was no way Saddam could comply, if the inspections were tough enough. The problem was that the resolution that created the new inspection group that Blix headed was much weaker than that of the UNSCOM authorities. The OSD and Cheney's staff understood this from the experience of UNSCOM. If no one else, certainly I made the case privately and publicly that inspectors in Iraq were at a severe disadvantage.

The White House directed that a new resolution be drafted and introduced to force tougher inspections and give Blix more power. Baghdad did not know what would fend off the United States and the United Kingdom in the Security Council. Iraq began a series of meetings with the UN in March, May, and July between senior Iraqis, including Foreign Minister Sabri, and Kofi Anan and Hans Blix. The first two sessions were held in New York, and the July meeting took place in Vienna. It was a process by which the Iraqis were testing how intrusive the inspections might be while seeking an explicit deal on limiting inspection duration and a more concrete commitment to lifting sanctions.[12]

President Bush gave the commencement address at West Point on June 1. In language that echoed his State of the Union message, he said that the United States could not tolerate growing threats. He explained that containment was not possible when "unbalanced dictators with weapons of mass destruction can deliver those weapons on missiles or secretly provide them to terrorist allies." This speech raised no flags in Baghdad. It did not use the word *Iraq*, and years later, senior regime officials said that they assumed it was more aimed at North Korea. This East Asian state had both WMD and a really unbalanced dictator. When Saddam heard reference to unbalanced dictators, he had no clue that someone might have him in mind, and no one around Saddam thought to tell him.

Bush's speech did not motivate the Iraqis to move forward on inspections in the July meeting with the UN in Vienna. That meeting produced nothing, and the dialogue went cold afterward.

During 2002, there was substantial public interest in Iraq WMD. I received requests to appear before congressional committees as an expert witness. I also received continuous requests from the media for comments. I had been accepting many of these and had made a practice of keeping Ryan Crocker and the Near Eastern Affairs press officer informed.

In one of my periodic meetings with Crocker on April 12, I asked specifically if there was any concern about my public activities. I had been extremely careful to characterize my views as my own drawing on my background as a former UN weapons inspector and a visiting scholar at the Center for Strategic and International Studies. Crocker and his press guy assured me they had no problem, as long as I was identified as an outside expert. He said there was utility in having an outside person the press could turn to for an informed view.

I emphasized to Crocker again that in my view, inspections would not be sustainable in any effective manner and Saddam was a threat, in any case. Crocker seemed relaxed about my views, but he also never really asked any questions. He always ended our meetings encouraging me to stay in touch, but I always had the feeling it was a waste of time for him. He was either disconnected from the Iraq decisions, or "outside facts" were irrelevant. His daily bureaucratic battles depended only on facts and views circulating in the interagency community. Nevertheless, I made occasional appointments to see Crocker and discuss what I saw happening.

Through the summer of 2002, I was also in regular touch with Will Tobey in the NSC Non-Proliferation Office, and John Hannah and I got an occasional call from the Near East office in the OSD. In each of these cases, they were probing on the experience of UNSCOM inspections and the likely interactions between Iraq and future inspectors.

In June, I went to London for an International Institute for Strategic Studies conference on Iraq WMD. I took the opportunity to catch up with an old friend who worked political military affairs in the Foreign and Commonwealth Office, Tim Dowse. He had been assigned to the Cabinet Office, but was able to spring free for some "bangers and beer" at lunch.

We caught up on the state of play over Iraq. I gave my view on the futility of inspections as a real solution and my sense that a change in

top management in Baghdad was necessary before sanctions completely disintegrated. Dowse was less free to express his views, given
his position, but we ran through the pros and cons and risks of
"regime change." He made the well-understood point that the United
Kingdom needed an international legal rationale, namely, noncompliance with UN resolutions. He mentioned that his office had been
preparing a proliferation threat white paper that addressed three
countries, Iran, Iraq, and Libya, but had now turned the project into a
paper only addressing Iraq. Dowse was well versed in the previous
UNSCOM work. The British had provided some of our best investi-
gators, including biological-weapons scientist David Kelly.

I had seen Kelly the previous week, but did not know, nor did
Dowse mention, that Kelly had been feeling some pressure to bolster
his analytic judgments on Iraq's biological-weapons status. A year
later, there would be a grinding political scandal about the biological
weapons and other assessments. As of 2002, I was blissfully unaware
of the defectors who were making claims about Iraq's biological
weapons (including the infamous "Curve Ball" source in Germany).
My own views were shaped simply by the UNSCOM experience and
were thus more tentative.[13]

During the summer of 2002, Washington, like London, was mustering the data concerning Baghdad's WMD and its relationship to
the UNSCOM inspections. In August, I spoke a couple of times with
Hannah concerning UNSCOM's findings and experience with Iraq.
He only said that he was working on something for the vice president
and wanted to be sure he had the facts correct about the commission's
difficulties in Iraq. We met on August 22 to discuss the work in
greater detail. Four days later, I realized that he was gathering information to help draft Cheney's speech to the Veterans of Foreign Wars
(VFW) in Nashville on August 26.

The speech made explicit the preemption theme that President
Bush had mentioned generally during his West Point commencement
address. Cheney took on Iraq specifically.

In hindsight, this speech has been sharply criticized. But as the rationale for a strategic decision that it is too risky for the United States
to wait for Iraq to do something concrete before acting to change Bagh-

dad's management, it does not look too bad. The consequences of allowing a resurgent Saddam to emerge with WMD were too great to allow. Moreover, the common wisdom in virtually all countries back then was that Saddam did have some (albeit unclear) WMD capability. There was also the unalterable history that WMD had been extremely useful to Saddam, and that if circumstances were favorable, he would build an arsenal and, if necessary, use it. "The risks of inaction are far greater than the risk of action," Cheney emphasized in his speech.

Cheney declared that Iraq had "been enhancing its capabilities in the field of chemical and biological agents. And they continue to pursue the nuclear program they began many years ago." This was more than I would have guessed. At the time, using strictly my own UNSCOM experience, I figured that there was some residual capability to produce biological and chemical weapons fairly rapidly if Saddam wanted to. I guessed there were a few long-range missiles available. And on nuclear capability, it seemed that Iraq had clustered its nuclear experts at five specific locations, where I assessed they worked to retain their knowledge base, if not to do selected small development projects relevant to nuclear weapons. I was unaware, however, of the defector reports of biological-weapons activity and the information concerning Iraq's clandestine import of high-strength aluminum tubes, which some argued were suitable for uranium enrichment centrifuges.

Cheney highlighted the tortured "hide-and-seek" process between UNSCOM and Iraq during the previous decade. This known track record certainly did not bode well for the future intentions of Saddam. The vice president also made a point that I considered accurate: Inspections would not provide security for the United States. In fact, they might provide a false sense of security.

Where the speech is weak is the discussion of the aftermath. In only the most general terms, he touches on what would happen: "The Middle East expert Professor Fouad Ajami predicts that after liberation, the streets of Basra and Baghdad are 'sure to erupt in joy in the same way the throngs in Kabul greeted the Americans.'"

Cheney went on: "With our help, a liberated Iraq can be a great nation once again. Iraq is rich in natural resources and human talent, and has unlimited potential for a peaceful prosperous future. Our goal would be an Iraq that has territorial integrity, a government that is democratic and pluralistic, a nation where the human rights of every ethnic religious group are recognized and protected."

Saddam's hard-line vice president, Taha Yasin Ramadan, was in Damascus three days after Cheney's speech. Ramadan was given to tough talk and tough positions. He often disagreed with Tariq Aziz for being too accommodating. In public comments he made in Damascus, Ramadan seemed to agree with Cheney. He saw no purpose in the return of UN inspectors. "What purpose would there be for a goodwill gesture or an initiative for the return of spies?" Ramadan told reporters. He went on:

> The U.S. administration says day and night that the issue is not related to whether the inspectors return or not, it has to do with changing the regime by force. This is an issue on which we shouldn't waste our time.
>
> What's new in the U.S. threat? We are taking the threat seriously. It is a despotic administration; it is an insane, criminal administration. Its logic in relations with the states of the world is the logic of force.[14]

And so the harsh voices on each side were raised.

Baghdad did have its equivalent of Colin Powell in the form of Tariq Aziz and Naji Sabri. They continued to argue that admitting inspectors sooner was better. The Iraqi ambassador to the UN, Mohammed al-Duri, was reporting that the Security Council would be passing a new resolution that would only make things much more difficult. This line was supported by messages from the Russians, that is, if the Iraqis should accept the existing team under Blix, this would diffuse the effort by Bush to create a more stringent resolution.

In Washington, the internal debate over how far to proceed along the UN track regarding Iraq was fought out in the lead-up to the UN

General Assembly. There, President Bush would give his annual address on September 12, 2002—almost exactly a year after 9/11.

Colin Powell, in response to Cheney's speech at the VFW, had asked to see the president privately. The secretary had discussed Iraq with the president over dinner a month earlier. Powell wanted to delay the movement to war, and he wanted reassurance that Bush was committed to going through the UN and its inspectors. The president said he would, though he doubted the inspections would work.

Powell's goal was to counter Cheney's opposition to going through the UN. For a year, President Bush had said Iraq must accept inspections. Still, Cheney and the OSD opposed going into the UN, where a quagmire of debate would ensue. There was an ongoing battle between the staffs of these offices. In the end, the speech given steered the United States through the Security Council before going to Baghdad, but Powell would have some very onerous work ahead of him.

President Bush set some tough standards in his speech, making it clear that the council would have to act forcefully or become "irrelevant." He said that "if the regime wishes peace," it would have to do five things:

1. Comply with the WMD disarmament objectives.
2. End all support for terrorism, and act to suppress terrorism.
3. Cease the persecution of its civilian population.
4. Release or account for all Gulf War personnel whose fate was still unknown (a long-standing issue remained over several hundred missing Kuwaitis and a U.S. pilot who was shot down), return stolen property, and accept liability for losses resulting from the Kuwait invasion.
5. Immediately end all illicit trade outside the Oil-for-Food program, and accept UN administration of those funds.

President Bush reminded the assembly of some of the acts of mass killing by the regime and went on to say, "We will work with the UN Security Council for the necessary resolutions. But the purposes of the United States should not be doubted. The Security Council resolutions will be enforced—the just demands of peace and security will be met— or action will be unavoidable. And a regime that has lost its legitimacy will also lose its power."

Only Bush's WMD measure attracted any sustained attention. Iraqi Foreign Minister Sabri was in New York to attend the General Assembly. After President Bush's address on September 12, Sabri held two meetings with Kofi Annan on September 14 and 15. He sought Annan's commitment to relieve sanctions. Annan could not agree to anything concrete, since the Security Council, over which he had no control, directed the sanctions. Two days later, Sabri sent a letter to Annan, saying Iraq was prepared to accept inspectors unconditionally. State Department spokespeople said this would not affect the U.S. effort then under way to create a new, much more stringent resolution to empower the inspectors in Iraq.

This was a time of very tense conflict between Powell and Armitage at the State Department, on one side, and Rumsfeld and Wolfowitz at Defense and Vice President Cheney, on the other. I was a minor casualty caught in the crossfire.

While I had been keeping Ryan Crocker and his press office informed and they had assured me that the "seventh floor was OK" with my public activities, all of a sudden, I was told I had to occupy an office at State Department (initially in the library). And in rapid order, I was threatened with being fired from the department three times. First, I was called by Assistant Secretary John Wolf, who had learned I was going to speak at a brown-bag lunch seminar at CIA headquarters about UN inspections. This was a classified session, so I was amazed when Wolf told me that Armitage had said that if I did this, it would be incompatible with continued government service.

The next time, shortly thereafter, a *Washington Post* article by Walter Pincus quoted me as saying something about the futility of inspections. This also caused Armitage to tell Wolf that I should be fired. I explained to Wolf that I had not spoken to Pincus. After some research, I found that Pincus had simply taken quotes out of a long journal article I had written earlier.

Then, a couple weeks later, on October 3 (and after checking with the Near Eastern Affairs press guy), I did a short appearance on CNN with Wolf Blitzer. Armitage told Marc Grossman, the undersecretary for policy and third-ranking in the department, to call me in. Grossman told me I would not have any contact with the press, or I would be terminated. I discovered that the bureau office would not acknowledge that it had, in fact, encouraged me to be public. Silence from all these great Foreign Service officers. I was furious, but had come to accept this from the State Department and the bureaucracy, generally. It was "save yourself first." Powell and Armitage wanted to argue that inspections would work. The last thing they wanted was the former head of UNSCOM, the guy who had been exposed as pursuing all sorts of extraordinary inspection techniques, to say that they still wouldn't work. The Powell argument depended on the inspections' being a good approach, and he did not want any reports to the contrary.

Others, however, did. Deputy Secretary of Defense Wolfowitz asked to meet with me the next week, and I described the history and dynamics of the UNSCOM inspections. Later that week, I was invited to a meeting of the Defense Policy Board to detail the past work of UNSCOM. The National Security Council staff, in the form of Will Tobey and presidential special assistant Bob Joseph, asked me for thoughts on how to make a tougher inspection regime and what might be some early test events to gauge Saddam's intentions to cooperate. Tobey absorbed the complicated details of the UNSCOM inspection history and procedures. He was working on a new draft resolution for submittal at the UN Security Council. I highlighted to him that in my opinion, the key was being able to talk to the Iraqi experts without their being subjected to regime pressure. I strongly suggested that a new resolution include some mechanism to allow free speech by the Iraqi scientists and engineers.

Even then, I reminded Tobey, it was very hard to find WMD in Iraq and that finding something substantial might not happen under any circumstances. I repeated a serious proposal that Aziz had made in 1998: He would allow UNSCOM complete access anywhere with all the inspectors it wanted, but only for six months. At the end of six months, Aziz would demand that if nothing was discovered, the sanctions would be lifted. Aziz might have been bluffing, but then maybe not.

In retrospect, he wasn't.

Tobey and I also discussed how a search for WMD would be conducted in the event an invasion happened. I believed a *CSI: Crime Scene Investigation* approach was the most useful. Tobey said he shared the view, but that planning for WMD searching was assigned to CENTCOM military planners. They were more inclined toward a World Wrestling Federation approach.[15]

For CENTCOM, the priority was to protect its forces. It developed war plans based on the assumption that Iraq had large stocks of chemical weapons. That is what the best intelligence predicted. They deployed troops with full chemical-protective suits, and they required the vaccination of troops for anthrax and smallpox. For CENTCOM, WMD was not an analytic exercise, but one of finding potential threats (i.e., chemical weapons stockpiles) and destroying them. In the end, it was an unrealized threat. But the analytic question about WMD remained.

CHAPTER 11

The New War

Regime change is a political activity first and a military activity second. Military action can make regime change possible, but then what? The State Department had large groups of "experts" and Iraqi expatriates identifying various problems, but it offered no serious solutions. Since Powell was primarily trying to impede any military action, the lower levels were not charged with really trying to solve the problems of a postconflict government. And, of course, they were disconnected from the real planning at the Pentagon.

The Pentagon thinking for postwar Iraq was informed by and implicitly guided by Ahmad Chalabi. The OSD was persuaded that he would incite support in Iraq. Chalabi's idea was to establish a sanctuary in southern Iraq among Shia and around the southern airfields. Once the U.S. military could secure this area, Chalabi supporters and other Iraqis would have a safe haven to "defect" to. In Chalabi's pitch, he asserted that Iraqis would swarm to such a safe haven. This was, in essence, the same scheme advocated in a January 26, 1998, letter to President Clinton. The letter had encouraged regime change and was signed by most of the key players now involved in Iraq policy for President Bush.

A strong view held by Richard Perle, among others, was that a government in exile with Chalabi heading it should be recognized immediately to show the Iraqis in Iraq that the United States was serious. Wolfowitz supported this view, but it did not get off the ground. While the president seemed genuinely taken by the expressions of support by exile Iraqis, he was cautious about installing Chalabi and the Iraqi National Congress (INC). This did not deter the OSD.

The State Department was not convinced by Chalabi's argument, but had no concrete knowledge to counter it. The department had acquired no direct experience in Iraq in over a decade. While the State Department recoiled at the OSD's leading the political decisions for a new government in Iraq, the OSD, understandably, did not trust the State Department, since it was doing everything possible to undermine the goal of regime change. Again, it was like Sunnis and Shias in Washington.

Independently, from 2000 on, I had been working on a project to identify Iraqis inside Iraq who would support new leadership. Only gradually did I come to appreciate how little was known about *Iraqis in Iraq* by official Washington.

I was convinced by my experience inside Iraq that regime change made sense and could be done at relatively low cost, especially considering the potential upside. But it was increasingly unnerving to see the enormous gulf within the U.S. administration. War was not unifying our bureaucracy. The president, whether he realized it or not, was going to be out there by himself, eventually. He had made a tough, but, in my view, respectable strategic decision. The United States could not accept the threat presented by Saddam in Iraq. But Bush could not make his American team unify to solve this problem in a coherent, informed way.

Further complicating the situation, intelligence about Iraq had taken a nosedive after UNSCOM left. With the end of the commission's access in December 1998, the intelligence community was bankrupt. A former head of the intelligence community's Nonproliferation Center, John Lauder, invited me to a large conference that brought together the whole range of collectors and Iraq analysts for an off-site two-day conference from July 31 to August 1, 2001—two and a half years after UNSCOM was last in Iraq.

The analysts highlighted the paucity of knowledge they had about the Iraqi nuclear program. As an illustration, someone mentioned that while he knew that the key leader of the program was Jafaar Dhia Jafaar, he did not know where the Iraqi was working—knowledge that would have helped the analysts understand the nuclear programs. There were dozens of representatives from the various U.S. intelligence components. Lots of very technical ideas were discussed. Sensors on satellites, communications-intercept techniques, new widgets on the ground—all sorts of creative ideas—none of which seemed likely to get a reliable answer.

I was asked if I had any thoughts. Not entirely facetiously, I suggested, "Why not just call him up? His former wife is probably in the UK, and you could ask her for the number. Or, his brother Hameed runs a trading firm called Crescent Holdings. Ask him. Hell, he must travel all the time. It would be easy to contact him."

For whatever reason, there was an emphasis on technical collection and not human collection. There was a matching absence of information about the internal political and social situation in Iraq. Without much in the way of intelligence sources inside Iraq, the opinions of external groups gained more credibility. They could state or make up anything, and it would appear credible.

During the previous seven years, I had spent a lot of time with living, breathing Iraqis—inside Iraq and outside. I had never presumed myself to be an expert on Iraq (Iraqis were the real experts), but since the United States had not had an embassy in Iraq for over a decade, and I had been going to Baghdad in the interim as a senior UN official, it turned out I was as much of an expert as the United States had. The analysts at CIA and elsewhere got the bulk of their information from computer screens.

Throughout my years at UNSCOM, I had become friends with some Iraqis outside Iraq who had extensive contacts with Iraqis back home. We had long, ongoing discussions about life in Iraq, the actions of the regime, and, particularly, the dealings pertaining to Iraq's oil business. For example, OPEC met multiple times during the year. These were ready-made opportunities to see Iraqis. There were also professional conferences that senior Iraqis sometimes received permission to attend. These were open windows into the regime. As I was with the UN and later with the Center for Strategic and International Studies (CSIS), I was unencumbered by the taint of representing Washington and mixed freely.

At the same time, nothing had diminished my sense that our intelligence-collection organizations made things too difficult. It seemed easier for someone to get a contract to design a new widget that could detect a high-speed centrifuge from the other side of the planet than it was to simply call up a contact and ask, "What's going on?" Our intelligence from human sources (HUMINT, for HUMan INTelligence) seemed pathetically limited.[1] To me, it just didn't seem that hard to contact real Iraqis. But CIA and other intelligence analysts were ensnared in the system they operated. They were unable to simply call up some Iraqi or wander around conferences and hear what was going on in the real world.

So, I sustained these dialogues with various Iraqis during my work at CSIS, and they helped inform my writing there. I also stayed in close contact with CIA officers responsible for Iraq and WMD.[2]

As a visiting scholar at CSIS, I could interact widely among various groups and conferences. At one conference in Prague, the organizers intended to bring Middle East and American scholars together to "look for common ground" in the Iraq dilemma. When they could not attract an Iraqi from Baghdad, the organizers asked me to play the role of the Iraq regime. Tariq Aziz would have been surprised. After years of listening to Aziz, I found I could make a pretty convincing case from his perspective—perhaps more convincing because I lacked his habit of chain-smoking Cohibas and hacking phlegm into a tissue. The other regional participants were also surprised—I had been widely known in region as the American pushing UNSCOM in its confrontations with Iraq—to hear an American who understood the Iraqi arguments well enough to present them credibly.

In February 2001, Ahmad Chalabi contacted me at CSIS to discuss the incoming administration. He knew many of the prominent players, like Richard Perle, very well. Chalabi wanted me to meet someone who he thought would be involved in the Iraq issue. He thought we would get along and perhaps I could help this person with background on Iraq and WMD. It had been in this way that, on February 8, I first met John Hannah at my office at CSIS. We began what became a continuing discussion on Iraq. Hannah was destined to become Vice President Cheney's top aide on Iraq.

Chalabi was correct about one thing. I did like Hannah. I found him a thoughtful, solid guy. And over time, I never revised that first impression. He worked very hard to understand a subject and define the best options.

In this first meeting, Hannah quickly said that he had no official position in the administration and did not yet have his clearances in place. Nevertheless, we spoke at length about Iraq and WMD. I offered my strong view that UN inspections would not work over the long term.

I also shared my view that the majority of Iraqis I worked with were talented, sophisticated technocrats who had had the misfortune to be born in a horrendous regime. In general, I found Iraqis energetic, Westward leaning, secular, and great builders. Their regular army was basically competent and professional. The Special Republican Guard was the elite, and its leaders were committed to Saddam. The civilian Iraqi ministries were not bad for a third-world country. You had to give credit to Saddam for building up the education and health sectors. There was a very strong professional class in Iraq. I knew many Iraqi professionals quite well, and perhaps this colored my strong view that the difference between what Iraq could be and what it was under Saddam's rule was enormous. The difference between the waste of the present-day Iraq and the potential of a future Iraq boiled down to one person—Saddam.

Hannah seemed to agree with the tone of my comments, but was cautious in expressing his views. He was stepping into a new issue and a very sensitive position: I learned weeks later that he would be working on Vice President Cheney's staff under Scooter Libby. I took it that Chalabi knew more and was introducing Hannah to those in Washington he thought could be useful or influential.

Hannah epitomized the best characteristics of those who collectively became identified as the energy behind the administration's decision to depose Saddam militarily. He was motivated by a sincere desire to shape the future in a way that would allow Iraq to blossom. There was a rational judgment that Saddam would become a threat again, if he wasn't already. Hannah and I remained in touch during the lead-up to the war and afterward. We would meet for coffee at what I called the "NSC Starbucks," located a half block away from the Eisenhower Executive Office Building, which was adjacent to the White House. The office building was where the National Security Council and the vice president's staff had offices. We discussed what UNSCOM had concluded about the WMD programs and what the UNSCOM data showed. Hannah knew I was in touch with various Iraqis who were not part of the INC group.

He also seemed to value my opinion on the prospects for future UN inspections under UNMOVIC. He repeatedly asked whether inspections could detect a carefully reconstituted WMD program. As he tested my case repeatedly, I offered a combination of practical aspects of monitoring and my own observations concerning the willpower of the Security Council to force compliance. I also expressed my view that the administration's "smart sanctions" were clear evidence that containment of Iraq in the UN was doomed; it was only a question of time. I recalled the meeting I had with Martin Indyk at the White House in 1993, when he drew two lines with his fingers, one indicating support for Saddam and the other support for sanctions. He had been correct in understanding that support for sanctions would not last forever. It was, to me, a surprise that sanctions lasted as long as they did.

My contact with Ahmad Chalabi continued even after UNSCOM left Iraq in December 1998. He would share information from occasional defectors who claimed to have knowledge of Iraq WMD. Chalabi obviously had an interest in opposing Saddam, and I didn't expect him to provide an individual who would say there was no remaining WMD in Iraq. His goal was to influence Washington to support getting rid of Saddam.

Still, given his broad interests in finding knowledgeable Iraqis coming out of Iraq, there was no reason in my mind to ignore the individuals he came across. UNSCOM had pretty good data by which to determine if someone was spinning a tale or not. But since UN-SCOM had published openly available UN reports with extremely detailed information about Iraq's WMD facilities, it had become pretty easy for someone—particularly Iraqis—to appear knowledgeable. An Iraqi would naturally have much ground truth about facilities and locations and people just from growing up in Iraq. Combining that natural background with the extensive detailed technical data UNSCOM put on its Web site allowed Iraqis recently out of Iraq to construct a credible and even convincing WMD tale.

In the time since UNSCOM left Iraq, a series of Iraqis had made claims about Iraq WMD. These defectors made themselves known to Chalabi and a variety of news organizations and governments. Their tales fell on fertile ground. The conclusion of UNSCOM's work had been that Iraq had not convincingly accounted for its WMD programs. UNSCOM had demonstrated that parts of Iraq's declarations were wrong. The unanswered questions about the disposition of various WMD items seemed better explained by a decision on the part of Saddam to retain such capabilities rather than the feeble-sounding explanations Iraq offered—especially given the long track record of deception. So defectors, claiming knowledge of Iraq WMD programs, were stating things intelligence agencies and many political leaders around the world expected to hear.

As defectors came out of Iraq with public claims about WMD, I would frequently get calls from journalists concerning their veracity. On occasion, there were individuals who came out with documents.

An example was an engineer who worked on facilities for the Iraqi Military Industrial Commission (MIC)—the organization responsible for all Iraqi military production, including WMD. Chalabi's INC had contacted Judy Miller of the *New York Times*. Miller had long been following the WMD and INC stories. She kept close tabs on UNSCOM's work and knew nonproliferation issues as well as many academics or government officials did. It had been the practice of the commission, under both Ekeus and Butler, to be quite open with the press. UNSCOM's Scottish public affairs officer, Ewen Buchanan, knew the issues in depth. When journalists wanted more, they would have access to the chairman and me, as well as our technical staff.

Miller knew our experts, especially the biological-weapons experts, very well. She also knew the Washington policy and intelligence experts. When she was offered the opportunity to see this defector, Miller contacted me to see if it would be worth the trouble. In her call, she was very cryptic, but I said it sounded potentially interesting.

Miller made her trip, and when she returned, she asked to come by with some documents. She had copies of Iraqi documents that described construction issues and appeared to be on authentic letterhead and with authentic signatures. They did not, as I recall, indicate WMD activities, but did seem to show that her source did work on some MIC facilities. I learned later that U.S. analysts debriefed this individual and issued a large number of reports based on his reporting. Sometimes what he said was correct; sometimes he was inferring too much. For example, his description of entering a facility only in a special protective suit may not have been because he was entering a place that could contaminate him, but because it was a gyroscope-test facility with a clean room, where individuals suit up to prevent any contaminating material on the individual from getting into sensitive equipment.

Journalists were quite anxious to get their hands on a new defector. It was good business. I received many hopeful queries about defectors whom journalists found in Amman or Europe and who claimed to have been involved in or witnessed WMD work. I *never* received a call from any journalist saying he or she had a defector who claimed there was nothing going on with WMD in Iraq. In retrospect, journalists were behaving in the same way that the intelligence agencies had behaved. Journalists got headlines for reports of WMD. No headlines for "no WMD" stories. Too often, they were basing stories on single sources. The goals, incentives, and problems for journalists are much the same as those for intelligence analysts and collectors. The difference is, journalists are not accountable to anyone except their editors, who may or may not care more about selling newspapers than accuracy. Journalists do not have to take polygraphs, testify before Congress, or be subject to inspector general investigations for not getting a story. On the other hand, intelligence analysts do not go to jail if they do not reveal their sources, as Miller did. Intelligence officials can go to jail if they do reveal them.

As some journalists found, many defectors were fairly credible. *Credible* is an important word. In the intelligence business, it means that an individual's information is technically feasible and consistent with other known facts. It does not mean the statements are known to be true. When journalists shared their defector debriefing materials with me, I would, on the basis of my own knowledge or that of other former UNSCOM colleagues, see if the information was credible. Many defectors were credible, but that was not saying we could verify their statements. They were plausible, but unprovable.

Some defectors said they had been present at secure facilities in Iraq and heard that something very secret was concealed there. Their direct knowledge would end at just the point where a definitive WMD link would start. These Iraqis were not necessarily fabricators, but the combination of the proclivity in Iraq to believe and spread conspiracy theories, combined with the anxiously tuned ears in the United States to hear such witnesses, gave these defector stories more prominence than they deserved.

Chalabi is smart and persuasive and knows what his interlocutor wants to hear. He has energy. I also knew that whatever I heard from Chalabi, there was more to the story. Ambassador Richard Butler used to have a standard question he would ask experts briefing him: "What are you not telling me?" This was a chronic question in my mind with Chalabi.

When I saw Chalabi in Washington we discussed the political events in Washington, not in Iraq. He would describe his efforts to unify the external opposition, but had nothing to say about contacts inside Iraq. While I appreciated his dynamism and bravery and his efforts to build a coalition among the range of opposition groups—Kurds, Monarchists, and others—I was skeptical of his ability to overthrow Saddam. I knew from my own UNSCOM experience how tough the regime security services could be. And I doubted that there was much sympathy for the INC among serious Iraqis in Iraq. Why would anyone in Iraq act to depose Saddam so that Chalabi, who had left Iraq before Saddam even came to power, could take over?

For his part, Chalabi never felt the State Department was completely fulfilling the intent of the Iraq Liberation Act, and of course, the department was not. It was obligated to fund the INC as a part of the congressionally mandated Iraq Liberation Act of 1998. The INC was using the funding to facilitate the collection of information from Iraqi defectors and other organizational efforts. The INC maintained an office in London not far from Harrods in Knightsbridge.[3]

I traveled through London at the end of October 2001 on my way to a conference in Istanbul. On Monday afternoon, the 29th, I took the opportunity to visit with Chalabi at his INC offices. While the location was pricey, the furnishings were scruffy—a bit like used IKEA furniture. A bunch of Iraqis were sitting around smoking cigarettes and drinking tea.

Chalabi was his usual bundle of energy. We spent three hours discussing his plans and his sources of information. I enjoyed talking with him. He was very quick and could shift ground rapidly while keeping his overall objective in mind. But I could never convince myself that he would be the key to successful regime change. Nevertheless, we certainly both agreed that Iraq had great potential, but for Saddam.

Chalabi had a longtime colleague with him named Arras Karim Habib, who was, among other things, Chalabi's guy for collecting information from defectors and other sources. I had met Habib years before, when UNSCOM had discussed reports offered by Chalabi from defectors. For example, in 1997 Habib had shared with UNSCOM a report from a defector claiming Iraq retained three nuclear weapons.

On the day I happened to visit, Chalabi said Habib had just received information from Iranian intelligence (the Ministry of Intelligence and Security, MOIS) that Saddam had sent two tons of VX salts to Osama bin Laden in Afghanistan two years earlier. (VX is a very advanced nerve agent; VX salts are the final chemical precursor to producing the highly lethal agent.) I knew Chalabi had maintained contact with MOIS, especially while he was based in Kurdistan. The MOIS had been quite active in Kurdistan during the 1990s, when Chalabi had a small opposition operation going there.

Chalabi said his relationship with Iran was good. He accepted assistance where he could get it. Chalabi reminded me that in 1997, he had offered to broker a meeting between Scott Ritter and the MOIS to discuss information on Iraqi WMD that could assist UNSCOM. When Ritter proposed this to me, I had said no. It was one of the few initiatives Ritter proposed that I nixed.

Later, when I was directing the Iraq Survey Group in 2004, the continuing close relationship between Habib and Iranian intelligence would be problematic. It was a surprise to some that the INC was very close to Iranian intelligence, when in fact the relationship was neither new nor surprising. What truly surprised me was that U.S. authorities would tell INC anything sensitive, considering that the information could be passed on to Tehran or anyone else.

We discussed the notion of links between Baghdad and the 9/11 attacks and the subsequent anthrax incidents. I said, "There are no obvious links that would stand up in court."

Chalabi responded, "But if it walks like a duck, talks like a duck, it's a duck."

I insisted Saddam would not do something like this. It was not his style to confront the United States secretly. He would do it directly as he had for years. "And why would he support a terrorist he could not control?" I asked.

I went on with my sense of Washington: "The dynamic of the current discussion in Washington has led to an artificial standard that *only* if proof of Iraqi involvement is found in the nine-eleven attacks, could the United States act against the regime. Otherwise there was insufficient cause." It was not what Chalabi wanted to hear. We discussed a couple other defectors who reported they had knowledge of Iraq WMD and the activities of UNSCOM inspections. One claimed to have worked with the Iraqi intelligence at a location called Salman Pak, which is south of Baghdad and a facility quite familiar to UNSCOM. Iraq had conducted biological-weapons work there, and we had inspected it many times. There were Mukhabarat facilities there, and training took place—including training on the airframe of an old Russian airliner. The Iraqis claimed it was antiterrorist training. It could easily have been the opposite, but we could come to no conclusions.

According to Chalabi, another defector reported that he had seen A. Q. Khan in Baghdad as recently as January 2001. Khan was the father of the Pakistani nuclear weapon and had been selling his expertise and centrifuge designs to the likes of North Korea, Libya, and Iran. Chalabi's source said Khan had made several trips to Baghdad since 1999. Although he gave me a two-page paper on this report, even Chalabi did not seem to expect me to believe it.

I asked Chalabi, "How do you respond to the skepticism over your ability to operate inside Iraq?" He led me to another room with a large Iraq map on the wall. He pointed to four southern cities, Amarah, al Kut, Karbala, and Najaf.

"We have strong supporters in these cities, especially Amarah," he replied. "There are two hundred who will act on a moment's notice." He described a plan whereby they would rise up once they had weapons—the southern enclave plan. A chunk of territory would be excised from central Baghdad control, along the lines of Kurdistan in the north, and then there would be safe locations to which Iraqis in the middle could defect. In this way, the INC could mobilize a larger and larger force, or so the idea went.

This idea was wishful thinking at best. Saddam had already demonstrated he could control the southern Shia areas when he crushed the Shia rebellion in 1991. I doubted the southern Shia would try that again. I also doubted that the influential clerics in the south would risk supporting such a scheme. From my many discussions with Iraqis in Iraq, I had a strong sense that changing the existing management without changing the existing structure was the least risky because it required the least uncertainty.

Chalabi had a different view, which amounted to an assumption that external dissidents could attract sufficient support to create an internal revolution. Maybe it sounded good outside Iraq, but I could not imagine that most of the key Iraqis inside Iraq would bet their lives on it—particularly for someone who was either not known at all inside Iraq or known quite negatively. Iraqis inside Iraq seemed to be familiar with Chalabi's felony conviction in absentia in Jordan for embezzlement after the collapse of the Petra Bank, which his family ran in Amman.[4] But Chalabi was making the best case he could. At that time, I don't think even he dreamed that the United States would muster a full invasion. He seemed to be tailoring his plans to suit a modest U.S. military commitment.

I asked Chalabi about one further point. Some in Washington had expressed concern that the INC was penetrated by the Mukhabarat. There had been a debacle when Iraqi forces slaughtered INC supporters in northern Iraq in 1996. Previous actions by the INC had been compromised, and his office in Knightsbridge seemed like a good and easy target for regime intelligence. He said he was confident the INC was secure and that rumors of Mukhabarat spies having been included in the training programs funded by the United States under the 1998 Iraq Liberation Act were untrue.

We discussed a range of Iraqi personalities, including some prominent scientists, like Jafaar Dhia Jafaar, the head of the Iraq nuclear program. Chalabi knew them well and their outside business relations. I would not have been in the least surprised if he himself had direct dealings with their companies, as he conducted complicated and intertwining business deals. In these areas, I had much greater confidence in Chalabi's knowledge.

As I was preparing to leave, he asked me to meet an Iraqi whom Habib was currently debriefing. The defector was visiting London from another European country. The man said he had been tasked with following UNSCOM, and he claimed to recognize me. When I asked when he was following UNSCOM, he said 1991–1992. I wasn't there until 1993. Such was the reliability of some of Chalabi's defectors.

Aside from Chalabi, the two truly powerful groups of Iraq opposition were the two Kurdish organizations: the Kurdistan Democratic Party (KDP) under Massoud Barzani and the Patriotic Union of Kurdistan (PUK) under Jalal Talabani. Both groups had something to lose, unlike Chalabi. The PUK and KDP had stopped fighting each other and had made deals with each other and the Baghdad regime over the flow of oil through Kurdistan. The United States, through the no-fly zones, protected the two organizations, so they were enjoying independence already.

The PUK was far savvier around Washington, especially through the work of Qubad Talabani, the son of Jalal Talabani. Barzani's KDP had better relations with Baghdad, but was feeling its way around Washington. In my own discussions with representatives of both the KDP and PUK, they voiced a deep concern that there would be talk about taking action on regime change, but Washington would not follow through. They were very leery of the vagaries of Washington. From their perspective, they had been sold out in 1991. Washington had encouraged the postwar uprising against Saddam, but did nothing when Saddam cracked down and the Kurds had to flee to the mountains. Now, they were not easily persuaded to commit to an antiregime course, especially since they had a much-improved position already. It would not be until after 9/11 that the Kurds would be convinced the United States was serious about dealing with Saddam.

CHAPTER 12

Getting Inside Iraq

To the U.S. intelligence community, Baghdad was a very hard target. The regime was authoritarian and had multiple layers of security. The United States had no diplomatic relations, and its embassy was empty. Once UNSCOM inspectors left in December 1998, the flow of information on Iraq WMD, or anything else, diminished to an irregular drip. Consequently, the occasional pieces of information had disproportionate importance. Making assessments became progressively more uncertain. It was like trying to connect dots in the correct pattern but there were only a few dots—and the lights were out. Still, various windows into Iraq offered some perspective.

One open window was through the oil business. The most valuable thing the regime had was its oil, and it had to interact with the international markets to sell it. The oil industry in Iraq was the premier technical field—with the possible exception of the WMD programs. Both areas attracted Iraq's best and brightest. Usually the best oil engineers, geologists, and financial people had studied in Europe or the United States. They came from the same top slice of Iraqi professional elite that the WMD scientists came from. Likewise, they were also tuned into the top leaders of the regime. It was a relatively small population, and all these people knew one another. For example, Saddam's WMD presidential advisor, Amer al-Saadi, has a brother, Radwan al-Saadi, who was named the director general of economics and finance in the Ministry of Oil in June 2002. Radwan, like many of the senior

Ministry of Oil technocrats, was quite helpful in running the ministry after the invasion.

Saddam also had to permit the top oil executives to travel. That was how business was done. Most obviously, there were regular, semiannual OPEC meetings, usually in Vienna where the OPEC Secretariat headquarters building is located. Additional, extraordinary meetings often addressed Iraq-related issues. (OPEC was created in Baghdad in 1960. The five original members were Iraq, Iran, Kuwait, Saudi Arabia, and Venezuela.) Especially from the mid-1990s on, the OPEC meetings focused on Iraqi oil coming to the market through the Oil-for-Food program. The meetings and deals that were made at these events were great opportunities to learn what was going on in Baghdad at very senior levels.

During my years at UNSCOM, oil industry executives and analysts stayed in touch with me because they wanted to know the prospects for Iraq's complying with the UN Security Council resolutions and, hence, the council's prospects for lifting sanctions. Any hint of Iraqi oil coming on the market drove futures prices berserk—millions could be made or lost on the basis of rumors. In fact, in the lead-up to the Iraqi acceptance of the Oil-for-Food program in December 1996, several traders alleged that the Iraq government and those close to, or supporters of, the regime were generating revenues this way, since they could take a position and then make the appropriate public statement to generate a healthy price swing. The result was they could bank a quick profit for themselves.

I became close to a couple of analysts in particular. One, Alexander, was a most thoughtful and reflective oil expert. He spoke fluent Arabic and had years of experience living in the region, including in Iraq. Alexander was interested in Iraq not only for financial reasons but also because he had developed close relations there over the years. His depth of expertise was recognized by other Gulf States, and he provided advice and counsel to senior levels of oil ministries in the Gulf. Since the other Gulf States shared family and other ties within Iraq, Alexander had solid lines into connections with Iraqi counterparts. Another oil expert, Youssef, was an Iraqi expatriate but had family and business ties in both Iraq and the United States. He maintained close contacts with Iraqi technocrats in the Oil and other ministries. Youssef and I got into the habit of speaking regularly when I was at the UN. The workings of the Oil-for-Food process were complicated and had a significant impact on oil markets during this period.

Youssef was attuned to the complex issues of oil pricing and the transactions that went on between states and individual oil companies. I was surprised the first time he mentioned something that was so obvious to him, but unknown to me—that the United States was one of the biggest importers of Iraqi oil. There were many intermediaries, but oil was a fungible commodity, and once it was on the market, it went wherever the market took it. Of course, the market was by no means a free one, as far as Iraqi oil was concerned. The UN was involved in the pricing, and because Iraqi oil had risk associated with it, the price was set at a discount to the market. Therefore, those who acquired the right to lift Iraqi oil stood to earn an instant premium over the market price. Baghdad quickly learned to dispense "oil allocations" to individuals, companies, or countries that could then trade that right to others who might exercise it by actually lifting the oil. For example, if Iraq wanted to reward person X for some favor, it could assign X the right to lift a million barrels of oil from one of the export points. The individual might have no knowledge about the oil business, but X could sell the option to some trading company that did—for a handsome price.

Such trading was the talk of OPEC meetings, occurring regularly at the key OPEC hotels such as the Continental in Vienna, just around the corner from the Iraq Embassy. The Intermezzo lobby bar of the Continental was filled with cigar smoke and analysts, traders, oil company representatives, press, and so forth. In the suites occupied by oil ministry officials of member countries, deals were made with huge implications. OPEC meetings are a fascinating kaleidoscope of international traders—some licit and some illicit—where wealth moves rapidly among various parties.

Being in the oil business, Alexander had been going to these meetings regularly for many years. From what he and others readily observed, the illicit trading was clearly burgeoning well before the war, but governments chose not to do anything. Certain illicit practices, such as Iraqi attempts to impose surcharges separate from the UN fixed-pricing mechanism, were raised in the Security Council, but the council could not agree on measures to address that or any other manipulations.

Among the oil trading community, it was natural to discuss the political situation in Iraq. Youssef sustained dialogues with his relatives, former classmates, and other colleagues who traveled regularly to Iraq. The Iraqi officials he met viewed him as another Iraqi who understood their position. He was not a foreign government official. Youssef could lend an ear and a hand in finding positions for the children of officials looking for jobs or university positions outside Iraq. He could help with the complexities of getting by in the Saddam regime. Importantly, Youssef knew the regime thugs from the regime technocrats. Like other Iraqi oil industry analysts, he had a good window into the regime, though at times, it was a kaleidoscope.

Even before Iraq agreed to the UN Oil-for-Food program, Iraq participated in all OPEC meetings and was exporting oil to Jordan. Dialogue in the oil business context was regular, and information flowed out of Iraq to the oil community. And there were some oil dealers who were quite close to the regime—some making the illicit deals. From such individuals came many of the reports of regime events, such as the attempted assassination of Saddam's son Uday in December 1996, just as Iraq was finally agreeing to the UN Oil-for-Food program.

The word among oil experts and traders was that Saddam believed the Oil-for-Food program would be a symbol of weakness. It turned out to be a powerful tool of corruption. Over the next six years, oil exports considerably strengthened the regime. The convoluted deals and relationships (especially banking) between the regime and all manner of other parties typify the unfathomable complexity of Iraq. Deals were made between the regime and not only its friends, but also some who are now members of the new government.

It was obvious to my contacts and others in the oil-trading business that a number of companies and individuals had particularly close ties to Saddam. They were allegedly involved in dealing with Saddam's (or the regime's) funds outside Iraq. Oil traders were quite aware of who was obtaining Iraqi oil allocations. There was speculation, sometimes well informed, on how the allocations were obtained. One prominent name was the commodities trader Marc Rich, who fled the United States in 1983 to avoid prosecution (by then prosecutor Rudy Giuliani) for tax evasion and trading with Iran. He was pardoned by President Clinton just before the president left office. (Rich, ironically, was represented by former vice presidential aide Scooter Libby, who was an attorney at Dechart, Price and Rhodes in Washington.) Rich's wife, a prominent socialite, had made large donations to the Clinton campaign and presidential library. Rich was also a major contributor to Israeli interests, and former Prime Minister Ehud Barak called President Clinton twice at the end of his presidency to lobby for Rich's pardon.[1]

A second prominent individual closely tied to Saddam was Oscar Wyatt, a Texan oilman who founded Coastal Corp. Ten years after Alexander and I first discussed these relations, Wyatt was charged and convicted in New York for paying bribes to Iraq for oil allocations.[2] There were many other businessmen and politicians around the world who were similarly prosecuted for sanctions violations after the regime fell (with the notable exception of anyone in Russia).

During 2000–2002, OPEC meetings were held with great frequency to deal with the ongoing crisis over Iraqi oil. The sanctions and Oil-for-Food programs were being debated in New York, and Baghdad kept threatening to end its oil exports. OPEC had agreed to keep oil pricing within a band of twenty-two to twenty-eight dollars per barrel, and the Saudis and a couple other countries with excess capacity were ready to compensate for any output reductions from Iraq. But many countries were cheating on their quotas. Despite all the high-paid analysts, even staff analysts at the OPEC Headquarters in Vienna did not really know how much oil was being put on the market. Add to this the growing Russian influence and the increasingly likely war, and Vienna became a scene of great frenzy, avarice, and sometimes desperation.

Vienna was a place where Iraqi elite could temporarily escape and vent. It was also a location where senior Iraqis looking for a legitimate excuse to get out of Iraq would look for jobs. It was possible to hear some candor from senior Iraqis that was never expressed in Baghdad. The scenes that could be watched in Vienna were a mix of tragedies, mysteries, spy stories, and soap operas.

Among the vignettes were the senior oil officials' complaining about the increasingly corrupt business patterns in Baghdad. Iraq's oil technocrats could not run an organized process for selling permitted oil when random orders from regime leaders were issued directing additional oil allocations to favored parties—irrespective of what had already been committed. One technician complained, "I just received an instruction to issue an allocation to a company that was agreed in a deal between the son of the top Kurdish leader and Uday."

He went on, "So I had no choice. I issued the allocation. But in fact, there are already too many allocations issued for that particular phase. We are making allocations for oil we cannot pump! And it is getting worse the longer this situation goes on. How can we operate as a serious country when there is no control over these allocations?"

Other Iraqi technicians and business executives who regularly traveled to Baghdad to obtain contracts to provide material under the Oil-for-Food program would compare notes on dealing with Iraqi ministries and individuals. They all were attracted to the prospects of business, and as the tensions grew in Baghdad, the fever to get deals grew as well. A frequent comment was, "Saddam knows the money does him no good if the war comes, so he is spending now to get influence. And everyone around him is making his own deals." They pointed to Saddam's son Uday and his colleagues saying they behaved like mafia dons and extracted payments amounting to between a 7 and 10 percent tax on most businesses.

Saddam Hassan al-Ziban was almost always on the Iraqi delegation to OPEC meetings and was clearly identified by the oil traders as "Saddam's Bagman."[3] An intellectually unimpressive relative of Saddam, he served as the direct link to Uday and the family. Ziban received and paid the bribes. Rumors swirled about him, and his close association with an attractive Western woman working in the oil business in Switzerland was classic. In retrospect, investigations after the war confirmed he had a central role in distributing the illicit oil trades.

Other Iraqi Oil Ministry delegation members inquired about jobs for their children or themselves in other countries. They were looking to get out. The trend grew as international tensions grew.

Gossip was rampant. A senior Iraq Foreign Ministry official said that former UN Ambassador Hamdoon was falling under a cloud and had been sidelined completely by the new foreign minister, Naji Sabri. The same was said about another former UN ambassador, Riyadh al-Qaisy.

The inner problems of Baghdad came to light in Vienna. Foreign Minister Sabri (who had previously been Iraq's ambassador in Vienna) was deeply involved in the oil issue because it was so closely connected to UN Security Council deliberations over sanctions. The council could not agree on alterations to sanctions or to pricing mechanisms. Sabri had to contend with sustaining Russian support. The Russians were delinquent in paying the surcharges Saddam demanded for Iraq's Oil-for-Food allocations. This became a bigger issue in 2002, since Russia found it harder to support Iraq after 9/11. Moscow wanted its surcharge fees forgiven or reduced. There was tension between Tariq Aziz and Naji Sabri on this and other issues, according to the complaints of Iraqi delegation members. Corridor conversations revealed that Zaid Aziz, the son of Tariq Aziz, was having business disputes with Saddam's sons. This became public in September 2001, when Zaid was arrested by the regime (and later released).

In June and July 2002, OPEC swirled with rumors about the UN. Foreign Minister Sabri had come to Vienna to discuss with UN Secretary General Kofi Anan the prospects for returning weapons inspectors. The minister also discussed the ongoing matter of UN pricing for Iraqi oil. Virtually nothing was agreed on, and more rumors rippled around Vienna. Sabri met with many individuals and delegations during his trips. Baghdad had not replaced him when he left Vienna to become foreign minister the previous year. His deputy, Ahmed Abouallah al-Duri, remained as acting ambassador. The two were close, and Sabri was happy to have in Vienna some eyes and ears he could trust.

Many Iraqis said that once he became foreign minister, Sabri became a much harsher advocate of the regime's position. Some commented then that Qusay, who ran the top security organizations, extended his influence to the Ministry of Foreign Affairs through Naji Sabri. Still, Sabri's predecessor, Mohammed Sahaf, was much coarser and concealed his intellect well. (Sahaf became the information minister later known as "Baghdad Bob" and known for his declarations that the American army was in retreat from Baghdad in April 2003.)

At OPEC, this kind of information from inside Iraq was available from the social networks of the Iraqis who were present in Vienna. Iraqis in government, former government officials tossed out by Saddam, professional elites—all these people became more talkative after the January 29, 2002, State of the Union message (the "axis of evil" speech) and still more so after the visit of Saudi Crown Prince Abdullah to Texas in April. It was beginning to look as though President Bush had made up his mind. Iraqis wanted to know—it was their lives at stake—was the United States serious this time?

The conflicting perspectives offered by Colin Powell, pushing the UN angle, and Vice President Cheney, emphasizing that Saddam had to go . . . period, were not lost on the Iraqis. This divide in the U.S. government was closely scrutinized. Saddam used it to argue that the United States was not serious. A common refrain heard at discussions around OPEC was that the United States had abandoned the Shia in their rebellion against the regime in 1991. Counting on Washington could be fatal.

As the debate about President Bush's intentions grew, senior Iraqis tried to discover when the American invasion might happen, because they were concerned about their own futures. Some senior Iraqis, under the right circumstances, became loquacious with Americans who were thought to be informed, but not part of the government. I found it progressively easier to find Iraqis who wanted to speak, but they were also more concerned that the pervasive Iraqi intelligence services would discover them. In this atmosphere, opportunities to meet in plain sight were often the most comfortable—like OPEC meetings.

The CIA Near Eastern Division has an office dedicated to Iraq called the Iraq Operations Group (IOG). I had been in touch with the group for years. Its objective was to get inside Iraq. I had been going into and coming out of Iraq since 1993 and knew many of the top Iraqi leaders. IOG helped with several useful activities. For example, IOG had assisted in arranging for my UNSCOM colleagues and me to meet with some Iraqi defectors who appeared to know things that would be useful for the commission's work in Iraq. It was natural that I stay in touch with the IOG office as well as with the Non-Proliferation and Iraq Analysis offices at CIA headquarters. A new chief of IOG arrived in August 2001, and with him, a new mission. The new chief was immediately tasked to consider how to change the regime, assuming there was a full commitment by Washington to see it through.[4] That was why he took the job. His activism was immediately apparent, and we concurred on the lay of the land in Iraq. Although I only saw certain slices of the emerging activities, it was clear to me that he understood that changing the Saddam regime would not be done through coups dreamed up by outside opposition groups. When I first met him, I was taken with his energy and how rapidly he figured out the steps involved to get to a given objective. He was results-orientated and willing to take risks so long as they were understood and worthwhile. The chief also seemed to be able to see beyond the limited secret world that operations officers inhabit. He saw the big picture and he was a good leader for what would be a very complicated job.

I offered my description of the Iraqi landscape—in particular, the lack of internal support in Iraq for outside opposition groups. He readily agreed. A further point on which the new chief and I agreed was that changing a regime was fundamentally a political activity, not a military activity. The military may create the conditions for a change, but there has to be a political substitution of control.

From August 2001 until the war, the chief and I had frequent conversations, and I worked progressively more closely with his group. We discussed particular individuals and pathways into Iraq. We also discussed the political environment around Washington. In some ways, these conversations mirrored the ones taking place in Vienna and even in Baghdad. Would the United States really do it this time? IOG was making plans that would require increasingly large commitments by people in the field. These people would be betting their lives that the United States would not pull the rug out from under them. Unfortunately, the United States has a long tradition of not sustaining its efforts or making good on its implied promises. The chief did not want to be another example of that tendency (his father was an alumnus of the Bay of Pigs Invasion).

We talked about Iraq WMD, but only in regard to Washington's policy decision to handle Iraq through the UN Security Council. The chief saw the decision to go through the UN as a major impediment to recruiting support in the region. To the Kurds, letting the Iraq WMD issue play out in the UN looked a lot like the same old wobbly U.S. policy of regime change, but ultimately letting Saddam off the hook. The Kurds now had a lot to lose if the United States backed away from regime change in favor of some UN-driven outcome to police Iraq. Both Massoud Barzani's KDP and Jalal Talabani's PUK were currently getting sizable oil revenue streams in tacit deals with the regime. The IOG chief needed to convince them the regime was going to be gone, since he needed their support to set up bases in the Kurdish part of Iraq that was beyond the regime's control.

The chief said, if Washington puts the Iraq issue in the UN's hands, the United States will not look serious about regime change. Clinton had done that for eight years, in addition to two lame coup attempts by external Iraqi opposition. I could offer no solace. Given an opportunity, if Iraq accepted inspectors, then the case for military action was as good as over. UNSCOM had aggressively inspected Iraq for seven years, with increasingly small returns—certainly nothing that would justify an invasion. Nevertheless, the chief, who went to White House meetings with the president regularly, developed increasing confidence that this time, with this president, Washington would be serious—especially after 9/11.

I had been scheduled to go to IOG at midmorning on that bright, clear Tuesday, September 11, 2001. I was driving up Route 123 from the Chain Bridge and approaching the CIA headquarters entrance when I concluded that the meeting was pointless; I had heard the radio news reports and was unable to call anyone on my cell phone.

After 9/11, it became clear that the momentum at the top levels of the administration was in favor of "doing Iraq." It was a question of how and when.

I was at IOG regularly to discuss what I'd learned from various Iraqis and other contacts that could be important. As time went on, I shared a cubicle in the IOG rabbit warren, which was teeming with officers night and day. From my perspective on the range of IOG operations, it was clear that the goal was not WMD elimination but how to undermine the regime and build an Iraqi capability inside Iraq for that purpose.

CSIS was supportive of my range of activities. Like many other think tanks, CSIS attracted foreign visitors who shared their views with resident scholars. The center also has many corporate clients who wanted to hear what people were expecting in various regions, but especially the Middle East. Oil companies were very tuned in to what the prospects were for Iraq, and CSIS had a strong energy analysis team.

Not being a regular denizen of the Washington think-tank circuit, I was surprised by a couple of things. One was how quickly a new idea expressed at a roundtable or conference could be appropriated by someone else and appear in some op-ed or be parroted on a cable news program filling time with babbling "experts." There was much repackaging of ideas and information and much less original work.

It was amazing to watch cable news on September 12, 2001. I don't think there were any terrorism experts at CSIS on September 10. But on the 12th, when every news channel in the universe wanted "experts" to fill air time, CSIS and every other think tank were filled with people who would go on air having just mastered the pronunciation of *al-Qaeda* and speak knowingly about the intricacies of global terrorism. The relationship between think tanks and media was mutually supportive. The media needed to fill air time, and the think tanks found publicity for experts a big plus. The same happened in a more gradual way with Iraq.

It is easy to forget now that, in 2001, almost no one in Washington had any recent (within less than a decade) experience in Iraq. Few officials or policy experts knew much about the geography, the sectarian composition, the regime structure, or even the key people of Iraq. If you could name five towns in Iraq, you were an expert. Iraqi expatriate dissidents had become the primary source of political information. This perplexed me, to say the least. What did it matter what people outside Iraq thought? The people who would decide issues critical to changing the regime were Iraqis inside Iraq. They would decide how hard to fight an invading force. It was their opinion about who should take charge after Saddam that mattered.

In the fall of 2001, I began assembling a list of senior Iraqis in Iraq who I could contact one way or another. I was also able to get some ideas of their basic views on the United States. This list grew. With my contacts, including Youssef and Alexander, I began to consider how this information could be used. In some cases, we could elicit views on current thinking in Iraq. Some of our contacts spoke very guardedly on the phone from Iraq, whereas others had the opportunity to travel outside Iraq—for example, some midlevel ministry officials came to California for a wedding. Very frank conversations took place outside Iraq. Over time, between these conversations and the discussions in the OPEC environment, I felt I was getting at least a partial sense of how Iraqis were seeing the emerging crisis.

Conversations are two-way. These individuals were thirsty for information about what the United States was going to do. It was an opportunity to transmit a message of U.S. intentions if that were judged useful at an appropriate time.

A third general question repeatedly came up in these discussions: Who would be a good leader after Saddam? Youssef and I reviewed various suggestions, and we also got many recommendations for other senior positions in Iraq. Separately, I discussed this with the IOG chief, who was interested, and it gradually evolved into an extensive project for me.

By the end of November 2001, there were open conversations in Iraq about risks of an impending American attack. The conventional wisdom in Baghdad was that Iraq would be the next Afghanistan.

Author in Chad with C-130A transport aircraft given to the country to support their army against Libyan invasion in the 1980s. Chad had only one qualified pilot at the time. (Credit: Author's collection.)

Author in Chadian camp at presidential compound. An assortment of small arms was provided to the Chadian forces in the 1980s. (Credit: Author's collection.)

Author with Dr. Amer al-Saadiin in March 1996. Saadi was a top presidential advisor on WMD and a preliminary interlocutor with the UN weapons inspectors. Dr. al-Saadi turned himself in to coalition forces on April 12, 2003, stating publicly that the world would see that Iraq had, in fact, disarmed. This was a significant statement since he was in a position to be knowledgeable about WMD and had no incentive to dissemble. (Credit: Author's collection.)

UNSCOM missile team chief Nikita Smidovich with author in Iraq in 1996. (Credit: Author's collection.)

The "dogs of war" that were found at the VIP terminal at Baghdad International Airport (BIAP) in April 2003. These two lucky animals were adopted by the first team to arrive at BIAP. They were brought back to the United States and, as one Iraqi professor noted, they obtained residence status in the United States, a status that is denied to talented Iraqi professionals who have risked their lives in the war effort. (Credit: Photo by author.)

UNSCOM headquarters at the "Canal Hotel" building in Baghdad, as viewed from the adjacent communications tower. This building was attacked by a truck bomb on August 19, 2003, killing twenty-two people including UN Secretary General Kofi Annan's representative Sergio Vieira de Mello. (Credit: UNSCOM photo.)

The United States provided the services of a U-2 "spy plane," which flew at the request of UNSCOM to cover designated targets. For UN missions, the aircraft was given a UN call sign and UN tail markings. (Credit: UNSCOM photo.)

The three-hundred-foot communications tower used by UNSCOM monitoring teams. It was a healthy climb to the top and the reward was a great view of Baghdad. (Credit: UNSCOM photo by Henry Arvidsson.)

The author on a cot at VVIP in May 2003. The laptop was a more important tool than the M-4 rifle. (Credit: Author's collection.)

An IED attack on a HMMV, May 26, 2003. One of the first such attacks on Airport Road (called "Route Irish" by the U.S. military). One soldier was killed during the attack. (Credit: Author's collection.)

An Iraqi-built Al Fat'h missile abandoned along the road to Samarra. Missiles of all sizes could be found scattered around Iraq in 2003. (Credit: Photo by author.)

The ISG explosive ordinance demolition team was busy destroying the thousands of tons of abandoned munitions. Here, Captain Brett Carey prepares to destroy one stockpile of artillery shells with sticks of C-4 plastic explosive. These artillery shells are the type frequently used to make car bombs and other IEDs. (Credit: Photo from the collection of Captain Brett Carey.)

One of two trailers initially, and wrongly, thought to be the mobile biological weapons production facilities. In fact, they were mobile units for the production of hydrogen to fill weather balloons. (Credit: Photo by author.)

The ISG chemical and biological disablement team (DT-4), dressed for success. (Credit: Photo from the collection of Captain Brett Carey.)

Author's armored Suburban vehicle after the attack on Airport Road, November 8, 2004. (Credit: Photo by author.)

Author's deputy, John, after the attack on Airport Road, November 8, 2004. (Credit: Photo by author.)

Pulitzer Prize–winning photo taken in the aftermath of the ISG inspection of the Al-Abud laboratory on April 26, 2003. An accidental explosion of chemicals stored in this building killed two and seriously wounded five people. It was a hostile neighborhood and residents celebrated in the aftermath. This iconic image marked a turning point in the understanding of the depth of the conflict in Iraq. Ironically, the burning HMMV was not the direct result of insurgent action. (Credit: AP Images.)

Author meeting with President Bush on the ISG results, December 21, 2004. In President Bush's left hand are medallions he gave the author to give to the families of soldiers killed and wounded in an attack a month earlier. (Credit: White House photo.)

Iraq Ambassador Nizar Hamdoon addressing the Security Council on December 16, 1998, following the bombing campaign initiated by the United States and United Kingdom in response to the standoff between Iraq and UNSCOM. (Credit: UN Photo/Evan Scheider.)

Secretary General Kofi Annan meeting with the Iraqi delegation chaired by Tariq Aziz on November 13, 1997. The Iraqi side includes (from left to right) Dr. Riyadh al-Qaisy, Deputy Prime Minister Tariq Aziz, Ambassador Nizar Hamdoon, and Ambassador Sayeed Hassan al-Musawi. Flanking Annan are Rolf Knutson to his left and Lakhdar Brahimi to his right. (Credit: UN Photo/ Milton Grant.)

Saddam with a sword presented to him by "the Iraqi people" on August 10, 2002. Presidential Secretary Abed Hamid Mahmud is, as usual, beside Saddam. Abed was the closest, and arguably the most powerful, of Saddam's lieutenants. Note Abed is carrying a pistol on his belt in Saddam's presence. Saddam had a pouch specially tailored inside the front of some of his pants to allow him to carry a small concealed pistol. (Credit: AP Images.)

ISG explosive ordnance officer Captain Brett Carey setting up an X-ray device to image the warhead of an Al Samoud missile. These missiles exceeded the UN range limits and were evidence of Saddam's intention to sustain his WMD options for the future. (Credit: SSG Ricardo Zamora.)

The security detail that gathered to unveil a memorial to Sergeant First Class Clint Wisdom and Sergeant Don Clary at the National Guard Armory in Atchison, Kansas, on November 8, 2005. Front row, left to right: Sergeant Jon Johnson and Specialist Bradley Berkstresser. Back row, left to right: Sergeant Steven Sprawka, Specialist Nathan Gray, the author, Specialist Steven Nelson, and Specialist Michael Finnegan. (Credit: Photo by Jeff Hower.)

Relatives in Iraq were telling cousins in the United States that neighbors were building shelters. As it turned out, the Iraqis were ahead of Washington in their thinking. It was only in November that President Bush very confidentially first asked Rumsfeld to examine the military options for removing Saddam.

In October 2001, I met in London with another Iraqi expatriate, Fadhil Chalabi, who was a very distant cousin of Ahmed and executive director of the Centre for Global Energy Studies. He was a former undersecretary in the Iraq Oil Ministry in the 1970s and the acting secretary general of OPEC in the 1980s. He had been highly recommended to me as someone who had a deep and balanced view of Iraq and its context in the region. Moreover, Fadhil Chalabi had no cause to promote. In his seventies by my estimation, he lived a very wealthy and very comfortable life in London. He conveyed calm gravitas and certainly had nothing to prove—he was quite unlike his distant cousin.

Fadhil Chalabi understood the Iraq situation in detail, as well as the Saudi situation. We discussed the history of the containment policy and the views of current Iraqi ministers whom I knew well. He was guarded in his comments, I think waiting to understand what my predispositions were.

I mentioned that a strong focus of the official Iraqis I knew was to supplant the Saudis as the leaders of OPEC. I recalled conversations I had with the Iraqi oil minister, Amer Rasheed, who strongly argued that Iraq would increase its oil production to compete with Saudi Arabia. This seemed to be a concerted goal on the Iraqis' part to help shed the constraints of sanctions, and it struck a resonant chord.

Fadhil Chalabi thought that the Saudi government faced problems of stability and Iraq would seek to benefit from such problems. I went further: "The Iraqis I spoke with were more explicit. They sought to actively weaken Saudi Arabia. They calculate that if Saudi Arabia is threatened, then the United States will have to come to terms with Baghdad, inevitably allowing sanctions to fall. In fact, if the regime were to support terrorism overseas, it would not be against us, but against the Saudis—not for political reasons, but for economic."

Fadhil Chalabi agreed that the oil economics could be radically affected by Saudi weakness, which would increase the importance and influence of Iraq. We went on to discuss the future prospects for the regime. He thought a slow transition from Saddam to the son, Qusay, was under way. People loyal to Qusay were being rewarded. Conversely, senior army officers were being shot for suspicion of treason. He said that the external opposition groups, including his distant cousin, did not have any prospects for success, as they had no internal support. He said the United States really had two options. It could decide to negotiate with the regime or act militarily to remove it.

He said, "If the U.S. puts forces on the ground and demonstrates it is truly serious this time, then the main Iraqi forces will not offer major resistance. However, there is not much chance of Washington doing that based on the quite limited actions taken by the U.S. over the last ten years." And he added, "There is also the matter of WMD, which is vital to the regime's survival. They used it extensively against Iran, and Saddam has said that if he were replaced, only stones would be left in Iraq." Fadhil Chalabi referred to a recent event reported in Najaf, where helicopters reportedly dropped flour from the skies as a warning that worse would happen if rebellion broke out.

When I queried him on who might replace Saddam, he said that a military governor would make sense and that a quickly established military government would be a proper transitional arrangement. I asked about the prospect for civil war; he did not think this was a great risk if a strong Iraqi government was quickly in place. Nor did he think that retribution would necessarily be widespread in the aftermath. (Of course, at the time, neither he nor anyone else would have predicted that the United States would occupy Iraq and then issue the first two orders eliminating the army and any role for former Baathists, who constituted the secular middle of the country as well as Saddam's loyalists.)

Fadhil Chalabi was quite sensitive to the suffering of Iraq's people and the wasted opportunity. He asked if I had been to Basra, where, he heard, there was now raw sewage in the streets. I said that I had not been there, but that clearly, the decay in Iraq was eroding the country physically and its society was becoming increasingly corrupt.

We parted in the early evening, and as I walked back to the Grosvenor House Hotel on Park Lane, I thought that his sort of balance and experience was wholly absent from the Washington interagency discussions. In my mind, he was a senior tenured professor with an established reputation and nothing to prove. In Washington, U.S. policy was being formulated by college freshmen. By the end of the war, they would be graduate students, and rebuilding the wreckage of Iraq would be their graduate master's thesis in political science.

In the New Year, I began a dialogue with another Iraqi expatriate in the Washington area, Dr. Salem, often accompanied by his younger brother, Ahmed. Their father had been a senior government officer dismissed by Saddam in the 1970s. Dr. Salem had been an ambassador, but left Iraq in the 1970s. The family stayed in touch with one another and events in Iraq, where they had both relatives and friends in positions that allowed them to pick up current thinking among senior or influential Iraqis. We met occasionally for coffee or lunch—once at the Baltimore Harbor, but more often at Georgetown Park. Dr. Salem was one of a large number of highly educated Iraqis with ties to the West and Baghdad. We discussed the prospects for the INC, and he expressed strong doubts about INC support inside Iraq. He thought an alternative to the INC might have greater support in Iraq, but he had found that the Pentagon was strongly supporting the INC. From his perspective, the Pentagon appeared not to listen to other voices. I could offer no solace on this point. We also discussed the prospects for Saddam's accepting weapons inspectors. After President Bush's "axis of evil" State of the Union message, Dr. Salem called me to arrange another meeting. He informed me that Saddam had spoken to a regional commander of the Baath Party and said that he would agree to accept weapons inspectors and would begin a discussion with the UN. Dr. Salem and I had discussed the prospects for another round of UN inspections. We both figured Saddam would agree to them if the United States became serious about regime change. Dr. Salem's information turned out to be exactly correct.

Through family ties, Dr. Salem also knew about some members of the Revolutionary Command Council (RCC). His family knew Huda Ammash, who in May 2001 had been named the first woman member of the RCC. Dr. Salem mentioned that she had been treated for cancer, and I knew this to be accurate. I had become familiar with Ammash because she had been a scientist with some potential involvement in the biological-weapons program. Her family was close to Dr. Salem's, and her father had been executed by Saddam.

Three years later, Dr. Salem and I would meet at the Adnan Palace in Baghdad, where he had his office in the new transitional government. I met with him to coordinate some work on searching for WMD. It was a long way from Georgetown Park. And the Iraq he found himself in was nothing he had ever imagined.

Following the "axis of evil" speech, Iraqis everywhere began to be persuaded that President Bush was serious about regime change. The frequency of my conversations with a range of Iraqis increased, as did my visits to the IOG office in CIA headquarters. I established a practice of writing up significant conversations that conveyed the tone and themes that were circulating in Baghdad.

With my contacts I continued to employ the lines of communication we had with Iraqis in Iraq, and to compare notes. To the extent that there were policy analysts following the Iraq situation, they concentrated on divining what the regime was doing and whether WMD were present. Understanding of latent, sectarian competition or conflict was minimal at best. There was virtually no consideration of the effect of a sudden absence of a strong, authoritarian government. The notion that without tough security services, Baghdad would become a radical Islamist magnet was not part of the official Washington debate.

Iraqis in Iraq were experts who *did* debate the dynamics that would be unleashed if Saddam dropped out. Conversations with Iraqis in Iraq contained some common themes. First, stability was important; they understood that Saddam's regime did hold the country together. They wanted to keep order, but without Saddam. To minimize the conflict, many Iraqis strenuously said that it was vital to declare in advance that there would be amnesty for Baathists. This point was made by senior Iraqis and other professionals—including many non-Baathists and Shia. Certainly, with time, the criminals and thugs would be pursued, but the vast majority of managerial and professional people needed to know that their interests *were not* the same as Saddam's.

There were also suggestions of who should follow Saddam. An illustrative (and common) recommendation was a former senior general who had been dismissed by Saddam because he was held in too-high regard. He had been a hero in the battle of al Fao at the end of the Iran-Iraq War. Now he was living a quiet life on a farm well outside of Baghdad. Another regular suggestion was to form a council of military and civilian members. I never heard any Iraqi from inside Iraq recommend that an outside opposition-group leader be placed in charge. Some thought that certain exiled military leaders (former Army Chief of Staff Nizar Khazraji was one) might be brought back to lead the military immediately after Saddam was gone.

The view that came through all these discussions was that Iraqis in Iraq would be able to distinguish between the thugs of Saddam's regime and the top-level professional technocrats under Saddam. There was also a clear sense that for the professional classes, it would be a relief to be without Saddam and his cronies.

At a special OPEC meeting convened in Osaka, Japan, during September 2002, Alexander met with the senior Iraqi official present, Saddam Hassan al-Ziban, an undersecretary in the Oil Ministry.[5] Hassan, who was a relative of Saddam and close to the ruling members, said that the United States should come in "like it means it. If America attacks on ground, then the Iraqi forces will not fight because they will understand, this time, the U.S. is serious." He added, "The U.S. just bombed many command-and-control centers in August. This is good. The Americans must bomb the communications centers. This is important because then the military leaders will have a reason for not fighting. They can say they did not receive instructions. This provides them the excuse to do nothing." When asked why he stayed, Hassan said, "How can I walk out on the children?" Of course, he would have difficulty matching his influence and wealth outside Iraq where being a relative of Saddam did not convey importance.

OPEC deferred taking actions on quotas, but set the next meeting for mid-December 2002. The thought was that Iraq would be "done" by then and there would be more certainty over oil availability. The expectation was that President Bush would wait only until after the November elections, and then the war and Saddam would go very quickly.

Still confusing to Iraqis was the consideration of UN weapons inspectors. For Iraqis in Iraq, there was no concern or interest in WMD. Their focus was on Saddam. The decision for the United States and President Bush was to get rid of him or let Iraq continue to suffer under him. Mention of UN inspectors was just confusing.

By July 2002, the chief of IOG decided that my informal accumulation of names and connections of Iraqis in Iraq should be developed further. He wanted to take advantage of my connections inside Iraq. I began a systematic process of identifying and evaluating both inside and outside Iraqis who could play a role after Saddam. IOG provided support, including an experienced officer named Kyle who could help record and structure the results of the work to suit IOG. Kyle was a tall man who reminded me more of Art Garfunkel than a CIA operations officer. He had an academic bent and enjoyed writing. We spent a lot of time together over the coming years in many countries, and it was always pleasant.

I had been briefing Ryan Crocker on my project in general terms during our episodic meetings. The State Department at senior levels did not want me to do anything other than perhaps park cars in the garage. Still, I met with Crocker to let him know what I was doing. He never offered any suggestions nor supported me with the secretary. Still, Crocker at least knew Iraq. He agreed in principle that if the United States were serious about regime change, that this would be useful. Crocker said the State Department postconflict work was limited to Iraqi exiles who had little connection with Iraq. He also said, "The fact of the matter is that the Pentagon ignores this effort, anyway. So even if we could develop useful contacts and plans, they would not be used."

Kyle and I continued to build a group of contacts who touched on all the key elements of the Iraqi government, meeting with Youssef, Alexander, and others in the United States and Europe. We assembled two contact lists—one of Iraqis outside Iraq and one of Iraqis inside Iraq. The key list was for contacts inside Iraq, but those outside could lead to key people inside.

We divided the lists into categories of expertise, such as oil industry, financial, electricity, intelligence, and military. For the internal contact list, we either knew each person directly or knew someone who knew the person. Between August and November 2002, I had compiled with my IOG colleague a list of about forty senior Iraqis whom we could reach. I assumed this would provide a basis for communicating intentions before and during an invasion. It would also establish a way to keep the basic government services and functions operating after Saddam's departure.

We found good opportunities to meet Iraqis traveling outside Iraq and made several trips that provided interesting insights.

Youssef knew Naji Sabri from years past. They had the opportunity to meet during OPEC meetings. Even after Sabri became foreign minister late in 2001, Youssef remained in contact. It was normal for Sabri to discuss issues with an Iraqi living outside Iraq who was a prominent oilman and whom he had known for many years. It was important for Sabri to know as much as possible about what was happening outside Iraq—particularly in Europe and the United States—since it obviously affected what was going to happen to Iraq.

Sabri was not a technocrat. He was, at heart, an English professor and enjoyed the cultural offerings of Vienna. By virtue of his position in Vienna and the proximity of OPEC, he had become involved in Iraq's oil issues. The Oil-for-Food issues also demanded that he become an expert in oil issues. He was not, however, a WMD expert; nor would he have any direct connection to any of the WMD programs past or present. Reports have surfaced alleging that before the war, Sabri stated that Iraq had completely disarmed. This is what he said publicly to the UN, as well as privately to a range of delegations, including the French and Russians. The problem for WMD analysts was that Sabri would not have been in a position to really know, and his instructions would have been to deny their existence, in any case. His statements on WMD from an intelligence perspective would have been irrelevant.

In November, Youssef traveled to New York to meet with Iraqis there. Youssef knew the UN ambassador, Mohammed al-Duri, and had several meetings and meals outside the Iraqi mission. The ambassador was a professional diplomat who had succeeded Sayeed Hassan al-Musawi. Al-Duri had been an English student of Naji Sabri, who brought him into the Foreign Service after he had become a lawyer. It was rumored that al-Duri had been forced to divorce his Austrian wife twenty years earlier by the regime and he was not, at heart, a Saddam supporter.

Al-Duri was under constant observation and implicit threat by the regime. He had personally suffered under Saddam's system, as had his family. Trapped by the system he was in and unable to leave it, he would clearly not miss the leadership of Saddam. Nevertheless, he gave the party line in the UN and, when required, to the press. Al-Duri was on edge because some members of the Iraq mission had defected while he was ambassador. While he would not be blamed directly by Baghdad for this, it made the Iraqi UN Mission in New York subject to very close scrutiny by the Mukhabarat, as well as the FBI. It was no wonder all his hair was falling out.

By the time Hans Blix's team went to Baghdad in late November 2002, Kyle and I had confidence that the bulk of senior Iraqi technocrats in major ministries (and even in the military) would welcome a forced U.S. removal of Saddam and his leaders. They wanted a change in management at the top—without upsetting the foundations of Iraqi society.

We assumed that the logical way to proceed would be to make contact with those individuals we had identified (after some vetting) and provide some guidance on what to expect. Not knowing the specific plans for the invasion or other preparatory work by the IOG, we simply provided the best information and opportunities possible to communicate with sympathetic senior Iraqis. The logic of such work seemed compelling, and Kyle and I made trips to Istanbul, Ottawa, Vienna, London, and other locations in this connection. Moreover, within the limits of security, much could be done over the phone. Iraq was not a hermetically sealed environment.

In January 2003 one of the most knowledgeable and experienced senior Iraqi officials, Ambassador Nizar Hamdoon, came to the United States. Arriving in New York for cancer treatments at Sloan-Kettering, he stayed at the Iraqi ambassador's official residence. Hamdoon had been granted a special visa for the trip. His cancer treatment was expected to require a few months. We spoke on the phone once he arrived, and we agreed to meet for lunch after he had recovered from his first chemotherapy session. Hamdoon was very cautious and used a cell phone given to him by his New York lawyer. The former ambassador did not respond to calls placed to the Iraqi UN Mission or the residence of the present Iraqi ambassador. I think he had a pretty good idea about what phones could be monitored by the government inside the United States.

Hamdoon understood the United States better than did any other senior Iraqi. He was, however, exiled by Sabri from the Foreign Ministry in Baghdad. Hamdoon was at the end of his career. His country was about to be invaded and its government replaced, and he had a life-threatening disease. And he was alone; his wife and two daughters were left behind in Baghdad. The regime would not permit families to accompany important officials who travelled outside Iraq. The families were required to remain in Iraq to ensure good behavior and the return of those officials. They were effectively hostages.

Hamdoon had studied architecture and was attracted to the arts; he had been in the Cultural Ministry at one point. Arranging a meeting would be sensitive for him. I was certainly known by the Mukhabarat in New York. Of course, Hamdoon and I had often met before in New York, but it was under different circumstances. When I was a UN official, lunch was simple and acceptable. I liked meeting at the Metropolitan Museum of Art. It is anonymous, and certain halls have favorable entrances and exits. There was one grand hall, the Mary and Michael Jaharis Gallery, which held Greek and Roman sculpture and was rarely crowded. A statue of a wounded Amazon warrior from the first or second century made a good rendezvous point. The Met publishes a postcard of this hall, and it was a convenient aid for coordinating a meeting without confusion.

We met at key moments during the period leading up to the war. At our first encounter, I noticed he was diminished. Never physically imposing, Hamdoon now looked shrunken in his heavy black overcoat. His handshake was perfunctory. The cancer treatment had taken a toll. I did my best to set him at ease. My goal was to listen and learn. Each meeting was informative concerning the issues that the United States would face in Iraq. Hamdoon made clear he would not be disloyal to his country, but would discuss the dynamics in Iraq. He was a source of information that proved to be quite accurate concerning the circumstances the United States would encounter in Iraq. During my conversations with Hamdoon, I could not help but imagine how useful it would have been for President Bush to have such a candid meeting. President Bush was making critical decisions based on no direct knowledge of the Iraqis in Iraq. It would have been impossible, but if he could have heard and evaluated for himself the views I got from Hamdoon (or others), it could have made an enormous difference in his judgments concerning U.S. actions.

By the end of January, I felt we had identified reliable individuals inside the key ministries, especially the Oil, Finance, Electricity, and Trade ministries, and even Iraqi intelligence. We had established routes to communicate with them. It seemed like a useful mechanism that would help make the invasion and transition to new leadership smoother.

What I did not know at the time was that all this effort was for nothing. I did not know what else IOG was doing to establish contacts with Iraqis in Iraq. I assumed it had developed more extensive links with senior officials. Certainly when I spoke with the chief, he agreed that taking out Saddam and keeping the rest of the mechanism running was the way to go. What you don't break, you won't have to fix later. What the chief could not tell me then was that the president had signed a top-secret intelligence order on February 16, 2002, that authorized a range of CIA actions, including sabotage, disinformation operations, attacks on regime finances, and other potentially lethal activities, to depose Saddam. But the CIA proposal to also prepare for "day-after" activities was not approved. The White House, through National Security Advisor Condoleezza Rice, explicitly removed this proposed authority.[6]

This protected the lead role of the Defense Department. This also killed any prospect for managed regime change, since the Office of the Secretary of Defense (OSD) was supporting Ahmad Chalabi and his transition plans for Iraq. Reliance on external opposition groups like the INC was doomed, in the view of anyone who listened to Iraqis inside Iraq. Of course, the OSD knew that the CIA assessment of the INC under Chalabi was low. The OSD also knew that the State Department did not subscribe to regime change. Therefore, the Defense Department simply cut out any options other than its own.

It was an unbelievably ill-informed approach. It reflected a strongly divided government in Washington and the OSD's disregard for some explicit directions from the president. In January 2003, the president directed that Chalabi and the INC would not be promoted by the United States in a postwar environment. The OSD did the opposite and flew Chalabi into Iraq in April. The president, who took a bold strategic decision regarding Iraq, led a fractious team that would not play assigned positions. In the post-9/11 environment, the Defense Department acted unilaterally in areas where its knowledge was minimal.

The prospect that postconflict chaos could have been minimized through contact with Iraqis in Iraq and even in the regime is illustrated by the experience with the Oil Ministry, where the OSD did not wholly control the postwar planning. Because of the singular importance of the Oil Ministry, the National Security Council staff became directly involved. They had been using contacts developed by Alexander and me and gave direct attention to the goal of protecting the ongoing functions of the ministry. During the invasion, the Oil Ministry was protected by the military, and senior Iraqi technocrats stayed at their job. This could have been the case for other ministries as well. However, the OSD placed its bet on Ahmad Chalabi and effectively blocked virtually all other efforts to work with the existing structure in Iraq.

The OSD elected to act boldly on knowledge gleaned carefully from selected sources. The lack of knowledge about WMD was understandable by comparison. To go into Iraq and not find WMD is one thing. To go into Iraq and not find any support for the external opposition and to find that the internal dynamics of the country were completely different than one assumed was inexcusable. These were readily knowable facts. The OSD pursued its objective with a theological zeal that did not admit contrary indicators. The disaster of Iraq did not stem from miscalculations of WMD; it stemmed from complete ignorance of what dynamics existed in Iraq. This was a miscalculation of Saddam-like proportions.

CHAPTER 13

The Beginning of Regime Change

President Bush made the decision to take the Iraq issue through the UN Security Council before the annual UN General Assembly meeting that he addressed on September 12, 2002. There had been strongly differing views between Vice President Dick Cheney, Secretary Donald Rumsfeld, and Secretary Colin Powell. Also, a powerful voice came from British Prime Minister Tony Blair.

The decision by President Bush to include the UN in his solution to the Iraq problem was the defining decision that established the dynamics of the debate leading to the war six months later. By placing the issue in the UN, he accepted the risk that council members would seek primarily to contain the United States, not Saddam. He also accepted that the debate would center on WMD and Iraq's compliance with the UN resolutions. Set aside would be the other risks of Saddam's regime—his record of aggression, internal repression, and support of terrorism.

In support of the decision to go through the Security Council in dealing with Iraq, a further decision was made that a new, much more stringent disarmament resolution would be tabled in the Security Council. The intent was to create terms that would make clear that Iraq had one final chance to demonstrate a strategic decision to disarm.

It was also intended to provide provisions that would visibly show that Iraq was either cooperating or not. The idea was to remove ambiguity about Saddam's compliance.[1] If I could predict one thing confidently from my work at UNSCOM, the outcome would still be anything but clear.

In Baghdad, Saddam was reconciled to the reentry of UN inspectors if done in a way that guarded Iraq's prestige. Foreign Minister Naji Sabri traveled to New York to represent Iraq at the General Assembly. Kofi Annan met with Sabri and Arab League president Amr Moussa twice during the weekend of September 14–15. This provided a graceful way for Baghdad to reverse position, and on Monday, September 16, Sabri provided Annan a letter accepting, without condition, the return of UN inspectors. In his address to the UN General Assembly on September 19, Sabri read a text written by Saddam. Sabri told me later that he took it upon himself to edit the speech, which was far too long and inflammatory. But it was clear that Baghdad understood that unless Iraq agreed to inspectors, it would face a Security Council united against it. Both Sabri and Aziz said afterward that their goal during this period was to divide the council. Baghdad was well aware of the ongoing military buildup in the Persian Gulf and that the United States and the United Kingdom were drafting a much tougher resolution.

After the decision, Hans Blix began discussions with Iraq over the practical implementation of inspections. This took some weeks, during which time the Security Council debated the new, tougher resolution proposed by Washington. He assured Iraq that his team would not be under the influence of any single member state—a clear reference to the previous UNSCOM team. It would not utilize spying techniques and would have a geographically diverse staff. Blix was surprised by some elements that the United States was intending to put into a new resolution, and he tried to soften the content. Believing that Colin Powell was being forced to suggest very tough measures, Blix could help the secretary argue that they should be removed.[2]

Blix agreed with Washington that since a new resolution was pending, it would not make sense for his team to enter Iraq until the new resolution was in place. The path through the UN Security Council was going to be very bumpy and would require Powell to perform as a contortionist. But it was the path Powell wanted, and he got what he asked for. On November 8, 2002, the UN Security Council passed Resolution 1441.

The new resolution was much more demanding on Iraq and caused the Iraqis to accept conditions they would never have faced had they immediately accepted the return of inspectors the previous February. Among the key new features were these:

1. The resolution clearly stated Iraq was, and had been, in material breach of the original ceasefire resolution of 1991, UNSCR 698. In the past, a statement by the Security Council that Iraq was in material breach of the ceasefire resolution was interpreted as being sufficient for a renewal of military actions. The text also reiterated that the council had warned Iraq previously that the country would face serious consequences as a result of its continued violations. On this basis, Washington believed it had authority under the council to renew military actions, even without any further council approval. Others (the Russians and French, notably) would argue otherwise.
2. There was a requirement for a new, written, and complete declaration of all WMD programs within thirty days of the passage of the new resolution. False information or omissions would be considered a further material breach of its obligations.
3. UNMOVIC could interview anyone and, at its discretion, take individuals out of Iraq for interviews (the intent being to protect them from regime pressure).
4. The resolution eliminated the previous restrictions agreed between Kofi Annan and Tariq Aziz in February 1998 for access to presidential sites.
5. It required Blix to report immediately any case in which Iraq interfered with inspections or otherwise failed to comply.

During the period that the United States was working on the new resolution, I had been asked to comment on some issues in the media as a former UN inspector. I commented that UN inspections could wind up to be a complicated matter in the Security Council and could work in Iraq's favor. This was tame compared with the comments of Ari Fleischer, the White House press secretary. He said inspections under the current resolution would be a "fool's errand," and inspectors would be "nothing more than tourists who get a run-around." On the same day that the Senate began considering the resolution authorizing the use of force in Iraq, the Iraqi vice president, Taha Yasin Ramadan, suggested that instead of the United States going to war with Iraq, Saddam Hussein and George Bush should have a personal duel.

The Iraqis accepted the new resolution a week after it was passed. The inspectors arrived at the end of November and began visiting sites and reestablishing procedures and techniques for inspecting.

The first major test for Iraq under the new resolution was to provide a new, complete written declaration of all its WMD programs and their disposition. After the war, top Iraqi scientist and presidential advisor Amer al-Saadi described the process of creating it. He said the Iraqi side took the previous material provided to UNSCOM and then surveyed it for any matters that were left out. He mentioned a nitric acid facility that the Iraqis had not previously declared, because they needed it for civilian purposes. They were concerned if they informed UNSCOM, it would be destroyed (he was right; we would have destroyed it). There were also some issues related to the range of the al Samoud ballistic missile. It did fly beyond the permitted range of 150 kilometers.

The documents were provided to UNMOVIC in Baghdad on December 7 in a single copy that numbered roughly twelve thousand pages. UNMOVIC brought the material to New York on Sunday evening, December 8, and by prior agreement, it was given to the United States, which flew the report by helicopter to CIA headquarters where staff churned out multiple copies for the five permanent members of the Security Council. UNMOVIC then had the task of redacting any proliferation-sensitive information that it deemed should not be made public.

The CIA reviewed the twelve thousand pages and found there was little new information. It concluded that the report was still not a full, verifiable disclosure. In principle, that was sufficient to declare that Iraq remained in material breach of the new resolution and had punted on its final chance. But others in the Security Council were not so sure, and as is usually the case in the council, what was reality for one was not necessarily the reality for the others. Blix and his team certainly were not pronouncing on the declaration one way or another. Hence, Washington was again in the bind of having its military forces cocked and ready to go but finding a squeaky Swedish lawyer who spent his life on arms-control negotiations—almost a caricature of the arms-control advocate—with his finger on the trigger. Kofi Annan was lending moral support to Blix, and the Russian and French ambassadors wanted a major violation in neon lights before they would go along with any military action.

The UNMOVIC inspectors did what they could and, to my surprise, even found a few bits of undeclared material. Nevertheless, Saddam's cooperation was grudging at best. After the war, in discussions with Saddam and his top aides, they explained that Iraq was reluctant for reasons of pride and because Saddam felt the war was inevitable. Tariq Aziz said that the reason they cooperated at all, including the reason they reluctantly agreed to destroy the al Samoud missiles (which would have had some use in the inevitable war), was to keep the Security Council split. On this point, they were successful.

Blix could provide no flashy evidence of Iraqi WMD (nor could he declare Iraq clean), so it fell to Powell to conjure a briefing for the UN Security Council to show U.S. evidence of WMD. On February 5, 2003, he gave his now-famous performance, wherein he declared that his statements about Iraqi ongoing WMD programs and stockpiles were "facts"—and this was a term he personally introduced to his text. Fellow UNSCOM alumni I spoke with afterward were dubious about his case. The commission had received reports similar to what Powell was describing, often from the CIA, and we had investigated them. Invariably, we would find some very weird and entirely unpredictable Iraqi reason why the evidence observed by U.S. intelligence was not WMD-related. With American logic, analysts staring at computer screens in Washington would connect dots in a way that made sense to them. Often, the reality on the ground was quite different. The problem was exacerbated by the lack of dots to connect.

In talking with my former UNSCOM colleagues about the Powell briefing, I found an informal consensus that at least 50 percent of what he said would turn out wrong—but we had no idea which 50 percent. Some of the material seemed to key off the uncertainties UN-SCOM had about the Iraqi accounting, and some fit with previous reports received. For example, UNSCOM had received reports of Iraqi mobile biological-weapons trailers in 1997. UNSCOM had mounted very aggressive, but ultimately inconclusive, inspections to investigate the reports. We reported these efforts in detail in our public reports to the Security Council.

The consensus view among my UNSCOM colleagues, and certainly mine, was that Saddam probably retained the capacity to produce chemical and biological agents, if a decision were made to do so, in fairly short order. I also suspected that Iraq retained some ballistic missile capability since UNSCOM could never fully account for the total SCUD force. On the nuclear side, the UNSCOM data indicated that the former scientists and engineers seemed to be congregating under Saddam's guidance at five key establishments. Whether they were actively working on nuclear weapons or simply staying active for some future time, we could not say. Before the war, I had an advantage in my own personal assessment, because I had *no* knowledge of the defector known as Curve Ball. His reporting fit with many of the UN-SCOM expectations, and that was at least part of the reason his accounts were given such credibility.[3]

Powell did a fine job presenting a picture that turned out to be wrong. It sounded good, but to careful listeners, there was nothing conclusive. That was the whole problem with the inspection process. Powell learned firsthand the difficulty, long experienced by UN-SCOM, of making the case to a skeptical council. UNSCOM had done this for years. We could sometimes prove that Iraq's declarations were wrong, but we could not prove that Iraq retained weapons. And while that technically wasn't the commission's task—it was Iraq's task to prove it had disarmed—the Security Council wanted to see evidence that Iraq had weapons, to justify sustaining the sanctions on Iraq. To justify regime change, Powell had to show the council that Iraq had weapons—that was the standard he set for himself and the administration in choosing to handle the Iraq problem within the Security Council context.

So, Secretary of State Powell spent an hour and fifteen minutes describing a reality that existed for him and for many analysts who had never been to Iraq. Looking on were the Director of Central Intelligence, George Tenet, and the then–UN ambassador (but future Director of National Intelligence), John Negroponte. Both seemed to be slumped in their chairs, but I know those UN seats, and they are difficult to sit in for more than a half hour. It all made sense. It matched previous reporting and actions by Saddam. When I watched Powell, I thought back to my previous experience accompanying Ambassador Jeanne Kirkpatrick as her intelligence analyst playing the communication intercepts of the Russian fighter aircraft shooting down the Korean commercial flight KAL 007. That was hard, solid intelligence that did not require leaps of faith on the part of the audience. We had the Russians cold. Powell did not have anything of the sort. Moreover, Blix and his team weren't coming up with anything compelling, either.

At the end, key council members would still not go along with the United States and the United Kingdom. There was an attempt to build a consensus for a final UN resolution declaring Iraq in noncompliance and subject to consequences, but the French and Russians would not participate. The effort had been more important to Prime Minister Blair, who was on thin legal footing without an explicit resolution authorizing military actions. In the end, Iraq was found guilty on a technicality. The comparison made by some in the administration was that it was like getting the Chicago gangster Al Capone off the streets for tax evasion, not murder.

As this play was unfolding in the UN, the State Department in Washington was engaged in an effort called the Future of Iraq Project. This was largely guided by Deputy Assistant Secretary of State for Near Eastern Affairs (NEA) Ambassador Ryan Crocker and NEA Special Advisor Tom Warrick. Their effort produced papers on various government subjects for a post-Saddam Iraq. They drew on meetings of Iraqi exiles. No one I spoke to at the Pentagon, NSC, or CIA thought it was useful. Even Crocker, when I met with him, despaired that even if his group produced something interesting, the powers behind regime change were at the Pentagon and would not let the State Department, which they considered disloyal to their objectives, become involved. It was an unbelievable impasse that the NSC could not adjudicate, because the NSC, and Condoleezza Rice, in particular, could not knock Powell's and Rumsfeld's heads together, even if Rice knew how dysfunctional the postwar planning was.

I was sympathetic to the president's strategic decision that Iraq with Saddam was a threat to the United States and containment via sanctions was doomed. Iraq without Saddam, but with a government that behaved closer to international norms and was responsive to the will of its people, was achievable with reasonable risk and cost. The Iraqis I knew in Iraq all agreed that the upside was tremendous without Saddam at the top. The work I was doing with the CIA seemed to me to be the most valuable work to make such a transition possible. I also knew that I was aware of only part of the CIA's work. I assumed that my efforts tracked with other actions to identify key leaders in Iraq for postwar leadership positions. I did not know that there was or would be a presidential decision that the entire Iraqi political and military infrastructure would be eliminated within days of removing Saddam. The premise of the work I was doing was to break as little as possible; keep the ministries, army, and even intelligence bureaus going with the existing staff. The idea was to create as few enemies and keep as many allies as possible. We certainly did not need more enemies.

This was the theme I conveyed to Iraqis I knew. This was the theme they derived from senior administration officials like Rumsfeld. For example, on September 18, 2002, Rumsfeld responded to a question from Jim Lehrer about whether disarmament could be achieved in Iraq without war:

If Saddam Hussein and his family decided that the game was up and we'll go live in some foreign country like other leaders have done—I mean, clearly the Shah of Iran left, Idi Amin left; "Baby Doc" Duvalier left. There have been any number of leaders who have departed recognizing that the game was up, that it was over, that they had run their term. So that could happen.

It's entirely possible that the people in that country, a lot of wonderful people who are hostages, they are hostages to a very vicious regime. They could decide the time was up and change the regime from inside. It's a repressive regime. It would be a very difficult thing to do. But clearly the overwhelming majority of the people—even the army—don't want Saddam Hussein there.[4]

On February 3, 2003, the White House press spokesman, Ari Fleischer, responded to a question about the president's views on the exile of Saddam:

Well, as the President said, if Saddam Hussein were to leave Iraq and to take, as the President put it, his henchmen with him, that would be a very desirable event. That would save the lives of many. It would improve the lives and the fortunes of the Iraqi people and give them, for the first time in decades, the freedoms that they are entitled to. And the President views that, if it were to happen—and the President holds no high hopes that it would happen—but the President, of course, and I think people around the world would welcome that event, no matter how evil Saddam Hussein is.[5]

On February 20, 2003, Rumsfeld, again on the *NewsHour with Jim Lehrer* program, said basically the same thing:

To the extent he [Saddam] is persuaded that it's inevitable that he's going to lose his position and his regime is going to be cast out, it's at least possible . . . is it one percent? I don't know. But it's not zero percent that he might leave. The second possibility is the people in Iraq might decide he should leave—and help him. And so that's a possibility. If that happens, if that were to happen, as remote as it may be, it would only happen because the people in Iraq—he or the people around him who decide they would prefer he not be there— were persuaded that it was inevitable that he was going to go either voluntarily or involuntarily.[6]

President Bush expressed similar sentiments in a news conference on March 6, 2003:

> So, in the name of security and peace, if we have to—if we have to—we'll disarm him. I hope he disarms. Or, perhaps, I hope he leaves the country. I hear a lot of talk from different nations around where Saddam Hussein might be exiled. That would be fine with me—just so long as Iraq disarms after he's exiled.
>
> . . . And our intention—we have no quarrel with anybody other than Saddam and his group of killers who have destroyed a society.[7]

These messages were interpreted by Iraqis as meaning Saddam and his top aides were at risk, not the entire government infrastructure. The administration did not mention anything about amnesty, except the point that if Saddam left, the United States would not seek his prosecution.

For Iraqis in Iraq, this struck exactly the right chord.

My discussions with Nizar Hamdoon touched on many of these themes. I had lunch with him on March 7, the day after President Bush said the United States' quarrel was with Saddam, not the Iraqi people. Hamdoon said that President Bush's theme was good, but that Saddam would not leave. "Still," he added, "there are many good people who will continue to operate the ministries if they have guidance. There cannot be a vacuum. But I assume you will tell them in advance. They will expect order."

Hamdoon criticized one part of Bush's press conference: "President Bush highlighted that the United States had stockpiled enough food to feed civilian Iraqis. This is not good to say. The Iraqi people will not want to be fed by the United States. This will make them recoil. It is symbolic of being subservient. You must avoid the tone that you are ruling Iraq. There must be a quick shift to a new Iraqi leadership mechanism. If you do not do this, the United States will be blamed for all that follows." He went on to say, "There are many good members of the government who will continue to function under some sort of temporary leadership council, perhaps mixing a senior military officer with civilian leaders, from inside Iraq. You just need to tell them to continue to work, and they need to know they are working for Iraq, not an invader."

Hamdoon was a shrewd enough observer of Washington to recognize that there were competing factions. He worried that the reaction in Baghdad would be quite different if the U.S. invasion was seen as part of a Zionist-linked effort: "Saddam is saying to his people that the invaders are working with the Zionists. This has an effect on the Iraqi people. Saddam knows the Iraqi people and how to affect them. I have no sense that Washington understands this." Hamdoon could not have imagined how dysfunctional the Washington planning had been. He knew I shared his views with Washington, and he obviously hoped they would affect U.S. actions. While Hamdoon was a part of the regime and many would have dismissed his perspective, he had more direct knowledge of how the influential Iraqis would react and he had less personally to gain or lose, given his personal health predicament.

Hamdoon at this point appeared to be earnestly thinking of how to improve the outcome for the Iraqis and Americans. He said the objective of allowing democracy to grow in Iraq would be well received, but he said that Baghdad identified the civilian part of the Pentagon with Israel. This would make cooperation more difficult on the day after, if Pentagon civilians were seen to be in charge. He also said that Iraqis would be very reluctant to cooperate with the United States, in that case. Hamdoon asked, "Where were the Arabists?," whom he knew from his period as ambassador in Washington. I replied that Washington, as he understood, was not always well coordinated. We discussed a number of factors that would affect postwar Iraq. He did not say so, but it was clear that he considered Saddam to be gone even then. The former ambassador had said he was committed to his *country*. He did not say he supported *Saddam*. Hamdoon did point out, however, that the Iraqis had achieved much. His major criticism was the vast resources poured into the military—resources that could have been used for other purposes.

I told Hamdoon the immediate problem would be who would run the ministries once the United States was in Iraq. Hamdoon said they would run themselves for a while, so long as it was clear Saddam was gone. He strongly recommended that the United States should not press for immediate changes. Things would sort out over time. He was concerned about articles he had read about various individuals being placed in charge of parts of Iraq. He noted in particular that the announcement that former U.S. Ambassador Barbara Bodine would be "Mayor of Baghdad" was a bad idea. "She may be a very talented and excellent representative of the United States, but to put her in charge of Iraqis would be a big mistake. Iraqis would resent and fight against this. Washington seems to be making many mistakes like this." He was right.

Our sessions became more frank as time ran out. I knew Hamdoon was concerned about his family. His two daughters, then about eight and thirteen years of age, spoke English with a New York accent and with the vocabulary of American teens. I asked him to identify his house on an aerial image so it could be put on the no-strike list. While I did not have particular faith in this mechanism, it was better than nothing. Hamdoon was able to identify his house in Yarmouk, helped by the fact that it had a white trailer parked in the front to help distinguish it.

Our last meeting was on March 10, at the Fives Restaurant at the Peninsula Hotel on the corner of Fifty-Fifth Street and Fifth Avenue. We had a somber and poignant conversation. The food came and went with scarcely any notice. War was in the air, and that occupied the mind. His body was ravaged by the caustic chemicals pumped into him by the doctors at Sloan-Kettering.

Hamdoon described the situation in the Security Council as he saw it. He said the French would veto the draft resolution authorizing force that Washington and London were pushing. But it did not matter. Hamdoon had watched Saddam's speeches and said Saddam saw the war as his destiny. It was inevitable. Hamdoon said Saddam believed he could survive somehow, just as he had following the Kuwait war in 1991. He did not care about Iraqi casualties. Iraqi suffering was to be followed by Iraqi suffering. Saddam would make Iraqis pay the price for his self-glory. He would not leave Iraq as Bush had demanded as the only way to avoid war.

I had known Hamdoon for many years. His career had many turns, as had mine. Now we sat at a table, not on opposite sides, but at a corner. For how long? Would the opportunity to work with Americans for a common purpose emerge? The regime would finally end, and soon. But Hamdoon did not know if his health would permit him to live to see the new Iraq. He did not know if he would see his family. I asked him if he was comfortable at the Iraqi ambassador's residence. "Yes," he said. "I have my own living area with its own kitchen. It is comfortable." He went on, "Your FBI just threw out two Iraqi guards who were Mukhabarat. I hope they will not throw out the entire mission. It would not look good in Baghdad."

I also asked if he was able to deal with all the medical expenses, and he said yes, that was not a problem. We discussed the situation in Iraq, and again, time ran out before our conversation did. The closer the invasion came, the more he had to say. When he asked to meet again, I said I would, if I was in the area. He had to return to the residence so that his absence would not be remarked on. He put his heavy black overcoat over his diminished frame. The chemotherapy had taken a toll; he had eaten almost nothing.

"You leave first," I offered. He nodded and walked out, as I waited a decent interval before exiting by another door. I never saw him again.

In Baghdad, the war planning on the part of Saddam was as bad as, or even worse than, the OSD's postwar planning. Saddam chaired Revolutionary Command Council meetings, but they lacked focus, according to one participant. His key diplomatic goal was to keep the Security Council divided. He refused all suggestions that he step down—including one from Russian foreign minister Yevgeny Primakov.

Saddam knew war was coming and believed it was inevitable. He offered no strategy to his military, other than requiring his commanders to defend for a couple of weeks while the irregular forces of Fedayeen Saddam could disperse and take up an insurgent battle.[8] His military lacked a cohesive strategy, and worse, Saddam had no system for maintaining command and control once an invasion began. He would not use telephones or radios, because of concern they would be targeted for intercept and attacked. He sent messages by courier and he moved regularly. This meant he could not maintain direction during the war. He had no solution for this problem, but did not admit the fact to his military commanders. Saddam's military commanders understood there was no Iraqi "postwar planning" as well. They had been generally informed that there were no WMD to save them. They were just expected to fight the Americans and buy some time. But for what? Saddam had no answer. The large Iraqi Army and even the elite Republican Guard were a receptive audience for the United States. With the right message for the postwar Iraq, they could have been prepared for a role in maintaining order.

The clock was running out. The contacts I had been maintaining were making preparations to ride out the war. Efforts to win high-level defections before the war were slipping away. Lots of options were offered and turned down. I found that senior Iraqis were not particularly loyal to Saddam, but were loyal to their country. They understood that the goal of the invasion was regime change, but it was still an invasion of their country. When there was an Iraqi leadership in place, they would be glad to support the United States in Iraq. I heard this clearly from several Iraqis. It was a point that Hamdoon had emphasized. There must very quickly be an Iraqi at the top—and probably, for constancy at the beginning, a Sunni, but a Sunni well known by all Iraqis. I had gathered a list of oft-repeated names. Later, I would discover that some of these same individuals were put on a *blacklist* assembled by intelligence analysts (based on the same quality reporting that produced the WMD estimates). They were blacklisted, in essence, simply because of their official positions—not based on any knowledge of their personal political leanings or individual history. Some had been jailed by Saddam. It would get worse. Once U.S. forces were in Iraq, they used the lists as targets. Those named would find their homes raided, and they would be thrown in jail. I met with more than one who had been jailed by Saddam and then jailed by us. The treatment in American detention was better, but it was small thanks. We continued to make more enemies.

By the middle of March, war was widely recognized as inevitable. The IOG was buzzing twenty-four hours a day. There were dozens of ongoing activities in Iraq and outside. Much effort was focused on trying to get a fix on Saddam, but there were dozens of other actions under way as well.

On Wednesday, March 12, I was meeting with the chief of IOG along with Kyle, the officer I had been paired with for working contacts for the last several months. The chief asked, "You want to deploy with Kyle?" I had assumed I would go out, but it was a question of when. The utility of my contacts with Iraqis was going to diminish swiftly once the invasion began. I still harbored the hope that the individuals I had identified as useful supporters could be brought into a postwar government. I did not know the CIA was prohibited from any such work at the time, nor did the chief of IOG tell me.

"Sure. When do I need to go?" I replied quickly.

The chief said, "That will be determined by when the airspace will be closed. I know that will be fairly soon. Talk to John M. [his deputy] and the logistics people."

I replied, "You know you will have to fix this with the bureaucrats at State Department."

He replied as any case officer would have, "Sure, we'll take care of that."

I suspected that this would not happen and that it would be a mess to be dealt with later. My role with IOG did not fit any existing mold. That was the utility of it. I had much more flexibility in what I could do, given my peculiar status . . . or perhaps my lack of any status. I was a senior guy who had been an assistant-secretary-general-level official at the UN and who knew a broad range of Iraqis in Baghdad. Moreover, I could drive from one side of Baghdad to the other without getting lost. Also, I could operate on my own and did not have the constraints of a normal operations officer. Linked with my colleague, Kyle, the chief figured this could only be good.

The downside to me was I could see close up the horrendous mistakes made by the United States. And I would see the effects on the Iraqis I knew, understood, and, in many cases, highly respected. But I had absolutely no authority to do anything about it. I could not even be sure the effects I recorded would be passed to policymakers in Washington.

I checked in with the logistics team, who had a routine for people deploying. I had very little time. I was told if I didn't fly out on that Sunday night, I might get caught in a sudden closure of airspace to commercial aircraft. The IOG had a list of gear that was authorized for purchase—boots, backpacks, sleeping bags, water packs, and so on.

I had some other meeting obligations the rest of the week, including meetings with some NSC staff and with Secretary of Commerce Don Evans (who was also a friend of President Bush's from Texas) in the White House situation room to discuss prospects for management of the Iraqi Oil Ministry. Pam Quanrud was the NSC officer charged with preparing for the postwar Oil Ministry. Alexander and I had been consulting with her regularly and had provided detailed information about key individuals in the Oil Ministry. The OSD staff had their own ideas, largely fomented by Ahmad Chalabi. Evans appeared to be a very thoughtful guy who could perhaps offset the drive by the OSD to control the Oil Ministry future. Quanrud used her position at the White House with some effect, despite the opposition of the OSD. She gave serious thought to which Iraqis were qualified and located *in* Iraq to run the ministry. The OSD fought this usurpation of control over the construction of a new Iraq government.

At the meeting at the White House that Friday morning, I briefed Evans on the talent pool at the Iraqi Oil Ministry and what recent retirees were still in Iraq and potentially available. I told him I knew the Iraqi oil minister very well and was quite certain that he would be helpful to me once I was in Baghdad. The final decisions, however, had to be made in Washington.

I left the meeting with some hope that there might be a useful consensus built around a set of Iraqi Oil Ministry leaders and that we could keep the ministry running with minimal disruption. In the event, the one example of a ministry that did not disintegrate was the Oil Ministry. It was protected, and senior technocrats stayed at their job. I had expected a similar process for all key Iraqi ministries, but that was not to be.

I attended to some mundane errands, like buying a large supply of contact lenses and spare eyeglasses. I was facing substantial uncertainty since I was deploying without any clear support structure and I had absolutely no idea how long I would be gone. Weeks, months, who knew?

The IOG had a checklist of things that were "required" before you could deploy. I did some of them, including a short training course on using the gas mask everyone was issued and using atropine injectors. I realized that I probably did not think Iraq had chemical weapons when they had trouble finding a mask that fit my face properly. I shrugged and said, "I don't think it really matters." Still, I brought one with me.

I made a tactical error and delayed going to the Office of Medical Services until the very end of the Friday before I departed. With a piece of paper saying what shots I needed, I found the nurse anxious to begin her weekend. I had not looked at the list before, but the nurse said there was a bunch of shots and the later on Friday it got, the more they would hurt. I *think* she was kidding. I told her to skip the anthrax shot, as I could get that later, and you needed a series for it to be effective, anyway. I wasn't really concerned. I also skipped the smallpox inoculation. I frankly saw no point in that. Tetanus and a couple of others seemed worth the pain.

On Saturday, I bought a bunch of camping gear and, on Sunday, flew to Kuwait. I arrived on Monday, March 17, the same day that Kofi Annan ordered the inspectors to fly out of Iraq. I linked up with Kyle, and we both stayed at the Messilah Beach Hotel—an inexpensive hotel away from the heart of Kuwait City. It had few Americans and almost no press.

Kuwaitis were leaving, while Americans and the press arrived. The streets were not crowded. The concentration of American military personnel was not visible in Kuwait City. They were at the assorted permanent and temporary bases, which included Camp Doha, a huge former warehouse facility now preparing all armor to go north (M-1A1 tanks, Bradley fighting vehicles, HMMVs, command vehicles, and more). There were also sites farther north, where convoys were mustering for the march into Iraq. Many had been waiting for weeks or even months.

Kuwait was weird. It had the air of a ghost town. I noticed a number of pet canaries and other birds at the hotel and other locations. It

gradually dawned on me that these were not pets, but had been purchased to constantly test the atmosphere for chemical agents Iraq
might launch.

At the government facility where I worked, I continued to stay in
touch with Iraqis I knew via contacts in the United States. My dialogue continued with those trying to continue to assure a smooth
transition for the Oil Ministry.[9] There were individuals who were
identified and who were considered able to run the Oil Ministry.
Quanrud asked if I thought I could contact these people once I got to
Baghdad. I said that should be no problem—once I got to Baghdad.

On Wednesday, March 19, I visited a team of CIA counterproliferation experts who were positioned inside the military zone close to
the Iraq border. They had been living in very dry, dusty tents for
weeks. They were not part of CENTCOM's WMD team called
XTF-75, which was part of the overall war plan to find WMD and
eliminate that threat. This separate CIA team was apparently going to
try to locate key individuals who were involved in WMD activities.
This made sense to me. The individuals could provide information on
where potential WMD material might be located, and ultimately,
these were the people who we did not want to be marketing their skills
elsewhere. The only problem I could see was that other than a few top
individuals, the CIA team did not seem to know who they were going
to look for or where to find them. I wished the group well and told
them I would see them in Baghdad.

On Thursday morning, March 20, U.S. strikes began. Later that
day, I paid a visit to a few people I knew to be involved in the postconflict reconstruction planning centered at the Kuwait Hilton. It was
one of the strangest assemblies I have ever seen in government.

The Kuwait Hilton had been occupied by the opposing forces of
the OSD and State Department. Dozens of U.S. bureaucrats and "experts" assigned to the Office of Reconstruction and Humanitarian Affairs (ORHA) were forward deployed to Kuwait to prepare to go into
Baghdad. The effort was led by the OSD, but unity of command was
in name only. There was no unity of purpose. I visited with State Department people I knew who did not want to be seen by OSD civilian
staff. I met with OSD civilian staff who tolerated the presence of State

Department staff, but assumed the State people were working against them. It was a Washington bureaucratic battle deployed to a hotel in Kuwait and overseen by retired Army Lieutenant General Jay Garner.

One of the oddities of watching this scene was that apparently, there was an ORHA regulation that all personnel had to have gas masks with them at all times. Everyone walked around with a green canvas satchel containing a gas mask strapped to their leg.

Secretary Rumsfeld had selected Garner to run the postconflict Iraq effort. Garner's only relevant prior experience was that he had run the relief effort to Kurdistan after the 1991 war. Otherwise, his background included commanding the U.S. Army Space and Strategic Defense Command (working mostly on the Star Wars development programs) and working on Patriot Air Defense batteries.

I offered to meet him through Dennis G., his intelligence liaison officer. Garner showed up with some aides. He was very polite, but he had absolutely no idea who I was. I described my background of work at UNSCOM, noting that I had known many Iraqis inside Iraq for close to a decade now. He politely asked what I thought would happen when the United States went in.

"I suspect the Iraqi Army will fight . . . for a while. Their command and control will go dead quickly, and if they have the opportunity to do nothing and go away, they will." I continued, "They will have no connection with Saddam, and with no commands to follow, the army, and even the Republican Guard, will dissolve. The key problem will be the loosely organized Fedayeen and the Special Republican Guard. The former may continue to conduct disorganized attacks. The latter is much more disciplined and may be able to act cohesively, simply based on the commitment of its leader, to Saddam."

Garner asked my thoughts on post-Saddam governance. I took the opportunity to express my deep concern about promoting the INC and Chalabi. "As far as I can tell," I said, "no one in Iraq supports Chalabi. Iraqis in Iraq will welcome the U.S. move to dislodge Saddam. They will not welcome our bringing outside Iraqis in to take over the wealth of a country they previously abandoned. No outside opposition leader will have the respect of those inside. Chalabi, in particular, is seen as a crook. My view is to break as little of the organizational structure as

possible when we go in. Let those who have been running ministries
continue to run them. If people keep their jobs, they will keep busy and
not want to shoot Americans. There are respected Iraqis in Iraq who
could take on temporary leadership roles—former military leaders and
others dismissed by Saddam but who remained in Iraq."

I was wasting my breath. Garner had no experience with what was
going on in Iraq. And he seemed to have little knowledge or control
over what was going on with OSD planning. The Hilton Hotel was a
squabbling mass of bureaucrats who had forward-deployed their interagency fights. The OSD and State Department staffs did not coordinate and work together to achieve a commonly defined and
agreed-on mission. Far from it. They divided into factions and lived
and worked separately. There was an unofficial, but palpable division
between those who were on board with Chalabi and those who were
not. This was the planning of the last superpower to replace Saddam.
I felt helpless and sorry for the Iraqis.

Besides seeing Garner, I met with Ambassador Barbara Bodine.
Although she had been told she would be the "mayor of Baghdad," the
OSD was having none of that. She was not seen as supporting the war
and certainly not supporting Chalabi. Bodine was strong-willed and
did have the experience of being in Iraq in the 1980s. She had low tolerance for what she saw as ideologically driven OSD staff.

The OSD staffers I talked to were committed to what they saw as
the mission—expunging the complete regime of Saddam and installing democracy. The Baathists had to go and would be replaced by
untainted Iraqis. The OSD people had a theory that sounded altruis-
tic, but they had virtually no knowledge of Iraqis. Removing Saddam
did more than create a vacuum; it removed the gravity holding Iraq together. Without an immediate central figure to hold the existing
structures together, the existing centripetal forces in Iraq would cause
things to fly apart. Adding Chalabi to the mix was in fact adding an
even more divisive force.

Over this writhing mess of well-intentioned, but bitterly fighting
Washington staffers watched General Garner. It was an impossible
situation—he could not even organize his team in the Kuwait Hilton.
So how was he going to organize a country—especially when his lead-

ership at the OSD was intent on smashing the existing Iraqi management, not just Saddam and his top commanders, from top to bottom, as Rumsfeld had previously declared?

The lunacy of this reconstruction effort was apparent even before U.S. forces crossed the border. Someone passed me a set of briefing charts on how ORHA would handle the Iraq financial system. A key point was to immediately get rid of Iraqi dinars (because they had Saddam's picture on them) and substitute dollars for the legal currency. This was unbelievably stupid. The United States was invading Iraq to liberate it, but the Iraqis were supposed to use our currency? That would do nothing to counter the street rumors that the United States was just moving in to take Iraq's oil and set up a puppet government for Ahmad Chalabi.

Using dollars was also a practical nightmare and betrayed complete ignorance of what things cost in Iraq. In dollar terms things were cheap. A 250-dinar note (the most common denomination) was worth about thirteen U.S. cents in 2003. How would you pay for the many things that cost 500 or 1,000 dinars? Had anyone calculated how to get U.S. currency to Iraq? Cash is bulky. The CIA has experience in moving cash, which is usually done in one-hundred-dollar bills, and even then, it is very awkward. A U.S. bill weighs about 1 gram. There are 454 grams in a pound. A million bills is 2,204 pounds, or about a ton. So, a million dollars is, literally, a ton of money . . . in one-dollar bills. But Iraq would need billions in currency. The population of around 24 million people did not use credit cards. Was ORHA planning on importing thousands of tons of one-dollar bills or just hoping inflation would solve the problem?

The level of ignorance was incredible. It was also bizarre that there was no connection between ideas on PowerPoint charts and Iraqis. The Americans' charts on the Finance Ministry made no mention of Iraqis who currently ran the ministry. I happened to know some who were very competent. Some members of the ministry studied in the United States, and a former official ran a bank in New York.

In my conversation with Garner, he seemed focused on setting up quick elections—as though that would be possible. I could not respond to that. I simply reiterated that the less we broke of the existing government, the less we would have to fix or do ourselves. I reminded him that this was the message that Iraqis had been hearing—Saddam and his top aides had to go. The rest we did not mention. The more we let the ministries continue with existing mechanisms, the better. Garner asked if I thought there would be much retribution killings. I said, "There may be some killings. The Iraqis may cleanse the worst offenders out of the system, themselves. We should not try to get in the middle of that. We do not know how to run Iraq, and anyone we pick from outside Iraq will only survive if he draws the United States into a bigger internal conflict."

Garner seemed to agree, but I think he was stuck with direction from the OSD to support the external opposition groups. His key hope was to have quick elections. I left feeling sorry for him. He was in an impossible position. He probably had lots of people telling him all sorts of things, and he had zero personal experience upon which to judge. I was just another "expert" and was completely out of his food chain. General Garner politely listened, but I am sure he moved quickly on to his next meeting. I doubt he would even remember our discussion.

I left the meeting with Garner convinced that the occupation of Baghdad was going to lead to a total vacuum of power unless, somehow, there emerged from Iraq a leader who could swiftly take control. But this would probably not be permitted by the OSD.

While U.S. forces were moving northward to Baghdad, I continued to stay in touch with my contacts who knew the Oil Ministry officials. They had even arranged for a former senior oil official to travel to Washington to meet with Pam Quanrud at the NSC and other officials. They discussed in detail what would be required to sustain the operations. They also discussed candidates they would want me to contact in Iraq. This activity seemed at least headed in a positive direction, even if it was about two months late. We should and could have been contacting officials in Iraq with explicit ideas before the war. Still, this appeared more constructive than the chaos at the Kuwait Hilton.

The office I used in a Kuwait City building was extremely busy supporting agents in Iraq. Some came out to Kuwait and were debriefed. One guy I knew in Iraq had seen on CNN some pictures of a massive high-explosive bomb tested on March 11 at Eglin Air Force Base in Florida called the Massive Ordnance Air Blast Bomb (MOAB). It had over twenty thousand pounds of explosive and created a huge, mushroom-shaped cloud (but was not nuclear). The Iraqi kept saying, "Use one of those 'mushroom bombs'; then everyone will quit fighting."

The bureaucracy grinds on, even during war. On March 26, I received an e-mail from the State Department, telling me I was being put on leave without pay since no other agency had indicated it would be reimbursing the State Department for me. I was also informed that my annual financial disclosure form was due immediately, or I would be fined $250. As a member of the senior service, I was obligated to fill out annual financial disclosures. This was like doing IRS form 1040, but worse. I did have the foresight to arrange for my accountant to send in my tax forms while I was away.

I contacted the IOG and pleaded with it to deal with the State Department. I was glad to be heading into Iraq, but felt I would be earning my salary, not going on leave. The IOG people said they would talk to the department and sort the problem out. They were busy running agents and paramilitary teams into Iraq. Calling up the State Department personnel people would probably not be a priority.

On the financial disclosure form, no one could help. I had forgotten about it. It took me a day to get the data and complete the form. I used the hotel fax to send the forms to the correct State Department office. The communications lines were highly irregular because of the military actions. It took much of one night and two hundred dollars in faxing fees to get the form in—slightly less than the fine for being late. Compared with the problems average Iraqis were about to have, mine were nothing.

The war did come to Kuwait in a halfhearted way. Iraq managed to launch some ballistic and cruise missiles. The launches produced warning sirens, and within the facility, a recorded voice would yell through the speaker system that an attack was under way. "Gas! Gas! Gas!" it shrieked. This meant you were supposed to put on gas masks. I admit, the first time this happened, it got you thinking. The first time, people really put on gas masks. Then there was an all-clear.

On occasion, you could hear a distant explosion. It was impossible to tell if it was from a Patriot defensive missile or an Iraqi missile headed in the general direction of Kuwait City. Iraq fired several missiles, but the accuracy was terrible, with one exception.

One night at 0200, there was a large explosion, clearly in Kuwait City. It turned out that Iraq had successfully launched a Chinese HY-2 Silkworm cruise missile, which approached Kuwait City from the sea and hit Kuwait where it would hurt—in a big shopping mall. The Sharq Mall is a slick, modern shopping mall that matches those in the United States. In fact, many of the stores are the same chains. The HY-2 hit the outside wall of the mall, causing some limited damage under the location of the movie theater. Possibly, Iraq had hoped to hit the Emir's palace, which is also on the coast but perhaps a half-mile away. That seemed to be the extent of damage to Kuwait for the entire war. Far different from 1991. The war was in Iraq this time.

CHAPTER 14

Baghdad

Baghdad International Airport (BIAP) was taken on April 4. Fighting in Baghdad did not turn out to be the horror some had feared. The opposition was relatively limited. The palaces fell quickly. There were isolated fierce fights, but for the most part, the Iraqi Army melted away as U.S. M1A1 tanks ground forward and U.S. Air Force jets and U.S. Army helicopter gunships crisscrossed overhead. This reflected success in separating Saddam's interests from the Iraqi Army's. It also reflected the successful dissection of Iraq's command and control. The forces were separated from the leadership. The only communication was via the international press.

Mohammed al-Sahaf, the information minister (and former foreign minister), gave regular briefings to the press from the Information Ministry, declaring that the Americans were being defeated. On April 7, he said famously, "Their infidels are committing suicide by the hundreds on the gates of Baghdad. Be assured, Baghdad is safe, protected." Sahaf left Iraq shortly thereafter. As did the head of the Mukhabarat, Tahir Habbush.

By mid-April, Baghdad was fairly quiet. I flew into Baghdad International Airport and rejoined my colleague Kyle at the Special VIP terminal building, which was dubbed the VVIP (presumably for Very VIP). It was intended for heads of state and held a store of large flags for a variety of nations. Colleagues raised an American flag on the pole in front of the building, which would be home for the foreseeable future.

The airport was filled with the debris of the recent battle. There were burnt hulks of aircraft and vehicles. An Iraqi Airways Boeing 727 lay on its side, largely burned out. Around the grounds of the airport were dozens of covered trenches prepared for fighting but mostly abandoned when the attack came. Stepping down inside these dugouts was to step into an earthen cell. I went in cautiously, as booby traps were a possibility. Inside were the remnants of recent occupants—teapots, sandals, weapons, and ammunition.

There was no communications between these trenches. The fear that must have existed in the dark nights waiting for the inevitable arrival of American forces must have been gnawing. Once the American forces arrived, in darkness, there must have been panic. Most of these fighting holes were quickly abandoned. I examined several of these trenches quite carefully. Tactically, they made sense in defending against dismounted troops in daylight. They were level with the surface of the ground and difficult to spot from above. At night, without night-vision goggles and against armor, they would be tombs.

I found no expended cartridges in or around these positions. The Iraqis in them did not fight; they fled, probably to the surrounding neighborhoods. Around BIAP (which is a very large area, approximately six square miles) and the surrounding areas that included the Special Republican Guard headquarters, it was common to find discarded uniforms. There were also a large number of discarded army boots. There were virtually no bodies. It looked as though the United States had expended a lot of ordnance, but the Iraqis had not. They withdrew. The passenger terminal building was untouched, and the runways were clear.

There were lots of unused weapons. If you wanted to pick up an RPG-7, all you had to do was walk in any direction for a couple hundred yards and you would find one. The explosive ordnance teams whose job was to clear areas of abandoned ammunition and other explosives would be busy for months.

The VVIP building was substantially damaged during the American assault. It had no working plumbing, and most of the windows had been shot out or shattered by nearby explosions. In a garden area behind the building, there was one broken pipe, which had water flowing out of it. This became the source of water for showering. In April, when the temperatures were still cool, we would heat some pans of water on a propane stove and pour them on our heads for bathing. Under the circumstances, it was not bad.

A generator had been among the first things flown in to provide electricity for communications, computers, and limited lighting in the evenings. A large, domed room was the general reception area. We had thirty-five folding cots set up. There were also a few separate rooms. I shared one with Kyle and a logistics officer, Roy, who looked as if he stepped off a movie set. Roy was in his late twenties, the son of a minister. A former marine, he was muscular and had piercing blue eyes under a growing mop of black hair and a lengthening beard. He was a pleasant, intelligent guy who had a positive attitude under any circumstances. He was kept very busy as we built a livable base from nothing. Eventually there were housing pods, secure offices, and portable aircraft hangars. It was Roy's job to manage the efforts of local and contract truck drivers who transported supplies from Kuwait and other locations. I can still see him standing on the hood of a HMMV, giving instructions to a group of local drivers who were forming a convoy. The sun was setting behind him, highlighting his long hair and beard. He looked like a prophet out of the Bible or Koran.

Sunsets at BIAP were stunning. I made a habit of jogging a couple of miles down the access road each evening, when temperatures were lower. Frequently, Blackhawk and Apache attack helicopters were taking off from their nearby location, and they would skim the ground in front of the setting sun, producing a striking silhouette. It was beautiful.

The BIAP area itself had been carefully cultivated before the war. Two of Saddam's most expansive palace areas adjoined the airport, and the grounds, behind heavily guarded walls, contained beautifully maintained gardens. There were herds of gazelles and a wide range of bird life. I had visited these palace areas in 1998 as leader of the UNSCOM inspection of presidential facilities. As the U.S. occupation proceeded, eventually all the trees and vegetation were destroyed: The greenery provided cover for insurgents and improvised explosive device (IED) concealment. Gazelles stood no chance among youthful Americans with M-16s and M-4s. The last gazelle I saw was in June 2003.

More fortunate were the dogs of war. Amid the debris of the battle were a dog and her four (cute) puppies, about three weeks old. They must have been terrified during the assault with the explosions in and around the airport. But they were in luck now. If anybody should have welcomed the United States as liberators, it was these guys. Dogs in Iraq are not seen as pets, more as nuisances. Markets don't sell dog food in Baghdad. Dogs tend to roam in packs and are regularly killed by cars on the roads. Some inventive IED makers were hiding roadside IEDs in dead dogs for a while.

There was also the frog of war. In a small concrete pit that was constantly filled with water, I found a frog that seemed to have found its own private pond. I had no idea how the creature got to that small oasis, but at least while Kyle and I were around we kept the water level up.

The VVIP building where we set up was filled with dirt, dust, and debris. The rooms were filled with heaps of documents and broken furniture and glass. Expended 20 mm cartridges from Bradleys were everywhere. There were also unexploded cluster munitions rounds littering the surrounding rose gardens. There was a kitchen area, where we set up some tables and chairs. The military prepackaged meals (meals ready to eat, or MREs) were the basic fare, but were soon supplemented with cereal, granola bars, and a range of other food that could be flown in on occasion.

The key logistical requirement was water, and our guys were on top of that. Every one of our aircraft supply flights had pallets of bottled water. We had water purification tablets, but never had to use them.

We had vehicles of various types—none were armored. Some SUVs had been driven up from Kuwait. There were some sedans that blended in with the types of cars common in Baghdad. We also had a few HMMVs. And there were some Toyota Land Cruiser pickup trucks that had been used in the western desert by CIA paramilitary officers before the war. I inherited one of these. The guys out west had put a lot of mileage on it—and rarely on paved roads, judging from the condition.

My Toyota Land Cruiser was virtually identical to the ones provided to Chad in 1986. In the bed, there was a pintle mount for a machine gun. The vehicle was painted in desert tan, and all reflective surfaces had been taped over. Tied to the hood was a dayglow orange canvas that identified the vehicle as friendly to aircraft. On the front was a winch that I never had to use. I became fond of that truck even though it was not in the best of shape. The front-end alignment was so bad that if you hit a bump at anything over forty miles per hour, a violent shaking would start and would stop only by decelerating to under twenty miles per hour—not good if you were trying to move quickly. Still, I was familiar with the vehicle and could change the tires quickly—a key skill, because in Baghdad, a flat tire was inevitable.

The vehicle had parachute flares, smoke grenades, a medic kit, a heavy-duty jack, gas cans, cable tie-downs, and two gas tanks (main and reserve), and I kept a few blocks of wood in the back. There were always a few liters of bottled water. The truck had air-conditioning, but no radio. I installed my own GPS on the dashboard. It did not have a Blue Force Tracker (BFT), a small transceiver that emits a signal picked up and relayed by satellite, providing your geolocation to be constantly recorded by a command center. The trackers served two purposes. They emitted a signal indicating that you were a friend, not a foe. So-called friendly fire has been responsible for more than a few casualties. The second function was to transmit a signal in an emergency. Push all three buttons at once, and you send a Mayday notice that gives your exact location—or so they say. I had seen the command center where such signals were monitored in Kuwait before the invasion, and I came away with the impression that these individual BFTs for CIA guys were the modern version of shark repellent in World War II—no effect on sharks, but made you feel better.[1]

Without a BFT, I had to assume I was on my own. I did have one tool that was useful. FalconView was a computer package that linked aerial imagery of Baghdad and surrounding area with GPS coordinates. Although I knew my way around the major Baghdad roads, addresses and specific locations were difficult to describe. A laptop with GPS coordinates allowing you to "zoom in" to identify individual buildings was a help in planning routes and helping Iraqis identify buildings of interest. Years later, with GoogleEarth, this software was all unremarkable, but in 2003, this tool was innovative.

One of the most important tools in Iraq was commercial Thuraya satellite phones. Iraq had no cell phones when we invaded, and landlines were spotty at best. Thurayas were slightly bulky phones that not only provided voice communication but also had built-in GPS monitoring. Saddam had made unauthorized possession of Thuraya telephones a capital offense. Not only was the regime worried about communications coming out of Iraq that were difficult for it to monitor (as compared with the Iraqi landline telephones), but it also feared the GPS capability. Thurayas could provide (and did) precise locations for military strikes or other purposes. The only drawback to Thuraya phones was that they worked poorly indoors. If it rang, you were better off running outside before answering.

The population at the VVIP Building grew rapidly, as a number of missions were operating out of it. The initial small group grew to include officers from the CIA, military special operations, and the FBI. A major early focus was to track down key regime members. A special military unit (called TF-20) focused on capturing "high-value targets." These were Iraqis on the blacklist drawn up before the war, and they included the fifty-two highest-priority members whose faces were printed on decks of cards. Saddam was the ace of spades. The other aces were his two sons; the ace of diamonds was his presidential secretary, Abed Hamid Mahmud.

The CIA counterproliferation WMD team I had met near the border in Kuwait had now also set up shop at VVIP and was tracking down key WMD personalities. Concurrently, a small military team was looking for Captain Scott Speicher, a U.S. pilot shot down in the 1991 war and never accounted for.

I became a resource for all these groups at various times. I also simply reported what was going on in the streets—the kind of reporting that the State Department might have done if it had an embassy or personnel on the ground. The State Department people who showed up at the Green Zone were not reporting what was happening in Iraq outside the Green Zone. They rarely left the Green Zone. I rarely went in.

Kyle and I made contact with a number of Iraqis we both knew. Over the course of the next few weeks, I met and had extensive conversations with former Mukhabarat officers, Directorate of General Security officers, police commissioners, military officers, sheiks of prominent tribes, doctors, nurses, former Finance Ministry officials, former and current Oil Ministry officials, former Ministry of Foreign Affairs officials, Iraqi journalists, businessmen, soldiers, and the wives and children of all the above. They were mostly Baathists, both Shia and Sunni. Some were people I knew before the war. Some were officials I had identified with my contacts as being good candidates to participate in a new government.

One thing was quickly clear: By May, Baghdad was at a tipping point. In the immediate period after the fall of Saddam, there was euphoria colored by huge uncertainty. The United States did not fill the vacuum of leadership once Saddam fell. In all my conversations, the Iraqis would ask, "What's going to happen? Who is in charge?" In April, there was a great curiosity toward the Americans. There was the expectation that the last superpower could fix Iraq. The expectations were high.

Satellite television receivers blossomed on roofs at a miraculous rate. And yet, there was no message about who was in charge. There was no single Iraqi voice. There was no voice from the United States. After decades of Saddam's rule, Iraqis were used to receiving government direction. Now there was nothing. There was no authority. There was complete freedom—to do absolutely anything, good or bad. In the absence of clear information, rumors and conspiracy theories flourished, drawn from whatever limited facts appeared.

When the United States (OSD) flew Ahmad Chalabi and a few hundred of his militia (he called them the Free Iraqi Forces) to Tallil air base near Nasiriyah, Iraq, on C-17s on April 6, 2003, the Iraqis interpreted this action as meaning the United States was going to install Chalabi. This created concern among Iraqis in Iraq, but they still believed that the U.S. president meant only to remove the very top leaders. Chalabi was given special treatment because he was opposed to

Saddam, not necessarily because the United States was going to install him in Baghdad.

The move by the OSD to fly him into Iraq surprised Iraqis in Iraq and, apparently, President Bush as well. The president had asked on more than one occasion who was paying Chalabi. At one meeting in early January 2003, no one knew, except the CIA chief of the Near Eastern region. The chief stated factually that the Department of Defense was paying Chalibi's INC group about $350,000 a month. The president said the payment should end. This was not guidance that the OSD chose to execute.

The OSD could not, however, provide everything Chalabi wanted. He wanted to be at the head of the American columns entering Baghdad, much like de Gaulle was placed at the head of Allied forces taking Paris in World War II. This request was blocked by the military. The forces simply could not advance according to their plans and push or carry Chalabi and his supporters along. Chalibi would not be a hood ornament on their M-1A1 tanks.

Nevertheless, Chalabi and his militia swiftly got to Baghdad and quickly took over the prestigious (under Saddam) Hunt Club in Mansour for their headquarters. There was no legal authority to do this, but Chalabi knew that in the chaos after the war, no one could complain. The Defense Intelligence Agency (DIA), the Department of Defense organization paying Chalabi, had officers accompany him. The rationale for the funds provided to the Iraqi National Congress was that they were to support INC intelligence collection for the DIA.

The other external opposition groups took their lead from the INC and seized buildings and facilities. These events were broadcast widely, and Iraqis in Iraq saw that the external groups were helping themselves to the property of the previous regime—often at the point of a gun. This quickly became the norm.

One of the first people I visited was Dr. Assad, a prominent physician in Baghdad and in medical circles around the world. We had met once before in New York when I was at the UN and he was visiting for business reasons. An independent, thoughtful observer of Iraq, Assad was able to provide many insights into what was going on in Iraq, particularly among the professional classes. We would get along well.

Like many Iraqis I met, he would invite me to his home to share meals and meet his children. We sat outside and had tea and talked about Iraq and what was happening to the people. It was an endless conversation that went on for months and, in fact, continues to the present. One evening as we spoke and as the sun dropped lower in the sky, an elderly relative named Jawad was tending to a small garden. Jawad was a thin, academic-looking gentleman in his sixties, by my guess. He had round horn-rimmed glasses, and to me, he resembled the pictures I knew of Alfred Stieglitz at that age. Jawad was methodically sorting out the seeds from various flowers. I inquired about his purpose, and he said, "I would like to have this section contain only red flowers next year, and I am separating the seeds that come from red blossoms. Those I will plant, and the others, discard."

I was taken by his attitude toward the future. I was not sure what I would have been doing in his circumstances. Perhaps planting seeds was a way of dealing with the uncertainty of the moment. I hoped the flowers would bloom and be enjoyed, but given what I was seeing on the U.S. side, I found little cause for optimism.

When I did not have other responsibilities, I would meet with Assad and explore Baghdad. We spent much time driving around the city, and he showed me what was happening in areas he knew well. He introduced me to other doctors, journalists, artists, and professors. Some became friends as well. Together we witnessed the decay of Baghdad and the growing hatred and chaos.

One day in May, I spent a day at a private hospital with a couple of doctors who had several patients with various problems, many related to the war. One was a victim of severe burns. The doctors decided to graft some skin from his thigh to a burned area around his neck and chest. Medical materials and physicians were in short supply, so only the more severe cases were treated. Supplies were looted and not replaced. Doctors were targets of crime and hostage-taking by gangs. The private clinics would soon close—another victim of the spreading chaos.

The surgeons invited me to join them in their efforts. While the patient, a young male, was being prepped, we had some rotisserie chicken and rice. We then walked around the corner to what was the operating room. It was austere by American standards. The patient was anesthetized and laid out naked on a simple operating table. There, a nurse and another doctor monitored the anesthesia. The surgeon had simple tools, but highly skilled hands. He trimmed off some of the thickening scar tissue that seemed to be compressing the man's throat, and using a small steel instrument that looked like a cheese slicer, he peeled patches of skin off the thighs and laid them out on the desired areas of the throat. Such was the status of medical care postinvasion.

This was a very lucky man. A month later, there would be far fewer hospitals in Iraq. There would be fights over who would control them—particularly among the religious groups. The doctors who were mostly secular drifted away as the "turbans" fought for control over major hospitals. Controlling hospitals would become a source of power. One of the good things that happened during the Saddam regime was the development of health care in Iraq, especially Baghdad. Now, health care was rapidly in decline.

The "turbans"—Assad's term—were also inciting groups to get rid of liquor stores. "Turbans" was shorthand for any of the various religious leaders who were now seeking to extend their religious leadership into political control over geographic areas and civil institutions. With Saddam gone, this was another element pushing to fill the vacuum. I visited a Christian family that ran one store near Mansour. The store had been burned out in May (as had several others in the area), and a note left warning that if they reopened, they would be killed. The family gave me the note as if I could fix the injustice. Freedom. They were free to sell liquor. Others were free to kill them.

When driving together through Baghdad in my Land Cruiser, Assad and I would observe all sorts of absurd behavior. In Amiriya in late April, a car drove directly at us on the wrong side of the road. Assad asked, "Is this freedom?" The phrase became a leitmotif to direct at all the chaos that gained momentum in late April and May 2003. Watching looters tear down metal fences, Assad would say, "Look, see, freedom!" Then we would see people stealing cars in broad daylight with pistols: "Freedom!"

Cars often represented the entire life savings of Iraqis, because banks and the Iraqi dinar currency had collapsed. I saw several Iraqis who were inconsolable after their cars had been stolen; it was all they had. There was a particular square in Baghdad where stolen cars were taken and street hoodlums would sell them to Kurdish gangs, who would drive them north. From there, the vehicles would be taken out of Iraq and sold. Real estate was also free. The records of ownership were destroyed, and there were no courts to try complaints. Freedom in action.

The incongruities of an American in Baghdad were glimpsed one very hot June day as friend Professor Shakir and I were driving through Mansour. We had just passed the building bombed by the United States when it was thought Saddam had been there two months earlier. Shakir suggested stopping for an ice cream at a popular shop on the main street. We got a couple of paper dishes of ice cream and ate them with plastic spoons, finishing them as we were driving past more damaged buildings.

I carefully, but awkwardly, put the empty cup, plastic spoon, and bunched-up paper napkin on the floor of the LandCruiser. The professor looked at me. Then he rolled down his window and tossed his cup out. I cringed momentarily. Littering. The professor glanced at me, reading my mind, and I instantly saw the absurdity. We were passing some government buildings destroyed in the bombing. Looters were pulling down fencing around the buildings. The city was in chaos and I hesitated over a piece of litter.

Another Iraqi whom I knew well from my UNSCOM days was a former senior UN official and colleague. He was a lawyer by training with broad international experience. We had spent many hours across the table from one another during the 1990s and had developed mutual respect. His home was close by, and he welcomed me to visit. Samir was the head of a highly educated family—all university graduates. His wife and children were extremely articulate and spoke perfect English.

One daughter was seeking to study abroad when the war intervened. She was in the process of applying to graduate schools outside

Iraq and needed to take a standardized test in Iraq and obtain her school transcripts. The Department of Education could not conduct the appropriate tests. Moreover, Baghdad University was in disarray and she could not get her records. It was symptomatic of a simple, apparently minor problem, which had the capacity to ruin a person's life. And a million such problems were affecting an increasingly unhappy country. Add to that a growing security problem in which women and many men chose not to leave their homes out of fear, and the U.S. inability to offer the prospect of it getting better, and you have a very resentful population. The more educated and highly trained Iraqis considered how to get out of Iraq, not how to build its future.

The situation worsened as the United States failed to agree on any path forward. The vacuum of power spawned wider chaos. There was no penalty for committing crimes; there was no reward for going to work. To Iraqis, it looked as if external Iraqi opposition groups, who had not suffered through the regime (as they tended to see it), had been brought in by the Defense Department to seize power, government buildings, and businesses. Animosity against the United States grew rapidly on the streets.

More than one Iraqi commented that the only place brightly lit up at night was the Republican Palace, where the United States had set up its headquarters. Just like under Saddam.

Watching events in Iraq from New York was Nizar Hamdoon. His chemotherapy had been progressing well. He had one final course of chemicals to endure during the first week of June. Then he hoped to return to Baghdad. At the end of April, he wrote a nine-page paper setting out his views on reestablishing a government. The report could have been very useful to American planners before the war, had anyone with authority been willing to listen and had the United States not predetermined to support external opposition groups, especially the INC under Ahmad Chalabi. Hamdoon's paper described a methodical, gradual process for removing the Baath Party and a like approach for reconfiguring the army, the Republican Guard, the police force, and the internal security forces. He emphasized weeding out the leadership but keeping the bulk of working-level members employed and on the job.

The paper reflected the discussions we had in New York, but which he could not write down at the time. He called me and asked for e-mail contacts at the new Coalition Provisional Authority (CPA) to send his paper to. I provided names, including a senior State Department representative, David Dunford. I know several people who received it, but they were powerless to alter the decisions that were about to be made by the CPA.

Driving around Baghdad, I came to judge various neighborhoods by watching the kids around U.S. soldiers. If the kids were hanging around army tanks, playing, then the neighborhood was not bad. The kids took their lead from their older brothers. If the teenagers and former military enlistees at home were condemning the Americans, the kids would not loiter around the U.S. checkpoints. As the weeks went by, I found the army positions becoming lonelier.

Still, in early May, there was not yet the outright animosity that would soon emerge. I had driven by my old UNSCOM office in Baghdad at the Canal Hotel and was crossing through what had been called Saddam City but is now known as Sadr City. It was a very poor and very crowded Shia neighborhood. During one UNSCOM inspection, our inspectors were examining some artillery fields of fire that Saddam had planned. The commission was checking to see if the firing plans included any chemical-weapons rounds. They did not. It was interesting, however, that the planned fields of fire were to lay down crossing barrages over Saddam City. The Iraqi Army was planning for a contingency of unrest in that segment of Baghdad. This was considered the most dangerous threat by Saddam. I shared some of Saddam's concerns when I suddenly had a flat tire. A year later, I would never have driven through Sadr City—it would have been fatal. As it was, I did not want to linger there.

With its gun mount and desert paint scheme, the Land Cruiser did not look like a civilian vehicle. I quickly got out the heavy-duty jack and found that it had so much sand in the ratchet mechanism, it would not operate. I dug around under the driver's seat for the small, typical Toyota hand-crank jack. It worked, but the Land Cruiser suspension was high and the jack could not lift the chassis high enough. I was glad I kept blocks of wood in the truck bed, as I used them to support the jack and got the vehicle lifted.

By this time, I had attracted a bunch of neighborhood kids—a good sign. They were all smiles, watching a dopey American change a tire. A month later, I would not have presumed that an episode like this would end so uneventfully. The awe of American power was being eroded by the growing realization that the United States had no idea what it was doing in Iraq. Iraqi society was fracturing quickly. There was no government to preserve order, so groups formed to protect themselves or grab power or money or both.

There was a window of time during which the United States could have, even at that late date, restored the order of the existing ministries. Unfortunately, the window was slammed shut by the arrival of Ambassador L. Paul Bremer III.

Washington had realized, as much due to reports of chaos in the press as from government reports, that Garner's ORHA was a self-contained vessel of complete confusion. Iraq was disintegrating, and ORHA was doing nothing to stop it. The White House decided that it needed to install a higher-ranking person reporting to the president to replace General Garner. By this time, the Oval Office was hearing opinions that the OSD approach was not working out.

Unfortunately, while Bremer is a talented, bright, and experienced Washington hand, he had no background in Iraq. He succeeded in bringing order to the Americans in the Green Zone, but could not bring order to Iraq. Like every other American who went to Baghdad, he was trying to do something good. There is a deeply rooted American attitude that we can fix things. If we apply effort and analysis, we can fix something, including Iraq. ORHA, which became the CPA on Bremer's arrival, was teeming with people who wanted to do good and be involved in this great experiment. Most had absolutely no knowledge of Iraq. Iraqis in Iraq came to feel they themselves were guinea pigs for American graduate students who would spend a few months abroad and return home and be considered experts.

Iraqis found it very difficult to get their views across to the CPA. Only a few members of the CPA made real decisions, and these people had no idea whom they should speak or listen to. In the critical first months of the occupation, the Iraqi opposition groups had better lines into the CPA because they had already been organized as parties and had existing contacts with Americans now in the Green Zone. Most Iraqis in Iraq did not have political parties, or funding, and therefore started from a distinct disadvantage in the internal squabbling over power and resources let loose by the sudden dissolution of government. Those groups from the outside came in with objectives and external support. For example, Chalabi's INC quickly seized the bulk of the records of the Mukhabarat, a natural source of power. The INC retained complete control over those documents for over a year before finally ceding them to the United States. It was said that the INC would pay former Mukhabarat staff for their assistance. I know at least one case in which a former Mukhabarat employee asked if he could work for the United States, because otherwise, he would have to take a job with the INC.

To Bremer's great credit, it did not take him long to appreciate that Chalibi and the INC had no particular constituency in Iraq other than himself and those he could buy. This put Bremer crossways with the OSD.

The two major Kurdish parties were different. They were outside Saddam's control, but maintained close financial connections via the export of oil through Kurdistan. They had resources and an existing infrastructure for their region. They could enter Baghdad politics from a position of strength. Their politics were quite flexible. KDP leader Massoud Barzani and his son had particularly close business dealings with the regime (and in fact, when Saddam's forces entered the Kurdish region in 1996, it was with the acquiescence, if not the invitation, of Barzani). They had joint interests with the regime (Mukhabarat) in a company called Sharekat Asia, which, in turn, dealt with a company called Petroline, in which Benazir Bhutto had a major interest. Petroline figured prominently in the oil liftings under the Oil-for-Food program. This is illustrative of the convoluted dealings that would come to dominate Baghdad political battles.

However, both the Kurdish groups (the KDP and PUK) were skilled in survival in a hostile environment and elected to assist the United States when they became convinced that President Bush was really going to invade. The Kurdish forces, working with CIA teams, kept Saddam's two Iraqi northern corps occupied so that he could not redeploy them to the south, where General Tommy Franks planned his approach to Baghdad. After Turkey denied U.S. forces transit to get to northern Iraq and keep open a second front, the role played by the Kurds was vital. They had contributed in a major way to the over-throw of the regime—and with some justification believed they de-served a piece of the pie.

The majority of Iraqis had no affiliation with the empowered par-ties. There were millions of poor and politically inexperienced people who were effectively seduced by the likes of firebrand Moqtada al-Sadr. Free elections of one person, one vote, sounded great in Wash-ington, but few stopped to consider how vast was the number of Iraqis who had no experience in the responsibilities of citizenship. These Iraqis would do whatever their religious leader told them. Premature democracy empowers the rabble-rousers. Bremer arrived in Iraq with the premise that the majority Shia should be empowered, but he did not know how to deal with leaders like Moqtada al-Sadr.

The Sunnis had no organization to represent them and saw the new government being closed out to them by Bremer, who on sev-eral occasions pointedly said the Shia constituted the majority. Of course, on hearing this, a Sunni immediately feels screwed. On the other hand, the Shia exile groups that had relied on Iran for support during the Saddam years naturally became immediate strong players in Baghdad.

The simpleminded democracy that the CPA attempted to install was the polar opposite of what existed under the regime. One person, one vote, is a great ideal. So is world peace. A more modest goal of shepherding a "government more responsive to the will of the people" would have been a more practical and achievable standard. In the post-Saddam chaos of Iraq, the emergent "political" groups were not political parties, as the Washington-trained denizens of the Green Zone thought. They were groups that participated in Iraqi politics as a method of getting a piece of power. But they also were militias and business enterprises. Both the INC and the Supreme Council for Islamic Revolution in Iraq (SCIRI; but in 2007 it became known as the Supreme Islamic Iraqi Council, SIIC) had militia forces and were busy establishing business deals to build and control revenue. Control over cell-phone licenses was an early battleground. Lost in all this "democratization" was the secular middle, including not just Sunnis, but Shia.

This dynamic was brought home to me through my contact with a group of senior representatives from the Jibury clan. The clan extends from north to south in Iraq and, while it is predominantly Sunni, also includes Shia. It is a good mix of "Iraq." The representatives described to me a tribal meeting they had with representatives from all over Iraq. The Jibury members had drafted a manifesto of goals for what they thought might become a political party. They wanted other clans to join with them and thus bring their talents to the new government. They did not know how to approach the CPA. When I said I would try to help arrange a meeting, they offered a luncheon at one of their homes in Karada.

I went to people I knew in the CPA political section and had great difficulty finding anyone interested or anyone who had the time to meet with the Jibury clan. These were proud Iraqis from one of the most important tribes. They were gathering influential tribal leaders from all over Iraq and wanted to meet with a CPA official who had authority. They wanted to meet with Bremer, but I knew this would never happen. I finally got two people from CPA to agree to see them. The senior was Ambassador Hume Horan, who was known for his excellent Arabic and was a former ambassador to Sudan. Among the Jiburys were Dr. Malik Dohan, a former minister from the pre-Saddam era; a former general who had been jailed by Saddam; and several powerful local sheiks.

Horan listened politely and spoke in generalities that offered nothing concrete. The Jiburys could have delivered a big block of support in an organized way. They made a very carefully considered presentation that was the result of many meetings among themselves and with other tribes. Their premise was that the United States must have been acting on poor information when it provided support to Chalabi. They said 95 percent of Iraqis still wanted the United States to succeed, but there had to be an Iraqi government. The clan had considered how to do this and suggested that a conference be quickly convened with attendees from each province and the numbers based on population, perhaps one representative per hundred thousand. In addition, to account for the external Iraqis, an additional few participants could represent them. A process like this could quickly yield an Iraqi government.

They went on to describe the forces creating instability. They highlighted the Badr Corps and Dawa militia. The Badr Corps was made up of Iraqis who had been forcibly exiled by Saddam to Iran and had fought on the Iranian side during the Iran-Iraq War. The corps was aligned with SCIRI. The Badr members were not numerous, but "because they have guns, they can cause problems." The Dawa militia, the Jiburys claimed, was also bent on revenge, not unification.

The Jibury representatives received polite words and were told to stay in touch with an earnest young woman named Yael, who had been given the task of acting as liaison with the tribes. They took her phone number with the expectation that further meetings would be arranged to discuss their evolving ideas. In fact, she was only in Iraq for a short time, and when she left, no one from the CPA contacted the Jiburys again.

They kept calling me to ask what was going on, and I tried to make some explanations, but I had none. By July, it was probably too late, anyway. Groups had formed to fight against the occupation. My contacts were telling me about meetings in late May and June by new outfits such as New Dawn, the Coalition of Iraqi People, the Gathering Sons of Iraq, and the Black Banner Group. There were reports of training in the Fallujah area with rocket-propelled grenades (RPGs) and other weapons. People would tell me these things with the expectation that the United States would do something about it, but the United States was incapable of doing anything at this point. From where I stood, it seemed events came to be understood by the CPA and Washington with a six-month lag time. What was happening in May would finally be understood, and a response considered, in November. Of course, by November, the situation had evolved in some other way, so the response was no longer appropriate. This cycle of education was costly.

During the first week of May, the former oil minister, General Amer Rasheed, turned himself in. He was one of the HVTs on the deck of cards. I went to meet with him on Saturday, May 10, at the HVT detention site on the other side of the airport. It was a very rudimentary site with some old barracks buildings and tents surrounded by concertina wire. There was an office with a large whiteboard showing who was in detention, who was debriefing, and what the evaluations were. The office had an air conditioner that kept grinding away. Outside, the heat poured onto the canvas tents, and dry dust was everywhere. The noise of generators was constant. Anyplace there was a U.S. presence, there were generators. My ears became deaf to them. The persistent droning was only noticeable when it suddenly stopped for some reason.

I did not know how Rasheed would react to seeing me. I did not relish the role of victor over vanquished. The difference between where I was and where he was had as much to do with serendipity as actions taken by individuals to shape their own destiny.

The officer in charge of the camp led me to the tent where they had brought Rasheed, and he left me alone. (This was before there were strict rules about all contact with detainees requiring more than one person present.) The tent was about nine feet wide and twelve feet long. The sides were partly rolled up to allow movement of air. The ground was dirt and sand. There were two folding chairs inside, nothing else.

Rasheed had not been informed who was going to see him. When I stepped out of the bright sun into the tent, it took him a moment to recognize me. I was backlit by the sun. I also looked nothing like the last time he had seen me. I had not shaved in a month and was dressed in dirty khaki pants and a similar shirt, with hiking boots. Rasheed was in a yellow jumpsuit and sandals, but otherwise looked about as scruffy as I did.

Then he recognized me, "Mister Duelfer! I was wondering when you would arrive." He smiled. I stepped forward and shook his hand. It was a respectful greeting. The moment of uncertainty passed. I shrugged, not knowing what to say, but thinking that little needed to be said that wasn't already apparent about our circumstances.

Rasheed, who was never fully able to contain what he was thinking, said, "You don't look so good."

I replied, "Well, neither do you. Please, sit," and we both sat in folding chairs that sank into the dust.

Rasheed and I knew each other well. We were alumni of the same recent history. I had respect for Rasheed and even liked him. He had been through a great deal with the regime. By virtue of his previous position heading Iraq's Military Industrial Commission (MIC, the state organization responsible for all Iraq weapons development, including WMD), he was one of the constant counterparts for UN inspectors. By this point, I had known him and his wife, Dr. Rihab Taha, for a decade. We had spent long hours in meetings at MIC headquarters in Iraq during the 1990s. We had traipsed through various inspections of Saddam's palaces. Ironically, the detention site was adjacent to a missile facility that had been the site of a contentious inspection site years earlier. All those inspections and Security Council crises meant nothing now.

I had last seen Rasheed at the final OPEC meeting before the war the previous December in Vienna. That had been a very delicate moment for Rasheed. He was at the center of attention, as the future of Iraq and its oil seemed to hang in the balance. We had met in his suite at the Intercontinental Hotel for over an hour. He had been accompanied by his delegation colleagues. Back then, he knew by my presence that, if he chose, he could have arranged to leave Iraq. But he had his wife and family to consider. In the end, like many Iraqis drawn into the regime structure, he had no choice but to stay.

We discussed this for a moment. He said he understood fully what I had been communicating in Vienna.

I asked briefly about WMD, knowing that others would be putting detailed questions to him for a long time. "General, is it possible there were WMD activities that you were not informed about? If so, who would know?"

He responded, "Mister Duelfer, what I would tell you here and now is no different from what I told you before. There were some small matters that we had not revealed before Blix came. For example, there was a nitric acid plant which we wished to preserve for commercial uses . . . but weapons, no." He continued, "I doubt that there could be anything else. I suppose it is possible the security services might have something small. But to answer that, you would have to find Abed or Qusay." By Abed, he meant the presidential secretary Abed Hamid Mahmud; Qusay was Saddam's younger son, who headed the SSO.

I turned to other matters regarding the Oil Ministry and the transactions during the regime. He readily provided the basics of how Iraq utilized the Oil-for-Food program to build support for Iraq. He offered to give the full details. Rasheed also angrily described how the professional operation of the Oil Ministry and its marketing organization, the State Organization for Marketing of Oil (SOMO), became corrupted by those around Saddam including Saddam Hassam al-Ziban. They were directing certain deals not just on the basis of political influence, but also on the basis of personal profit. Rasheed emphasized that he himself was a poor man, while those around him had grown wealthy.

Rasheed's description of this web of greed and influence was the first by anyone on the Iraqi side. It was a fascinating first insight into the Oil-for-Food program, as seen from Baghdad. The tragedy for Rasheed was that he knew too much about the widespread corruption. He could implicate Iraqis and foreigners in senior positions—including those in the new Iraqi government. Once authority for Rasheed's detention was transferred to the new Iraqi government, some of those he knew to be corrupt had responsibility for his imprisonment. And of course, the United States supported the new government.

As of this writing, Rasheed still lingers in prison—a technocrat who knew too much. It was not WMD that trapped him, but the UN Oil-for-Food program. I regularly raised with the White House the plight of many detainees. The White House either elected to do nothing or deferred to the OSD, which in turn deferred to the judgment of the new Iraqi government. So, Rasheed, who had the opportunity to get out of Iraq before the war, but did not out of concern for his family, now shuffled back to his cell.

I passed through the office of the detention camp on my way out and scanned the whiteboard showing who else was there. I noticed the name of someone I had identified before the war as a potential candidate to participate in the immediate post-Saddam government. His name had been included in the interagency process that generated the blacklist—based on what, I do not know. He had been in jail under Saddam and was again in jail under the United States. The notation on the whiteboard from a debriefing of May 8 was quite simple: "Waste of three MREs a day. House arrest since 95. Most info on him is incorrect. No job since 94."

This did not surprise me. This was all perfectly consistent with what I had learned before the war and what other senior Mukhabarat guys had told me since. I thought he would be released soon. I was wrong. In spite of not being worth "three MREs a day," he was held for over two years. I raised his case many times. However, between Iraqi politics and the U.S. bureaucracy, he remained in prison and his home was taken over first by U.S. troops and then by insurgents. I compared him to the character "Joseph K" in Kafka's *Trial*. Amazingly, when this Iraqi was finally released, he still wanted to help the United States, but not the "outsiders" running Baghdad. I doubt he will find support and probably will be the target of one of the political or militia groups. His story is not pretty, nor unique.

The United States was vulnerable to being misled by Iraqi sources who would provide reports on individuals acting against U.S. forces. Such reports were sometimes motivated by a desire to settle old scores or for other reasons to suit the source. A former INC supporter told me he had provided such reports to cause suspicion or generate raids by the United States against political or business rivals. In 2003, raids were initiated on some very thin, uncorroborated information. By 2004, however, procedures for more rigorous vetting of sources were being implemented, according to the DIA.

On Wednesday morning, May 28, I was visiting again with my former UN colleague Samir, and we were joined by a retired former deputy head of the Iraq Central Bank, Ahmed Munir. Munir was on my unused list of accomplished individuals who could have played an immediate role as the United States occupied Iraq. He had studied and lived in the United States in upstate New York. I believe he was even married to an American. He certainly knew our system and the Iraqis. He was a professional and no supporter of Saddam. That morning, we had a long discussion about what was happening in Iraq and what groups and individuals were making money and how.

A couple of days later, I was shocked to hear from Samir that American soldiers had raided Munir's home in the middle of the night, breaking in and taking him to jail. Every night, raids were conducted against all sorts of Iraqis—raids based on the flimsiest of intelligence. Units had been set up to conduct nightly raids to capture or kill suspects. They then pressed intelligence and targeting officers to come up with suspects. The system demanded targets. I heard of many raids that did not capture real insurgents, but had the effect of creating outrage toward the United States from people who would have been supportive. Munir's family was terrified, and he was humiliated by being bagged and tied. He was released some days later. Apparently, someone in the system thought Munir might know something about where Saddam's hidden money might be.

On May 26, I was driving down the airport road to go to a meeting at CPA with Dennis G., now the intelligence officer to Bremer. It was late in the afternoon, and the temperatures were cooling. The airport road was still landscaped with palm trees and still had guardrails. It was a divided highway with three lanes in each direction and perhaps twenty yards of groomed plantings between the lanes. I had passed the turnoff that led to Amiriya, where I often went to get some rotisserie chicken. I was approaching the next overpass that carried the highway that went north intersecting Abu Ghraib Highway and Jordan Street. To the south, it became a regular city street, but connected to the highway south to Hilla. There was the usual flow of traffic, not heavy, but not light, either.

Ahead of me, perhaps a hundred yards, were a couple of HMMVs. They were in the right lane, slowing to exit to head south. Traffic was passing on the left. Suddenly, with a crack and a flash, there was an explosion. One of the HMMVs spun wildly around. Cars were screeching to a halt and driving off the road to the left. The road was soon blocked with cars, and from where I was, it looked as though one of the occupants of the HMMV had gotten out. The other HMMV had stopped to help. The attacked HMMV quickly went up in flames. I drove down the center. The soldiers were waving traffic off and leveling weapons at approaching vehicles. I imagined ammo was cooking off and would seem like incoming fire. I turned off to the other side of airport road.

The HMMV that had been hit had armored doors, but not enough to protect those inside. I had first thought the HMMV had been hit by an RPG, but the next day, I saw a small crater in the roadway. It was one of the first IEDs on the airport road (possibly the first). One man was killed. There would be plenty more. Two weeks later, I was returning to BIAP and passed a Blackhawk helicopter that was landing adjacent to where another U.S. vehicle had been destroyed. We had won the battle for Baghdad International Airport easily enough but somehow failed to secure the main highway to it.

CHAPTER 15

The Generator

The failure of good American intentions to produce good results in Iraq can be seen in stories like this one.

There is a man who epitomizes all that is good in Iraq. I call him Professor Shakir. The professor taught postgraduate students and had the opportunity to mix with the top academic and professional classes of Iraq. He was the best in his field and, though not a Baathist, was consulted by senior government officials. His home was modest for an Iraqi man of his stature. It was in the Jihad area of Baghdad, a neighborhood that would be considered upper middle class. Saddam was in the process of building an array of larger homes in this district for some of his guards, but the war intervened.

Seen from above, neighborhoods of these homes appear as a pack of rectilinear plots and blocks. I have spent hours staring at aerial imagery of various neighborhoods locating homes and streets. It is a difficult task. An aerial image of almost any neighborhood in Baghdad would make a very challenging jigsaw puzzle. Curved lines are rare. Roofs will have a water tank for storage, but even these tanks are usually boxlike. It is very difficult to see where one residence begins and another ends.

Baghdad is not an easy place to navigate, for other reasons. The Saddam regime had its own motives for controlling navigation and location information. It shared the concerns of the former Soviet Union about accurate maps: They were considered sensitive security information.

I had visited the home of the professor many times—sometimes several times a week. It was a place I escaped to when I had unencumbered time. A black metal gate rolled aside to allow a car to pull into the otherwise walled perimeter. A small yard contained a few bushes and some gardenias, which scented the air and were often brought inside to do the same.

Mounted like a statue in the yard stood a large, faded blue industrial-looking generator. Roughly a rectangular block, it was about five feet long, four feet high, and three feet wide. A long, black exhaust pipe extended about two feet above the top. It had a German motor and a Chinese armature. When running, the generator sounded industrial, and it was impossible to have a conversation nearby. Usually, however, it was silent.

Generators are a vital part of modern life in Baghdad. The city has had irregular electrical power since before the war in 1991, when sanctions were imposed. Generators have been a fixture in the homes of the well-to-do for decades. Most were acquired to fill in the gaps in service during periodic blackouts. The recent war has made an existing problem worse. Other than in the Green Zone, the power was off in Baghdad far more than it was on. Electricity was insufficiently regular to sustain a refrigerator without a supplemental power source. Thus, foods requiring refrigeration were available only to those people with generators. Air-conditioning—in the summer days, temperatures are normally well over 120 degrees Fahrenheit—depended on a generator.

Having a generator does not solve all problems. Generators run on fuel. Iraq, a country with enormous proven oil reserves, could not provide its own gasoline. Its refineries were decrepit, and looters and saboteurs were keeping them that way. Before the war, the regime was at least able to produce and provide inexpensive gas to its people. One of the most immediate and annoying consequences of the American presence was the daily problem of obtaining gas. Lines could be hours long at times. Iraq had to import refined oil products like gasoline, liquid petroleum gas, and other products to shrink the lines. The Iraqi Oil Ministry, which runs the gas stations, had no money to do this with any regularity.

I saw an opportunity to make life better for the professor, who epitomized all that is good in Iraq. I asked him, "You don't seem to use your generator very often. Is this because of difficulty in getting fuel?"

"Well," he replied, "partly because of the fuel problem and also because my immediate neighbors do not have generators." I had not anticipated a problem with the neighbors. I dismissed it as merely a matter of not wanting to flaunt a luxury that those on either side did not share. Clearly, I thought, the major problem was simply the physical one of obtaining fuel—a problem that I felt I could fix. We had brought with us a logistics machine to support the presence of thousands of vehicles and people. On the American bases were fueling points with free access and no lines. I had many jerry cans available and thought I would simply fill a couple and bring over fuel for the generator.

Later, I would realize that the professor's second reason for the stagnant generator was more important and somewhat more complicated than simply not wanting the neighbors to be jealous. In Iraq, there is a cultural expectation of hospitality and sharing. Visits between friends and neighbors are far more common than in the United States. This became even more the case with the collapse of the telephone system after the war. His neighbors would all expect to come by and visit, as long as the generator was operating. The professor did not want to attract company who would repeat endlessly the same conversations heard all over Baghdad concerning all the current problems.

So now, it was with classic American enthusiasm that I believed I could solve a problem for a good man and, in a small way, make his life much better. Not insignificantly, I would make myself feel better as well—perhaps in some measure atoning for the huge suffering the entire city was undergoing.

Standing before this blue shrine to the industrial age with its thunderous noise and hot, lightly colored exhaust rushing out into the sky, I offered to bring him fuel for the generator.

"Well, that's not necessary," he said. "I can send Mohammed, my driver, out to get fuel."

I was not put off with this simple parry. "But no, it's no trouble and quite easy for me to fill a couple of jerry cans with fuel. Does it take gasoline or diesel?" I asked.

"Diesel," he said, "but really, don't bother."

That evening, I asked a colleague involved in logistics where the source was for the diesel fuel that powered so many of the American vehicles. I told him I needed a couple of cans for a very good friend. The next morning, when I finally spotted my friendly logistics man, he looked busy. Nevertheless, I reminded him of the two cans of diesel.

"Oh, shit. I got caught up with an aircraft arrival that had three pallets to be unloaded . . . You need them right away?"

"Well, yeah, I'm supposed to see the guy at eleven hundred."

He scurried among the clusters of jerry cans, picking them up and trying to make sense of the arrangements. There were two basic questions to the problem he (we) were facing. The first part was relatively simple—sorting empty cans from full ones. The second part of the problem was less obvious. Did the cans contain unleaded gas or diesel? Some vehicles took gas, while others ran on diesel.

"I am not the guy who manages these gas cans. The communications guys are in charge of them. They have to keep diesel for their generators going twenty-four/seven, or else they are really hosed. What a mess. I want to make sure I give ya diesel. Maybe they're all diesel, but I don't know." He looked at the array of jerry cans and at the same time looked around for someone who might know the answer.

Then, he thought of a solution: "HMMVs run on diesel. We'll just take a couple cans off the back of one of them and replace them later."

"Great."

We unhooked the jerry cans from a dusty HMMV, carried them to my LandCruiser pickup, and strapped them in the back. Off I went, not more than a half-hour late, eagerly anticipating the happiness I would deliver.

The professor was waiting for me. I got out and quickly directed his attention to the jerry cans in the back. "Diesel," I declared. "For the generator."

"Really?" This was his regular response to good news, and I was pleased to confirm it.

I then brought out from the truck a funnel that I had borrowed for the purpose of filling the tank at the top of the generator. We jointly took the items to the generator and, without speaking, divided the tasks. He held the funnel, and I lifted the jerry can to pour the fuel into the now opened tank.

The day was hot, and the electricity was, of course, off. This made the anticipated starting of the generator even more tantalizing. Soon he could run the air conditioner with abandon.

I lifted the jerry can with one hand on the handles at the top and supported it from the bottom with my other hand. Slowly, I tipped it toward the funnel my friend was now holding steadily in the tank opening. A steady flow of brilliant, clear fluid splashed into the tank. Seconds passed. Something odd was triggering an alert in my mind, and at the same time, the man who epitomizes all that is good in Iraq said anxiously, but politely, "Isn't that water?"

It was.

Normally extremely polite and astonishingly tolerant, my friend was at a loss for words. His perfect English no doubt included all the appropriate expletives. I heard none. It was more devastating to watch his upper lip quiver at the stupidity before him and consider the implications that this large generator had just been rendered useless by an American ignoramus. Once the pain and shock of the initial realization had worn off, I began the process of analysis. The tank had a drain plug on the bottom.

"It would seem that we could open the plug on the bottom and drain the contents into a bucket." One was nearby.

Another uncertainty remained. "What about residual water in the system?" the professor asked.

"That would depend on what is heavier, water or diesel." My thinking was that if water was heavier, it would have gone to the lowest point, hence toward the motor intake . . . an area not drainable by the tank plug.

I wondered aloud, "If we refill the tank with diesel and just run it, will it work through the water?" Neither of us knew. We were both reluctant to take further chances in the absence of more information or expertise. No doubt recalling the adage that a physician should first do no harm, the professor felt we should let things alone. He was, I felt, gently trying to "will" me away from the generator.

We were able to conduct a simple experiment to see whether water was heavier than diesel. Pouring some water into a glass containing some diesel fuel, we discovered it sank to the bottom. My spirits went down as well.

With this suspicion confirmed, we decided to let the tank dry out and then refill it with diesel the following day. The vacuum furnace–like parching heat of Baghdad would in this case prove beneficial. It seemed that as long as the tank was left open, it would quickly become bone dry. I hated the delay before seeing if it would work. The Iraqi was less concerned about the slippage of time. He had quickly accepted the turn of fate that put water into his very valuable generator, rendering it useless. He laughed and said the next day would bring better results.

That evening, I found the logistics guy. I explained the experience with the generator and the water. "Why," he asked himself, "would they keep water strapped to the back of the HMMVs? Especially in jerry cans?" Water was found in plastic bottles everywhere. It was completely unexpected to find water in something other than clear plastic bottles. He was obviously dismayed as well. He promised to get me new jerry cans and personally fill them with diesel. "There was a whole tanker truck with diesel in the lot out back. I will fill three jerry cans first thing in the morning."

I thought ahead to what else might be needed. I scavenged around a workshop area and borrowed the funnel, hose, rags, and anything else that might be necessary for the next day's operation. I wanted to be as prepared as possible for a smooth restart of the generator.

The next day arrived, and I drove through the Baghdad streets to the house of the professor. I backed my LandCruiser into his drive, hesitantly, as always. Despite the previous day's fiasco, he greeted me with his usual quiet warmth. I lifted the jerry cans from the back of the truck and experienced a sudden doubt that maybe he would not want to try putting this fuel into the generator. Maybe I was being presumptuous. As I was setting the cans on the ground near the generator, his driver, Mohammed, appeared.

Mohammed was a very thin Iraqi about twenty-seven years old. He was fortunate to work for the professor. The job was simple; he had the use of the vehicle for his own purposes, and the pay was sufficient by Baghdad standards. As things turned out, Mohammed was quite experienced with petroleum products. His nose for fumes might be compared to that of some French sommelier sorting Bordeaux wines. Likewise, he had a practiced eye for color and clarity. Mohammed also had some knowledge about motors. It seemed that it was not an accident that Mohammed was present.

With the added supervision, I proceeded to insert the funnel into the opening of the fuel tank. We had all concluded that the water would have evaporated in the past twenty-four hours of withering heat. The professor said he had explained the predicament to someone who was very knowledgeable about generators. I lifted the can of diesel as my friend held the funnel and Mohammed looked on from a step further back. I began to pour. Not more than a cup or two had flowed from the five-gallon can when Mohammed said something in Arabic and the professor snapped, "Wait!"

I stopped suddenly.

"Are you certain this is diesel?" he asked.

"Yes . . . I think. I explained the problem to a guy in logistics, and he said he would fill the cans himself with diesel. What else could it be?"

Mohammed stepped forward and looked carefully in the can. He put his nose close to absorb the fumes. He put his finger in, but did not exactly taste it.

"This is not diesel," he declared, and held it to his lips.

I was not about to protest. If it was not diesel, what was it? Something was amiss that I did not understand.

The professor filled the silence by offering, "Well, you know, maybe this is benzene . . . you know, the fuel you use for cooking."

I did not have a clue what the fuel was you used for cooking. To me, there are three ways to cook. One, on an electric stove (takes too long to heat up, a nuisance to clean the burners, and you're hosed if the electricity goes out). Second, you can cook on a gas stove, which uses gas that is a gas, not a liquid. Third, you can microwave. Whatever the professor was referring to, it was not in my databank, nor at the local Safeway in the Washington, D.C., suburbs.

"It looks clearer than diesel, so maybe it is the fuel for airplanes by mistake," Mohammed pondered.

I was defeated and deflated. I proceeded without discussion to open the drain plug at the bottom of the fuel tank and, spilling a substantial amount, drained what I had just poured into the tank. I suggested that Mohammed just put what remained in a separate can of the fluid he knew to be diesel back in the tank and run the generator. Whatever slight impurities were introduced by the variant of petroleum product I brought would be negligible. At least it was better than pouring water in. Now what? I gave the three jerry cans to Mohammed. He could dispose of the contents in some fashion, no doubt to his profit, and fill the cans with the substance he was convinced was diesel.

A few days later, I watched the communications people drive the tanker truck labeled DIESEL to the generator that powered our telephones and computers. They pumped its contents into the generator tank. I seized this moment and a jerry can to fill it exactly with the diesel that fueled the American generator.

The next day, with no expectations of a favorable judgment, I delivered the diesel to the professor. Mohammed was there. He rendered his judgment quickly. "No diesel."

The generator continued to chug when the professor chose to risk attracting neighbors. Mohammed retained the responsibility of standing in line for fuel, his importance amplified by the failure of the American.

The mystery in this endeavor remains. An almost existential question has been posed between Iraqis and Americans: "What is diesel?" Mohammed knows it when he sees it. He also knows it when he smells it. Whatever I brought over to the generator was not the diesel that made the Iraqi generator function.

Was it a language problem? Was fuel refined in Iraq just different from that which we had? Why did I initiate this fiasco to begin with? I should have known that something so simple could easily go wrong. I was fixing what I thought was a problem. The professor did not know he had a problem before I helped. He certainly had a problem after I began my effort to help.

Weeks later, I visited the man who embodied all that is good about Iraq at the home of his sister. It was a pleasant, if worn-down, residence in the Khadra section of Baghdad. A family of four or five would have been comfortable there. At the time of my visit, four generations were present, and the numbers, while varying, seemed to average around eleven.

We sat on some old folding chairs in a garden that was well tended by the husband of his sister. It was evening at the end of a very hot Baghdad day. A niece brought out some Turkish coffees and glasses of water to drink. With the darkening day, my eyes were relaxing from the strain of bright sun during the day. The greens of the garden were pleasant.

The conversation we had was light, touching on only simple subjects with long periods of comfortable silence. It was a way of allowing the tension of a summer day in Baghdad to subside. The normal activities of driving around Baghdad, trying to contact people, trying to arrange meetings, trying to purchase simple things, inevitably involved many unanticipated frustrations. Working through an average Baghdad day was like receiving a couple dozen splinters. Sitting in this yard was healing.

I noticed that an area adjacent to the flower bed had been poured with concrete during the day and was drying. It formed a four-by-five-foot flat, square surface.

Since the end of the war, the professor had endured more hardships than during the war. His work was virtually finished. The building where he worked was looted. The staff was afraid to come to work. Colleagues had had their cars stolen, one within plain sight of the building and a U.S. military patrol.

In early June, the wife of his cousin came to him one evening very distraught. Her husband had been missing for a day, and she and her brother, while looking for him, had found his car but not him. They spoke to the Americans, but no one could help. The man who embodied all that is good about Iraq then did what was usual in Baghdad: He went to the hospitals and then to the Baghdad Post-Mortem Center. No results. Two days later, they learned that the cousin's body and a few others were found in Yussifiya, south of Baghdad. He had been shot in the back by an automatic weapon.

"He was a very pleasant and amiable man. He was gentle," the professor said later. He did not even bother to ask how this could happen. Such things had become quite normal in a country with total freedom—freedom from consequences for any actions.

Three weeks later, the home of the professor was robbed. The door was broken open with a crowbar after padlocks were cut with bolt cutters. Inside, interior doors were kicked in. Clothes were cast about everywhere. Televisions, computers, jewelry, clothing, appliances, and the like were all missing. Sentimental items were taken or broken. A large amount of cash was taken. Since banks have been looted, Baghdad citizens must keep cash at home. Thieves knew this.

The professor felt responsible to his wife and daughter for the loss. They were in Amman and had left things in his charge. Before the war, he had enjoyed some control and influence over his environment. There was no chance of recovering the stolen items. His daughter had asked him to take her jewelry to the home of his sister, her aunt, where she felt it would be safer. He had not yet done that, and now it was too late. He felt guilty for having been robbed.

I looked at the drying cement and suddenly knew what it meant.

I got up to leave, since it was getting quite dark and driving across Baghdad with no lights was quite risky. Many cars in Baghdad had no lights but still coursed the roads in the blacked-out nights. Car thefts, though prevalent in daytime, were even more so at night. And there was the ever-present risk of being stopped by American patrols. Many of their friends had been victimized, and there were no police to take a report, much less respond. This was after Iraq had been liberated. This was freedom.

The professor's wife and daughter had concluded they could not return and could no longer just wait with their lives on hold in Amman. They had recently obtained visas to the United Kingdom and had decided to go there. On the day that I watched the cement hardening, they had flown to London.

I was reluctant to depart. This man had become my friend. So we stood next to the new concrete, and I said what he had been waiting for me to say. "This is for the generator?"

"Well, yes."

"So you have decided to leave?"

"Yes. I have been offered a position outside Iraq."

I looked at the dark gray slab and bent over to pick up a stick. It was a sarcophagus for his hopes for Iraq. I inscribed my name and date as though on an empty gray canvas.

He said, "Oh, that is good."

The professor had been offered a comfortable situation in one of the booming Emirates. He would have all the resources he desired. It would be a clean and orderly environment. The man who embodied all that is good in Iraq decided to leave Iraq. He may return, but not soon. He planned to have someone guard his house. It was eventually taken over by insurgents, after being broken into and searched by U.S. forces.

The generator would be of no use there and would probably only be stolen, so he had promised it to his sister. It would easily supply her house and the three neighbors who had already strung electrical lines to his sister's home to share her wealth. He needed to give it to them. Those with whom he had been living could not leave. They did not have travel documents. They did not have a country that wished to accept them. Certainly, they could not go to the United States. The United States still has particularly tough standards for Iraqis—even visitor visas. Iraq, though occupied, was still treated like an enemy and terrorist state. I had once made the mistake of mentioning to the professor that a colleague had arranged to take home one of the puppies that was living at the airport base. He observed without animus, "So, America will accept dogs, but not Iraqis."

Years later, this same gentleman was invited to the United States to visit. He obtained the appropriate American visa and flew to Kennedy Airport in New York. Immigration officials spotting his Iraqi passport instructed him to go to an office, where he waited while two officers discussed their lunch. Then they questioned him at length about his occupation, his family, and his intentions for his visit, with the clear implication that they were debating refusing to allow him entry. The professor told me later that it was just like being in an Iraqi police office under Saddam.

The professor would still support his family financially as best he could. He would stay in contact. But he would not be there to try to solve their problems. They would hope for his return. He would keep his house and keep the thought that he would one day return. But no one knew if he ever would. In Baghdad, no one ever knew if one would return from even the shortest journey.

So the concrete would harden. In ten days or so, the Iraqi workman would move the generator. Hopefully it would not be stolen en route. It would cover the gray concrete canvas with my American signature.

CHAPTER 16

Governing in the New Iraq

Ambassador L. Paul Bremer III arrived in Baghdad on May 12, 2003, with two draft edicts that he, as the president's designated envoy and with the president's full authority, would issue within days of his arrival in Iraq. In magnitude, they were on a par with the decision to base the action to remove Saddam upon the UN resolutions addressing WMD. These two immediate postoccupation decisions doomed prospects for a controlled post-Saddam transition. They were based on avoidable ignorance.

On May 16, a week after Bremer arrived, he signed Coalition Provisional Authority Order Number 1, which was designed to extinguish the Baath Party and Baathists from Iraqi government and society. Somehow, in the previous two weeks of background briefings on Iraq, Bremer had been persuaded that Baathists were equivalent to Nazis in Germany.[1] Just before he had departed Washington, Bremer had been given a draft of the de-Baathification order by Doug Feith in the OSD.[2]

Excising Baathists hollowed out the entire Iraqi civil service and professional control over the ministries. The intent of the OSD had been to open all key ministerial positions to people blessed by Chalabi and the other external opposition groups vying for power.

No one who spent any time listening to Iraqis in Iraq would have concluded that this would create anything other than chaos. Of course, the Baath Party was the mechanism of control used by Saddam. Bureaucrats and technocrats had great pressure to join, at least in name, if they were to hold responsible positions. This was more akin to the Soviet Communists than the Nazis. The public comparisons with Nazi Germany were especially provocative in Iraq because it was seen as a line of argument that derived from Israel, a conspiracy theory that easily and destructively abounded in Iraq.

I was dumbstruck when I heard about the edicts. I had spent much of the previous year grooming contacts in Iraq who believed the United States would excise the senior leadership and not destroy the entire system of government. The most talented Iraqis were often, by necessity, members of the Baath Party. They knew how the ministries worked. They were waiting for the direction to go back to work and resume business under temporary U.S. direction. They had assumed, as had I, that the governing thesis was that rot came from the head of the regime. I had convinced many good Iraqis to bet on the United States. Now they were confronted with a monumentally wrong decision. They had been cheated and could not understand how the United States could make such a decision except to empower the external opposition leaders.

One year later, in April 2004, when the White House was belatedly considering slightly revising its de-Baathification policy, Ahmad Chalabi declared that this was akin to putting Nazis back in charge of Germany.[3] He said it would endanger any new government and cause it to fall. In the temporary Iraqi Governing Council, Chalabi had also chaired a committee charged with keeping Baathists out of government. In essence, he had to clear potential government appointees.

Therein lay the only explanation that most Iraqis I met could see to explain the Bremer declaration. Without destroying the existing government structure, there was no lever of power for Chalabi to grasp, since he had no existing support inside Iraq.

But its effect was greater than a simple blocking action to create room for Chalabi or anyone else. Excising Baathists, particularly in a way that impugned their dignity, made enemies of the secular part of the Iraqi government, upon which the normal functioning government depended. Each Baathist had an extended family. When the person lost income, the effect was compounded. Iraqi officials pleaded with me, "Why on earth would you do that? Why would you insult and make enemies of the professionals who can run the ministries? Why could you not just remove the bad apples one by one? Instead, you leave no ambiguity. You declare to their faces that they are your enemy? This is not what your president said he was going to do! He said his quarrel was not with the Iraqi people but with Saddam and his immediate group."

Then the mistake was compounded by a second blunder, in effect a coup de grâce to any hopes for an organized transition in Iraq. Bremer signed the second edict of the CPA, disbanding the army. He later said the Iraqi Army had already melted away. This was not an accurate assessment. The army had largely melted away per the assumed direction of the United States. They took off their uniforms and went home. But they all would have returned to their units if the word had been put out.

This decision brought even greater disbelief among Iraqis. There were many youths in Iraq without jobs. The army was a mechanism to keep them busy, with jobs and with dignity. The army members also supported their families, so the effects were multiplied across the number of family members. In a country where employment is going to be scarce, to tell everyone with a weapon that he is not on your team is idiotic. It created another few million enemies.

With these two decisions, the United States had committed irreversible damage. Bremer was doing what he thought was right, on the basis of four weeks of experience. But his ignorance and that of those who pushed him to that action for whatever reason were colossal mistakes that would deny the United States the potential of a major success. The president's decision and his guidance about removing just Saddam and his top people were subverted, and Iraq was doomed to years of turmoil and chaos.

Although I spent most of my time meeting with former regime members to understand what was going on politically, I also met occasionally with the team searching for WMD scientists and material. There was great excitement when trailers loosely fitting the description of mobile biological-weapons production units (described by Powell at the UN) were discovered. They were brought to the BIAP area. I was asked some questions about my UNSCOM experience, but

I steered them to some of my former colleagues who had deep knowledge in biological weapons. NBC had gotten on to the story and sent David Kay as a consultant to examine them. For the cameras, he confidently concluded that the trailers were, in all probability, for biological-weapons production. This turned out to be wrong, but the trailers would require close examination before anyone could conclude they were not what everyone expected them to be.

Among the WMD experts, there was a big difference between those who read about stuff and wrote reports and those who had actually made things, like biological weapons. Both sorts of experts have value, but someone who had made anthrax would look at the trailers and see things with a very different eye. He or she would see what was *not* there as well as what was there. An analyst would tend to see only what was there.

These trailers were a classic case. An analyst might examine the piping and imagine how a fermentation process could take place, given the layout of the piping and tanks. Someone who had hands-on experience might notice that the only drain hole on the tank thought to be used for fermentation was on the side, not the bottom. This would make it almost impossible to clean the tank after a fermentation run. Cleaning a tank before another batch was essential. Also, someone with practical experience might notice that the fluorescent lamps inside the trailer were of a special type. They were expensive units, specially configured to eliminate any possibility of an electrical spark. This would be essential for safety in a hydrogen environment (remember the hydrogen-filled zeppelin *Hindenburg*), but unnecessary in a fermentation unit. The Iraqis did indeed state that the trailers were for filling hydrogen weather balloons.

On another occasion, toward the end of May, one of the CIA WMD nonproliferation guys I had worked with when I was at UNSCOM came up to me.

"Guess who I am meeting with?" he asked.

This guy was usually pretty serious, so I said, "Saddam Hussein."

He looked disappointed. "No. Obeidi." He had me.

"The centrifuge guy?" I asked.

"Yup."

Mahdi Obeidi was a respected nuclear scientist, not a regime hack. He directed much of the centrifuge enrichment program. The IAEA and UNSCOM inspectors had met with him extensively. He was one of the top three nuclear scientists in Iraq. Unfortunately, a second key nuclear scientist had been killed. Khalid Ibrahim Said, who had been in charge of weaponization (i.e., designing how the implosion device would work), was killed by U.S. soldiers in early April as he was driving toward a checkpoint. I do not know the exact circumstances, but it was easy to imagine. The young kids who manned security checkpoints could be jumpy and decide to "light-up" any approaching vehicle that they may have signaled to stop. I was glad Obeidi was alive.

"That's great. What's he saying?"

My friend said, "Well, he's scared. The DIA [Defense Intelligence Agency] grabbed him and took him to the INC, and he thought they were going to lock him up. I think I have that sorted out."

He was containing a half-grin. There was more to the story.

"He has documents."

"Really!" The UN inspectors—UNSCOM and IAEA as well as Hans Blix's group, UNMOVIC—had been pressing Iraq for documents constantly. We had been convinced that documents remained, but we could not prove it.

He continued, "And he has some centrifuge parts."

"That's great! You now have something tangible . . . probably the only thing tangible . . . and someone who will be credible."

He said Obeidi was really frightened and wanted to get out of the country. That is always a big issue. Contrary to what one might think, offering to bring someone to the United States is very difficult. The bureaucracy of the immigration part of government makes this extremely difficult, and there are concerns over the cost.

"Well, maybe you can just get him out of Iraq," I said.

"I am working on it, but it is tough. He doesn't want to talk without some commitment."

I wouldn't, either. I said, "Look, it's not my issue, I know, but I can express a view to the NSC for whatever that is worth." Later that day, I called Will Tobey at NSC. I had spoken to him on occasion using

my Thuraya satellite phone late at night, Baghdad time, as I wandered around the tarmac and watched the stars. The black night
closed in and was pleasant if you walked away from the lights of the
building. It was also pleasant to get away from the incessant racket of
the generators.

I was lucky to catch Tobey at his office. I could not say a lot on an
open line, but after he asked the usual "How's it going?" I said, "The
guys here have someone who has documents and materials, but needs
help. If you ask around, you will know who. Will, it's not my business,
but my gratuitous advice would be to get this guy out and declare success. This is probably as good as it will get on the WMD front."

I said this largely on the basis of one event. Dr. Amer al-Saadi, the
presidential advisor who had been responsible for organizing the production of the 12,000 page Iraqi WMD declaration for Hans Blix the
previous December, had turned himself in to coalition forces when he
learned he was on the list of "high value targets." He had done this
quite publicly. Just before presenting himself to U.S. forces, he spoke
with German television and said that the world would see that Iraq
had eliminated its WMD.

I knew him very well. He had been a top level technocrat for
decades and worked extensively with the UN and IAEA inspectors.
This action made me doubt whether there would be anything to find.
Saadi was a very smart and shrewd. He would not have said this if he
was concerned that there were substantial WMD programs of which
he had no knowledge. He was going to jail. Why would he publicly
make a false claim once the United States had occupied Iraq? I had
the strong view that we would learn the most about the Iraqi WMD
from people, not by searching sites or even examining documents.
Hence, with Obeidi's materials, there was at least a tangible reminder
that Iraq had the intellectual capacity to recreate its nuclear program
and that this was a very real threat under Saddam.

It took time, but my colleagues eventually got Obeidi safely out of
Iraq. He knew a great deal about Iraq's former nuclear-weapons program but saw no evidence that it was being sustained.

❖

I met on Saturday, May 17, and again, several days later, with a former senior officer in the Iraqi Directorate of General Security (DGS), the organization responsible for security within Iraq. The man was a thoughtful colonel who made a well-organized presentation on how the DGS worked and, by implication, how Saddam controlled the country. I wish I could have brought the guy back to the United States and put him in the MIT Political Science Department.

Before the war, the DGS was run by Major General Rafi Abdul Latif Tilfah. There were many directorates involved in all sorts of monitoring, including the bugging of what seemed like everything. The Political Directorate was run by Major General Shakir al-Duri. Under him were departments that focused on the assorted vectors or divisions that made up Iraqi society. There were offices for the various geographic regions, political parties, religious sections, and sectarian elements like clubs and universities. The colonel described in detail how each of these parts in Iraqi society was monitored. There was no meter that measured satisfaction or threat levels, but through a complicated and deeply entrenched system, the central government could address emerging problems.

The system recognized that Iraqis had multiple identities or affiliations. In the first instance, surprisingly to some Americans, there was a strong national identity under the Saddam regime. Iraqis thought of themselves as Iraqis. Saddam promoted this with some success. Only secondarily did they tend to have other affiliations, and those were not simply the three the United States assumed, Shia, Sunni, or Kurd. There were other identities, such as clan and local village identities. The colonel stressed that under Saddam, there was an almost instinctive balancing that went on to satisfy Iraqis. For example, an individual may feel disadvantaged because he is a Shia, but may accrue prestige by virtue of membership in a proud tribe. The individual or clan may get benefits from the central government, or benefits may flow to a region.

Of course, in back of this was fear. The colonel emphasized that the Iraqi population had to believe that the central government would know what was going on everywhere and that it would exercise great punishment (or reward) based on that knowledge. The regime did exercise this power, and the people of Iraq behaved with carefully nurtured fear.

The colonel's analysis pointed out that Saddam was the force that kept Iraq together. Then the colonel made a comment that stayed with me thereafter: To rule Iraq, you must become Saddam. Some other force had to replace Saddam, and the colonel thought the United States did not understand that fact. He asked, "Why does the U.S. think Chalabi can rule Iraq? He has no power among Iraqis. If he tried to, he would be killed. The DGS and Mukhabarat also followed Iranian activities very closely. It was the highest priority and threat. We had agents here and in Iran. The Badr Corps that Hakim brought into Iraq was one of our major targets, especially after you UNSCOM people left. The U.S. must have the Mukhabarat files. They had extensive information on the links between Hakim, Chalabi, and Iran."

(The Badr Corps was the militia connected to the Supreme Council for Islamic Revolution in Iraq—SCIRI—which was based in Iran during the Saddam years. Its leader was Ayatollah Mohammed Baqr al-Hakim, who was assassinated in a car bombing in Najaf three months later. This group was strongly supported by the clerics in Iran.

I knew no one in Bremer's office who had any real sense about how to rule Iraq. They sure were not going to be able to apply the sometimes nuanced and sometimes brutal judgments about Iraqi society that the colonel was describing.

Between my first meeting and the second a week later, the two disastrous coalition edicts became publicly known. The colonel was perplexed: "You must be very committed to placing these outside people in power, because these steps will cause all the Iraqis who lay down their arms during the invasion to now pick them up. This was not what they thought the U.S. was going to do. Your president said Saddam had to leave. Now you have fooled us. After he is gone, you say the rest of Iraq is your enemy as well. Forgive me for being so blunt; you have been very kind to me and I wish I could help you avoid mistakes. But when you say one thing and then do another to put a puppet in power, we Iraqis will not accept this."

He was correct. We had said one thing and then, once in Iraq, done something completely different. The Iraqi Army had not fought as it could have. The U.S. invasion went easily because the Iraqi institutions thought they would be better off with new leadership. They did not imagine that the United States would declare the Iraqi Army its enemy and try to install someone from outside.

One of the last things this thoughtful colonel said was a dire prediction: "Mister Bremer has created an insurgency. There are many small groups and gangs and criminals. Now they will come together. Now they can have a principle to fight for." The colonel was baffled. The mighty United States must have some clever strategy, but he could not see it.

On a Saturday morning, May 24, and again on the following Monday morning, May 26, I had similar long discussions with a couple of senior retired officials, one from the police and the other from the DGS. Both had Ph.D.s, and both had been members of the Baath Party. The DGS official was well into his sixties and spoke slowly and carefully. He had been arrested under Saddam and sentenced to death, though later released.

The police official was about ten years younger and quite proud of his international credentials for law enforcement studies. He had written a book on law enforcement.

They described the long relationship between the opponents of Saddam and Iran, including the relations with the Iranian Embassy in Baghdad. They pointed to Iraqi Shia who were disaffected by the Saddam regime. But, they said, the problems would come from the organized groups that had fled to Iran. Key among these was the Badr Corps militia.

The two former officials also correctly predicted the rise of Moqtada al-Sadr. One of my interlocutors, a friend of an uncle of Moqtada, noted that Moqtada derived much of his power from an ayatollah in Iran. This cleric had the authority to issue *fatwas*—decrees with religious authority. Sadr used this connection to obtain legitimization for his youthful supporters' actions, including killings. Some of Sadr's supporters were believed to be responsible for the April stabbing death of a respected Shia cleric, Sayyid Abdul Majid al-Khoei, who was returning to Najaf from exile in London. Moqtada could have prevented the killing, even if he did not order it. Sadr's supporters had also distributed leaflets demanding the closure of liquor stores and insisting that all women must follow Islamic tradition and clothing. They were trying to enforce strict Islamic traditions at the universities, where leaflets were also distributed warning women about their presence at university. There were leaflets directing the killing of prostitutes. Moqtada, the retired officials emphasized, was dangerous. He was "unstable, like Uday." Moqtada had inherited his fame from his father, who was a respected Shia ayatollah killed by the regime in 1999, and his great uncle, Mohammad Bakr al-Sadr, a founder of the Shia Dawa Party who was killed in April 1980 by Saddam.

The former DGS official said his former colleagues were being solicited by Chalabi. They were being paid for their information about the other groups, like al-Hakim's SCIRI. Chalabi, they claimed, was then providing edited versions of this information to the United States and Bremer. This information was used for raids by the U.S. military. He also said that sometimes, former DGS colleagues had declined to help Chalabi's people. These colleagues then had their homes raided by the U.S. military and were put in Abu Ghraib prison. Either the United States was consciously helping Chalabi root out competitors, or the United States was exceptionally ignorant. He also said that Chalabi was offering protection from American raids.

The veracity of his claims was difficult to establish, but they represented views widely held among Iraqis. The DIA was handed the responsibility for managing the U.S. relationship with the INC via the Intelligence Collection Program. It was not a program initiated by the intelligence community but one mandated by the OSD.[4] When President Bush, in challenging the continuing relationship with Chalabi, asked if the CIA had received any useful information from the INC, George Tenet said he was unaware of any. The OSD representative at the meeting said he would have to get back to the president. Subsequently, the OSD claimed that the military received tactically useful information.

My two interviewees also knew many of the individuals who were leaders of the Badr group and said that this group, founded largely by

Shia exiled by Saddam, had undergone long training and indoctrination by Iran. Many had married Iranian women. They had been well trained in Iran in military and insurgency tactics. For years they had been trying to infiltrate and conduct sabotage against the Saddam regime. Now they would use those same tactics to obtain power.

The man who had been jailed by Saddam said, "The *U.S.* must appoint Iraqi leaders. And the U.S. must stay in Iraq. There cannot be elections now. The Iranian-supported groups are much too powerful and would take over in an election because they have organization, money, a militia, and the ability to coerce their will in Baghdad. How can voting work in these circumstances?"

The two men presented the case against de-Baathification in an organized list:

1. The United States must have been persuaded to do this [de-Baathification] by the external opposition groups, who are small and trivial in numbers. Only by completely eliminating the existing structure and forcing themselves into new jobs could they achieve power.
2. De-Baathification denies millions of people of their rights. The workers lose their positions, whether they are competent or not and whether they did anything wrong or not.
3. Some external opposition groups wanted the Baath Party eliminated because it was secular.
4. De-Baathification undermines the lives and dignity of many millions of people. Each family has roughly five members, so if one million Baathists are removed, it means you have punished five million secular Iraqis.
5. The Baath Party has been around Iraq for thirty-five years. Most professionals and technocrats are members. This does not mean they supported Saddam. Most, maybe 95 percent of them, hated Saddam.
6. It is obvious that the Baath Party did not fight the Americans. Why treat them the same as Saddam? Before the war, the United States said only Saddam and his top staff were guilty. Why has the United States changed?

7. Why does the United States want to radicalize the secular middle of the country? These people will not just go away.
8. De-Baathification will only help the religious extremists. They are fragmented now, but they will coalesce.
9. Before this order, many Iraqi professionals wanted to help. Now they will stay home. They have lost dignity and pensions. What do they tell their families? They are not guilty. De-Baathification would make the United States hated by many Iraqis.[5]

The two men were sorrowful in stating their complaints. They had wanted to be part of a new government and a new Iraq. Now they were blocked from that.

Of course, some would say that by their presence in the government of Saddam, the Baathists had supported Saddam. I heard this complaint more from those who had not been in Iraq than from those who went through the Saddam regime in Iraq. And, one could reasonably ask, why was the leader of the KDP, Massoud Barzani, welcomed into the new government when he had established such business connections with the previous regime? He had enlisted the support of Saddam when he was fighting the PUK and Jalal Talabani in 1996. Talabani had drawn on assistance from the Iranian Revolutionary Guard forces to fight the KDP. Barzani drew on the regime to offset this—the regime that had gassed thousands of Kurds in the 1980s. Both the PUK and the KDP enjoyed the income of the regime oil exported through Kurdistan. Iraq was a land of shifting alliances. Washington and particularly the OSD did not seem to appreciate this fact.

The groups vying for power were viewed as crooks, thieves, religious zealots, or surrogates for Iran by most of the secular middle class I met. Iraqis saw that the parties brought in by the U.S. invasion were using every possible means of leverage to get and hold power. These perspectives did not fit the predisposition of the OSD, which had chaired a couple of meetings in the early months of 2002. The CIA Iraqi Operations Group representative made a case for a bottom-up approach to the postwar world, recommending working through tribal leaders, who were the underpinnings of Iraqi society. The OSD argued that a top-down approach was the way to go. It argued that replacing the government at the top with Chalabi would force down a modern democratic government. Rumsfeld expressed the view that the tribal system was outdated and should not be perpetuated. The CIA was not invited to any more OSD meetings.

With the two CPA orders in May, the insurgency, which the Bush administration banned from its lexicon until the following year, became inevitable. Bremer has explained that these orders were not his ideas alone. The impetus for the de-Baathification order was clearly in the OSD, and the dissolution of the army, he notes, was not opposed by anyone he asked.

In an opinion piece for the *New York Times*, Bremer explained the chain of responsibility for the de-Baathification order: "On May 8, 2003, Secretary of Defense Donald Rumsfeld gave me a memo titled 'Principles for Iraq—Policy Guidelines' that specified that the coalition 'will actively oppose Saddam Hussein's old enforcers—the Baath Party, Fedayeen Saddam, etc.' and that 'we will make clear that the coalition will eliminate the remnants of Saddam's Regime.'"[6]

This explicit guidance from the OSD was based on profound ignorance of the situation in Iraq. By the end of May, the United States had committed itself to a path that guaranteed a long and bloody transition.

As spring turned into summer, I came to know many people and parts of Baghdad. I had a favorite restaurant called Finjans, which was not far from the Karada section, and dined there occasionally. In the past, it had been popular with the Mukhabarat. I also arranged some out-of-Green-Zone experiences for friends who would otherwise never go out of the CPA building in the Green Zone. Ambassador Robin Raphel had expressed an interest in seeing some of the art in Baghdad. I asked my friend Professor Shakir if he would mind joining us for an afternoon excursion. We had lunch at his home in Jihad and then visited the home and studio of artist Suded Khalil in a southeastern Baghdad section called al Ma Ri'fah. We finished with a stop at some galleries on Abu Nawas Street, which passes behind some of the major hotels, like the Palestine and the Tigris. In the 1990s, this was a pleasant area to dine and overlook the river.

At another time, I brought a couple of senior State Department people to lunch with Samir, a highly trained lawyer who knew the history of Iraq's law from the British period. Since the CPA was beginning to consider a process for creating a new constitution, the contact seemed potentially useful. Samir was making plans to establish a law firm with a partner in Baghdad. He judged that there would be a need for legal services, especially with the arrival of new foreign firms.

Another acquaintance, a former Mukhabarat officer named Khalil, said he was anxious to help the United States, but he had been offered employment by the INC for three hundred dollars a month. Khalil said he had spoken to the INC, but did not want to work for it. He said it had looted the Mukhabarat files with particular attention to the Jordanian section. He claimed this was to protect Chalabi, who had been convicted of embezzlement in Jordan after a bank he ran, Petra Bank, had failed.[7] According to the Mukhabarat officer, Chalabi wanted incriminating information about the Mukhabarat activities with the Jordanians so that he would have leverage with the Jordanian government.

Then Khalil mentioned a story that really made him angry. Just after Saddam fell, Khalil had purchased a gold Rolls Royce that used to belong to Uday. My acquaintance had bought it from a guy who lived near a farm Uday owned south of Baghdad along the Tigris. Khalil had it put on a trailer and brought it back to Baghdad. As the trailer was passing through Baghdad, some INC militia seized it and took it to INC headquarters at the Hunt Club in the Mansour section of the city. They apparently figured they could use it.

Khalil went to the Hunt Club with a friend and found Tamara Chalabi, Ahmed's daughter, who had recently graduated from Harvard. He told her that they had his Rolls Royce in the compound. According to my acquaintance, Tamara replied that she would agree to raise the matter with her father if Khalil paid her ten thousand dollars. Khalil was struck by the injustice. Whether all this was accurate or not, in postinvasion Baghdad, it was entirely possible. It certainly showed how some Iraqis would work whatever angles they could.

By late June, WMD information was also turning into a marketable item. There were many reports of WMD, especially as word got around that the United States might pay rewards for such information. I steered clear of this for the most part, since scamming was becoming a minor industry. But one of my colleagues had a Kurdish contact whom she knew pretty well and who had a pretty convincing WMD tale, or so she thought. She was sharp and experienced, so we drove to one of the villas that the Kurds were occupying to meet with her contact. He had been in touch with the United States in Kurdistan from before the war. He grandly called himself the "drunken master." I was prepared to believe half of that description straight away. We listened to him at length as he went on about the Iraqi nuclear program and its staff. He knew a lot about the previous program, but everything he said had been published in UN reports.

His punch line was that he knew where there was some VX agent. It was in an ampoule thirty centimeters tall and hidden in a Baath Party member's house.

"What color is it?" I asked.

The question made him pause. At least he did not say it was green. He said it was dark and he could not see the color.

I had the distinct feeling this guy had been selling information for a long time. I shook my head and dared him: "If you bring it here, I will drink it."

Lucky for me that was as far as this caper went. While I was certain there was not VX involved, there were plenty of other liquids that would not have been good to ingest.

One of the improvements that had been made to the Special VIP building was the creation of a bar. This did not take long, since there was a small, detached building and some of our crew built the necessary shelves and counters. Decorations came from the assorted palaces and other sites that were raided. The walls were adorned with a small arsenal of RPG launchers, gold-and silver-plated AK-47s, and assorted other trophies. A roulette wheel appeared from somewhere. Beer and liquor were readily available in Baghdad. It could be purchased, but there was also a large stock of Johnnie Walker Blue Label found in Uday's villa. The bar was dubbed the HVT (high-value target) Bar, since in that period, most patrons spent their time finding senior Iraqis. Because the military lived under a complete restriction against the consumption of alcohol in theater, the HVT Bar attracted some interlopers.

Taking advantage of the looser civilian rules, the intelligence office chief held a couple of barbeques, for which some steaks were flown in from Amman. At one of these events in early June, Bremer showed up and I had the opportunity to speak with him. I had known him in the 1980s, when he ran the State Department's counterterrorism office. When he asked me what I was doing, I said simply that I spent all my time out around Baghdad.

He asked, "So how are things going?"

I replied, "You won't like the answer."

Bremer said, "Tell me."

"It's not going well. I meet with Iraqis every day, and they don't understand why we bring in these outside groups. They think we have made fatal mistakes in firing the Baathists and the army."

Bremer responded confidently, "Well, you aren't talking to the Shia. They are the majority, and that's what counts."

That was the extent of the conversation, and I am sure it left no impression on Bremer whatsoever. But I remember how simple Bremer's calculation seemed to be: The Shia are the majority and have been repressed by the minority Sunni regime. We will fix that.

By the end of May, Kyle and I were writing up notes based on my conversations with former intelligence officials, the police, the educated professional elite, and others from a variety of neighborhoods. There were increasing reports of people gathering and hiding weapons. The incidents of crime were growing. Soon there would be an intersection of crime and attacks against the United States.

In another long afternoon meeting with a former retired police chief, he pleaded for the reconstitution of some of the Iraqi Special Police (akin to undercover cops in a large U.S. city—but with more latitude to use force). He recalled that a few months prior to the war, Saddam had released tens of thousands of known criminals, many from Fallujah and other hotbeds, from Abu Ghraib prison. The Special Police would know these criminals by sight and could pick them up. If nothing were done, the released prisoners would form gangs—many already had—and wreak havoc.

Those who set U.S. policy in the CPA were strictly opposed to any reconstitution of law enforcement groups, since the police were deemed instruments of the past regime. The U.S. military would not and could not enforce civil laws. They were not trained for it. As a result, outrageous crimes often could be committed right in front of U.S. troops, who were powerless to stop them.

Criminals had the freedom to do as they wished. Virtually every Iraqi I met with wanted to obtain a permit to keep a weapon to protect their property. They were afraid to be stopped by a U.S. military checkpoint and found with a weapon; they could be put in Abu Ghraib prison. On the other hand, they wanted to be able to defend their cars and homes. These were the dilemmas we imposed on the average Iraqi.

It was easy to make a long list of the security and political calamities that were pointing inexorably to an insurgency. I wrote up a draft report with such a list and said there would be, for all practical purposes, an insurgency by July 4. I spoke to the intelligence office chief about it. He said he understood and agreed, but added, "There's no way I can send something like that to Washington. OSD would kill me."

He was right. The word *insurgency* was still banned. A couple months later, in August, his successor sent to Washington a report known as an *aardwolf*. An aardwolf is a personal assessment that the intelligence office chief bases on his experience in country. In the aardwolf message, he used the word *insurgency*. This message was circulated among some officials in Washington, and the point on insurgency leaked. President Bush was very upset, believing that the CIA was purposely undermining his policy and had purposely leaked the message. The interagency suspicions were not getting any better. The OSD's complete distrust of the CIA became even more pointed. This poisonous atmosphere undermined any cohesive action. The CIA was still being blamed for the failure to find any WMD. In fact, we were about to discover that the prevalence of conventionally destructive weapons was a much more serious problem than the phantom WMD.

One Sunday, I drove north out of Baghdad through Taji up to Samarra. I had never been to the spiral minaret or the Great Mosque there. Along the road, I found abandoned, destroyed tanks still full of ammunition. I spotted several abandoned FROG (Free Rocket Over Ground) rockets on their mobile launchers in a grove of date palms. These are thirty-foot-long unguided rockets that can carry a thousand-pound warhead about forty miles. About halfway to Samarra, a large white missile just lay in its cradle not far from the road. It was an Iraqi-produced al-Fat'h ballistic missile. As the temperature in Iraq rose, it was clear to me that if there wasn't an insurgency, it would not be for lack of weapons. If you could find missiles lying around with a range of thirty miles or more, there would be plenty of other weapons and explosives to be picked up.

In early June, I got a message from Nizar Hamdoon in New York asking me to call him. We spoke briefly. He was in bad shape and wanted me to see his family. His house, located near the Yarmouk Hospital just outside the Mansour section of Baghdad, had escaped unscathed from the bombing. Hamdoon's wife, Sahar, was anxious to obtain visas to take their two daughters to visit their father in New York. She had gone through the process of entering the Green Zone and located the appropriate State Department officer. She explained that when her husband left to go to New York for treatment, the former government had confiscated their passports to make sure Hamdoon came back to his family. This was standard for the regime. Now they needed to go to New York because he was near death. The State Department officer said there was nothing she could do. If they had no passport, they could not get a visa (which would be very difficult to obtain, anyway). Sahar pointed out that there was no government to issue a new passport. There was only the U.S. government. The family was distraught. I had heard from other sources just how critical Hamdoon's condition had become. He had been very close to completing a successful chemotherapy course, but just at the end had contracted pneumonia. He had been through a chemically induced coma. When he spoke to me, it was in a very weak, whispery voice.

I called the people I knew at the CPA, but no one who was inclined to help, could. I never heard anyone say it out loud, but the sense I got was Hamdoon was part of the former regime that had caused plenty of suffering. Now he had to suffer in his turn.

Hamdoon died before anyone could solve the visa problem. I attended the funeral for Hamdoon in early July at his home. There were a few Iraqis I knew, but I stood out as the only American. Hamdoon had genuinely wanted to make Iraq better and did his best within the limits of his government to connect Iraq with the United States. He had taken personal risks, but, like many others, did not live to see how these events would play out.

Visitors paying their respects gathered outside the Hamdoon house. The white trailer that had served to help pinpoint Hamdoon's house in the aerial imagery we scanned four months earlier remained in the same position. I spoke briefly with Sahar and the daughters, Lula and Sama.

A few days later, I was visiting with Samir, who had also known Hamdoon. We talked, as usual, about the evolving tragedies in Iraq and what was going on at the Ministry of Foreign Affairs during and after Saddam. There had been substantial changes when Saddam named Naji Sabri to replace Mohammed al-Sahaf as the minister of foreign affairs. In the midst of this discussion, a former Iraqi ambassador whom I knew also happened to stop by to visit Samir. He had been an assistant to Tariq Aziz in the 1990s, and when the war broke out, he was serving overseas. I had spoken to him on the phone from Kuwait, and I knew him to be a solid professional. The ambassador had a son in the Houston area and was a *Star Trek* fan at one point. He had returned to Baghdad to explore the prospects of retaining a position in the new government's Foreign Ministry. I had recommended him to the CPA staff.

He had been told he would have to get an exception from the no-former-Baathist edict. At this point, Bremer had told the CPA staff he would consider making exceptions. However, when I inquired of the people monitoring the Iraqi Foreign Ministry, they said that frankly, the prospects for any exceptions were slim to none. There was too much pressure from the outside groups like SCIRI and the INC to exclude former Baathists. These groups saw jobs as opportunities to place their own loyalists and were not going to accept regime holdovers, no matter what anyone at CPA said. Competence was interesting, but irrelevant. Loyalty was the dominant criterion.

The ambassador asked me for my advice. Should he stay in Baghdad or return overseas and try to make a new life separate from his country and the new government? I knew that Samir was recommending that he come back and make a new start with the new country. The question caught me up. I suddenly had to tally all the things I had been seeing on the streets of Iraq and the dynamics in the CPA and the forces of the Kurds, SCIRI, Dawa, and INC. I was pessimistic: "I know Iraq is your home. I wish I could tell you that I saw a path ahead where Iraq would come together. The institutions have been destroyed, and there arc too many devious groups trying to achieve power. I don't see things getting better. I wish I did. I think things are going to get much worse and the INC and SCIRI and the others will do everything possible to block any former government members from getting jobs. It's not so much about being Baathist. It is just that they want to put their people in positions. You already have what more and more Iraqis desperately want—a visa to another country."

Samir was surprised, I think, at my answer to the ambassador. In fact, *I* was surprised at having verbalized my pessimism. In any case, the ambassador left Iraq to take a series of teaching positions in various other countries. It was difficult, but he and his family were safe.[8]

Samir's optimistic plans for a law firm in Baghdad became another example of lost dreams. Within a couple weeks, he learned that his name was on a death list being circulated by the Dawa Party that had returned to Iraq and was rapidly asserting itself. I had heard of other death lists being circulated by various groups. Some were more serious than others. Samir conducted due diligence on the level of the threat and determined that it was real. It stemmed from his involvement in the Iraq government during the Iran-Iraq War, and in particular the negotiations to end the war, nearly fifteen years earlier. Other people had been murdered already. After much anguish, he and his family decided to pack up their home and leave Baghdad—probably forever. It was the correct decision for him. The area where his home was located was later occupied by insurgents, including some purportedly aligned with al-Qaeda in Iraq.

In October 2003, a U.S. Army team conducted a raid based on intelligence that a senior former regime official was at a house not far from the Mansour neighborhood of Baghdad. As usual, in the middle of the night, soldiers surrounded the home using their night-vision gear, swiftly broke through the door, and swarmed in to secure the site and round up the inhabitants. They found only a terrified woman and two petrified girls. Their interpreter demanded to know where the men were, thinking they were hiding or had escaped. The woman answered in English; there were no men there. The soldiers challenged them, saying they knew Nizar Hamdoon lived there and they wanted to know where he had gone.

The last superpower had raided this home to capture a man who had died in Manhattan four months earlier after enduring six months of chemotherapy at Sloan-Kettering Hospital. The man they targeted had written and forwarded to the CPA a very insightful analysis of how a new government could evolve. Nevertheless, the last superpower sent soldiers to break down the door of his widow's home—the same woman who had pleaded with the State Department representative at CPA to arrange some sort of passport to travel to the United States with her children to see him before he died.

By the middle of July, it was clear that I could do little in Baghdad. The Iraqis whom I identified as potentially useful to lead ministry operations were ignored because of the rigidity of Bremer's two decisions. Additionally, the CIA had formally been shut out of the postwar planning, such as it was, in Washington and so my recommendations carried little weight. The Defense Department still trusted the advice of the largely Shia exile groups rather than anyone who had recent experience of working and living, let alone governing, in Iraq. I could see no role for the class of professional Iraqis I knew.

That which was best about Iraq was destroyed along with the leadership of the regime. Instead, the United States provided an opportunity for various groups to try to seize power and resources in the resulting vacuum. There was nothing I could do that made any sense, so, like many of the secular professional Iraqis I knew, I left.

I had no position to return to in Washington. I took early retirement after twenty-six years in the Civil Service. The Woodrow Wilson Center in Washington offered me a spot as a visiting scholar, and I returned to begin an academic project comparing the disarmament provisions of the Treaty of Versailles with those of the UN toward Iraq. I stayed in contact with my former friends and colleagues involved in Iraq. It was difficult to watch the ongoing series of blunders and tragedies. The United States continued to dig a huge hole for itself, and no one seemed to have any idea how to climb out or even the wit to suggest that it stop digging.

CHAPTER 17

Iraq Survey Group

I had been back from Iraq for barely four months when I received a call from John McLaughlin, the Deputy Director for Central Intelligence—George Tenet's number two. I knew McLaughlin by reputation as a superb analyst and manager. He said that David Kay, who had been leading the Iraq Survey Group (ISG), which was charged in June 2003 with investigating Iraq's WMD programs, was resigning. They were considering candidates to replace him. Would I be interested in discussing that?

In October 2003, Kay had reported to Congress that the ISG had found some new, but limited WMD information and material. I had seen Kay once or twice out in Baghdad, but I had never discussed what he thought about the prospects for the WMD search. I had more extensive discussions with some of the experts on his team (who had been colleagues in earlier UNSCOM efforts) and had a general understanding of their progress during the last few months. They were having a difficult time coming up with anything tangible.

The ISG had been created to replace the military unit called XTF-75, which was created as part of CENTCOM war planning and prosecution. XTF-75 unit's primary objective was to find and eliminate the WMD threat to U.S. forces, not to conduct an ongoing investigation.

By the time I left Baghdad, it was obvious that there was no WMD threat to U.S. forces. The president had asked George Tenet to take the lead in looking for WMD. Tenet quickly decided to pick Kay, who happened to be consulting in CIA headquarters the day the question came up.

When Kay was given the leadership of the ISG, his guidance to the staff was to develop investigative leads and find key Iraqi scientists. This approach produced substantial information and background, but no WMD stocks. Kay, who had been convinced that Iraq had stockpiles of WMD before the war, now had to deal with the constant questions, "Where is the WMD? When are you going to find it?"

The WMD subject was also getting heated in Washington. The longer that militarily significant stocks were not found, the more closely the prewar estimates were examined. The number and pressure of Iraq WMD skeptics was building. The political atmosphere became incandescent as the security situation in Iraq deteriorated. The administration was in the difficult position of trying to sustain support for the stumbling efforts to establish a new government in Baghdad while political opponents in Washington were claiming that the WMD issue was a case of intentional deception, not by Saddam, but by President Bush. The administration's credibility was further strained by its insistence that the situation on the ground was not an insurgency when it was increasingly obvious to the press, and certainly the Iraqis, that it was.

I had not intruded on the WMD issue and had been blissfully unaware of the prewar assessments, including the October 2002 National Intelligence Estimate (NIE) on Iraq's WMD. The debate after the war, especially the splash by Ambassador Joe Wilson (concerning the false prewar reports of Iraqi attempts to acquire Niger uranium), seemed to be politics at its worst on all sides. Righteous statements thinly veiled a desire to harpoon opposing political sides.

The WMD controversy in 2003 struck me as *secondary* in importance to the immediate problems caused by *new* mistakes being made shaping post-Saddam Iraq. The assessments about WMD were wrong, that was pretty clear. It would be interesting to know how this happened so as to learn from the errors. But the faulty knowledge about WMD was looking pretty good compared with the faulty assessments that seemed to form the basis for the Defense Department's plans for post-Saddam Iraq.

Still, when McLaughlin called me, I was interested because I had invested close to a decade on the question of Iraq's WMD program and I had a deep curiosity to know exactly what had happened and how, within the regime. I also wanted to do what I could to improve the process and status of the intelligence community and its relation to policymakers and the public. The WMD question was separate from the deepening mess of postwar management. That was a catastrophe that would be fought out in Washington as well as Baghdad. Blame would be distributed in Washington; destruction in Iraq. By comparison, the WMD matter seemed much simpler, and the goals, I thought, would be clear.

McLaughlin invited me to meet with him at CIA headquarters on Thursday, January 15, 2004, and we had a discussion on the background of the ISG, its mission, and its configuration. McLaughlin spoke in prose that was crisp and efficient. He did not fill time with extra sentences and words. He had spent his career in the analytic side of the CIA and reflected its best qualities.

McLaughlin also looked the part—slightly bookish behind wire-rimmed glasses. And he was dressed conservatively, like a banker or a successful academic. He might have walked out of J. Press in New Haven or Cambridge. He did not look like a bureaucrat.

I went through my background on WMD and my recent experiences in Iraq. I asked why David Kay was leaving and got a polite answer that seemed to indicate that McLaughlin wasn't really sure. Kay had departed Iraq almost two months earlier, but only recently had declared that he would not return. I did not press for a fuller explanation, thinking maybe there were personal reasons. Later I learned that there was friction between Kay and both the CIA and the military.

This was a unique opportunity to finally understand the Iraqi side of the issue. The world had been focused on the UNSCOM inspections, and we had done our best to unearth the true story. This was a chance to obtain and record the real answers on both sides. An idealist might even suppose there would be an opportunity to learn from the past. McLaughlin said he would get back to me after talking to some other candidates.

The following Monday, the Martin Luther King holiday, I met with Tenet, McLaughlin, and John Moseman (Tenet's chief of staff) in the DCI's office suite on the seventh floor of CIA headquarters. McLaughlin was dressed casually by his standards—no suit, but neat and unwrinkled. Tenet was without a suit jacket to cover his wrinkled shirt and slumped in his chair. He was the opposite of crisp. Moseman was somewhere in between, straddling the two styles. He was the thoughtful and steady guiding hand in the seventh-floor executive suite who reached out to the various staff offices on many of the wide range of delicate issues concerning Tenet.

Tenet led the conversation, and we talked about the state of WMD knowledge and work. He said Kay had done an interim, highly classified report that found some new things, but nothing like a militarily significant stockpile. Kay had been following people and organizations as well as inspecting sites. Tenet emphasized that this was a high priority and had the full support of everyone in the bureaucracy. Resources were not an issue. He was careful to note that the ISG was not seeking to justify the recent NIE.

Tenet and I had worked on the Iraq WMD issue while I was at UNSCOM. He knew me, and my style. He would also know me from the agency officers who supported UNSCOM. He was going to get an activist who knew the Iraqi side, perhaps better than the U.S. side. Tenet knew I had deployed into Baghdad during the invasion and worked with the intelligence office in Baghdad on non-WMD business. After some general discussion, I simply asked, "George, what do want out of this?"

He looked up at me and said, "The truth." After a pause, he said, "Look, you're independent. You steer where you want. You'll get the resources. What we want is simply the truth." That was good enough for me, and Tenet made good on his commitment.

The Iraq WMD issue had confounded the international community for years. I had been a direct participant for over a decade and felt that there was probably no other American better positioned to investigate and record the regime's programs. I had confidence in my background. But inside, I knew the truth would not be simple. I had spent seven years at UNSCOM trying to sort out the truth on WMD. "Just finding the truth" sounds clear-cut. I had learned, however, that there were inevitably multiple levels of truth. You could dig very deep for facts and reasons, but there were always more. Moreover, searching for truth implied trying to understand the meaning of the facts, and that could depend upon the observer.

My thoughts turned quickly to the practical side. While I figured that resources would be available, the one thing that would be in short supply was time. I would need to hustle.

I made one immediate request: "There will be some specific people I will want out there. I know the ISG has lots of people who work hard. But the number of people who know anything about Iraq WMD is very small. I will want to get some of them. And I would like a couple of guys I have worked with in the past to come out—one of them you know, Larry Sanchez, and a guy I have worked with in IOG."

Tenet said, "Sanchez?!" He smiled. Sanchez's history of working on the intrusive UNSCOM inspections had earned him a reputation on the seventh floor of CIA headquarters for getting things done at the cost of conflict with the system. Tenet readily agreed, "Sure, we should be able to arrange what you need," and looked to Moseman to nod his assent.

Four days later, on Friday, January 23, I was back in Tenet's office being sworn into government service again. Taking the oath to uphold the Constitution is a powerful thing that is too often forgotten in the daily grind of government service. Even to someone with a strong cynical streak, nurtured through decades of government service, it is a potent ideal.

During the next two weeks, I met with the various WMD experts at headquarters. It was my first real exposure to some of the highly tendentious issues like the trailers thought to be for biological weapons, remotely piloted drones, the al Samoud ballistic missiles, and aluminum tubes that had been assessed to be for nuclear centrifuges. McLaughlin had warned me that the aluminum-tubes issue had taken on theological dimensions and I should keep that in mind in listening to the various presentations.

Survival in Washington also required that I make some introductory calls on key congressional players. I knew I would have to be testifying to Congress very soon, and I wanted them to know where I stood going into this politically charged issue. This was time well spent. Most had not read the NIE on Iraq WMD before they voted to support the war, but they had certainly read it afterward. Senator Carl Levin, in particular, was well versed in the controversial elements of the WMD assessment.

I had decided not to read the NIE yet. I wanted to work with the facts the ISG had developed on the ground. I told the legislators that my objective was to put together the full picture of the Iraqi WMD programs, not to verify or analyze the NIE. Frankly, I did not care what the NIE said. I would later spend much time reining in analysts who came to Baghdad trying to investigate their prewar assessments. It took continuous attention to focus the effort on developing the story from the evidence in Iraq, not prewar assumptions in Washington.

As soon as I accepted the position, I found that my predecessor was making the rounds on television and radio, declaring the results of his WMD investigation. Five days after I had been sworn in, David Kay accepted the opportunity to testify before the Senate Armed Services Committee and declared, "We were all wrong." He sounded conclusive, even though Kay himself had been declaring that Iraq was violating the UN weapons resolutions throughout the 1990s and in the lead-up to the war. Prior to the war, Kay spoke authoritatively on the Iraqi WMD deception. Now he was declaring a new conclusive truth to the world, despite the fact that seventeen hundred members of the ISG were still doing the methodical work of exploring all credible lines of investigation.

Aside from angering the staff he left in Iraq, Kay's declarations made it much more difficult to collect information from Iraqi sources. Once the world had heard the decrees of the former ISG leader, why should any of the Iraqis provide further information? I was annoyed, to say the least. It was as though one of the participants in the 9/11 Commission preemptively resigned before the report was completed and made the public rounds declaring his personal answer.

During my preparations, I spent time on the phone with Major General Keith Dayton, the military commander of ISG. It wasn't ideal to meet him telephonically. A good working relationship would be vital, and I had been warned that he could seem a little stiff and had a suspicion of the CIA (not necessarily an unhealthy reaction). Dayton had been around since the beginning of the ISG. He built it as a military organization, first in Qatar and then moving it to Baghdad International Airport (BIAP).[1]

Dayton made a plea that I live out at the ISG facility with the rest of ISG. Kay had lived in the Green Zone and made visits to ISG from there. I readily agreed with Dayton. That's where the people doing the real work were, and besides, I would get claustrophobic staying in the Green Zone.

Dayton also mentioned that there was an existing obligation for the ISG to report to Congress in March 2004. Kay had promised a report six months after the interim report he gave in October 2003. In Kay's absence, Dayton had requested that the analysts start a draft report. He sent me the lengthy draft text and I quickly concluded that I would not be in a position to understand fully and defend this document by March. Moreover, I disagreed with the approach it took on addressing WMD segments and issues piecemeal.[2] I did not want to make incremental pronouncements. The conclusions would be made at the conclusion. I had in my mind the goal of producing a substantial, comprehensive report that would record the range of Iraq activities, decisions, and policies. For now, I could not anticipate providing anything other than a status report to Congress in March.

I squeezed in two meetings at the Pentagon with Doug Feith, the undersecretary for policy, and Steve Cambone, undersecretary for intelligence. Both underscored their support of the ISG, and we had general discussions. Although both suggested ideas, I did not take the suggestions as anything other than free advice.

Then, on Friday, February 8, Tenet and I met with President Bush. He thanked me in advance for my service and offered his support. I was grateful and told him there was a large team in Baghdad who would like to hear that as well. Perhaps he could sign a note that I could take out to the ISG. He readily agreed. I described briefly my strategy and asked his support to implement it. I said I would keep everyone, including Condoleezza Rice, informed. I also made the usual joke about going out to Baghdad, where things were safer than in Washington.

I planned two stops on my way to Baghdad. The first was in London, where I met with MI-6 (the U.K. Secret Intelligence Service), the Defence Intelligence Staff, the Foreign and Commonwealth Office (the U.K. "State Department"), and Prime Minister Tony Blair and some of his cabinet staff. I arrived on Monday morning, February 9, and just had time to change at the hotel before the full round of meetings. The United Kingdom had a big stake in the ISG work. Prime Minister Blair was as exposed domestically as President Bush on the WMD issue—perhaps more so. Whatever I wrote or concluded would affect the British government deeply. I had worked for many years with the British both at UNSCOM and before, on an assortment of political-military issues. I knew many of the U.K. individuals quite well. They could be very helpful, especially MI-6.

My meeting with Prime Minister Blair lasted forty-five minutes. He greeted me in his office, where we sat before an unlit fireplace. He was in a blue shirt with red tie and no jacket. His aides arrayed themselves around his office in a far more relaxed mode than that of the Bush Oval Office. The prime minister went into substantial detail concerning the WMD hunt so far. Blair was very well informed on the WMD issue, and I had the opportunity to go into greater depth about my plans and tactics than I had with President Bush or Condoleezza Rice.

I said I intended to provide a short status report on ISG work and its direction to Congress in March. I explained that I would somewhat broaden the work of ISG. I highlighted that I felt it was important to take this historic opportunity to record the *reasons* for Saddam's decisions on WMD and to understand where the regime was headed. Since we had the top decision-makers in our custody, we should find out their strategic intentions.

Prime Minister Blair asked questions about the sources of information and how I would arbitrate between the views of differing experts. He did not make any strong suggestions, but carefully inquired where I was headed and asked about rough estimates on timing. I said I felt I had a clock running and that when sovereignty was returned to Iraq on June 30, this would greatly affect ISG operations. I promised to keep the U.K. government fully informed.

The day finished with meetings at the U.S. Embassy on Grosvenor Square. There I spoke with the ambassador and the chief U.S. intelligence representative.

I made it a point to stop in London on each trip to or from Washington. The United Kingdom was very helpful in providing support, as it had helped me when I was at UNSCOM. It was time well spent, and London was always a great break from Baghdad and Washington. It was easier to avoid the press and escape the whole WMD issue for some brief moments there.

The next day, I flew to Doha, Qatar, arriving on a Tuesday evening. On Wednesday, February 11, I visited the part of the ISG that was not located in Iraq—the Document Exploitation (DOCEX) facility. A warehouse there was the destination for documents collected by U.S. forces during the invasion and occupation. From my experience, collection of documents was a low priority during invasion. When I first arrived in April 2003 at the VVIP terminal at Baghdad International Airport, heaps of documents had been left exposed to the elements. The VVIP had been operated by Saddam's elite Special Security Organization (SSO), and most of the documents were on SSO letterhead. They were eventually put in garbage bags, and after some weeks, they disappeared, possibly sent for intelligence exploitation.

The documents that arrived at DOCEX sometimes had some data describing where they were collected, but often did not. More than five hundred linguists were charged with reviewing them. The process was limited to creating a very short one- or two-sentence summary of a given document and entering that in a database. If an ISG analyst found something of interest (the database was accessible at ISG in Baghdad), then a full translation would be requested. The DIA supported this activity, which was quite important, if tedious, work. Although I regretted that attention to locating and collecting documentation was not systematically pursued during the invasion or even during the early WMD search, at least in the aftermath, an organized approach was being taken. The documents could serve many purposes. For example, the OSD had a very strong interest in the documentation pertaining to regime crimes and any links to terrorism. But as long as the ISG was operating, WMD had the highest priority.

There were a range of fascinating documents in the DOCEX holdings. Iraqi intelligence documents were one obvious category of interest to ISG and others. Considering the range of Mukhabarat activities around the world, including in the United States and Europe, there would be tales to tell. Unfortunately, there seemed to be some gaps in the types of Mukhabarat documents obtained—for example, concerning Iraqi operations in Iran. The United States was not always the first to get to important Iraqi document archives. For instance, according to a former Mukhabarat officer I met in 2003, the INC had seized many Mukhabarat documents and was not fully sharing them with the United States. It would be easy to imagine other groups in Iraq being quicker to seize, read, and/or destroy regime records.

One special category of sensitive documentation had to do with Iraqi efforts to influence Americans. These documents could eventually be used for counterintelligence purposes and even criminal prosecutions.[3]

However, my main area of interest was the collection of documents related to the state organizations in charge of weapons development or acquisition. Over time, that body of documentation grew and helped fill out and support the debriefings of Iraqis in Baghdad. We picked up organization charts, procurement documents, presidential orders, and so on. One particularly interesting find were audio tapes of some of the Revolutionary Command Council (RCC) meetings Saddam chaired. These gave a fascinating window into some discussions over key decisions made by Saddam. For example, there is a recording of Saddam ordering the preparations for use of biological and chemical weapons before the Kuwait war. The Iraqis had admitted this to me in September 1995, and with the recording, those chilling discussions and decisions came to life. Remarkably, the description the Iraqi ministers gave to me in 1995 was completely consistent with the recorded Saddam directives.

On another occasion, Saddam spoke at length with his top defense technocrats on approaches to camouflage and ways of defeating U.S. bombers and cruise missiles. He was convinced that through the clever use of camouflage, U.S. missiles would miss valued assets. The Iraqis had learned a great deal about American cruise missiles over the years. Many missiles had been fired at Iraq, and some had not exploded. Saddam mentioned that Iraq had provided a cruise missile to Russia and that the Russians had learned more about the weapon's operation.

While we could not process all the documents, they were a very important tool. The high-value detainees (HVDs) and other Iraqis we questioned knew full well we had regime documents. If for some reason the interviewee elected to dissemble, it would be at the risk of our having a document proving the person was lying.

Sometimes provocative, but forged, documents made their way into the system. A couple of Iraqi memoranda indicated that Iraq had WMD, but we found convincing evidence that they had been forged. We were never able to take the time to track back the sources of these fabrications, and that remains a tantalizing unanswered question.

I had one other objective while in Qatar. The former foreign minister, Naji Sabri, had taken up residence there, as had many other Iraqis I knew. Sabri agreed to meet with me to discuss the UN inspections and Iraq's WMD activities. Contrary to what some supposedly informed intelligence officers have claimed since, Sabri was stating privately what he was charged with saying publicly about WMD, namely, that Iraq had fundamentally rid itself of WMD in the 1990s. It was his job to get this message out. However, as foreign minister and in his previous jobs as ambassador in Vienna and a university professor, he was simply not in a position to have direct access to WMD programs. He could describe the actions and rationale for various Iraqi positions in the UN, but he would not have known about any clandestine, retained WMD in the normal course of his duties. Conversations he had before the war were aimed at supporting the Iraq goal of keeping the UN Security Council split.

My discussion with Sabri centered on the Baghdad strategy in the
UN and the general attitudes expressed by Saddam and the senior
ministers around him. Sabri confirmed that the absolute priority had
been to get out of the UN sanctions. He noted that Iraq was making
great progress. The sanctions were falling apart, and Baghdad was
using the Oil-for-Food program to accelerate the decay.

Our conversation helped me get a feel for the series of steps that
Saddam took and that ultimately led to his downfall and execution.
Sabri also helped me understand the dynamics and tensions among
the top Saddam aides, especially the presidential secretary, Abed
Hamid Mahmud, and the "quartet" or "gang of four" top lieutenants:
Vice President Taha Yasin Ramadan, Deputy Prime Minister Tariq
Aziz, Vice Chairman of the RCC Izzat Ibrahim al-Duri, and Ali
Hasan al-Majid ("Chemical Ali").

Sabri did not have a close relationship with Saddam, nor did he
have control over any Iraqi resources. He was not liked by Abed
Hamid Mahmud, who, as presidential secretary, was the gatekeeper to
Saddam. But while Sabri's role in the regime was limited, he still had
an interesting perspective on the regime operations and the actions by
other council members trying to derive favor from Baghdad.

I told Sabri, "It is my goal to try to record the regime's actions and
directions. We have been through a lot of turmoil over the last
decades. Part of this tragedy is the result of Saddam. But there is also
the role played by mistaken perceptions. Perhaps some of those can be
understood in retrospect." I would have a follow-up discussion with
him later to test some of the themes that would form the basis of the
Comprehensive Report. He was skeptical when I told him the United
States wanted to record the truth. He replied, "We'll see."

On February 12, I boarded a C-130 with Major General Keith Day-
ton and two officers who would serve as my deputies in Baghdad.
Two and a half hours later, I was back at the Baghdad International
Airport.

Unlike the last time I arrived, there was infrastructure in place and
lots of people who wanted to make my life easier. Dayton had seen to

that. I was taken to what would be my quarters at Camp Slayer, where ISG was headquartered in a small (by Saddam's standards) palace. There was a single-room separate building on the edge of the lake that Saddam had constructed at the southeast part of the airport. The building was about thirty-five by twenty feet and was surrounded on three sides by the lake. A small walkway surrounded the building. Inside were a bed, a closet, shelves, a shower, and a television. It was air-conditioned, and an Internet terminal was promised. Compared with my last Baghdad living arrangements, it was indeed a palace.

A cluster of similar adjacent buildings were all occupied by sizable groups. Directly adjacent was the military team that provided personal protection for Dayton on his trips off BIAP.

The vast majority of ISG staff lived in a housing area that comprised dozens of living "Pods." These were rapidly fabricated trailer boxes that had air-conditioning and beds. Some had bathing facilities, but there were common showering areas as well.

Being on the lakeside was soothing. In 1998, during the UN-SCOM presidential site inspections, I had seen this area before the lake was filled. It had been a dusty, beige expanse without life. Now it was the opposite. The water was cooling and in constant motion. There was the mystery of what lay beneath the surface. Many birds were attracted to the water, which had also been stocked with some (now large) fish by the regime.

I spent many hours staring into the shifting reflected images on the water. During the day, the sky and clouds would wobble on the surface as the wind brushed by. At night, the black surface reflected the stars. Beneath the surface, I could only imagine the debris that littered the lake bottom. The regime had made a habit of disposing of some of its grimmest material in bodies of water.

Only one aspect of my quarters bothered me. The three sides of the building facing the water were almost completely glass. It was not difficult to imagine a nearby mortar impact having the effect of a fléchette round. I never opened the heavy curtains covering the windows (it would have been too hot, anyway.) The other unlucky aspect of the location was its proximity to the palace dome. That seemed to be a convenient aim point for insurgents who wanted to lob an occasional mortar at us. One evening, a couple rounds did land about a hundred yards away in the lake. They were loud, loosened some plaster, but did no lasting damage.

Mortars were a regular, sometimes daily, event. They were random and poorly aimed. They were never a concentrated barrage, just occasional shots by insurgents who knew that their launch location could be very rapidly fixed by American surveillance and possibly taken under return fire. Therefore, insurgents might fire one or two and flee. A mortar hit the side of the ISG palace one evening and did little damage, but it was very loud if you were indoors or, as was the case for one female biological-weapons expert, you happened to be using a nearby portable toilet.

One ISG staffer who lived in the Pods left for a few days and, when he returned, gradually noticed light coming in through a small hole, no more than three inches wide, in the ceiling. Then he noticed a matching hole in the floor of his Pod. That was very odd. He went outside and looked under the space between the Pod and the ground and found an unexploded 60-mm mortar round. In this vein, I learned later that our adventurous British deputy commander, Lieutenant Colonel Henry Joyson, would take the precaution of leaving his heaviest set of body armor around his most valuable bottles of wine and whiskey when he went out on operations garbed in his lightweight body armor.

Metal dropping out of the sky also included bullets. Celebratory gunfire from nearby neighborhoods was the biggest risk (when the Iraq soccer team defeated Saudi Arabia, the skies were lit with tracers). A famous story I could never confirm told of a round landing on a table directly in front of someone eating in the mess hall.

Despite falling metal, it was great to be back in Baghdad. Life was interesting, and the frustrations of Washington traffic and lines at the supermarket and everything else that sapped energy in the United States were lifted. The new problems brought a new perspective.

I had just unloaded my gear in my quarters, taken the tour of ISG, and had dinner with Dayton at the dining hall when DCI George Tenet arrived with his entourage for a visit. We met for forty-five minutes and discussed a range of issues.

George asked, "How's it going? When did you get here?" Jet-lagged from his flight from the United States, he was departing shortly to Afghanistan. He would be on the ground only a few hours.

"I got here this morning, and it's going fine, but I need helicopters," I replied. "The way ISG plans and executes site visits with military convoys of HMMVs is a cumbersome process. It takes a week to request a movement, for it to be approved, planned, and executed. We will only be able to visit around fifty places between now and June when sovereignty transfers back to the Iraqis."

I didn't really think this idea would be approved, but I wanted to make the point that greater velocity in inspections would help. I also wanted him to know that site inspections would be limited unless we did them with agency resources.

To my surprise, the Baghdad intelligence office chief said, "Well, George, you know we are trying to get some helicopters in here and we could obviously jointly use them." The chief was quick. He had not missed an opportunity to quickly bring my request into his request, enlisting the momentum to his cause.

George replied, "We'll work it," which was as much as I expected. I did want to get better mobility. My highest priority was to find key people, and they weren't all in jail. Some we had to go find, almost door-to-door in Baghdad's neighborhoods. It would be impossible if we arrived with a convoy of HMMVs.

We then went downstairs to the open area where the analysts had their cubicles. Dayton had announced that Tenet would visit, and the DCI wanted to say a few words. It was well after 2200, but perhaps a couple hundred of the staff gathered.

George stood in the middle of the round room, clearly very tired, but in a strong voice introduced me in a flattering and lighthearted manner. He then thanked everyone for their efforts and urged them on to "find the WMD."[4]

The lack of real experts was the biggest problem I had. The various government agencies would send people out, but most of these people would come out for only a couple months. I even gave serious thought to asking some Iraqis to do some of the report writing. There were a lot of very knowledgeable people at the detention site at Camp Cropper. Some spoke and wrote very good English and had nothing else to do. And they sure weren't going home to rearrange their lawn furniture or attend to any of the other home crises that regularly caused many civilians to depart Baghdad.

Tenet left later that night, assuming he had solved one of his many problems, getting someone to finish up the WMD work of ISG. I went to my new quarters that night wondering how I could generate and record as much information as possible by the date of sovereignty change, and whether it was in fact possible, in a few short months, to learn the truth about WMD in Iraq.

CHAPTER 18

Plato's Cave

David Kay's preemptive public declarations that Iraq had no WMD stocks and that everyone was wrong made great headlines. To simply conclude, however, that there were no significant stocks in May 2003 was to miss the larger picture. Many important details about the Iraqi WMD programs and policies were not yet understood. And in fact, some UN inspectors, both UNSCOM and Blix's team, doubted that large inventories of WMD remained in Iraq. So while some may have been all wrong, not everyone was as completely wrong. Those statements were too simple.

To spend all this effort on ISG and simply report the disposition of the WMD programs was to miss an historic opportunity to look inside the regime and figure out why these decisions about WMD and other critical issues were made. I did not really care about the hotly debated aluminum tubes and alleged biological-weapons trailers. I was quickly convinced they had nothing to do with WMD; I did not want to waste time on them. I did want to build a robust understanding of the overall program over the duration of the Saddam regime.

In my first few days, I met with the leaders of the existing ISG teams who covered chemical, biological, and nuclear weapons, and political-military, procurement, and delivery systems (meaning ballistic missiles and unmanned vehicles). They told me where their work stood. The teams had been working hard, gathering data through interviews and visiting possible WMD-related sites. However, they were without overall direction and had a tendency to be testing the prewar intelligence estimates as their point of departure. It was possible (though I certainly did not think so) that all the issues prominent in Washington (alleged centrifuge tubes, unmanned aerial vehicles, Niger uranium, mobile biological-weapons trailers, etc.) could be proved wrong, but Iraq might still have a concealed WMD program. I wanted a comprehensive picture of the WMD programs Iraq *had* developed and their disposition, not long expositions about why some decrepit hydrogen-production trailers were *not* related to a biological-weapons program. We could discuss a lot of things in Iraq that were not related to WMD.

The ISG had gathered much information that was related to real WMD efforts and decisions. More was needed, but I also wanted to better arrange what we already had. I thought we could learn more from the information, if only we could find the correct viewpoint. We needed to see the world as Saddam saw it. We needed to know what he knew and how his logic worked.

Also, we had to create a dynamic, not static, picture of the regime, reflecting that things changed by the day. In the abstract, I wanted to be able to take any given moment during the Saddam regime and show the key things that shaped his view at that moment and, within this continuum, plot the points where key decisions were made on WMD. By analogy, I wanted to make a motion picture by stacking a pile of static images and flipping through them so you would see the apparent motion. The dynamics would show through. An advantage of this approach would be that analysts without broad or deep knowledge of Iraq could constructively contribute to plotting and describing the individual events that would form the frames that made up the movie. That was the idea, anyway. I had no idea if I could pull it off.

In an ideal environment and with time, I could envision a computer database that would serve this function, but not one that would be created in time for the ISG. Instead, a low-tech method would be to build a big paper timeline. I wanted analysts to be able to stare at this large plot and place whatever subtask they were studying in the context of Baghdad's perspective—not Washington's.

I knew that the majority of analysts studying Iraq WMD before the war spent their entire professional lives staring into computer screens. These people were completely disconnected from the reality in Iraq. They had no tactile feel for Iraq. The system for analyzing Iraq WMD was very much like Plato's cave, as described at the beginning of Book 7 of *The Republic*. Socrates describes a group of prisoners shackled since birth so that they can only view the rear wall of a cave. The only illumination comes from a constantly burning fire, well to the back of them. Between the fire and prisoners is a path along which various people and objects are transported, thereby creating shadows on the rear wall.

The prisoners' only experience in life is shadows formed on the wall. Socrates notes that to the prisoners, it is reality. He goes as far as to imagine that one prisoner later in life is permitted to see outside the cave and concludes that the sun-illuminated world is not real and he returns to the position where he sees the shadows that have become his reality. The hundreds of cubicles in Washington containing analysts before the war was the present-day version of Plato's cave. Now the prisoners had a chance to venture outside the cave. The whole of Iraq was open to them. Some seemed to have bouts of agoraphobia and were dizzy with boundless new information. They grasped for a handrail, and the handrail was to test their prewar assessments. I wanted to take their hands from the rail.

During my first week at ISG, I called a general meeting with the team leaders to lay out my priorities and perspectives. I also wanted to make clear that while I had some pretty firm ideas on methodology, the conclusions would come from whatever we learned. Nothing was politically predetermined. I emphasized that I wanted a report that told the whole story of the regime's relationship with WMD. I did not care what the story was, but wanted it to be comprehensive. I wanted it to be rich in facts and data. I also wanted to describe the evolution of the WMD programs over time. I drew my concept for a timeline tool on the white board in the conference room, explaining that it would serve as a mechanism to organize our work and thinking. We could plot on a timeline all the events that affected the regime's WMD programs, decisions, tests, political events, funding, Monica

Lewinsky, UN actions, and so forth. Anything that would have shaped Saddam's thinking or program decisions concerning WMD.

The line would start with Saddam's becoming president in 1979 and go forward to the present and, conceptually, point in the direction Saddam planned to go in the future. I used a mathematical analogy that I repeated many times: "If all we investigate and record is the existence or nonexistence of WMD in Iraq in May 2003, then we have described a single point on the curve. It is an interesting point. We could provide that bit of truth and be successful."

I went on, hoping I wasn't droning or sounding like the usual new guy who arrives all spun up with some bright idea that will never work.

"I think the opportunity we have deserves more than that. I want calculus, not algebra. We should be able to describe the inner dynamics of the regime's relationship to WMD. Saddam elected to have and use WMD at one point. At another, it looks as if he chose not to use or perhaps have WMD. Why? To answer those questions, we need to analyze the area under the curve."

Turning to a mathematical analogy again, I said, "What equation, with what functions, was Saddam solving in his head, whereby at certain values for certain factors the coefficient of WMD was zero and, at other times, greater than zero? I want to answer that question." That would be our gift to the historical record, and maybe future policies would be improved by recording these events.

I knew some of my audience pretty well and had discussed my notions before, so it wasn't an entirely cold presentation. I made sure that Bill M., an old colleague from UNSCOM, was present. He had the most encyclopedic knowledge of Iraq and its WMD program of any non-Iraqi I knew. Bill could begin to fill out a timeline with the data in his head, and he began to do just that.

Moving further from the abstract to the concrete, I said, "I would like to create a group that focuses on the strategic intent of the regime. This group will dig into the minds of Saddam and his top aides."

I continued, "And I want to dissect the regime's decision making by opening up the finances. We have two very key features bounding our problem. First, to understand the regime, we have one key guy to understand—Saddam. Second, if the regime was going to do something on WMD, it would take resources. Iraq's resources were limited, and I think we can probably track most of them. Under the Oil-for-Food program, we can look at the flow of money and what happened to it."

Shaping my thinking was my own experience in Washington with the Office of Management and Budget. This agency forms the president's budget each year. Governments can have lots of policies, but real decisions and priorities are determined by how the budget is allocated. I also knew the Iraqi Oil Ministry people well and was confident we could get all the oil records. There had to be a story there.

Finally I added, "To accomplish this, I would like to create a new team called the Regime Strategic Intent (RSI) team. This will subsume the current political-military team and give it sharp focus."

I wanted to be able to document what Saddam's objectives were and tie them to the actions we saw in all the other areas. To get at his objectives, I wanted to form subteams within the RSI group for debriefing select individuals. There were key Iraqi officials who would know key parts of the Saddam regime. I wanted to go after their experiences in a coordinated way and record the regime goals and methods.

This was a broad agenda. I did not know if we would get through to the end. The team leaders did not throw anything at me but questions. The natural reaction to anything new is usually negative. I had been on the other side of the table many times. If I had been listening to me, I probably would have been rolling my eyes. They were more polite and soon, I think, even became enthused. They also improved on my skeletal strategy in their implementation. The new methodology overlay all the ISG's regular activities.

I made several trips a week from our headquarters at Baghdad International Airport (BIAP) to the CPA and embassy offices downtown. I had a weekly meeting with Bremer to update him on ISG work. It was frustrating to be such a close witness to the ongoing chaotic efforts by the CPA. My lane was WMD, however, and I restrained myself from offering unsolicited advice to Bremer on the overall direction of the CPA.

Things were clearly getting worse. Our teams were at greater risk operating in the field. The accumulating wreckage of vehicles attacked along the airport road to Baghdad was a tipoff that things were not right.

Although I had seen what may have been one of the first IED attacks on the airport road the previous May 26, there had obviously been many more since then. The guardrails and beautiful palm trees were mostly gone—they had been too convenient for hiding IEDs. The airport road was now a combination of a drag-racing strip and demolition derby. You did not want to linger to study the statue of Ibn Firnas, a famous Arab poet and inventor who attempted flight in the ninth century in Andalusia. When you passed him, you knew you were getting close to BIAP. Six months earlier, I had regularly driven myself to visit Iraqis in nearby neighborhoods and to have my favorite rotisserie chicken at a place in Amiriya. That was a thing of the past. So were my visits to Iraqi friends. Even if it were safe for *me*, it would not be safe for *them* to have the best-known CIA officer in Iraq visiting them. As it was, during the past six months, many of them had left Iraq.

Odd things happened every day at ISG. Boredom was never an issue. The day after I arrived, an operation called Stunned Mullet was under way. A team of underwater sonar specialists had been brought to Iraq to systematically examine all bodies of water where there were reports of concealed materials having been dropped. The team operated from semirigid boats. Among the reports they were investigating was that of large missiles in containers dropped into the Tigris River.

There was a long-standing tradition of throwing all sorts of junk into the Tigris. UNSCOM had commissioned divers to retrieve a lot of missile gyroscopes that the Iraqis had tossed there. The divers came upon other things as well, including a plastic bag of body parts on one occasion.

The Stunned Mullet team recorded images of six metallic boxes on the riverbed just downstream of a bridge. The objects were not big enough to hold missiles, but were a couple of feet per side. The team decided to conduct other surveys, including one at Lake Habbaniya about fifty miles west of Baghdad, before returning to examine the boxes. By the time the team returned, the boxes were gone—forever to remain one of the unsolved mysteries of the Iraq story. My favorite hypothesis was that they contained the gold reserves that Saddam had ordered to be accumulated prior to the war. Saddam was concerned that Iraqi accounts outside Iraq would be frozen, and so as a preparatory measure, he had given instructions to buy gold and bring it to Baghdad. There is a lot of gold someplace.

My second week in Baghdad, I was organized enough to spend some concentrated time working with the new RSI group and planning an overall intelligence collection campaign for the spring. The RSI team had a delicate task. It had to collect and assess information about how the regime acted and why. Most of this would come from the top leaders. We set up dedicated teams for key detainees like Saddam's presidential secretary, Abed Hamid Mahmud; Vice President Taha Yasin Ramadan; and head of the Military Industrial Commission, Abd al Tawab Huwaysh. For Saddam, we had a unique approach, given his circumscribed incentives and future. The goal was to understand the inner workings and rationales for the WMD decisions and where the regime was headed.

I also wanted to put as much primary data in the comprehensive report as possible. If readers chose to disagree with any conclusions, at least they would have all the data available. I was fortunate to get another former UNSCOM colleague, Steve Black, to join this effort. He had several years' experience working with senior Iraqis (and he also knew the Iraq chemical-weapons program in depth). At UNSCOM, Black served both as the historian and as an inspector who directed a successful series of inspections of Iraqi concealment activities by their security organizations. He understood how the regime operated in its most sensitive parts and the power and structures of Saddam's security apparatus. On top of this, Black was a swift and good writer.

Black was not the captain of the RSI team, but he was the coach (and he backstopped the chemical- and biological-weapons team). With Black on board I also had another team member whom Tariq Aziz or other senior Iraqis could not bullshit about previous Iraqi WMD claims. There were a few of us who had been through much of this before. Stated more positively, the Iraqis knew when they spoke to certain experienced ISG members, they would be understood and did not have to waste a lot of time explaining background on circumstances of being in the regime. The RSI section of the report would not have been nearly as successful without Black.

Closely aligned with the RSI team was a separate, smaller team that was charged with investigating and documenting the Mukhabarat. This effort was successful in revealing the various components and missions of the Mukhabarat. This Iraqi intelligence service played a vital role in the acquisition of weapons-related materials through front companies and their contacts outside Iraq. Mukhabarat officers were also major actors in bribing and influencing foreigners. I took a personal interest in this part of our investigation because I had come to know and debrief many of the Mukhabarat officers. Some were solid professionals, and some were despicable thugs who would appear very cooperative and seek to kill you the next day. They were a substantial tool of the will of Saddam, and, like the financing and procurement, to the extent we could understand how Saddam used the Mukhabarat, we would understand his objectives.

We developed and recorded useful information about Mukhabarat activities in Iran and with well-established terrorist groups (but *not* al-Qaeda). We plotted out the range of its activities, from surveillance to assassination, money laundering, setting up front companies, and establishing overseas bank accounts. I was amused to hear that Mukhabarat officers often favored bribing officials and would compete for the opportunity, because in the process, the bribers could usually skim off a percentage for themselves.

Unfortunately, the head of the Mukhabarat, Tahir Jalil Habbush, was long gone from Iraq and we could not debrief him. I used to drive by his house (not far from BIAP) and that of his son (also not far from BIAP, but on the other side of the airport road) once in a while just to see what was going on. They were nice homes, but there was no sign of Habbush. He left Iraq several days before U.S. forces arrived in Baghdad and, as near as I could tell, did not risk coming back. If he ever turns up, I would still like to get his assessment of the detailed Mukhabarat annex in the comprehensive report.[1]

❖

The collection planning for ISG required tying together the efforts of almost every imaginable intelligence-collection capability: DIA collectors, CIA operations officers, imagery collection from satellites, unmanned aerial vehicles of various sorts, indigenous operations officers, money to pay informants, and a range of other technical collection capabilities. The one additional request I made of Washington was to have a senior National Security Agency (NSA) person at ISG. The NSA director at the time, Lieutenant General Michael Hayden (later the director of the CIA), readily agreed and sent out a series of good officers. NSA effectively collects all sorts of communications and other electronic emissions and has an historical database of which our analysts could make direct use through asking the NSA representative. I am convinced that NSA's data is regularly underutilized simply because analysts are unfamiliar with what exists. NSA also has a tremendous capacity to collect for both local and longer-range strategic targets. We applied all elements of NSA's capacity to our task.

If we conducted a raid, or even a cooperative interview, it could be useful to know whom the subject was speaking to before and especially afterward. We would often apply the same strategy with optical or physical surveillance. We had the ability to watch sites or people before, during, and after raids. It could be very useful to see whom our subjects contacted and what was said. This could provide additional leads, or the absence of some reactions could tell us something else.

One of the things I kept reminding the analysts (and myself) was to look for what was not there. A photograph shows some things, but it may also be important to notice what is not there (e.g., an image of a facility that had no vehicle tracks near it may indicate lack of use). Likewise, it is important to note what is not said. Identifying and recording negative information is difficult in our intelligence system, but it's a critical task. Another example would be the absence of a reaction when a reaction might be expected. ISG officers interviewed a number of Iraqi engineers and scientists who were likely to have had contact with clandestine WMD activity—*if it had been taking place*. If it had been taking place, they probably would have taken steps to alert others or move materials. This did not happen. It was important negative information. Sherlock Holmes's observation about a non-barking dog hits this point.

Another source of information and analysis came from the British. I met with the head of the Joint Intelligence Committee, John Scarlett, in London and stayed in contact with him and his office throughout the process. Like Tenet, Scarlett had had a hand in the UK prewar assessments. Also like Tenet, he was emphatic that the ISG should report the facts of the situation as completely as possible. He wanted to be certain that the ISG had access to the same data that the United Kingdom had. The British had an intelligence support team for Iraq known as the Rockingham Group, which had been working the Iraq WMD matter for many years. I was familiar with the group through its support to UNSCOM. The United Kingdom had some human sources who were unique, and their analysis was often somewhat different than Washington's.

I valued the direct involvement of Scarlett. Some questioned his suggestions for ISG. I found it helpful to hear and evaluate his ideas. I knew he had long and valuable experience in the collection and perception of intelligence. Scarlett had been the case officer for one of the most important Soviet defectors in the early 1980s, Colonel Oleg Gordievsky of the KGB. From long experience, Scarlett knew the process of receiving and reporting information directly from a source. He understood the strengths and weaknesses of various reporting and knew the unexpected and completely different perceptions of events that another government might observe. The filter of a different bureaucratic system for gathering and reporting information often produces another perspective.

Scarlett had been handling Gordievsky during November 1983, when Moscow—under the leadership of a very ill (unbeknownst to the West) Yuri Andropov—went to a high state of nuclear alert as a result of the misperception and misapprehension of a NATO exercise called Able Archer. The world was the closest it had been to nuclear war since the Cuban Missile Crisis, and the West had had no idea except, eventually, from the reporting of Gordievsky. From this part of

Scarlett's background (as far as I knew), I judged that he could appreciate that other governments inevitably have their own logic that would be unknowable from the outside. Nevertheless, analysts are obligated to make assumptions about those governments—assumptions sometimes completely wrong and, perhaps, dangerously wrong.

During the Able Archer exercise, the Soviet intelligence system was reporting that the United States might be preparing a first strike against the Soviet Union under the guise of the NATO exercise. The Soviet intelligence system, we later learned, was calibrated to report positive information, which tended to reinforce this hypothesis. Their intelligence system, like ours, suffered from this "confirmation bias." And Andropov ordered all the nuclear forces to be ready to launch. This completely wrong interpretation of the situation on the part of Moscow was not unlike Washington's misinterpretations of Baghdad, or Baghdad's erroneous assessments of Washington. The potential to assemble data in a way that forms a logically correct, but quite wrong picture of reality was something that Scarlett had seen happen. The Soviet Union had collected detailed information about U.S. and NATO nuclear strike plans and then observed an exercise that seemed to conform to such a plan to conduct a first strike. And this seemed to conform to the rhetoric of President Ronald Reagan. While the assumption was utterly logical, it could have been disastrous. Experience with these fundamental aspects of intelligence collection and analysis combined with the reactive steps taken by policymakers is invaluable. Few people have it; Scarlett was one of them.

In early March, I discovered one feature of ISG's intelligence collection that I immediately sought to terminate. ISG had an existing relationship with the INC at its headquarters at the Hunt Club in Mansour. The DIA had been using the INC to locate Iraqis of interest to the ISG. I was very uncomfortable with using an Iraqi political body to round up other Iraqis for ISG questioning. I had two concerns. First, the U.S. government's use of one political party in Iraq for intelligence-collection purposes would send a bad signal to those individuals we wished to find. Second, I was concerned that by just telling the INC which Iraqis were of interest to us, we could put those very Iraqis (who were often simply former scientists and engineers in the WMD program) at risk. The INC could use its role in various ways, including skewing the information we received on WMD. In my opinion, the INC had a track record of providing information to "influence as well as inform," as the intelligence jargon goes. I recalled the reports Chalabi and his INC intelligence assistant, Arras Karim Habib, had given to me in London; their reports strained credulity. Consequently, I asked Keith Dayton to carefully restrict the INC channel and be certain that information flowed in one direction only. He readily agreed.

As it was, I was regularly asking about the documents that we knew to be in the possession of the INC and had not been conveyed to the United States. The INC had its own agenda, determined by Chalabi. Increasingly, his agenda and the U.S. agenda were obviously diverging. For example, the INC held thousands of boxes of documents, which it only provided to the United States beginning in mid-2004. I have no confidence that all the documents the INC seized throughout Iraq were ever shared with the United States. (The official DIA relationship with the INC was finally curtailed in mid-June.)

There were a lot of moving parts at ISG. Every day, there were teams traveling to sites in convoys, high-level debriefings, operations officers out with teams to locate WMD, scientists and engineers to question, visiting congressional representatives, consultations with the intelligence shop of the "big army," some counterterrorism work (many of the ISG techniques and capabilities were applied to terrorism issues), explosive ordnance removal, and more.

A routine quickly established itself. Weeks were filled with team meetings, weekly sessions with Bremer, biweekly meetings with the downtown office to coordinate resources and some operations, and daily "all hands" ISG meetings at 1800 to review the day's operations (battlefield update briefings, or BUBs in military jargon). The meetings took time, but provided essential structure. Keith Dayton and his military team did a great job of making sure the ISG machine ran smoothly. There were significant logistics, personnel, and safety issues. ISG cost tens of millions of dollars a month to sustain and operate.

There were seventeen hundred ISG personnel in the war zone with weapons. Many of these were young men away from home, perhaps for the first time. There was a mix of civilians who had varying degrees of discipline and maturity.

Dayton kept things running securely and smoothly, as you would expect in a fundamentally military unit. I allowed myself to be slightly iconoclastic, but without undermining the need for order. I could not bring myself to wear boots in the hot weather when Teva sandals were just as practical and much cooler (assuming I wasn't going outside the base). I also took some liberties in not wearing body armor within our compound during periods when mortars became more prevalent and the military ordered personnel to don armor and helmets. I cannot recall ever having or putting on a helmet.

One of the most enjoyable aspects of the work was having a team of young, enthusiastic operations officers who were anxious to get out on the streets and find Iraqis or materials. I had no luck in getting helicopters in a timely fashion, but I did get additional armored civilian cars that our officers, teamed with paramilitary guys, could use at short notice. These young men and women enjoyed the action and the ability to shape their own missions in direct support of our analysis. They learned some useful skills in the process. Not surprisingly, the better ones would be stolen by the CIA office downtown for other missions. As time went on, the office downtown also stole (my term) some of our armored cars.

Once, I was being driven back from the Baghdad office during a dust storm. The security team was driving like hell, as they usually did. Suddenly, we heard a large *crack!* and the BMW lifted into the air and landed with a crash. I felt my spine compress but suffered only a large bump on my head from where it had struck the roof. We had not been attacked; we had hit a curb at a high speed and wrecked the axle, effectively writing off a $350,000 car.

Worse was the fate of a brand-new Mercedes that was flown to Baghdad and taken for a test drive by a young mechanic down a road at BIAP. He got up a head of speed. Unfortunately, an Iraqi bus pulled out in front of him, and the mechanic could not stop. Stopping an armored car takes much longer than normal because of the substantial weight of the armor. I later checked the odometer of that totaled Mercedes—it had fourteen miles on it. Armored BMWs and Mercedes were being purchased wherever possible and brought to Baghdad. We could not get enough of them. And when they broke or were shot up, we could not readily repair them in Iraq.

It was very easy to work sixteen- or seventeen-hour days. On the one hand, it was always interesting, and on the other, there wasn't much else to do. For my part, I would go jogging around the facility, which was large enough to do a circuit of three miles. Alternatively, a gym with treadmills and weights was available and stayed open until midnight.

The best moments were late at night, midnight or later, when I could sit outside in a chair looking over the lake. The stars were strikingly sharp, as long as there wasn't a dust storm. And the occasional tracer fire was beautifully reflected in the dark water.

Explosions happened with some regularity. Apart from mortars and rockets, which quickly got your attention if they were close, there were also regular detonations conducted by the explosive-ordinance disposal (EOD) teams at fixed times, usually ten minutes before, or twenty minutes after, the hour. And there were the loud, distant explosions of car bombs in Baghdad or IEDs on the airport road. Automatic-weapon firing was also a common sound, but it was usually from the military M-16s or M-4s at our range. AK-47 firing (which has a more distinctive clatter) was heard in surrounding neighborhoods. Sometimes, the cause was celebratory; other times, it was quite the opposite.

Out of this sensory-data-rich and turbulent environment, our goal was to produce a silent, written text that would reside in libraries and in the ether of the Internet. The data was all around us. We just had to capture and record it in a way that would be useful. Individuals found their own ways to focus and work in this environment. Late at night, I would see analysts in their cubicles with headsets listening to music that would transport them from the surrounding Iraqi chaos to some more balanced state. Somehow, they were seeking to create a rational exposition of the reality we and the Iraqis perceived, trying to reconcile their own world with the one they now found themselves in.

Each war has its music. It is a constant in modern wars that music is frequently playing—in vehicles or through headphones. I have found, as have colleagues I have asked, that there is an involuntary memory of a war with certain music. Like the memory imprints of smell famously described by Marcel Proust, soundtracks can trigger a visceral memory shudder. David Bowie's "Ricochet" was often playing in my headphones in a jeep in Chad. Jefferson Airplane's "White Rabbit" echoed in my mind and headphones as I drove around Baghdad in 2003. Late nights at ISG, I often played the soundtrack of David Mathews' "Oh."

By March, I had constructed a short interim report to take to the various committees in Congress. The message was simple since I had been on the job for only four weeks. I provided an update in each of the functional areas on what had been found or not found. I highlighted areas that I still believed required further investigation, and noted that I would be including an analysis of the regime's intentions. Further, I made clear that I wanted to make a single comprehensive report and not a series of conclusions. Finally, I emphasized that the conditions under which we had to work were very difficult and made progress slow. At that point, we had armored cars shot up but no casualties yet.

I had previewed this message to governments in Canberra, London, and Washington and asked for comments. I did this in our weekly secure videoconferences, which took place each Tuesday afternoon. I made clear that although I would appreciate suggestions, it was my report and it would do no one any good if it appeared to be anything other than an independent report. John Scarlett asked if I was not forgetting elements that David Kay had mentioned in his highly classified report the previous October. Scarlett thought some might wonder what happened to these "nuggets" that Kay had referred to.

Scarlett was referring to inconclusive evidence that Kay had referred to concerning possible WMD activities that had been discovered. Scarlett and I had spoken in person in London and I had requested that he bring to my attention any aspects that I might have overlooked. The particular points he recalled from the earlier Kay report had been further investigated since their publication and found to be without consequence. The nuggets were fool's gold, but I was reassured to have examined them.[2]

I briefed the Senate Intelligence and Armed Services committees on March 30 and the House on the 31st. On April 1, I saw Tenet and John McLaughlin to catch up. I also saw Condoleezza Rice and filled her in on where we were headed. The next day, I went to New York to meet with Ambassador John Negroponte and explained how our work was going and the implications for the UN. I had lunch with Demitri Perricos and some old colleagues from the UN. Perricos was the acting head of UNMOVIC, having replaced Hans Blix.

The following day, Keith Dayton and I flew to Sydney. In my career, I have had several opportunities to work with Australians. They contributed a great deal and often got less credit than they deserved. I wanted to recognize their contribution to the ISG—a contribution that included a sizable military contingent and some excellent civilian intelligence officers.

We arrived in Sydney, and to my surprise, the Aussies seemed to think there was some potential threat against me. They had decided to provide a twenty-four-hour security team. It was flattering, but unnecessary.

Dayton wanted to meet with the Australian military chiefs to thank them for their military support at BIAP. Among other missions, the Aussies ran the control tower at the airport. While Dayton saw the military side, I met with some intelligence groups. Then we both met with Minister of Defense Robert Hill in Canberra, Foreign Minister Alexander Downer in Adelaide, and then staff from Prime Minister John Howard's office back in Sydney. It was a long way to go, but they deserved to hear our prospectus firsthand. I also wanted to hear any ideas or concerns they had. I was lucky to see some friends from the U.S. Embassy and have the opportunity to go to the Sydney Opera House. There happened to be a ballet performance of a selection of Balanchine's work, and for some reason unknown to me, there were fireworks over Sydney Harbor after the performance. They looked a lot like tracers.

Then Dayton and I made our way back to Washington and London and Amman. And then, home to Baghdad.

CHAPTER 19

Abed

During my 2004 meeting with President Bush before I left for Baghdad, I had one substantive request. It was my strong view that in order to elicit an accurate accounting of Saddam's WMD, I needed authority over debriefing and some flexibility in dealing with the senior Iraqis just under Saddam. I personally knew the Iraqis who would know the answers. Important as it was to inspect sites and gather documents—and we certainly did that—my best bet for getting at the truth was to talk to those key officials who had the best knowledge of Saddam and his WMD program directives. Saddam, of course, was a special and different case.

Saddam had very limited incentives. He had been debriefed after his capture a few weeks earlier and had not made any revelations about WMD stocks. President Bush knew this. Even if Saddam talked more, we needed to be able to test what he was saying. In effect, Saddam was an important source, but not the most important to understanding the regime. My main target would be the guy under Saddam—the presidential secretary, Abed Hamid Mahmud.

I knew Abed from UNSCOM days, when we met for long discussions over the course of a series of presidential inspections. He was the closest to Saddam and a former Murafaqin—one of the select few to be a presidential guard. As presidential secretary, he controlled everything that went to or from Saddam. Abed was "the man." If I could get him, and I was pretty confident I could, I could accomplish my task. Of course, I would collect as much data as possible from others for the historic record, but if nothing else happened and I got to Abed, I would have the story.

"Sir," I said during my discussion with President Bush, "there is one thing about my approach that I believe will be essential. Saddam's top people will know the answers about WMD. I need them to talk candidly to me."

In retrospect, Tenet and Rice and a couple others in the Oval Office for this session may have started wondering where I was headed with this. Tenet cocked his head in my direction and started looking at me closely. He had been managing, with explicit presidential approval, the "rendition" program, whereby al-Qaeda leaders were captured and brought to locations where "enhanced" interrogation methods might be applied. I spoke informally with various people I knew who had knowledge of these techniques. The opinions were not clear-cut, though in some cases tough interrogations seemed to work. Maybe this was appropriate for the al-Qaeda thugs, but not for my targets. I had a completely different group of people. They were high-ranking government officials and scientists. Although they may have been part of a horrendous government, they thought of themselves as senior elite.

I needed carrots, not sticks. My subjects were in jail with the prospect of being handed over to a new Iraqi government. The new Iraqi officials would probably not value their long government expertise. There would be trials of some sort and punishment. When Clinton was elected and his team wanted to put a political appointee in my job, I was sent to the UN, not the gallows. The tradition in Iraq was different. Each change in government was traumatic for the predecessors. The detainees would already be sweating at the prospect of the worst possible rendition—a transfer from U.S. custody to the new gang running Iraq. I wanted to be able to offer them a way out, and I needed President Bush's authority to do so.

"Sir," I said. "I know the people closest to Saddam who will know where the weapons are or were. I would like to be able to materially affect their future if they cooperate with me."

Bush replied, "You mean like set Betty Germ up with a condo in Sarasota, Florida?" (He was referring to the well-known Iraqi female biological-weapons scientist Dr. Rihab Taha, known in the press as "Dr. Germ.")

"Well, that's the idea, though I am more focused on one particular guy, Abed Mahmud. He's sort of like Doctor Rice . . . well, not exactly, but he's the guy who controlled access to Saddam on all security and military matters. He's usually standing in back of Saddam in pictures. I know him from when I was at UNSCOM."

When I said I knew him, I saw a quizzical expression pass across Bush's face. But he quickly agreed: "Well, I guess that makes sense."

From my work before the war, I knew that the White House was willing to offer serious money and relocation to senior Iraqis who would defect. It would be consistent to offer get-out-of-jail-free cards to people who would help me now. That was the tool I wanted when I saw Abed again, and that was the key thing I took away from that meeting with President Bush.

It was odd, but I thought of Abed while I was sitting in the Oval Office. I had met him when we were inspecting Saddam's palaces. We had inspected Abed's office, which was like Rice's office in the West Wing of the White House, except much bigger. Abed's office was in the Republican Palace close to Saddam's office (though Saddam was never at his office—he kept moving). I could not help but think about Abed and the gang around Saddam. What a different scene that would be. They did not wake up at night worried about the press or Congress, or election results. They worried about failing to satisfy Saddam, who had complete control over their lives.

Oddly, I knew Saddam's team better than I knew the president's people. I did not like nor respect Abed, but we got along in the past and I let him think that we were kindred types when we met in Baghdad. Now he was in jail while I sat on the sofa in the Oval Office. At that moment it dawned on me what my strategy with him would be. I would become his new Saddam. There are people who relish the reflected authority derived from being an executive to a leader. He was one of them. Weak alone, he needed to be attached to someone with power. For a while, it would be me. Without me, he needed to be thinking about the view from the gallows and missing his wife and (more importantly to Abed) his two sons.

❖

I contacted some Iraqis I knew to gather data I could use in debriefings. Naji Sabri offered poignant and enlightening views that provided a context to the decisions leading up to the war. He described a sense of inevitability overhanging Baghdad and the frustration felt by some senior Iraqis at their inability to influence the decisions of the leadership: those of Saddam or even of the so-called quartet of top advisors around him—Taha Yasin Ramadan, Izzat Ibrahim al-Duri, Tariq Aziz, and Ali Hasan al-Majid ("Chemical Ali"). I also gathered some information about Abed from an Iraqi contact who was now out of Iraq, but who knew Abed and his family. He knew Abed had a girlfriend who had gotten out of the country with some money—enough money that, apparently, it took up most of a room in the apartment she occupied. Sabri offered more details that I could use at the right time. Abed would understand that I knew more about him than did his previous debriefers, who, I suspected, knew barely anything at all. In fact, it turned out to be worse than that.

When I met with the Regime Strategic Intent team to discuss my strategy for focused debriefings of the key senior Iraqis, I included the chief of the ISG team that managed detainee debriefings. A separate unit ran the debriefings of all the high-value detainees (HVDs) and was called the Joint Debriefing and Interrogation Center (JDIC). The staff there were military and civilian officers who were trained to interrogate people, but had no expertise in the subjects they were to be asking about. The military doctrine was that it was important to have a debriefer who knows how to debrief, not necessarily who knows anything about the subject—in this case, Iraq. And these folks didn't. They were doing their best and learning on the job, but needed direction.

I explained my goals for the overall ISG report, to describe the WMD program and the regime's decisions concerning WMD and to include why they made decisions and their strategic intentions. I emphasized that we had little time, but a unique opportunity to record for history the inside decision making of a regime.

I then turned to my immediate goal. I wanted teams of subject-matter experts and debriefers to go after selected key leaders and build the story of the regime's decisions on WMD and its overall conduct. If anyone knew about remaining concealed WMD programs, it would be one of these guys. We should scrutinize any past debriefing records and build on them.

Further, I said we would need to adjust the existing process, and on this point I was glad the JIDC chief was fully supportive. He understood the limitations of the existing system for our purposes. The debriefing system limitations were symptomatic of the overall Iraqi occupation. Staff turned over regularly after very short deployments. The same topics would be explored many times by new debriefers. Record keeping was sporadic. The detainees would get visibly frustrated at having to answer the same dumb questions every time a new twenty-something debriefer showed up so that he or she could say he or she had questioned Tariq Aziz or some other notable. I suspect these senior Iraqis felt like they were speaking to a government suffering from dementia—you could have the same conversation every fifteen minutes, and it would be just as new and exciting each time.

To offset this, I brought in four or five people who I knew truly knew their stuff and created teams for Vice President Ramadan, Mullah Huwaysh, "Chemical Ali," Tariq Aziz, and, of course, Abed.

I asked the JDIC chief, "How are the prisoners segregated?"

He replied, "Well, they aren't. They have cells, but they can meet in the common ground during exercise periods."

We had the top political, security, and intelligence officers of Saddam's regime all in one place, and they could all discuss what we had been asking them. We were amateurs dealing with the world's best dissemblers, manipulators, and, in certain cases, torturers. In lumping them all together, we had additionally mixed up potentially helpful technocrats, who had welcomed the U.S. invasion, with unreconstructed thugs. They all looked alike on the U.S. blacklist, because our intelligence on Iraqi individuals was as bad as, or worse than, that on Iraq WMD. Worse yet, the intelligence often came from sources that definitely had their own agendas, like the INC.

I asked that a wall be built down the middle of the camp so that we could at least divide the detainees into two sides. Getting the military to do this was ultimately too hard. These were the elite prisoners, whose prison at Camp Cropper was nothing like Abu Ghraib. Camp Cropper was small, populated by dozens, not thousands of prisoners at that time. (The camp was subsequently greatly expanded to deal with the influx of prisoners from ongoing counterinsurgency operations.)

I moved to my most immediate issue—Abed—and my game plan for him. I said I wanted to know about his debriefings so far and that I would debrief him personally. "Abed is the key," I said. "We have Saddam, but he has limited incentives and we have limited flexibility with him. I can't see saying to Saddam, 'Hey, dude, tell us where you put your WMD, and we'll let you go.' But Abed is a weasel who is only a big man when he is attached to a bigger man. Now he is unattached. I am going to become Abed's new Saddam." It sounded odd. I added, "When the U.S. Special Forces guys captured Abed last June, he asked them to contact me. Now he'll get his chance."

Abed was number four on the ridiculous "deck of cards." He was the fourth ace, the ace of diamonds. (Saddam was the ace of spades; Qusai, clubs; and Uday, hearts.) I inquired how his previous debriefings had gone in the interim. What I learned should not have amazed me, given the way the rest of the occupation had been handled. It turned out that the debriefer (a pleasant young woman) found him very cooperative. He did not have much to say about WMD, but had many good ideas about the new government. The debriefer had eventually given Abed the impression that he would probably find himself an important position in the new government!

Like so many aspects of the occupation, it was incredible. It was almost immoral how incompetent we were. Abed had only slightly better prospects of becoming a member of the new government than did Saddam. The secretary's more likely future was at the end of a rope.

This was one of endless instances where inexperienced people were assigned tasks for which they were unprepared and unguided. Abed had been encouraged to think he was going to get out of jail at some point when the new government took over. He would wait out some time, endure some questioning, and be out to rejoin his sons and wife. This was wildly misleading—to no good purpose. Little made me angrier about my experiences during the occupation than the listing, capturing, and treatment of the HVDs. Something else made the prospects for HVDs even worse. As part of an almost theological zeal to punish the former regime, the Defense Department established the Regime Crimes Liaison Office (RCLO). This institution ensured that a bureaucracy was in place to make sure that former regime members were processed, and reprocessed, for any connection to previous regime crimes.

In effect, the RCLO made it virtually impossible to release anyone from Camp Cropper. I would have to go to President Bush to get someone out, if it were necessary. ISG could propose someone for release, someone who served no intelligence value, had been in prison under Saddam, and perhaps had family members killed by Saddam. But to be released under the procedures established by Deputy Secretary Paul Wolfowitz in an August 2003 memorandum, several offices, now including the RCLO, which would also consult the new interim Iraqi government, had to agree. The problem was that personnel in Iraq turned over so frequently that there was always someone new who had not interviewed prisoner X for his purposes and therefore did not want to let the opportunity go.

This system was immoral, bad U.S. policy, and wrong for Iraq and created many enemies. I raised the issue regularly at all levels of the government, including with Rice, on multiple occasions. Nothing was ever done. This process was watched carefully on the Iraqi side by Ahmad Chalabi and his nephew, Salaam. Some of the most potentially helpful Iraqis were still in prison and could not get out. Later, the new Iraqi government would have its own political and personal reasons for keeping some good Iraqis jailed long after the United States agreed that their detention served no purpose.

Abed, however, was not a good person caught in a bad system. He was a thug. The absurdity was that while some of the talented Iraqis were losing hope, Abed believed his future was bright. I told our team, "Well, I will need to recalibrate Abed's thinking radically and quickly." It was difficult to be polite, and my language included much color in addition to the basic point. We were jailers, and with being a jailer comes a huge responsibility. I was very angry at how we had performed so far.

Over the next couple days, while setting up work programs for site inspections and document exploitation, I worked out a strategy for my first encounter with Abed. It would be six days after I landed in Baghdad, on Thursday, February 19, at 1400.

The plan was to have a debriefing session begin with a regular debriefer and a linguist. The debriefer would have a list of questions, as was often the case, prepared by analysts, often in Washington. They would talk for a while, and I would watch via the pinhole video monitor mounted in the room. At a given point in the middle of their discussions, I would open the door to the debriefing room and sit down next to Abed. I had pretty carefully worked out in my mind how I would play this out.

In discussing my plan with the JDIC chief, I said I wanted to do one additional thing. I wanted to be wearing my Glock, albeit unloaded. I thought the chief's brains would fall out. Certainly, his jaw dropped. I explained that in Abed's world, only an elite few could carry weapons in the presence of Saddam. It was a mark of importance. Abed carried a semiautomatic around Saddam. When Abed and I met at the palaces in 1998, we had discussed his pistol in a sort of guys-like-us, macho discussion. If I carried my weapon, it would silently communicate a lot to him.

It was too much for the JDIC chief. Having a weapon around any of the prisoners was wrong—against the rules—he would have to go back to Washington, and so forth.

I tried again: "Look, the goal is for Abed to understand quickly that his future is grim and that I am the only guy who can conceivably improve his future. In Baghdad, nothing communicates that like a gun."

He shook his head. In retrospect, he was absolutely right, and he saved me from my own bad idea. Abed was in the U.S. system now, not Iraq's. Any deviations from U.S. standards would be wrong. So, I would have to jar Abed out of his erroneous complacency with the force of personality—augmented by the truth.[1]

The debriefing rooms were as pathetic as the rest of the system for HVDs. There were a half dozen mobile trailers like those you see at construction sites for new buildings. One was an office, and one had some recording equipment and video monitoring tapes. The rest were empty rooms with a table and some stiff chairs. The trailers had noisy air-conditioners. If you turned them on, you could barely hear anyone speak. You certainly couldn't hear or record the conversation in the monitoring room. Of course, the taping equipment usually didn't work, and there was no system for storing or filing any recordings, so usually no one bothered. It was just another unbelievable example of our absence of planning or simple incompetence.

The day of the debriefing was relatively warm. I had on a light fleece sweater and sat in the darkened monitoring van as Abed was escorted from his cell to debriefing room 2. I watched on the video screen, which offered a downward-looking view. Abed had a beard and skullcap and seemed pretty fit. He was in regular clothes, not a prison jumpsuit. I made a note to myself that he should have a regression in privileges, to include a return to a jumpsuit.

I watched his body language for a while. He was confident. Though not fluent in English when I last saw him, he understood some. I suspected he knew more than he let on. After twenty minutes, I was getting anxious to start and walked over to the debriefing van, pulled open the wobbly aluminum door, and stepped in from behind him. His head snapped around, and he was surprised to see me. He started to stand and offer a hand. I just said, "Sit." To the debriefer, I said, "Keep going."

I roughly pulled up a chair and sat very close to him on his left side. He did not smell bad, so I assumed he had regular showers. I could see the hairs in his ears and the smoothly shaven hair follicles around the edges of his mustache. His brown eyes were shifting, not fearful, but not confident. Questioning. He wanted to be with the Duelfer he had met in 1998—two important guys talking about guns—but this wasn't happening.

I tried to visualize the images he saw in the debriefing room. I imagined how a noose would fit around his neck just above the hair on his chest at the top of his shirt. The hard loop of rope would pass just under and in back of his earlobes. I noticed that they had a slight fold. The ears were not large. He had bushy eyebrows, but it looked as though he trimmed them.

These eyes would probably see a last blurring image as a trapdoor released under his feet, and his neck would snap. Those brown eyes would bulge out of his head, having gathered some last image and thought. For

Abed, death was something that happened to others. He was not a guy who thought about his own death. That needed to change.

The debriefer droned on through his next questions. I grew more agitated and impatient. I was looking hard at Abed, who kept twisting his head between the debriefer and me. After a couple more methodical questions and hesitant, but empty answers from Abed, I exploded.

"This is bullshit! You are giving us bullshit answers to bullshit questions. You know what I want to know." I pounded the table.

"Do you have any idea what's going to happen to you?" I was loud and leaning into his face. The interpreter was struggling to keep up. I stopped and stared at Abed. I grabbed his arm. He quivered, which triggered my next semiplanned rant.

"Every picture of Saddam has you in back of him. Here's Saddam. Here's you!" I put my hands up in sequence, one for Saddam and one for Abed. "Saddam and Abed! Here's Saddam, here's Abed! Saddam and Abed! " I repeated in his ear.

Louder still, I said, "What happens to Saddam is going to happen to you!"

I said it twice to let the interpreter catch up.

Then I made my point, "Sovereignty goes back to Iraq in a hundred days. You and I have one hundred days." My math was wrong, but the point was the same. "In one hundred days, you're on your own."

I grabbed his arm again and suddenly, very quietly and slowly, said, "Your life can get better . . . or it can get worse." I let a few of my heartbeats go in silence. Then finished, "You know what I need to know. And you know that I know you." I was looking as far into his eyes as I could, imagining the back of his skull. And then I got up and walked out.

I wanted to create an impression on Abed, and a tightly wound up (slightly crazed) anger was what I was trying for. It came all too easily for me. Baghdad had that effect on me and, I suspect, most others. I was glad the JDIC chief had talked me out of the pistol idea. I hadn't been all that serious about it; there are strict limits on handling prisoners, as is proper. I had made a point of spending some time with the CIA chief legal counsel before coming out, so I would have a good sense of where legal limits extended regarding prisoners and other operational issues. Things would change once sovereignty returned to an Iraqi government.

Ironically, in Abed's case, his jailers had been too nice to him for his own good. He had been in fantasyland.

I walked back into the monitoring room, and Bill D., who was my senior staff guy and an analyst, said that I gave a good performance.

"Bill, that wasn't an act," I said. "That was the truth."

And it was, for Abed and me. I was his new Saddam. And back in his cell, when he reran in his mind this encounter, I hoped he would consider that his fate with the new Iraqi government may not be a happy one and could include a noose, and that I might be his way of avoiding that fate—although he would have observed that I had never promised him anything.

Over the next couple days, our "Team Abed" met to discuss strategy. We had a new debriefer named Nako, who was now energized. We decided to reduce Abed's status in the prison. Abed, I found, had been given certain privileges that had encouraged him to assert himself as the top dog in the prison. He would frequently debrief the prisoners after their meetings with our debriefers. Abed tried to carry his regime status with him to the prison yard, and many of the prisoners automatically accepted that. Since I couldn't divide up the prisoners, I decided to take advantage of the fact that everyone would know that Abed had been brought down a few pegs.

I decided not to see him for three weeks. Nako would meet with him, and Abed knew that Nako was in regular touch with me. That gave Nako leverage. When the "Team Abed" group met with me, we also compared notes with the debriefings of the other top regime members, though I was most directly involved with Abed and Saddam. Although in my first meeting with Abed, I had told him he knew what I wanted, Nako wasn't at all sure what it was.

I spelled out some objectives to Nako: "First, we need to know whatever Abed knows about the disposition of WMD. If he claims he doesn't know, he's lying. If he claims there may be some things he doesn't know, he's mostly lying. We need to know who at top levels was involved, and how. Much of this may deal with the money flow through the presidential office [Diwan] run by Ahmed Hussein al-Samarrai.

"Next," I added, "we want to know where Saddam was headed. We know the Iraqis wanted out of sanctions. Abed can tell us who they were paying and how they manipulated the Security Council. We need this data to illustrate the intentions of the regime. Abed has historically valuable information and unique insight into the strategies Saddam was applying. That would be great to record.

"Finally, I would like to know what they were doing with the UN-SCOM inspectors and inspections all this time.

"Oh, and Nako, anything else that you think is interesting. Just as long as he is scared not to tell the truth, but also so he isn't making stuff up. He has to be worried that we can check this stuff."

After a couple weeks of Nako's separate sessions, Abed was still being guarded in what he said. It was getting close to when I had to depart for congressional hearings in Washington. I thought maybe he was holding back until he could meet with me personally. We decided I would meet with him again and, this time, give him some written questions and some paper to answer them on, if he chose. Homework. It would be due the day before I left for Washington.

The idea of written responses turned out to be a useful approach, which we soon used with some of the other top detainees. Some responses were quite eloquent.

On Sunday, March 21, I had my second meeting with Abed, who was now wearing an ill-fitting, yellow jumpsuit. I greeted him coldly. Abed asked if he could address me.

I ignored that and began by saying slowly and deliberately, "Saddam has no future. He thinks he is president of Iraq. He is president of a prison cell. Saddam can only affect his legacy." I continued, "You, however, may possibly have a future."

Abed jumped in and said, "I know Saddam is finished. Did you know that I provided information that helped capture him? Senior officers thanked me."

I ignored the last bit. Why would anyone tell him his information helped capture Saddam? I doubted that it did.

I reiterated that Abed was "inextricably linked to Saddam."

He said, "I am only the presidential secretary. The group of four around Saddam made all the decisions."

I looked back at him. "Even if that were true, no one in the world would believe it, including me. I am leaving for Washington on Wednesday. I will be seeing very senior officials who will want to know if I am finding the truth about Saddam and WMD. I have told them that I was personally talking to you because I know that you know the most, besides Saddam. I would like to be able to say something positive that you have contributed."

Then I let Abed speak. "I will tell you anything you want to know, Mister Duelfer. I am your friend. You know I could only do so much when you were in Baghdad before. I was limited, but wanted to help." He went on to distance himself from Saddam's decisions: "I was not present during many of the key decisions Saddam made, because he would only speak outside and privately with the others and Abd al Tawab Huwaysh [the former head of Iraq's Military Industrial Commission]. Saddam thought all the palaces were bugged after your presidential inspections. Therefore, I did not hear many of the decisions."

"But," I said, "the others would have told you what happened."

Abed declared, "No! It was forbidden to tell anyone what Saddam discussed privately. You would be punished. They would be very careful not to tell me, because I would inform Saddam and they would be severely punished." This sounded believable.

At this point, I had a specific matter on which I needed his help. We had come across a presidential document that reported on a meeting with Saddam. There was a transmittal page with Abed's signature. The memorandum described a meeting in March 2003, just before the war. In the very last sentence in the memo, Saddam is said to have asked Tahir Jalil Habbush, the former Mukhabarat chief, how the United States might react if Iraq used chemical agents against their forces. We had received a few documents that were suspicious in the past. This one was very suspicious to me, and it came to us from Mukhabarat documents that were originally captured by Chalabi's group and then passed to the United States.

I gradually walked Abed through the meeting, which he acknowledged did take place. Then I showed him a paper (without letterhead showing) containing just the last paragraph. Abed studied it, but looked puzzled. He said, "No official memorandum would refer to Saddam in the way that document did. It was as if a White House document referred to 'Bush,' not 'the president.'"

When I finally showed him the entire document, he reviewed other parts, including a report about someone in the Pentagon who had obtained information for Iraq. This was true, he said. "This is all accurate, but for the last part." He implied that the last part was forged. I had to agree, as did our experts who subsequently studied the paper. We never had the opportunity to try to track down the origin of this and other forgeries, but I had deep suspicions about the INC. In this case, I found myself trusting Saddam's presidential secretary more than I trusted the Iraqi opposition.

The conversation warmed a bit, and I wanted to encourage Abed some. I told him a joke that Saddam had relayed about the Baath Party leaders. Abed no longer found Saddam's humor funny. In fact, Abed immediately declared that he renounced the Baath Party on June 25, 2003, the date of his capture.[2]

I had one other goal for the meeting. I wanted Abed to know that I knew more about him than he thought. I showed him some pictures I had taken of a house that a very good source had told me Abed used in the Mansour neighborhood. The presidential secretary was vaguely familiar with it, but not conclusive. Then I asked him if he knew a particular woman. He immediately said yes without thinking and then realized why I asked. He explained she was a senior person's wife, who had gone to Jordan. Abed was twisting his pencil. He was surprised I knew about his affair. Then he said without prodding, "You see, I am being honest with you. She was divorced." I shrugged. The point I wanted to make was that I knew people who knew about him. If he was going to lie, he could get caught out.

Finally, I ended the session with my written list of questions. I told him he could answer them over the next day or two. I would visit him again before I left. Any final things he might wish to add he could tell me after I had read his responses. "Yes, of course," he said gladly.

I said, "Write carefully. I would like you to be precise in separating what you know to be fact from your opinions, but please include both." Then I reminded him again, "Sovereignty returns to Iraq at the end of June. Time is running out." I got up to leave and was about to shake his hand when he said he would like to ask me something.

"They have taken away my regular clothing and even my book and I have been kept by myself for a long time," he said. "Can't this be reversed?"

I became angry. "No! You have less than a hundred days left before your fate changes radically, and you want to discuss clothing? Do you have any idea what lies ahead? You and Saddam are still linked." And I walked out.

Abed did his homework well. He wrote explicitly about Saddam's objectives regarding WMD and the Security Council. He began to mention how Saddam influenced key Security Council members, especially the Russians: "Saddam Hussein desired for Iraq to possess WMD, nuclear, biological, and chemical, because he always said that he desired for balance in the Middle East region and there are countries in the region that possessed such weapons (Israel) and countries on their way to possessing these weapons, like Iran." He went on to say that Saddam had instructed Tariq Aziz in 1991 to deal with the UN to get out of sanctions. Aziz would head a committee of four, called the quartet, consisting of Taha Yasin Ramadan, Ali Hasan al-Majid, and Izzat Ibrahim al-Duri. Abed said that Saddam expected that the sanctions would be gone in three years and that it would be a step-by-step process whereby Iraq would give something to the UN and the UN would give something to Iraq. Abed quoted Saddam as saying to Aziz, "You gave everything to the UN, but did not get anything back." The rest of the quartet also criticized Tariq for this outcome, according to Abed.

In another comment, Abed quoted Saddam as instructing Aziz to "tell the scientists to preserve the plans in their minds and that there must be a day in which we will get out from the siege [sanctions] and we will continue the activity in manufacturing of weapons and we will achieve the international balance and protect the dignity of Iraq and Iraqis and the Arab Nation." He also wrote, "If the sanctions are lifted and there is no UN monitoring, then it is possible for Saddam Hussein to continue his WMD activity and in my estimation it would be done in total secrecy and concealment because he has learned from

1991 and the UN decisions." Abed had been well aware of the deception activities in response to the UN inspectors and seemed to be confident that clandestine WMD programs would be possible after the sanctions were removed.

The former presidential secretary also noted that Saddam derived revenue from the Oil-for-Food program. He said income came from "the 10% taken from oil companies in the Oil-for-Food program." As Abed did not run this program directly, his knowledge of the exact mechanism was weak. However, he clearly expressed the policy that the cost of doing business with Iraq was a roughly 10 percent kickback on any given deal. I had heard this before the war anecdotally from oil dealers who lurked around the OPEC meetings.

Abed was aware of the priorities Saddam established for influencing the Security Council: "Saddam Hussein's instruction was that first preference was given to the Russian companies because Russia's stance was good and favorable to Iraq. Special preference was to companies nominated by the Russian government, the Russian President Putin, the Russian Foreign Minister Ivanov, and the Russian Ambassador in Baghdad." Abed highlighted that companies' oil allocations would be accorded to companies nominated by the Communist Party leader Gennady Zyuganov and the Russian Duma president, as well as companies identified by Russian intelligence. A second level of preference was given to French companies.

These were *very* interesting statements. And Abed knew we would talk to Aziz, Ali Hasan al-Majid, and Saddam. We could cross-check his statements. In these circumstances, I was beginning to acquire more confidence in the themes that were emerging for the direction of the final comprehensive report. In a way, I intended to get the Iraqis to write the report for me.

I went to see Abed the morning I was flying out of Baghdad, on Wednesday, March 24. We met with Nako and the linguist in the same flimsy trailer, debriefing room 2. I shook hands with Abed, and he smiled.

We went over many of the topics in his written paper, and Abed provided more details. He said the Russians were quite emphatic about getting oil allocations for their companies. According to Abed, the Russian ambassador in Baghdad met with Vice President Taha Yasin Ramadan twice a week on this and other matters. Foreign Minister Ivanov had come to see Vice President Ramadan to inquire about allocations for Russian companies. Similarly, the Russian ambassador saw Tariq Aziz to request that Russian companies get oil allocations and contracts.

Aziz was in close contact with the French. He had called Jacques Chirac directly and had gone to Paris for medical treatment. Abed said there was substantial interaction with the French, and it was through Aziz.

Abed then volunteered something more on the Russian influence: "I will talk about the Russian intelligence, on their financial transactions. They were done through Tariq Aziz and the Iraqi ambassador in Moscow, who is a Shiite. The ambassador in Moscow was the contact with Russian intelligence. There was a woman colonel in the Russian intelligence who wanted Aziz to accommodate companies named by Russian intelligence. She said they wanted contracts and cash for fifteen to twenty million dollars, and they should be in six-month installments." Abed knew this woman because he had also met with her in Baghdad.

I asked Abed about the role of Yevgeny Primakov, the former Russian foreign minister, who was close to Saddam. Abed said, "He is considered Saddam Hussein's most important friend. In the 1970s, Primakov was a journalist and met Saddam Hussein. But his close relationship with Saddam ended when he brought a letter from the Russian President Putin to Saddam Hussein shortly before the war. I was at the meeting. Putin was asking Saddam Hussein to step out of power and remain as the secretary general of the Baath Party. By this move, he would be able to convince the United States not to attack Iraq. Saddam Hussein walked out of the room, leaving Primakov in it. Saddam instructed me to summon Doctor Hammad Sadoun, Taha Yasin Ramadan, Tariq Aziz, and maybe Ali Hasan al-Majid. When they assembled, Saddam Hussein returned to the room with Primakov still standing there and asked him to read the letter from Putin in front of them all. When the letter was read, they showed their extreme displeasure with the letter and their strong support for Saddam."

There were some other sensitive areas of discussion, including Abed's relationship with Syria. He had close contacts there with senior officials close to the President Bashar al-Asad.

Abed discussed former UNSCOM inspector Scott Ritter. The Iraqi said that the head of the Mukhabarat stayed in touch with Ritter either directly or through an intermediary. Abed was familiar with the documentary film Ritter had made in Iraq: "Ritter had the assistance of an Iraqi American man called Khafaji of Detroit. Tariq Aziz and the Mukhabarat were involved, but I do not remember who made the coordination."

Abed went on about Ritter: "In August 2001, Ritter was in Iraq, and later, he came again and explained how the UN inspection teams would work." Other sources also commented on how the Iraqis benefited from these early briefings by Ritter, helping to prepare them for UNMOVIC inspections.

I asked how Saddam would order money paid.

"Saddam Hussein would instruct me to direct the head of the Diwan, Ahmed Hussein al-Samarrai, or the finance minister, Hikmat al-Azzawi, and tell them who to transfer funds to."

I knew about the bizarre withdrawal of $1 billion in cash from the Iraq bank during the night of March 29, 2003, in advance of the American invasion. Abed described his role in witnessing Saddam's written order instructing that the boxes (reported to be 250) of hundred-dollar bills be moved to safe houses. I could only imagine the Iraqis hurriedly loading boxes on trucks and careening through Baghdad in the middle of the night with a billion dollars in the back.

In this case, Saddam issued a written order. Abed said that in other circumstances, Saddam instructed that there should be no written record of orders or discussions. The secretary said, for example, when discussions about UNSCOM inspections took place between Qusay (head of the Special Security Organization) and other members of the quartet, they were instructed not to write anything down.

Our conversation had been relaxed, and Abed seemed to be enjoying telling some of the more sensitive matters. He had one last offering before I left. He described a very sensitive document Saddam had written and signed in three copies. It was a presidential decree Saddam created immediately after the bombing by Clinton in December 1998. The decree declared that Iraq would not comply with nor recognize the Security Council resolutions, and would no longer recognize Kuwait. The order was not to be distributed nor read by anyone other than a few key officials. There were three copies made. Abed said he kept the original in his office desk until he moved to an alternate location in the al-Ja'maa area during the war. He brought the document with him and then gave it to the general director of his office, Jasim Mohammed al-Mimari, on April 7, 2003. A second copy of the decree was given to the head of the Diwan, Ahmed Hussein al-Samarrai. And the third was given to the vice chairman of the RCC, Izzat Ibrahim al-Duri. Abed said that on the day the order was issued, Ramadan, Aziz, al-Samarrai, and two others were in the meeting with Saddam, and he instructed that this was for their knowledge but they were not to speak of it to anyone.

Abed said Saddam's intent resulted from anger provoked by the U.S. attacks. To Saddam, these attacks demonstrated that the United States felt unbounded by the UN resolutions. If the United States no longer felt restricted by the resolutions, then Iraq should not feel limited either. Abed's account revealed a great deal about the regime's operations and intentions. It was very clear that Saddam complied with the UN disarmament restrictions only as a tactic. His strategy was to reconstitute his weapons programs. Unfortunately for Abed, this information was too subtle and we did not, so far as I know, recover the original documents. The only thing that would have been worth intervention by the White House to save Abed was if he could come up with a sizable stockpile of chemical or biological weapons. Abed could not create such facts.

I was still not absolutely certain there were no weapons stockpiles. I wanted to confirm much of what Abed said with others who would be in a position to know. And I wanted to complete the picture of when and how the weapons were destroyed. Abed had given me a great deal, but it would not be enough for him to buy his way out of facing the new government.

On Thursday, April 1, 2004, I met with Condoleezza Rice at 1500. I brought Kyle, the colleague I had worked with in Iraq when the

invasion first got to Baghdad. Otherwise, I was alone. With Rice were
Steve Hadley and my friend on the National Security Council staff,
Will Tobey. I explained to Rice my discussions with Abed. I told her
that what he had provided so far was very interesting, but did not
show that there were weapons stockpiles to be found.

I also made the point that while Abed was probably deserving of
whatever he got, the United States was holding many technocrats who
would probably be strong supporters of the United States. Still in jail
were people who had been in prison when I was in Iraq the previous
spring. One was the man whose note in his debriefing record read, "not
worth three MREs a day." After being in jail under Saddam, he was still
in jail under the United States. The HVD process was not working.

Rice nodded politely. Nevertheless, nothing was ever done to correct the problem. I raised the issue every time I visited Washington,
progressively becoming less polite. Nothing was ever done, as I
learned later, because the issue was run by Paul Wolfowitz, who had
strong views on anyone who may have been involved in the previous
regime. Moreover, Wolfowitz was informed on the subject by Ahmad
Chalabi, who exercised control in Iraq by limiting the freedom of former regime members.

Rice brought the conversation back to the prospects of finding
WMD: "I understand one suggestion is that perhaps Saddam did not
know what his scientists were doing. For example, the nuclear scientists were promoting projects as being related to WMD because they
could attract funding. Did you see evidence of this?"

I said, "Do you mean, well, like if Iraq invaded the United States
and the Iraqis were investigating U.S. defense programs and discovered that defense contractors had been scamming the White House
on ballistic-missile defense schemes for decades?"

I realized too late that she might not appreciate this analogy, since
ballistic-missile defense and extracting the United States from the
ABM treaty had been the highest priority of the administration—
until two airliners, not missiles, were used to destroy the World Trade
Center in Manhattan.

Thankfully, Rice allowed herself to smile. I gather that when Rice
smiles, it is similar to laughing among less-disciplined individuals. In

any case, I said I did not think so. Unlike in the United States, it would be pretty risky to try to promote a program in any way that Saddam might consider duplicitous.

I did highlight one aspect of the picture that seemed to be coming together, including information from Abed. It looked as if Saddam certainly had the intention of getting WMD as soon as he could get out of the UN constraints.

Rice asked repeatedly if there was anything I needed, and I said no. She never hinted at any outcome that would please the White House. There were only expressions of support for whatever I judged to be necessary.

When I returned to Baghdad, I met with Abed twice more. "Team Abed" continued to work with him. Nako left Iraq, and another debriefer was assigned to Abed. The debriefer was a nice guy. Too nice. I thought of him as a Quaker. He seemed to see only the good in people, and from what I could see, Abed worked him perfectly. I was less directly involved in Abed's case once I got some fundamental features of the regime documented. I was amazed, however, when I was asked about a request for Abed to be allowed a family visit. The question propelled me to go see the debriefer.

"I am perplexed," I said. I was trying to be polite and clean up my language. "I see you have requested a family visit for Abed." A family visit was a big privilege. HVDs would get a phone call once in a while, but a visit was huge. I asked, "Is this part of a strategy to isolate Abed from the other prisoners? I guess I can see where you might instill distrust of Abed among the fellow detainees if he were seen to be getting special privileges from us. They would figure he was really giving up something."

The Quaker quietly said, "Well, no. I just recommended Abed for a family visit."

I did not get it. "But why? You must have a reason."

He did. "I think everyone should have family visits," he said simply. I thought to myself, "This guy is too good to be in Baghdad. Hell, he's too good to be in Washington."

Abed is a guy who wouldn't dream of family visits for the Saddam opponents he incarcerated in his time in power. Yet Abed happens, through the luck of the personnel draw, to be assigned a debriefer who thinks everyone should have family visits and all people are basically good. In the next cell is someone who tried to help us *before* the war, and it is his luck to be stuck with a debriefer who thinks Baathists are Nazis and Wernher Von Braun should have been shot. There were too many problems with the U.S. system to fix.

Maybe, in the end, Abed deserved his family visit. He did provide a lot of detail about the regime. Abed described a fascinating aspect of Saddam's direction for the defense of Iraq before the war. Saddam exercised control and passed authority through the regional offices of the Baath Party. This circumvented the normal command and control of the regular army. This basic point explained much of the mystery concerning the defense (or lack thereof) for Iraq.

Abed also provided essential background for debriefing of Saddam. With Abed, we could understand Saddam's perspective and test some of his statements. I had studied Saddam's behavior and used that knowledge with Abed. Saddam described Abed as a loyal but fundamentally weak and not particularly brilliant individual who derived his power from Saddam. I agreed completely with Saddam's assessment of Abed.

I also suspected that Abed might not share the same fate as Saddam in the end. It had been Abed's practice to make deals for the regime. He did this with Syria, and I suspect he did this with some who are in the Iraqi government. It is possible that some of these people may still come to his aid. I would be surprised if his family had not brought large sums of money out of Iraq when they fled. Still, I have difficulty picturing him as an old and weak man. He is a person who should not have a peaceful old age surrounded by grandchildren with whom he would never discuss his past. But the vagaries of Iraqi deal-making are impossible to predict.

CHAPTER 20

Saddam

I knew exactly where to find essential facts about Iraq's WMD programs. There was a simple concrete block room, approximately eight by eight feet, that held the answers to the questions that gnawed at the world. The room was in a nondescript, one-story building at Baghdad International Airport. I could drive there in twenty minutes. It was Saddam Hussein's prison cell.

Like Abed, Saddam was kept in Camp Cropper, the U.S. military prison established specifically for HVDs. It was filled with Iraqi celebrities of a sort, and they were treated well. We called it the "petting zoo."

Unlike Abed and the other detainees, Saddam was placed in a cell in a separate building and never mixed with or saw the other HVDs. We could search hundreds of military facilities, weapons depots, intelligence buildings, safe houses, and laboratories. We could sort through millions of documents from all over Iraq. We could capture and debrief dozens of top scientists and military and intelligence officers. But the essence of what was important to know was in Saddam's head.

Saddam was the Iraq regime. To understand the regime and how it operated, one had to understand Saddam. This was both a complicating factor and a simplifying one. On the one hand, to understand the government's actions, you only had to understand one man and the system around him. On the other hand, that man was not your average Joe.

The decisions to have and, later, not have WMD were Saddam's. The decisions to use and not use WMD had been his. If we were to understand those decisions and learn from them, it was vital to understand Saddam. He was central to the tragedy of Iraq. How Saddam acted and reacted to events and policies would show how things had gone so wrong and might again elsewhere.

So it was imperative to record how Saddam saw the world. I wanted to get as far into his mind as possible. Many decisions throughout the past three decades had been based on a cartoonist's impression of Saddam. He was not a cartoon. He was catastrophically brilliant and extremely talented in a black, insidious way. Saddam understood what motivated people at their basest level. He had a visceral talent for using power. He would mix reward and punishment in ways that controlled an explosive country. Saddam was narcissistic, deadly, and without any conscience as understood by most modern Westerners. But he compelled Iraq to obey him for almost a quarter century. He compelled the world to attend to him, as well. We had an historic opportunity to dissect that process.

On December 13, 2003, in a moment of misplaced bravado, Ambassador L. Paul Bremer III famously crowed at a press conference, "We got him!"

Saddam Hussein was finally captured following an intensive hunt by U.S. Special Forces that began with the invasion nine months earlier. He had been literally holed up outside his hometown, Tikrit. Saddam looked haggard and disoriented in the videos made public to the world after his capture. He had been tracked down by a combination of human and technical collection. An informant from his hometown identified a farm with a very obscure small hut. U.S. forces arrived at night and almost missed the concealment cover to Saddam's hide site. When they lifted the cover, Saddam's first words were something like, "I am Saddam Hussein, the president of Iraq. I am prepared to negotiate with President Bush."

Getting to the informant in Tikrit had not been easy. Through the fall of 2003, CIA and military teams had been tracking down and debriefing individuals who were close to Saddam—especially the inner circle of his guards known as the Murafaqin and others who were physically closest to Saddam, such as his personal valets. Curiously, these tended to be Christians because they had beliefs that would have inhibited them from attempting to murder Saddam (or so Saddam thought).

This process was very successful—an unheralded success—and yielded very interesting details about Saddam's private life. For example, one of the Murafaqin (call him Naseer) had been abandoned by Saddam and left to fend on his own, with no money, as the Americans occupied Baghdad. This was not a smart move by the ungrateful Saddam. This guard was in his forties and well fed to the point of having a belly that forced his belt buckle to twist out at a forty-five-degree angle. Naseer was balding and had the characteristic strut that conveyed power and importance in the former regime—except he now found himself without either. All he had were stories about Saddam. Saddam left too many like him behind, and they provided directions to finding the man himself.

Another individual we found was a personal valet who served Saddam his morning tea, laid out his clothing, etc. The trusted manservant was well aware of who may have been in bed with Saddam. This led, in turn, to a particularly poignant debriefing of a Ministry of Foreign Affairs official (call him Fahad) who was unwittingly closely connected to Saddam. His relationship illustrated some of the intricacies and blindness of those drawn into the regime. Fahad was not terribly bright or effective, according to the professionals around him. But no one told Fahad this, and it did not occur to him that he did not achieve his position in the Ministry of Foreign Affairs on merit. He had been appointed by Foreign Minister Naji Sabri at the request of Saddam, and at the request of Saddam he was sent on many missions outside of Iraq—in itself an honor and a sign of privilege.

What he did not know until Americans informed him was that Saddam took a personal interest in his absence. The Iraqi president had an ongoing relationship with Fahad's wife—and the young daughter of Fahad was in fact not his, but Saddam's. When this was conveyed to Fahad in an undeniable way, he seemed physically shocked. He had, like so many in the regime, rationalized the gifts and special treatment accorded by Saddam to his wife and her father. Indirectly, it was a seduction of him as well as of his wife. It shows how those around Saddam could incrementally bend to his desires without confronting some hard facts about the ultimate end. This minor event also illustrates why the regime had such difficulty understanding how the Monica Lewinsky controversy nearly brought down the Clinton administration.

And, finally, the valet noted that Saddam endured substantial scolding and teasing from the woman.

In Washington, expectations were high that Saddam's capture would be the turning point for the occupation. The violence that had been growing in Iraq after the invasion and the destruction of all existing elements of the former government would plummet. The assumption was that the violence was caused largely by a limited number of former Baathists, Special Republican Guard and security services, or so-called former regime elements (FREs, in the vernacular of intelligence PowerPoint charts). "Dead-enders," Bremer called them.

President Bush addressed the nation on Sunday, December 14, 2003: "The capture of this man was crucial to the rise of a free Iraq. It marks the end of the road for him, and for all who bullied and killed in his name. For the Baathist holdouts largely responsible for the current violence, there will be no return to the corrupt power and privilege they once held. For the vast majority of Iraqi citizens who wish to live as free men and women, this event brings further assurance that the torture chambers and the secret police are gone forever."[1]

The hope was that once people realized Saddam would not return, they would give up their fight. The White House, Defense Secretary Donald Rumsfeld, and Ambassador Bremer still refused to call the resistance an insurgency. Nor did they see the growing fractures that would become outright sectarian conflict. What they saw was Saddam in U.S. custody. They had "cut off the head" of the "resistance" . . . or so they thought.

Bremer and others directing the occupation still did not understand that they had eviscerated the secular, technical, and bureaucratic infrastructure of Iraq without establishing any clear hope that there would be any future for those displaced. And the displaced included virtually the entire army and the thousands of bureaucrats who knew how to run the normal systems of government, including those that provided water and electricity.

What slowly became apparent—too slowly—was that neither Saddam nor the favored groups like the INC had much effect one way or the other on the indigenous opposition elements that evolved into an insurgency. The insurgency did not have unity of organization or unity of purpose. From the American standpoint, it might have been better if the insurgency had had some unity—at least then you would have a known counterpart to either fight or negotiate with.

The capture of Saddam did nothing to address the fundamental problem. We had created enemies of the Iraqis themselves—and they knew where all the explosives and guns were. By the time of his capture, Saddam was already detached. The Iraqis who had learned that there was no hope of reconciling with the occupying power also learned that the last superpower's military could be attacked fairly easily with minimal risk. They did not need Saddam for inspiration or direction.

This disappointment became pretty clear as the initial debriefings of Saddam proceeded. The CIA had the lead in the first series of debriefings, and a team was rapidly assembled. The group included a military officer who spoke Arabic and served as translator, a senior polygrapher (who had long experience in trying to understand if someone is dissembling—though Saddam was not given a polygraph), two longtime Iraq analysts who had followed Iraq for many years, and a couple of "reports officers" who wrote up the proceedings in highly restricted cables. While the team was expert, only one analyst had spent much time in Iraq and personally knew senior Iraqis. Still, they recorded Saddam's responses to the vital questions that were pressing at the time. They also methodically recorded Saddam's descriptions of his decisions from the beginning of the Iran-Iraq War to the present day.

While Saddam would have viewed the team as junior in rank (compared with his position as a head of state), they conveyed to Saddam that whatever he said would go to the highest levels of the U.S. government (and it did). While this message was meant to give Saddam a stronger rationale for talking, his incentives still were limited.

The CIA team quizzed Saddam on the matters of immediate interest to Washington—WMD, the insurgency, and links to terrorism. They got few revelations on WMD or the insurgency, but a long, detailed recitation of Saddam's version of history—fascinating in its own way. Saddam was highly controlled and cautious. The debriefings produced a long series of cables that someday will be invaluable to historians. Not many dictators survive being deposed long enough to relate any of their opinions and judgments.

While interesting, these discussions did not fully convey the inner workings of Saddam. He was a tough customer—a former dictator who was conducting his own war of wits with interrogators. This was slim pickings for official Washington. Still, Saddam knew that the debriefers had access to other senior Iraqis and documents. He knew his deputies would be spinning history in their own ways. The team also worked to induce his cooperation by providing limited comforts such as books by Naguib Mahfouz (the Noble Prize–winning Egyptian author) and a thin mattress for his standard army nylon and aluminum frame cot.

Back in Washington, the bloom of hope that Saddam would reveal the location of WMD and that the insurgency would collapse in advance of the upcoming U.S. election wilted quickly. Saddam's comments on WMD were terse. He said Iraq had none and added, "If you can locate a traitor to find me, why shouldn't you find a traitor to locate WMD?" Saddam had some respect for U.S. and UK intelligence. In the fall of 2002, following the release of a British "white paper" describing Iraq WMD and following U.S. pronouncements about Iraqi possession of WMD, he was prompted to ask at an RCC meeting if anyone there was aware of capabilities that perhaps he, Saddam, was not. Could the CIA be right? Saddam was asking. The RCC members of course responded that such an event would be impossible; it would be impossible for Saddam not to know something . . . but Saddam was not so sure.

By mid-January, it became apparent that there would be no sudden revelations and the focus shifted to matters that could ultimately be used in a court of law. This opened the possibility that those conducting the debriefings might be subject to testifying, a possibility that was anathema to the CIA. At this point, the lead in debriefing Saddam would have to shift to the FBI.

It was obvious to me that Saddam was different, so debriefing him had to be different. When I met with President Bush before departing for Baghdad, he had conveyed his support of my strategy for controlling the debriefing of senior Iraqis. My best target for insights to the regime was Saddam's presidential secretary, Abed. At the same time, I had been thinking about Saddam and had read some of the reporting cables. When I arrived in Baghdad, I did not yet have a strategy for Saddam, and neither did I have much hope that more information would be forthcoming from him. Still, whatever he said would be important, and to the extent that we could induce some candor, this would be valuable.

Saddam was in a special solitary cell. It had an army cot, a prayer rug, and nothing on the walls. He was able to use a mirror and razor twice a week. Saddam had ruled the 440,000 square kilometers of Iraq. Now he paced, prayed, and slept in about 9 square meters. Saddam had a bad back, and so a board was placed under the mattress to provide a firmer surface. It was quite a change from one of his bedrooms I inspected in 1998 in his Tikrit Palace. That room was large enough for a basketball game.

Whatever was done with Saddam would eventually be scrutinized by the international community. It was also clear that what happened ultimately to him would be decided by whatever new government was constituted in Baghdad. The United States would only be a temporary custodian. Saddam had to be treated very carefully.

Time was limited. Once sovereignty was returned to Iraq, so too would control of Saddam. Until then, we had complete control of his environment. His only non-American visitors were from the International Red Cross, with the exception of a single visit by a group of representatives of the interim Iraqi government, including Adnan Pachachi, Mowaffak al-Rubaie, Adel Mehdi, and Ahmad Chalabi. They visited briefly the day after he was captured. Unlike the other HVDs, the information Saddam received about the outside world was carefully controlled. He had no contact with the other HVDs (although they were aware he was present).

Saddam knew he would face some sort of trial. Anything he said could be used against him. He could not claim to have been simply following orders. Saddam was a very shrewd and cagey individual, which he demonstrated in his initial debriefings from December to January. He was in a contest with his debriefers, and he knew he could simply outwait them, if he chose.

Saddam had survived for decades using his ability to interrogate and intimidate others. He had a controlling presence. When Saddam gazed upon you, he conveyed the sense of decrypting you. His eyes focused not on the plane of your face; they seemed to focus two or three inches beyond. Perhaps consciously, Saddam did this to appear to see into you. It was a commonly expressed fear that "*he* knew you were considering disloyalty before *you* knew you were going to be disloyal." His stare was unnerving to his lieutenants. It was even unnerving to his captors.

The initial CIA intelligence debriefings ended in late January 2004. Recognizing that a trial was coming and the need for material that could potentially be used publicly, an FBI team was dispatched to Iraq. A senior FBI officer initially directed the team, but he soon left. The effort then fell into the hands of a crafty thirty-six-year-old Lebanese American, fluent in Arabic, with sparkling intelligent eyes and a calm, winning manner. This was Special Agent George Piro.

Piro arrived on January 13, 2004. It was his second assignment to Iraq. He had also been in Iraq during the early days of the occupation, when he had been involved in efforts to track down wanted terrorists and HVTs. One HVT was Abdul Rahman Yasin, a fugitive from the first World Trade Center bombing in 1993. Before joining the FBI, Piro had been a detective for ten years in California.

Piro came to the United States as a child when his father, a successful Lebanese businessman, moved his family to California. He entered seventh grade not speaking a word of English, but he picked it up quickly and today speaks without a trace of accent.

As a detective, he successfully investigated and prosecuted over thirty cases—including capital cases. Nearly all resulted in convictions. He knew how to get things done in the field, but also how things had to fit together to build a case in the courtroom. And he knew how to deal with people in a natural, but purposeful, way. Piro has the quiet confidence of someone who knows he can take charge of a situation physically and mentally. He seemed perfectly pleasant with only the best interests of his subject in mind, while at the same time, he was extracting information to help condemn his prisoners. I was delighted to have him on the ISG team.

Piro had some colleagues who helped in writing and research. One co-worker, Todd, had worked terrorism issues and had been a field agent in California, where he had recruited Piro into the bureau. Todd had also been a professional tennis player. Another colleague, Tom, was a brilliant profiler. He had experience profiling mass murderers. He excelled in trying to get into psychopaths' heads, which was just where we wanted to go. And there was a sharp CIA reports officer who would keep track of and report useful intelligence material. She was young, bright-eyed, and earnest. She had also been in the CIA Iraq Operations Group before the war and had solid knowledge of the Iraqi regime.

While Piro met one-on-one with Saddam, there was usually a pinhole camera by which others on the team could observe and take notes. Saddam had to assume there was a camera, given his security services' broad use of video surveillance. The Rasheed Hotel was notorious for its video system. I remember being amazed when I read a *Washington Post* story about the preparations made by CBS news anchor Dan Rather before a very rare interview Saddam granted him a month preceding the invasion on February 24, 2003. The article quoted Rather describing how he practiced his questions before the mirror in his hotel room. "I sat in front of the mirror and pretended he was on the other side and tried out the questions." Given the wiring in the Rasheed Hotel, Saddam might as well have been on the other side.[2] The strategy we developed for getting Saddam to reveal himself had a few entry points. Saddam was realistic enough to realize his future was limited.[3] This did leave one incentive on his part—to shape his legacy. We could play on that. He knew his senior ministers and his presidential secretary were in custody. It was made clear to him that the legacy of his regime was being written in the course of our work, and unless he offered his views, it would be shaped strictly on the basis of "those weasels around him who were now blaming him for everything wrong with Iraq." This argument had some traction with him. It was also decided that the approach would be to get close to him psychologically and not be aggressively confrontational.[4] Saddam was an extremely controlled and disciplined individual. Curiously, he seemed content in the confines of his cell. Having had so many palaces and servants, one might be surprised at his placidity in confinement. A couple of factors may explain that.

First, he was safe for the first time in years. He did not have to move from one location to another regularly to thwart attempts to kill him. Nor did he have the demands of all the devious characters who had surrounded him.

Finally, he had a self-mythology that he was engaged in a long epic struggle, often alone, dependent upon his wits for survival in the desert. His present incarceration was a continuation of the storyline that included his escape from Iraq after his participation as a young Baathist in the failed attempt to assassinate General Abdul Karim Qasim in 1959. Lonely struggle was part of his psyche. He had also been in jail before in Iraq from 1964 to 1966.

To implement our strategy, Piro would spend hours every day with Saddam. Piro would be the only person Saddam would see and talk to regularly—apart from medical care. If Saddam wanted something, then he had to ask Piro. They were going to be inescapably close, and Piro would have complete control over how to manage the situation. I have to admit, I had to overcome a strong desire to meet with Saddam myself. But this would not have advanced our work and would have undermined Piro's position with Saddam. The prisoner Saddam had to see Piro as his only channel to the rest of the world.

Piro and I met regularly to review progress and discuss tactics for both Saddam and the other key HVDs. I wanted Piro to be fully aware of all the other ISG work; it was quite possible he could stumble across something with Saddam that would be useful. Piro needed to learn everything that we were doing to understand WMD in the context of the overall regime. He had to become expert in all the WMD issues as well as all the criminal matters, so that he could shape his dialogue with Saddam to the most pivotal issues.

Piro also helped the ISG members who were working with the other HVDs. Different perspectives on events, like decisions at Revolutionary Command Council meetings, were collected in this way and gave a tangible picture of the workings and atmosphere of the regime's operations and decisions. We regularly tested our working hypotheses on senior Iraqis concerning decision points. And ultimately, through Piro, we tested them with Saddam. With this approach, I worried about the fundamental risk that Saddam, a master manipulator, would string Piro along until we ran out of time and sovereignty was returned to Iraq at the end of June. One possibility, however, was that Saddam might see Piro in terms of a son. The American was about the same age and physical appearance as Qusay. This too carried some risk: We were not sure how vengeful Saddam would feel about the deaths of his own two sons. On the other hand, Saddam might also allow his interest in his legacy to manifest itself through a surrogate—Piro—if he got past any anger over the loss of his own progeny.

As it turned out, Saddam was not consumed by the deaths of Qusay and Uday. He seemed peculiarly untroubled. When Piro raised, explicitly, the subject of his sons and their role, Saddam displayed no particular feelings and certainly no pride. It was a strange reaction. Cold. He evidenced no anger toward the United States for their deaths. It was almost as though he thought they were not strong enough to survive (and succeed him). Nevertheless, Saddam did express some paternal pride that they had gone down fighting. In the earlier debriefings, he had expressed anger only once—when the CIA team questioned him about his illegimate son Ali (whose mother was one of his mistresses, Samira Shahbandar). He snapped, "So you want to kill him, too?"

Saddam acknowledged that Uday was a dangerous misfit who had not earned his position. Qusay was more trustworthy and was semi-competent in running the security services, but Saddam knew he was weak and could make bad choices. The son could also be manipulated by those around him.

While I proffered the notion that Saddam might implicitly use Piro as the surrogate son to shape his legacy, something slightly different seemed to occur. Saddam saw himself in Piro as a younger man. That was even better. For Saddam, who could be a better image than himself?

One salient risk in this strategy was that Piro would be won over by Saddam. I had to trust Piro and his reports. Piro knew this and used his team and others to make sure he stayed grounded. Still, it would not be without personal cost to develop the necessary bond with Saddam to lead the Iraqi to share information and views that Piro knew could be damaging to himself. Piro entered this process with his eyes open. It turned out he was very good at allowing Saddam to believe he was capturing his sympathy. It was high-stakes deception.

Piro and I also reviewed the work with Abed. Anything we could get from Saddam to leverage Abed or validate the former secretary's statements would be valuable. In the end, I expected to get more hard information from Abed than Saddam. As it turned out, this was the case. However, much truth came from the Saddam dialogues.

The early days of Piro's meetings with Saddam were not smooth. Saddam was making demands. He still thought he was the president of Iraq and wanted to be treated that way. Of course, it did not happen. He was "Mr. Saddam," not "Mr. President." It was to be a period of testing by Saddam (similar to his early testing of UN inspectors in 1991). Both Piro and I had been separately questioning other key members of Saddam's government (like Tariq Aziz) to gain background. We began to build an understanding of Saddam and his tangible and intangible exercise of authority. But it was uneven progress, and we had a long distance to go to understand the full relationship of Saddam to WMD, past, present, and future.

While I knew our strategy with Saddam required patience, I was getting more anxious as time elapsed. Piro's relationship with Saddam was building, and we were gaining considerable knowledge, but we needed some concrete statements as well. While this part of ISG's work risked no lives, it was one of the major elements that kept me up at night.

In one way, I was envious of Saddam. He seemed to have no trouble sleeping. He was regularly sleeping six to eight hours through the night (we would get regular information on Saddam's health and habits). He was doing a lot better than I was.

As the relationship deepened, Saddam began to derive psychological benefit from his meetings with Piro. The military police who brought Saddam his meals were supposed to pass them through a slot in the door. Saddam demanded that they open the door and bring the tray in. The soldiers had been complying with this request. When Piro learned this was going on, he told them to stop and only pass the food trays through the slot. Saddam rebelled by going on a hunger strike. It lasted five days.

Finally, Piro found a way out. "Mister Saddam, you as a leader must know that it is impossible for me to change this rule. If I were to concede this exception to the rules, what would my men think? They would see weakness. What would the other prisoners think? They would make demands. It is impossible, and you of all people should know this."

Saddam saw the point and resumed eating. It proved to be an incremental step in their relationship. Saddam had accepted Piro's superiority.

They spent much time discussing nonthreatening subjects. For example, Saddam spent many hours talking about women. Saddam reputedly had many women besides his wife. Nothing he said to Piro contradicted that. He enjoyed female company mentally and physically. He did not approve of the vicious track record of his psychotic son Uday, who notoriously abused women.

Saddam's Iraq had maintained a relatively liberal attitude toward the role of women in a Muslim country. Saddam had fostered the education of women, and professional women were common. He had named a woman, Huda Ammash, to the Revolutionary Command Council in May 2001. (Ammash, a microbiologist, had studied at the

University of Missouri and was suspected of involvement with the biological-weapons program.)

But Saddam's discussions of women were more often less academic. He acknowledged multiple mistresses to Piro.[5] Although his dissertations on the female of the species were not crude, they tended to be earthy. But even these discussions allowed Piro to get closer to Saddam and to the facts we sought. They revealed much about Saddam and his secular nature. He indulged his senses, but controlled them. He drank alcohol regularly, but not to wild excess.

By late March, Piro and Saddam grew more comfortable in their discussions. Saddam told Piro, "Mister George, you know that in fact, I am a simple man. My confinement to this cell is not a hardship. I have few needs."

Piro responded casually, "Come on, you had thirty-seven palaces, dozens of cars, helicopters, boats . . . Are these the tastes of a simple man?"

But Saddam said, "The palaces were to confuse the enemy. You know the Americans wanted to bomb the leadership. With thirty-seven palaces, they could not locate the leadership at any given time. This was successful."

He had a point . . . sort of. He had to work to preserve his security, and it was a real burden. The threat came not just from the United States. There had been plenty of attempts on his life by Iraqis. He confirmed to Piro that he felt safe in his cell. He had also admitted that he never touched a telephone again after 1991, recognizing the risk that it could compromise his safety. This ironic feeling of security in the hands of his captors worked favorably with the approach Piro took to get close to him.

In 2003, one of the people we came across in Baghdad was Saddam's tailor. He had made and altered suits for Saddam. Some were still in his shop, uncollected by Saddam's staff. I picked up an Italian suit, a Romanini Uomo of gray gabardine. The pant waist was about forty-two inches, and the inseam thirty-two. The tailor had altered the trousers to add a small pocket concealed behind the front of the waistband of the trousers. It was for a small pistol. I could not resist the temptation to put the suit on. It was very big on me. Saddam was a heavy man before the war. He was much thinner at Camp Cropper.

By April, Saddam seemed to realize he had been giving up some information that could be used against him in a trial. He declared that he would no longer submit to further questioning, claiming status under the 1949 Geneva Convention III. Saddam knew that Secretary Rumsfeld had declared that he was considered an enemy prisoner of war. Saddam had become knowledgeable about the Geneva Protocols—he had a copy and read them. Significant to us during this period, however, was that Saddam wished to *continue his meetings* with Piro.

This was a turning point. Saddam had formed a dependent bond with Piro. He rationalized in his mind that his dialogue with Piro was proper. This was a significant mark of success.

Saddam knew it was Piro's job to question him. It was clear that Saddam also needed to talk with Piro. Piro adjusted his tactics—he scheduled formal sessions, when he would question Saddam about specific events. This scheduling implied that the rest of the time when Saddam was with Piro was somehow different. In the scheduled sessions, Piro had notes and prepared topics. The rest of the time, topics flowed in any direction. Saddam could be guarded in the formal sessions and still let his need for human contact flow in the unstructured time he spent with Piro. It was in those moments that some key revelations were shared.

Piro carefully measured what he would allow Saddam to have. But first and foremost, Saddam had to ask. Anything he wanted, he had to ask Piro, and Piro would decide. Saddam asked for paper and pencil. Piro agreed. It was a concession, and Saddam knew it. By asking, Saddam was also acknowledging his dependency. Saddam knew this as well. Piro could give or take it away, on a whim if he desired. Piro could be like Saddam used to be.

It was not lost on us that in our positions of absolute authority over Saddam and the other detainees, we had powers that were Saddam-like. Could we become Saddam? That dark question floated silently over our work. What made Saddam extraordinary? What was in him that was not in any of us? Or was it in us, but buried? Such ruminations floated through my mind on nights when I stared into the black water surrounding my quarters at Saddam's former palace. When he had stared at the same water, what did he see? Was it different?

In one of Piro's formal sessions, Piro questioned Saddam about war crimes committed by an Iraqi tank crew in 1991. Civilians had been tied to the front of tanks as human shields. Piro was pressing Saddam about his knowledge of such tactics committed under the leadership of his military commanders, including "Chemical" Ali Hasan al-Majid.

Saddam parried by questioning Piro, "How do you know this? Who told you? What was the weather like at the time?" He continued with other spurious points to deflect the line of questioning.

Piro pressed on, stating flatly that he must have been aware. "How could you not know these tactics? You are the supreme military commander at the time. Weren't these officers under you following your lead? Did the great Iraqi Army not report up the chain of command as all modern military systems do?"

Saddam countered, "Many times, subordinates are afraid to report to the president." He slipped into the third person to discuss his role. "Officers are particularly reluctant to report information that is not good. They are afraid that their superiors may punish them."

This was a recurrent theme of Saddam's, and it held some truth, though it was self-serving. The terror he emanated inhibited his receipt of accurate information. The picture he saw was distorted by those reporting to him who feared for their positions and their lives either from Saddam directly or from some of the surrounding guards. Unlike Saddam, President Bush had not shot any of his subordinates, but I had to wonder if he didn't experience similar doubts about the information provided to him, perhaps especially about Iraq.

I watched Saddam's exchanges with Piro. The former dictator spoke as though he was discussing events in a novel someone else had written. He was distant in a way that went beyond feigned ignorance. These atrocities seemed trivial to Saddam in relation to the greater good that Saddam saw himself embodying.

With the paper and pen that Piro had allowed him, Saddam took occasional notes during this questioning. At one point, Saddam, by his attitude and gestures, assumed the air of president. It looked like he was about to respond dismissively, "Well Mister George, I can't understand why you waste my time with this trivial matter. But I respect you, and if it is important to you, Mister George, I will have someone look into it." And he extended his left hand with the paper (he wrote with his right hand) blindly, as if he were passing it to an invisible aide whom he assumed would scurry off and attend to the matter. But Saddam caught himself. He was not in a palace office with surrounding Diwan and presidential staff. There was no one there but George Piro. Piro was the only human mirror in which he saw himself. And Piro was the only recorder of what he may have wished to communicate.

There was much to learn from Saddam's "management style"—good and bad. He was able to consolidate power and build a powerful organization from disparate groups. As an organization, it worked—for a while. Saddam was able to overcome many obstacles that hobble more representative organizations and governments. But he was also trapped by it, and ultimately, it killed him as well as those he purported to lead to a greater Iraq. Watching Saddam paw at the questions put by Piro helped illuminate some of these features of his regime. They were also apparent in the explications of his lieutenants. The WMD programs—their birth, use, and hibernation—were also reflective of Saddam's style of management. It became clear that many of his key directions were conveyed implicitly rather than explicitly. The fact that, in the previous fall, Saddam felt it necessary to ask his senior ministers whether there were any WMD programs that may not have been brought to his attention was evidence of a critical flaw in his ruthless leadership.

After a month, Piro's team expressed a view that Piro was not pushing vigorously enough and that time was seeping away. Piro had to balance those views with his own gut feelings about his understanding of Saddam. He felt he was getting somewhere. It was a seduction, and only Piro would know where it stood. Push too hard for too much, and Saddam would recoil into a mode of enduring and giving nothing. Saddam had revealed that one of his favorite books was Hemingway's *The Old Man and the Sea*, a tale of a fisherman named Santiago who goes out alone and catches a large, beautiful fish, which he struggles to bring back before marauding sharks can decimate it.

We did not want Saddam to slip into the role of Santiago. I bet on Piro's instincts. If anyone could charm Saddam, I figured Piro could.

Saddam began to open up with Piro in April, at least in his informal meetings. He loved to talk about the early days of his revolution. He retold many times the story about how he had attempted to assassinate Abdul Karim Qassim in 1959, was wounded, and escaped on horseback and by swimming the Tigris. This tale had become folklore in Iraq, and no doubt, the tale got better each time Saddam retold it. Still, it built more of a bond with Piro. These stories also allowed Piro the opportunity to draw out important details on Saddam's perspectives. For example, among his lieutenants, Saddam clearly distinguished those who were with him at the beginning, like Izzat Ibrahim al-Duri and Taha Yasin Ramadan, from those who came later, like Tariq Aziz. Saddam placed more trust in, and rewarded more, those who had been with him the longest.

Saddam provided useful anecdotes about those around him. He related his version of the frailties of his highest aides, like Watban Ibrahim al-Tikriti, one of Saddam's three half-brothers, who had been serving as minister of interior. Almost looking for sympathy, Saddam related his frustration with both Watban and Uday's intoxication and womanizing.

Another time, when Saddam was having a blood sample drawn for routine tests by a U.S. Army National Guard nurse, Saddam was commenting in Arabic to Piro that she was quite attractive. Piro said, "You're too late. Watban saw her, and he asked her to marry him!" Saddam laughed.

Saddam was also scathing in his assessment of another half-brother, Barzan al-Tikriti. Barzan had been the former head of the Mukhabarat, and his daughter Saja had the misfortune to be married to Uday. Saddam said simply, "Barzan is an asshole." Saddam would probably not have been disturbed to know that when the Maliki government executed Barzan by hanging, it demonstrated its incompetence by dropping him so far that Barzan's head was ripped off. But by then, Saddam was dead.

Saddam's perspectives on where Iraq stood in modern Arab history were enlightening. He argued that the Arab states were weak in the

1960s and had no international standing and little respect before he came to power. He, Saddam, built Arab pride. Saddam viewed himself as the latest of great Iraqi leaders like Hammurabi, Nebuchadnezzar, and especially Saladin, who recaptured Jerusalem from the Crusaders in the twelfth century. Saddam was sensitive to his legacy. But consistent with his long view, which differed from the Western view, he thought about how he would be remembered hundreds of years in the future, not just by the next generation.

Coming closer to current issues, Saddam explained to Piro how he had tried to resolve the issues with Kuwait before invading in August 1990. He made rightful (in his mind) demands for financial payments from the Gulf States, which he had defended by defeating the Persians at the cost of Iraqi lives. He explained that the emir insulted Iraq by the emir's declaration to the Iraqi foreign minister that Kuwait "would not stop selling oil under the OPEC set limits until they turned every Iraqi woman into a ten-dollar whore." Saddam said he did not particularly want to occupy Kuwait, just take its wealth.

Saddam had told the earlier CIA debriefers that a key goal was to negotiate the acquisition of Warba Island—he wanted a port on the gulf—but the emir would not talk. Also in discussions with the earlier debriefers, Saddam had remembered that in his prewar meeting with U.S. Ambassador April Glaspie, she had said Iraq and Kuwait should settle their own differences and the United States would not get between two Arab states—even though he had told Glaspie that the Kuwaiti aggression was very serious.

Throughout his rule, Saddam promoted the arts in Iraq. He saw himself as a great patron and connoisseur. He wrote a great deal; most of his long florid speeches, he composed himself. He continued to write in his cell. He kept a diary and wrote poetry. This provided a window into his thinking. Piro discussed Saddam's interests in literature and art and writing. This became a useful discussion that later led to a key insight in one of their formal conversations.

I happened to be very well acquainted with an Iraqi who was both one of the best physicians and most-accomplished artists in Iraq. He was steadfastly nonpolitical and had no ambitions beyond healing and his art. Perhaps because of this, Saddam had recognized him as a great national asset. This was a decidedly mixed blessing, but a dilemma all talented Iraqis faced. If you were distinguished in your field, you would naturally come to the attention of the leadership.

In the case of this physician, he was called upon to minister to the health of Saddam and his family. His medical specialty was reconstructive surgery. He addressed the vanities of the leaders—rhinoplastic surgeries and other elective processes, as well as emergencies caused by Uday and others during various outbursts. The doctor also had the perspective of treating the mangled soldiers returning from Saddam's wars.

Saddam allowed himself, by necessity, to be dependent upon the doctor for medical care. He also saw the doctor as a confidante. I knew of no other person with whom Saddam had been so open. So I arranged a meeting in late May so that we could compare impressions. Piro was focused on the immediate problems of validating his understanding of Saddam and testing certain tales that Saddam had related. We also discussed deeper notions of how Saddam thought. I was convinced that Saddam did not think in abstractions, and the doctor agreed. Saddam saw physical objects and power. He had an exceptional sense for manipulating people through base fear or reward. He saw glitter and he built glittering palaces, not ideas—despite his interest in the arts.

One particular insight was helpful in guiding Piro's remaining time with Saddam. The doctor predicted that Saddam would be looking forward to his trial. It would be an opportunity to retake the stage that he had lost. Irrespective of the outcome, Saddam could again stand before the world and behave as the leader of Iraq. Piro had been treading lightly on the pending conduct of a trial. This would be an event out of our control. But with the idea that Saddam might be anticipating it, Piro could pose questions and discussion shaped to elicit his views.

Piro would suggest to Saddam, "You know the prosecution will be asking you about the Anfal Campaign . . ." and Saddam's response could fill in some data.[6] Piro began to use the pending trial as a mechanism to facilitate further discussion.

Following a break he had for a few days, Piro was surprised that Saddam greeted him like a returning friend, in the traditional Arab custom. Saddam had missed Piro and had a pent-up desire to talk.

By May, less than two months remained before the transition from the authority of the CPA to the new transitional Iraq government. Piro had accumulated much knowledge of Saddam's actions and thinking. But the next couple weeks would determine if the strategy could actually deliver. Saddam would see the end coming and either edge toward candor or not. It was time to close, and I was especially anxious to get Saddam's words on key WMD issues.

Perhaps the most important question was that of Saddam's intentions regarding WMD in the future. We now understood from Saddam and his lieutenants that in 1991, Saddam had established a clear priority of getting out of UN sanctions. This was his most important objective, and he made this explicit. To the extent that he could retain WMD expertise and production capacity, he would, as long as it did not interfere with getting out of sanctions.

It was also clear, however, that Saddam had a very long view and his ambitions remained. Like Hemingway's Santiago, he saw nobility in a long struggle. He would not give up anything except as a tactical retreat. I wanted to know for certain his ambitions with respect to WMD. We had varying bits of evidence from his key military leaders and technocrats. His presidential secretary, Abed, could provide the best informed judgment about where Saddam was headed. But I wanted it from Saddam himself, if possible.

This was an issue around which there would be heated debates—often driven by political objectives on all fronts. I wanted to be as solid as possible in my report's description of the regime's intentions. I knew that once Saddam was under the control of the Iraqis and spent all his time focusing on an upcoming trial, the prospects of getting any more information would end. And it would probably end forever, given the Iraqi propensity to kill former leaders.

Piro was warming up the subject with Saddam in his informal and formal meetings. In early June, the American FBI agent got Saddam to open up on his planning for the 2003 war. Piro kept asking him about his military planning for what Saddam himself said was the inevitable invasion.

"I told my commanders that their duty to Iraq was to defend against the invaders with all their power, pride, and dignity for two weeks," Saddam said. "This would make it costly for the invaders. After two weeks, I instructed that the commanders were to conduct an insurgency against the occupiers. Iraq would absorb and destroy the invaders." This may have been what Saddam thought he did, but military commanders debriefed after the war did not recall this instruction. There could be multiple explanations for the differing versions of history. Saddam may have given an order to be passed on, and it wasn't. He may have lied, or he may genuinely not have recollected the event as it happened. Events, as seen in Saddam's mind, could be quite different.[7]

Saddam had also indicated to senior Iraqis like Aziz that perhaps the Russians and French would force a halt to U.S. military actions after some time. This statement was not contradicted by others.

Piro was unable to elicit any more details, such as how command and control would operate in the insurgency. It was apparent that Saddam had done very little postconflict planning. The insurgency was not well planned or well organized.

At one session, Piro recalled for Saddam a speech he gave to the Military Industrial Commission—the state organization responsible for all weapons production and acquisition—on June 12, 2000. This speech was reported on Iraqi television and addressed weapons and potential disarmament in the Middle East.

In his speech, Saddam said emphatically, "If the world tells us to abandon all our weapons and keep only swords, we will do that. We will destroy all the weapons, *if* they destroy their weapons. But if they keep a rifle and then tell me that I have the right to possess only a sword, then we would say no. As long as the rifle has become a means to defend our country against anybody who may have designs against it, then we will try our best to acquire the rifle."[8] The broadcast video shows Saddam examining a brand-new rifle given to him by Abd al-Tawab Mulla Huwaysh.

This was a thinly veiled reference to the presence of WMD in the Middle East. Saddam's language seemed deliberately ambiguous. It suggested that *until* Iraq's neighbors gave up their WMD, Iraq would also *retain* WMD. To Washington, this speech sounded like Saddam's declaring flat out he had WMD even while claiming that Iraq was complying with the UN disarmament resolutions. The most benign reading of the statement was that Saddam was declaring his intention to have WMD if others did not get rid of their WMD.

Piro raised this subject with Saddam: "Mister Saddam, you remember the speech you gave in June of two thousand? I have the text here. I have listened to it, and I know you write your own speeches. This does not sound like you." The last point Piro made to provoke a response. In fact, it did sound very much like Saddam.

Piro continued, "It also doesn't make any sense to me. Why would you say something that suggests Iraq has WMD stocks when, as you say, you had been trying to convince the UN Security Council that Iraq had complied?"

"Mister George," Saddam replied, "you in America do not see the world that confronts Iraq. I must defend the Arab nation against the Persians and Israelis. The Persians have attacked Iraq regularly. They send missiles and infiltrators against us. If they believe we are weak, they will attack." Saddam continued, "And it is well known that both the Israelis and Persians have nuclear bombs and chemical bombs and the biological weapons. I made this speech to warn the Persians."

Iran had indeed sent agents and missiles against Iraq. On April 18, 2001, it had launched a combination of about sixty conventional missiles into Iraq. There was virtually no news coverage of that event in the United States.[9] Of course, Iraq was also sending agents into Iran, and Saddam allowed the anti-Iranian Mujahidin-e Khalq (MEK) to remain in closely controlled camps in Iraq. These were Iranians dedicated to the overthrow of the Iranian regime and had been listed as terrorists by the U.S. State Department, but their terror was aimed at Tehran.

The point that Saddam made explicit in this discussion with Piro was that he was at times deliberately ambiguous about his WMD capabilities. This intentional message reverberated through the government in Baghdad, as well as Tehran and Washington. Many of Saddam's own senior military and civilian leaders were uncertain about whether Iraq secretly possessed WMD before the war. This attitude, stemming directly from the president, was a fundamental contributing factor to the world's misreading of the presence of WMD in Iraq at the time of the decision to go to war.

But did this not also say something about the importance of WMD to Saddam? Piro continued this theme with Saddam in a conversation later in relaxed surroundings, on the ostensible subject of his poetry. Piro would ask the meaning of certain of his writings and elicit his views on things like the prominence of the threat from Iran. In this way, Piro got closer and closer to Saddam's intentions.

It was the second week in June when Piro came to me, beaming. Something was up, because Piro generally was more measured. He related a thoughtful discussion on WMD by Saddam. In the discussion, Saddam clearly stated that it would be his goal to reconstitute his WMD, especially nuclear, to reassert Iraq's place in the region and because it was necessary to match the military capabilities of Iraq's neighbors.

This was the clearest statement of his intentions we could have asked for. It was consistent with much of the physical and financial evidence we had collected. It was consistent with the opinions of many of the key ministers. In Saddam's government, however, there was no tangible exposition of planning or intentions on security issues the way they exist in the West. What counted was what Saddam thought. After months of dialogue and the investment of his own physical and especially psychological energy, Piro had become close enough for Saddam to share his views on this pivotal subject. This was success.

Long after the completion of the comprehensive report, more direct evidence of Saddam's intentions was found on a recording of an RCC meeting (which probably occurred in 1997). The tape was not transcribed and translated until 2005–2006. It includes a brief but telling dialogue. Saddam says, "We do not have WMD," in the course of a discussion on the UN Security Council. An unidentified male then says, "We don't need it." Saddam rebuts with "Why don't we? If they would have come and attacked Baghdad, don't you think we would have needed it to send to Israel?"[10]

During this period and the impending shift of custody to the Iraqis, Saddam's appreciation of reality sharpened. He and Piro began to discuss the upcoming trial and even the likelihood of his execution. Saddam said he wanted to be executed by firing squad, as a soldier. He did not want to be hanged, as this was for criminals. Piro sensed that he was planning out his last acts in his mind.

The first appearance of Saddam before a magistrate to initiate some sort of formal legal process occurred on Thursday, July 1, 2004— two days after sovereignty was returned to Iraq. Saddam was in the legal custody of Iraq, but the U.S. Army still provided physical custody. Saddam was looking forward to his appearance and discussed his approach with Piro in advance. Piro listened. Saddam was pumped. He groomed himself carefully and put on a suit but no tie. Saddam understood appearances. Piro accompanied Saddam to the courtroom, which was located in the Green Zone.

Saddam and Piro had made several trips to the Green Zone, mostly for medical checks and procedures. Saddam was treated at Ibn Sina Hospital, which was in the Republican Palace area. When he was in power, he had been treated there by his doctor, among others.

To get to the Green Zone, Saddam and Piro went by a U.S. Army Blackhawk helicopter. The prisoner Saddam was required to be blindfolded and handcuffed, so it was an intimate experience: Piro was Saddam's guide until he was permitted to see.

At one such visit to the hospital for some relatively routine work, Saddam had an interaction with a female nurse he found attractive. The nurse asked Saddam to roll up his sleeve so that she could take a blood sample.

Saddam replied through Piro as translator something to the effect that "you may begin with the sleeves and continue as far as you want . . ." Piro did not fully translate, but the nurse got the message and the banter continued throughout the examination and tests.

On the way back to the helicopter, Saddam asked Piro, "Hey, do women like beards?" Saddam had been clean-shaven, save his moustache, since his capture the previous December. He did not look at all like the last public pictures of the haggard vagabond pulled from the spider hole.

On the other hand, Piro had a tidy goatee that was in style and fit well with his visage. It looked good.

Piro replied jocularly, "Oh yeah, women love beards."

"I am going to grow my beard back!" Saddam declared. And he did.

This came to mind while watching the CNN coverage of Saddam's appearance at the court in Baghdad that hot summer day. One of the "experts" who had been consulting for CNN on Saddam and who purported to analyze his psychology was brought on air for commentary. He stated quite profoundly that the presence of a full beard on Saddam indicated that he was trying to reach out to the religious elements in Iraq to broaden his support. The expert (who had worked in American intelligence) said that Saddam's regime had been mostly secular Sunnis but Saddam was now seeking to attract the support of the more religious Shia.

This conclusion was humorous, but it also reflected how far off the mark reality could be from an intelligence assessment, given the paucity of direct interaction with the regime.

As the end of June approached, Saddam asked if he could continue to see Piro once the transition occurred. Initially, Piro demurred, saying it would depend on the government of Iraq. In fact, Piro knew that his contact would end shortly. It would be emotional for both men. Toward the end, Saddam said, "George, you have become like a son to me." Saddam gave him a pair of sandals.

Piro had helped record history that would otherwise have been lost and hopefully will help inform the future in ways to avoid the horrors of Saddam. I recommended, and Deputy DCI John McLaughlin endorsed, the largest award I could request for Piro—twenty-five hundred dollars. It was a paltry sum by Saddam's standards. He would have been shocked and insulted if he knew that the person to whom he revealed his secrets was so poorly compensated.

The award the CIA presented in 2004 was put to good use. Piro is a serious marksman and understood weapons—this was also a topic of conversation with Saddam. After taxes, the twenty-five-hundred-dollar award left him just enough to purchase a .45-caliber Springfield Armory 1911 pistol, with thirty dollars left over for a leather holster. That is now his standard sidearm. Saddam would have identified with this decision. He often bestowed as gifts gold- and silver-plated pistols and rifles.

The FBI wanted Piro back. He had been gone and doing nothing that concerned them for months. They did not care about Saddam or WMD, and they had no interest in what Piro was doing. In classic Washington bureaucratic style, it was only years later, in 2007, that FBI management took notice that one of its officers had accomplished something noteworthy. At a time when the FBI was being pummeled in Washington, Director Robert Mueller belatedly gave Piro an award and promoted him in the press as a great FBI success story.

In 2006, Piro and I met for dinner at a restaurant in Reston, Virginia. Saddam had just been hanged. It would be hard to imagine a greater opposite to Baghdad than the synthetic plastic suburban environment created by the developers who manufactured Reston. But during that dinner, much of Baghdad and Saddam came back. There were few people with whom I felt that I could speak candidly about my disappointment at Saddam's hanging. The gang that now passed for a democratic government in Iraq was salivating at the prospect of demonstrating their control, and so they did what every new government seizing Baghdad has always done—they killed their predecessor.

Piro said that in a way, he was proud of how Saddam had comported himself on his way up to the gallows. He had dignity when those who would kill him did not. It was now done, and any unasked questions would remain so. It was the end of the story for Saddam, an end that all of us, including Saddam, knew would come. Piro and Saddam had discussed it—many times—and that was a measure of the effectiveness of the interrogation strategy.

It is impossible to forget the horrors Saddam presided over. But he was charismatic. Tariq Aziz once anxiously asked me what Saddam said about him. The prime minister was looking for affirmation. Later, Aziz testified at Saddam's trial for an hour with nothing but praise for Saddam, who sat just yards away. Aziz is an intelligent man who was completely subsumed by Saddam.

In the end, both Piro and I came to have a deeper understanding of the man, and perhaps Man. Saddam embodied ambition unfettered by societal norms of good and evil. He was an individual with energetic intensity, a tragic aspect, and even humor. He was a complex man who had accumulated much knowledge and experience—albeit in a very twisted way. We did our best to record the facts and details of Saddam's rule. But to convey the nature of the man requires going beyond objective facts.

For use in potential prosecution, Piro wrote a long Narrative of Offense report. It addressed certain selected atrocities. Piro included the admissions he elicited from Saddam during their long conversations. In addition to the goal of extracting Saddam's WMD perspectives, Piro had used his charm to get Saddam to admit many incriminating facts concerning his ruthless leadership. Piro's smiling banter was also carefully managed to build the case that would help snap Saddam's neck.

I tried to imagine the world, literally, as Saddam saw it. How he viewed the scenery at the palace at the end. What he saw in people's faces. I tried to imagine the images he saw as he was steered up the gallows scaffold: a rabble, an inferior gang of thugs who now had seized the government. They would not last or be remembered as he would. In Saddam's mind, he would know there would be no massive crowds to celebrate these thugs' rule the way crowds filled the parade grounds on his birthday each April 28.

We treated Saddam differently because he was different. I hope he was a lot different, but I worry that he wasn't. Saddam was a reminder that darkness exists. Looking into the darkness that was Saddam was unnerving. Things were visible that you did not want to see about humans and society. And, the edge of the abyss is never very far off.

CHAPTER 21

The Al Abud Network

On Monday, March 29, just two days before I testified before Congress, a unit from the U.S. Army First Cavalry Division was carrying out a raid (called Iron Promise) on a building where a tip-off suggested they might find an anticoalition bomb manufacturer. The building was located in an area of northwest Baghdad near the Saddam Military College. The strict civil order associated with Saddam had long since disappeared; instead of the despotic head of state, power had passed to the chaotic insurgency, and to improvised, highly mobile, and potentially very destructive cabals. The First Cavalry thought it had found one in a premise called the Al Abud Trading Complex, which included many shops and businesses specializing in chemicals and was known as the "chemical souk."

Soldiers stumbled across assorted barrels of various chemicals and what appeared to be a rudimentary laboratory. They took sixteen individuals into custody. Thirteen were released very quickly—perhaps too quickly, as it turned out. Among the three kept for questioning was a twenty-something, slim, academic-looking Iraqi named Ali, who owned the laboratory. Ali called his laboratory the Al Abud Company.

Ali's office was situated among buildings littered with barrels, bags, jugs, and simple piles of chemicals—some chemicals were labeled, many were not. It was evident that the chemicals were probably looted from various military and industrial locations. It was a spice market of chemicals. The aroma was more ominous than enticing. There were no safety standards: Almost certainly, carcinogens wafted in the dusty air. Much of Iraq had become an industrial wasteland filled with all manner of hazardous chemicals. The First Cavalry intelligence officers suspected there was more to Al Abud, so they contacted the ISG.

On the morning of Wednesday, March 31, the head of ISG's chemical- and biological-weapons team, Rita, sent an Australian chemist and intelligence analyst, Vanessa, to investigate the site. Vanessa returned with photographs, an inventory of equipment, and other documents, including a copy of the mujahedeen "recipe book" for chemical agents. Her assessment was that the First Cavalry raid had uncovered an ongoing effort to produce the toxin ricin.

Vanessa's findings triggered a cascade of events that would nearly cost her life. Ali, under interrogation, admitted that he was producing ricin for money. Ricin is a highly toxic poison that can be made from castor beans. Before Iraq, it was best known as the poison used in the pellet fired from a device concealed in an umbrella tip to assassinate a Bulgarian defector named Georgi Markov in London in 1978. In Iraq, the Mukhabarat had experimented with ricin as an assassination tool. It was also one of the chemical agents that Iraq admitted developing to the UNSCOM inspectors. In the 1990s, Iraq had told UNSCOM chemical-weapons inspectors that it had produced ricin as part of its chemical-weapons program at the huge Muthanna State Establishment—the enormous facility that had developed and produced the massive chemical-weapons arsenal Saddam used against Iran and the Kurds.

The more Vanessa learned, the more alarmed she became. At the Al Abud lab, she found a container that was labeled triethanolamine (TEA), a chemical known as a precursor for the production of a nerve agent (among other purposes in the chemical industry). Debriefers discovered that Ali was only one part of a larger insurgent effort— apparently backed by serious funding and intentions. The discovery raised more questions: How long had these efforts been going on? Who was linked to the program? Did ISG already have information connected with this effort that we did not appreciate fully?

Rita's team and associates in Washington studied connections with past reporting and looked for new information from ongoing operations. They ran the usual name traces on the detainees and on other individuals identified by the detainees. The outlines of a picture began to emerge. Ali continued to cooperate but could only provide limited information about the customers who commissioned his efforts to make ricin. He had been approached by a middle-aged man named Dr. Zayeed (always referred to by Rita's team as Dr. Zo), who was also a chemist, for help in producing the ricin. Zayeed had funding from a man named Nazar Abdul Amir Hamoudi al-Ubaydi. According to Ali, Nazar was part of Jaysh Mohammad, a group opposed to the coalition.

The name traces finally paid off. Unbeknownst to ISG, sitting quietly in Abu Ghraib was the very same Nazar. He had been picked up in a raid on February 27, 2004, at his office, where a lot of chemicals and explosives were also found. Further checks revealed that he had worked at the Muthanna State Establishment under Saddam. Routine debriefings had not produced any information on WMD—but it was also evident such questions had not been asked. Nazar potentially seemed to be a critical link in an entire weapons-procuring network.[1]

Rita's analysts initially focused on whether Nazar, Ali, or their contacts would lead to hidden regime WMD stocks. As they conducted further debriefings, it was clear Ali had been financed by anticoalition forces composed of former regime members—including a brother of Nazar. During the first two weeks of April, the chemical-weapons team had been chasing down the elements of the former regime's chemical-weapons programs; now the team was gathering information about ongoing chemical-weapons efforts. It was unclear if these would intersect.

ISG had a lot of information about chemical-weapons activities conducted by the Iraqi Intelligence Service, or Mukhabarat. These activities had been carefully concealed from the UN inspectors. The Mukhabarat section M-16 (which was called the Directorate of Criminology, but which served as a technology center for a variety of Mukhabarat goals) had conducted extensive work at various covert labs—including the testing of agents on human subjects. As far as we knew, the aim was limited to small-scale killing, not military purposes. We also knew that the M-16 Directorate had cooperated with the M-14 Special Operations Directorate, which conducted assassinations.

M-14 was also involved in suicide bombers, training for Mukhabarat officers going abroad, and a special department to operate against Iran in Iran.

A truly despicable, vastly overweight, oily character named Muhammed Khudayr al-Dulaymi ran the M-14 section. I happened to be around when he was captured and debriefed in 2003. He would have traded anything and anyone to save his large, fat, infected ass (when picked up, he had huge boils that needed to be soaked in a big tub of water). To me, he epitomized the worst of the regime and, indeed, the worst of humanity. If the likes of him had access to chemical weapons, there was going to be a real problem. He had held several positions in the Mukhabarat and clearly knew as much as any single individual knew about its most insidious actions over the years.

Some in Washington at very senior levels (not in the CIA) were concerned that Khudayr's debriefing was too gentle; they asked if enhanced measures, such as water-boarding, should be used. The executive authorities addressing those measures made clear that such techniques could legally be applied only to terrorism cases, and our debriefings were not, as yet, terrorism related. The debriefings were just debriefings, even for this creature. I hated sitting in the same room with him. He contaminated the air; air molecules that had been in his lungs were in mine and I feared becoming infected by him. He embodied the worst elements of the regime.

As the connections were found, Rita's analysts were trying to understand the pattern and its significance—between the insurgents, former Mukhabarat, and former chemical-weapons production programs. The ISG followed leads and used detainees to fill in this gap in the concealed portion of Iraq's WMD activities. It was certainly possible that further concealed Mukhabarat chemical and perhaps biological resources could exist and be tapped by the insurgents. It was a particular concern that the area of the greatest insurgent activity—west of Baghdad through Fallujah, Habbaniya, and Ramadi—included most of the major chemical-weapons facilities that had been built by Saddam.

❖

On the afternoon of Saturday, April 17, 2004, when I returned from hearings in Washington and consultations in Canberra and London, I met with Rita and her group in our conference room. It seemed clear there was an ongoing effort to acquire chemical agents for use against coalition forces. What we did not know was how advanced this effort was, how extensive it was, and who ultimately was directing it. Nor did we know if there was any connection to existing chemical-weapons stocks. *If these were former regime insurgents and they were try-ing to concoct new agent, then this would say something about the presence (or absence) of concealed chemical weapons.* We did know that the head of al-Qaeda in Iraq, Abu Musab al-Zarqawi, had expressed interest in chemical and biological weapons and, indeed, had acted to obtain the capability. Zarqawi was bad, and I (among many others) wanted him captured or killed.

There was a lot we did not know. And what we did not know could kill us and many others. Since the invasion, the risk and threat of chemical weapons had faded from the consciousness of those charged with military operations in Iraq. Too many people were dying in too many other ways. The Al Abud events served to remind people that the ongoing risk was still there.

In his speech in Cincinnati on October 7, 2002, President Bush had warned that Iraqi weapons of mass destruction could come into the hands of terrorists. It was one of the major concerns he high-lighted before the critical congressional vote authorizing the use of force against Iraq. At the UN briefing of February 5, 2003, Colin Powell referred to Ansar al-Islam, the group that had carved out a small piece of Kurdistan prior to the war and populated it with their version of jihadists. They had been working on chemical and biologi-cal weapons. Videotapes of tests they had conducted on animals had been recovered. There were ample reasons to be worried about the spread of chemical-weapons expertise, given the presence of such ded-icated and ruthless groups.

Could it be that, belatedly, it was now happening under our noses?

Rita reviewed the financial connections. Nazar had revealed some information about his business connections. It became clear that funds came from Nazar's brother, Asa'ad Abdul Amir Hamoudi al-Ubaydi.

We also learned that Nazar ran a company called Al-Nathir and he had business relations with the Military Industrial Commission (MIC) of the former regime. There were also connections to a businessman named Sattam Hamid Farhan Najaris al-Gaaod, whose family had been involved with, and prospered from, smuggling prohibited weapons into Iraq through Syria before the war. One of the companies they ran, the Al Ayman Company, was a front company for the MIC.[2]

From Ali, we also learned that the chemist Zayeed had been trying to produce chemical agents for months. He had attempted to produce tabun—a nerve agent—the previous February.

Rita is a sharp analyst and would shape her presentations in a way that you knew what conclusion you were supposed to arrive at. In the agency, manipulating people is an art form. Operations officers are taught this to elicit cooperation from potential spies. Analysts learn this in the course of briefing and impressing superiors.

I did not need to be convinced this was serious. The leads were real and growing. I asked Rita to form a team from the full range of ISG experts, including the counterterrorism experts, and to pursue the investigation as a top priority. Clearly, this was what Rita and her team wanted to do; my only reluctance was that it took talent away from the task of building the comprehensive report of Saddam's WMD programs. We would just have to do both.

The Al Abud team began a daily routine with an 0830 meeting in one of the ISG conference rooms. The team had many night owls—invariably, civilians—who had to be enticed with coffee, baked goods, and soda. Starbucks coffee was never in short supply, thanks to families who mailed care packages to ISG members.

The morning meeting began with a summary of the activities planned for the day—trips to Abu Ghraib, debriefings at local detention facilities, coordination meetings with MNF-I, and so on. The team also reviewed a link chart, which was usually updated overnight. Priorities and tactics would be discussed and often argued.[3]

Some of the Al Abud team were great and blossomed during deployment. Some quiet, but brilliant individuals found an opportunity to shine in the nonbureaucratic ISG operation. Back at their headquarters, they may have been stunted by competitors more vocal or by insecure supervisors, or they may simply have seemed like misfits. In Baghdad, things were different. Here, several gifted individuals could apply their talents without constraints. One nerdy guy remembered everything—names, connections, even phone numbers—of suspect insurgent operatives. Quickly dubbed Abu Brain, he was a great resource.

Another example was Zach, known to the team as "Good Will Hunting," after the movie by the same name about a bright Boston kid who makes his way through MIT. Zach was a graduate of Notre Dame with a master's from MIT in aeronautics and astronautics. I remain amazed that the government could attract such talent, given the insurmountable frustrations and political inanities it imposes. Returning to the real world (if that is what Washington is, compared with Baghdad) was a letdown. Bureaucratic layering and squabbles produced little action and consumed much time. That is all too depressing when one has been active, doing things independently in the field. Zach left the CIA not long after returning from his work in Iraq.

Rita's team prepared a concerted plan to quickly capture individuals connected to Ali's Al Abud effort. The First Cavalry and the marines were actively pursuing insurgents—but the regular military units were not focused on WMD per se. ISG needed to know the metes and bounds of the WMD activity and, with luck, follow this thread back to the top leaders, maybe even Zarqawi. This required a rapid, but systematic collection plan before word got out among the bad guys.

In this case, a critical element of collection was identifying, capturing, and debriefing people linked to those we had in custody. Raids were conducted every night in Iraq by forces trying to run down insurgents. Too often, it was with bad information. (I kept reminding myself of what had happened to Nizar Hamdoon's family months after he was dead.) Within ISG, we had analysts, technical collection, and operations officers, but when it came to conducting capture/kill operations, we had to reach out to either regular army or marine elements or special operations forces. It was not simple.

I asked Larry Sanchez (who was a senior CIA officer—ranking equivalent to a general officer in the military) to perform this role. He linked up with a specialized military unit that had been operating in Baghdad since day one (and in fact, before). Their unit designation changed regularly, and their personnel rotated between their continental U.S. (CONUS) base and either Iraq or Afghanistan. These guys were calm professionals who regularly ran capture/kill missions—virtually every night. They were not cowboys. They were mature, intelligent professionals who had every tool and resource for their work. They lived in their own deadly and grim world and had extraordinary freedom to select missions from the too many tasks that Iraq provided.

Before 9/11, they were constantly on training exercises all over the world, keeping their skills honed and developing all manner of new tactics, techniques, and technology. Since 9/11, they had been constantly on operations. It was an insular life, and the teams live in a world that can never be appreciated fully by outsiders. Psychologically, it is difficult. Given the rapidity of movement today, one could be doing a night operation taking down a suspected insurgent hideout, killing or capturing suspects, risking or taking casualties, and within hours be walking down a street in the United States, past local supermarkets, pawnshops, barber shops, and all the trivia of modern America. There was no time for gentle transitions.

These teams live literally in their own time zone. No matter where they happened to be geographically, they operated in Zulu time (Greenwich Mean Time). This caused confusion for me in confirming meeting times. To them, 1600 was four hours earlier than it was on a Baghdad clock.

Larry worked well with the specialist team. He knew Iraq from the days when he helped support UNSCOM inspections. Larry's background made no sense in the traditional intelligence bureaucracy. He trained as an operations officer, but was currently on the analytic side of the house. Part of the attraction of the intelligence business is the mix of characters in it. Larry's background included being skipper of a fishing vessel in Alaska. He had also been a bouncer. He had been accepted to medical school, but had opted not to go. He spent a year at the Naval Academy. At the CIA, his job was to provide support to UNSCOM, and then he became Ambassador Bill Richardson's intelligence assistant. When Richardson became the Secretary of Energy he asked Larry to become the head of the intelligence section at the Department of Energy. Larry had a weird background—perfect for our operations in Iraq.

Larry took an early and independent look at the information we had collected from the detainees so far and put together a link diagram to show who was connected to whom.[4] Good, experienced analysts make informed judgments about these links. Unfortunately, good, experienced analysts are scarce. In the hands of the inexperienced, these link analyses can be useless or worse. The charts can rapidly look like nuclear fission reactions if you simply connect cellphone calls, relatives, bank accounts, and name variations. Poorly worked charts can divert your energy to chasing a huge number of false leads. I would be surprised, given all the Iraqis I have been in touch with over the years, if I did not appear on many such link analyses. It is no wonder there are tens of thousands of people listed on airline watch lists, which grow endlessly with contributions from all sorts of intelligence analysts and contractors.[5]

Larry and I met in my office on Saturday morning, April 17, and went through all the connections. Larry spoke almost uninterrupted for about fifteen minutes, explaining various links at a very fast pace. My head soon hurt, but this early work seemed to lead tantalizingly close to Zarqawi. This was the hook that could bring in the support of the military units we needed. Larry had his sales pitch for the special military unit, and it was a winner. Together, the team members worked up a strategy of technical collection and raids. They scoped out the next group of individuals we wanted to target. Like everyone else in the CIA, we wanted to get Zarqawi. Larry went off to begin coordinating and clearing a plan of "capture" operations.

The ISG had a critical advantage. It was not burdened by layers of bureaucratic supervision. We could select our direction and go with remarkable flexibility. But I was not entirely free of adult supervision. I reported weekly to senior levels in Washington by classified SVTS (rhymes with *rivets* and stands for *secure video teleconference system*). I knew I would have to inform Washington of our plans and discoveries, but I faced the classic dilemma of all field operations, how much to tell headquarters and when. Washington is seething with bureau-crats who all want to preen themselves before political masters.

The Washington analysts and staffers would inform seniors of news, in full recognition that the higher-ups would usually remember who told them, but not who actually did the work. I could readily imagine somebody getting wind of the Al Abud work and spinning it way out of proportion. Washington, under any administration, could get way ahead of the known facts. It was easy for me to imagine Washington blurring the difference between what we were concerned *could* be the case and what we *knew* for a fact at that moment. The Iraq WMD story was replete with instances of these discrepancies.

Tuesday, April 20, 2004, was a typical day, mixing the planned with the unplanned. In the morning, I made one of my usual runs from BIAP down the airport road to the downtown office in the Green Zone. Larry and I were meeting with the head of the intelligence of-fice to brief him on our goals for investigating insurgent activity and to get support for some of the human collection activities. We needed to use local assets to develop leads and apply their local area knowl-edge. There were many competing and shifting demands for these capabilities. At ISG, we made the best possible use of locals who could move about the streets readily. However, these individuals, who would be risking their lives to help us, were not numerous and would only be used for very important objectives. For this mission, we got what we needed.

That Tuesday, Keith Dayton and I held our weekly 1730 SVTS with all the senior players involved in Iraq WMD. I briefed the Al Abud activity, trying to balance between facts and concerns. Chairing the meeting, as usual, was the CIA deputy director, John McLaughlin. He was the one person I would always want to know absolutely every-thing, and I would make certain he did, in private discussions.

The videoconferences were helpful, but had a broad audience. All the key organizational participants in the ISG effort were present in the SVTS meetings. The Office of the Secretary of Defense, CENT-COM, Joint Chiefs of Staff, Defense Intelligence Agency, the downtown U.S. intelligence office, Australian intelligence, and British intelligence all were party to these discussions. Each organization tuned in from a classified room with a television camera that showed the key speakers. You never knew who else was in any particular location off-camera, so it was never certain how many people were listening in. Typically, McLaughlin chaired at the Washington end, though on occasion George Tenet would sit in at the CIA site. McLaughlin expressed his interest, gently asked some probing questions, and then offered support, as always. I knew McLaughlin briefed the president regularly on our activities. The Al Abud investigation was something that the White House would have been very interested in. Yet, it was highly uncertain and I definitely did not want our activities to be spread around Washington. There was a huge risk it would find its way to the front page of the *Washington Post*, and such publicity would kill our collection opportunities. To this day, I am amazed that it did not happen. I think McLaughlin's calm and skillful management at the Washington end had much to do with avoiding that pitfall. It was entirely up to him what he shared with the White House and in what terms. He was very careful to separate the policymakers at the White House from my activities in Iraq. I appreciated this, though I never felt any pressure from the White House, just anxious curiosity.

I described in general terms our plan for a coordinated nighttime raid designed to capture key individuals in one pulse. Timing was critical because once the raid went down, word would get out and other potential cell members would be warned. We wanted to be able to observe the results of the raid, as well as rapidly debrief captured detainees and quickly plan for another pulse. The date had not yet been set. We were still trying to confirm some residences and get to know the movement patterns of some of the targets to be sure we could get them. There was agreement in the SVTS on the importance and direction of this plan.

Then, a weird, even by Baghdad standards, thing happened. And it was not good. There was a mortar attack on Abu Ghraib prison, and Nazar was killed. Abu Ghraib is huge and had thousands of detainees. Nazar was in a tent area, and according to one story picked up by an ISG reserve army officer who regularly debriefed detainees, the rounds were fired from a nearby highway overpass and seemed to "walk in" on Nazar's location. Whether he was targeted intentionally or not is yet another unresolved mystery, but the more we learned about Nazar, the more we realized what we had lost when he died.

The family of Nazar was in thick with the insurgents and with previous regime WMD activity. Nazar had several brothers. One brother, Asa'ad, had been identified as a key financial guy for the group. He had connections with former regime elements that we would still have to unravel. Iraq was a family affair. It turned out that Nazar's daughter was married to the son (named Hasan) of Abd al Tawab Huwaysh, the most recent director of Iraq's MIC. Abd al Tawab Huwaysh was one of Saddam's two or three top technocrats and directed, among other things, the development of the al Samoud ballistic missile. He was in custody at Camp Cropper and had long regime ties and interests in all the many front companies and accounts in Iraq, Jordan, Syria, and elsewhere.

I knew Huwaysh pretty well from my years at UNSCOM and now, during his time in jail. He was a smart technocrat who savored the rewards and power of being a top minister to Saddam. He was arrogant, and those under him were treated cruelly. In his meetings with UNSCOM, when he was a top figure in Baghdad, he would lean back in his chair, eyes narrowed to slits, and puff on a cigarette in an ostentatious cigarette holder held between his thumb and forefinger. He enjoyed the power and wealth bestowed by Saddam.

Huwaysh presented quite a different picture in jail at Camp Cropper. There, he affected a hurt and harmless creature, a deflated balloon lying limp in a chair. To his unknowing debriefers, he offered the image of a meek, innocent human who was, like others, a victim of Saddam. I suspected he had already moved substantial wealth out of the country and he and his cronies would happily fund attacks against the coalition. There were good senior technocrats in the former Iraqi regime. In my opinion, he was not one of them.

Coordination is no easy matter with, and among, the military. This was distressingly apparent when we learned that a U.S. Marine unit, acting independently, raided a chicken farm on Thursday, April 22, in an operation called Rio Grande. The marines found a small laboratory, some chemicals (including the chemical-agent precursors TEA and chlorine), and some documents that appeared related to chemical-agent production.

Rita had a way of informing me of such bad news events. Typically she began with, "You won't believe what just happened!" I am certain she enjoyed my reaction during the interval of time between that statement and the denouement that she controlled.

I had no trouble believing almost anything in Iraq. My reaction was still one of frustration, and I responded impolitely, "What the f— are they doing out there?" It seems they had been conducting a normal sweep operation.

The marines thought they had done well. In addition to the laboratory materials, they found some 120-mm mortar rounds that had been crudely modified to carry chemicals. Swell, but their operation would have alerted individuals who were the targets for an operation we had in the final stages of preparation. So, instead, we rushed a team to join the marines and investigate the laboratory materials. But when our team arrived, the marines had already explosively destroyed much of what they had found. Nevertheless, samples taken from the site indicated traces of various chemicals that could be precursors for nitrogen mustard or nerve agents. There was also a handwritten formula for tabun (although it was incorrect in a minor way).

The problem raised by the raid was that it would have tipped the rest of the people in the cell and they might go into hiding in ways that we were not prepared to observe. We are frequently our own worst enemy. As a result, we had to accelerate plans for a key capture mission that became known as Operation Hull. This operation would use the special military units recruited by Larry for some targets as well as regular army units integral to ISG for larger sites.

The regular army forces in ISG included teams of U.S. Army (mostly National Guard) as well as Australian and UK military components. ISG had its own military units, which provided base security and operated armored convoys for inspection operations in daytime. These teams could get ISG team members to selected inspection sites and provide perimeter security during the inspection work. However, they were not trained for nighttime assaults or capture operations.

The other tools we used daily included technical intelligence collection, both signals intelligence and imagery. We had the ability to task the full range of national systems in support of particular missions. Tactical collection included drones (the now well-known Predator) that could provide a loitering surveillance over inspection targets. Finally, we had clandestine human collection teams. All were brought to bear.

We had a collection plan that reminded me of the collection activities surrounding UNSCOM inspections. The goal was to observe activity before, during, and after the inspections or, in this case, raids. This was simply logical. We wanted to know who did what after the raid. We assumed people would flee, and it would be interesting to see who returned afterward.

Near simultaneous raids were planned for three residential sites, and a morning raid was planned at a location known to have labs and offices in the area of the "chemical souk." The latter site would be difficult, because it was relatively large, would require a large team to secure the site, and would have to be conducted in daylight for ISG experts to survey the buildings. The residential sites were smaller, discrete targets that would be raided at night by the small special military teams. Larry coordinated with them, while Rita's group worked on the larger chemical souk sites.

The chemical souk was a large, built-up area; the raid would have to be done as a cordon-and-search action. Because the site was in an increasingly unsettled area of Baghdad, we set a time limit of forty-five minutes to be on site. The longer we stayed, the longer it would give the bad guys time to react.

It was essential to avoid conflicting with other ongoing military operations. If we were going to conduct an operation, we had to clear it with the overall military unit that owned that area of responsibility. This is a vital activity and mistakes can be fatal. Friendly-fire incidents are all too common. We had had none so far and wanted to keep it that way. There was also the risk that normal army security operations and counterinsurgency operations would blunder into sites or people we were watching, before we could conduct the raids. With all the various operations going on in Iraq, especially the Baghdad area, the odds of not intersecting with another U.S. military or some other operation was akin to driving ten blocks in Manhattan without hitting a red light.

As Rita's team developed more information about individuals and locations, it became clear that operations would be required in the areas then controlled by the First Cavalry (then in charge of greater Baghdad) and the First Marine Expeditionary Force, under Lieutenant General James Conway, who controlled the Fallujah area west of Baghdad. Conway had his own round-the-clock counterinsurgency operations, and he agreed to have his operations and intelligence teams coordinate with ISG. Keith Dayton kept lines open with the First Cavalry at the top, and Rita had her intelligence links to the First Cavalry intelligence teams.

Larry and his special operations unit were a different story. He had persuaded David, the CIA liaison to the Special Forces, to work with him on these operations. David was quiet, confident, and affable. He had the confidence of his military counterparts and understood their special circumstances. Though he was in Iraq on a contract to the CIA, he was not doing it for the money. He had a twenty-five-thousand-acre farm in Oklahoma. He simply enjoyed the mission and the people and had an ample store of quiet patriotism. With his quality of character and intellect, he could easily have been a successful CEO of a major corporation. Larry and David made regular trips between the downtown office and our headquarters at BIAP and the Special Forces headquarters located at a distant part of the airport area. These trips were common, but dangerous, especially at night.

In this way, final plans for the night of raids called Operation Hull were made and approved.

On Sunday morning, April 25, a dawn ANZAC Day ceremony was held on a clear point jutting into the lake surrounding ISG headquarters on Camp Slayer. ANZAC Day is the most important memorial day for Australia, marking the day when Australian and New Zealand troops landed at Gallipoli in 1915, launching a vain attempt to knock Turkey out of World War I. Australian troops fought a stalemate for eight months and lost over eight thousand killed.

At ISG, the Australians gave much and asked little. The value of their contribution to ISG was high. An Australian lieutenant colonel was in charge of our military operations. Quiet competence was the rule, and all ISG was proud to stand by their Aussie comrades in this ceremony. The flags of Australia, the United Kingdom, and the United States—the three countries of ISG—were the backdrop for a somber service commemorating ANZAC Day. Bagpipes played "Last Post" to commemorate the fallen. This long military tradition was celebrated by ISG, as it was at locations throughout Iraq. It reinforced the fact and feeling that we were a coalition effort.

Later that morning, I reviewed my e-mails on the CIA classified computer system. I had a message from McLaughlin. In his inevitably polite tone, he apologized for not sending his personal notes more frequently, but found weekends at the office the best time to write. He knew our days in Baghdad were all the same—there were no weekends. A tradition of working less on Sunday was attempted . . . with partial success sometimes. The message from McLaughlin was one of support for our efforts. He noted that in his daily intelligence briefings with President Bush, the president regularly asked about what we were doing.

I hoped that I would be able to forward some good news to McLaughlin the next day, after our planned raids. I put off answering his message, since the initial results of the raids would be known well before Washington got to work on Monday morning.

Operation Hull took place during late Sunday night to early Monday morning on April 25–26, 2004. The day that began at dawn with a memorial service would last long into the night and the next day, as the raids went on.

Larry had done such a good job selling the special operations team on the targets that they invited him along to one of the sites in southeast Baghdad. Night operations are almost spiritual. The blackness and quiet are otherworldly. The power to see and not be seen is mystical. The control of being able to select the moment when chaos will erupt touches some primeval pleasure.

The adrenalin burst when they blew the door open in pitch-black conditions. Screams and blood, and then a return to order once the house was secured. Larry, who lacked night-vision goggles, shared the experience as the Iraqis saw it . . . or didn't see it. He entered and made his way to a sofa in the dark. He sat down and felt a large object under him. It was warm, soft, and wet—a detached foot, blown off in the initial explosive entry. The mind does odd things in odd circumstances. He recalled a mother's admonition to never put his feet on the furniture. Ugly circumstances yield dark humor. But the raid was a success. One key individual was captured. One key individual target was not there— Asa'ad, the money guy. We would continue to pursue him.

The raid on the chemical souk and adjacent chemical-supply store began with the departure from Camp Slayer at 0930. Transit time to the site would be at least forty-five minutes, probably longer, given traffic and the coordination of the convoys. There were two convoys of armored vehicles and HMMVs. Vanessa, the Australian analyst, was present to inspect the site for chemical-weapons evidence and documents.

The plan had been carefully designed; Keith Dayton kept a close eye on that. Lots of things could go wrong. Worrisome to me was a bridge crossing (the Ahdamiya Bridge). The convoy would get in OK, but withdrawing could be more difficult if insurgents could react quickly.

The morning dragged at ISG headquarters. We awaited word. When news came, it was not good. At 1120, there was a report of fighting at the chemical store. At 1145, we got a report of ISG vehicles burning. At 1210 came word of casualties. There is an old adage that the first reports are always wrong, but when the first reports are bad, they seldom improve, however wrong they are. It would not be until late afternoon that the pieces could be put together. And then we could watch a videotape taken by the Predator.

Everything appeared to go well until there was a huge explosion, which virtually leveled a building being searched. Watching imagery from surveillance, one can see two pulses of smoke appear—a small one followed by a huge puff that is eerily silent on video. The reality on the ground was of tension and adrenalin burst by an unexpected explosion—huge, which ignited not just the chemicals, but the latent anger in the neighborhood. Suddenly, this was not arms inspections;

this was war—chaos, fire, burns, and a disorderly retreat to hospitals and safety.

Five ISG soldiers positioned defensively around the buildings were badly burned. Sergeants Sherwood Baker and Lawrence Roukey of our military escort team were killed.

Vanessa had been examining chemical stores in the basement and felt nothing as the explosion tore over her head. The ISG military teams quickly evacuated. Accounting for everyone took time as some injured were brought to local hospitals and communications became uncoordinated. Crowds quickly gathered, and youths celebrated the destruction of American HMMVs by jumping on them. The next day, the military newspaper *Stars and Stripes* featured a full front-page photo of Iraqis gleefully jumping on a burnt HMMV. It became an early iconic photograph of the Iraq war, one that highlighted the depth of the struggle we found ourselves in just a year after taking Baghdad. Listless youths found glory and manhood strutting on burning American vehicles. The AP photographer won a Pulitzer Prize.

The contrast with the silent, emotionless video of the Predator that I watched rattled the sense of reality and purpose. Predator images showed a puff and the rapid scattering of small figurines, like ants. It was an antiseptic image. This was a clear example in which simultaneously two pictures of one event conveyed two completely different realities. To make judgments about Iraq from either picture alone was incomplete.

It was the worst incident to date for ISG. The investigation determined that the explosion was from the accidental detonation of dust from chemical bins stored haphazardly around the buildings. Smoldering embers remaining from a high-speed portable saw used to break into locked doors were probably the source of ignition. The dangers to ISG staff were not just from insurgents, but from the industrial wastelands that had to be investigated.

It was a somber debriefing Monday afternoon. The successes of the nighttime raids were overwhelmed by the loss and pain of the Al Abud explosion. But work continued alongside the mourning.

Debriefings of the Iraqis captured were conducted by military debriefers aided by ISG experts. We got many of the individuals we targeted, including Zuhair Abdul Amir Hamoudi, another brother of the late Nazar, and the elusive financial guy, Asa'ad. Larry's team also captured Dr. Zayeed at his residence. Zayeed would prove very helpful since he straddled the technical chemical-weapons knowledge and the senior direction of the network we were unraveling. It was a key capture.

At 0730 on the following day, Wednesday, April 28, a memorial service was held with hundreds of the ISG team present. It was just three days since we had assembled at the same location to commemorate ANZAC Day. Major General Dayton and the ISG chaplain presided. Wind blew the American, Australian, and British flags. At the base of the flagpoles stood the worn boots, rifles, and helmets of Sergeants Baker and Roukey. The ANZAC ceremony three days earlier had been somber, but was a general moment of reflection for the sacrifice of strangers. This day, the loss and pain were immediate and proximate.

The "Last Post" was piped again before we somberly returned to our mission.

Later that week, we were reminded that there were still chemical rounds lying around Iraq. On May 1, an IED made from what turned out to be an old nerve agent round was found on the airport road. Three days later, an old, leaking mustard round was found at one of the gates to BIAP. It seemed as if WMD were finding us and not the other way around.

I took it on myself to see former MIC director and now detainee Abd al Tawab Huwaysh that week. He could not bullshit me the way he might others. I was accompanied by an analyst and an army debriefer. I wanted to get more from him on the prewar smuggling that might be ongoing. Huwaysh described the close cooperation with Syria to support the smuggling of prohibited goods into Iraq. He noted especially the Syrian company SES, with an office in the Mansour section of Baghdad. Key people in the company (Asif Shalish and Dhu al-Himma Isa Shalish) were very close to Syrian President Bashar al-Assad. Firas Tlas, the son of former Syrian Defense Minister Mustapha

Tlas, had visited Baghdad as the guest of Uday. The Syrian had facilitated deals and assisted in obtaining the necessary false import/export certifications, which allowed countries like Russia to export to Syria prohibited materials that were, in fact, bought by Iraq.

Huwaysh also described the use of the Mukhabarat and various front companies. It was very complicated and very extensive, and he avoided incriminating himself. We would continue to debrief Huwaysh. He and his family certainly had prospered from the regime, but I could not prove that they were now financing the ongoing anticoalition operations.

In the midst of this, during the evening of May 4, there was a total lunar eclipse over Iraq. The full moon passed into the earth's shadow and took on a magnificent coral color during the late-night hours. Anyone in Iraq who looked up would have been taken in by the beauty of that moment that night. But the problems on the ground did not slow down.

Rita's team focused on getting information from detainees. Simply getting access to detainees was a problem. There were arguments about who had custody of detainees, who was authorized to speak to them, and indeed who was in fact detained. ISG had to persuade others in charge of detainee debriefings that much critical information would be lost if we were not present when the interrogations took place. There were also complications in just getting to the detainees. Military units had their own detention facilities, but only to hold individuals temporarily. This made sense, because there had to be a general system for treating detainees in accordance with all rules and laws. The Army First Cavalry division detention facilities at BIAP could be used only to hold a detainee for thirteen days, whereupon either a high-level exception was sought, the prisoner was released, or he was moved to the huge Abu Ghraib detention area.

Abu Ghraib was a long and unsafe distance from ISG headquarters, so ISG debriefers had to make complicated, often multiday trips. Putting prisoners in the general population at Abu Ghraib also exposed them to the knowledge that circulated there.

We faced this problem with the late Nazar's brother Zuhair. He was cooperative and not stridently anticoalition. We were learning much about the network and its financing—particularly the role of the brother Asa'ad, who had eluded us in Operation Hull. Tantalizingly, Zuhair noticed the picture on a matchbook cover one of our debriefers had with him. Zuhair said he had seen the man at a Fallujah farm with Asa'ad and others. The matchbook was one of a series printed up to help willing citizens turn in wanted people. I always thought it was a pretty lame idea, until Zuhair identified this particular picture—of Zarqawi.

We tried to delay Zuhair's transfer, but on May 11, he was sent to Abu Ghraib, where he would soon learn his brother Nazar had been killed. We wanted to continue questioning him and others before he learned about the lethal mortar attack. We did not want him to know that we could not check some of his statements with his brother. The failure to rationally segregate and debrief prisoners was a costly one. For the most part, detainees were just rounded up, good and bad, and mixed.

Many of the individuals in prison were not committed insurgents, but educated, middle-class Iraqis caught in a world turned upside down. What always struck me about the Iraqis I met both before the war and, later, in custody was the enormous sense of fatalism that imbued their character, understandable, given the system under which they had lived. Iraqis did not grow up with a sense of responsibility for their own condition. They did not have the sense of being a citizen and that they were a constituent part of the system of government. They did not own the government; the government owned them. Things happened to them, and often, inexplicably. Only those Iraqis who were part of the regime felt some sense of control over their own destiny, and even that was precarious. Being invaded and occupied by the United States was just the most recent disaster.

An indication of how unreliable and outright chaotic our information about the detainees was came on May 13. Just before lunch, a message was received from the ISG debriefing group (the Joint Interrogation and Debriefing Center, JIDC). Zuhair, brother of the missing financial guy Asa'ad, was reported to have left a debriefing session with chest pains. He was taken to a clinic and then rushed to a combat support hospital, where he died of a massive heart attack. This was really bad.

434 HIDE AND SEEK

After lunch, the news improved, as did Zuhair. At about 1400, a second message announced that "reports of death were premature. Zuhair is fine in the hospital." Shouts of "He lives!" were heard among Rita's team.

From the link analysis of the known Al Abud figures constructed and analyzed by the Al Abud team, we were able to identify the financiers, the chemists, and some known anticoalition insurgents. One central financial guy named Ghadban was the son of a sheik. He, like others, ran a car dealership. It highlighted the role of car dealers in the postwar Iraq. In some ways, car dealers were like bankers. There were no bank accounts, and for many Iraqis, most of their tangible wealth was embodied in their cars. Buying and trading cars was one of the methods of trade.

In addition to the broad anticoalition group Jaysh Muhammad, there was a small cell calling themselves "God's Lions." The name was apparently drawn from a passage in the Koran addressing martyrdom: "The memory of battles and martyrdom aroused my longing for the lasting abode of eternity. The roar of God's Lions in the fields inflamed my desire for jihad. My soul's ardor for jihad, what grief for all that has gone before."

By the third week in May, Rita's team had concluded that this insurgent cell was clustered around a few key families of influence under the former regime—notably the Al-Gaaod family. This family had run a collection of companies we dubbed the Al-Eman network. The Al-Gaaods had ties with Saddam's notorious son, Uday, and Saddam's former son-in-law, Hussein Kamel. Through its banking and business connections, the family had ties to assets in neighboring countries; resources would not be a problem. These individuals were closely tied to the wealth of the former regime—largely generated from the UN Oil-for-Food program.

Sattam Hamid Farhan Al-Gaaod was a key Saddam operative. He worked closely with the MIC and the Mukhabarat to set up front companies aimed at procuring banned materials. He traveled on an Ecuadorian passport and, as late as March 2003, traveled to Sweden and Ukraine on behalf of Saddam's son Qusay. Two of Sattam's brothers, Hasan and Mohammed, were identified as being active in anticoalition activities in the Fallujah area. They also had business interests, including a car dealership, there.

Sattam Gaaod was in custody after his capture in April 2003. Among his many transactions involving the MIC were some involving Asa'ad Abdul Amir Hamoudi al-Ubaydi, to obtain contracts with many of the MIC establishments, including Al Qa Qa, a huge facility where all sorts of explosive testing and storage had taken place.

Links to Abu Musab al-Zarqawi were still inconclusive. It was also an unresolved question whether these former regime actors were connected to the foreigners. Nevertheless, the information assembled from this second "pulse" of collection had been very productive and illustrated the nature of much anticoalition activity at the time. We were also shutting down a potentially very dangerous cell.

On May 18, I met with George Tenet at the Four Seasons Hotel in Amman. I brought Larry with me, since one of the topics I wanted to cover was the Al Abud effort. As Larry ran through his link analysis chart, Tenet, who was jet-lagged, predictably glazed over—until Larry pointed to a dotted line representing a possible link to Zarqawi.

Tenet looked at me and said, "Charlie, does this make any sense?"

I said simply, "If the insurgents can't find or make WMD, then that tells us something important. Of course, if they can, that is really bad."

Tenet appeared to be concerned that I was running operations at the expense of looking for WMD.

I reminded him of the 152-mm binary sarin round that had been made into an IED and planted on the airport road and a mustard round that had been placed at an entrance to BIAP. "George," I said, "my approach now is to drive up and down the airport road as much as possible, and the WMD will find me." At the time, this was grim humor. Tenet was persuaded that our methods made sense, nonetheless.

Much as we wanted to pursue more fully the potential insurgent efforts to get chemical weapons, time for collection against our primary mission was running out. I had decided that all ISG intelligence collection efforts to support the comprehensive report on the regime's WMD programs would have to end by June 30. There were two reasons. First, to get our massive load of data into a report by the end of September would require undivided attention by experts. Second, sovereignty over Iraq was scheduled to be returned to a caretaker Iraqi government on June 30. Our ability to operate in the field, as well as the control over detainees, would change.

For the final weeks before the June 30 cutoff, ISG analysts developed new targeting packages. Various collection techniques were used to identify key sites and individuals. Planning for a final pulse of raids was accelerated. Support for ISG was at its highest at this point. All agencies in Washington and the military in the field understood the importance of getting to the bottom of the WMD question. The military was also concerned that there may have been an ongoing threat, given what we had discovered investigating the Al Abud network, and no one wanted to begin carrying chemical-protection suits.

Our Al Abud team pressed on. They now had a pretty good picture of the range of people involved in the network. We were uncertain just how far these Iraqis had gotten, but it appeared we disrupted them before significant chemical-weapons capability was created. We did not know, however, if other groups would try similar tactics.

Two final pulses of collection and analysis were planned for June. On May 23, a meeting was held to review the target set for the first pulse, which to my annoyance was dubbed Operation Rubber Chicken. Sixty pages of PowerPoint charts laid out the set of targets that covered the known sites in the Fallujah area. Chicken farms and businesses (including a car dealership) of financial supporters were targeted. Specific individuals were identified for capture.

On May 25, I was scheduled to meet with Major General Stanley McChrystal, who headed the Special Forces elements we had been working with (and was the head of the Joint Special Operations Command, JSOC). I needed his buy-in. His guys had a lot of competing missions. The meeting was at McChrystal's local headquarters on BIAP, not far from Camp Cropper. Accompanied by Larry and Keith Fennell, a newly arrived senior officer who would be my latest deputy, I was driving a Toyota Land Cruiser SUV to the meeting. Keith Dayton was ahead of me, being driven by his staff. The roads at BIAP, like everywhere else in Baghdad, were dusty and rutted. I got a flat tire. Dayton's driver apparently did not use his rearview mirror much and never noticed that we were no longer behind him. So, with temperatures in the nineties (it could have been much worse), we pulled out the jack, removed the lug nuts, and changed the tire. Metal gets very hot in Iraq, and as I had left my Nomex gloves elsewhere, my fingers were scalded and covered in grease. When we arrived at McChrystal's headquarters, we looked as if we had just changed a tire in the heat. Shaking hands was skipped. Dayton looked at me, and his expression said "typical civilian."

I was pretty spun-up by the time I got there and started with a bit of a rant about the usual bureaucratic sludge you had to wade through to get anything out of the massive bureaucracy at MNF-I headquarters at Camp Victory. It was as if they had transplanted the entire Pentagon to a chunk of BIAP. It seemed like every useless colonel floating around the army was there so he could require staff to write reports that they would then carry waddling up to general officers. These types never left the confines of Camp Victory, but would get credit for serving in the Iraq war. I continued on about large, useless, oxygen-wasting colonels.

I was seated next to a very large and very muscular guy. And, like everyone in the room with the exception of Dayton, he was dressed in civilian clothing. A civilian, I stupidly assumed, even though the rest of McChrystal's staff was dressed in civilian clothing. McChrystal, I thought, would be sympathetic to the issues of bureaucracy. His guys were not into process; they were into results. They did not even wear uniforms. He nodded in the direction of the massive guy next to me and said, "What's your opinion on that, Colonel?"

The colonel let me live, and McChrystal provided the support we needed.

❖

Operation Rubber Chicken took place from the night of June 8 to the morning of June 9. This series of raids captured a number of targeted participants in the Al Abud network, including a couple of key individuals in the Fallujah area—Juma'a abid Mehdi and Jamal al-Wani. Jamal had worked at the huge Al Qa Qa munitions facility located southwest of Baghdad. We learned that many of the chemicals at the chemical souk had been looted from Al Qa Qa. At this facility and adjacent ones, Iraq conducted missile development, munitions testing and storage, and other similar activities. This was the facility where among the huge stocks of explosives were eight bunkers containing an explosive called RDX, which had been acquired for testing of the trigger portion of the Iraqi nuclear weapon. These bunkers had been visited by the International Atomic Energy Agency when its inspectors were in Iraq. We found rudimentary laboratories and materials for making bombs and various IEDs.

Ten days later, on June 19, a last raid (named Razorback) was conducted in the Fallujah area, but it was uneventful and not terribly productive. The cell we pursued had dissipated.

So the Al Abud investigation ended with a whimper, not a bang. This was success. At the end, there was no more to find. The financiers were in prison. Sattam Hamid Farhan Al-Gaaod and his family, who had made a fortune for the regime importing weapons and other materials in violation of sanctions, were, at least for the moment, in prison. The limited numbers of true chemical-weapons experts were in jail or, in the case of Nazar, dead. We could never conclude if this branch of the insurgency, God's Lions or Jaysh Mohammed, was directly connected to Zarqawi. If not, they were very close. Like much of Iraq, it was probably a group with alliances that drifted on the currents of power and the tides of anger.

Zarqawi would live another two years before he was finally located and killed.

The Al Abud effort was a successful case of rooting out and eliminating a pending threat. The investigation was also vital for our understanding of the limits of what WMD remained in Iraq, both in physical material and in intellectual capital.

Some comfort was derived from the rudimentary quality of the insurgency's WMD efforts. Further comfort could be derived from our observation that they clearly did not have knowledge of, or access to, hidden WMD stocks. What was unsettling was the clear desire to obtain such weapons. We staunched the efforts of 2004, but the aspiration to use chemical and other WMD remained. In 2007, other insurgents exploded chlorine trucks as rudimentary chemical attacks. The use of chlorine in truck bombs was the natural and predictable evolution. To date, Iraq still has lots of chlorine, lots of explosives, and little governmental control.

The Al Abud investigation saved lives, in addition to building knowledge. It is the sort of quiet endeavor that can be accomplished with bright, young, and energetic operations officers, military officers, and analysts who have yet to develop bureaucratic mind-sets that thwart innovation and responsiveness. It was government at its best. The team had a unifying mission, resources, and minimal second-guessing. We employed every possible intelligence tool imaginable, from sophisticated communications and technical collection to agents in the street.

In the end, the Al Abud effort confirmed that the threat of hidden WMD stocks was small. The fact that the insurgents were trying so hard to procure chemical agents was evidence that they did not already have any hidden away. This was a solid piece of information to reinforce the comprehensive report.

CHAPTER 22

The Comprehensive Report

In the middle of 2004, key events upped the pressure to get the report done sooner rather than later. On June 28, 2004, Ambassador L. Paul Bremer presided over a brief ceremony yielding sovereignty over Iraq to the Governing Council created under the CPA. The ceremony was conducted two days early with the idea that if insurgents had been planning any mayhem for the transition day, they would be preempted by an early move. The importance of the transition to those of us in ISG was that our ability to collect and run military operations became legally uncertain. The authorities and controls on U.S. operations posttransition were unclear. Whatever was agreed would involve UN mandates, U.S. military authorities, and whatever the presumptive Iraqi government wanted. This would remain unclear for some time.[1]

A second major change was that George Tenet, my direct boss, was resigning. Tenet was my strongest supporter and had the most invested in producing a correct factual presentation of the Iraq WMD program. He had been in back of Colin Powell during the UN Security Council briefing on WMD before the war. The DCI was emphatic that a complete, credible report should now be produced; it was necessary to restore confidence in the U.S. intelligence community.

Tenet had been the DCI for seven years and had moved the agency and the rest of the intelligence community from a world where threats and intelligence objectives were largely defined by the competition between the United States and the Soviet Union, to a world where threats did not come conveniently packaged in geographic areas with attendant governments in charge. This was a true paradigm shift. Tenet recognized it and worked hard to restructure the intelligence bureaucracy to deal with the new, more amorphous threats.

Tenet had been caught up in the storm over Iraq and the mischaracterizations of its WMD programs. While the CIA performed very well in the Afghanistan war, that success was quickly forgotten with the controversy over Iraq's WMD. The White House and others were laying responsibility for the incorrect assessments on Tenet and the intelligence community he led. Now he decided it was time to pass the baton.

I flew back to Washington to meet with both Tenet and John McLaughlin, who would be acting DCI. There was a relatively small group dinner for Tenet at CIA headquarters on July 7. He was genuinely admired for what he had done for the agency and would be missed. McLaughlin, however, was also highly regarded and would lead the agency well. I was as comfortable as I could be, given that the individual who hired me to create the complete record of Iraq WMD was now leaving. McLaughlin recognized my position and stepped in to make sure I was not left dangling. He would provide, as he had been all along, direct personal attention to the ISG on an almost-daily basis.

Another major factor driving my decisions on timing was the upcoming U.S. election. I was convinced that for the report to be considered an objective compilation of data and analysis, it had to be produced before the elections. If the report were issued after the elections, it could too easily be dismissed as a politically driven product. Too much had been sacrificed to build this knowledge, to risk that fate.

Before returning to Baghdad, I had another meeting at the White House with Condoleezza Rice and Steve Hadley to inform them of my plans and the schedule for the report. I made clear that I had now completed most collection efforts and would be concentrating on building the comprehensive report that would be ready at the end of September. Rice appreciated the update and asked questions about the investigations and nature of the regime as we had found it. Again, she offered full support and made no requests with regard to either the format or the timing of my report.

I also met with the Australian ambassador to bring the Australians up to speed, and I stopped in London on my way back to Baghdad to give the British the same briefing. Canberra, London, and Washington had a large political stake in the outcome and had all provided substantial resources and expertise.

Other management factors drove the need to bring the ISG work to closure. In June 2004, Major General Keith Dayton finished his tour. I would miss him. Picking up his role as senior military officer at ISG was Marine Corps Brigadier General Joe McMenamin. He was another solid officer, but he saw his mission as managing the disassembly of ISG. There was a real war on, and while all senior parties said I could have all the resources necessary to do my job, they deeply coveted the assets of the ISG. The vultures were circling.[2]

Finally, the ebb and flow of analysts into and out of the ISG was continuous. Analysts would arrive, and some would suddenly depart for any number of reasons. I tried to plan for a ramp-up of talent toward the end of summer to complete the report for September release. Even then, I had major staffing problems and surprises—among them, the head of the biological- and chemical-weapons teams, Rita, left in mid-August, leaving behind no coherent draft material. Again I was reminded that I would be left holding the bag at the end.

In June, the report existed as piles of drafts and redrafts that filled my office. They were heaped everywhere. Reading and rereading, writing and rewriting these long, complicated texts and tracking for consistency across volumes was an endless process that began each morning and went well past midnight. Saving me from complete despair, McLaughlin temporarily sent out some very talented analysts and writers, including Andrew H. and Tim K. Together with my deputy, John, we sorted the data and assembled what would be the longest U.S. intelligence report then produced.

The multiple piles of text were several inches thick. At one point, we considered taking the first complete draft text out to the range and testing how deep into the report a standard NATO 9-mm (metal jacketed) round would penetrate. Much debate was had over whether the bullet would make it through the Regime Finance and Procurement section and into the Delivery System section, and perhaps even into the Nuclear section.[3]

Such ideas were born of the frustration of dealing with shifting analysts of varying quality. When I got crap text based on crap analysis from crap collection, it was hard for me to gently understand that the team members couldn't help it. They had been shipped out to ISG with zero relevant experience. By August, my patience was running thin. Those closest to me in this process, Andrew, Tim, and John, had to provide a buffer between me and these earnest analysts. I was not polite while reviewing the text and susceptible to midnight rants to my deputy John.

"Who the f—— writes this stuff? Monkeys could have done this. No, monkeys would be an improvement. Can we get monkeys? John, call Headquarters and ask them to send out monkeys. They would be cheaper than the four hundred thousand the DIA pays some Beltway bandit to send some grad student out here!"

John was particularly good at massaging my message. In the end, I would make remarks that were more constructive and would try to find work-arounds for the absence of resident expertise.

The analysts and even the team leaders could get up and leave before the text was done. And this happened. It was ultimately my problem to generate the report and to convey it to Congress and the rest of the world. It had to be a product that was worthy of all the resources that had been expended—including the lives of those who died in ISG service. And then it had to receive any criticisms from Washington and other capitals, the Iraqis, the United Nations, and even the experts who floated into and out of ISG, but who may have had their own opinions or areas of emphasis.

So, we worked with what we had. The Nuclear team was headed by a pleasant reserve navy captain who had been on a nuclear submarine. He had a couple of contractor support team members who worked in U.S. nuclear labs. They were bright, methodical guys who arrived knowing nothing about Iraq or its nuclear programs. They were reviewing previous work. I discovered that they had gone out and debriefed just one Iraqi that summer—and, then, only when I pressed them. Fortunately, they were thorough in examining all the previous reporting, and there was a significant body of work done by previous ISG experts who had come and gone. The text eventually matured, often helped by other experts in other capitals who reviewed and submitted sections. I also indirectly got a pretty candid description of the program as described by the former head of the Iraqi nuclear program, Jafaar Dhia Jafaar.

Yet the biggest problem was the combined biological- and chemical-weapons team. Rita and her team had been focusing heavily on the Al Abud investigation and put off other work such as producing draft text. When she suddenly departed in early August, there was no replacement. Tim K. filled half the gap by assembling a draft for the chemical area.

The biological-weapons area remained a problem. We had conducted a thorough investigation and had collected much data. The task was to assemble it into a coherent picture. I turned to some former UNSCOM colleagues to help, including Rod Barton of Australia, Hamish Killip of the United Kingdom, and Americans Robert Kadlac and Richard Spertzel (who was the lead biological-weapons expert at UNSCOM and worked closely with the late British biological-weapons expert, David Kelly).

Dick Spertzel had devoted an extraordinary amount of his life to the Iraq biological-weapons question during the UNSCOM years. Aside from his expertise, I wanted to have him present at what would inevitably be the last chapter in this tragedy. Spertzel had massive background data, most of which he kept in his head. He seemed to know every detail from every conversation he ever had with the Iraqis during his work at UNSCOM. He knew which Iraqis had been at any given facility at any given time. Spertzel had one other key advantage. He had worked on the U.S. biological-weapons program in the 1960s and had personally made biological agents for the United States in the 1960s and tested them as weapons (before the United States abandoned the program and signed the Biological Weapons Convention).

Killip, who lived on the Isle of Man, had massive data about the Iraq biological-weapons program—data that he kept in his personal laptop computer. He had data about the various sites and inspections from UNSCOM and he added to it during his work at ISG. He chose to share this knowledge selectively.

Both Barton and Killip had great disdain for the U.S. intelligence community.[4] They were independent contractors paid by their respective governments, but believed they had no obligation to contribute to what they saw as a CIA text if they didn't feel like it. Until the very end, they withheld judgment about whether they would participate in the final product. They each had their own personal versions of the truth and did not want to sully themselves with anything less perfect . . . or so they came across to me. It was, as the expression goes, like herding cats. The experts were as quirky as they were talented, and there were moments when getting a product that they would agree on seemed utterly remote. I found myself regularly wishing I could just go out to Camp Cropper and get the Iraqis to write the sections themselves, since they would be easier to manage, would not suddenly leave, and certainly knew the subject matter.

In the end, I really enjoyed the weirdness of this group of difficult, opinionated scientists who had been seeking to decipher the Iraq biological-weapons puzzle for years. They knew as much as anyone else in the world knew about the Iraqi biological-weapons activities, and I was fortunate to have access to all these minds for one last time. They tended to disagree on many particulars, but the overall picture of what had been done was pretty well agreed on.

The missile team was a delight. The team leader, a Brit named John Harlow, had worked for years with UNSCOM. He stuck it out with the ISG until we had a complete product. Harlow knew the Iraqis and got the full, verifiable details on the program from them. Another talent of his was getting the best work out of the experts he had at ISG and tapping the expertise from contacts he knew around the world. Harlow produced some excellent background on the extensive support Russia was providing to the Iraqi missile programs being conducted despite sanctions. For example, we made a point of getting into the guest registry at the main hotel in Iraq, the Rasheed Hotel. Harlow found out which Russian missile experts and suppliers were in Iraq and when. (The registry was useful in other areas as well.)

Harlow detailed the Iraqi ongoing missile production[5] and development plans, which were premised upon the continued violation of sanctions by the provision of various components and technology from Russian sources. The strength and momentum of the ballistic missile program was silent testimony to the fundamental long-term goals of Saddam for building a capability that would be ready to go as sanctions ended. Even before the war, Tariq Aziz had stated publicly in Jordan that the United States had bombed permitted missile facilities in 1998 because "they know that if anyone can produce a missile of a 150 km range, they can produce one with a 1,000 km range."[6]

The material on the missile program developed by Harlow's team dovetailed elegantly with much of the data collected by the Regime Finance and Procurement team under Marine Reserve Lieutenant Colonel Steve Zidek, who was on the State Department's Intelligence and Research staff. He did an incredible job assembling a team of financial and other experts from the UK Customs and U.S. Treasury departments.

When I arrived in Baghdad, I knew the material on regime financing would be rich and a major part of the ISG report. I had met with former oil minister Amer Rasheed in a dirty tent a year earlier, when he had described the details and the documentation concerning how Iraq used the Oil-for-Food program to buy influence. The senior people, governments, and objectives were stunning. The oil industry data, banking and financial records, and clandestine procurement data would contain a latent image of the regime's intentions and programs, which could reveal an image like a developing photograph. I got early access to the Oil Ministry records and cross-matched them with records from the Central Bank.

This was data that would allow us to track any WMD efforts as well as the overall goals and objectives of the regime. We also decrypted the Mukhabarat and Military Industrial Commission joint efforts at procurement through front companies around the world. While our mandate was focused on the WMD aspects of the regime, I wanted to make public all the data that would be of interest for many other reasons as well. Zidek's collection and analysis provided firm data to support the understanding of the political decisions on resources directed to weapons areas. It also firmly supported the conclusions concerning the intentions of the regime. Finally, by making public these records, many other investigations by governments around the world were touched off. The United States, the United Kingdom, France, India, and others conducted investigations over illicit trade and bribery. The United Nations commissioned its own investigation of its Oil-for-Food program, and I provided copies of records to them and also ensured them access to detainees under American control.

The one exception to this trend of accounting, of course, was Russia, where there apparently have been no investigations of the Iraqi funds going to key Russian officials and offices.[7]

The Regime Finance and Procurement text was by far the longest and most complicated. It revealed much about the regime and the countries supporting the regime. It was also the only section about whose content Washington raised questions, especially about its declassification.

From my earlier conversations with her, I was confident I had support from Condoleezza Rice, but I double-checked with Will Tobey at the National Security Council. The problem was with the State Department. My CIA colleagues who were running the declassification process, including Bruce Pease, chief of the Weapons, Intelligence, Non-Proliferation and Arms Control Center (WINPAC), and my former deputy Keith Fennell, had been doing battle with regional offices at the State Department. The department argued that important relations would be damaged if the report revealed the information about countries and top officials who had been violating Iraq sanctions and profiting through the Oil-for-Food program. Powell himself disagreed with revealing information about such activities—especially those involving Russia. He raised the matter with McLaughlin, who said Powell should talk to me if he had a problem. In a conference call (after midnight my time on September 2) that included Rice, McLaughlin, and Richard Armitage, Powell asked, "Is it really necessary to publish the information about the relationship of Putin's government to illicit trade with Iraq? Does that have anything to do with WMD?"

In essence, I said: "The information about the oil vouchers and who was being rewarded goes to the question of regime intentions.

We are making the case that Saddam's strategy was to erode sanctions. He was having success, and the Russians were helping him."

Powell responded, "But you are implicating Putin. You list a Russian state company [Rosoboronexport], in which Putin has a position, as being involved in illicit trade. That does not mean Putin was directly involved."

I responded by referring to some information we had collected, but Powell still objected, saying that it was not conclusive data. We adjusted the text to take Putin's name out. Still, the involvement of the Russian government at the highest levels was inescapable, and Powell remained concerned about the political implications.

Unstated in this dialogue was the underlying question of whether sanctions were working. The State Department and Powell had been advocates of pursuing the UN inspection process as an alternative to war. The success that Saddam was making in eroding sanctions with the support of other Security Council members tended to undermine the "sanctions were working" ex post facto arguments.

Powell added one parting shot, perhaps meant as advice: "You'd better be correct on your data. There are going to be a lot of very angry people, and you will be all alone."

Sometime after that conference call, at 0245 in the morning in Baghdad, McLaughlin called again to report that Powell had not given up. The general had separately called McLaughlin again without Rice on the line. In classic bureaucratic fashion, Powell was trying to erode the decision outside the formal process and to get McLaughlin to remove the data. Since the CIA was printing the report, it would be a CIA publication. It was my report, but I was the DCI's special advisor on Iraq WMD. Powell argued that McLaughlin should take the material out.

McLaughlin called to inform me of that dialogue and wanted to know my reaction. I did not say what I thought about Powell. I simply said that for my report, this information was essential to the overall message. However, if someone judged it necessary to remove the data, it would be fine by me, but the CIA would also have to remove my name from the report. I would quietly go away, but it would not be my report.

In the back of my mind, I was thinking about the irony of it being Powell who so strenuously was trying to manipulate CIA reporting on Iraq in ways that did not support another side of the Iraq debate. I later discovered that Powell's people continued to try to eat away at the report—requesting a little change here and there. For some reason, the State Department wanted to remove some references to the direct involvement of individuals close to Syrian President Bashar. It was a typical game played out by bureaucrats who will fight eight hours a day to protect their ability to say they were right all along. In the meantime, Iraq was imploding.

I did take Powell's warning to heart. If there was fallout from the publication of the illicit trading information, at least as far as Powell was concerned, it would be directed at me personally. Suddenly, I could envision lawsuits and legal bills that I certainly could not afford. Immediately after hanging up with Powell, I called the counsel general's office at headquarters to ask about professional liability insurance. The staff gave me the name of the Washington firm that provided such coverage to government officials. I called them and bought as much coverage as I could on the spot. This did not reflect a lack of confidence in the report, but lawsuits, even if ill-founded, could be an expensive mess and I had zero confidence the government would help. I also did not want to be in a position where I had to stay on government rolls indefinitely to retain their legal support in the event some lengthy case came up. In the end, although there were initially strident howls from certain governments they became muted as the concrete evidence laid out in the report was validated.

The portion of the report that would set the tone and context for the whole picture was the assessment of the regime's strategic intent. I had been keeping a very close eye on this aspect of the report, as it would give meaning to the whole effort and, potentially, some understanding for the tragedy around Iraq WMD. I had worked closest with this team because it depended on the debriefing of some senior key Iraqis, including Saddam and Abed. It was also an area I found fascinating from a historical perspective. We could record the actions and dynamics of the secret, innermost workings of the Saddam regime. The majority of the key participants were available for extensive discussions, and we could test our hypotheses with the actual participants. There were many lessons to be learned about how Saddam's government operated and how the intelligence community perceived the regime.

By the first week in August, I knew I needed to do something to get critical text drafted and reviewed in time to meet the September 30 target. I decided to have a conference with current and former ISG experts the first week of September. I figured it would be easier to get people to go to London than to Baghdad. From August 30 through September 3, our most experienced hands gathered to review drafts and create text where needed. We scrubbed data and conclusions during five days of intensive effort. At the end of the week, we returned to Baghdad with a nearly final version for review and production.

I had one last critical test for the draft report. I asked the teams to review their respective sections with some of the best-informed critics on the planet—the high-value detainees. I wanted to test the key features of each section with the relevant Iraqis—possibly even asking them to examine selected draft text. If they agreed or disagreed, I wanted to know why. In my mind, I imagined how the former regime members would read the descriptions of their actions and their government. I spent time myself testing the general themes of the comprehensive report with detainees. I had been doing this since I arrived. In the end, I had confidence that the underlying dynamics of the regime were reflected as best as anyone could lay them out, recognizing that there would be differing interpretations, even among Iraqis. One senior Iraqi told me some of the report's observations of the regime were enlightening because they showed the Iraqis facets of their own system that they themselves had been too close to see.

By early September, the number of analysts at ISG was shrinking rapidly. The "mosh pit," as I called the area under the palace dome filled with cubicles, was pretty sparsely populated. If there were any problems left now, there weren't many of us left to fix them. John and I were spending every night until well after midnight working the final details.

CIA headquarters was in turmoil producing the report. It had never published anything this large (now well over a thousand pages), and what was worse, everything in it had to be declassified.[8]

I was convinced that the report had to be completely unclassified, or there would always be suspicion about its validity. To begin to restore some confidence in the intelligence community, I wanted to lay out all the data. If others chose to draw other conclusions than I did, that was fine. Everyone would have the same facts to debate; the data was all open. There was no secret annex. Tenet had agreed with this approach back in May, and now the system at headquarters had to deliver, by reviewing all the referenced intelligence reports and declassifying them. Declassifying alone took three weeks of long days and nights.

Nor did I want the report to tell people what to think up front: There was no executive summary with a predetermined conclusion. The story of Iraq, sanctions, and WMD was too intricate for that: It deserved to be seen in its entirety, without single aspects being taken out of context. It was a complicated story—that was the point. The truth, which Tenet said was my goal, was not simple and could not be abbreviated. But the content, unique methodology, and comprehensiveness of the report I was very satisfied with. I believe no such analysis has been created before. We had a unique opportunity to record for history the inner workings of a regime that had been the cause of international crises and tragedies for decades. There is a lot of raw data in the report, and it has fueled much subsequent academic work, as well as the investigations spinning out of the Iraqi manipulation of the Oil-for-Food program. But I still had to present the report to the U.S. Congress, and I had no idea whether the legislators would tolerate that much unprocessed truth.

Moreover, the truth I would present was not black-and-white, but included many shades of gray. In a political season with the presidency in balance, I had no confidence that anyone wanted more truth than could be inscribed on a bumper sticker.

Washington had informed congressional committees that the report was nearing completion. Congress expected that hearings would be scheduled for the first week of October, one month before the 2004 presidential elections. While I did not closely follow the election campaign, it was evidently tense, and Iraq and WMD would be an issue. At the same time, I was beginning to appreciate more fully the political context in which I would be reporting. Congress, the press, and others were looking for an event. I was coming a bit late to the realization that this would be a solo mission. While the comprehensive report comprised the efforts of hundreds of people, by the time I testified to Congress, the ISG would have largely vanished. There would be no back row supporting me. If a senator questioned any of the dense details I had purposely included in the thousand-plus pages, either I knew the answer or I didn't.

I found myself asking what had all these contributors to the report worked so hard to create? For all my complaints about the quality of analysts, short terms of duty, lack of sustained effort, and diversions of investigation, these individuals had, nevertheless, contributed to a mission with a singular purpose. They had given a lot. Some had died. Iraqis had contributed as well. Presenting the report was the opportunity to bring this effort together to a result and conclusion. I suppose I hoped that if there was a single objective reality, that the report would closely reflect it. It was as close to Tenet's instruction "find the truth" as I could come.

In the September evenings, when I was trying to commit to memory the facts and themes of the text, the Water Palace and its previously buzzing mosh pit echoed with emptiness. If I had a question, it was mine to answer. When I returned to my quarters, I could sleep only briefly. The viral fever of worry about the report and its delivery had only brief remissions. Habitually, around three in the morning, I would be awake with doubt and angst. I envied Saddam's ability to sleep peacefully through the night. I would go outside and stare at the black Baghdad skies.

I arrived in London on Wednesday afternoon, September 29. I paid calls to my usual British colleagues to let them know what I intended to say to Congress in Washington. I spent the weekend reviewing testimony and traveled to Washington on Sunday. Then it was an endless round of meetings until the hearings on Wednesday and Thursday. On Wednesday morning, October 6, I had a closed hearing with the Senate Select Committee on Intelligence. It took place in the secure hearing room of the Senate at the Capitol Building. I was glad to have my first encounter with the Senate under conditions where there was no press and the proceedings were all classified. The senators would not be performing for the cameras, but, presumably, simply asking questions that genuinely concerned them. I began by summarizing orally my written introductory comments. It was easy, since I knew the material and the themes cold. In a way, I was describing something that had occupied my professional life for a decade, not just the previous nine months. The senators had some prepared questions, but no one had had time to read the voluminous report.

The one complaint I recall was from a senator who opened by saying, "Mister Duelfer . . . your report . . . your report . . ." She paused, not quite sure how to phrase the comment. "Your report has, well, it has a lot of words in it."

I bit my tongue. I could easily have said any number of things that I would have regretted. The accusation she was trying to make, I think, was that perhaps I was trying to bury a simple truth in a mound of detail.

I gave her the justification for the report's length—that I wanted her and others to read the evidence, not to be told what to think: "I apologize for the length, but the issue is very complicated and the ISG expended a lot of effort to collect the data. I wanted to record the data and show what happened to Saddam's WMD over time and why. If you or others do not agree with the themes included in this long report, the data is still there for you to examine. You may extract another conclusion."

The afternoon hearing with both the Senate Armed Services Committee and the Senate Foreign Relations Committee would be the more challenging event. It was public. WMD was then the big political issue. The hearing began at 1400, and I arrived a bit early with the head of the CIA Congressional Relations office, Stan Moskowitz. Stan had been extraordinarily helpful and had the wisdom of many years of service in the agency; he was trusted on the Hill.

The hearing room was jammed with press. Virtually every senator showed up. I made a point to say hello to all of them beforehand, not knowing if I was about to be skewered by them in a ritual political sacrifice.

They were an odd assortment of individuals. I could not fathom beforehand who was driven by politics and who might really care about the issues. I did know that Senator John Warner would be a very polite chairman. I had seen him in Baghdad more than once, and he was very serious about the issues. Senator Carl Levin always accompanied Warner on trips to Baghdad, and I knew he seriously tried to understand the facts. I recalled the words of caution he had given me before I went out to run the ISG. He anticipated that this would be a pivotal political issue that would put me squarely between the White House and the CIA.

Senator Joe Lieberman was as serious and polite as John Warner. He had attended the same high school as I had attended, only some years earlier. We both hailed from the same town in Connecticut.

I greeted others who were all outwardly friendly. I shook hands with Senator Hillary Rodham Clinton and found her reluctant to let go. The handshake just seemed to go on longer than usual. Then I figured out it had to do with photographers who were positioning themselves to take pictures. Finally, I retreated down to the lower table, where witnesses were obligated to look up at the elevated semicircular dais of senators.

The session was formally called to order, and two and one-half hours of televised hearings began. The senators made statements that often reflected their views on the administration. The questioning was basically earnest and reflected a respect for the work of the ISG. As I sat there carefully considering how to respond to various questions, I was gradually, and perhaps cynically, concluding that both political parties had decided it was in their interest to accept the report as credible. By selectively lifting various parts of the report, the senators could declare that it supported their political positions.

Some (John McCain in particular) asked detailed questions, which I answered in detail. The only testy exchange I had was with Senator Ted Kennedy. He read his question/statement about the waste of resources I had consumed on a "wild-goose chase" looking for WMD to justify the administration's decision to go to war.

With all the sacrifices and efforts made by the ISG in mind, I recoiled at his dismissive characterization. I replied: "Senator, I must come back on your comment. My task was not to find WMD. My task was to find the truth. I am quite proud of our work to delineate the program, and anyone can examine it. This was not a wild-goose chase. People put great effort into this. People died. This was a worthwhile effort to understand a complex situation. . . ." I moderated my tone, recognizing that it would do no good to embarrass a prominent senator in this extremely public forum. I bit my tongue. The senator later went on to point out that the report talks about the regime's intentions, but that was not how the administration sold the war. The ISG was searching for weapons that did not exist, while real bombs were being used by insurgents. This was a line of dialogue for the cameras, not me.

At the end, I felt the report (and I) had endured the process. There was far too much data in the report for any senator or senator staffer to analyze fully. The press headlines ranged all over the map. Some journalists dug through the report and found many of the buried pieces of data that could become stories in themselves. The list of Iraqi oil vouchers provided grist for many articles. There was some frustration that the report didn't simply declare the intelligence about WMD was wrong. It was, of course. All intelligence is wrong to some degree. The prewar WMD estimates were way off, but there were many reasons. There were also many reasons why Saddam's intelligence assessments were wrong. It was underlying incorrect assessments by *both* Baghdad and Washington that produced catastrophic results.

I returned to Baghdad with some relief. I found I missed Baghdad—I still do. But when I returned, the energy for the ISG activities was almost completely extinguished. As the election approached, I was focused on tying up some loose ends.[9] The presidential election took place on November 2, 2004. The returns would start to be reported at 0400 on Wednesday morning in Baghdad. Washington was far away from my mind, and I did not stay up to hear the results.

Nevertheless, I would be called back again as a result of the report. It had sparked congressional interest in the Oil-for-Food program corruption. Two new hearings were requested by the Senate Government Affairs Committee and the House International Relations Committee for November 15 and 17. I would have to prepare for them. At the same time, my deputy, John, and I were working to develop more information about the Syrian question. The pace was slower. The temperatures were cooler, and my corner of Baghdad seemed relatively pleasant.

The challenge was to obtain support for any further investigations. John McLaughlin had supported the idea of working to collect more information to close out the remaining uncertain issues. The White House had also wanted this to continue. However, the remaining staff in ISG at the Perfume Palace was largely focused on the burgeoning insurgency. The one key thing John and I wanted to do was to contact some Iraqis in the Mosul area who knew about the Iraqi trucks traveling to Syria before the war. I needed to meet with officers in Baghdad to try to set this up, and both John and I had other issues to discuss with several other officers.

On Saturday, November 6, we tried to go downtown, but had to cancel the meetings because we could not get transportation. On Monday, November 8, the ISG protective service detail was available and we arranged to depart at 0900. As I described at the beginning of this book, that gray, cool Baghdad morning would end with the deaths of Clint Wisdom and Don Clary and the critical wounding of Nathan Gray.

I was able to return to my quarters that day, only because these fine Kansas National Guardsmen took an action that cost them their lives. I needed to be certain that I did my best to finish the work of the ISG and assure that it was a lasting product. And I rapidly realized that whatever I did for the rest of my life, I owed it to these colleagues. That would be a stringent mark to measure my choices by.

John and I completed annexes to the report, drawing upon the archived data we had already collected. After the attack on November 8, it was decided in Washington that further collection under the decaying conditions in Iraq was not worth the risk. Thanksgiving was somber. The dining facility served turkey, and the staff, largely Sri Lankans (earning seven dollars a day from Kellog-Brown-Root) were given Pilgrim hats to wear. Lots of cardboard decorations, of the sort you might find in a Wal-Mart, were placed on the tables. It was absurd.

On December 13, senators John Warner, Carl Levin, John Cornyn, and Evan Bayh visited Baghdad again. I spent the day with them, although they were no longer interested in WMD, but rather in how the military and the embassy were planning on dealing with the growing chaos in Iraq. They were briefed by Iraqis, General George Casey, Ambassador John Negroponte, and others during their day-long visit. I respected their effort to travel yet again to Iraq, but I did not see that they got much in the way of answers to their basic question, "Where is all this going?"

That was not a question anyone was asking me. My task was officially over. I could only look at the chaos of Iraq and think what might have been.

I began packing up my things. John and I turned in our weapons and boarded our small transport aircraft to depart Baghdad on December 16. I was sad to leave. I had invested much of my life there and had many friends. On reflection, I had stayed in Iraq longer than many Iraqis who could get out. Most Iraqis could not leave. When I tried to help Iraqis who had been very helpful to me come to the United States, I was told it was virtually impossible. I could never explain this to those who had helped me and the United States. There are millions of other immigrants in the United States from countries we have not invaded. How could I explain why they could come to the United States and the Iraqis, some who risked their lives on our behalf, could not?

In Washington, just before Christmas, I made a round of calls to the White House, Pentagon, and DIA. I met with the newly named head of the CIA, Porter Goss. Goss had been the chairman of the House Intelligence Committee, where I had met with him previously. Since he was now my boss, I stopped by his office to brief him on the report and the work of the ISG and our methodology. I thought he might be interested in the work since it was now the definitive statement on an issue that had previously vexed the agency. The methodology and lessons in the report could help in future work. I also brought back something that would fit easily in my pocket from Baghdad to present to Goss.

One of the locations inspected by the ISG was Ashraf, a militia camp of the Mujahidin-e Khalq (MEK), the anti-Iranian group harbored by Saddam. ISG inspectors came across some interesting capsules in small leather pouches that hung by a cord around the neck. Upon analysis, they turned out to be cyanide capsules. I thought one might make a good present for the new CIA director (or the CIA Museum). I gave it to Goss; he fingered it and then asked what it was. I told him. He put it down. Carefully. He seemed neither amused nor interested.

He had the same attitude about the report. I saw Goss on occasion after that meeting, and he never seemed to be enjoying the job or steering the organization according to a clear vision. At the very start of his tenure, he reportedly declared to his immediate staff that he did not "do personnel." Others would handle those issues. This comment spread rapidly through the agency. The CIA is extraordinarily dependent upon its people. Staff must pass rigorous security clearance checks; they need to be expert in their fields and trained regularly. Operations officers have a completely separate and more convoluted set of issues concerning living undercover and all the complications associated with operating overseas. The agency is all about people, and for the new director to say he didn't "do personnel" was evidence that he was the wrong man to lead it.

At the same time, Goss was confronted with the creation of the new Office of the Director of National Intelligence. This new layer of senior management was created by Congress in the middle of the election season (when rationality is in particularly short supply in Washington) as a response to the desire to "improve" intelligence capabilities. Goss had to deal with a new organization of people who would coordinate and supervise the range of intelligence agencies. The first head of the DNI was John Negroponte, a longtime Foreign Service officer and the current U.S. ambassador to Baghdad. Negroponte's running the new DNI was eerily similar to Bremer's creating and running the Coalition Provisional Authority. I was reminded of other administration appointees who were bright, good individuals but who were occupying the wrong jobs. Goss lasted eighteen months in his job, Negroponte less than a year.

On December 21, I had a final meeting with President Bush. I had asked Will Tobey if he could arrange for the president to provide a note or some other memento for the families of Clint Wisdom, Don Clary, and Nathan Gray.

I briefed the president quickly on the ISG results and mentioned that the only reason I was there was because of the actions of three National Guardsmen, two of whom had died. The president gave me small presidential medallions with his respects for the families. He must have had to do that a lot. We talked some about the situation in Iraq. I said that the Iraqis who were working with the United States were at least trying to build something. The foreign terrorists, like Zarqawi, who had sent the suicide bomber against my car, were only promoting destruction. Eventually, it seemed to me, the Iraqis would eliminate the foreign terrorists. What I did not say was that the internal conflict was growing and that the United States apparently had no idea what to do. It was not my job to offer advice on that subject. He presumably had the Iraq experts he wanted handling that matter.

The president thanked me for my service, and I left the Oval Office. He would have four more years to try to come up with a winning strategy and team for Iraq.

CHAPTER 23

Kansas

Observers and participants—especially participants—in the long-playing Iraq tragedy ask the simple question: Why? It is a question that has been asked repeatedly: in the 1980s during the bloody Iran-Iraq War, in 1991 following the invasion of Kuwait, and now after the removal of Saddam and a costly occupation. Complete answers are not simple, nor static, nor certain.

Nevertheless, there are identifiable elements of the answer that may be picked up and examined so that when we see them again, we will recognize them. This reflective process points to the miscalculations on both sides. It points to miscalculations about the opposite side and also of one's own capabilities. There was ignorance in Washington about Iraq. There was also ignorance in Washington about its own ignorance and its own capabilities. The same condition was true in Baghdad.

I sat in a bland, fluorescent-lit office on the sixth floor of the CIA headquarters building just before Christmas 2004. Life in Washington was strangely empty, compared with the incandescence of Iraq. It was very difficult to return to shopping malls, swarms of frantic people clawing their way ahead in traffic, and the consumer frenzy of Christmas. Iraq had changed me.

There was one thing I knew I wanted to do that December—meet a group of people who, more than any policy experts, would be consumed

461

with the questions of what happened and why: the families of Clint Wisdom and Don Clary and Nathan Gray. It had been only a few weeks since the attack that had killed Wisdom and Clary and that had severely injured Gray, who was now recovering at home after a month in a hospital. All three men were from Kansas: Wisdom from Atchison, Clary from Troy, and Gray from Lancaster. Struggling with uncertainty, I handwrote short letters that expressed my gratitude, sympathy, and a request to come meet the families if that would not be an intrusion. I did not know if these strangers who had lost so much would hate me or whether I would be interfering with their private grieving. Yet I felt I was connected by circumstances and wanted to explain our objectives and activities in Iraq.

A month later, I bought tickets for my deputy, John, and me to fly to Kansas on the last weekend of January 2005. On Saturday afternoon, January 29, we drove up to the home of Virginia Clary—Don Clary's grandmother—where his sister Kristi had invited relatives. It was a small home in a small town in Kansas. The median household income of Troy, I later found, was under forty thousand dollars. Towns like this provide the manpower for much of the U.S. military.

As I walked up to the door, I was glad to have John along. I couldn't help but think that we would be seen as the men from Washington, with all the negative baggage that implied. John's garrulous nature would hopefully offset that image.

Before I could knock on the door, it opened and a young man came out to investigate the strangers. Introductions were made, and it did not take long to feel welcomed into their informal home. A constant flow of relatives passed through the kitchen. It seemed that half of Troy was made up of the extended Clary family. Don Clary's sister Kristi greeted me warmly. Young, in her twenties, she had just been through a lot of turmoil she did not deserve. She was Don's designated next of kin and had received the official visit and notification that Don had been killed. As we talked about Don, she wanted to know what happened on the airport road on November 8. She had been told next to nothing by the army. I was amazed, but learned that families generally were provided very little information about those who have been killed in action. These families, who gave such a commitment to the local national guard, received little more explanation than the statement that their loved ones had died serving their country. I gave Kristi the president's thanks, as I had said I would in my last meeting with Bush, and one of the small presidential medallions.

In the living room of this home were pictures of other family members who had been in the military. The small plastic- or wood-framed photos hung on the most prominent wall in the house—this home that would sell for less than what many New York Wall Street traders or Washington defense contractors would spend on one of their cars, but a home that was worth so much more. The Clarys and their neighbors were earnest people who had more in common with the average Iraqi than with the average Washingtonian. While Troy, Kansas, was definitely not Baghdad, it also was not New York or Washington.

This family and the others like it supported their country. They believed in contributing to America. They were not cynics simply trying to make money or get power or manipulate the system to their own benefit. They did not talk about wine or art or whether the stock market was up or down. They had other problems and priorities. The thought that I shared a common bond with them made me glad. The thought that I had spent my career, with its risks and sacrifices, with comrades from this home reassured me. I was especially proud to serve this part of America. Walking the streets of Manhattan, I often felt that the people there would have considered me a sucker for wasting my time on efforts that got me nowhere and earned so little.

I asked Kristi Clary if I could take a little time to explain to the gathering what we had been doing in Iraq and why. John and I stood in the crowded kitchen, which opened into a joint living room and dining area. I began by explaining that, yes, John and I were in the CIA and it was our job to lead the effort to investigate Saddam's WMD programs. We had built a detailed analysis, and I had brought them copies of the multivolume report. It was a unique record that would help future decisions. We had all learned from it. Questions were gently asked about why we were in Iraq. What was Saddam like? What did the CIA do? How did we spy? When would the war be over? What was President Bush like?

A year and a half earlier, I had met regularly with Baghdad families whose lives had also been upended through no fault of their own. They asked many of the same questions, but the clear difference was that the Iraqi families felt no attachment to their government. Iraq and the government were two different things. In Kansas, the tone was "our government," and I was a piece of it standing in their living room. The questions went on until food was ready to eat and everyone grabbed a plate of hot dogs, pork and beans, and some vegetables. It was so much better than the CIA cafeteria, and I told them so. If honesty had a flavor, this was it.

That evening, John and I drove to Atchison to the home of Janet Wisdom, Clint's widow. There, a much smaller family gathering welcomed us. Mrs. Wisdom, two of her children, and Clint Wisdom's father were present. Mrs. Wisdom was very gracious in welcoming us into their living room. We sat in the chairs and the surroundings that had been so familiar to her husband, to which he would never return. We talked about the family and the activities of the children. In my mind, I recalled how my childhood home echoed of my father long after he died. Awkward tension gradually relaxed. We got on to the topic of the ISG mission and activities, and in no particular order, I described what we had accomplished and gave them a copy of the report. John and I explained why the report was important and unique. Then we both outlined what we did in government, and without forethought, we talked about why we personally did this work. Somehow, Janet Wisdom, without asking in words, elicited this conversation.

At the same time, Clint Wisdom's father's eyes were hard on me or at the floor. He was judging me and clearly had no reason to believe or trust what I said. I felt this was a man who disliked Washington and the two CIA guys, who had something to do with the death of his son in a war he did not support. He was polite, but said little.

I went on to the broader topic of the war and what I felt were the basic objectives and risks of the endeavor. Saddam was a genuine risk, in my judgment. His track record was bad, and nothing in our work indicated that he would reform. I saw skepticism in Clint's father's eyes. I could not answer, and did not try to answer, the questions I felt he most wanted to ask: "But was it worth this . . . the death of Clint, my son? Is the war worth it? Are you worth it?" These were words I felt, but did not hear.

Janet Wisdom appeared more supportive of the effort, but this was not a discussion of politics or policies. It was a discussion of purpose and meaning. It was a meeting of the souls who had been drawn together by fate. In the end, I think, Clint's father at least appreciated the ideals of the ISG mission.

As we were getting up to depart, Clint's father asked one question, "Did the government send you fellows out here?"

I was caught off guard. "No, sir. We are here because we wanted to be. The government has nothing to do with it." He nodded and, I thought, softened a bit.

Janet Wisdom, who conveyed both strength and intelligence, expressed appreciation for our visit. As we rose to depart, I gave her the presidential medallion and told her of the president's thoughts. She then pulled out, from somewhere, Clint's ISG identity card. We both looked at his picture. I could not imagine the wave of feelings she felt in looking at the picture. She handed it to me, and there was a silence and suspension of time between us before I could move. Then, I put the card in my wallet, where it has remained ever since.

We stepped through the entranceway of this sturdy Kansas home and onto the front porch. The door light gave a soft illumination to the steps leading down to the silent road. The night air was clear. I was conscious of breathing the air that night as John and I made our way to the car and the hotel.

The next morning, we made our way to Lancaster to see Nathan Gray, then twenty-four, and his wife Amelia, their six-year-old son, and their infant daughter. It was another small home, but in a wide-open farming area. The surrounding fields were bare on this snowless winter day.

His wife led us into their living room and past many of the usual toys found in a house inhabited by a small child. Nathan was seated in a chair. He wore a neck brace and an immobilizer on his right leg, but otherwise looked remarkably well on the outside. Nathan was recovering at home and still needed extensive treatment. He spoke slowly and, it seemed, with some effort.

We talked about his care. The army had not been helpful, and he was having trouble getting to Texas for required medical help. The bureaucracy made it difficult, not easy. His family was consumed with coping with the calamity of his injuries and the loss of his civilian job. Amelia had been working as an assistant in a school, but now had to help Nathan convalesce. The local community was raising funds to help them.

Nathan talked about the rest of his unit that was scheduled to return to Kansas the next month. I spoke a little about the ISG report and its importance in Washington and gave them a copy. It was just so much paper to them. I gave Nathan the presidential coin, and this made an impression. I told him the president personally asked me to express his thanks for what Nathan and his team had done. This carried much more meaning for Nathan. Amelia looked to be consumed with trying to cope with the cascade of problems. After a while, I felt that Nathan was tired, the kids needed attention, and the presence of John and me was another complication. We took our leave and began a slow drive through the Kansas countryside and across the Missouri River to the airport in Kansas City. John and I spoke little.

In America, there is a conviction that we are a nation founded upon ideals. There is also a tendency to believe there are universally correct ways of doing things. We recoil from the notion that our ways may not always be the best or even an improvement. This was evident within the well-intentioned effort to replace the Saddam regime.

Universal ideals exist, but often those universal ideals can be most successfully realized by local efforts. No single way of achieving them suits every situation. A government responsive to the governed is a fine ideal. American democracy provides a government that is responsive to the will of the governed—in America. It is not the only way.

Clearly, by any modern standard, the Saddam regime was insidious for Iraqis and a threat to others—including the United States. The policy of containing Saddam was crumbling by 1998, never mind 2001. Something had to be done. President Clinton's wait-until-hedrops-dead strategy had failed; the problem was passed on to his successor. Saddam was edging his way back using the power of Iraq's increasingly valuable oil. President Bush chose to remove Saddam militarily and create a new government. This was a rational strategic calculation—especially in light of the vulnerabilities exposed by the 9/11 attacks. Saddam was a reemerging threat, and President Bush did not believe the regime could be reformed, moderated, or removed by anything less than the use of force.

But two critically flawed decisions to implement regime change were made successively. The first was the decision to go through the UN Security Council, assuming Saddam would categorically defy the WMD resolutions and thus solidify a consensus in the council for his forced removal from power. This would have been ideal—and it certainly suited our allies—but it was a major miscalculation of the Security Council and of Iraq's WMD status. It ignored the reality that the UN route was exhausted after ten years of decaying sanctions and diplomatic carrot and stick. Moreover, it too narrowly defined the problem in terms of WMD. Iraq was much more dangerous than its weapons systems: It was a rogue state, run by a rogue regime. There was no need to send a Swedish arms inspector to try to find a test tube and a missile to make the case for deposing Saddam.

The second error was the premise that changing the fundamental principles of the government from Saddam's brutal dictatorship to a representative government required the complete destruction of all parts of the former government's structure—including the Baath Party and the army and other security structures. These actions were, in effect, damning the broad secular central mass of Iraqis, with no substitute to provide the necessary gravity to hold the country together. There was some ill-considered expectation that external opposition groups, like the smooth-talking Ahmad Chalabi, could form the catalyst of a new government. These fundamental missteps dramatically and predictably raised the horrible cost of President Bush's basically sound calculation that action was necessary to resolve the Saddam regime threat.

For his part, Saddam blundered (fatally for him) in not immediately accepting inspectors in early 2002. This would have defused the

U.S. effort to build a much tougher resolution by which to measure compliance with UN mandates. The spring and summer of 2002 became a period of debate over Iraq's WMD, because the UN resolutions containing Iraq were tied, in 1991, to its WMD activities—not the other threatening or vicious aspects of the regime. So, like the UNSCOM inspections of the 1990s, WMD issues were again a surrogate for national policies between Washington and Baghdad. In the 1990s, containment depended on Iraq's failure to satisfy UN inspectors. In 2002–2003, the Bush administration's desire for international support for its goal of regime replacement by force hinged on Iraq's failure to satisfy the disarmament provisions of UN resolutions. By his actions, Saddam was never convincing in his claims to have forsaken WMD forever; nor did he ever appear to have reconsidered his aggressive domestic and regional policies. But Saddam was also not in such blatant noncompliance as to sway all members of the council to support war. France and Russia would not go to war on a "technicality" when they had so much to lose.

An alternative and more transparent course in the UN Security Council would have been to create an entirely new UN resolution not cast strictly in WMD terms, but in the terms that Secretary General Kofi Annan introduced in his speech to the UN General Assembly in September 1999.[1] Annan introduced the idea that, in select circumstances, the international community could be justified in intervening in another country. This was a bold statement in the UN context and one that deserves to be pursued.

A new basis in international law for intervention with a much broader foundation than just WMD would have been a more honest and ultimately more convincing reason for deposing Saddam. Secretary of State Colin Powell would have had a very difficult task pushing through this sort of resolution, but on the other hand, in the immediate post-9/11 period, there would have been greater receptivity. And, he would have avoided the subsequent contortions over WMD in the Security Council.

The UN, and particularly the UN Security Council, will need to adjust to the viral risks and threat dynamics that can rapidly spread well beyond the geographic borders that define who is in charge of what chunk of the earth's surface. Globalization blurs the sanctity of sovereignty.

The UN has always had a role in setting international norms of behavior. Within its mandate are international legal standards of various sorts. While the UN has a multitude of faults, there is no alternative to the UN for many international matters. Looking ahead, one could expect times when the behavior of sovereign states is either so egregious or so potentially threatening that the international community should act against one of its member states. Circumstances like Iraq will recur. Darfur currently raises some of these same issues. If the council cannot act, individual nations will move unilaterally to preserve their own security, as they are entitled to do under the terms of the UN Charter. The result would be a less consensual world, but that may be the inevitable future.

It is becoming more difficult to envision a consensus among the permanent five Security Council members required to pass tough enforcement actions. With China becoming an economic superpower with global economic needs and a resurgent Russia with pride to recover since the collapse of the Soviet Union, U.S. leadership in the council will be challenged more often. Indeed, there may be no leadership.

Today's Russia would have been a much more powerful and successful advocate of Saddam's Iraq during the prewar debates. Saddam's purchase of Vladimir Putin's support in the Security Council was insufficient to save the Iraqi leader in 2003. The outcome today might be different. The equations of power are changing. And as has been the longtime habit, each member of the Security Council can choose its own version of facts. Certainly, the American version will no longer dominate.

Errors in the picture of reality drawn by the U.S. intelligence community occurred for many reasons. The WMD assessments, and especially the October 2002 National Intelligence Estimate prepared in response to congressional queries, drew on limited supporting data. The information was collected and put into reasonable but incorrect hypotheses born out of the previous behavior of the Saddam regime.

These assessments were not designed to deceive the president or the American people, but responded to the questions being asked at the time. The cycle of Iraqi challenges and deceptions that took place during almost eight years of friction with the UN inspectors had the effect of conditioning our senses to hear or see only evidence of weapons. The process of cognition is limited to identifying things that we have seen before. If we have never seen truth from Iraq, how will we know it when we do see it? There were so many reasons to expect to see WMD that we construed even limited pixels into elaborate WMD pictures. The bias to confirm our expected image was overwhelming. This is part of the way the brain operates.

Still, while Iraq did not have stockpiles of WMD, as the world was given to expect, neither was it in compliance with the UN disarmament resolutions. Iraq did pursue a prohibited missile program and was clearly laying a base for future work. Saddam certainly made statements that exacerbated the uncertainty, and he did that intentionally. Saddam retained the goal to reacquire WMD once Iraq was free of sanctions.

"Intelligence" will always be incomplete. It is only a question of how, and to what degree. Some knowable facts may be missed. Incorrect meanings may be attached to known facts. Insufficient energy may be devoted to delving into the reasons for facts.

The Bush administration, which has been criticized for pushing the intelligence community toward a conclusion, was behaving the way any official does in asking pointed questions about potential threats. Senior Bush administration officials who challenged intelligence assessments had every right to do so. Clearly, some of the assessments were founded on weak underlying information. The tension occurs because the act of asking the question shapes what the intelligence community is poised to look for or see. If no one asked about a nuclear-weapons program in Mauritania, no one would ever look. Yet, if they do not ask, it may be a reflection of faulty forward vision.

The case of "Curve Ball," the single person who was the source for over one hundred reports about Iraq biological-weapons programs that did not in fact exist, is a good example of seeing what you expect to find, even when it isn't there. That source turned out to be very wrong, and although some former CIA staff members now assert that they knew he was a rotten source and they waved red flags about him, these same people appear to have been astonishingly ineffective in saying so during meetings when real decisions were being made. It was a tale without any heroes. Curve Ball told people what they expected to hear and wanted to hear. His reports were not adequately scrutinized, and they ballooned into unsubstantiated headlines.[2]

In the end, it is the responsibility of political leaders to judge what to do with the intelligence community mechanism and its products. The Bush administration was inclined to use the CIA assessments of Iraq WMD—assessments that were largely incorrect. On the other hand, the administration chose not to use the largely accurate CIA intelligence and assessments of the political situation in Iraq, especially as they related to support for opposition groups and postwar reactions. The administration also challenged the assessment that Saddam was not connected to al-Qaeda. And although it used CIA covert operations to facilitate the removal of Saddam, the administration blocked the agency from using its internal resources and knowledge in replacing Saddam. To use the agency for half the time, and not consistently throughout a major foreign-policy adventure, seems reckless in retrospect.

President Bush's foreign-policy team, at least with respect to Iraq, was much less than the sum of its parts. The president gave general guidance by his strategic decision that it was unacceptable to the security of the United States to have Saddam remain in control of Iraq. Beyond that, there never seemed to be an adequately coordinated approach to implement regime change. While changing a regime is fundamentally a political—not military—activity, primary decision authority was, de facto, given to the Office of the Secretary of Defense (OSD).

The administration failed to operate as a team with an agreed-on set of objectives. On the contrary, members of the administration worked in opposition. The State and Defense Departments represented sectarian warfare in Washington. The White House and particularly National

Security Advisor Condoleezza Rice could not exert control over the OSD or State Department through the interagency process. The OSD ran the political activity of replacing Saddam and was clearly supporting the president's larger objective of getting rid of the dictator. Secretary Powell, who reportedly argued against regime replacement, was never trusted to be fully working for the president's objective. This factor underlay the assumption of control for postwar planning and actions by the OSD, where Iraq expertise was circumscribed at best.

Though incapable of coordinating its own policy and actions regarding Iraq, Washington was convinced that it could create a functioning government there. There is no satisfactory answer to the question "How could we presume to run Iraq if we couldn't run Washington?"

Senior Iraqi academics, diplomats, and other professionals whose lives and homes were devastated would ask me to explain American actions after the United States ejected Saddam. Politely, but pleadingly, they asked, "Why had you Americans not just eliminated Saddam and his top couple dozen aides? That is the message you conveyed before the war. Why the sudden change?"[3]

I was silent. There was no satisfactory answer to that question, either. I could not explain that the last superpower could act with such tremendous effect and with so little knowledge. I did not say that the number of things that our government can do is getting smaller rather than larger. I bitterly realized that even if there were a clear and necessary objective for the United States to pursue, our ability to mobilize and coordinate all the myriad tentacles of government to generate popular support and to organize all the interested parties has become progressively limited.

My brain was reluctant to admit that our government's reach was shorter than our vision. Like a recent amputee, we lived with a "phantom limb." We could see something and try to reach for it, but the physical limb, or lack thereof, did not match the muscle memory in the brain. Personally, I was confounded. I had been convinced there was a practical path for removing just Saddam and his top lieutenants and leaving the rest of the structure for case-by-case revisions over time. Instead, the decision to destroy all existing structure and make no plan for replacement other than bringing Chalabi and his small militia into Iraq was summarily and disastrously applied. Inside Iraq, I spoke to no Iraqi who thought this could have ever succeeded. In the spring and summer of 2003, I found it painful to stand before Iraqi professionals whose lives had been ruined. They were now terrorized by criminals. They were threatened by religious groups or Iranian-backed parties whose return to Iraq we facilitated.

They would ask incredulously, "Who is advising President Bush? You must tell him about Iraq!" I could not disclose that the CIA's postwar advice had been deliberately shut out. It was impossible to explain that in Washington, ignorance does not disqualify someone from responsibility. In 2005, a new special assistant to the president and deputy national security advisor for Iraq was named, the most senior policy official in the White House on Iraq. Senior Iraqis would ask me about this person: "Who is it? Do they know Iraq? What is the person's experience? Is this the person directing President Bush's plan for the future of Iraq?"

Implicit in these questions were, no doubt, sentiments more contentious: "What gives this person the right and wisdom to be making decisions affecting our lives? What is the experience that allows this person to judge us in Iraq? This person will be affecting the lives of millions of us and we did not elect this person." Iraqis could understand how the dictator Saddam gained control over their lives. They could not understand how Meghan O'Sullivan, a bright and articulate American who gained her only firsthand knowledge of Iraq as an aide to Bremer in the Coalition Provisional Authority (CPA), could become President Bush's top official on Iraq.

Like Ambassador L. Paul Bremer, who was given charge of the occupation despite having no experience in Iraq, O'Sullivan took a vital position at the White House with minimal experience. Such individuals learned on the job by trial and error. They had laudable goals, but it would cost many Iraqi and American lives as Washington educated its policymakers. Their ideals, combined with ignorance and power, could result in substantial damage. And it seems not to have occurred to such individuals to say to the president: "Look, Sir, I know you need someone to take this job, but I have absolutely no clue about what needs to be done and I do not know anything about Iraq. And I have never run anything, much less a country."

In Baghdad during 2003–2004, it looked as though the United States was running some sort of social science experiment at the CPA and the Iraqis were the lab rats. We had academics and graduate students experimenting with the homes, businesses, and livelihoods of 26 million people, in a country loaded with the weapons that had once made its army the fourth-largest in the world. Ignorance about Iraq was no bar to being part of the great adventure. Knowledge of the Washington process and being a trusted political ally, on the other hand, were essential. One bitter English-speaking Iraqi said the U.S. government was not a democracy or a meritocracy but an "idiocracy."

Our government incorporates checks and balances among its divided components. It is responsive to the views of its population, and those views are provided virtually continuously with modern communications. Elected officials who wish to win reelection must be sensitive to those increasingly immediate views. Combined with the lengthening electoral campaign seasons, the *political* impact of any policy initiatives has grown. The political cycles for congressional elections and presidential elections now seem to leave only brief moments when a pending election does not drive decisions to be considered in terms of their very short-term political impact. There is now ceaseless caterwauling from congressional representatives playing to the television and Internet audiences, who respond with almost real-time thumbs-up or thumbs-down in electronic polling.

Not unrelated, the quadrennial practice of submitting for Senate approval the now very lengthy lists of political appointees has become a slow and tortuous process that hobbles the ability to start a new administration. The process for new leaders to develop their own systems and learn the existing issues is lengthened. Combining this start-up phase with the inevitable lame-duck period of the prior expiring administration results in a long period when Washington is unable to act in a considered way. With luck, an administration will not have to face major crises and may even be able to try out some initiatives before it has to begin worrying about the soon-to-come midterm congressional elections.

One effect of this politically induced coma is the increasing tendency to do nothing to address problems—especially problems that occur over a long term. In some ways, this was the essence of the Clinton Iraq policy. That administration did not want to spend its political capital on an inherited problem that offered no electoral advantages. There's little place for action that has near-term political costs but whose benefits occur in the long term. There is no incentive for a politician focused on the omnipresent elections to risk an awkward present for an uncertain future. It is always safer for a politician to do nothing.

Other dynamics work against Washington's flexibility and ability to act shrewdly and strategically. Political appointees with little or no experience are placed in critical positions. The regular flushing of key staff to be replaced with new political appointees assures that experience does not accumulate. This was one of the reasons behind the failure of the Bush administration's Iraq policy. The number of political appointees has grown, as has the size of the government. Neither increase has made governing any more effective.

For these reasons, America stumbled badly in Iraq both because it didn't do enough and because it did too much. The lack of satisfactory results from attempts by two administrations pursuing very different courses in Iraq does not imply the problem is insolvable. That's not the case. Iraq was, and remains, difficult. It requires expert and sustained attention. Our strategic objective for Iraq should be that it emerges as a stable, independent, and democratic state. That is not going to be achieved quickly.

The future of Iraq is still unpredictable. While its future is mostly in the hands of the Iraqis, Iran has substantial influence and Tehran is capable of taking a longer view—to sustain long-term objectives—than Washington. The leading political parties have strong ties to Iran. Both the Dawa Party and the Islamic Supreme Council of Iraq were harbored in Iran for decades prior to the fall of the Saddam regime. The Kurdish leaders, especially Iraq President Jalal Talabani, have long historical connections with Iran, which has gained from this transition. Iraq's threat to Iran has now vanished. Beyond that, Iranian leaders may be able to steer Iraq further in the direction of an Islamic state rather than a secular, Westward-leaning democracy.

On the other hand, the secular core of Iraq will not easily be extinguished. Iraqi secularism might influence Iran in unexpected, but potentially positive ways.

The Iraqis, growing more accustomed to the notion that they—not Saddam or Washington—have responsibility for their own fate, will fight it out in the streets and, hopefully, at the polls. Competing interests will ultimately coalesce. Iraq will reestablish itself as a viable state. Iraq is not Afghanistan, but a country that has had sophisticated and extensive governmental agencies that have provided governance for its population. It has massive natural resources. Those who compare the American military actions in Iraq with those in Afghanistan should bear in mind a key distinction. The prospect of a stable, economically viable government ruling Afghanistan requires a significant departure from the historical norm. By comparison, one does not need such a leap of imagination to foresee Iraq as a stable, self-sustaining state. For Iraq, it is a question of time, cost, and what its regional role will be, especially with respect to Iran.

In general, it is no wonder that difficult problems fail to be addressed by our government. In foreign and national security issues, the checks and balances have progressively evolved to constrain action. The Intelligence Reform Act crafted during the 2004 election season was ignited in the aftermath of the Iraq invasion. In the heat of the moment, it was convenient for everyone to blame the intelligence community. The result was typical of Washington. The act added a layer of bureaucracy (the Office of the Director of National Intelligence and its staff of many hundreds), more funding, and more process. This is what Congress can safely do—add resources and organizations. Increased quality, however, cannot be legislated. The government got bigger and more expensive. I doubt it got better. In fact, the search for truth probably got harder.[4]

The most frustrating reflection on the limits of the U.S. government's abilities is the thought that even if it had correctly identified a way to ease Saddam from power—a policy of rapprochement with the explicit aim of getting close enough to him to maneuver him out, one way or another—U.S. politics make such a policy impossible. In theory, the United States could establish relationships with senior Iraqis who might be alternatives to Saddam. In theory, the United States could lay out a staged process of getting into Baghdad and working to undermine Saddam. This would avoid an invasion and the cost of thousands killed and hundreds of billions of dollars expended. But in Washington, it would have been impossible.

Such a strategic decision and long-term execution was not considered possible by either the Clinton or the Bush administration. Just imagine the political fate of any president who started a dialogue with Saddam. Moreover, in our transparent government, it is impossible to have a declared policy of one sort and a real policy widely different. Could any administration secretly brief Congress that while it was engaging in an overt policy of reconciliation, its real goal was to subvert and replace the regime? It would not be a sustainable gambit inside Washington. Such a low-cost option is simply not possible for the U.S. government. We are incapable of subtlety. Intentionally, the independent power of the White House is very limited.

It is difficult to admit that *we*, the most advanced nation in the world, have a government incapable of doing many things even if we have clear knowledge and understanding that they should be done. We the people have constrained our government by our democratically created processes.

One key part of wisdom is awareness of one's limitations. Can we admit to ourselves that our system of government is too prone to incompetence or clumsiness to address certain international problems, even if we know with confidence what should be done? I doubt it. We assume we can always muddle through. There is some strong American trait that says let's try to fix it, anyway.

Do the decency and morality of our objectives offset ill-informed, clumsy attempts to achieve them? There is a huge cost to innocents who may be eviscerated by such good intentions. After World War I, France's Marshal Ferdinand Foch said something along the lines that it costs fifteen thousand casualties to make a general. He highlighted a harsh reality of the military. But at least the military places decisions in the hands of generals, not the dilettantes who cycle through civilian positions in Washington.

While tragedies often repeat themselves, perhaps the Iraq experience will profitably inform future leaders in Washington. The political prohibition on opening a dialogue with Iraq was costly. Intelligence in every sense of the word was lost. While I personally had a fruitful dialogue with Nizar Hamdoon, Washington had no similar communication with Baghdad. The absence of communication was costly.

Incorrect intelligence and incorrect policy assessments are starkly highlighted in the history of U.S. actions in respect to Iraq, and vice versa. These historical inflection points offer classic case studies of the differing apprehensions of events at a given time by different actors. Washington's inability to realize that American logic and assumptions were not the same as Iraq's logic and assumptions was a major cause of the broken assessments.

Likewise, Baghdad's assessments of Washington were misconceived. The Iraqis, beneath Saddam, understood more viscerally that American thinking was different, and they tried to understand it and better predict Washington's actions. They failed as well. While Iraqis may have studied in the West and deeply understood American traits and logic, predicting Washington is difficult even for Americans.

Clearly, the aftermath of deposing Saddam did not have to be this costly. There is a list of "if-onlys" that are not difficult to imagine: If only the U.S. government could have acted as a team; if only the United States had been open to working with Iraqis inside Iraq, not placing all chips on a bet with Chalabi; if only we had pursued a strategy of breaking the Iraqi government as little as possible; if only we had assured Iraqis that the immediate change would be at the top and had stuck to that policy; if only we had used our channels to Iraqis in the government to keep the machinery of government, including the army and Republican Guard, intact; if only we had understood that "political" groups like the Iraqi National Congress would behave more like the mafia than like American political parties in jockeying for power; if only we had decided that Iraqis inside Iraq were the priority when we reached Baghdad, not the returning carpetbaggers who swiftly seized and occupied prime locations, government buildings, documents, and anything else they could leverage into power or profit; if only we had taken a measured approach of case-by-case removal of

Baath Party leaders—then we might have achieved a government responsive to the will of the people in Iraq with less chaos and blood.

Still, Saddam's regime is over, and that is good. Years from now, the basic decision to remove Saddam from Iraq will be seen in a more favorable light. The alternative future of an Iraq with Saddam in control and empowered by the growing demand for its oil resources would have been dangerously disruptive to the region in ways that we happily no longer have to imagine.

On November 8, 2005, John and I returned to Atchison for the dedication of a memorial to Sergeant Don Clary and Sergeant First Class Clint Wisdom at the local National Guard Armory. The night before the ceremony, the team from Baghdad gathered to rehearse the ceremony and then retreated to a local bar. To relive the events was painful, but there was reassurance in the group. We were a team, and I was certainly proud to be part of it.

The guardsmen insisted on buying me a drink, and before I could say, "Just a beer," John interjected, "He drinks martinis," which was true . . . on occasion. But this was Kansas. When the request was conveyed to the young bartender, there was hesitation. No one had ever asked her for a martini before. John yelled to the bar and said martinis were mostly gin. When the young army specialist returned, he carried a regular beer glass, but it was filled with gin. I worked on it over the course of the evening, with partial success.

We talked about Baghdad and events since. Conversations like these take place all around America now. Families have been torn apart, and relationships tattered. Some of the guys were having trouble readjusting. Some wanted to go back, as I did. One guy asked if I would call his commanding officer and get him assigned back to Iraq. There was peace in Kansas, but ironically, there was a degree of torment in the lives of all of us who have returned from Iraq. Throughout that night, I learned the depth of the term applied to the National Guard—*citizen soldiers.*

I spoke separately with the young man who was on the .50-caliber machine gun in the trail HMMV of our convoy. He had been placed in the horrible position of making the decision to fire on civilian vehicles if he judged them a threat. In his position, I told him, I would not have fired. The attacking car's intentions were not clear. The car was not obviously a threat until the driver detonated his bomb. The explosive was so powerful, the attacking vehicle did not have to be abnormally close. The scene with the explosion will play out in slow motion repeatedly in each of these men's heads, often during sleepless nights. The images will be different for each of them. I tried to see the scene as the .50-cal gunner would, frame by frame.

The next day, the ceremony took place at the exact time of the attack a year earlier. When I spoke at the ceremony, I included this thought:

> At this moment, a year ago on an airport road, the best and worst of humanity intersected. A youth whose mind had been fed some toxic ideas accelerated his vehicle toward us in a fit of destruction.
>
> Don Clary, Clint Wisdom, and Nathan Gray unhesitatingly reacted to preserve life and drove their vehicle to block the car bomb. The blast was huge, and chaos erupted as the impulses to destroy and to protect clashed.
>
> I have the rest of my life to try to understand this.

We found much truth in Iraq. There is much truth yet to be found.

NOTES

CHAPTER 1

1. Dr. David Kay had initially led the ISG in Baghdad from June to November 2003 and resigned officially in January 2004.

2. It was operated by Kellog-Brown-Root (KBR), which supplied much of the logistics for the overall military deployments. Logistics was extremely expensive. A case of soda was on the order of one hundred dollars, delivered in Iraq. With some pressure, this cost came down substantially, but to keep U.S. troops supplied via the convoys snaking their way up from Kuwait at great risk was very expensive.

3. The total personnel levels at the ISG fluctuated with the arrival and departure of various units and contractors. At its peak, it was around 1700.

4. It was also called the Water Palace, because it was primarily constructed to house a large indoor pool.

5. For most Iraqis, government was not something they did; it was something that happened to them. It was not their responsibility. They had no sense of the obligations of citizenship. There was absolutely no hesitation about looting—whether from government facilities or private. Unguarded property was un-owned property. So, with the invasion, they expected the imposition of a new order better and more secure than in the past. Iraqis did not think it was *their* job to restore order, and the U.S. military did not see it as its job. Within weeks, it was clear to Iraqis that the United States had no clue how to rule in Baghdad. They saw the United States dismiss (but not disarm) the army and declare all Baathists guilty of all sins of the regime—guilty unless proven innocent at some future time.

CHAPTER 2

1. Geologic history of that part of the earth now called Iraq is found in Farooq A. Sharief, "Permian and Triassic Geological History and Tectonics," *Journal of*

Petroleum Geology 6, no. 1 (July 1983): 95–102. See also Saad Z. Jassim and Jeremy C. Goff, eds., *The Geology of Iraq* (London: Dolin and the Geological Society of London, 2006). The last mass extinction of 65 million years ago is now thought to be the result of a meteor impact in the Yucatan.

2. While this is generally credited with being the first of written laws (and certainly the most complete set found), there are remnants of other, earlier law fragments from the ancient Iraqi city of Ur.

3. The Hammurabi Code was inscribed circa 1760 B.C. in ancient Babylon. Saddam quoted Hammurabi regularly and saw himself, like Hammurabi, as a "law-giver."

4. In his inaugural speech of January 20, 1977, President Carter stressed the pursuit of ideals in American foreign policy and the goal of eliminating all nuclear weapons from the earth.

5. Zbigniew Brzezinski, interview in *Le Nouvel Observateur*, January 15–21, 1998. An interesting assessment of the intelligence warnings prior to the Soviet invasion of Afghanistan is found in Doug MacEachin and Janne E. Nolan, cochairs, "The Soviet Invasion of Afghanistan in 1979: Failure of Intelligence of the Policy Process?" Working Group Report, No. 111, September 26, 2005, Institute for the Study of Diplomacy, Edmund A. Walsh School of Foreign Service, Georgetown University, Washington, D.C.

6. Saddam Hussein, "Voice of Masses," Speech, Baghdad, 1200 GMT, April 2, 1980, FBIS-MEA-80–066, 3 April 1980, FBIS E 2–3.

7. For a discussion of the number of expelled Iraqis, see Marion Farouk-Sluglett and Peter Sluglett, *Iraq Since 1985*, rev. ed. (London: Tauris Publishers, 2001), 355 and footnote 7.

8. In May 2007, the organization renamed itself the Islamic Supreme Council of Iraq (ISCI), presumably to recognize that it is no longer seeking revolution in Iraq, but is a major stakeholder.

9. The reporting cables of Rumsfeld's visits to Baghdad in December 1983 and March 1984 have been declassified and offer accounts of his meetings with Saddam and also Tariq Aziz. They are available in the George Washington University National Security Archive. George Shultz covers the same period in his memoir, *Turmoil and Triumph: My Years as Secretary of State* (New York: Scribner's, 1993). Shultz emphasizes his negative view on chemical-weapons use (see pp. 238–243), but from Baghdad the perspective was different.

10. Sensitive State Department memoranda and cables related to the Iraq chemical-weapons use in 1983–1984 have been declassified and are available on the George Washington University National Security Archive, Washington, D.C. See especially Information Memorandum to Undersecretary Eagleburger, 7 October 1983, "Subject: Iran-Iraq War: Analysis of Possible US Shift from Position

of Strict Neutrality"; Information Memorandum to: The Secretary, "Subject: Iraq Use of Chemical Weapons, November 1, 1983" (which notes "almost daily use of CW"); Action Memorandum to: Undersecretary Eagleburger, "Subject: Iraq Use of Chemical Weapons," 21 November 1983; and Cable of 14 December 1983, "Subject: Talking Points for Ambassador Rumsfeld's Meeting with Tariq Aziz and Saddam Hussein."

CHAPTER 3

1. For a lengthy discussion of the support provided to Iraq during this period, see Alan Friedman, *Spider's Web: The Secret History of How the White House Illegally Armed Iraq* (New York: Bantam Books, 1993).

2. We discussed President Reagan's Star Wars initiative of 1982. This was a case of huge unintended consequences that could have been catastrophic. Nikita pointed out that the Soviet reaction to Star Wars was to build a huge covert biological-weapons program, especially with smallpox. Delivery vehicles on SS-18 ICBMs were developed. Both of us marveled at the accidental and unpredictable outcomes that fall out of actions taken by governments.

3. For an interesting description of this incident, see Seymour M. Hersh, *The Target Is Destroyed* (New York: Random House, 1986).

4. One military deal with the United States was almost completed in the late 1970s. Qaddafi had purchased ten C-130 Lockheed transport aircraft, but the delivery was blocked by the State Department before the aircraft left their Marietta, Georgia, plant.

5. Interestingly, the French term for southern Chad was *Tchad Utile*.

6. Libya had been controlled by Italy, and Chad by France. The boundary between them had been the subject of lingering dispute. France had long been protective, or perhaps controlling, of its former African colonies. Paris asserted its primacy in Francophone African affairs among the Western powers.

7. In 1992, I made a trip with a small delegation to Moscow to discuss some arms control issues having to do with strategic defense systems. The foreign ministry provided us an escort officer who accompanied us in a van from the hotel to the ministry. The topic of Africa and Libya came up. The escort mentioned that his brother had been killed by Chadians in southern Libya.

8. In August 2003, Libya sent a letter to the UN Security Council, accepting responsibility for the actions of its officials in the bombing of Pan Am 103.

9. See George Shultz, *Turmoil and Triumph* (New York: Scribner's, 1993), 796. The name was picked to pose the question "Will he be good?"

10. Marion Farouk-Sluglett and Peter Sluglett, *Iraq Since 1958*, rev. ed. (London: Tauris Publishers, 2001), 266.

CHAPTER 4

1. Foreign Broadcast Information Service, Central Intelligence Agency, FBIS report (FBIS-NES-90-064), April 3, 1990, 3–36. See also Alan Cowell, "Iraq Chief Boasting of Poison Gas, Warns of Disaster If Israelis Strike," *New York Times*, April 3, 1990.

2. As I recall from the inscription, the photo was taken in November 1986, when Hamdoon visited Arkansas, a state doing big business in exporting agricultural products to Iraq using commodity credits.

3. U.S. imports of Iraq oil grew from eighty thousand barrels per day in 1987 to 1.1 million barrels per day in July 1990, according to CIA data quoted in Alan Friedman, *Spider's Web* (New York: Bantam Books, 1993), 163.

4. George Shultz, *Turmoil and Triumph* (New York: Scribner's, 1993), 243.

5. James A. Baker, *The Politics of Diplomacy* (New York: Putnam's, 1995), 264.

6. Ambassador Glaspie's entire reporting cable on her July 25, 1990, meeting with Saddam Hussein has been declassified. This reference is from paragraph 21.

7. Foreign Broadcast Information Service, Central Intelligence Agency, FBIS report (FBIS-NES-90-137), July 17, 1990.

8. These references are from Glaspie's reporting cable (noted above). The segments reflected here are from paragraphs 14, 22, 23, and 24.

9. See ibid., 355–363, for his detailed account of meeting with Tariq Aziz in Geneva on February 9, 1990.

10. According to one Iraqi oil expert, the key Iraqi player was Ramzi Salman, who had been head of the Iraqi State Oil Marketing Organization. He was understood to have had a long and lucrative business relationship with Wyatt.

CHAPTER 5

1. On July 11, 1995, in the absence of Ambassador Ekeus, I had the task of informing the Security Council about our decision to destroy a substantial amount of valuable equipment that Iraq had used in its WMD program (of particular concern was an expensive radar China had sold to Iraq for its missile development program). Iraqi Foreign Minister Mohammed al-Sahaf was in New York to meet with Security Council members. Ambassador Hamdoon invited me to dinner with Sahaf, with whom I had a long argument on this point. Although Hamdoon largely kept silent, Sahaf became agitated. I wasn't quite sure, but it struck me then that Sahaf was not very bright. (Subsequently, other senior Iraqis informally agreed that he was a burden for them, as well.) The facts of this particular case had become pretty clear. We established that the equipment had been purchased by the organization in charge of developing missiles and that the equipment had been used for those purposes. China, it is worth noting, was

completely unhelpful in providing any information. To the Chinese, it was a spectator sport.

2. The U-2 surveillance aircraft (or "spy plane" as it is often called) was originally designed to fly over the Soviet Union before the advent of spy satellites. (Updated versions still provide very high-altitude surveillance imagery over key areas.) This aircraft had two features that were useful to UNSCOM: Its images covered broad areas, and it could find unknown Iraqi facilities. In addition, because it flew relatively slowly and could loiter for extended missions, it was capable of detecting Iraqi reactions to UNSCOM inspections; for example, it could capture on film convoys of vehicles evading approaching UNSCOM inspectors.

3. Calutrons were inefficient but relatively simple devices used to enrich uranium. They were developed in the U.S. Manhattan project in the 1940s by Ernest O. Lawrence of the University of California (hence the name *Cal. U. Tron*). They were soon abandoned by the United States in favor of other more complicated, but more effective enrichment techniques. The huge magnets required for calutrons were so out-of-date that American intelligence analysts did not even recognize them at first.

4. James A. Baker, *The Politics of Diplomacy* (New York: Putnam's, 1995), 432.

5. Ekeus made it a practice to have extensive notes taken at virtually all official UNSCOM meetings, including those with foreign governments and representatives as well as UN officials and, of course, Iraqis. This is a very interesting archive that provides insight into the dynamics of the UNSCOM effort. Ekeus personally approved (and edited) the minutes of his meetings. This very rich, albeit sensitive, archive is found in the UN.

CHAPTER 6

1. The formal acceptance was transmitted in a letter to the president of the Security Council, dated November 26, 1993. UN document S/26811.

2. This had been a training facility for hotel staff and management and was located next to the Army Canal in northeast Baghdad. It became the headquarters for all UN activities, including the humanitarian aid work. In 2004, a truck bomb destroyed the facility.

3. Shortly before we finished the report, I had dinner with Iraq's deputy ambassador to the UN, Sayeed Hasan al-Musawi. (Nizar Hamdoon had returned to the United States as the UN ambassador.) Musawi, a Shia from al Amarah in southern Iraq, and I met often for coffee in the UN delegates lounge. Over the years, we became friends, but at this point, he was still very cautious around me. He had clearly been given the task to try to fathom the American thinking on UNSCOM. Musawi probed how long it would take to complete the UNSCOM inspections and finish the monitoring project. He played up the theme that

thousands of Iraqi children were dying because of sanctions and that this was a direct result of UNSCOM's not getting its work done quickly. I gave him no reason to be optimistic that we could quickly complete our task, given the grudging cooperation we received from Iraq.

4. For example, on March 7, 1994, the French ambassador Jean-Bernard Merimee invited both Ekeus and me to lunch at his residence on Fifth Avenue. France held the rotating presidency of the Security Council that month, and Iraq was the most prominent issue. Merimee wanted to move the process forward. He asked if Ekeus would object to providing a monthly briefing to the Security Council rather than just written reports semiannually. Also, in an attempt to put words in UNSCOM's mouth, he congratulated Ekeus on completing the disarmament part of the task. Now all that remained was a couple of months to put in place the monitoring system. Ekeus agreed to monthly reports, but did not agree with the French attempt to declare the disarmament questions finished.

5. The idea of meeting a defector in northern Iraq was unusual in the UN context. It was not something the IAEA would have done, and Ekeus was breaking more new ground in approving this move. It was also a very unusual request for me to put to Washington. I got support from the White House NSC to have the U.S. military fly the three of us into northern Iraq, and other U.S. officers on the ground set up the meeting.

6. There were continuing reports of such transactions. For example, see Seymour Hersh, "Annals of Espionage: Saddam's Best Friend," *The New Yorker*, April 5, 1999.

7. UNSCOM, under Ekeus, had a policy of accepting information relevant to the UNSCOM mandate from virtually any source. This led to a number of dialogues with many sources, some of which were more accurate than others. Journalists also came to UNSCOM with reports they wished to check.

8. This was Madeleine Albright's last point on a two-page list of "Talking Points" handed to UNSCOM after a meeting on June 28, 1995, at her office in the U.S. mission building across the street from the UN just before Ekeus left for Baghdad to see Tariq Aziz.

9. The French UN ambassador, Jean-Bernard Merimee, was one of the prominent individuals who had been designated to receive oil allocations under the Oil-for-Food program by Iraq.

10. Sergei Lavrov, the Russian ambassador to the UN at the time and later Russian foreign minister under President Putin, called on Ekeus on June 8, 1995, to check Ekeus's views on the upcoming UNSCOM report. Russia was pushing three points: Iraq had made progress in the chemical-weapons area by admitting sizable VX production, there were no major outstanding chemical-weapons issues, and, since the monitoring system was now operational, it would provide a "safety net" for anything that had been missed. Lavrov passed over a personal

message from Deputy Foreign Minister Sergei Ivanov that there was much internal debate within the Iraqi government over whether to continue to cooperate at all with UNSCOM. Russia believed that now was the time to recognize progress, because, if not, Iraq may cease cooperation entirely. Lavrov asked whether the United States would find it possible to move on the matter of the oil embargo and sanctions when UNSCOM did report sufficient Iraqi compliance. Ekeus referred to discussions he had had (the previous day) with Acting Deputy Secretary of State Peter Tarnoff. Ekeus told Lavrov that while the State Department had previously been aloof on the UNSCOM issues, Tarnoff had been briefed on the tensions in Baghdad and said that once UNSCOM reported that Iraq had completed its tasks satisfactorily, it would be difficult for the United States to hold out on its own against implementation of paragraph 22 of Resolution 687 (lifting the oil embargo). This implied that the United States would not use its veto alone, making the position of the United Kingdom important, Ekeus added. This discussion was illustrative of the sort of dialogues UNSCOM was drawn into at political levels.

11. One other disagreement was discussed by Ekeus. He confirmed to Tariq Aziz that UNSCOM would require Iraq to destroy certain unique production and test equipment used by Iraq in its indigenous program to manufacture SCUD-like missiles. This effort, called Project 1728, was only recently admitted to by Iraq. We knew the Soviets had sold Iraq 819 SCUDs, and we were trying to account for those only. The indigenous production capacity made accounting much more complicated and produced uncertainties we could never resolve fully. Baghdad was upset about the demand that it destroy such irreplaceable equipment—including the Chinese tracking radar. At Ekeus's last meeting, Aziz requested that Ekeus not confirm or execute that decision until later . . . that is, until after the biological-weapons deal was complete. Aziz told Ekeus that it was a very sensitive time. (Iraq's chief of military industry and Saddam's son-in-law, Hussein Kamel, was said by Aziz to be furious. Indeed he was.)

12. We were concerned that Iraq would have second thoughts and seize back the documents. Iraq subsequently regretted not having copies of the documents to refer to in our subsequent discussions. We had a strong advantage by being able to refer to their documents to test their statements. The Iraqis regularly requested copies of their own material (which we did not accommodate).

13. It became my task to conduct what passed for counterintelligence work for UNSCOM. I detest counterintelligence work—too much depends on snooping on your own people and continuous suspicions. It may be necessary, but can be very imperfect and very ugly, with much collateral damage to innocent people. Security investigations and attendant polygraphs create an atmosphere that inhibits interaction with foreigners, journalists, and others outside the cleared community. This constrains access to experiences and information that may be

quite useful. Security measures to protect information can come at the cost of limiting information. It is a difficult balance. Leaks and spies cause real damage. So do mistaken suspicions. And even the routine security investigations into every aspect of intelligence officers' lives repel many otherwise talented people from government work.

14. Kamel had thought the United States would give him support to replace Saddam. After it became clear that this would not happen, he became very morose about his lack of status and future. He was an unwanted guest in Jordan, but had no other place to go. His decision to return to Baghdad is not quite so bizarre when seen from that perspective and the sometimes mercurial ability of Saddam to accept former opponents. Still, the magnitude of Kamel's transgression was clearly unforgivable by Saddam.

CHAPTER 7

1. Thomson-CSF was later privatized and, in 2000, renamed Thales.

2. I delighted in listening to French Ambassador Alain Dejammet in the Security Council. He could go on forever (UNSCOM staff took to betting on how long his interventions would last when the president of the Security Council would recognize his request to speak). I remember one particularly telling speech, when he went on about the need for pragmatism in the council's efforts regarding Iraq. Dejammet said something close to this: "We in the council have created UNSCOM as a tool for implementing our resolution. One must recognize the impracticality of complete disarmament and that no inspection monitoring can be 100 percent effective. These UNSCOM inspectors, while I am sure they are acting with purely honorable, objective intentions (although Iraq has frequently raised questions about the fact that the most intrusive inspections were always directed by an American or other Anglo-Saxons and complains that they are not objective), are not broadly representative of the council members. I have no doubt about their sincerity. But they are perhaps too fastidious. Do they wish to find every piece of metal or screw that goes into one of these SCUD missiles? Must they find every scrap of paper that Iraq ever had on weapons? It is natural that many things are lost. We must accept that. After all, as long as the sanctions remain, millions of Iraqis are suffering. We should be balanced in our treatment of Iraq. Is it not possible to allow the monitoring system, which we have heard UNSCOM describe so marvelously, to do its job and let the natural business of Iraq recommence? Of course, the government of Iraq finds it difficult to deal with these inspectors. That is quite normal. They have natural security needs, as we all do. We should recognize this and accept that we have, in fact, achieved our goals."

As Dejammet was speaking, I kept thinking that this sounded exactly like a guy in a French movie explaining away a mistress to his wife. The bounds of the resolution were not meant to be so categorical as to prevent that which is necessary in life. This was clearly an attitude that Iraq could appreciate. Dejammet was eloquently and professionally expressing the views of the Chirac government. Unlike his predecessor, Ambassador Jean-Bernard Merimee, he was never tainted by allegations of personal involvement in Iraqi influence peddling. In later discussions with Mukhabarat officers (and in their documents), they claimed to have substantial influence with the Chirac government in Paris.

3. John O'Neill was relentless in pursuing a case or a threat. He was one of the people who recognized the al-Qaeda threat before it was fashionable to do so, and he worked the case hard. As happens to many workers in a bureaucracy, O'Neill got to that point in his career where talent, energy, and vision exceed what the bureaucracy will tolerate. You can be bitter, retire in place, or get out. In 2001, O'Neill left the FBI and became the chief of security for the World Trade Center, knowing it was still a target. He died there on September 11, 2001.

4. At the time, UNSCOM was seeking Security Council approval of an elaborate export-import mechanism that would be part of the monitoring net. This system would require that governments notify UNSCOM of planned exports to Iraq so they could be reviewed for impact on WMD monitoring. The system was essential as Iraq conducted more international business under the Oil-for-Food program. It would also be vital if there was to be any hope of even a mildly credible monitoring system after sanctions on Iraq were lifted.

5. Ekeus and the rest of UNSCOM staff had no such concerns. He thought nothing of an excursion I made while on a UNSCOM visit to Moscow to make a parachute jump at the North Pole as part of a Russian arctic exercise. UNSCOM experts also organized skydiving "off-site" meetings.

6. The Iraqis kept extremely good and accurate records of all U.S. and UNSCOM U-2 flights over their territory. They considered the U.S. patrols over the no-fly zone illegal and reported them to the UN in formal notes. The numbers and dates of flights were quite accurate.

7. We had a parallel series of quiet inspections that also targeted sensitive sites. They produced some pretty clear evidence of Iraqi concealment activities. During an inspection in September 1997, U-2 imagery showed a convoy of UN inspectors approaching Saddam's hometown of Tikrit (imagery shows a quite distinctive archway over the road at the entrance to the town). At the same time, and not visible from the ground because of an intervening ridge, the imagery showed a small convoy of Iraqi vehicles fleeing Tikrit. The Iraqi convoy circled up on the other side of the hill. The drivers stood around smoking cigarettes (actually, you can't see the cigarettes, but the men are standing in a circle, and if they

are breathing, they are smoking). When the inspection team had passed, the Iraqi cluster of vehicles dispersed.

8. In one case, we received advance knowledge of a planned November 1997 clandestine meeting of Iraqi missile experts seeking to procure components from a Romanian aerospace company. With help from non-American intelligence services, the meeting was videotaped and briefcases examined. We had visions of playing such tapes in the Security Council. But although the Iraqis were clearly seeking ballistic-missile components, it was not definitive that the missiles would exceed the range permitted by the UN resolutions. The countries involved also did not want to go public with this material, since it was an illegal transaction on the part of the individuals doing business with Iraq, but not a major violation by Baghdad that would carry much weight in the Security Council.

9. Ritter was energetic and creative, and while he was on the UNSCOM team, he gave his all. There was one big problem, however. He had lost his U.S. security clearance. While a marine, he had served in the former Soviet Union, conducting arms-control inspections in support of the Intermediate Nuclear Forces Arms Limit. He became involved with a Soviet (Georgian) woman, and they eventually married, moved to the United States, and had twin daughters. At one point, he applied to join the CIA clandestine service and was not accepted. He flunked his polygraph badly, as he described in Peter Boyer, "Scott Ritter's Private War," *New Yorker*, November 9, 1998, p. 56. For whatever reason, he set off alarm bells about his work with foreigners. This ignited an FBI investigation into him. So not only did Ritter find himself excluded from the U.S. national security community, but he was also investigated for potentially very serious breaches against the United States. From my perspective, this made things complicated. Ritter and I would brief our inspection plans and strategies in the White House situation room and seek continuing support from the U.S. national security community. At the same time, the intelligence community had suspicions about him. This was awkward, to say the least.

CHAPTER 8

1. He was fairly pleasant and seemed to enjoy living in New York at the UN's expense; he subsequently became a senior staffer for Hans Blix.

2. Not all the diplomats were of the UN stereotype. Ambassador Ryan Crocker—who years later became U.S. ambassador to Baghdad—had an adventurous streak. As we were completing the final visits, I happened to be spending some time in the small exercise area of the Baghdad monitoring center. Accompanying me was our operations chief, a tall, strapping Royal Marine named Chris Cobb-Smith. In walks Crocker, who was the designated American diplomat to observe the presidential-site inspections. He was a chronic runner and in

good shape. I got it in my head to make a suggestion. "You guys want to get some exercise and a great view of Baghdad?"

"Sure," Crocker answered, thinking I was going to suggest a jogging route. "OK," I said, "let's climb the communications tower. Wait here while I get the gate keys from the communications guys."

The tower was a typical hundred-meter, wire-stabilized tower that served as our microwave link to the videocamera monitoring sites we had in a few locations around Iraq. I led the way up, and in a half hour, we had a great view of Baghdad, although when the wind blew, there was a bit of swaying to the tower. There was also a dead bird that apparently expired in an effort to build a nest at the base of one of the navigation warning lights. It was a memorable view of Baghdad before the chaos of 2003.

3. The bombings were in reaction to a decision by Iraq to prohibit UNSCOM aircraft from Iraq. Incidentally, one of the Tomahawk missiles went off track and struck the Rasheed Hotel, killing a prominent Iraqi artist and two other civilians.

4. Roger carefully handed me an empty Pepsi can. It was Abed's, and he thought maybe we could get something off it. He was thinking fingerprints. I took the can carefully back to our offices at the end of the day and put it on a desk I was using. I later found one of our German inspectors using it for an ashtray.

5. Aziz had made a proposal to Butler months earlier to resolve, once and for all, the accounting of Iraq's WMD and the controversy over access to sensitive sites. He said Iraq would permit inspectors, of all types, to have complete access anywhere in Iraq for six months. However, at the end of six months, UNSCOM would have to declare Iraq in full compliance unless it found weapons material. Aziz's point was that Iraq wanted closure, not an endless process. He wanted UNSCOM to report to the Security Council so the council would have to confront the issue of removing sanctions. We did not give the idea serious consideration at the time because we thought it was simply a tactic to divide the Security Council.

6. In fact, the western Iraqi desert looked a lot like Mars. In 1997 a NASA probe called *Sojourner* landed there and sent back images that looked indistinguishable from the Iraq desert. On a lark, I substituted a NASA picture of Mars (in an internal UNSCOM report) for a picture of the Iraq desert taken during an inspection. No one ever noticed.

CHAPTER 9

1. There was an open letter dated February 19, 1998, to President Clinton emphasizing that containment of Saddam was an inadequate response to the Saddam threat. A systematic approach to regime change was necessary, and the letter

proposed a series of steps, beginning with support of the Iraqi National Congress's principals and leaders. It recommended what had been Chalabi's idea of creating U.S.-protected safe havens where the INC could govern. Sanctions would be lifted in these "liberated" areas. Among the forty signers were Donald Rumsfeld, Richard Armitage, Doug Feith, John Bolton, Richard Perle, Zalmay Khalilzad, Paul Wolfowitz, Dov Zakheim, and Peter Rodman—all individuals who would come to be major players in the Bush administration.

2. The Iraqis had retrieved some dud missiles, and our inspectors had even found the Iraqis running the Williams International Corporation turbofan engine on a stand at one of their missile plants called Karama. The Iraqis told us that they had also provided recovered cruise missiles to Russia for analysis. The Russian-Iraq missile exchanges were extensive, sanctions or no sanctions.

3. As Ritter's comments about UNSCOM hit the papers, the French ambassador would quote Ritter to support the French position in the Security Council. This was quite a switch. The Iraqi government Web site came to praise Ritter, especially after he began declaring that Iraq had complied and the prolongation of the sanctions was the fault of the United States. The Web site even solicited other UNSCOM inspectors who were of a like mind to contact Iraq via a posted e-mail address. In 1999, I half kiddingly asked Nizar Hamdoon if he was paying Ritter. He shrugged. He did not understand Ritter, either.

4. Jeff Smith had been covering the UNSCOM events for several years. He was well informed and accurate, with a good sense of judgment. Smith went on to cover Kosovo during the worst of times there, and in my opinion, his reporting was gripping. Barton Gellman, a young reporter presumably anxious to make his name, called on Ritter and informed him that he was replacing Smith and that anything Ritter would normally tell Smith, he should now tell Gellman. This apparently spawned several *Washington Post* articles about Ritter and his inspections in August 1998, including Barton Gellman, "US Fought Surprise Inspections," August 14, 1998, A-1; Barton Gellman, "US tried to Halt Several Searches," August 27, 1998, A-1; and Barton Gellman, "Inspector Quits UN Team, Says Council Bowing to Defiant Iraq," August 27, 1998, A-1. On October 11 and 12, 1998, Gellman also ran a couple of detailed stories based on Ritter and the concealment inspections. The stories concerning UNSCOM collection techniques appeared on January 8, 1999, and March 2, 1999. George Tenet and I both engaged the *Post* management and Gellman to limit aspects of the story that would risk the individuals involved. Not surprisingly, an ambitious reporter cloaked with the bulletproof mandates in the United States—the public's right to know—went forward. Dumb luck put him in the position of being able to write stories that stirred the political pot, excited the public, and allowed him to promote himself. In the United States, journalists have an enormous incentive to promote themselves by exposing government activities, good or bad.

They have a built-in justification with freedom of the press. I have encountered some, usually more experienced, journalists with established reputations who opt to limit disclosures, especially when it puts people at risk. Other reporters rationalize their self-promotion with a righteous proclamation of freedom of the press. The Iraqis would never understand this—for them, such stories somehow could only occur with the connivance of the government.

5. As luck would have it, the key individual involved in this smuggling operation turned out to be the son of a former minister in Iraq. I met the former minister in May 2003 and had occasion to speak with the son on unrelated business. Later, it was not unusual to find that those involved in smuggling weapons or other material had also found good contacts with the governments that succeeded Saddam.

6. Dejammet spoke at the 4084th meeting of the UN Security Council, which approved UN Security Council Resolution 1284. The statements by members are recorded in UN Security Council document S/PV.4084.

CHAPTER 10

1. Much was made of the Iraqi offer to pay $25,000 to the families of Palestinians killed in attacks against Israel. Senior Iraqis in private conversations with me revealed that implementing this was not simple and that, in fact, there were many cases of the equivalent of insurance fraud. The Iraqis were receiving numerous fraudulent applications from families of individuals who had died of more common causes, like traffic accidents.

2. Foreign Minister Ivanov traveled to Baghdad carrying a personal letter from Vladimir Putin to Saddam on November 13, 2000. Two days earlier, Zhirinovsky had arrived on a "humanitarian" flight, in defiance of the air transport limitations.

3. It was shot down on March 27, 1999, by a Serbian SA-3 GOA air defense missile system—the only F-117 ever shot down in combat. These aircraft were retired from service by the US Air Force in August 2008.

4. The Iraqis and the Yugoslavs had also long shared information on air defense. Iraq had purchased weapons from Yugoslavia, and Iraqi air-defense experts traveled to Yugoslavia to assist and learn techniques in tracking U.S. aircraft. This was important for pride and the potential leverage of a captured pilot. American and British pilots had been captured in the 1991 war and treated badly as prisoners. In 1995, Nizar Hamdoon discussed with me the potential loss of a U.S. pilot during no-fly-zone missions. This conversation was provoked by the experience of U.S. Air Force F-16 pilot Scott O'Grady, who bailed out and survived for six days, eluding capture in Bosnia operations. Saddam was pushing his air defenses to score a hit.

5. Khalilzad had been on the Bush Department of Defense transition team and was one of the signatories of a Republican letter to Bill Clinton, dated January 26, 1998. Khalilzad had been born and raised in Afghanistan, but studied at the American University in Beirut and received a Ph.D. at the University of Chicago. He was director of strategy, doctrine, and force structure at Rand Corporation. During the Reagan administration, he served as an advisor on Afghanistan while the United States was supporting the mujahedeen against the Soviet occupation.

6. In a long interview with a group of editors-in-chief of Iraqi newspapers (led by Hani Wuhayyib, editor-in-chief of the newspaper al-Qadisiyah) that was broadcast on Iraqi TV on May 23, 2001, Tariq Aziz gave the Baghdad perspective on a range of issues including the end of UNSCOM, the weakness of the United States, the growing support for Iraq from Europe, and the role of France and Russia. He was quite explicit about Iraq's use of its economic influence over Security Council members.

7. Uday commented to his doctor later that this was similar to the injury he caused Saddam's brother-in-law, Watban, when Uday shot him in August 1995 in a fight over a woman.

8. The enforcement of the no-fly zones had become more aggressive over the previous few months, even in the absence of any clear new Iraq policy. The Defense Department was acting more aggressively to attack air-defense sites that were illuminating patrolling aircraft. There was no longer the limitation to wait until an air-defense site fired. Targets also expanded to include not just missile launchers, but also the radars and the command and control facilities. The command and control facilities were being upgraded. Improvements to the communications systems included the use of fiber-optic cable from China. This was apparently procured under the Oil-for-Food program. If the Iraqi air-defense communications were shifted to fiber, then interception of communication would be impossible and there would be increased risk to patrols. The attacks forced the Iraqis to use radio links or none at all. In Baghdad, Saddam too was at war. Throughout the 1990s, the Iraqis regularly stated that they remained at war with the United States. Aziz repeatedly said to me that the UN resolution was not a peace treaty; it was a ceasefire. In Baghdad's view, a state of war remained. Aziz pointed to the sanctions as economic warfare and the continuing no-fly-zone patrols as well as the strikes against Iraqi air-defense sites as ongoing conflict. Washington, on the other hand, asserted that Saddam's attempts to shoot down U.S. and British aircraft patrolling over Iraq were acts of aggression.

9. In my conversations with John Hannah (a national security advisor to Vice President Cheney) and others who were in the administration at the NSC and OSD, it seemed there was a desire to avoid the UN. Perhaps this was my own prejudice, because after almost seven years of working at the UN to accomplish

NOTES TO PAGES 198-204

the inspections, I was firmly convinced that they would not work over the long term and that Saddam could divide the council against the United States. I had been asked for my views on inspections by OSD staff, including a lengthy session with Doug Feith, the previous May. I also met regularly with Will Tobey, an old friend and now an NSC staffer for nonproliferation. He wanted to know the details of UNSCOM's previous work in Iraq. Tobey had the energy and patience to examine the details of the Iraq WMD experience. While he rarely shared with me the direction the White House was going, he regularly asked for historical UNSCOM information and views on how to force a credible inspection system on Saddam or create conditions that would demonstrate the limits to his cooperation. I also connected Tobey with other UNSCOM alumni who were scattered around the United States and had deep knowledge of the Iraqi programs and practices.

10. Charles Duelfer, "Inspectors in Iraq? Be Careful What You Ask For," *Washington Post*, January 9, 2002, A-19.

11. It is easy to forget the emotions in the nation at the time. The president declared that terrorists "who once occupied Afghanistan now occupy cells at Guantanamo Bay," and there was strong applause. The costs had only begun to escalate. Bush outlined these early costs: "It costs a lot to fight this war. We have spent more than a billion dollars a month—over $30 million a day—and we must be prepared for future operations." (Iraq would cost over ten times more a month in 2006.)

12. An amusing aspect of the second meeting was that the large Iraqi delegation included a number of senior Iraqi scientists who had management roles in the previous WMD programs—including Jafaar Dhia Jafaar, the head of the nuclear program. Since their travel routes were knowable (and they had to apply for visas to enter the United States when they got to Amman, Jordan, from Baghdad), the United States took the opportunity to try to "pitch" to some of them in transit and in New York. Jafaar was quite vocal in complaining about this to the press. Naji Sabri later said that these clumsy attempts were the reason the last meeting in the series was moved to Vienna. To my mind, this was a far better location to make a pitch. The irony in these blatant and pretty lame attempts at recruitment was that even if they had succeeded, these individuals would have had a tough time convincing debriefers that there were no WMD left, although it might have generated enough doubt to recalibrate the WMD assessments.

13. Kelly, a genuine biological-weapons expert with long Iraq experience, was a scientist to his core and found it difficult to make declarative statements beyond his view of the evidence. That was what the political scientists who were steering the government wanted. UNSCOM had a few very talented biological-weapons experts (from the United States, the United Kingdom, and Germany, and sometimes a guy from Russia). These scientists would argue endlessly over the facts, their importance, and what they meant. It was a relief when they all

agreed on something. When they did, I felt much confidence, but it was a painful process to get there. Still, they bonded as a group, and Kelly was highly admired. A year later, in the midst of a parliamentary investigation of the British prewar intelligence presentations, Kelly was caught in a maelstrom of political science, and he apparently saw no way out. The savage attacks of politics and the press were too much for the quiet scientist. He was obligated to testify before the British foreign affairs committee publicly on July 15, 2003, and the intelligence committee on July 16. On July 17, he took a walk from his home in Oxfordshire to a field about a mile away. According to the subsequent inquiry by Lord Hutton ("Report of the Inquiry into the Circumstances Surrounding the Death of Dr. David Kelly, C.M.G."), he committed suicide. At the time, Kelly had been preparing to travel to Iraq, where he was to join the efforts to investigate Iraq's WMD programs. He would have been safer in Baghdad.

The alumni core of UNSCOM inspectors is a tight group. The members span many nationalities, but have a long background in dealing with the UN, host governments, and Baghdad. It remains a sad mystery why Kelly could not endure the temporary humiliation of the summer of 2003. His former colleagues, whose opinions he truly valued, had only high regard for him. We all understood the political systems that surrounded individuals at the UN and in nations' capitals, including even Baghdad. Governments were one thing, and individuals another. Kelly's death was another tragedy tied to the Iraq conundrum.

14. Reuters, from Damascus, August 29, 2002; available at http://www.ctv.ca/servlet/ArticleNews/print/CTVNews/20020829/iraq_war_react_020829/20020829/?hub=World&subhub=PrintStory.

15. Tobey and I had discussed the possibility of not finding significant WMD either because the inspection tactics were flawed or because they weren't there. The president, after all, would want to find WMD. Between Tobey and me, it seemed as if there were the elements of a wager here, but it was far too serious. Toby would experience the real thing in 2004, when he came out to Baghdad for a few days with the Iraq Survey Group. We drove in the vicinity of Baghdad International Airport in the pitch black of an unlit, unmarked Iraqi road. He was one senior policymaker who genuinely acquired a feel for the difficulties in the field.

CHAPTER 11

1. Subsequently documented in Laurence H. Silberman and Charles S. Robb, commission cochairs, "Report to the President by the Commission on the Intelligence Capabilities of the United States Regarding Weapons of Mass Destruction," March 31, 2005, available at http://www.wmd.gov/report/index.html.

2. While at UNSCOM, I had been the conduit for both the regional office and the nonproliferation office on the analytic side. It turned out that even after

leaving the UN, I was able to retain access to a nongovernment organization—access that was valuable on both sides of the CIA house.

3. In 2001, the State Department was getting pressed to do more with the external opposition from the NSC and indirectly from the new team around Rumsfeld, including Paul Wolfowitz and Doug Feith. To them, the State Department was a noodle that they were trying to use to push regime change forward. The department reluctantly organized some international meetings of the disparate Iraqi opposition groups, and Chalabi tried, with some success, to bring unity of purpose and organization to these groups. During the summer of 2001, these activities went forward by fits and starts.

4. A long discussion of Chalabi's banking and his felony conviction is presented in Aram Roston, *The Man Who Pushed America to War* (New York: Nation Books, 2008).

CHAPTER 12

1. Michael Issikoff, "Terror Watch: The Paper Chase," *Newsweek*, December 22, 2004; Michael Issikoff, "Scandal Still Going," *Newsweek*, September 16, 2002; and Michael Issikoff, "Pardon Mess Thickens," *Newsweek*, March 1, 2001.

2. Wyatt pleaded guilty on October 1, 2007, in Federal District Court in New York.

3. Saddam Hassan al-Ziban is variously referred to as Saddam Hasan or Saddam Ziban in Iraqi documents. "The Comprehensive Report of the DCI's Special Advisor on Iraq's WMD with Addendums" (September 30, 2004) discusses his role in a range of illicit oil deals and procurement schemes. See Volume III, pages 19–53, of the section titled "Regime Finance and Procurement."

4. Previous guidance during the Clinton administration was far less categorical, and halfhearted activities were started and then ceased—including a short experience supporting Ahmad Chalabi and his Iraq National Congress. For a discussion, see Robert Baer, *See No Evil* (New York: Crown, 2002).

5. The oil minister, Amer Rasheed, was not permitted to leave the country at that time for security concerns.

6. This presidential order is described in Bob Woodward, *Plan of Attack* (New York: Simon & Schuster, 2004), 108, but the prohibition of CIA work in the postconflict period was not mentioned.

CHAPTER 13

1. As the White House was drafting a new resolution to table in the UN Security Council, Will Tobey solicited my views and suggestions drawing on my UNSCOM experience. He asked about features that would test Iraqi compliance

and be useful to energetic inspectors. My strongest suggestion was some mechanism to provide candid interviews with Iraqis who had been involved in the WMD programs. People with direct knowledge and access would be the best source, but they had to be able to speak freely. I suggested a provision that would allow them to be interviewed outside Iraq—even providing for them to leave permanently.

2. For Blix's perspective, see Hans Blix, *Disarming Iraq* (New York: Pantheon, 2004).

3. In retrospect, I suspect that "Curve Ball" read the very detailed UNSCOM inspection reports that were posted on the UN Web site. These reports gave extensive detail about Iraq WMD programs, people, and facilities. It would not be hard to weave convincing stories from these reports, and Iraqis could take the data, combine it with their own area knowledge, and make exciting reports. I suspect this was a practice of multiple Iraqi defectors who were encouraged to make themselves attractive to Western intelligence agencies.

4. Donald Rumsfeld, interview with Jim Lehrer, *NewsHour with Jim Lehrer*, PBS, September 18, 2002, transcript available at www.pbs.org/newshour/bb/middle_east/july-dec02/rumsfeld_9–18.html.

5. The press briefing record transcript can be found at the White House Web site: http://www.whitehouse.gov/news/releases/2003/02/20030203–17.html.

6. Donald Rumsfeld, interview with Jim Lehrer, *NewsHour with Jim Lehrer*, PBS, February 20, 2003, transcript available at www.pbs.org/newshour/bb/middle_east/jan-june03/rumsfeld_2–20.html.

7. George W. Bush, National Press Conference, March 6, 2003, transcript available at www.whitehouse.gov/news/releases/2003/03/20030306–8.html.

8. An effort to record Iraqi military perspectives was conducted by the Joint Center for Operational Analysis of the U.S. Joint Forces Command. Material from debriefings and selected documents is assembled to describe the regime's military planning, guidance, and execution in a report. See Kevin M. Woods et al., *Iraqi Perspectives Project: A View of Operation Iraqi Freedom from Saddam's Senior Leadership* (Joint Center for Operational Analysis, U.S. Joint Forces Command, March 2006). This is a good collection of some firsthand views. However, I would disagree with some of the categorical conclusions drawn about Saddam's intentions and plans. There seems to be a Western bias to interpreting statements and documents. Moreover, some of the definitive conclusions about Saddam's views are at odds with some of his own postwar debriefing statements. It is likely that the senior participants held differing and even contradictory views—often at the same time, and including Saddam. Definitive recollections of the Iraq war planning and top-level directions will remain elusive.

9. While the CIA was explicitly not permitted to do postwar planning, the NSC staff could, and did, take steps regarding the Oil Ministry. On their guid-

ance, I was able to provide assistance for postinvasion planning and actions related to that ministry.

CHAPTER 14

1. Julia Child, before becoming famous as a chef, worked for the OSS in a number of ways, including trying to concoct something that would repel sharks.

CHAPTER 16

1. If a comparison were necessary to provide some instant knowledge, the comparison should have been to the Communists in the former Soviet Union. Bremer was in no position to evaluate any of the advice he received, and he had little time to develop any understanding of Iraq before signing the most momentous decision of the postconflict period. It was about a month between when he was first asked about the job and when he landed in Baghdad for the first time in his life. Only in Washington would someone with absolutely no regional experience be considered the perfect person to assume an extraordinarily difficult job determining the fate of twenty-four million people.

2. For Bremer's own discussion of these events and his rationale, see L. Paul Bremer III, *My Year in Iraq: The Struggle to Build a Future of Hope*, with Malcolm McConnell (New York: Simon & Schuster, 2006).

3. Reuters Report by Khaled Yacoub Owels, "Chalabi Compares U.S. Policy on Baathists with Nazis," Baghdad, August 23, 2004.

4. The Intelligence Collection Program came from congressionally mandated support to Iraqi opposition groups, specifically the INC. The DIA is very sensitive about this dubious activity. See the subsequent congressional investigation, U.S. Senate, Select Committee on Intelligence, "The Use by the Intelligence Community of Information Provided by the Iraqi National Congress," report, 109th Congress, 2nd Session, September 8, 2006.

5. I saved this list from my contemporaneous notes.

6. Paul Bremer, "How I Didn't Dismantle Iraq's Army," *New York Times*, September 6, 2007, available at http://www.nytimes.com/2007/09/06/opinion/06bremer.html?pagewanted=print.

7. See Aram Roston, *The Man Who Pushed America to War* (New York: Nation Books, 2008), for a thorough discussion of Ahmad Chalabi's financial machinations and his felony conviction in Jordan stemming from the Petra Bank collapse.

8. Four years later, much to my surprise, he sent me a note saying that he had lately been named an ambassador of Iraq to the country in which he was then resident.

CHAPTER 17

1. In my discussion with Dayton, I got the impression that there were some strange circumstances about Kay's departure. I never fully understood what happened, and no one could ever really explain why Kay left when he did. Dayton said that Kay had complained about a reduction in resources and had keyed his departure on that point. But Dayton also said that no resources had been taken away. Moreover, Kay had left several weeks earlier, and while he completely cleared out his quarters, he never informed anyone at ISG that he was quitting. I also spoke with some of the other experts at the ISG. They said that he had been distant from the work, just coming out for occasional meetings while living in the Green Zone.

2. Dayton was not a WMD expert, so he turned to an Australian and former UNSCOM biological-weapons inspector, Rod Barton, to begin drafting a report. Before leaving the ISG, David Kay had requested the services of Barton and John Gee, another Australian expert. They arrived after Kay departed and so had no guidance. Dayton figured Barton would be a good person to lead the report-drafting exercise and suggested that I might want to look at the draft. I did. It was over a hundred pages long already. It made declarations "to close issues" on high-profile matters like the aluminum tubes and the trailers. I was very concerned that I would have to appear before Congress and defend a position I had not yet internalized, if in fact I agreed with their views. I asked Dayton to suspend the drafting despite the fact that much work had been done. We could probably use the text at a later time. However, I did not want to make piecemeal pronouncements. The conclusions would be made at the conclusion. This angered the Australians, who assumed I did not like their text either for political reasons or because it did not agree with prewar CIA assessments. No matter how much I explained this to Barton and Gee, they held to their own view on my motivations. Still, they knew a lot about Iraq's programs, and I wanted non-American views to keep the analysis honest.

3. The sorting process for incoming documents included a primary screening done by personnel with security clearances. Sensitive documents would be separated and translated by U.S.-cleared linguists. For example, there were documents of current intelligence value, such as sources in other countries (including the United States) or assessments of other countries.

4. I don't think Tenet realized that the crowd, while mostly American, also included British and Australians. In any case, his pep speech was heard by the delicate ears of at least one Australian, the biological-weapons expert Rod Barton, as conveying instructions to find WMD, not find the truth. Tenet had not been trying to convey any guidance on the direction or goals of ISG. He was simply giving a short ad hoc talk after a long flight to Baghdad. Barton, in later writing,

refers to this talk by Tenet as evidence that the CIA was pressing ISG for a political conclusion about Iraq WMD. That, and Barton's statements about the political direction of the ISG, or actions to falsely validate WMD assessments, are completely wrong.

CHAPTER 18

1. A 2008 book by Ron Suskind (*The Way of the World: A Story of Truth and Hope in an Age of Extremism*, published by Harper) claims (among other dubious things) that Tahir Habbush was assisted in escaping Iraq by Western intelligence services. This is contrary to my direct experience and that of many colleagues, including in the UK service. Moreover, I am unaware of any direct or productive contacts with him.

2. Some outside critics and certain former ISG members thought Scarlett was pressing me to include more dubious evidence about possible WMD. In fact, I had asked the United Kingdom, and specifically John Scarlett, to suggest any and all bits of data that could be considered. I did not want to be in a position afterward whereby critics faulted us for overlooking any credible evidence. Scarlett was not overstepping any bounds so far as I was concerned. We examined the data he pointed to and it amounted to nothing important.

CHAPTER 19

1. Later, after they had talked me out of the modest idea of carrying an unloaded sidearm, it was jokingly suggested that if I really wanted to become the new Saddam for Abed, I could enter the debriefing room and listen to the debriefer go through his stupid list of questions for a while and then, with predictable exasperation, pull out a pistol, saying, "Those are some of the dumbest fucking questions I have ever heard." And shoot the debriefer . . . with blanks, but Abed won't know. That would quickly recalibrate Abed's thinking. That was humor, but it was quite clear our debriefings were guided by Geneva Convention rules and we were able to achieve our objectives staying well within such limits.

2. Abed was captured during a night raid when Blackhawk helicopters delivered a capture team to a site in the town of Bayji north of Baghdad. The site had been specified in a tip from an informant.

CHAPTER 20

1. George W. Bush, "Remarks on the Capture of Saddam Hussein," Washington, D.C., December 14, 2003, available at http://www.whitehouse.gov/news/releases/2003/12/20031214–3.html.

2. Howard Kurtz, "Rather Says Saddam Asked Questions," *Washington Post*, February 26, 2003.

3. There were, however, early notations in his journal referring to nearby mortar or rocket explosions, and he would comment that maybe "they" were coming to rescue him.

4. At the first FBI debriefings, there was an attempt to play on guilt by recalling for Saddam all his former close associates whom he had eliminated as necessary. This went nowhere, given Saddam's absence of remorse or any consideration that he may have erred.

5. One mistress I corroborated. In late April 2003, I had gotten to know a former Mukhabarat officer who claimed to have had an ongoing relationship with one of Saddam's mistresses. This sounded dicey to me. One day in May 2003, I challenged him. I got in his car, and we drove to the Mansour house that Saddam had provided for her. She was not home, but the Mukhabarat guy seemed to know his way around there. Interestingly, he said that Saddam was with their shared mistress at that house on the afternoon of Monday, April 7, when an Air Force B1-B bomber had been quickly diverted to drop four precision-guided bombs on a nearby house (very close to the popular Mansour restaurant Al Sa'ath). This quick strike was allegedly in response to U.S. intelligence that Saddam was meeting with his two sons at the targeted house. (In fact, three or four looked to be destroyed, considering the huge hole in what had been a row of houses just off the main north-south street in Mansour.) From what the Mukhabarat guy said, Saddam's ears must have been ringing that day, given the proximity.

6. By "Anfal Campaign" Piro meant the genocidal attacks using chemical weapons against the Kurds largely during 1987–1988. Ali Hasan al-Majid, Saddam's cousin, received the nickname "Chemical Ali" for his ruthless direction of this atrocity.

7. There were many debriefings of senior military commanders after the war. Kevin M. Woods et al., *Iraqi Perspectives Project: A View of Operation Iraqi Freedom from Saddam's Senior Leadership* (Joint Center for Operational Analysis, U.S. Joint Forces Command, March 2006), presents their conclusions.

8. My source for this quote is an FBIS report date/numbered 122115Z, serial number GMP20000612000293. Also see Baghdad-datelined Associated Press article (No. AP-NY-06–13-00 0814 EDT) by Waiel Faleh titled "Hussein Willing to Reduce Arsenal." The latter article includes a slightly different translated version of the same quote.

9. For a discussion of this event and the overall Iran-MEK conflict, see Amin Tarzi and Darby Parliament, "Missile Messages: Iran Strikes MKO Bases in Iraq," *Nonproliferation Review* (summer 2001): 125–133.

10. In the collection of RCC recordings this is tape number 6893. DOCEX materials, including transcripts of RCC audio recordings, were posted on the

Web site of the Foreign Military Studies Office at Fort Leavenworth (http://fmso.leavenworth.army.mil) from March until November of 2006. The idea was to make the Iraqi materials available to the general public for review. However, among the documents were a few that were judged to have proliferation-sensitive material, and the archive was removed from free public access. (See William Broad, "U.S. Web Archive Is Said to Reveal a Nuclear Primer," *New York Times*, November 3, 2006.)

CHAPTER 21

1. The First Cavalry had picked him up in a raid on his office as part of their efforts to contain the Jaysh Mohammad group. At this point in time, MNF-I (Multi-National Force–Iraq) intelligence was just beginning to understand the cohesiveness and potency of this group of insurgents centered in the Fallujah area. (Curiously, I first heard of the group in May 2003 while meeting with old Iraqi friends after the United States first occupied the country—at that time, the group was characterized by the Iraqis as a few Saddam supporters . . . and was ignored.)

2. The al-Gaaod family and its ties to the Mukhabarat procurement are described in volume 1 of the comprehensive report—specifically, on pages 88–91 of the "Regime Finance and Procurement" section.

3. It is inevitable that tensions will grow in a group on deployment. They were analysts for the most part, not operators trained to function as a unit. Rita brought in a few additional members from Washington to keep up with the workload. These were individuals in a very stressful environment for which they had no training. They worked very long hours and had little to do besides work. Three individuals in particular illustrated the problems of analysts on deployment (even for only a couple of months). They became known as the Bermuda Triangle. Each analyst was competent, aggressive, and ambitious. These individuals were also arrogant and overconfident. Over a month, tensions grew. Arguments erupted based on emotions, more than facts and theories. Life on deployment was different from commuting to headquarters in the green Virginia suburbs and worrying about rearranging the lawn furniture at the end of the day. Some individuals became more trouble than they were worth and moved out or were sent home. But eventually, they were a team. They certainly had a mission.

4. Link analysis is a classic tool supporting counterterrorism efforts. It is logical and can help in visualizing networks. Like so many tools, though, the quality of information backing the display can vary. If known al-Qaeda person A telephones unknown person B, does that make B bad? And if B calls C, what does that mean?

5. The potential for screw-ups is enormous once names are linked for the slightest reason. One database can be accessed by others unfamiliar with its

meaning or reliability. In circumstances that I cannot fully describe, I found myself in a hotel room in New York with an Arabic person who had risked his life to help the United States. There was a pounding on the door and FBI agents appeared with the clear intent of seeking to haul away both the guy I was meeting and me. It was a mistake along these lines that put me in that situation.

CHAPTER 22

1. Initially, I was concerned that all our collection operations would then fall directly under Iraq's legal control. However, the UN Security Council mandated authority for the Multi-National Force–Iraq (MNF-I). It gave MNF-I legal authority in Iraq. With the impending transition, the ISG was moved under the authority of MNF-I, with the explicit understanding that General George Casey, then the four-star general in charge of MNF-I, would not interfere in any ISG operations or resources as long as I remained at the head of ISG. This was an agreement between George Tenet and Donald Rumsfeld. This legal arrangement allowed the ISG to continue to run operations, including raids and capture missions, after transition. As a practical matter, however, I had requested that all teams plan on completing major collection activities by June 30 and concentrate on organizing and recording the results during July and August.

2. From the perspective of MNF-I and even the CIA in-country, the ISG had a lot of assets focused on archeology. They had a war on and coveted any assets that could be taken over by the MNF-I machine and distributed among the various brigadiers and colonels. In the ISG, Dayton had created a unique military tool combined with civilian intelligence. In my opinion, the ISG could have directly shifted its mission from WMD to either the IED threat or foreign terrorists in Iraq. It was a unique capability—a concentrated task force of deployed analysts, all types of intelligence collectors, and indigenous maneuver units. It was lean and agile. Naturally, the regular army would disassemble it as quickly as possible. The ISG did not fit the army's normal order of march. McMenamin was charged with dismantling this tool. Other generals and colonels were anxious to occupy the facilities that the ISG had built up.

3. By comparison, I found that a draft of this book of roughly six hundred pages was easily penetrated by the same type of round fired from about fifteen feet.

4. Part of their problem was that the team leader, Rita, had a role in the prewar biological-weapons assessments by the CIA and in the drafting of a July 2003 white paper that quickly offered an (incorrect) assessment that the trailers found in June were for biological weapons. Barton had already left the ISG once, but I requested the Australian government to inquire about his willingness to return for a month. The Australian government advised against Barton, but I wanted a diverse, knowledgeable group.

5. Even under sanctions, Iraq had successfully been importing hundreds of Russian-designed rocket engines. After the war, Harlow discovered that some al-Samoud rocket engines had made their way to scrap yards in Holland. Apparently, Iraqi looters had scavenged them for their valuable metal components and shipped them out of Iraq as scrap.

6. Reuters article, dateline Baghdad (No. 09:38 02–03–00) titled "Iraq Says West Destroyed Seven Missile Plants."

7. However, a Russian diplomat who once headed a UN budget oversight committee was given a fifty-one-month prison sentence in U.S. Federal District court in October 2007 for Oil-for-Food corruption.

8. The report was long, but we devised a structure that I hoped would tie together the massive amount of data into narrative sections that could be readily understood. The history of Saddam's regime and its relation to WMD were mapped with many other relevant factors such as available resources and outside events. To this end, I decided to include a copy of the huge timeline that we had built in a special room at ISG. I am convinced that this was a vital tool in helping our analysts gain some understanding of the reality perceived from Baghdad. We also included a reference system of mapping points in the timeline to points in the descriptive text. This was the suggestion of British Brigadier Graeme Morrison, who served as military deputy to Keith Dayton. Ideally, it would have been great to build in data links and publish it on CD with that capability. Unfortunately, we were pushing our luck getting the CIA to print both the text and a separate large foldout sheet for the timeline.

9. Close to the election in late October, a bizarre issue was raised by Senator John Kerry and supported by Mohamed El Baradei, the head of the IAEA. Seeking to criticize the Bush administration on Iraq, Kerry made a special note that some tons of RDX explosive had been left unprotected at the Al Qa Qa facility. RDX is a powerful conventional explosive that Iraq had procured years ago for its tests associated with its nuclear-weapons program. Iraq wanted to keep the explosive for non-WMD purposes, and the IAEA had allowed the Iraqis to retain it but had sealed the bunkers with tags. After the war, Al Qa Qa, a huge military development and test area filled with sites for rocket, artillery, and other developments, was looted like most places. Kerry expressed shock that the IAEA-sealed sites were left unprotected. El Baradei, venturing into U.S. domestic politics, piled on, saying this was a big problem, why hadn't the United States secured the RDX or destroyed it?

The administration did not have a good answer. From my perspective, whether the RDX was still there or not was irrelevant to understanding the WMD program. I suspected strongly that the RDX was not still there. In fact, a year earlier, my colleague Kyle had been in touch with an Iraqi who brought him a white substance that the informant swore was important to WMD. Bored that night, I set some of the material on the ground and lit it. We were impressed with the bright blue flame. Testing that was more scientific revealed that the substance was RDX, which I figured came from Al Qa Qa. My assumption was that the RDX was now just one more explosive in the hands of the newly freed Iraqis—like much of the six hundred thousand tons of munitions also estimated to have been in Iraqi stores.

The White House wanted the ISG to investigate the sites. I saw no point in it, but did see risk because any convoy going to Al Qa Qa would have to pass through areas with active insurgents. I did not want to do this just for a stupid political issue. I politely said no. The Office of the Secretary of Defense, in turn, put an order through military channels, and a military team went down to Al Qa Qa, fortunately without incident.

CHAPTER 23

1. See Kofi Annan, remarks, Fourth Plenary Meeting of the 54th Session of the General Assembly, September 20, 1999, UN document A/54/PV.4.

2. The "Curve Ball" experience highlights many of the characteristics that make intelligence assessments uncertain. In retrospect, it is easy to see the faults in relying on a single source of a liaison service. But in reading the intelligence reports of his debriefings even years later, one can find them pretty convincing— especially given the expectation, based on UNSCOM investigations, that Iraq would pursue mobile biological labs. I suspect that Curve Ball was aware of UNSCOM reporting and packaged his on-the-ground knowledge into tales that fit the UNSCOM reporting. U.S. intelligence analysts had so little to go on, they connected the few dots they had in a way that everyone expected, but it was largely guesswork.

3. Illustrative of the desperate views pressed upon me during the first weeks of the chaotic occupation were those contained in a letter written by hand (and in imperfect English) that one prominent academic implored me to pass on to the White House. (I conveyed it to NSC staff.) It read:

12 May 2003 Baghdad—Iraq
Mr. President of the United States of America,
the Honorable Mr. G. W. Bush

Dear Sir,

History will remember you as the leader who liberated Iraqi people from the dictatorship of Saddam Hussein. An achievement that needed a unique courage and will. You have them both. We are grateful to you and the American people for your gift to our land, that contains freedom, liberty and dignity.

Dear Sir, I come to you with true and honest voice, displaying the truth in front of you.

Depending on the noble goals of yours, that of freedom liberty and dignity in the frame of law and order [are not happening].

What is actually happening now in Iraq, that of total loss of law and order, and that of mutilation of principles of freedom and liberty, as it has now been granted to criminals and looters ant to these groups of fully armed parties who came and invaded the cities and the capital, leaving no space for the silent majority of Iraqis who are looking up for your help and only you to save them again and to let them enjoy the real taste of freedom and liberty and dignity.

In conclusion dear sir, the truth is that these organized fully organized, so-called [political] parties, they will hijack your achievement of liberation and freedom of Iraq and prevent the silent majority of Iraqis from expressing their voice forever if they are not stopped now. You can be sure of the above statements through trustful people and departments. The majority look to your good heart and wisdom. God bless you and your family. Please accept my apologies for things I mentioned that might be improper.

4. The quality of individual actions and analysis, in my opinion, would be most directly improved by reducing the number of people involved. There is far too much diffusion of responsibility for subjects and operations in the intelligence community. Bright individuals will not be attracted to a mammoth bureaucracy, in which they will have little direct responsibility and too many layers of oversight. In many cases, the intelligence community could be significantly improved with a serious reduction in staffing and a concomitant increase in individual responsibility—but that is an option politically unacceptable in Washington.

ACKNOWLEDGMENTS

A book about the search for truth is susceptible to criticism for failures of accuracy. To the extent I have avoided errors, I have many to thank. To the extent I have included errors in accuracy or emphasis, the responsibility is mine.

In the course of both living through and writing about the events in this book, I have benefitted from the knowledge, advice, support, and camaraderie of many individuals. I have also had the good fortune to be a member of, and sometimes lead, some great organizations.

The UN Special Commission of Iraq (UNSCOM) had some of the most talented and dedicated individuals in the world. I was fortunate to serve as deputy to both Ambassador Rolf Ekeus and Ambassador Richard Butler through the 1990s. The vitality and creativity of UNSCOM came from its core team of individual inspectors. They set the standard for weapons inspections anywhere across the globe. Illustrative of the range of talent involved were: from Russia, Nikita Smidovich and Igor Mitrokhin; from Britain, John Scott, Rachel Davies, Hamish Killip, David Kelly, Ewen Buchanan, John Harlow, Tim Trevan, and Lesley Barlette; from Germany, Horst Reeps and Gabriele Kraatz-Wadsack; from France, Didier Louis, Michel Saint-Mleux, Fouad el Khatib, and Eric Fournier; from Australia, Roger Hill and Rod Barton; from the Netherlands, Cees Wolterbeek; from Argentina, Gustavo Zlauvinen; and from the United States, Richard Spertzel, Bill McLaughlin, John Larrabee, Mark Silver, Steve Black, and Scott Ritter. There were many others from many countries.

At the Iraq Survey Group, I was also surrounded by dedicated and energetic colleagues. Our military, led by U.S. Army Major General

Keith Dayton and U.S. Marine Corps Brigadier Joe McMenamin, along with U.K. Brigadier Graeme Morrison and Major Henry Joynson, as well as Australian Army Lieutenant Colonel Steve Beaumont, made certain that the ISG military and civilian components blended into one team. Military and civilians were a well-integrated team under their guidance.

Unlike the UN inspection teams, ISG operated in a violent, hostile environment. Sgt. Sherwood Baker and Sgt. Lawrence Roukey died in an explosion at an investigation site known as Al Abud. Sgt. Michelle Hufnagel, Spc. Brian Messersmith, Sgt. Darren Miles, Spc. Ryan Owlett, and Sgt. Joseph Washam were badly wounded also at that site. Sgt. Don Clary and Spc. Clint Wisdom died, and Sgt. Nathan Gray was seriously wounded, in an attack on my vehicle on an airport road. Other members of ISG suffered the nonvisible wounds of service in Iraq—as did their families. Sometimes, the families were the casualties.

ISG was a unique team organized around a unique mission. It is an organizational model for the government's national security agencies when they have a specific goal. There were too many individuals upon whom I was dependent to list here. Each sub-team of the ISG accomplished its role under difficult circumstances for which there was little precedent.

To the Personal Security Detachment team, I owe my life. I was surrounded by the soldiers of Battery B, 2nd Battalion of the 130th Artillery of the Kansas Army National Guard. No one has ever been in better company.

To the rest of the ISG teams I am also grateful and honored to be among our collective alumni. ISG had great components: SOC & SAC, the Pol-Mil, CT-COIN, Nuclear, CBW, Missile, and RSI analytical teams; JAG, Special Staff, the U.K. and Australian components, the SCP-B, Ops-Plans, JIDC debriefers, DTK, CMPC-Baghdad, J-staff 1–6, CBIST, TEU, NGA, DET-B, CIA, Contracting, Garrison, and others. A few had to endure my direction at close hand and I am grateful for their tolerance and support. John D., Andrew H., Tim K., Kyle, Larry Sanchez, Commander Bob Kettle, Zach W., Keith Fennell, and Lois J. were close then and now.

At CIA, I had complete support from DCI George Tenet. He was in the midst of political turmoil and steering a growing organization, but he gave me both full assistance and complete discretion. Likewise, Tenet's deputy, and later Acting DCI, John McLaughlin, paid particularly close attention and guaranteed all possible help. I am indebted to him for his sustained guidance. Leslie Ireland provided a reassuring and indefatigable link to all parts of CIA and the rest of the U.S. intelligence community. John Moseman, Jim Pavitt, Jami Miscik, Bill Harlow, and the late Stan Moskowitz all threw the full backing of the CIA behind this effort with the simple goal of presenting the most accurate picture of the Iraqi regime and its WMD programs. CIA management all wanted to know where they went wrong and they wanted to rebuild confidence in the intelligence community.

The CIA's Iraq Operations Group, a team that seems to go on forever, deserves special mention. I worked closely with many IOG officers and in multiple capacities over the years. IOG has had some of the best operations officers, reports officers, and analysts. I have been able to say little here about their people and activities due to the security constraints. Suffice to say they did great work in a physically and politically dangerous environment. There was much knowledge about Iraq within the IOG that had been accumulated over many years. Not enough of it was used. I have touched on elements here, but someday I hope a more thorough rendition can be made public.

The Center for Strategic and International Studies provided me support during a key part of the time reflected in these pages. Judith Kipper graciously brought me into her Middle East Studies section at CSIS. Later, thanks to Lee Hamilton and Michael Van Dusen, I was fortunate to spend time at the Woodrow Wilson International Center for Scholars.

I must also acknowledge the role of my Iraqi friends, sources, counterparts—and even former enemies—both inside and outside the former regime. There were dozens of Iraqis over the last fifteen years who have spent time with me, sometimes at great personal risk, in an effort to share perspectives and knowledge. Their lives have been filled with challenges and decisions that Americans have never had to confront.

Much of what separated us was serendipity. I hope I have reflected their perspectives accurately here.

PublicAffairs founder Peter Osnos and I first discussed this project in the fall of 2003 following an introduction through the late Peter Jennings. Peter Osnos and Executive Editor Clive Priddle encouraged me to shape what I had witnessed in Iraq into the themes and perspectives necessary for a book. That effort was interrupted when I returned to Iraq to head the Iraq Survey Group. Peter and Clive demonstrated extraordinary patience as I spent 2004 in Iraq. A further test of their patience resulted from the requirement that I submit this manuscript for government security clearance, not just from the CIA (which has a relatively quick response time) but from the entire range of security agencies under the new Director of National Intelligence. Working at the speed of bureaucracy, the DNI review process took over nine months. I hope this book justifies the patience and sustained support of the PublicAffairs team.

A special thanks to my former professor and mentor, William W. Kaufmann at MIT. He taught me the ideals of analysis in the search for truth. And to Julie Davidson, who provided vital encouragement and who reviewed the text to assure my thoughts and words made sense.

Many others—family, friends, and colleagues—helped me and often suffered because of me during the events resulting in this text. I both thank and apologize to those caught up in this. I wish it could have been easier.

INDEX

Charles Duelfer served as the deputy chairman of the United Nations weapons inspection organization (the UN Special Commission on Iraq—UNSCOM) from 1993 to 2000. He was also the leader of the Iraq Survey Group, which was the CIA-led team charged with the search for weapons of mass destruction in Iraq. His name is commonly given to the final CIA report of the Iraq Survey Group, the Duelfer Report. He lives near Washington, D.C.

PublicAffairs is a publishing house founded in 1997. It is a tribute to the standards, values, and flair of three persons who have served as mentors to countless reporters, writers, editors, and book people of all kinds, including me.

I.F. STONE, proprietor of *I. F. Stone's Weekly*, combined a commitment to the First Amendment with entrepreneurial zeal and reporting skill and became one of the great independent journalists in American history. At the age of eighty, Izzy published *The Trial of Socrates*, which was a national bestseller. He wrote the book after he taught himself ancient Greek.

BENJAMIN C. BRADLEE was for nearly thirty years the charismatic editorial leader of *The Washington Post*. It was Ben who gave the *Post* the range and courage to pursue such historic issues as Watergate. He supported his reporters with a tenacity that made them fearless and it is no accident that so many became authors of influential, best-selling books.

ROBERT L. BERNSTEIN, the chief executive of Random House for more than a quarter century, guided one of the nation's premier publishing houses. Bob was personally responsible for many books of political dissent and argument that challenged tyranny around the globe. He is also the founder and longtime chair of Human Rights Watch, one of the most respected human rights organizations in the world.

·   ·   ·

For fifty years, the banner of Public Affairs Press was carried by its owner Morris B. Schnapper, who published Gandhi, Nasser, Toynbee, Truman, and about 1,500 other authors. In 1983, Schnapper was described by *The Washington Post* as "a redoubtable gadfly." His legacy will endure in the books to come.

Peter Osnos, *Founder and Editor-at-Large*